Contents at a Glance

List of Figures

Microsoft

Working with

Microsoft Dynamics® CRM 2011

Mike Snyder

Jim Steger

Kristie Reid

Published with the authorization of Microsoft Corporation by:
O'Reilly Media, Inc.
1005 Gravenstein Highway North
Sebastopol, California 95472

Library of Congress Control Number: 2011923689
ISBN: 978-0-7356-4812-8

Printed and bound in the United States of America.

Microsoft Press books are available through booksellers and distributors worldwide. For further information about international editions, contact your local Microsoft Corporation office or contact Microsoft Press International directly at fax (425) 936-7329. Visit our Web site at www.microsoft.com/mspress. Send comments to mspinput@microsoft.com.

Acquisitions Editor: Todd Merrill
Developmental Editor: Devon Musgrave
Project Editor: Valerie Woolley
Editorial Production: Christian Holdener, S4Carlisle Publishing Services
Technical Reviewer: Matt Cooper
Copyeditor: Becka McKay
Indexer: Jean Skipp
Cover: Twist Creative • Seattle

[LSI] [2012-07-27]

List of Tables

List of Sidebars

Table of Contents

Foreword

CRM continues to see accelerated growth and adoption around the world. As we move into a new phase of business computing, we have seen the retirement of complex, rigid, and inflexible CRM systems in favor of solutions that are simple, agile, and valuable to today's information worker. It is in this area that Microsoft Dynamics CRM continues to shine and leads organizations into a new world of empowerment and enhanced business productivity.

And we're only getting started.

Enter Microsoft Dynamics CRM 2011—a solution designed to amplify user adoption, help organizations discover new business insights, and fuel business productivity across your entire business network. Designed to meet the most comprehensive set of CRM needs across the cloud or in your own IT environment, Microsoft Dynamics CRM 2011 delivers the unparalleled flexibility, security, and scalability needed to manage crucial relationships, guide everyday interactions, optimize business processes, and deliver real-time business intelligence for every system user.

Mike Snyder, Jim Steger, and Kristie Reid yet again deliver the most comprehensive resource for Administrators and Developers of Microsoft Dynamics CRM 2011 to understand new concepts and master enhanced system capabilities. It seems that with every customer that I visit around the world, a copy of this resource has been used to enhance deployment success.

Working with Microsoft Dynamics CRM 2011 continues this tradition of excellence.

No matter where you find yourself in the system development life cycle—from solution envisioning, planning, developing, and stabilizing, this book provides a comprehensive reference for each project team member:

For users of Microsoft Dynamics CRM 2011, this guide provides comprehensive examples of mastering native functionality and enhanced capabilities.

For system implementers and customizers, this resource serves as a definitive guide to unleashing the full power of the solution framework to deliver tailored business applications.

For information technology administrators, this text provides an outstanding reference guide for planning, implementing, managing, and maintaining Microsoft Dynamics CRM 2011 across your organization.

Mike, Jim, and Kristie shine at explaining the essential topics, but also help readers see beyond the basics when it comes to customizing and extending Microsoft Dynamics CRM 2011 for unique system needs. The concepts and examples covered in this text are certain to accelerate your mastery of this innovative new release. Again, every deployment of Microsoft Dynamics CRM 2011—in the cloud or in your own IT environment—will greatly benefit from this resource guide. It has been a pleasure to work with both Mike and Jim in the development of this text, and I, like the readers who will follow me, keep this resource nearby when approaching each new business challenged to be solved with Microsoft Dynamics CRM 2011.

I look forward to hearing of your success in working with this new release.

Sincerely,

Bill Patterson
Director, Product Management
Microsoft Dynamics CRM
Microsoft Corporation

Introduction

We love Microsoft Dynamics CRM 2011, and we hope that by the time you finish reading this book, you will love Microsoft Dynamics CRM, too. We understand that you might be skeptical about the possibility of falling for a piece of software, but we want you to know right up front that our goal is to show you all of the wonderful and amazing benefits the Microsoft Dynamics CRM application can provide for your business.

Who Should Read This Book

We wrote this book for the people responsible for implementing Microsoft Dynamics CRM at their organization. If you're the person responsible for setting up or configuring Microsoft Dynamics CRM software on behalf of other users at your company, this book is for you. You might be an information technology professional or simply a Power User from the sales or marketing departments. You should be comfortable with technical concepts and understand the role of various Microsoft technologies such as Microsoft Exchange Server, Microsoft Active Directory, and Microsoft SQL Server. You don't need to be a coding expert to benefit from this book, but we hope that you can edit an XML file and that you understand how relational databases work.

This book can also help prospective customers with their software selection process as they evaluate the customization options that Microsoft Dynamics CRM offers. If you want to learn more about the software's capabilities before you make a purchase decision, we hope that this book provides some of the technical details you're looking for.

Who is this book not for? It's *not* for end users interested in learning how they will use Microsoft Dynamics CRM on a day-to-day basis because their company just went live with the software. If you don't have System Administrator rights, you won't be able to perform most of the steps in this book, so it probably won't provide much benefit for you. If you're not sure whether you have System Administrator rights, then this book probably isn't for you either. If you're interested in end-user topics, consider purchasing *Microsoft Dynamics CRM 2011 Step By Step* from Microsoft Press.

This book also *does not* tell you how to install the Microsoft Dynamics CRM software and troubleshoot any installation-related issues. We don't cover upgrading an existing Microsoft Dynamics CRM installation to Microsoft Dynamics CRM 2011. The Microsoft Dynamics CRM Implementation Guide gives excellent and detailed advice on the installation and upgrade processes, so we don't need to repeat that information here.

Organization of This Book

We divided *Working with Microsoft Dynamics CRM 2011* into 2 parts and 15 chapters. The two parts break down as follows:

- **Part 1, Overview and Setup** Provides a quick overview of the various components of Microsoft Dynamics CRM and explains how to configure some of the more frequently used areas of the software.
- **Part 2, Solutions** Goes deeply into how you can modify Microsoft Dynamics CRM to match the way your business works. Topics include adding new data fields, revising the user interface, creating reports and dashboards, and automating business processes by using workflow.

In resources such as the Implementation Guide, the software development kit (SDK), the User Interface Style Guide, and the online Help, Microsoft Dynamics CRM 2011 includes more than 1,500 pages of product documentation on how to use the software. This book is *only* 624 pages, so obviously it can't possibly cover every nook and cranny of how Microsoft Dynamics CRM works. Rather, our goal is to focus on the key areas most companies will need to set up, customize, and extend the software while providing plenty of examples and real-world advice. This book assumes that you can install the software and that you have a decent understanding of how to navigate the user interface. Consequently, if you want to learn more about using the software (as opposed to customizing the software), we recommend that you take advantage of the many Microsoft training options available for Microsoft Dynamics CRM, such as eCourses, classroom training, and the Foundation Library. Because of this book's space constraints, we decided not to repeat any information or samples already covered in the product documentation. Therefore, we frequently refer you to the SDK and the Implementation Guide.

One last thought regarding the organization of this book: We tried to eliminate any "marketing fluff" so that we could cram as much information as possible in this book. To that end, you will not read the reasons why customer relationship management (CRM) projects fail or read a discussion about the future of CRM software. We're straightforward and direct people, so we appreciate it when books present information in the same manner. We hope that you like this style, too.

Prerelease Software

We wrote most of this book using preproduction versions of Microsoft Dynamics CRM 2011. Microsoft released the final version of Microsoft Dynamics CRM 2011 just a week or two before we submitted the final copy to our editor, but we did review and test our examples using the final release. However, you might still find minor differences between the production release and the examples and screenshots included in this book.

Microsoft Dynamics CRM Online

As you learn in this book, Microsoft Dynamics CRM offers several different deployment options, including a Microsoft-hosted version of the software named Microsoft Dynamics CRM Online. Both versions of the software work identically in almost all areas, so our content and samples work for all versions of Microsoft Dynamics CRM, unless explicitly noted. If you're interested in Microsoft Dynamics CRM Online, we suggest that you check *http://crm.dynamics.com* for the latest information about that product.

System Requirements

We recommend that you refer to the Microsoft Dynamics CRM Implementation Guide for detailed system requirements. From a high level, you'll need the following hardware and software to run the code samples in this book:

Client

- Microsoft Windows 7 (both 64-bit and 32-bit versions), Windows Vista (both 64-bit and 32-bit versions), or Windows XP Professional SP3 operating system
- Microsoft Internet Explorer 7 or a later version
- Microsoft Office 2010, Microsoft Office 2007 with SP2, or Microsoft Office 2003 with SP3 (if you want to use Microsoft Dynamics CRM for Microsoft Office Outlook)

Server

- Microsoft Windows Server 2008 x64-based computers Microsoft SQL Server 2008
- Computer/processor: Quad-core x64 architecture 2 GHz CPU or higher such as AMD Opteron or Intel Xeon systems
- Memory: 8 gigabytes (GB) or more of RAM recommended
- Hard disk: 40 megabytes (MB) free space
- Network card: 10/100 megabits per second (Mbps) minimum, dual 10/100/1000 Mbps recommended

Code Samples

This book features a companion website that makes available to you all the code used in the book. The code samples are organized by chapter, and you can download code files from the companion site at this address:

http://oreilly.com/catalog/9780735648128/

Acknowledgments

We want to thank all of the people who assisted us in writing this book. If we accidentally omit anyone, we apologize in advance. We would like to extend a special thanks to the following people:

- **Bill Patterson** Bill sponsored the book project and helped make sure that all the pieces fell into place correctly. He also agreed to help us by writing the book's foreword.
- **Kara O'Brien** Kara did an amazing job (on a ridiculously tight timeline) of copyediting the initial drafts of each chapter and blending them together in a single cohesive product. We would never have completed this book on time without Kara's help!
- **Neil Erickson** We asked Neil, our Sonoma Partners network architect, to build and update more Microsoft Dynamics CRM environments than we care to admit. We want to thank Neil for all of his assistance.

In addition, we want to thank these members of the Microsoft Dynamics CRM product team who helped us at one point or another during the book project:

Abhishek Agarwal	Shamiq Islam	Nirav Shah
Inna Agranov	Raju Kulkarni	Manoj Shende
Andrew Bybee	Rubaiyat Khan	Derik Stenerson
Maureen Carmichael	Amy Langlois	Craig Ungar
Jim Daly	Nick Patrick	Praveen Upadhyay
Rich Dickinson	Manisha Powar	Sandhya Vankamamidi
Ajith Gande	Girish Raja	Mahesh Vijayaraghavan
Abhijit Gore	Venkata Ramana	Brad Wilson
Humberto Lezama Guadarrama	Michael Scott	Zhen Zhang
Peter Hecke	Vishal Sahay	

Thank you to the following Sonoma Partners colleagues who assisted with reviewing the content and providing feedback:

Brian Baseggio	Chris Labadie	Jeff Meister
Brad Bosak	Brendan Landers	Corey O'Brien
Jacob Cynamon-Murphy	Bob Lauer	Steven Oxley
Matt Dearing	Peter Majer	Jason Tyner
Mike Dearing	Sean Massa	Matt Weiler

Of course, we also want to thank the folks at Microsoft Press who helped support us throughout the book-writing and publishing process:

- **Ben Ryan** Ben championed the book project and he helped us through the process.
- **Valerie Woolley** Once again, working with Valerie has been a delight. She did a great job of helping us through the book production process, and she also helped fight for additional page count when it looked like we had written too much!
- **Christian Holdener** As our project editor, Christian did a great job of staying on top of the timeline and helping to get this book in print in time for the Microsoft Convergence conference.

Last but not least, we want to thank Matt Cooper. As the technical editor for the book, Matt worked around the clock to confirm the technical accuracy of the text. This included reviewing and testing all of our code samples and double-checking our facts.

Mike Snyder's Acknowledgments

I want to thank my wife, Gretchen, who tolerated the long nights and weekends that this book consumed over the past few months. Despite the fact that I kept disappearing into my office to sneak out some work, she supported me 100 percent from start to finish. Even though they won't be able to read this note for years, I want to thank my children, who provided me with the motivation to undertake this project. I also want to recognize my parents and my wife's parents who assisted my family with various babysitting stints. I would like to thank all of my coworkers at Sonoma Partners who helped pick up the slack created by my time commitment to this book.

Jim Steger's Acknowledgments

I would like to thank my wife, Heidi, and my children for their continued support in this undertaking. In addition to the Microsoft Dynamics CRM product team members we thanked above, I want to give an additional thank you to the following people who graciously spent time reviewing content and helping explain functionality: Matt Cooper, Ajith Gande, Nick Patrick, Jim Daly, Rubaiyat Khan, Richard Dickinson, Andrew Bybee, and Amy Langlois. Finally, I wish to express my gratitude to my associates at Sonoma Partners for their assistance during this process.

Kristie Reid's Acknowledgments

I first want to thank Mike and Jim for giving me the opportunity to help them with this project. They have both been an integral part of the successes that I have had implementing Microsoft Dynamics CRM solutions. Of course, I would not be able to do the work that I enjoy without my husband, Jon, who patiently took care of our remarkable kids, Maggie and Dylan, during the long hours I spent on my computer writing chapters. I also want to acknowledge my husband's parents, who entertained my family during our trips to see them while I hid out in their house working. Finally, I want to thank everyone at Sonoma Partners who helped me in so many ways during this process.

Errata & Book Support

We've made every effort to ensure the accuracy of this book and its companion content. If you do find an error, please report it on our Microsoft Press site at oreilly.com:

1. Go to *http://microsoftpress.oreilly.com*.
2. In the Search box, enter the book's ISBN or title.
3. Select your book from the search results.
4. On the book's catalog page, under the cover image, you'll see a list of links.
5. Click View/Submit Errata.

You'll find additional information and services for your book on its catalog page. If you need additional support, email Microsoft Press Book Support at *mspinput@microsoft.com*. Please note that product support for Microsoft software is not offered through the addresses above.

We Want to Hear from You

At Microsoft Press, your satisfaction is our top priority and your feedback our most valuable asset. Please tell us what you think of this book at

http://www.microsoft.com/learning/booksurvey

The survey is short, and we read every one of your comments and ideas. Thanks in advance for your input!

Stay in Touch

Let's keep the conversation going! We're on Twitter: *http://twitter.com/MicrosoftPress*

Part I

Overview and Configuration

Chapter 1

Microsoft Dynamics CRM 2011 Overview

In this chapter:

We know you're eager to get into the details of how Microsoft Dynamics CRM 2011 works and learn more about its great customization capabilities. Before we dive into those details, we need to cover some background information about Microsoft Dynamics CRM and introduce some of the core concepts and terminology used throughout this book.

Life Without Customer Relationship Management

Think back to a particularly bad customer service experience you had. Maybe you called a customer service phone number and were transferred to five different people, and every single person asked you the same questions so that you had to keep repeating the same answers. Or perhaps a salesperson pulled together a proposal for you but forgot to include your preferred customer pricing in the quote. Or maybe a credit card company mailed you an application for a new account, even though you've had an account with that company for 10 years. You probably thought to yourself, "Why doesn't this company know who I am?" Do any of these situations sound familiar?

As its name implies, the goal of *customer relationship management* (CRM) is to enable businesses to better manage each and every customer experience. More important, CRM strategy recognizes that customer experiences span over time and that a typical customer might interact with your business 50 to 100 times in the course of your relationship. Ideally, your company could provide each customer a personalized experience based on the customer's unique history of interactions with you. For example, when customers call your service department, you wouldn't have to ask them to answer the same questions over and over again; your most valuable customers would always receive preferred pricing; and you wouldn't ask longstanding customers if they would like to open an account.

Important The purpose of CRM is to enable businesses to track and manage all of their customer interactions over the lifetime of the customer relationship. CRM is a business strategy, and companies typically use a CRM software system as a technology platform to help implement their CRM strategy, processes, and procedures.

In today's competitive business environment, mistreated customers can easily find other vendors or suppliers that are eager to replace you. However, if you give your customers a personalized experience, they're more likely to value their relationship with you and continue to patronize your business. The CRM philosophy makes so much sense, so why do so many companies force good customers to suffer through bad experiences every day?

As you probably know, it's very difficult for companies to embrace a CRM strategy and create consistently great customer experiences. Some of the factors that make a CRM strategy difficult to implement include the following:

- **Multiple customer management systems** Almost every company uses more than one system (such as sales tracking, warehouse management, or financial accounting) to run its business. Most of these systems can't easily communicate with each other to seamlessly share data. Therefore, you can imagine how salespeople using a sales tracking system might not know that a customer just opened an urgent customer service issue in your customer service system.
- **Remote workers** Even if your company is lucky enough to use a single system to track all of your customer interactions, remote and offsite workers may not have the ability to access data in the customer management system.
- **Rapidly changing business processes** You may recognize the saying, "The only thing constant in life is change," by French author François de la Rochefoucauld. This expression really hits home in regard to the business processes of our Internet-enabled world. No sooner does a company finalize a customer management process than it must reconsider how that methodology will change in the next month, quarter, or year. Rapidly changing business processes challenge employees to adjust quickly, but most CRM systems can't react and do not adjust as quickly as the changing business requirements.
- **Multichannel customer interactions** Customers expect to be able to work with your company using their preferred communication channel. With the proliferation of different technologies, these customer communication channels can include websites, phone, mobile, fax, email, mail, and instant messaging. If a company wants to track all of a customer's interactions, its customer management system must work with each of these technologies.

- **Difficult and rigid systems** Adopting a CRM strategy usually requires a company to select a technology system as its customer management platform. Earlier CRM systems earned the reputation of being difficult to use and complex to install. Even worse, companies could only customize their CRM systems to their business needs if they invested large sums of money and time in consultants who could customize the software for them.

CRM isn't a particularly new concept and it has earned somewhat of a bad reputation among businesses. These are just some of the reasons responsible for its less-than-stellar track record over the years.

What would happen if a company *could* successfully implement a CRM strategy and software? What types of benefits would the company receive?

- CRM could track customer interests and purchase history over time, and then proactively generate new marketing initiatives for customers based on their unique histories.
- CRM could log a history of a customer's service requests so that a service technician could easily view all of those requests when the customer calls with a new issue. Reviewing a customer's service history might help the technician resolve the customer's new issue much faster.
- A manager could view all of the interactions with a customer across sales, marketing, customer service, and other functions. People typically refer to this cross-functional history as a *360-degree view* of the customer.
- Marketing managers could analyze and report on the effectiveness of their marketing lists and campaigns to determine how they should reallocate future marketing investments.
- An analyst could use business intelligence tools to segment customers and prospects to identify trends and create predictive models for sales and customer service planning.

This list doesn't include all of the benefits of CRM, but it's clear that a successful CRM implementation can provide many short- and long-term benefits for any business.

Introducing Microsoft Dynamics CRM

Microsoft saw the need for a better CRM software platform and created a solution called *Microsoft Dynamics CRM*. Microsoft designed this software for companies of all sizes to use as their technology platform for implementing CRM strategies. The first version of the software was released in late 2002 and Microsoft has since continued to update the software with new releases and features. This book covers the latest release of the software, Microsoft Dynamics CRM 2011, in addition to Microsoft's hosted offering named Microsoft Dynamics

CRM Online (available at *http://crm.dynamics.com*). This chapter gives you a brief overview of the Microsoft Dynamics CRM software to explain how it helps companies implement CRM strategies. We discuss the following topics:

- Distinguishing Qualities of Microsoft Dynamics CRM
- Licensing
- Connector for Microsoft Dynamics CRM
- System Requirements

After we cover Microsoft Dynamics CRM from a high-level perspective, the subsequent chapters explain how you can configure, customize, and extend the software to meet your company's unique business needs.

More Info This book explains how to configure and customize the Microsoft Dynamics CRM software, but we do not instruct you on CRM strategies because they can vary widely by industry and company size. If you're interested in learning more about the philosophies and methodologies behind CRM, we suggest that you read one of the many books that discuss these topics in a non-software-specific manner. We wrote this book for people who are responsible for managing and deploying Microsoft Dynamics CRM.

Distinguishing Qualities of Microsoft Dynamics CRM

Customers investing in CRM software have plenty of vendors from which to choose. The latest Forrester Wave report on CRM included evaluations of more than 20 different CRM solutions. Most of these solutions offer similar core functionality around sales, marketing, and customer service. So what makes Microsoft Dynamics CRM unique? Let's review some of the key points of difference of Microsoft Dynamics CRM compared to other CRM products. Unlike other solutions, Microsoft Dynamics CRM:

- Provides customers a choice of deployment options (on-premises, Microsoft-hosted or partner-hosted).
- Offers a better end-user experience through tight integration with Microsoft Office products.
- Uses existing investment in Microsoft cloud and platform technologies.
- Includes a highly configurable and extensible development framework.
- Offers simple and straightforward licensing and pricing.
- Lets your .NET developers use their existing development tools and languages.

Provides Customers a Choice of Deployment Options

One of the most obvious benefits Microsoft Dynamics CRM offers customers is the power of choice with regard to how you purchase and deploy the software. Customers can obtain and deploy Microsoft Dynamics CRM using one of three methods:

- Purchase perpetual software licenses and deploy the software on premises
- Pay for the software on a hosted basis through Microsoft Dynamics CRM Online
- Pay for the software on a hosted basis through a Microsoft hosting partner

For the most part, all three deployment options offer nearly identical functionality, so customers can select which model they want based on their personal preference. However, some differences do exist.

One of the main differences between on-premises and Microsoft Dynamics CRM Online deployments is that Microsoft Dynamics CRM Online uses Windows Live ID for user authentication, and on-premises uses Active Directory.

More Info Microsoft Dynamics CRM Online currently uses Windows Live ID as the authentication method, but we expect that Microsoft will eventually offer customers the option to federate their Active Directory security with their Microsoft Dynamics CRM Online deployment. By doing so, Microsoft Dynamics CRM Online customers could eliminate the need for Windows Live ID.

In addition, Microsoft Dynamics CRM Online and on-premises deployments differ by the level of access customers have to underlying servers running the application. Because Microsoft Dynamics CRM Online is a hosted offering and many customers share the same infrastructure, Microsoft restricts each customer's access to servers and databases for security purposes. This same access constraint applies not just to Microsoft, but to any hosted CRM software. Consequently, customer interactions with the application infrastructure must take place through the web interface or through the application programming interface (API). For most customers, this restricted access does not pose any issue because they don't need to access the application servers or database directly. However, customers with highly complex Microsoft Dynamics CRM needs should consider how this Microsoft Dynamics CRM Online constraint might impact them.

More Info One other difference between Microsoft Dynamics CRM Online and on-premises deployments is that custom SQL Server Reporting Services reports must use FetchXML instead of supporting SQL queries. Again, this constraint exists for security purposes so that customers can't run harmful SQL queries in the shared hosting environment. Refer to Chapter 13, "Reports and Dashboards," for more information on writing custom SQL Server Reporting Services reports in Microsoft Dynamics CRM 2011.

Microsoft's multiple deployment choices makes Dynamics CRM unique compared to competing CRM products. Most solutions offer only one deployment option, which limits customers' choices and flexibility. Microsoft Dynamics CRM also offers customers the choice to switch from one deployment model to another if their needs change. For example, a customer might start with a hosted deployment and then switch to on-premises software later. Because the products are nearly identical, Microsoft Dynamics CRM makes this type of transition possible.

Offers a Better End-User Experience through Tight Integration with Microsoft Office Products

Most customers select the Microsoft Dynamics CRM platform over competitors because of the tight integration it offers with Microsoft Office products. Earlier CRM systems forced users to track information in multiple systems because the CRM software didn't include all of the functionality that users need to complete their jobs, such as email, calendaring, task management, and spreadsheets. People performed their work using productivity tools such as Microsoft Office Outlook, Microsoft Office Excel, and Microsoft Office Word, but then they had to copy customer data into their CRM system. This extra step caused negative user feedback, and it's easy to understand why—it slowed down processes, created additional work, and forced users to learn an entirely new tool.

To address this problem, Microsoft Dynamics CRM works directly in Microsoft Office applications such as Outlook so that users can perform their usual job functions *and* track data in Microsoft Dynamics CRM at the same time. A special Outlook add-in, Microsoft Dynamics CRM for Outlook, allows users to access CRM records and perform key actions directly within Outlook. Many users prefer to access their CRM data by using this Outlook add-in instead of using the web client because they are already working in Outlook to manage email and perform other tasks. Figure 1-1 shows how you can access Microsoft Dynamics CRM data directly within Microsoft Office Outlook.

If your users know how to use Outlook, they already know how to use the key customer management tools in Microsoft Dynamics CRM, such as contacts, tasks, appointments, and email. Figure 1-2 shows the Microsoft Dynamics CRM toolbar used to compose an email message in Outlook. By clicking the Track in CRM button in the ribbon, users can quickly save a copy of the message to the Microsoft Dynamics CRM database.

This tracking concept applies not only to email messages, but also to appointments, contacts, and tasks. By offering this native Outlook experience to users, Microsoft Dynamics CRM lets users work with their usual tools *and* easily manage CRM data.

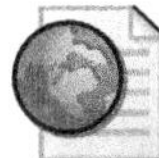

Real World Believe it or not, many companies still require their employees to copy information from Outlook email messages and paste it into their CRM systems. It sounds crazy, but this process is implemented at many companies, both big and small. Microsoft Dynamics CRM for Outlook eliminates the need for this extra work.

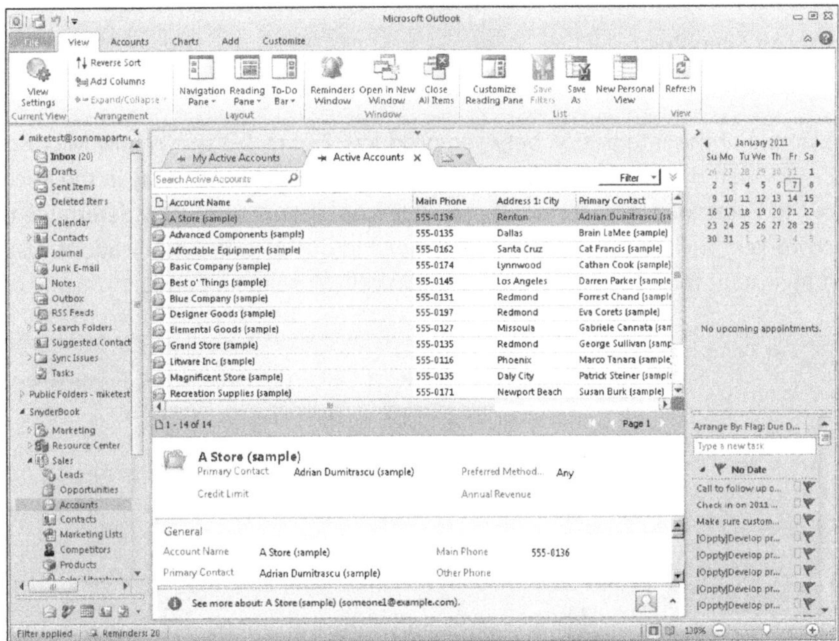

FIGURE 1-1 Tracking Microsoft Dynamics CRM data in Microsoft Office Outlook

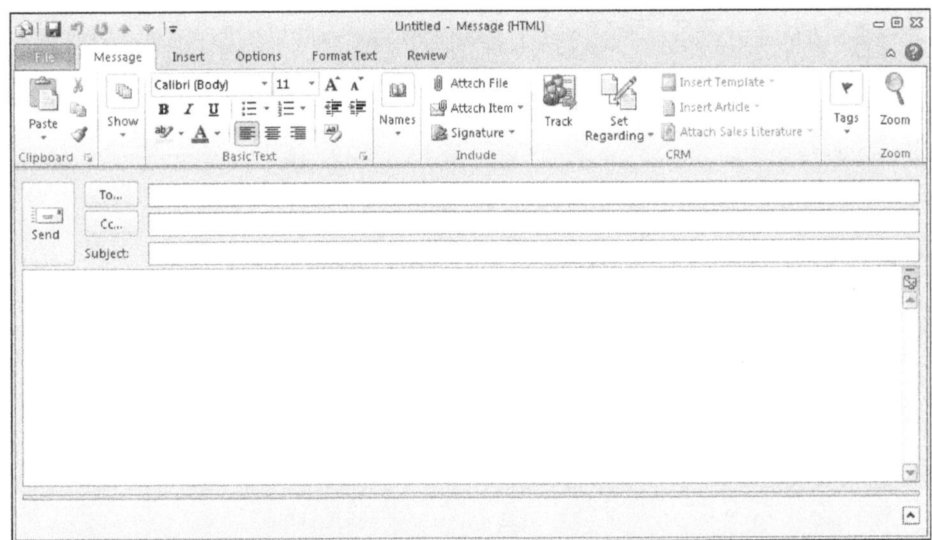

FIGURE 1-2 The Track in CRM button for saving data to Microsoft Dynamics CRM

Beyond Outlook, Microsoft Dynamics CRM also integrates directly with additional business productivity tools, such as:

- Microsoft Office Excel
- Microsoft Office Word
- Microsoft Exchange Server
- Microsoft SharePoint
- Microsoft Lync

As one example of this integration between products, Figure 1-3 shows how Microsoft Dynamics CRM can display the Microsoft Lync presence indicator directly in the Microsoft Dynamics CRM user interface. From the presence icon, users can quickly determine the status of their coworkers, including schedule availability and out-of-office notifications. Users can also start an instant message conversation, audio call, or online meeting.

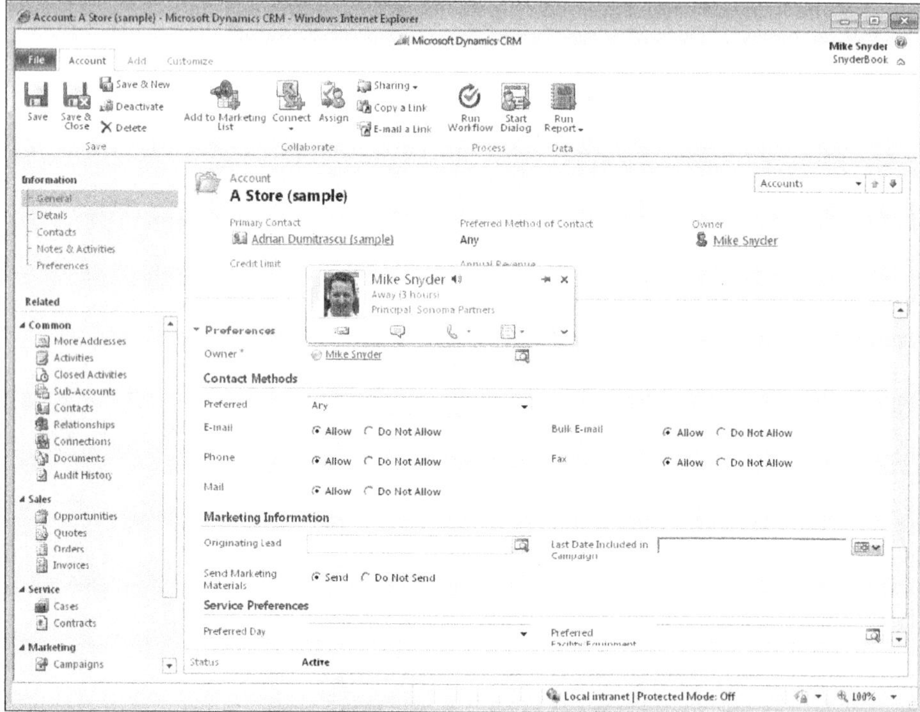

FIGURE 1-3 Microsoft Dynamics CRM integrating with Microsoft Lync to display user presence and additional actions

We explain the details of Microsoft Dynamics CRM integration with Excel, Word, SharePoint, and Exchange Server in later chapters.

By providing a tight integration with tools your users already know, Microsoft Dynamics CRM provides a more rapid learning curve to ensure maximum user adoption when compared to competing CRM products.

Uses Existing Investment in Microsoft Cloud and Platform Technologies

If you're in the information technology (IT) department, we're sure you've worked with some difficult systems. Maybe the software used a proprietary database format that only three people in the world understand, or maybe the software was so fragile that you didn't want to upgrade it for fear of breaking it. Microsoft Dynamics CRM is designed to work with the existing Microsoft tools, applications, and infrastructure that IT professionals use every day. If your organization is already running Microsoft's infrastructure technologies such as Windows Server, SQL Server, Exchange, and Active Directory, operating and maintaining Microsoft Dynamics CRM will be very familiar and comfortable for you. Beyond the typical Microsoft platform technologies, Microsoft Dynamics CRM also offers easy options to work with Microsoft's Azure cloud platform using the Azure Extensions for Microsoft Dynamics CRM.

For user authentication, Microsoft Dynamics CRM uses industry-standard network management technologies. The on-premises version of Microsoft Dynamics CRM uses Microsoft Active Directory services and Integrated Windows authentication for user and password management. This means users don't need a separate login and password to access Microsoft Dynamics CRM. By using existing security technologies, Microsoft Dynamics CRM simplifies access for users and minimizes IT's administration requirements. Most competing CRM products have their own proprietary user authentication technology that requires users to remember and maintain separate logins and passwords just for their CRM system.

Note Microsoft Dynamics CRM Online uses Windows Live ID for user authentication. Windows Live ID is a single sign-on service that you can use for many other online services such as Windows Live Hotmail and Messenger.

For its database, Microsoft Dynamics CRM uses Microsoft SQL Server. By doing so, Microsoft Dynamics CRM customers can benefit from all of the great functionality Microsoft SQL Server offers, such as:

- Enterprise performance and scalability
- Robust failover and disaster recovery options
- Excellent business intelligence and reporting capabilities

Customers that deploy Microsoft Dynamics CRM have a level of comfort that the underlying SQL database platform will satisfy the most complex and demanding requirements.

For its application server, Microsoft Dynamics CRM uses Microsoft Windows Server and Internet Information Services (IIS). IIS is a widely used web server technology that offers great security, ease of management, and high levels of performance. Administrators who already understand IIS can easily set up and troubleshoot Microsoft Dynamics CRM deployments. With Microsoft Dynamics CRM, you can split the various server roles (such as the Organization Web Service, Web Application Server, and Help Server) onto different servers to distribute the application load. Splitting the Microsoft Dynamics CRM server roles to different computers can be appropriate for customers with large or complex deployments.

For email, Microsoft Dynamics CRM provides integration with Microsoft Exchange Server, but also supports any Post Office Protocol 3 (POP3) email system for incoming mail and any Simple Mail Transfer Protocol (SMTP) email system for outgoing mail.

Finally, Microsoft Dynamics CRM supports a wide variety of automation, such as command-line install and Terminal Services. Microsoft Dynamics CRM also supports thin-client environments such as Citrix and roaming profiles.

Includes a Highly Configurable and Extensible Development Framework

Just like most of the competing CRM products, Microsoft Dynamics CRM offers excellent core CRM capabilities for sales, marketing, and customer service. Customers with core CRM needs can be up and running very quickly with Microsoft Dynamics CRM.

For customers looking to build more complex solutions with requirements that extend beyond sales, marketing, and customer service, Microsoft Dynamics CRM offers an excellent development framework compared to other CRM products. Some of the key customization capabilities in Microsoft Dynamics CRM include:

- Point-and-click customization interface for forms, fields, system views, dashboards, and charts.
- Plug-in model that allows customers to develop custom .NET assemblies to execute complex business logic.
- Web service interfaces to help simplify integration with external systems and applications.
- User interface customization tools that allow customers to streamline the system to meet their specific needs.
- Solution framework that supports ease of bundling, moving, and upgrading different customization sets across systems.
- Workflow engine and web-based workflow rule designer to automate business processes.

- Client extensions and scripting framework to implement business logic on forms.
- Custom reporting, visualization, and dashboarding capabilities that allow customers to provide powerful business intelligence and analysis about their Microsoft Dynamics CRM data.

Section 2 of this book, "Solutions," covers system customizations in exhaustive detail.

xRM Framework

Sometimes customers and Microsoft refer to customizations beyond the core CRM capabilities of sales, marketing, and customer service as *xRM*, or extended CRM. This name comes from the idea that although the *C* in CRM stands for *customer*, *X* is a variable that could be equal to any relationship that needs to be managed, such as vendors, employees, prospects, and dealers, as well as other types of business relationships including properties, assets, projects, grants, and legislation.

Please note that there is *not* a different product or SKU for xRM. Customers building these types of deployments use the exact same Microsoft Dynamics CRM product edition as customers deploying core CRM.

Offers Simple and Straightforward Licensing and Pricing

It might surprise you to learn that Microsoft Dynamics CRM offers some of the simplest licensing and pricing options in the CRM industry. For customers who want to purchase the software and deploy it on-premises, there are just two editions:

- Microsoft Dynamics CRM 2011 Server
- Microsoft Dynamics CRM Workgroup Server 2011

The Microsoft Dynamics CRM 2011 Server edition includes all of the available functionality, including support for multiple organizations, multiple server instances, and role-based server deployments.

The Microsoft Dynamics CRM Workgroup Server 2011 is limited to a maximum of five users. This limit means that very few customers will purchase this edition because they might outgrow it. Consequently, almost every customer who purchases Microsoft Dynamics CRM 2011 for on-premises deployment will select Microsoft Dynamics CRM 2011 Server. Other CRM solutions have complex edition options with varying levels of functionality and pricing. Many customers appreciate Microsoft's simple and straightforward approach to its editions. They purchase one edition and they know it will support all of their needs going forward without any surprises or upcharges later.

For customers that deploy Microsoft Dynamics CRM Online, Microsoft follows a similar licensing approach as the on-premises edition. Microsoft Dynamics CRM Online offers one pricing option called *Microsoft Dynamics CRM Online Professional.* This edition is currently priced at $44 per user per month, and it includes all available functionality, such as:

- 5 GB of storage
- Access to Microsoft Dynamics CRM for Outlook (both online and offline capable versions)
- Full integration capabilities
- Workflow and automation
- Customer support and training

Again, many competing CRM solutions have complex editions and pricing models that might require you to purchase an edition significantly more expensive than Microsoft Dynamics CRM Online. We'll discuss licensing of Microsoft Dynamics CRM in more detail later in this chapter.

Lets your .NET Developers use their Existing Development Tools and Languages

For Microsoft Dynamics CRM customers that develop programming customizations for their system, Microsoft Dynamics CRM offers a big benefit by using .NET technologies. Because .NET is one of the most widely used development platforms in the world, many customers already have employees with the tools and skills to develop Microsoft Dynamics CRM programming customizations in Microsoft Visual Studio. Many other competing CRM products require programmers to learn an entirely new programming language or markup syntax specific to their application. The proprietary and niche customization technologies used by competing CRM products can lead to a slower development cycle and higher maintenance costs.

More Info This book focuses on configuring and customizing Microsoft Dynamics CRM, but we do not cover the software installation and related troubleshooting because the Microsoft Dynamics CRM 2011 Implementation Guide provides more than 300 pages of information on these topics. You can learn more by downloading the latest version of the Implementation Guide at *http://www.microsoft.com/downloads/.*

Licensing

As mentioned earlier in this chapter, Microsoft Dynamics CRM 2011 offers straightforward licensing options. Let's take a look at the software's licensing in more detail, starting with the on-premises edition.

In addition to purchasing Microsoft Dynamics CRM 2011 Server, you will need to purchase Client Access Licenses (CALs) for each user who accesses the software. Every deployment must include at least one server license, and you must have one CAL for every active user in the system. CALs are typically referred to as user licenses.

Customers can purchase CALs under two models:

- **Named User CALS** The number of user licenses you need depends on the number of *named users* in your system. The CAL is tied to a specific user, and that user can access Microsoft Dynamics CRM from any computer.
- **Device CALs** Under this model, the CAL is tied to a specific device and different Microsoft Dynamics CRM users can access the system, as long as they access it from the same device. Device CALs fit best with multishift operations such as call centers and hospitals.

Important Named user licensing is different from many other software programs that base their licensing on the number of concurrent users. Every active user in Microsoft Dynamics CRM consumes a license, regardless of how often he or she accesses the system or how many users log on at the same time. But don't worry, a system administrator can easily transfer user licenses from one user to another when necessary, such as when a user leaves the company or if an employee takes an extended leave of absence.

Regardless of whether you select the named user or device CAL model, four types of CAL licenses exist:

- **Full** Users with a full CAL have access to all of Microsoft Dynamics CRM as defined by their business unit and security roles. Chapter 3, "Managing Security and Information Access," explains the details of configuring user access.
- **Read-only** Users with a read-only CAL can read data in Microsoft Dynamics CRM, but they cannot modify or delete any records. Some documentation refers to this type of CAL as a *limited user.*
- **Employee Self-Service** Users that need to access Microsoft Dynamics CRM data, but will not use the Microsoft Dynamics CRM user interface or Microsoft Dynamics CRM for Outlook. Employee Self-Service users would be able to access Microsoft Dynamics CRM data through a custom application, web portal, SharePoint, and so on. After they access the data, they are subject to limited privileges (for example, they cannot assign, share, or delete records).
- **Administrative** Users with an administrative CAL can modify the system settings and customize records, but they cannot modify any of the other records in the system. Administrative CALs are free of charge.

If your company deploys a web farm with multiple Microsoft Dynamics CRM web servers, you must have a Microsoft Dynamics CRM 2011 Server license for every web server running Microsoft Dynamics CRM.

Customers that purchase Microsoft Dynamics CRM Online do not need to purchase the Microsoft Dynamics CRM 2011 Server license. Instead, they only need to pay the Microsoft Dynamics CRM Online Professional edition monthly fee for each active user.

External Connector License

If you want to share Microsoft Dynamics CRM data with external users such as your customers or partners, you can purchase an *External Connector License* that allows you to share Microsoft Dynamics CRM data with an unlimited number of third-party users and systems. By using the External Connector License, you do not need to purchase a user license for each external user. For example, you can create an extranet where customers can log on and retrieve Microsoft Dynamics CRM data in real time. You also can create a special website for your partners to enter and update Microsoft Dynamics CRM data. It is important to note that the External Connector License does not apply to your company's employees; it applies only to external users such as customers, partners, and vendors. Internal employees need a Microsoft Dynamics CRM CAL to access data in Microsoft Dynamics CRM.

Important The External Connector License is only a software license—it does not include any software components. Therefore, you must create your own custom portal and authentication mechanism to allow external users to access your Microsoft Dynamics CRM data.

The two primary versions of the External Connector License are:

- **External Connector** Allows external users full read-write access to Microsoft Dynamics CRM data
- **Limited External Connector** Allows external users read-only access to Microsoft Dynamics CRM data

You will need an External Connector License for each server that hosts an external application. If you have multiple servers hosting external applications, you can mix and match the types of connector licenses as necessary.

The following types of users would not qualify for Microsoft Dynamics CRM usage under the External Connector License:

- All internal users
- External users acting in an internal capacity by using the Microsoft Dynamics CRM web client or Outlook client interface

These types of users need to purchase a CAL to access Microsoft Dynamics CRM.

Volume Licensing

You can purchase the Microsoft Dynamics CRM software licenses through various Microsoft licensing programs such as Open Business, Open Value, Select, Enterprise Agreement, and Full-Package Product. We don't go into the details of these programs because they are complex and subject to change, but the key point is that you can purchase the software using whichever licensing program makes the most sense for your business.

Important When you purchase Microsoft Dynamics CRM licenses, you will receive software updates and new version rights at no charge for a period of time after your initial purchase. The length of time that you receive software updates depends on the licensing program you use to purchase the licenses, but it ranges from one to three years. You can continue to receive software updates by purchasing Software Assurance for additional years. If you choose not to renew updates, you will still own the Microsoft Dynamics CRM software licenses in perpetuity.

When you purchase Microsoft Dynamics CRM software licenses through volume licensing programs such as Open Business, Open Value, Select, and Enterprise Agreements, you receive a product key to enter during the software installation. This product key allows you to add as many users as you want, regardless of the number of licenses you actually purchased. Therefore, you should periodically check the number of user licenses you have purchased against the number of active users in your Microsoft Dynamics CRM system because stiff penalties exist for non-compliance with software laws.

Connector for Microsoft Dynamics

Because CRM strategies revolve around tracking and managing customer interactions, CRM applications typically focus on customer touch points in departments such as sales, customer service, and marketing. Some people refer to these customer-interfacing departments as the *front office* of a company. Consequently, you can refer to the departments that support a business's operations but that don't interact directly with customers as the *back office*. Typical back-office departments include information technology, human resources, manufacturing, distribution, and accounting. Most people refer to software applications that help companies manage back-office operations as enterprise resource planning (ERP) applications. Just like CRM systems, implementing ERP applications requires careful and well-planned processes to maximize success.

The Microsoft Dynamics CRM functionality focuses on front-office features, so it doesn't really include any back-office functionality as part of its default installation. Of course, you could customize the Microsoft Dynamics CRM software to include your own back-office functionality, but developing ERP functionality can prove extremely complex and expensive.

Fortunately, Microsoft offers several ERP applications from the same division that created Microsoft Dynamics CRM.

Important In addition to Microsoft Dynamics CRM, the Microsoft Dynamics division offers several ERP software products.

Some of the current Microsoft Dynamics ERP products include:

- Microsoft Dynamics GP
- Microsoft Dynamics SL
- Microsoft Dynamics NAV
- Microsoft Dynamics AX

Each of these products provides rich functionality, and choosing the right ERP product for your business requires careful consideration—well beyond what we can explain in this book. We mention these ERP products so that you know Microsoft offers software for these back-office departments, in case you're interested in automating that part of your business. In addition, Microsoft offers the Connector for Microsoft Dynamics software so that customers can synchronize customer records, orders, and invoices between front-office CRM and back-office ERP systems, as Figure 1-4 illustrates.

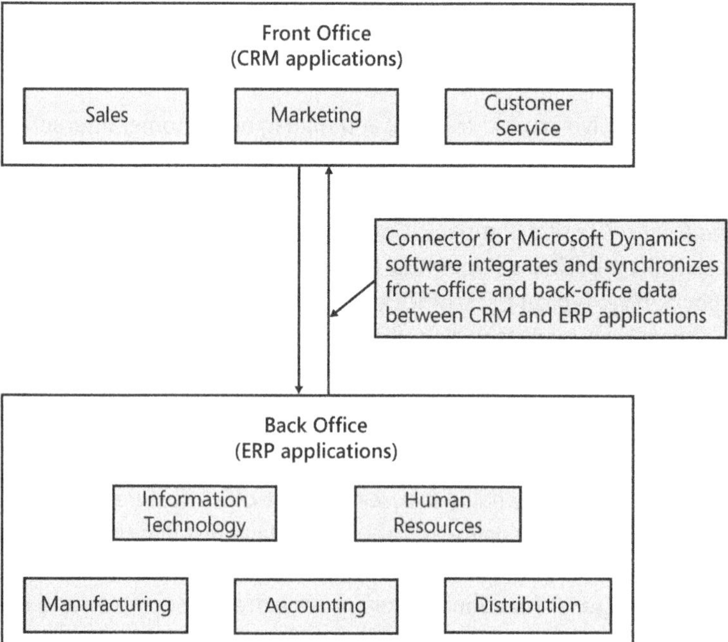

FIGURE 1-4 Microsoft Dynamics CRM synchronization and integration with a back-end system

Note Microsoft previously offered CRM to ERP integration software known as *Microsoft Dynamics CRM Adapter for Microsoft Dynamics GP*, which was developed on the Microsoft BizTalk platform. Microsoft replaced the Microsoft Dynamics CRM Adapter for Microsoft Dynamics GP with the Connector for Microsoft Dynamics. It is a new and different integration software platform, and it does not use Microsoft BizTalk.

In the previous version of Microsoft Dynamics CRM, the Connector for Microsoft Dynamics supported integration with the following ERP products:

- Microsoft Dynamics CRM 4.0, both on-premises and online (minimum Update Roll-Up 5)
- Microsoft Dynamics GP 10.0 Service Pack 4
- Microsoft Dynamics GP2010
- Microsoft Dynamics NAV 2009 R2
- Microsoft Dynamics AX 2009 Service Pack 1

The Connector for Microsoft Dynamics is free of charge to customers with active Microsoft Dynamics ERP Enhancement and Microsoft Dynamics CRM Software Assurance (SA) plans.

At the time this book went to press, Microsoft had not announced the exact timing regarding support for Microsoft Dynamics CRM 2011 or Microsoft Dynamics CRM Online, but we expect both on-premises and Microsoft Dynamics CRM Online will be supported within a few months after the initial software release.

System Requirements

If you use Microsoft Dynamics CRM Online, you don't have to worry about any of the server requirements detailed in this section because Microsoft includes everything you need as part of the monthly hosting fee. However, if you choose to deploy Microsoft Dynamics CRM on-premises or as partner-hosted software, you need to consider the design of your server environment. You have great flexibility in designing and configuring your Microsoft Dynamics CRM environment, and your final system design will depend on several variables, such as:

- The number of servers available and the hardware specifications of each
- The number of Microsoft Dynamics CRM users and their expected system usage
- The hardware specifications of your servers and your local area network performance
- Your network structure and security configurations, including firewalls and virtual private network (VPN) connections
- The amount of disaster recovery and failover systems needed in your deployment

The Microsoft Dynamics CRM 2011 Implementation Guide lists some recommended deployment configurations based on these variables. However, as a general rule of thumb, the Microsoft Dynamics CRM server environment requires the following components:

- Microsoft Windows Server 2008 x64 or Small Business Server 2008 Premium x64 Edition
- Microsoft SQL Server 2008 x64 SP1 or later with SQL Server Reporting Services

Of course, users accessing Microsoft Dynamics CRM must also meet certain minimum hardware and software requirements on their computers. Users need at least Internet Explorer 7 running on Windows XP with Service Pack 3 to access Microsoft Dynamics CRM using the web client. Internet Explorer 8, Internet Explorer 9, Windows 7, and Windows Vista also are supported. Microsoft Dynamics CRM for Outlook requires either Microsoft Office 2003 SP3, Microsoft Office 2007 SP1, or Microsoft Office 2010. We don't include the exact hardware and software specifications in this book because they vary over time as Microsoft releases new versions of its software. Please consult the Microsoft Dynamics CRM website at *http://crm.dynamics.com* or the Implementation Guide for the latest hardware and software requirements.

More Info Some customers ask us about using web browsers other than Internet Explorer, such as Mozilla Firefox or Apple Safari, with Microsoft Dynamics CRM. If you browse to a Microsoft Dynamics CRM website using a browser other than Internet Explorer, you get an error message stating that the browser isn't supported, or possibly even a useless, jumbled page. However, we did find a Firefox extension named IEtab (*http://ietab.mozdev.org*) you can use to render pages in Firefox using the Internet Explorer engine. This trick relies on installing Internet Explorer on the computer because IEtab simply displays an Internet Explorer window in a Firefox shell; therefore, you could argue this doesn't qualify as running Microsoft Dynamics CRM in Firefox. Of course, this configuration is not supported by Microsoft, so we do not recommend deploying it in a production environment. Unfortunately, we have not yet found a trick or workaround to get Apple's Safari browser to display Microsoft Dynamics CRM correctly.

What's New in Microsoft Dynamics CRM 2011

If you're already familiar with Microsoft Dynamics CRM, you probably want to know what's new in Microsoft Dynamics CRM 2011. The comprehensive list of new features is long, but following are some highlights of the key new benefits:

- **Improved Microsoft Office Interface** Microsoft Office 2007 introduced a new ribbon interface in products such as Excel and Word. Microsoft Office 2010 expanded the ribbon into other office products such as Outlook and OneNote. Microsoft Dynamics CRM 2011 also includes the contextual ribbon interface for improved ease of use and consistency with the other Microsoft Office applications.

- **Role-Based Forms and Views** Microsoft Dynamics CRM 2011 allows administrators to create multiple forms for each record type. By doing so, organizations can streamline the user interface so that users only see the data they need to access. For example, sales representatives might see a form filled with sales data about a customer, whereas customer service representatives could view the same customer record but instead see a different form that displays only customer service data.
- **Inline Data Visualization** You can now quickly create charts that display next to records in a grid. For example, you can view a list of opportunities and have a chart to the right that visualizes the estimated revenue of those opportunities. Microsoft Dynamics CRM 2011 also includes web-based tools for you to create and edit your own charts.
- **Dashboards** This feature allows users and administrators to configure dashboards with charts, grids, and possibly even data from external systems. Dashboards can be customized and tailored to each group's or individual's needs so that users can quickly access the information they need.
- **Better Office Outlook Experience** Microsoft Dynamics CRM for Outlook offers even deeper levels of integration with Microsoft Office Outlook. You can now use Outlook features such as filtering and conditional formatting on CRM data, in addition to other new benefits such as inserting CRM templates into Outlook email messages.
- **Contextual Document Management** With Microsoft Dynamics CRM 2011 and Microsoft Office SharePoint Server 2010, you can set up and associate integrated document libraries with specific records. For example, you could open an account record in CRM and access a SharePoint document library with the contracts and other documents related to the account.
- **Field-Level Security** You can toggle security on a custom field and then configure security so that only certain users can view or edit data in that field. This field-level security applies both to forms and data views.
- **Goal Management** Microsoft Dynamics CRM 2011 lets you specify the goals you want individuals or teams to achieve, and then track performance against those goals.
- **Interactive Process Dialogs** You can configure interactive dialogs that work like screen wizards to guide users from page to page, collecting information along the way.
- **Solution Management** Microsoft Dynamics CRM 2011 offers a new way for system administrators to manage their customizations. In particular, solutions allow administrators to group and bundle customizations so that the customizations can be transported to different systems more easily. In addition, solutions can be configured to prevent other users from modifying the changes.
- **Extensibility and Developer Features** Microsoft Dynamics CRM includes a number of new programmer enhancements, including a new programming model using

Windows Communication Foundation (WCF), extended use of Windows Workflow Foundation 4.0, and support for .NET Language-Integrated Query (LINQ).

- **User Interface Enhancements** Microsoft Dynamics CRM 2011 includes multiple user interface enhancements designed to reduce the number of clicks it takes users to accomplish tasks. Some of these enhancements include a recently viewed items list, the ability to tag specific records for quick access, and in-line filtering on data views.
- **Global Customizations** You can now create option sets of values that can be attached to multiple records. For example, you can create a single option set for a list of countries and use that option set on accounts, contacts, and leads (instead of managing three different country picklists, as you did in previous versions of the software). In addition, you can also create globally available JScripts that can be accessed from any entity.
- **Cloud Development** Microsoft Dynamics CRM 2011 includes Azure extensions that help speed development of cloud-based solutions.
- **Connections** This new feature replaces the relationship functionality from previous versions of Microsoft Dynamics CRM. Connections offer more flexibility, allowing users to create their own connections between records. Further, connections can be applied to many different types of entities.
- **Queues** Microsoft Dynamics CRM 2011 extends queue functionality to other record types, instead of limiting it to cases. Queues also now offer better security options and can participate in workflow.
- **Microsoft Dynamics Marketplace** The Marketplace is an online catalog of third-party solutions available for download that you can use in your Microsoft Dynamics CRM system. You can access the Marketplace directly within the Microsoft Dynamics CRM web interface.
- **Teams** Teams can own records in Microsoft Dynamics CRM 2011, whereas only users could own records in previous versions of the software. This opens new options for teamwork and collaboration in the Microsoft Dynamics CRM security model.
- **Auditing** You can now enable auditing on a field-by-field basis, in which Microsoft Dynamics CRM captures each change on a record. The audit feature also captures the date and time of the modification, along with the old and new values of the specified fields.
- **Web Resources** Microsoft Dynamics CRM 2011 allows you to store HTML, Jscript, and Silverlight applications as web resources. System administrators can then use the web resources in form customizations, as well as in the site map or application ribbon.

Although this list only contains a small set of the new features in Microsoft Dynamics CRM 2011, we hope you'll agree that this version of the software offers great new customization and end-user productivity enhancements.

User Interfaces

Microsoft Dynamics CRM is a web-based application built using the Microsoft .NET Framework technology platform. Because of this web architecture, users can access Microsoft Dynamics CRM through the Internet Explorer browser. Figure 1-5 shows the interface.

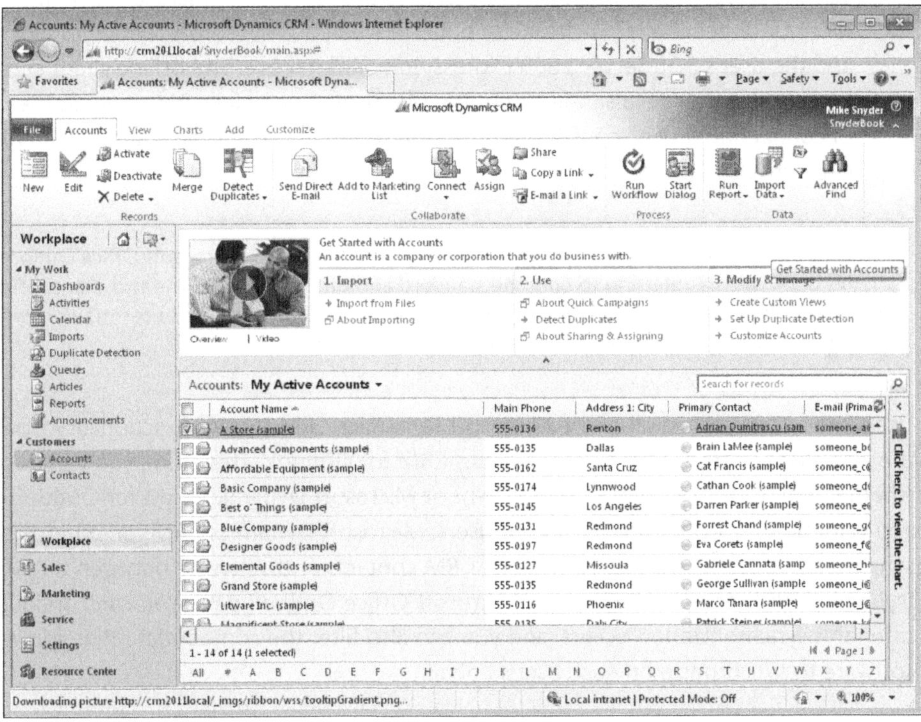

FIGURE 1-5 Internet Explorer interface to Microsoft Dynamics CRM

In addition to the web interface (also known as the *web client*), users can access Microsoft Dynamics CRM by installing the Microsoft Dynamics CRM for Outlook client on a computer running Microsoft Office Outlook. Because Microsoft Dynamics CRM for Outlook is optional, you can pick and choose which users should receive this software on their computer. You can deploy Microsoft Dynamics CRM for Outlook to all, none, or just some of your users. Earlier in this chapter, Figure 1-1 showed the Microsoft Dynamics CRM for Outlook interface. Microsoft Dynamics CRM for Outlook has two versions:

- **Microsoft Dynamics CRM for Outlook** Designed for use with desktop computers that will remain connected to the Microsoft Dynamics CRM server at all times. Use this client for online-only scenarios and when multiple users log on to the same computer using different profiles.

- **Microsoft Dynamics CRM for Outlook with Offline Access** Designed for users of laptop computers who must disconnect from the Microsoft Dynamics CRM server but who still need to work with CRM data when they are offline. The software copies data from the Microsoft Dynamics CRM server to a Microsoft SQL Server 2008 Express edition database installed on the user's computer so the user can work while disconnected. When the user reconnects to the server, the Microsoft Dynamics CRM client bi-directionally synchronizes data between the Microsoft Dynamics CRM server and the user's SQL Server 2008 Express edition database. The offline client can be used by only one user on a single computer. Microsoft Dynamics CRM refers to the processes of connecting and disconnecting from the server as *going offline* and *going online*, respectively.

Note When we reference the Microsoft Dynamics CRM client for Microsoft Office Outlook in this book, we are referring to *both* the standard and offline versions. The two clients offer nearly identical functionality, except the version with offline access allows users to work while disconnected from the Microsoft Dynamics CRM server.

Users can access almost all of the Microsoft Dynamics CRM system functionality from either the web client or from Microsoft Dynamics CRM for Outlook. Therefore, you can decide whether you want to deploy the web client or Microsoft Dynamics CRM for Outlook or if you want to offer both options to your users. Microsoft Dynamics CRM for Outlook can synchronize a user's Microsoft Dynamics CRM contacts and activities between the Microsoft Dynamics CRM server and the user's Microsoft Office Outlook data. You can configure how often this synchronization occurs, and you can also filter the contact data that you want the software to synchronize on each user's behalf.

More Info In addition to the user interfaces, Microsoft Dynamics CRM includes additional tools for administrators to set up and manage the deployment. We cover some of the tools, such as the Microsoft Dynamics CRM Data Migration Manager and the E-mail Router, in Chapter 2, "Setup and Common Tasks."

Microsoft Dynamics CRM also offers a mobile user interface known as Mobile Express. If you need to access your Microsoft Dynamics CRM system while you are out of the office or away from a computer, you can use the Mobile Express module to access the system with an Internet-enabled device such as a cell phone. Mobile Express displays web pages in a streamlined format specifically designed to work on small screens and with a wide variety of mobile web browsers so that you can access the system from most Internet-enabled cell phones—even devices that do not use Microsoft software. Figure 1-6 shows the Mobile Express interface.

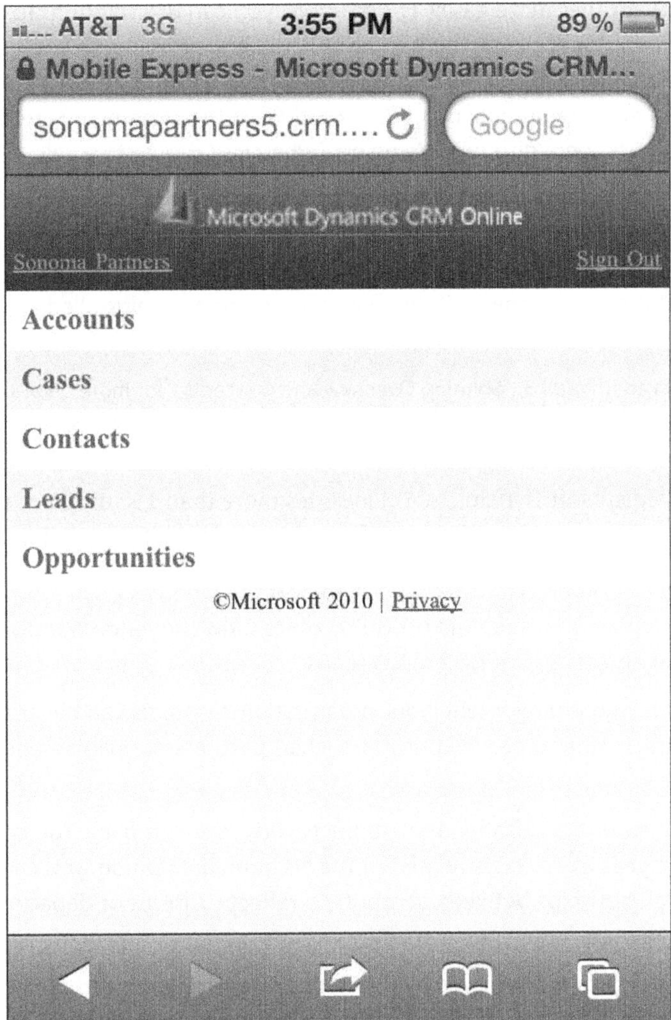

FIGURE 1-6 Microsoft Dynamics CRM Mobile Express interface

Entities and Solutions

Microsoft Dynamics CRM uses the term *entities* to describe the record types it uses throughout the system. The concept of entities is easily one of the most important concepts to understand before you can customize Microsoft Dynamics CRM. Some people use the term *objects* to describe the concept of entities.

Microsoft Dynamics CRM uses *solutions* to bundle and group system customizations in a single package. Solutions can contain many components, such as entities, dashboards, reports, security roles, and more. By using solutions, you can move your set of customizations from one deployment to another more easily. For example, you can use solutions to move customizations from development to staging to a production environment. In addition, by defining a solution as *managed* you can limit the customizations allowed within a solution. Although you can always edit the original managed solution on the system you created it on, installing a managed solution on a different Microsoft Dynamics CRM system will:

- Prevent the addition or removal of solution components.
- Prevent someone from exporting the managed solution.
- Delete all of its solution components if the managed solution is uninstalled.

More Info Please refer to Chapter 5, "Solution Overview and Concepts," for more details about working with solutions in Microsoft Dynamics CRM.

The initial installation of Microsoft Dynamics CRM includes more than 150 different entities bundled in the default solution. Some of the more frequently used entities include:

- **Lead** A potential customer that can be qualified or disqualified as a sales opportunity. When you qualify (convert) a lead, Microsoft Dynamics CRM can automatically create a related account, contact, and opportunity record.
- **Contact** A person who interacts with your organization. Contacts can be customers, but you can also track other types of contacts, such as partners, suppliers, vendors, and so on.
- **Account** A business or organization that interacts with your company. You can link an account's employees as contacts related to the account. In addition, you can create parent and child relationships between accounts to reflect divisions or departments within a single large account.
- **Case** A customer service incident your organization wants to track and manage until it's successfully resolved.
- **Activity** An action or follow-up item, such as tasks, phone calls, letters, and email messages. You can link activities to an entity to specify what the follow-up item regards.
- **Note** Short text annotations that you can link to various entities throughout Microsoft Dynamics CRM.
- **Opportunity** A potential sale for your organization. After a customer decides whether he or she will purchase from your company, you can mark the opportunity as won or lost.

Microsoft Dynamics CRM uses a *form* to display the data fields of a single entity record, as shown in Figure 1-7. Users can view and update entity records by editing the data that appears on the entity's form.

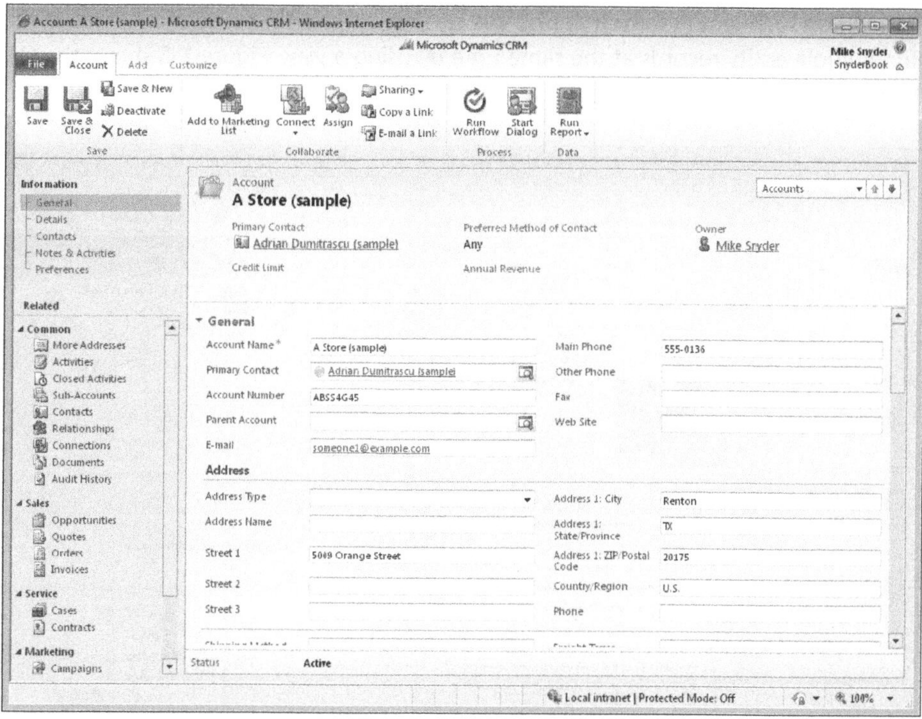

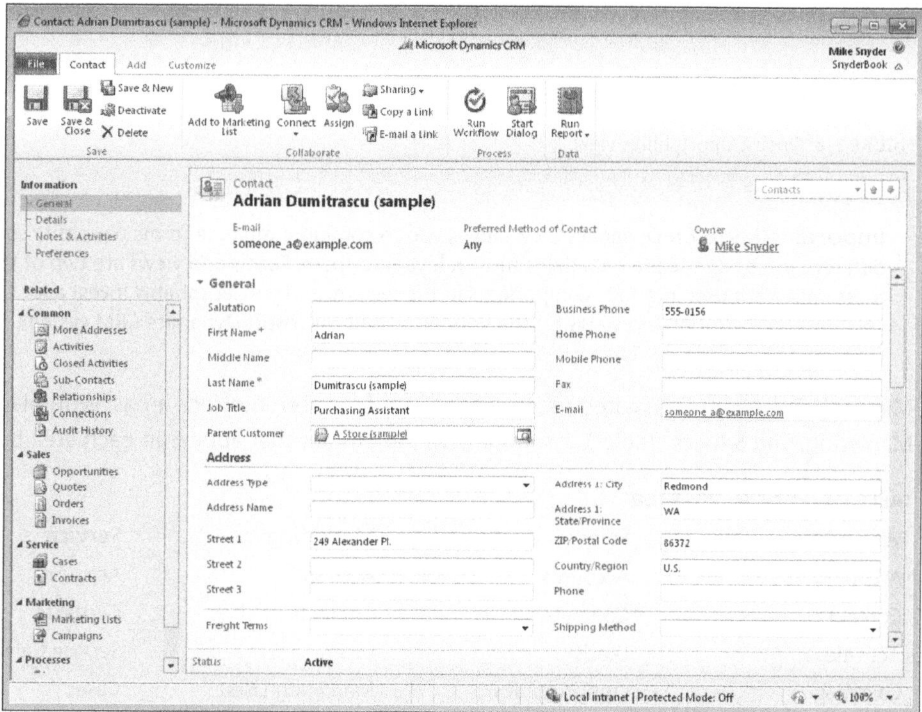

FIGURE 1-7 Account and Contact forms

In addition to an entity form that displays one record at a time, users can retrieve data for multiple entity records at the same time by using a *view*. Figure 1-8 shows the Open Opportunities view in the web client.

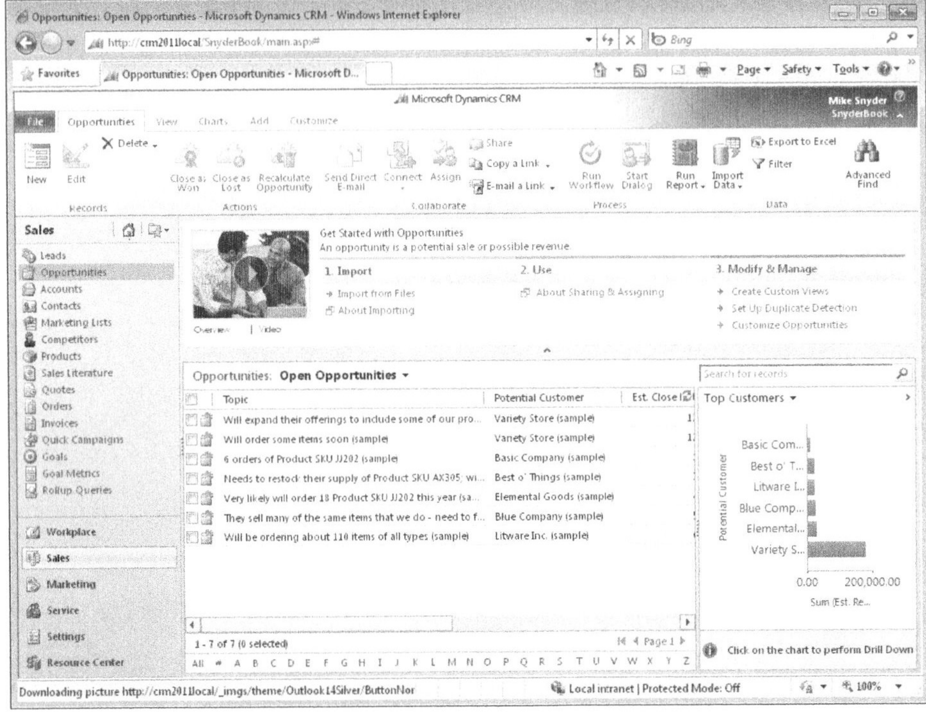

FIGURE 1-8 Open Opportunities view

> **Important** Microsoft Dynamics CRM allows you to configure multiple forms per entity so that different users can see the data fields most relevant to them. Forms and views are two of the most important user interface components in the system, and you'll probably invest a lot of time customizing the forms and views for the entities in your Microsoft Dynamics CRM system.

Microsoft Dynamics CRM categorizes entities into four user interface areas: Workplace, Sales, Marketing, and Service. Table 1-1 summarizes the entities that appear in each area by default.

TABLE 1-1 Entities by Area

Workplace	Sales	Marketing	Service
Accounts	Accounts	Accounts	Accounts
Contacts	Contacts	Contacts	Contacts
Activities	Leads	Leads	Service Calendar
Calendar	Opportunities	Marketing Lists	Cases
Queues	Marketing Lists	Campaigns	Articles

Workplace	Sales	Marketing	Service
Articles	Competitors	Products	Contracts
Reports	Products	Sales Literature	Products
Announcements	Sales Literature	Quick Campaigns	Services
Dashboards	Quotes		Goals
Imports	Orders		Goal Metrics
Duplicate Detection	Invoices		Rollup Queries
	Quick Campaigns		
	Goals		
	Goal Metrics		
	Rollup Queries		

Note You can create new areas in the user interface and change which entities appear in an area by editing the site map. For example, you could edit the site map so that the Announcements entity appears in the Sales and Marketing areas in addition to the Workplace area. Refer to Chapter 12, "Solutions: Client Extensions and Site Map," for more information about editing the site map.

Users primarily work with entity records by using the forms and views in the system. However, system administrators can review all of the configuration data related to an entity, such as its fields, forms, views, and any relationships to other entities in Microsoft Dynamics CRM. Administrators use a web-based solution editor to modify the system configuration data instead of making the changes directly in the Microsoft SQL Server database. By using the solution editor, Microsoft Dynamics CRM automatically performs all of the behind-the-scenes modifications necessary to ensure that the software continues to function properly. Figure 1-9 shows the solution editor.

Important Do not edit the Microsoft Dynamics CRM database directly in Microsoft SQL Server! Doing so will likely cause unexpected results such as loss of data or irreparable damage.

You can customize nearly half of the default entities included in Microsoft Dynamics CRM, but there are some entities that you cannot customize because Microsoft Dynamics CRM uses them to manage the inner workings of the software. Section 2 of this book, "Solutions," goes into great detail about how to customize new and existing entities to meet your business needs.

Important With Microsoft Dynamics CRM, you can customize entities, and you can also create entities to store additional types of data. System administrators use a web-based interface to create and customize entities without having to write a single line of programming code.

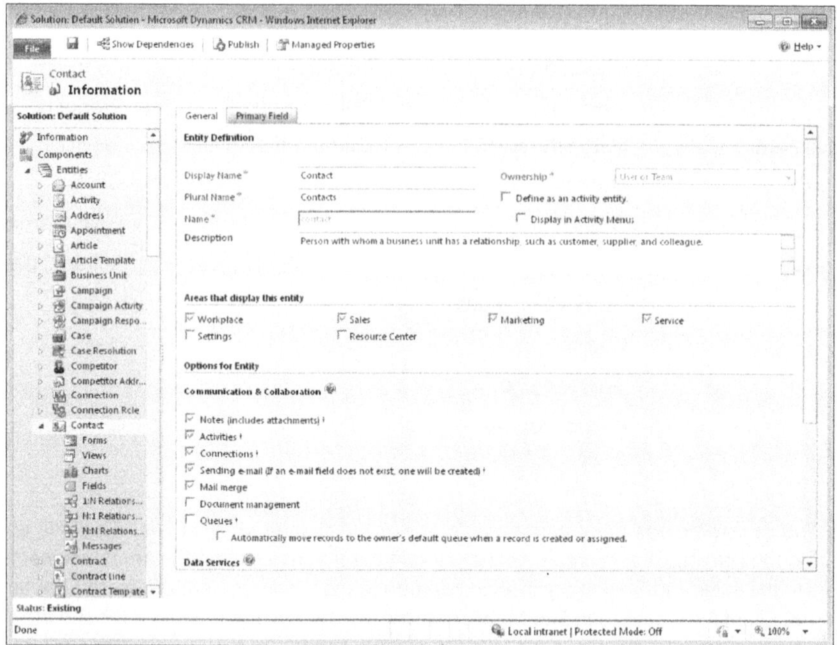

FIGURE 1-9 Solution editor

Supported vs. Unsupported Customizations

Although Microsoft Dynamics CRM provides almost limitless customization options, you might encounter scenarios in which you want to customize the software in a manner not described in this book or in the product documentation. You might hear that these types of undocumented customizations are "unsupported," but what does that really mean? Unsupported customizations could fall into one of three categories:

- Microsoft has not tested the change and can't confirm whether it will cause problems.
- Microsoft has tested the change and knows that it will cause problems.
- The change might not cause problems now, but it might cause problems if you update your software with hot fixes, security updates, or new releases of Microsoft Dynamics CRM.

Unfortunately, you can't really know into which category a particular customization will fall. Therefore, it's possible that an unsupported change won't cause any problems. However, it's more likely that unsupported customizations will cause problems sooner or later, potentially even months after the change is made. If you do experience a problem with an unsupported customization and then call Microsoft technical support, guess what they'll say? "That's unsupported, so we can't assist you." Of course, they are quite friendly people and they may give you a tip or two related to your request, but you should not expect any assistance from Microsoft technical support if you implement unsupported customizations. Some of the most obvious unsupported customizations include the following:

- Manually or programmatically interacting directly with the SQL Server database (other than through filtered views)
- Modifying any of the Microsoft Dynamics CRM .aspx or .js files
- Installing or adding files to the Microsoft Dynamics CRM folders other than those folders explicitly permitted, as defined in the Microsoft Dynamics CRM Software Development Kit (SDK)
- Referencing or decompiling any of the Microsoft Dynamics CRM .dll files

Even though many unsupported customizations are technically possible to implement, you should carefully consider the risks and rewards of doing so. You should anticipate that your unsupported customizations could *possibly* break with Microsoft Dynamics CRM 2011 hotfixes and that they *probably will* break with future versions of Microsoft Dynamics CRM.

Summary

Customer relationship management (CRM) is a strategy that businesses implement to improve the quality of their customer interactions. For companies using existing Microsoft productivity applications like Microsoft Office and SharePoint, Microsoft Dynamics CRM is an excellent choice as the technology platform for implementing CRM strategies. Microsoft Dynamics CRM is designed to address common user and IT complaints related to earlier CRM applications. In particular, Microsoft Dynamics CRM uses all of the common tools that employees already use every day, such as Outlook, Internet Explorer, Word, and Excel. It also uses industry-standard technologies from Microsoft, such as Active Directory, SQL Server, and Exchange Server, to minimize the time required by IT professionals to deploy and manage the software.

Customers have many choices for purchasing and deploying Microsoft Dynamics CRM. For example, customers can purchase perpetual licenses and deploy the software on premises, or they can use Microsoft Dynamics CRM through a web-hosted service such as Microsoft Dynamics CRM Online.

Microsoft Dynamics CRM uses entities as the data storage mechanism for the record types in the software. You can customize many of the default system entities, including modifying forms and views. You can also create custom entities to capture data about new record types unique to your business. In addition to entity customization, Microsoft Dynamics CRM offers a variety of customization and integration options.

Chapter 2

Setup and Common Tasks

In this chapter:

Now that you understand some of the background and benefits of Microsoft Dynamics CRM, we can delve into the details of setup and common tasks in the system. Because companies of varying sizes and industries use Microsoft Dynamics CRM, we'll concentrate on the information that applies to most businesses. At this point, we assume that you have already installed the software and that you can access it from the web client and through the Microsoft Dynamics CRM client for Microsoft Office Outlook. In addition, we also assume that you are at least somewhat familiar with using the Microsoft Dynamics CRM user interface and you understand how to work with records to add activities, notes, and so on.

Tip Installing the Microsoft Dynamics CRM software is a topic beyond the scope of this book. The Microsoft Dynamics CRM 2011 Implementation Guide provides excellent information on this topic. You can download the guide at *http://www.microsoft.com/downloads.*

We want to provide you with more information about the most common end-user activities so that you can help guide users to make the most of your organization's investment in Microsoft Dynamics CRM.

Microsoft Dynamics CRM for Outlook

Without a doubt, the integration that Microsoft Dynamics CRM offers with Microsoft Office Outlook generates the most excitement and interest among our customers and prospects. People love that they can work directly with their customer relationship management (CRM) data in Outlook without needing to open a second software application. Unfortunately, the integration between Microsoft Dynamics CRM and Outlook also generates quite a few questions about how the two systems work together. We expect that you'll get a lot of questions about how the systems work together, too; therefore, we want to give you a detailed look at the integration. We'll cover the following topics in this section:

- Standard versus offline client
- Integration points
- Data synchronization
- Remote workers

In the next section, we also cover how to work with email in Microsoft Dynamics CRM, which includes some overlap with Microsoft Dynamics CRM for Outlook.

More Info This section provides an overview of the Microsoft Dynamics CRM for Outlook client from an administrator perspective. For more details on the end-user experience in Microsoft Dynamics CRM for Outlook, please refer to the book *Microsoft Dynamics CRM 2011 Step by Step* by Microsoft Press.

Standard vs. Offline Client

As you learned in Chapter 1, "Microsoft Dynamics CRM 2011 Overview," Microsoft Dynamics CRM offers two versions of the Outlook client:

- Microsoft Dynamics CRM for Outlook
- Microsoft Dynamics CRM for Outlook with Offline Access

The add-ins offer almost identical functionality, but one version allows users to work offline while disconnected from the Microsoft Dynamics CRM server. Microsoft Dynamics CRM for Outlook with Offline Access uses significantly more system resources than the standard version of Microsoft Dynamics CRM for Outlook. Therefore, we encourage you to install Microsoft Dynamics CRM for Outlook with Offline Access only if you know that the computer and user definitely need to work offline.

With Microsoft Dynamics CRM for Outlook with Offline Access installed, users can click a button to *go offline*. When going offline, Microsoft Dynamics CRM for Outlook with Offline Access copies data from the server to a Microsoft SQL Server 2008 Express edition database located on the computer. The offline client automatically installs this database as part of its installation routine. Users see a progress window indicating the status of the synchronization process (Figure 2-1).

Once offline, users can continue working with Microsoft Office Outlook and Microsoft Dynamics CRM data as usual, but when they view Microsoft Dynamics CRM pages, only data from the local database is displayed.

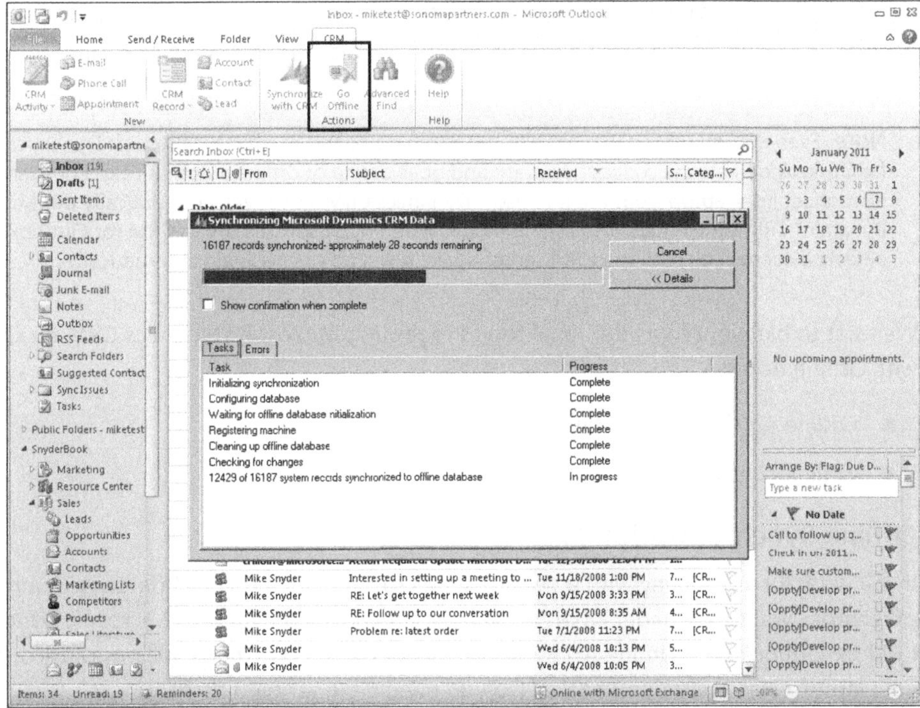

FIGURE 2-1 Users click the Go Offline button and Microsoft Dynamics CRM for Outlook with Offline Access displays a synchronization progress window

More Info When offline, Microsoft Dynamics CRM uses a local web server named Cassini to display the web pages. Cassini is a lightweight web server built on the Microsoft .NET Framework.

Microsoft Dynamics CRM for Outlook with Offline Access performs the offline synchronization process when users click the Go Offline button. If users forget to click the Go Offline button, they can still work with Microsoft Dynamics CRM data offline, but the data may be out of date depending on the last time it was synchronized with the offline database. To avoid this scenario, users can select a setting in the Local Data tab of the Personal Options of Microsoft Dynamics CRM for Outlook so that the system automatically updates local data in the background at regular intervals, such as every 15 minutes.

When users want to connect to the Microsoft Dynamics CRM server, they click the Go Online button. Microsoft Dynamics CRM for Outlook with Offline Access then performs another synchronization process. This process uploads data to the server that the user created or modified while offline. If Microsoft Dynamics CRM encounters a conflict scenario in which a user modified a record on the server while an offline user modified that same record, Microsoft Dynamics CRM uses the record with the latest modified date stamp to determine which record to keep. It automatically keeps one record or the other without prompting the user; it does not merge field-level changes of the two records. Microsoft Dynamics CRM will also fire any asynchronous plug-ins and workflow rules that apply to records created or modified while offline.

Note Even though users can manually choose to go online or offline, Microsoft Dynamics CRM for Outlook detects the connection state and goes online or offline automatically. For example, disconnecting a laptop from the Microsoft Dynamics CRM server will automatically put Microsoft Dynamics CRM for Outlook into offline mode. When Microsoft Dynamics CRM for Outlook detects a connection with the CRM server again, it will go online again automatically.

We want to highlight two additional topics regarding Microsoft Dynamics CRM for Outlook with Offline Access:

- Offline synchronization filters
- Offline constraints

Offline Synchronization Filters

If you work for a company with a very large Microsoft Dynamics CRM database (with millions of records), you may wonder what happens when you go offline with Microsoft Dynamics CRM for Outlook with Offline Access. Does the software copy those millions of records to your laptop? How long does it take? Do you need a bigger hard drive?

Fortunately, users can configure exactly which data they want to download to their computer using the offline synchronization filters. Microsoft Dynamics CRM for Outlook with Offline Access includes predefined filters for the default system entities, as shown in Figure 2-2.

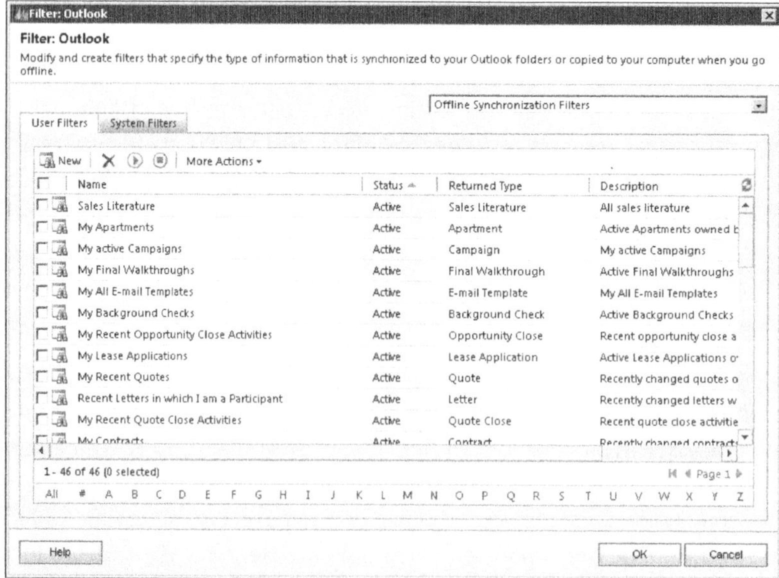

FIGURE 2-2 Default offline synchronization filters installed with Microsoft Dynamics CRM for Outlook with Offline Access

As you can see in Figure 2-2, Microsoft designed the offline synchronization filters to restrict the amount of data the system takes offline. For example, on the Account and Contact entities, the default settings download only active records that you own. Obviously, if you own millions of accounts and contacts, you should be careful about the amount of data you download when you go offline. As you would expect, very large offline data sets negatively affect system performance. To avoid downloading very large offline data sets, modify the offline synchronization filters to only include the records you need while offline.

In addition, the offline synchronization filter settings do not include *any* custom entity records. Therefore, if your users want to work with custom entities offline, you must instruct them on how to include the specified records in their offline synchronization filters. To access the Outlook offline synchronization filters, click the CRM button under File in Microsoft Office Outlook, and then click Outlook Filters under Synchronize, as shown in Figure 2-3.

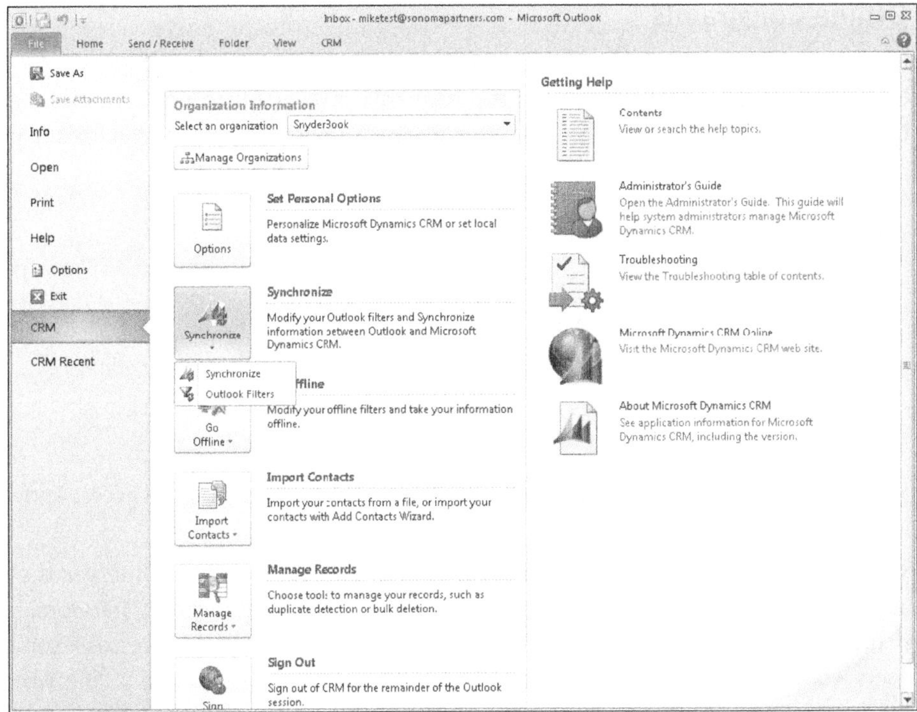

FIGURE 2-3 Accessing the Outlook Filters in Microsoft Dynamics CRM for Outlook

To add filters, click the New button on the grid toolbar. The New Filter form appears, in which you can design a filter using the familiar Advanced Find user interface. Note that there are two types of Outlook filters:

- Outlook synchronization filters
- Offline synchronization filters

As you would expect, the offline synchronization filters determine which data gets copied into the offline database on the client computer. The Outlook synchronization filters specify which records Microsoft Dynamics CRM should copy from the server to your Outlook file. By default, Microsoft Dynamics CRM for Outlook includes Outlook synchronization filters that will copy contacts, phone calls, tasks, and other records that you own from the Microsoft Dynamics CRM server into your Outlook file.

Important You must manually include custom entities in your local data groups if you want to work with those records while offline. Unfortunately, Microsoft Dynamics CRM does not include a web-based tool or mechanism for administrators to modify offline synchronization filters for multiple users at one time. However, this functionality is exposed in the Microsoft Dynamics CRM application programming interface, so you could accomplish this with custom programming.

Offline Constraints

For the most part, both the standard and offline versions of Microsoft Dynamics CRM for Outlook provide nearly identical user experiences. However, Microsoft Dynamics CRM for Outlook with Offline Access does include a few constraints when running in offline mode:

- Workflow rules do not run offline.
- Asynchronous plug-ins do not run offline.
- Duplicate detection does not work offline.
- You cannot import data when offline.
- You cannot access the system settings or customize entities while offline.
- You cannot access the Resource Center when offline.
- You cannot access the service calendar when offline.
- You cannot modify the knowledge base when offline, but you can access knowledge base articles.

When users go back online and connect to the Microsoft Dynamics CRM server, the system applies the appropriate workflow rules for the new or modified records. Therefore, be mindful of creating workflow rules that implement business-critical processes if some of your users work with data offline. Similarly, asynchronous plug-ins do not run offline. Microsoft Dynamics CRM runs asynchronous plug-ins against the appropriate records when users synchronize with the server after working offline. However, you can create synchronous plug-ins that will run offline in Microsoft Dynamics CRM for Outlook with Offline Access.

Integration Points

Now we will review the details about how Microsoft Dynamics CRM for Outlook integrates with Microsoft Office Outlook. Many users prefer to access their CRM data by using Microsoft Dynamics CRM for Outlook instead of using the web client because they are already working in Outlook to manage email and perform other tasks. The Outlook client user interface is a little different from the web client. Figure 2-4 shows the components of the Microsoft Dynamics CRM for Outlook interface.

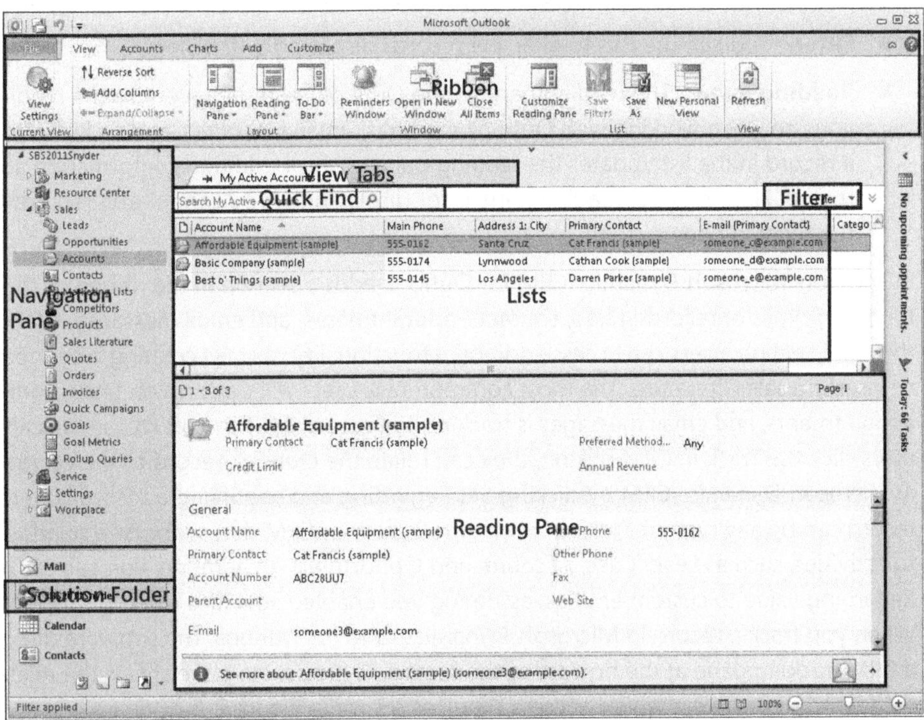

FIGURE 2-4 Microsoft Dynamics CRM for Outlook modifications to Outlook user interface

- **Solution Folder** You will see this button in Outlook after you install the Microsoft Dynamics CRM for Outlook client. Click it to access additional Microsoft Dynamics CRM functionality. The name that appears in this button will match the name of your Microsoft Dynamics CRM organization.
- **Ribbon** Just as in the web client, the ribbon displays different buttons and features depending on the context. For example, if you're viewing a list of accounts, the ribbon displays actions that you can take on account records. If you're viewing a list of contacts, the ribbon will display the actions available for contact records.
- **View Tabs** In this area, you can select the data views with which you want to work. In addition, you can use the view tabs to pin views that you want to quickly access in the future.
- **Lists** Similar to views in the web client, this area displays a list of records. Microsoft Dynamics CRM for Outlook filters the records displayed in the list depending on the view selected in the view tab.

- **Quick Find** Just as in the web client, you can enter a search term in the Quick Find field to search for records. However, unlike the web client version of Quick Find, the Outlook client Quick Find only searches for records in the currently displayed view. The web client Quick Find searches for active records across the entire database.
- **Filter** You can use this to filter the records displayed in the view.
- **Reading Pane** The reading pane in the Outlook client behaves like the reading pane you use when working with Outlook contacts, email messages, and tasks. Selecting a record in the list updates the reading pane to show additional information about that record. Note that the reading pane is for display only; you cannot edit records within the reading pane.

In addition, Microsoft Dynamics CRM for Outlook adds a section in the ribbon of the following types of records: tasks, contacts, appointments, and email messages. Within this CRM section, users can access additional functionality, such as creating a connection or inserting sales literature. The most common task users will perform on tasks, contacts, appointments, and email messages is tracking the record in Microsoft Dynamics CRM. When users click the Track in CRM button, they can relate the Outlook record to the correct record in Microsoft Dynamics CRM by clicking Set Regarding and specifying a record. The regarding record can be any type of entity in Microsoft Dynamics CRM that supports a relationship to activities, such as Lead, Case, Account, and Opportunity. In addition, you can set the Regarding value to custom entities, assuming you enabled activities when creating the entity. When you track a record in Microsoft Dynamics CRM for Outlook, the software displays a CRM tracking pane at the bottom of the record. This tracking pane shows the related CRM records so that you can quickly access them, as shown in Figure 2-5.

By linking email messages, appointments, and tasks to records in Microsoft Dynamics CRM, users can view those Outlook records in the list of activities related to that CRM record. Users can create records in Outlook and track them in Microsoft Dynamics CRM, or the activities can be created on the Microsoft Dynamics CRM server and then synchronized with a user's Outlook file. A typical example of this scenario is creating and assigning a task to a user using workflow (on the server), and then Microsoft Dynamics CRM for Outlook synchronizes that new task with the user's Outlook task list automatically.

Finally, Microsoft Dynamics CRM for Outlook creates an address book that users can access when writing email messages, shown in Figure 2-6. With this Microsoft Dynamics CRM address book, users can quickly access the email addresses of the contacts in the Microsoft Dynamics CRM database without having to open another application to look up that information. To access the address book, click the To or Cc button when creating an email message in Outlook and select the *Microsoft Dynamics CRM Address Book* option in the drop-down list. You can modify which records Microsoft Dynamics CRM for Outlook will synchronize with your address book by changing the settings in the Address Book tab on the Options menu.

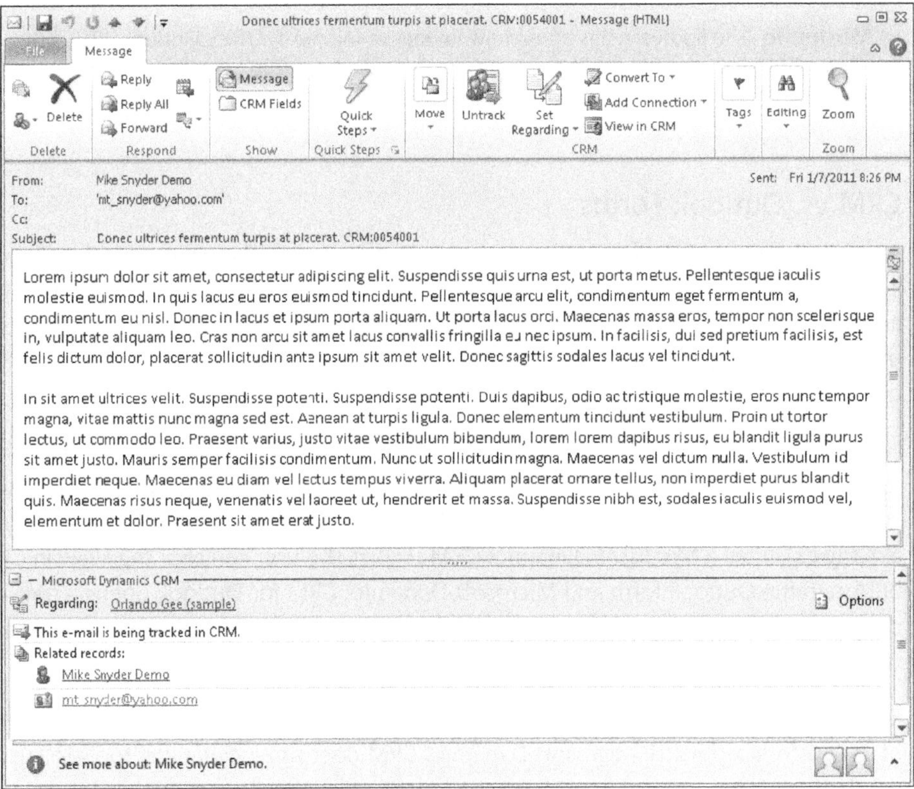

FIGURE 2-5 Tracking an email and setting the Regarding value

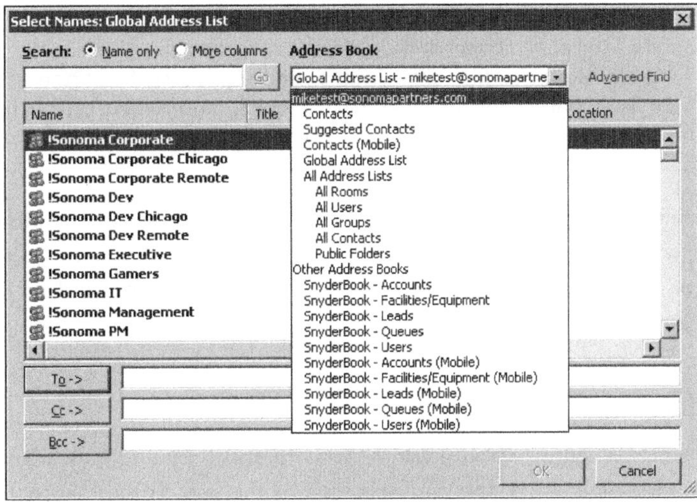

FIGURE 2-6 The address book of Microsoft Dynamics CRM records and email addresses

More Info The figures in this book show images of Microsoft Office Outlook 2010, but Microsoft Dynamics CRM for Outlook also supports Outlook 2007 and Outlook 2003. The user interface for Microsoft Dynamics CRM for Outlook is different for each version of Outlook.

CRM vs. Outlook Forms

As you can see, working with customer records in Microsoft Dynamics CRM for Outlook is really no different from working with standard Outlook records. As we indicated, these are just Outlook forms with the Track in CRM button added. Therefore, users can learn the system quickly and become comfortable tracking data in Microsoft Dynamics CRM right away.

However, some Microsoft Dynamics CRM customers ask about customizing the Outlook forms to capture additional types of data. For example, they might want to display some custom fields on the Microsoft Dynamics CRM Contact entity in Outlook. If the record is already linked to a Microsoft Dynamics CRM record, the user can click the View in CRM button in the Outlook form and Microsoft Dynamics CRM for Outlook opens a new window displaying the full Microsoft Dynamics CRM form, complete with custom attributes and other customizations.

Users should click the View in CRM button to view the Microsoft Dynamics CRM form with all of the customized fields. Microsoft Dynamics CRM does not include any tools to customize the Outlook forms using custom fields, and attempting this type of Outlook customization requires Outlook programming expertise.

Tip If you poke around on the appointment and email forms in Outlook, you'll see that Microsoft Dynamics CRM for Outlook adds a CRM Fields button. If you click this button, you will see any additional CRM fields that do not appear on the Outlook form, including custom fields that you created. The task and contact forms in Outlook do not include the CRM Fields button.

However, you can configure Microsoft Dynamics CRM for Outlook to display the Microsoft Dynamics CRM form when you create a new appointment, task, contact, or email record from the CRM toolbar. You can access these settings by clicking the Options button located under CRM after clicking File in the Outlook ribbon.

Activity Reminders

Outlook includes a reminder feature for tasks and appointments that automatically opens a message window on the date and at the time specified by the user. This reminder is intended to ensure that the user notices the event and doesn't accidentally overlook it. Microsoft Dynamics CRM for Outlook takes advantage of this Outlook feature by automatically creating reminder times for the tasks and appointments created in Microsoft

Dynamics CRM that synchronize with Outlook. The integration works in one of two ways, depending on how the user creates the task or appointment:

- **Activity created in Microsoft Dynamics CRM** Microsoft Dynamics CRM for Outlook automatically specifies the Outlook reminder time. For activities such as tasks and phone calls, the Outlook reminder time matches the activity due date and time. For appointments, Microsoft Dynamics CRM for Outlook will create the reminder time based on the default reminder settings configured for that user in Outlook (none, 15 minutes, 30 minutes, and so forth).
- **Activity created in Outlook and tracked in CRM** For appointments and tasks, users can configure the reminder to suit their preferences. For tasks, the reminder time does not need to match the task due date. For example, users might configure a reminder one day before the task is due.

Microsoft Dynamics CRM does not store the Outlook reminder date and time as attributes of the activities. Therefore, users cannot access the Outlook reminder time on the Microsoft Dynamics CRM activity forms. Additionally, users cannot turn off the automatic reminder for tasks, phone calls, letters, and faxes. Creating any of these activities with a due date creates a reminder in Outlook. The user can modify the Outlook reminder date and time after the activity synchronizes in Outlook, but updating the activity due date and time in the Microsoft Dynamics CRM web client resets the reminder time to match the activity due date and time.

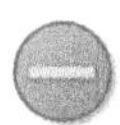

Caution Reminder windows only appear when you're using Outlook; they will not appear in the Microsoft Dynamics CRM web client.

Outlook Web Access

Microsoft Dynamics CRM for Outlook works with Outlook 2010, Outlook 2007, and Outlook 2003; however, it does not support integration with Outlook Web Access. Therefore, if your organization only supports Outlook Web Access, your users cannot access the Microsoft Dynamics CRM integration functionality we have described.

However, if Microsoft Dynamics CRM for Outlook is installed, users can log on to Outlook Web Access and view the Microsoft Dynamics CRM data synchronized with their Outlook file, such as CRM contacts, appointments, and tasks. However, the user will not see the Microsoft Dynamics CRM for Outlook user interface modifications such as the CRM toolbar, the Track in CRM buttons, and the Microsoft Dynamics CRM folders.

Caution Microsoft Dynamics CRM for Outlook does not support integration with Outlook Web Access. To track Outlook data in Microsoft Dynamics CRM and synchronize data between Microsoft Dynamics CRM and Outlook, each user must install Microsoft Dynamics CRM for Outlook on a computer running Outlook 2010, Outlook 2007, or Outlook 2003.

Data Synchronization

The Microsoft Dynamics CRM for Outlook software synchronizes Microsoft Dynamics CRM and Outlook data. Quite impressively, Microsoft Dynamics CRM for Outlook updates data bidirectionally so that users can modify records in either the Microsoft Dynamics CRM web client or Microsoft Dynamics CRM for Outlook. Changes made in either system update the other the next time Microsoft Dynamics CRM for Outlook performs a synchronization.

Data synchronization generates a lot of questions, so we want to explain the following topics:

- Configuring data synchronization
- Deleting records

Configuring Data Synchronization

Earlier in this chapter, you learned how to configure the offline synchronization filters that determine which Microsoft CRM data to copy into the offline database. Using a similar technique, you can configure which CRM data Microsoft Dynamics CRM for Outlook should copy into your Outlook appointments, contacts, and tasks. To access the Outlook synchronization filters, click the CRM button under the File tab in Outlook, then click Outlook Filters under Synchronize to launch the Filter dialog box, as shown in Figure 2-7.

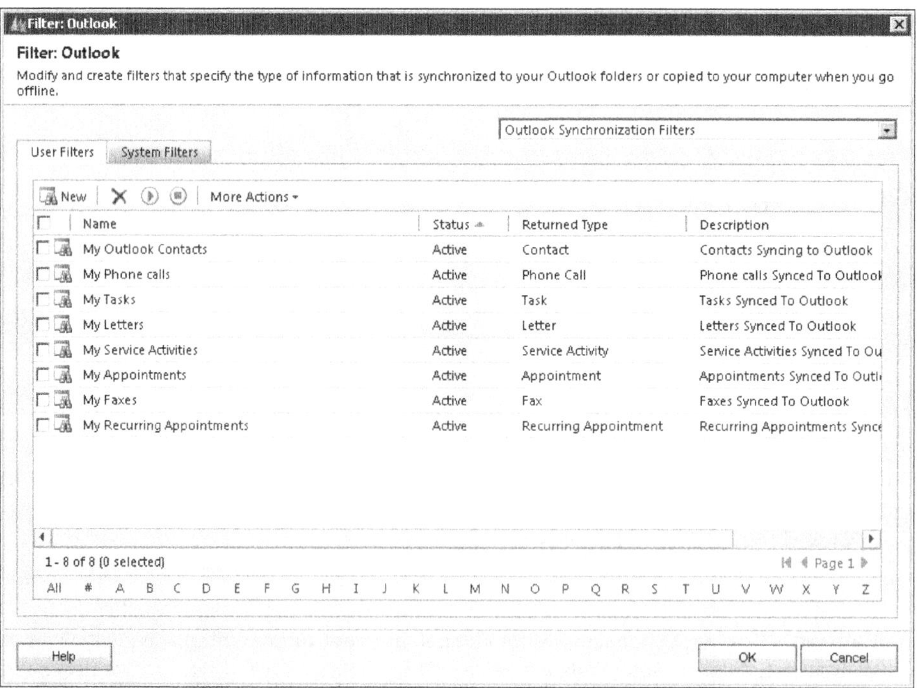

FIGURE 2-7 Microsoft Dynamics CRM for Outlook synchronization filters

In this dialog box, you can modify the default filters or add your own filters to determine which data you want to access in Outlook. By synchronizing the data into Outlook (instead of copying it into the offline database), you can access the data more quickly and easily via mobile devices such as your cell phone. For example, you might want to add a filter that synchronizes all of your customer contacts into Outlook so that when a customer calls your cell phone, the caller ID can show you who is calling!

Important Because Outlook does not contain records for phone calls, letters, or faxes, Microsoft Dynamics CRM for Outlook synchronizes those records into Outlook tasks. Additionally, any record that you create in Outlook and for which you click the Track in CRM button is also included in the synchronization process because you will own that record in Microsoft Dynamics CRM.

In addition to the Outlook synchronization filters, you can also configure the synchronization settings. To access these settings, click the File tab in Outlook, click CRM, and then click Options. When the Set Personal Options dialog box opens, click the Synchronization tab, as shown in Figure 2-8.

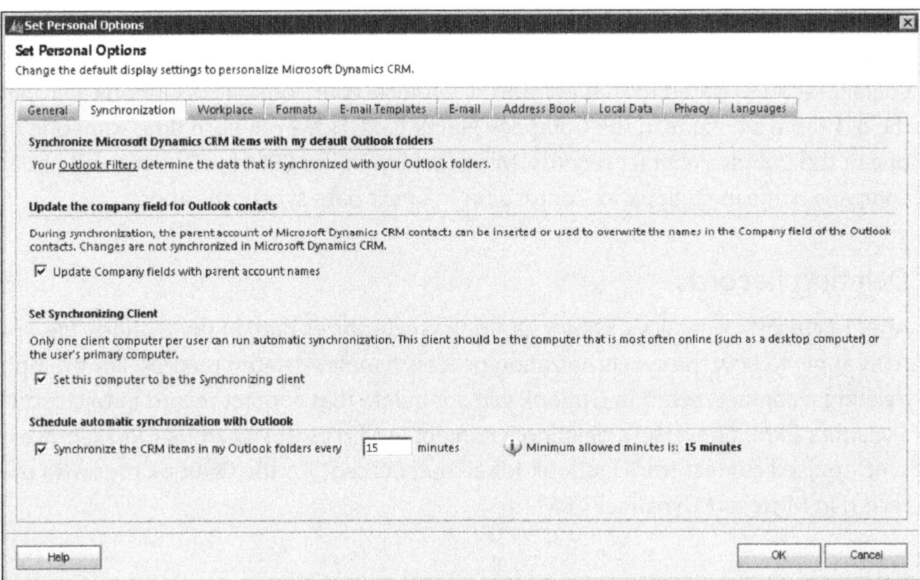

FIGURE 2-8 Microsoft Dynamics CRM for Outlook synchronization settings

If you select the *Update Company fields with parent account names* option, Microsoft Dynamics CRM for Outlook populates the contact's company name in Outlook. Unfortunately, the contact company name behaves differently from the other fields because Microsoft Dynamics CRM for Outlook does not perform a bidirectional synchronization of changes to the contact's company name. If you change a contact's company name in

Outlook, Microsoft Dynamics CRM for Outlook will overwrite that change with the contact's parent account name.

Figure 2-8 also shows that you can configure Microsoft Dynamics CRM for Outlook to synchronize automatically (the default interval is 15 minutes). This scheduled synchronization only applies changes from the server to your Outlook. Conversely, if you change a record in Microsoft Dynamics CRM for Outlook while online, that change will update the Microsoft Dynamics CRM server *immediately*. It does not wait for the next scheduled interval to make the update.

Important Scheduling synchronization applies only to downloading changes from the server to your Outlook file. Changes made to records in Microsoft Dynamics CRM for Outlook when online update the data on the server immediately.

One other important factor you should consider regarding data synchronization is that the Microsoft Dynamics CRM for Outlook software updates your Outlook records only if a record was modified since the last synchronization. For example, assume that an account named Fabrikam has 10 contacts associated with it. As a result of a merger, Fabrikam changes its name to Contoso, Inc. If you update the account name in Microsoft Dynamics CRM, Microsoft Dynamics CRM records a modification to the account record, but it won't alter the contact records related to that account. Therefore, your contacts in Outlook will still have the old Fabrikam name in the Company Name field. However, each time someone updates one of the Contoso contact records, Microsoft Dynamics CRM for Outlook will update the company name in Outlook to Contoso on the next data synchronization.

Deleting Records

After Microsoft Dynamics CRM for Outlook synchronizes data in the Outlook file, special rules apply to how the synchronization process handles deleted records. For example, deleting a contact record in Outlook will *not* delete that contact record in Microsoft Dynamics CRM. Conversely, deleting a contact in Microsoft Dynamics CRM removes the synchronized contact from Outlook for all users except for the Outlook user who owns the record in Microsoft Dynamics CRM.

Important Microsoft Dynamics CRM for Outlook uses different rules and conditions on deleted records to determine how the synchronization process should update Outlook and Microsoft Dynamics CRM.

Microsoft Dynamics CRM for Outlook processes deleted records, as outlined in Table 2-1.

TABLE 2-1 Microsoft Dynamics CRM for Outlook Deletion Processing

Record	Action	Record state	Result
Contact	Delete in Microsoft Dynamics CRM	Any	Deleted from Outlook for all users except contact owner. Remains in Outlook of contact owner.
Contact	Delete in Outlook	Any	No change in Microsoft Dynamics CRM.
Task	Delete in Microsoft Dynamics CRM	Pending (not completed in Outlook)	Deleted from Outlook.
Task	Delete in Microsoft Dynamics CRM	Past (completed in Outlook)	Remains in Outlook.
Task	Delete in Outlook	Pending (open in Microsoft Dynamics CRM)	Deleted from Microsoft Dynamics CRM.
Task	Delete in Outlook	Past (completed or canceled in Microsoft Dynamics CRM)	No change to Microsoft Dynamics CRM.
Appointment	Delete in Microsoft Dynamics CRM	Pending (open in Microsoft Dynamics CRM)	Deleted from Outlook if appointment start time is in the future.
Appointment	Delete in Microsoft Dynamics CRM	Past (completed or canceled in Microsoft Dynamics CRM)	Remains in Outlook.
Appointment	Delete in Outlook	Pending (open in Microsoft Dynamics CRM)	Deleted from Microsoft Dynamics CRM if deleted by appointment owner or organizer. Not deleted from Microsoft Dynamics CRM if deleted in Outlook by non-owners or non-organizers.
Appointment	Delete in Outlook	Past (completed or canceled in Microsoft Dynamics CRM)	No change to Microsoft Dynamics CRM.

When a user deletes a contact in Outlook (which will not be deleted from Microsoft Dynamics CRM), and someone subsequently modifies that contact record in Microsoft Dynamics CRM, Microsoft Dynamics CRM for Outlook will regenerate that contact in the user's Outlook file even though the user previously deleted it.

On a related note, deactivating contact records in Microsoft Dynamics CRM does not remove the contacts from Outlook. Users must manually delete the deactivated contacts if they don't want them to appear in Outlook any longer.

Email in Microsoft Dynamics CRM

As you would expect, Microsoft Dynamics CRM includes several features to help you track and manage email communications with customers. From a high level, Microsoft Dynamics CRM can send and receive email using one of two methods:

- Microsoft Dynamics CRM web client
- Microsoft Dynamics CRM for Outlook

The options available to you depend on your email infrastructure and how the network administrator installed the software. Microsoft Dynamics CRM supports a wide number of email platforms, including Microsoft Exchange Server and any Post Office Protocol 3 (POP3) or Simple Mail Transfer Protocol (SMTP)–compliant email server.

Microsoft Dynamics CRM includes a software application named Microsoft Dynamics CRM E-mail Router that acts as an interface between your email system and Microsoft Dynamics CRM. The Microsoft Dynamics CRM E-mail Router is *not* required for you to install Microsoft Dynamics CRM, but it does offer advanced email routing and tracking features. If for some reason your organization cannot use the Microsoft Dynamics CRM E-mail Router, Microsoft Dynamics CRM for Outlook will perform similar routing and tracking functionality on each client computer. However, because it is a client application, users must keep Microsoft Dynamics CRM for Outlook open for the software to process the email.

More Info Because configuring email and installing the Microsoft Dynamics CRM E-mail Router offer so many different deployment options, explaining these topics is beyond the scope of this book. Please refer to the Microsoft Dynamics CRM Implementation Guide for detailed instructions on how to install and configure the E-mail Router software.

After you configure Microsoft Dynamics CRM to work with your email systems, you should understand these important areas:

- Email tracking
- Email templates
- Creating and sending mass email messages

Email Tracking

After you've successfully configured the email options in Microsoft Dynamics CRM, you should configure automatic email tracking for both the organization and the individual users.

Important All of the email tracking settings we describe apply to the *automatic* tracking of email. Regardless of the settings you choose, users with Microsoft Dynamics CRM for Outlook installed can manually track email using the Track in CRM feature. Some customers prefer to rely on manual email tracking so that the database contains only key email messages, as determined by your users. With automatic tracking, Microsoft Dynamics CRM captures all of the messages, even if they are just short email replies, personal notes, out-of-office replies, and so forth.

Organization Settings

You can access the organization email settings in the E-mail tab of the System Settings dialog box, shown in Figure 2-9. To access the system settings, open the web client, navigate to the Settings area, and then click Administration.

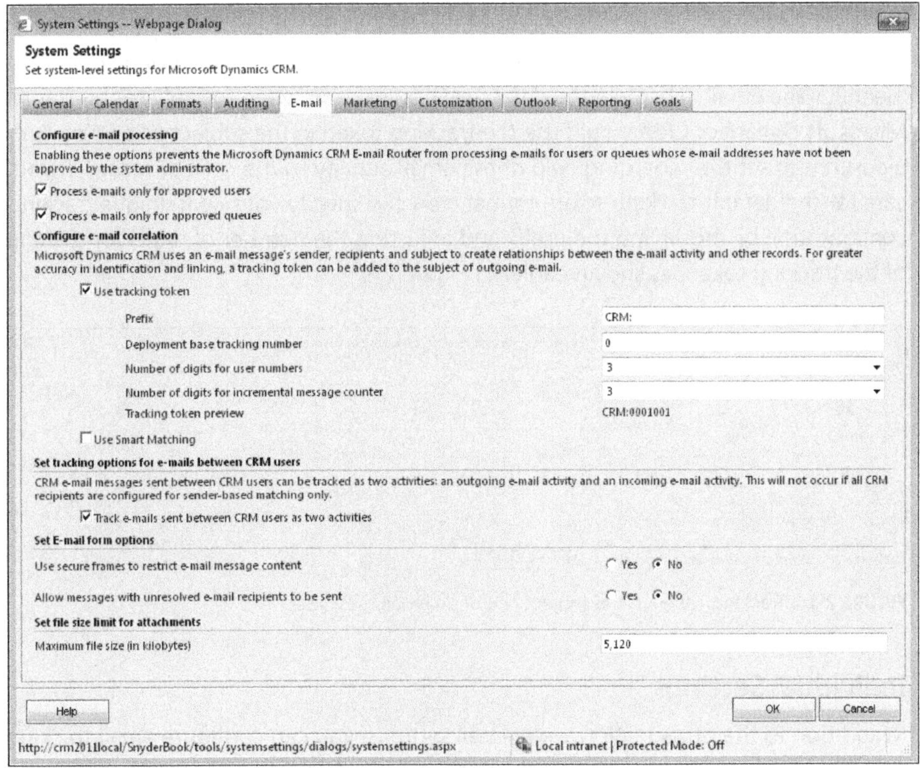

FIGURE 2-9 Configuring organization email settings

From here, you can configure the organization's email settings, and most of them are self-explanatory. For the email correlation portion of these settings, you have one of two options:

- Smart matching only
- Smart matching with tracking tokens

If you leave the Use tracking token check box clear, Microsoft Dynamics CRM uses the smart matching feature to correlate email messages automatically with the appropriate records. Smart matching uses an algorithm based on the email sender, recipients, and message subject line to determine which record to use as the email's regarding record (lead, opportunity, quote, and so on). When matching the email message subject, the smart matching feature ignores prefixes (such as RE: and FW:) in addition to capitalization.

In you find that the accuracy of the smart matching feature does not meet your needs, you can choose to include the tracking token feature, which increases the accuracy of automatic email matching. With the tracking token feature enabled, Microsoft Dynamics CRM adds a code in the subject line of email messages sent from Microsoft Dynamics CRM.

In Figure 2-10, you can see that Microsoft Dynamics CRM automatically appended the tracking code CRM:0054001 to the end of the email subject. This tracking code uniquely identifies the email activity in the database. If a customer were to reply to this message, Microsoft Dynamics CRM would use the tracking token in the subject as part of its matching algorithm to set the regarding field of the email activity to the correct record. If you don't care for the default tracking token format, you can specify your own unique tracking token configuration by modifying the prefix and adjusting the number of digits for the components of the tracking token, as shown earlier in Figure 2-9.

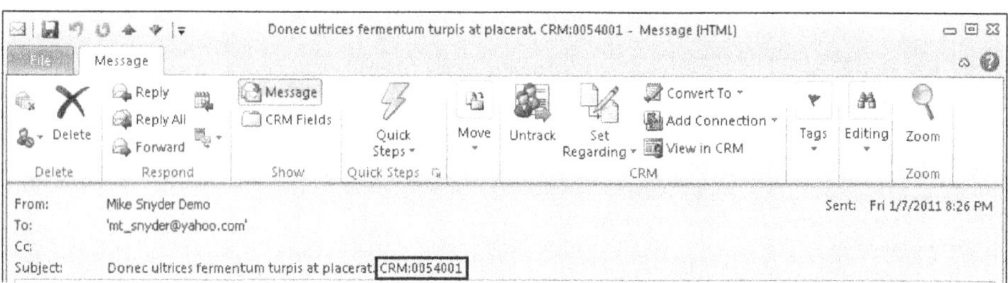

FIGURE 2-10 Tracking token in the subject line of an email message

Individual Settings

In addition to the organization-wide email settings, you can configure email tracking settings on a user-by-user basis. You edit individual email settings in one of two places:

- Personal Options E-mail tab
- Microsoft Dynamics CRM User form

In the E-mail tab of each user's personal options, users can specify which email messages they want to track in Microsoft Dynamics CRM, as shown in Figure 2-11. To access your Personal Options, open the web client, click the File tab in the ribbon, and then click Options.

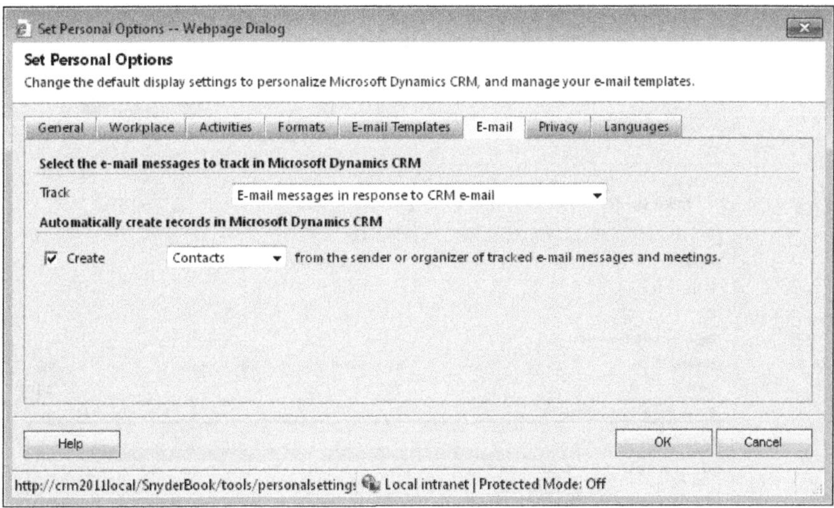

FIGURE 2-11 Configuring email tracking in a user's personal options

The four options are:

- *All e-mail messages*
- *E-mail messages in response to CRM e-mail*
- *E-mail messages from CRM Leads, Contacts and Accounts*
- *E-mail messages from CRM records that are e-mail enabled*

The other option on this screen allows you to configure whether contact or lead records will be created automatically in Microsoft Dynamics CRM for tracked email messages. When you track an email in Microsoft Dynamics CRM for Outlook, the software tries to match the email addresses against your existing CRM data to find matching records. If the software finds a match, it automatically links the email to that matching record. When you select the Automatically create records in Microsoft Dynamics CRM option shown in Figure 2-11, the software will automatically create contact or lead records only if it can't find matching records.

Finally, you might want to turn off automatic email tracking for a particular user. To accomplish this, administrators with the appropriate security credentials can modify the user's profile record in the Microsoft Dynamics CRM web client to set the incoming and outgoing email access type to None, as shown in Figure 2-12. The default Microsoft Dynamics CRM security roles do not allow users to modify their own system user records, so typically a system administrator is required to configure these email settings.

Tip Administrators can also use the Microsoft Dynamics CRM E-Mail Router Configuration Manager to update the user profile settings regarding incoming and outgoing email access types. With this tool, administrators can update the settings for multiple users at one time.

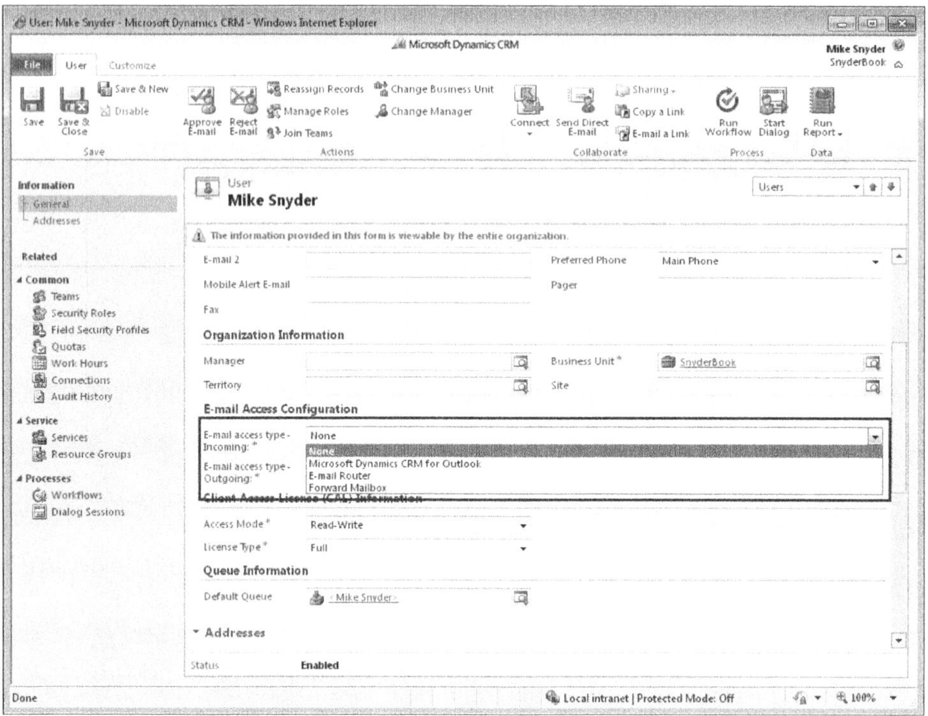

FIGURE 2-12 Turning off email tracking for a user by setting the E-mail Access Types to None

E-Mail Templates

As their name implies, with E-mail templates you can create pre-formatted email messages that you can reference in several areas throughout Microsoft Dynamics CRM. You can use E-mail templates in the following ways:

- **Insert templates into email messages** When users create email messages in the Microsoft Dynamics CRM web client or Microsoft Dynamics CRM for Outlook client, they can insert an E-mail template into the body of the message. Users can also insert multiple E-mail templates into a single email message if necessary.
- **Send direct email by using templates** Users can use E-mail templates to send the same email message to multiple records. For example, you could use the direct email feature (which uses E-mail templates) to send the same message to 500 contacts.
- **Reference E-mail templates in workflow processes** Users can reference E-mail templates in Microsoft Dynamics CRM workflow to accomplish many types of business process automation techniques.
- **Use E-mail templates in quick campaigns and campaign activities** When creating a quick campaign using email activities, you have the option to use an E-mail template.

In addition to being accessible from different areas of the Microsoft Dynamics CRM application, E-mail templates have the following unique features:

- **Data fields** You can insert dynamic data fields into E-mail templates that Microsoft Dynamics CRM will automatically populate when the template is used. For example, if you want to send an email message to 20 people and address each recipient by his or her first name, you can insert a first name data field into the E-mail template. When Microsoft Dynamics CRM sends the message, it will automatically populate the data field with the first name value for each of the 20 recipients.
- **Personal and organization ownership** E-mail templates can have individual or organization ownership, so security on each template can be set to specific users or all users.
- **Template types** For each E-mail template you create, you must specify a single entity (such as leads or opportunities) to which the template applies. You can also create a global template that can be used with multiple entities.

You can create and use E-mail templates for many different record types, such as leads, opportunities, accounts, quotes, orders, and service activities. You can also create E-mail templates for your custom entities. Next, we explain the details of working with E-mail templates.

Creating or Modifying E-Mail Templates

Now that you understand some of the ways in which you can use E-mail templates in Microsoft Dynamics CRM, we can discuss how you create E-mail templates. Microsoft Dynamics CRM includes more than 20 E-mail templates in the default installation, including a reply for leads who visit your website and an acknowledgment sent to a customer when a case is closed.

You can modify these default templates or create your own E-mail templates. To view the E-mail templates that are currently in your system, browse to the Settings area in the Microsoft Dynamics CRM web client, click Templates, and then click E-mail Templates. A grid displays all of the E-mail templates and their types. Double-click any record to view a template, such as the Lead Reply – Trade Show Visit template shown in Figure 2-13.

A template contains several attributes:

- **Type** Indicates whether the template is global or applies to only one entity.
- **Title** Short title of the E-mail template that appears when users select a template.
- **Description** Additional descriptive text that explains the function of the E-mail template. Users can access the description when they select a template.
- **Subject** The subject line of the email message.
- **Body** The body of the email message. It isn't labeled on the form, but this is the large text box below the Subject field.

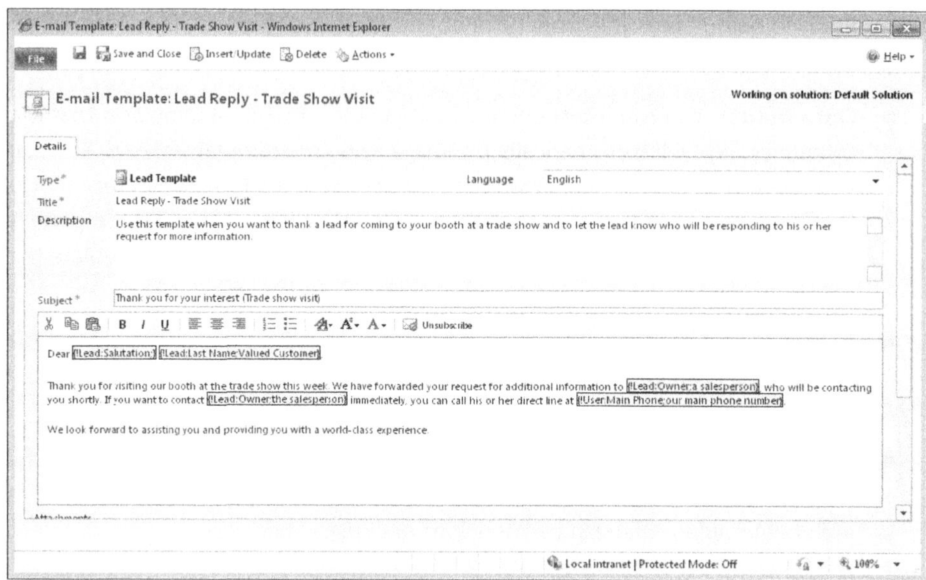

FIGURE 2-13 Lead Reply – Trade Show Visit E-mail template

Important You can also include file attachments to your e-mail templates. To add attachments, scroll to the bottom of the E-mail template form and click the New E-mail Attachment button.

One of the key benefits that templates offer is their ability to dynamically populate record-specific values in placeholder data fields. You can see in Figure 2-13 that the E-mail template includes a highlighted data field like the following:

```
{!Lead: Last Name; Valued Customer}
```

Microsoft Dynamics CRM automatically converts this data field to the lead's last name. The text before the colon refers to the entity, and the text after the colon specifies the field name. If a lead record does not have a last name value, you can include a default value for the data field by entering text after the semicolon. In this example, Microsoft Dynamics CRM would insert the text *Valued Customer* in the email message if there were no data in the Last Name field.

To add a data field to an E-mail template, click the Insert/Update button on the form toolbar. The Data Field Values dialog box appears, as shown in Figure 2-14.

When you click the Add button, another dialog box prompts you to select the Record Type and Field for the data field. Depending on the entity you selected for the E-mail template type, you can add fields from the primary entity or any related entities. For example, in E-mail templates associated to the Lead entity, you can add fields from the Lead and User entities. However, for opportunity E-mail templates, you can add fields

FIGURE 2-14 Data Field Values dialog box

from the Account, Contact, Opportunity, and User entities. After you select the field you want to add and click OK, the field appears in the Data Field Values list. Then you can specify the default value text (optional) by entering it in the Default Text box. When you click OK, Microsoft Dynamics CRM automatically creates the data field and adds it to the E-mail template.

Tip You can add data fields to both the subject and body of an E-mail template.

If you want to add multiple data fields to an E-mail template, you must add them one at a time, as in this example:

```
{!Contact : Salutation;} {!Contact : Last Name;}
```

These data fields will insert the following text into an email message for a sample contact, Mr. Brian Valentine:

```
Mr. Valentine
```

However, if you add both data fields at the same time by using the Data Field Values dialog box, Microsoft Dynamics CRM will create one data field in the template, like this:

```
{!Contact : Salutation;Contact : Last Name;}
```

This data field inserts the following text for the same Contact:

```
Mr.
```

As you can see, Microsoft Dynamics CRM allows you to enter a dynamic data field for the default value of a different data field. In this example, *Contact: Last Name* is the default value for the *Contact: Salutation* data field. However, because the contact record includes a value for the salutation, it does not need to output the default value of *Contact: Last Name*.

Creating an E-mail template is straightforward. Click the New button on the grid toolbar, select the entity type for the E-mail template, and then enter the appropriate information in the template fields. After you set up your new template with data fields, click the Save button on the E-mail template toolbar. Microsoft Dynamics CRM immediately applies your changes to the E-mail template so that users can access it.

Tip When you enter and edit text in the E-mail template body, pressing Enter on your keyboard adds an extra line. If you want a single carriage return instead of a new paragraph, press Shift+Enter instead.

Inserting Templates into E-Mail Messages

When you're writing an email message in either Microsoft Dynamics CRM for Outlook or the web client, you can click the Insert Template button to open the Insert Template dialog box, as shown in Figure 2-15. You must select at least one email recipient before you can insert a template because Microsoft Dynamics CRM must know which template types apply to the message based on the entity type of the recipients.

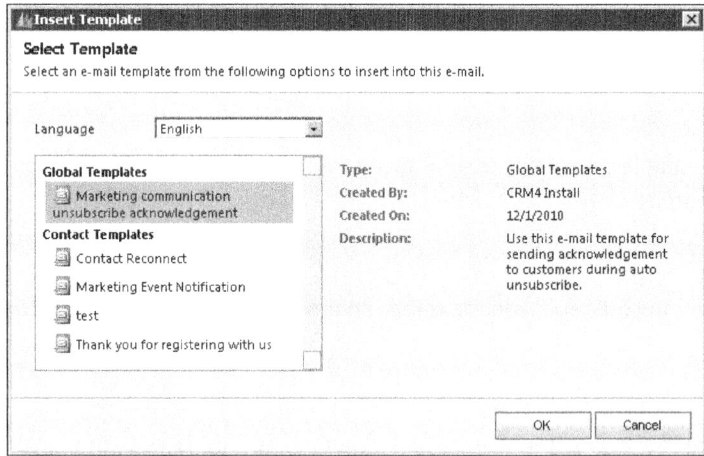

FIGURE 2-15 Inserting an E-mail template into an email message

After you select an E-mail template, Microsoft Dynamics CRM automatically populates the template content in the body of the message and dynamically fills out any data fields that the E-mail template contains. This is a convenient feature if you want to edit or add additional content to an email message before you send it, something you can't do with the direct email feature. If your email message includes multiple recipients, Microsoft Dynamics CRM prompts you to select one recipient as the E-mail template target when you insert a template into the message.

Caution Each time you insert an E-mail template into the body of an email message, Microsoft Dynamics CRM updates the subject line of the email message to match the subject of the E-mail template. If you insert multiple templates, the subject is determined by the last template inserted. This is very convenient for writing new email messages, but you should be aware of this behavior if you insert E-mail templates when you reply to messages.

Creating and Sharing Personal E-Mail Templates

The process we just explained creates an E-mail template that the entire organization can use. Users can also create personal templates for their own use.

Follow these steps to create a personal E-mail template:

1. In the web client, click the File tab in the ribbon and then click Options.
2. The Set Personal Options dialog box opens. Click the E-mail Templates tab.
3. Click the New button on the grid toolbar.

If a user decides that she wants to share an E-mail template with the entire organization, she can convert a personal template into an organization template at any time by clicking the Make Template Available to Organization link located under Actions in the menu bar.

Inserting Images and Hyperlinks into E-Mail Templates

After you create a few E-mail templates, you'll probably notice that the editing tools for the email message body are somewhat limited. For example, none of the buttons allows you to add a hyperlink or image to the message. If you want to develop a more sophisticated E-mail template with multiple images, links, and so on, you can create HTML code with a development tool such as Microsoft Visual Studio 2010. However, if you try to copy and paste your HTML code into the E-mail template, it is displayed as plain text; your recipient will receive a bunch of HTML code instead of the formatted version of your message! Fortunately, by using a little trick, you can easily copy and paste your custom HTML code into the E-mail template and still maintain the correct formatting.

For example, assume that you want to send a simple company newsletter to contacts in your database by using an E-mail template with the following requirements:

- Display the company logo in the message
- Display a hyperlink that readers can click to get more information

The following sample shows a company newsletter created in HTML using Visual Studio 2010. Next, you can copy (Ctrl+C) the sample newsletter and paste (Ctrl+V) it into the email message body. The trick is to copy and paste the rendered HTML output, not the HTML code. You can accomplish this in a couple of ways:

- Copy and paste the formatted message from the Visual Studio 2010 Design view.
- Copy and paste the HTML web page from a Microsoft Internet Explorer window.

After you copy and paste the contents of the message into the E-mail template body, you will see the properly formatted email message, complete with an image and a hyperlink. After you paste the code into the message, you can also add a data field to dynamically display the contact's first name in the newsletter. Please note that if you use images, you need to make sure that the image references a URL that the email recipient can access. This technique does not copy the image file into the E-mail template; it simply references the image URL from the HTML file.

Caution You cannot copy and paste HTML code from a text editor program such as Notepad into the E-mail template.

You can also try using the copy and paste technique with other HTML editor applications. We found that the success of this technique varies depending on the format that applications use to copy data to the Clipboard.

Creating and Sending Mass Email Messages

Many Microsoft Dynamics CRM users want to send an email message to a large group of their prospects or customers, and of course Microsoft Dynamics CRM includes several tools for mass email messages. One key criterion for mass email messages is that each message must be individually addressed to a recipient. For example, if you want to send an email message to 500 contacts, you want the system to create 500 copies of the message each addressed to an individual recipient instead of generating one email with 500 people in the To, CC, or BCC fields. The four methods for sending mass email messages in Microsoft Dynamics CRM are:

- Direct email
- Quick campaign
- Workflow process
- Mail merge

Each mass emailing method is explored in more detail in the following sub-sections.

Regardless of which option you select, Microsoft Dynamics CRM sends the email messages through the outgoing email server configured during the software installation. Therefore, use some discretion when sending a very large number of messages at one time because it can negatively affect the performance of your servers. Some factors that come into play include the hardware specifications on your servers, network performance, Internet bandwidth, and the amount of load on the server. Although no published specifications exist and the numbers can range widely depending on your infrastructure, if you need to send more than 10,000 or 20,000 email messages in one hour, we recommend that you explore the option of using third-party email engines instead of Microsoft Dynamics CRM. You should also be mindful of the latest laws and legislation regarding bulk email marketing, including the federal CAN-SPAM law. You can learn more about these laws at *http://www.ftc.gov/spam/*. Sending large numbers of unsolicited email messages from your email servers can get your system blocked or blacklisted.

Direct Email

By using the direct email feature, you can select recipients in a grid, and then choose an E-mail template that you want to send. As discussed, E-mail templates can include data fields that Microsoft Dynamics CRM dynamically populates with information specific to each recipient. E-mail templates can also include file attachments. You access the direct email feature from the ribbon for entities that support E-mail templates. Figure 2-16 shows the Send Direct E-mail button in the Contacts ribbon.

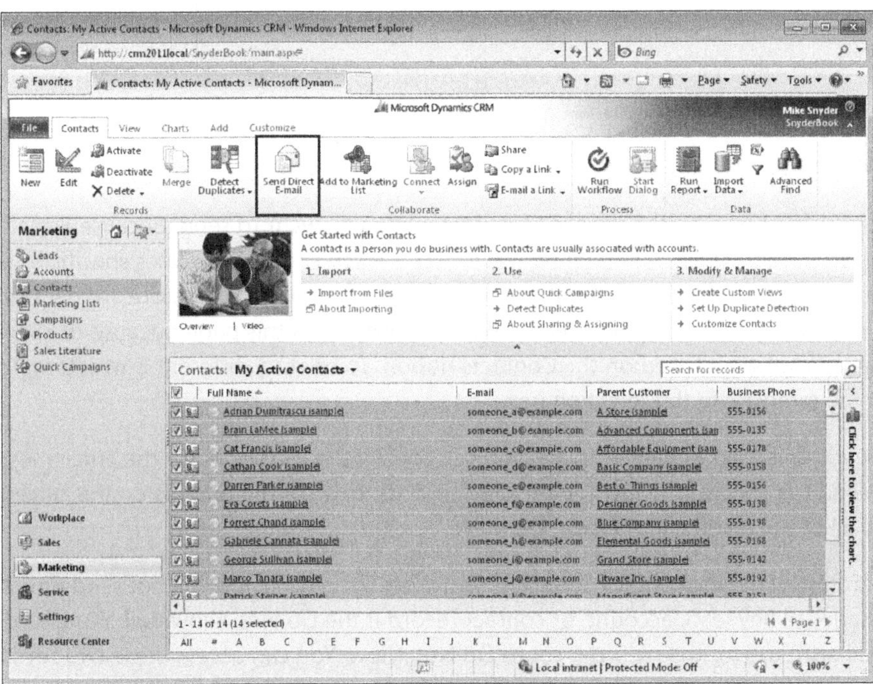

FIGURE 2-16 Direct E-mail button in the Contacts ribbon

When you click the Send Direct E-mail button, Microsoft Dynamics CRM opens the Send Direct E-mail dialog box, shown with sample data in Figure 2-17.

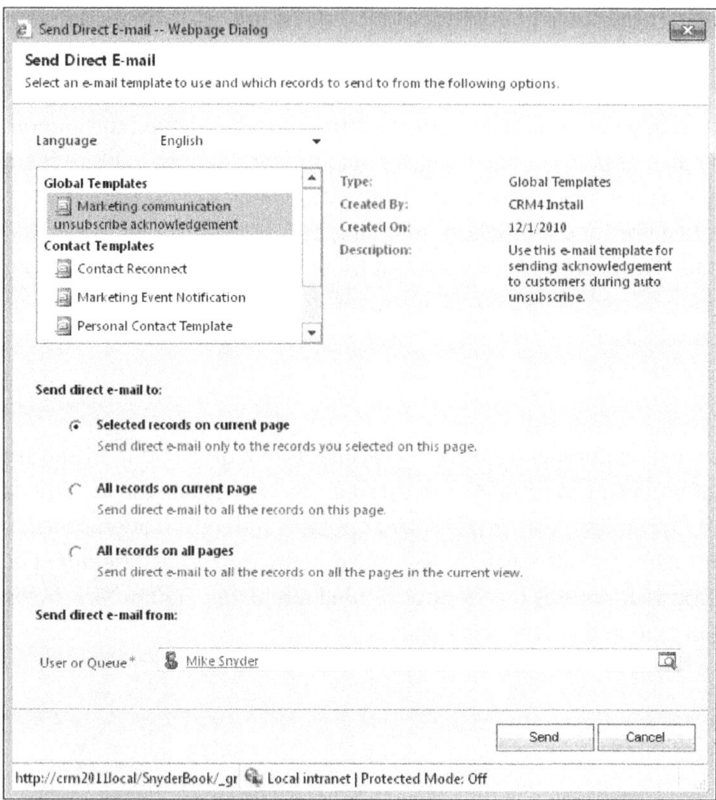

FIGURE 2-17 Send Direct E-mail dialog box

In this dialog box, you choose the E-mail template you want to send. Because E-mail templates are defined with an entity type, you can select only templates specific to the entity that you're working with or one of the global templates. Therefore, in this example, you cannot send an account or lead E-mail template from this page because the Send Direct E-mail button was clicked on the Contacts ribbon. To select a different E-mail template, click the template in the selection box.

After you select an E-mail template, you can specify the recipients for the email message. You can send the message to just the selected records, to all of the records on the current page, or to all of the records in the selected view.

Regardless of the value that you select, Microsoft Dynamics CRM will not send direct email messages to any lead, account, or contact record if the Do Not Allow Bulk E-mails or Do Not E-mail attribute for the record is set to Do Not Allow. You can access these two settings in the Administration tab on each of the forms if you want to modify their values.

By default, Microsoft Dynamics CRM sets the sender of the email message as the logged-on user. You can change this value by clicking the lookup button and selecting a different user or queue.

Warning Be very careful when using the direct email feature! When you click the Send button, Microsoft Dynamics CRM sends the message immediately. There is no preview or cancel option, so make sure that your message is ready when you click the Send button.

In summary, direct email offers the following benefits and constraints:

- You can send direct email messages to many different entities such as Lead, Account, Contact, Opportunity, Quote, and Order.
- Direct email uses previously created E-mail templates.
- You can send direct email messages to selected records in a view or all the records in a view, regardless of the number of pages in that view.
- You cannot preview your message before you send them.

Quick Campaign

By using the Microsoft Dynamics CRM quick campaign feature, you can send a large number of email messages to a group of recipients. To send a quick campaign email message, select a group of records in a grid, click the Add tab in the ribbon, and then click the Quick Campaign button in the Marketing section of the ribbon. You will need to select which records in the grid to include in the quick campaign. The options match the direct email options:

- For selected records
- For all records on the current page
- For all records on all pages

After you select the records to include, Microsoft Dynamics CRM starts the Create Quick Campaign Wizard that walks you through creating a mass email message. On the Select the Activity Type and Owners page, you can select the *Mark e-mail messages to be sent and close corresponding e-mail activities* option to send the email messages automatically when the wizard is completed, as shown in Figure 2-18. If you clear this option, Microsoft Dynamics CRM will create the email messages as open activities but won't send them to recipients until someone sends each message individually.

Quick campaigns also give you the option to record customer interest as *campaign responses*. A campaign response lets you record how a particular customer responded to one of your campaign efforts. You can create the campaign response record manually for each recipient, or you can use a data import process to load a larger number of records. In quick campaigns, Microsoft Dynamics CRM does not automatically create campaign responses for you.

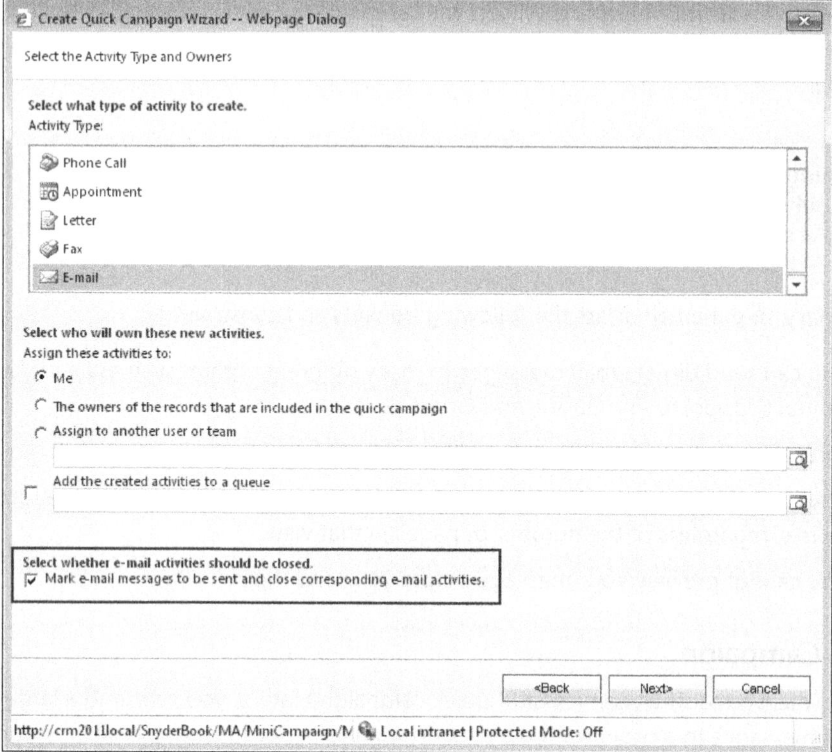

FIGURE 2-18 Specifying whether to send the quick campaign email messages upon wizard completion

In summary, quick campaigns offer the following benefits and constraints:

- They only apply to leads, accounts, contacts, and marketing lists.
- A wizard walks you through the creation of quick campaign email messages.
- You can use E-mail templates when you send a quick campaign, and templates can include file attachments.
- Quick campaigns save the group of records to which you sent the message in case you need to go back and reference that information later.
- You can create quick campaigns for non-email activities such as tasks and phone calls.
- You can capture response data using the Campaign Response entity.
- You can send quick campaign email messages to selected records in a view or all of the records in a view, regardless of the number of pages in that view.

Workflow Processes

If neither the direct email nor the quick campaign feature meets your needs, you can use the Microsoft Dynamics CRM workflow engine for sending mass email. Chapter 14, "Workflow

Processes," explains the details of configuring and running a workflow process to send email, so we won't cover that here. However, we do want to highlight workflow as a viable option for mass email because it offers one big benefit over direct email and quick campaigns. You can automatically send your workflow email messages based on different trigger events that you configure in the workflow process, such as updating a field or changing a record's status.

Unfortunately, using workflow for mass email does include one significant constraint: You can only manually apply a workflow process to a single page of records in a grid. Therefore, if you want to send 1,000 email messages, you must select all the records on a page, and then apply the workflow rule. Then, you must move to the next page of records and repeat the process. If you configured Microsoft Dynamics CRM to display 100 records per page, you need to repeat this process 10 times to send all 1,000 email messages by manually applying a workflow process. However, you could configure the workflow process to trigger automatically based on some other criterion in the record to avoid this constraint.

Tip You can display up to 250 records per page by changing the default configuration of 50 records per page. To access this setting, click the File tab in the ribbon and then click Options.

Mail Merge

When most people hear the expression mail merge, they immediately think of Microsoft Office Word and printing documents. However, Microsoft Dynamics CRM for Outlook allows you to also use the mail merge features to send customized email messages to a large group of recipients.

You can start a Microsoft Dynamics CRM mail merge from one of two locations:

- List of records in Microsoft Dynamics CRM for Outlook
- List of records in the web client

Regardless of where you start the mail merge, the final results should appear the same, but there a few different steps along the way. For this email merge example, let's start the mail merge process from a list of records in Microsoft Dynamics CRM for Outlook.

Tip Using mail merge for emails behaves a little differently than using mail merge for letters, envelopes, and other Microsoft Office Word documents. The next section in this chapter will cover using mail merge for letters.

First, click the solution folder in Outlook and navigate to the list of records that you want to include in the email merge. In the ribbon, click the Mail Merge button. The Microsoft Dynamics CRM Mail Merge for Microsoft Office Word dialog box appears, as shown in Figure 2-19. Because you want to conduct an email merge, select E-mail from the mail merge type picklist.

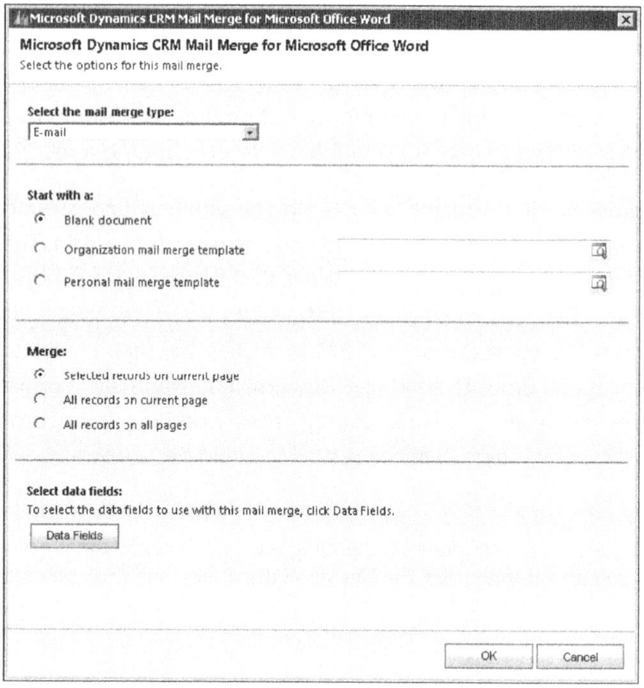

FIGURE 2-19 Microsoft Dynamics CRM Mail Merge for Microsoft Office Word dialog box

To create the email content, you can start with a blank document or you have the option to select one of the mail merge templates. Please note that the mail merge templates are not the same as the E-mail templates reviewed earlier in this chapter. Microsoft Dynamics CRM includes approximately 10 mail merge templates, and you can create others as needed.

You also select which records you want to include in the email merge process. Similar to direct email and quick campaigns, you can choose selected records only, all records on the current page, or all records on all pages.

Finally, you select which data fields you want to include in the mail merge. Microsoft Dynamics CRM includes several default data fields, but you can also add more data fields, most likely custom fields that you want to dynamically populate in your email messages. Note the following when you select data fields:

- You can select fields from the entity on which you're running the mail merge, including any custom fields.
- You can select fields from related entities, including custom entities and entities linked through custom relationships.
- You cannot select fields on a custom entity if that entity has an N:1 relationship with the Mail Merge entity.
- You can include a maximum of 62 data fields.

After you click OK, Microsoft Dynamics CRM will launch Microsoft Office Word with the mail merge recipients selected. Click OK to accept this list and start the merge process, as shown in Figure 2-20.

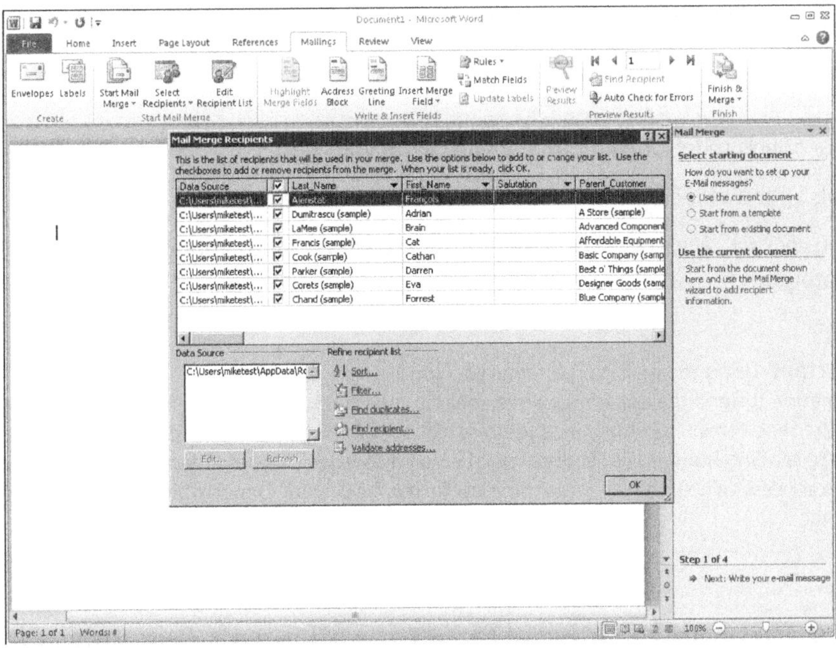

FIGURE 2-20 Selecting mail merge recipients

Note Explaining the details of setting up and using the Mail Merge feature in Microsoft Office Word is beyond the scope of this book. We assume you're already familiar with the concepts and techniques related to using Word Mail Merge.

Follow through the mail merge steps by adding your content and mail merge fields. In Step 4, click Electronic E-mail. The Merge to E-mail dialog box appears and you need to enter the subject line for your email, as shown in Figure 2-21.

FIGURE 2-21 Entering the email subject line

After you click OK, Microsoft Dynamics CRM launches one final screen that gives you some additional features, including:

- The option to create Microsoft Dynamics CRM activities attached to the recipients. You also have the option to customize the text and content of those activity details.
- The option to create a new quick campaign related to the email messages you're sending.
- The option to include an unsubscribe link in your email.
- The option to include multiple attachments to your email.

After you click OK, Microsoft Dynamics CRM for Outlook sends your merged emails immediately.

Important Using the mail merge feature to send emails uses your personal Outlook information to send the email messages, meaning that you will see these messages in your Outlook Sent Items. The email messages are not sent from the Microsoft Dynamics CRM server. If you're sending hundreds or thousands of email messages, please be aware that the email merge process will negatively impact the performance of your Outlook file until all of the emails are sent.

Third-Party Add-On: ExactTarget for Microsoft Dynamics CRM

Although the out-of-the-box options for mass emailing in Microsoft Dynamics CRM can meet most organizations' needs, a company named ExactTarget (*http://www.exacttarget.com*) offers an add-on product for Microsoft Dynamics CRM that includes many additional email marketing features and benefits. ExactTarget offers its email marketing services on a hosted basis, and it created an integration with Microsoft Dynamics CRM so that users can send email through the ExactTarget service directly from the Microsoft Dynamics CRM interface, shown in Figure 2-22.

By using the ExactTarget service for sending mass email, Microsoft Dynamics CRM users can enjoy the following additional benefits:

- ExactTarget sends the email messages through its servers, not through the outgoing email server configured for Microsoft Dynamics CRM. This allows users to send a large volume of email without affecting their internal network. Outsourcing the message delivery to ExactTarget also helps improve message deliverability because ExactTarget works with email companies to ensure consistent delivery.

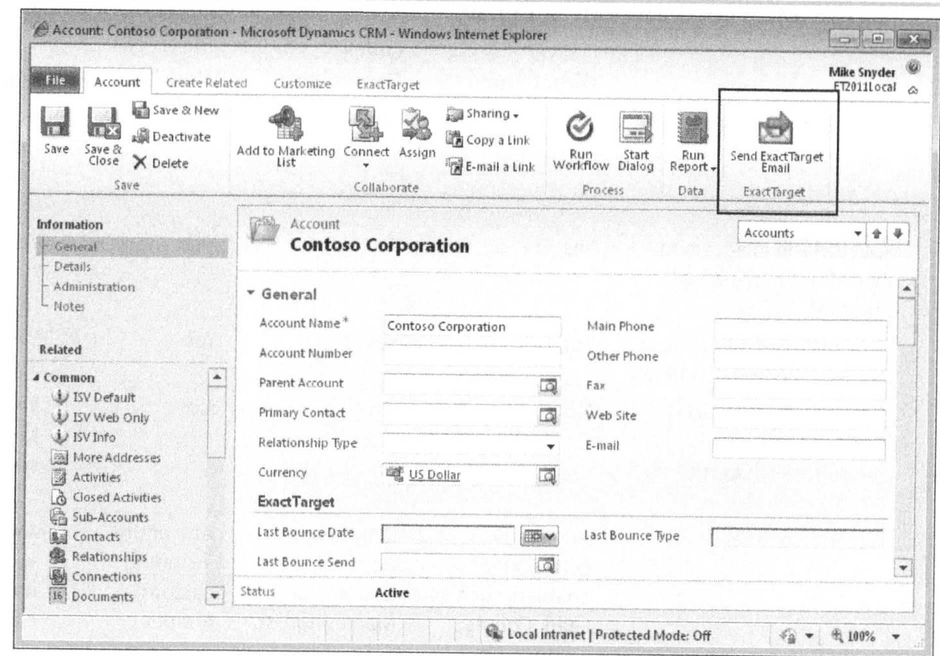

FIGURE 2-22 Send ExactTarget emails within Microsoft Dynamics CRM

- ExactTarget automatically captures response data, such as email opens, clicks in messages, bounces, and unsubscribes. Almost all of the response data downloads into the Microsoft Dynamics CRM user interface so that you can report on it, access it using Advanced Find, and so on. The default ExactTarget for Microsoft Dynamics CRM installation includes data such as unique opens, total opens, unique clicks, deliverability rate, and bounce rate.
- Users have more control over the delivery of their mass email messages because they can schedule a specific date and time to start the message send. In addition, users can throttle the email to send only a certain number of messages per hour.
- ExactTarget offers a proprietary user interface in which users can create and design their email messages to include images and hyperlinks.

Companies looking for more advanced email marketing in Microsoft Dynamics CRM should definitely consider the ExactTarget for Microsoft Dynamics CRM option.

Mass Email Summary

Table 2-2 outlines some key differences of the mass email options for Microsoft Dynamics CRM.

TABLE 2-2 Mass Email Options Summary

	Direct Email	Quick Campaigns	Workflow	Mail Merge
Can use E-mail templates	Yes	Yes	Yes	No, but can use mail merge templates
Can include images and hyperlinks in the email message	Yes	Yes	Yes	Yes
Can include dynamic data fields in the body content	Yes	Yes	Yes	Yes
Can include conditional content within the message (such as if/then/else statements)	No	No	No	Yes, with Mail Merge syntax
Available entities	Any entity with activities enabled, such as Lead, Contact, Opportunity, Account, Quote, and Order	Only Lead, Account, Contact, and Marketing List	Any entity, including custom entities	Any entity with mail merge enabled
Email recipient selection	All or some of the records in a view	All or some of the records in a view	Can only apply manual workflow to all records on a page (250 records max)	All or some of the records in a view
Can include a file attachment	Yes	Yes	Yes	Yes
Works with campaign responses	No	Yes	No	No
Tracks email opens	No	No	No	No
Tracks hyperlinks clicked in the email message	No	No	No	No

Mail Merge

As you just read about, Microsoft Dynamics CRM includes a mail merge feature that allows you to create mass emails. You can also use the mail merge feature to create a large number of letters, envelopes, or labels. Remember, you can start the mail merge from either the web client or Microsoft Dynamics CRM for Outlook. Note that running the mail merge from Microsoft Dynamics CRM for Outlook provides a few additional benefits, including:

- After completing the merge, you can create activities associated with the mail merge.
- You can upload the mail merge template back into Microsoft Dynamics CRM. This is helpful if you changed the template during the merge.
- You can create a quick campaign associated with the mail merge.
- You can run mail merges from quick campaigns.
- You don't need to use a mail merge Word macro, so you won't need to enable any security prompts.

The email example in the previous section showed how to start the mail merge from Microsoft Dynamics CRM for Outlook, so let's review how to run a letter mail merge starting from the web client.

First, browse to a list or view of records in the Microsoft Dynamics CRM web client, then click the Add tab in the ribbon and click the Mail Merge button.

Note To run a mail merge on a quote, you need to open the quote record and click the Print Quote for Customer button in the ribbon. Mail merge on quotes runs against one record at a time.

After you click the Mail Merge button, Microsoft Dynamics CRM launches the Mail Merge dialog box. In this dialog box, you can select the mail merge type such as letter, envelope, or label. Assuming that you want to send a letter, select that value in the picklist. From there, you can choose to start with a blank mail merge template or use one of the templates already in the Microsoft Dynamics CRM database, shown in Figure 2-23. By default, Microsoft Dynamics CRM includes mail merge templates for the Lead, Account, Contact, Quote, and Opportunity entities, but you can also create your own mail merge templates.

After you click OK, Microsoft Dynamics CRM will then launch Microsoft Office Word, as shown in Figure 2-24.

After you click the Enable Editing button, Word will update with a new tab in ribbon titled Add-ins. When you click the CRM button located within the Add-ins tab, Word runs a macro that loads the mail merge data into the document, and then you will see the recipient list like the one shown earlier in Figure 2-20. Click OK to approve the recipients, or edit the list as necessary. From here, the mail merge behaves the same as the standard Word Mail Merge feature in which you can insert mail merge fields, modify the document, add rules, preview your letter, and so on.

Important You might receive security prompts and warnings in Microsoft Office Word, depending on your macro security settings. Click the appropriate buttons to enable the macros.

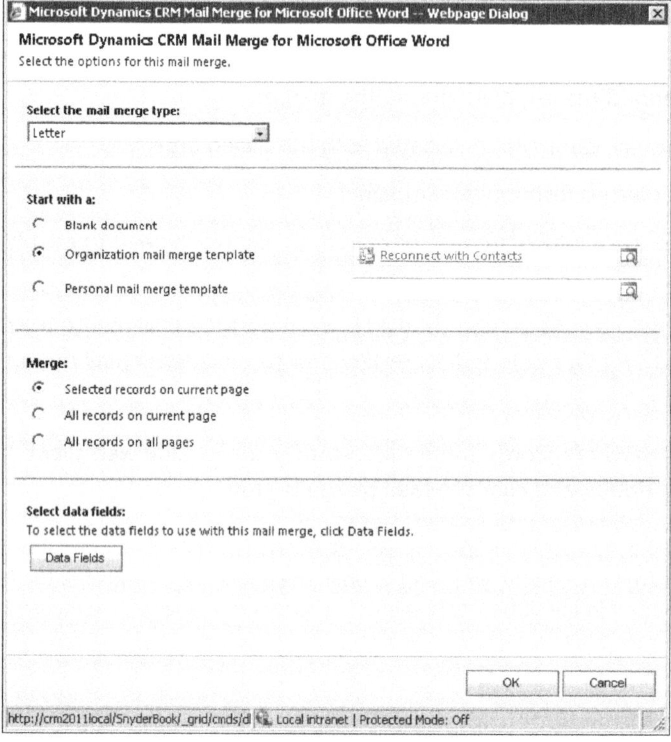

FIGURE 2-23 Selecting an organization template in the Mail Merge dialog box

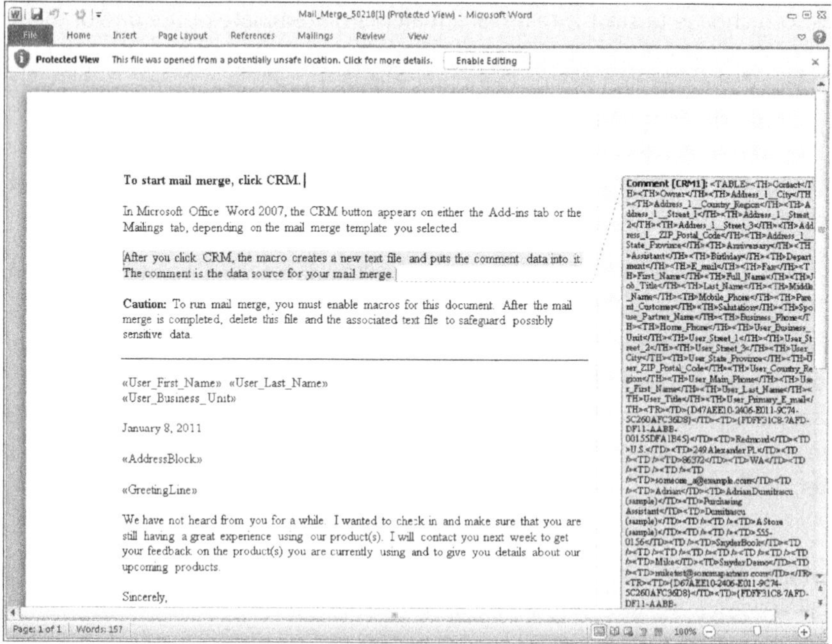

FIGURE 2-24 Microsoft Office Word document created when launching a mail merge from the web client

This example showed how to run the mail merge from the web client, so the mail merge process is complete. However, if you run the mail merge from Microsoft Dynamics CRM for Outlook, you have a few additional options. First, you can choose to upload the final version of the template to Microsoft Dynamics CRM. This upload can either create a new template or modify the template you selected when you started the mail merge, as shown in Figure 2-25.

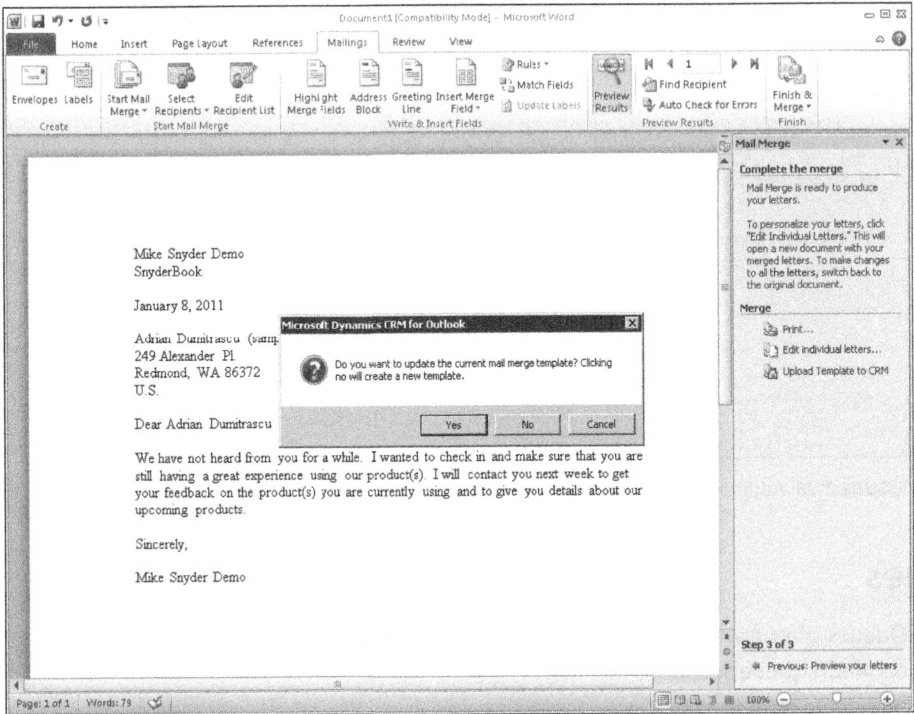

FIGURE 2-25 Uploading a mail merge template to Microsoft Dynamics CRM

Second, you can create letter activities in Microsoft Dynamics CRM to record the completed mail merge. When users click the Print or Edit individual letters links, the Create Activities dialog box opens, as shown in Figure 2-26.

You can click the Activity Details button to modify the subject of the completed letter activity to better describe the purpose of the mail merge. In addition, Microsoft Dynamics CRM automatically includes the final version of the Word document (with merged data) as an attachment to the letter activity.

Finally, you have the option to create a quick campaign that will be associated with the mail merge.

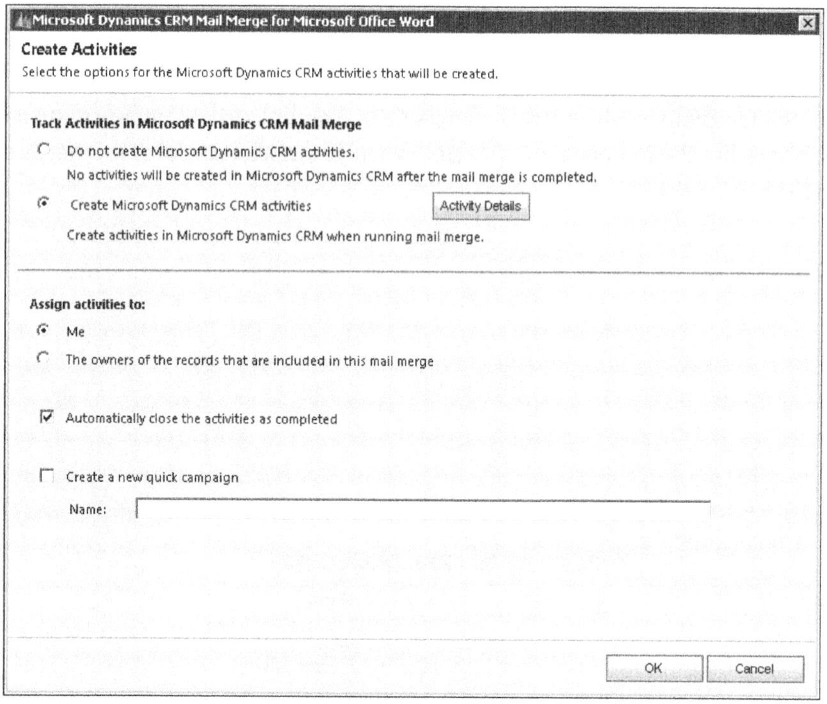

FIGURE 2-26 Additional features offered by running a mail merge from Microsoft Dynamics CRM for Outlook

Queues

Queues offer a way for your business to more easily share work across a team. Some common queue scenarios include:

- A customer service department receives a large number of cases each day.
- A sales team receives inbound leads from a website.
- A geographically dispersed team manages their project-based work items and tasks.

In each of these scenarios, the work that needs to be done could be completed by one or more of the team members. Furthermore, the team members' availability might vary because of differences in time zones and work schedules. For example, when the day shift ends, the night shift team members could take over the items that need completion. Queues are particularly useful for managing work items that require several hours or days to complete, but you can use queues to manage the process of completing any type of task or work item.

Creating Queues

By default, Microsoft Dynamics CRM sets up queues for each of your users and teams, but you can also create your own queues. To create a queue, navigate to the Settings area, and then click Business Management. Click on Queues and click the New button on the grid toolbar. Enter **Sales** for the Queue name and click the Save button in the toolbar, as shown in Figure 2-27.

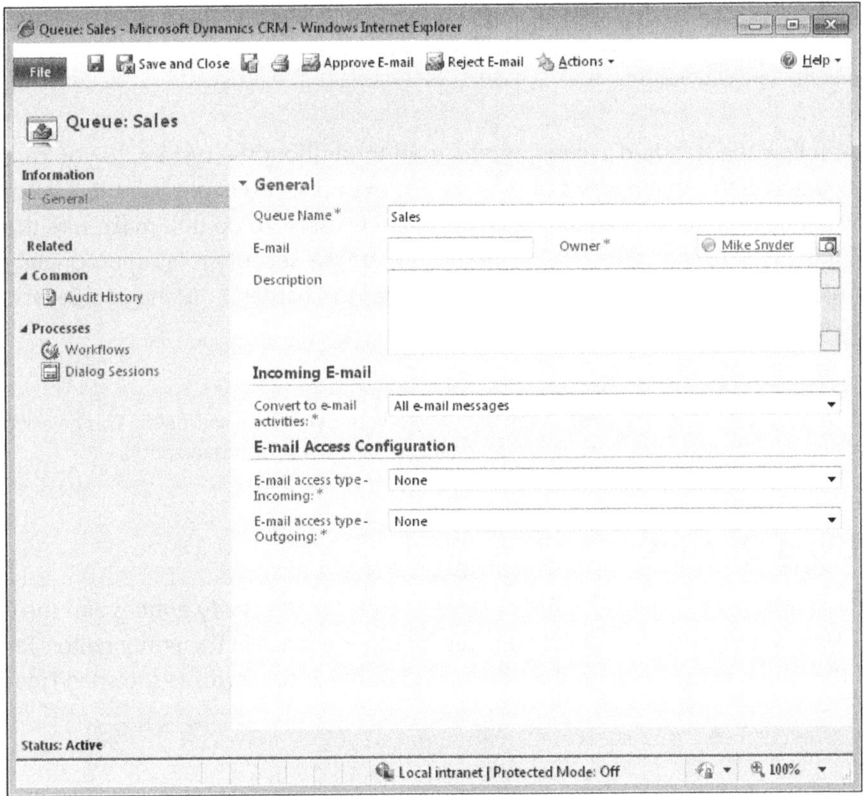

FIGURE 2-27 Creating a queue

Notice that you can configure a queue with an email address. By doing so, someone could send a message to the queue's email address and automatically create an item in the queue. The incoming email settings let you configure which type of email messages sent to the queue should create an item.

Imagine that a sample organization, Adventure Works Cycle, created the email address bikesupport@adventure-works.com to handle all incoming customer support requests. The goal of this support alias is to allow the Adventure Works customer service representatives to monitor incoming support requests in a single location so that they can resolve all requests in a timely manner. Adventure Works Cycle would create a queue called Bicycle Cases and configure the queue's email address as bikesupport@adventure-works.com. Then, every email message sent to bikesupport@adventure-works.com would create a queue item in the Bicycle Cases queue.

Important When you add or modify a queue's email address, you must approve the queue so that it works properly. If someone modifies the queue's email address, the queue moves to a Pending Approval status until it's approved. This approval step adds security so that someone does not change a queue's email address to gain access to a different email box. You can disable this additional security step by clearing the *Process e-mails only for approved queues* option on the E-mail tab of the System Settings dialog box, but we recommend that you keep this additional verification step.

Queues follow the standard security model used throughout the system, so you can set up queues with varying levels of security. For example, you might want to create a "private queue" that can be accessed by only a few users. To do this, make sure that you assign the queue to the correct owner and configure the security roles appropriately. For more information on setting up security roles, refer to Chapter 3, "Managing Security and Information Access."

Tip You can customize the queue item entity with your own views and fields. This gives you additional flexibility to use queues in a manner that best fits your organization.

Enabling Queues

By default, Microsoft Dynamics CRM enables queues for all activity entities and the Case entity. However you can also enable queues for other entities in the entity editor. To do so, select the Queues check box on the General tab of the Entity form, as shown in Figure 2-28.

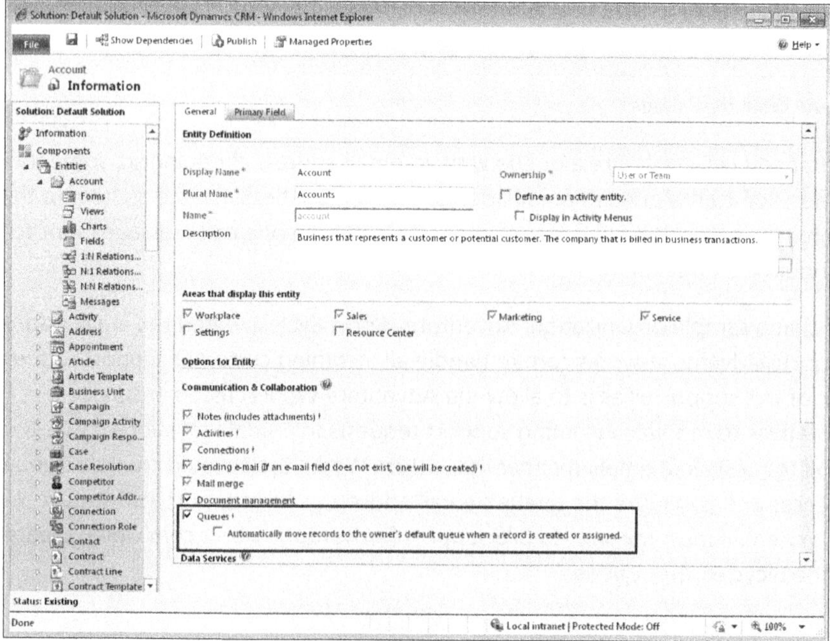

FIGURE 2-28 Enabling queues for an entity

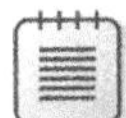

Note When you enable queues for an entity, you cannot disable the option.

When you enable queues for an entity, you also have the option to automatically move created or assigned records to the owner's default queue. For example, let's assume you enable queues for the Lead entity and select the option to automatically move records to the owner's default queue. Every time someone creates a lead or assigns a lead to someone else, Microsoft Dynamics CRM automatically adds the lead to the owner's default queue.

Working with Queue Items

After you configure your queues, you can start adding items to queues. The two main methods for adding items to a queue are:

- Manually clicking the Add to Queue button located in the ribbon
- Using Microsoft Dynamics CRM workflow processes to automatically create queue items

You can manually add items to a queue by clicking the Add to Queue button in the application ribbon, or by clicking the Add to Queue button located in the ribbon of the individual record. Figure 2-29 shows how to add leads to a Sales queue from the leads view.

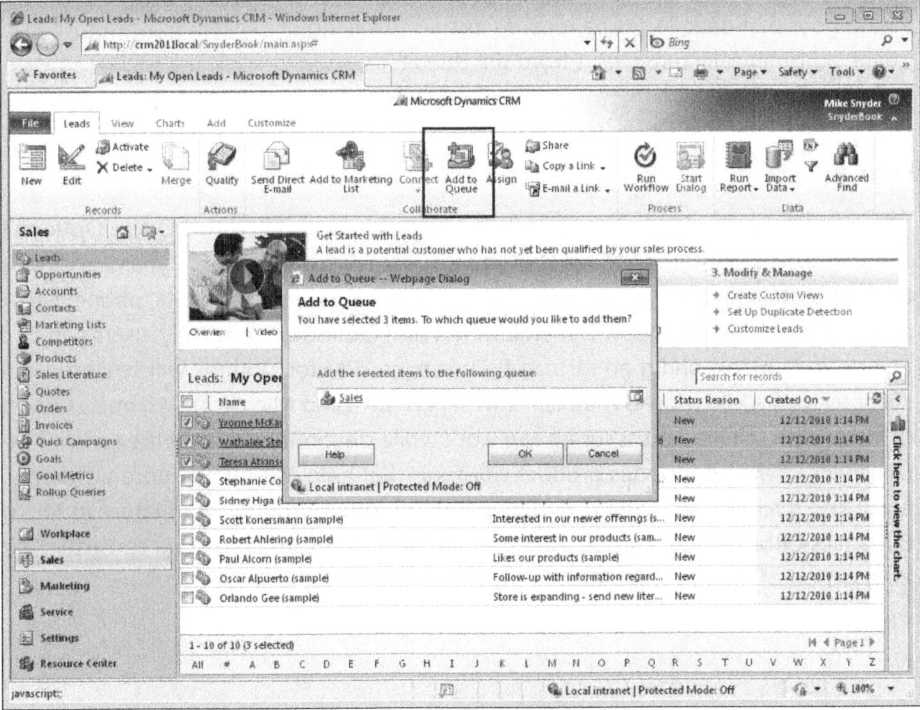

FIGURE 2-29 Adding leads to a Sales queue

After you add an item to a queue, you can view details about when the record entered the queue and when it was last modified by clicking the Queue Item Details button located in the record's ribbon. You can use the data in these details to look for items that have been stuck in a queue for a long time, or maybe find items that have not been modified in a while.

More Info For information about creating workflow processes, please refer to Chapter 14. Once you understand the basics of workflow, you can easily use it to create queue items automatically.

To review all of the items in a queue, browse to the Workplace area and click Queues. From here, you can easily access all of the queue items and create views and charts of the queue items. You can also take the following actions on queue items:

- **Routing** You can route the queue item to another queue. Alternatively, you can assign the item to a specific user or team.
- **Work On** You can choose to work on a queue item, which lets other users know they should work on other open queue items.
- **Release** When you're done working on a queue item, you can release it so that other users can continue to work on it.
- **Remove** You can take the item out of the queue entirely by clicking remove.

Please note that deactivating a record (such as resolving or canceling a case) while it's in the queue automatically removes it from the queue.

Summary

Microsoft Dynamics CRM offers excellent integration with Microsoft Office Outlook through the Microsoft Dynamics CRM for Outlook software. With Microsoft Dynamics CRM for Outlook installed, users can synchronize contacts, tasks, appointments, phone calls, letters, and faxes between Microsoft Dynamics CRM and Outlook. Conversely, users can update records in Outlook, and then Microsoft Dynamics CRM for Outlook will synchronize the changes to the Microsoft Dynamics CRM server. By using Microsoft Dynamics CRM for Outlook with Offline Access, users can work while disconnected from the server. Microsoft Dynamics CRM also includes productivity tools that help users work more efficiently with email and mail merges. Queue management is another productivity feature in Microsoft Dynamics CRM. Queues can be used to track work items that require a consistent process or long period of time to complete.

Chapter 3

Managing Security and Information Access

In this chapter:

If you've deployed multiple systems in the past, you already know that you must design your customer relationship management (CRM) solution to restrict information appropriately based on individual user permissions. Controlling how your users access customer data is a mission-critical component of any business application. Microsoft designed the Microsoft Dynamics CRM security model to support the following goals:

- Provide users with only the information they need to perform their jobs; do not show them data unrelated to their positions.
- Simplify security administration by creating security roles that define security user rights, and then assign users to one or more security roles.
- Support team-based and collaborative projects by enabling users to share records as necessary.

Microsoft Dynamics CRM provides an extremely granular level of security throughout the application. By customizing the security settings, you can construct a security and information access solution that will most likely meet the needs of your organization. The process to customize the Microsoft Dynamics CRM security settings requires that you configure your organization structure, decide which security roles your system users (employees) will have, and then define the security privileges associated with each security role.

Although you might not expect to, you will find yourself continually tweaking and revising the security settings as your business evolves. Fortunately, the Microsoft Dynamics CRM security model makes it easy for you to update and change your security settings on the fly.

Mapping Your Needs

For the first step in planning security settings for your deployment, we recommend that you create a rough model of your company's current operational structure (by using a tool such as Microsoft Office Visio). For each section of your organizational layout, you should identify the approximate number of users and the types of business functions those users perform. You will need this rough organizational map to start planning how you want to set up and configure security in your Microsoft Dynamics CRM deployment.

Important Your Microsoft Dynamics CRM business unit structure should not necessarily match your operational structure. You should configure the Microsoft Dynamics CRM business unit hierarchy to match your security needs, not to create an exact model of your organizational structure. Whereas the operational and Microsoft Dynamics CRM security business unit structures typically remain consistent for smaller organizations, midsize and enterprise organizations usually need to design a Microsoft Dynamics CRM business unit structure that does not match their organizational chart.

To put this type of organizational mapping into a real-world context, consider an example organization. Figure 3-1 shows the business structure for a fictional company named Adventure Works Cycle.

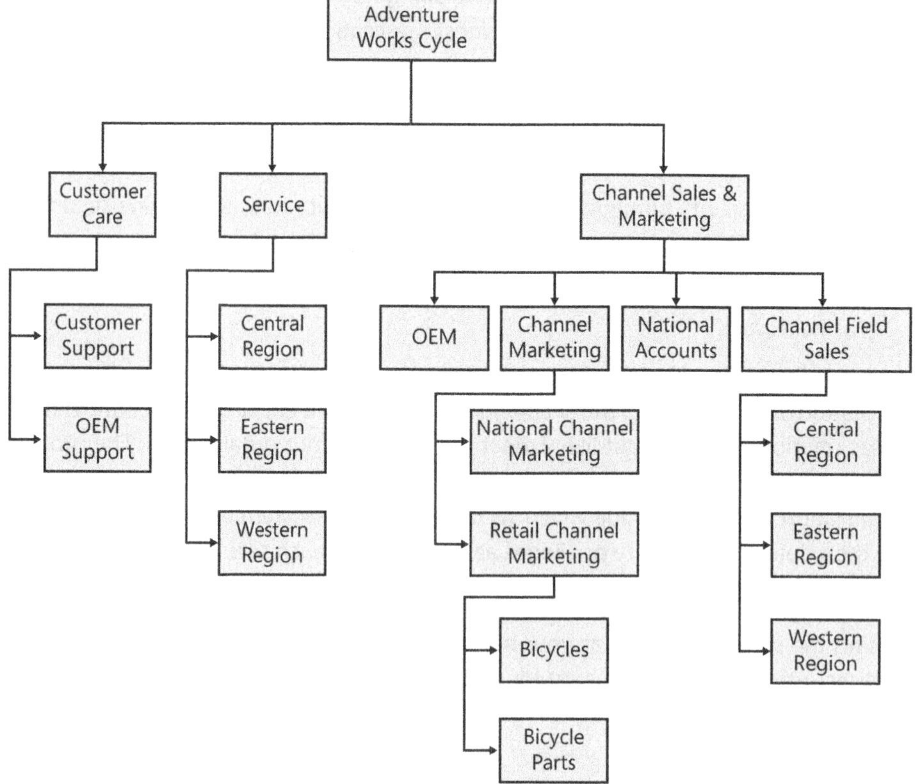

FIGURE 3-1 Organization structure for a sample company called Adventure Works Cycle

Each box in the figure represents a business unit in Microsoft Dynamics CRM, and you can structure parent and child relationships between business units. *Business units* represent a logical grouping of business activities, and you have great latitude in determining how to create and structure them for your implementation.

Tip Sometimes people refer to business units by using the acronym BU.

One constraint of configuring business units is that you can specify only one parent for each business unit. However, each business unit can have multiple child business units. Also, you must assign every Microsoft Dynamics CRM user to one (and only one) business unit.

For each user in your organizational structure, you should try to define answers for questions such as the following:

- Which areas of Microsoft Dynamics CRM will the users need access to (such as Sales, Marketing, and Customer Service)?
- Do users need the ability to create and update records, or will read-only access suffice?
- Will you need to structure project teams or functional groups of users that work together on related records?
- Can you group users together by job function or some other classification (such as finance, operations, and executive managers)?

As you map out your business units and users, you will probably find situations where users from different business units need to work together on a set of shared set of records. However the Microsoft Dynamics CRM security only allows you to specify one business unit per user. In these types of situations, you should consider the use of *teams* in Microsoft Dynamics CRM. Teams are a group of users that share and collaborate on records. Even though you specify a single business unit for a team, each team can consist of users from one or many business units.

After you develop a feel for how your organization and users will use Microsoft Dynamics CRM, you can start to configure the Microsoft Dynamics CRM application to meet those needs.

Real World For smaller organizations, mapping out your Microsoft Dynamics CRM organization model might take only 15 minutes. However, you may want to budget a few hours to map out the security model for enterprise organizations with hundreds of users spread geographically throughout the country. You should also not expect to get the security model *done* because it will constantly change over time.

Don't spend too much time trying to perfect your organizational model right now. The goal of the exercise is to research and develop more details about how your organization intends to use Microsoft Dynamics CRM so that you can configure the security settings correctly. This organizational model won't be your final version, but it can help you think through and consider the ramifications of the security settings you choose.

Security Concepts

After you've developed a rough organizational model with information about the different types of users in your system, you must translate that information into Microsoft Dynamics CRM security settings. Before we explain how to configure the security settings in the software, we explain two of the key topics related to Microsoft Dynamics CRM security:

- Security model concepts
- User authentication

After you understand these concepts, we can get into the details of configuring the software to meet your specific needs. Because of the many security customization options offered in Microsoft Dynamics CRM, very rarely do we see an organizational structure that Microsoft Dynamics CRM security settings cannot accommodate.

Security Model Concepts

The Microsoft Dynamics CRM security model uses two main concepts:

- Role- and object-based security
- Organizational structure

Role-Based and Object-Based Security

Microsoft Dynamics CRM uses security roles and role-based security as its core security management techniques. A *security role* describes a set of access levels and privileges for each of the entities (such as Leads, Accounts, or Cases) in Microsoft Dynamics CRM. All Microsoft Dynamics CRM users must have one or more security roles assigned to them. Therefore, when a user logs on to the system, Microsoft Dynamics CRM looks at the user's assigned security roles and uses that information to determine what the software will allow that user to do and see throughout the system. This is known as *role-based security*.

With this security model, you also can define different security parameters for the various records (such as Lead, Account, Contact, and so on) because each record has an owner. By comparing the business unit of the record owner with the security role and business unit of a user, Microsoft Dynamics CRM determines that user's security privileges for a single record. You can think of configuring access rights on the individual record level (not the entity level) as *object-based security*. Figure 3-2 illustrates this concept.

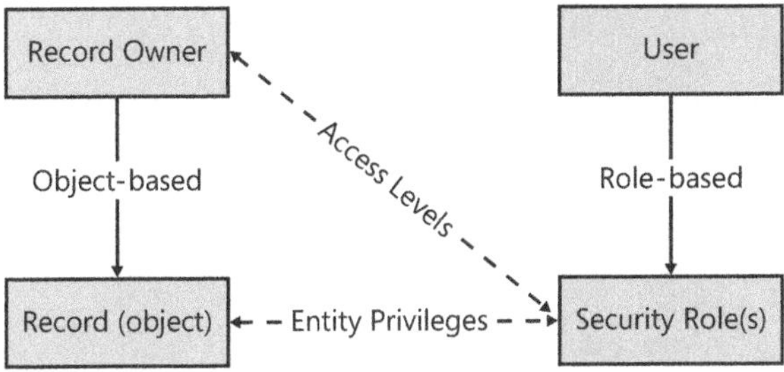

FIGURE 3-2 Role-based security and object-based security combine to determine user rights.

Important Both users and teams can own records in Microsoft Dynamics CRM 2011.

In summary, Microsoft Dynamics CRM uses a combination of role-based and object-based security to manage access rights and permissions throughout the system.

Organizational Structure

In addition to security roles, Microsoft Dynamics CRM uses an organization's structure as a key concept in its security model. Microsoft Dynamics CRM uses the following definitions to describe an organization's structure:

- **Organization** The company that owns the deployment. The organization is the top level of the Microsoft Dynamics CRM business management hierarchy. Microsoft Dynamics CRM automatically creates the organization based on the name that you enter during the software installation. You cannot change or delete this information. You can also refer to the organization as the *root business unit*.
- **Business unit** A logical grouping of your business operations. Each business unit can act as a parent for one or more child business units. In the sample organization in Figure 3-1, you would describe the Customer Care business unit as the parent business unit of the Customer Support and OEM Support business units. Likewise, you would refer to the Customer Support and OEM Support business units as child business units.
- **Team** A group of users that work together. Team members can belong to different business units.
- **User** Someone who typically works for the organization and has access to Microsoft Dynamics CRM. Each user belongs to one (and only one) business unit, and each user is assigned one or more security roles.

Later in this chapter, we explain how these terms relate to setting up and configuring security roles.

User Authentication

Microsoft Dynamics CRM supports three different types of security methods to authenticate users when they try to log on to the system:

- Integrated Windows authentication
- Claims-based authentication
- Microsoft Windows Live ID

Customers that purchase Microsoft Dynamics CRM and deploy the software on premises will use Integrated Windows authentication, and they have the option to deploy a claims-based authentication for Internet-facing deployments of Microsoft Dynamics CRM as well. For on-premises deployments of Microsoft Dynamics CRM, each user who logs on to the system needs to use a Microsoft Active Directory account.

Only customers who use Microsoft Dynamics CRM Online will use Microsoft Windows Live ID to authenticate and log on to the system.

Integrated Windows Authentication

Microsoft Dynamics CRM uses Integrated Windows authentication (formerly called NTLM, and also referred to as Microsoft Windows NT Challenge/Response authentication) for user security authentication in the web browser and in the Microsoft Dynamics CRM for Outlook interfaces. By using Integrated Windows authentication, users can simply browse to the Microsoft Dynamics CRM website and Microsoft Internet Explorer automatically passes their encrypted user credentials to Microsoft Dynamics CRM and logs them on. This means that users log on to Microsoft Dynamics CRM (authenticate) by using their existing Microsoft Active Directory directory domain accounts, without having to sign in to the Microsoft Dynamics CRM application explicitly. This integrated security provides great convenience for users because there's no need for them to remember an additional password just for the CRM system. Using Integrated Windows authentication also helps system administrators because they can continue to manage user accounts from Active Directory services. For example, disabling a user in the Active Directory directory service prevents him from logging on to Microsoft Dynamics CRM because the user's logon and password will not work anymore.

More Info Disabling or deleting users in Active Directory prevents them from logging on to Microsoft Dynamics CRM, but it does not automatically disable their user records in Microsoft Dynamics CRM. Because all active users count against your licenses, make sure that you remember to disable their user records in Microsoft Dynamics CRM to free their licenses. Also, if you change a user's name in Active Directory, you must manually update it in Microsoft Dynamics CRM. We strongly recommend that you deactivate the user in Microsoft Dynamics CRM before deactivating his or her Active Directory account.

Most companies install Microsoft Dynamics CRM on their local intranet in the same Active Directory domain that users log on to. By default, the User Authentication security settings in Microsoft Internet Explorer automatically log users on to any intranet site that they browse to, including Microsoft Dynamics CRM. This default setting will work fine for almost all of your users.

However, you may find that you want to alter the default security settings to change how the Internet Explorer browser handles user authentication. Typical reasons to modify the Internet Explorer security settings include the following:

- You want to log on to Microsoft Dynamics CRM impersonating one of your users during setup and development.
- Your Microsoft Dynamics CRM deployment resides in a different Active Directory domain (or on the Internet) and you want to change the logon settings.
- You want to trust the Microsoft Dynamics CRM website explicitly to allow for pop-up windows.

To view your Internet Explorer 8 security settings, click Internet Options on the Tools menu in Internet Explorer. The Security tab in the Internet Options dialog box displays web content zones, including Internet, Local intranet, Trusted sites, and Restricted sites, as shown in Figure 3-3.

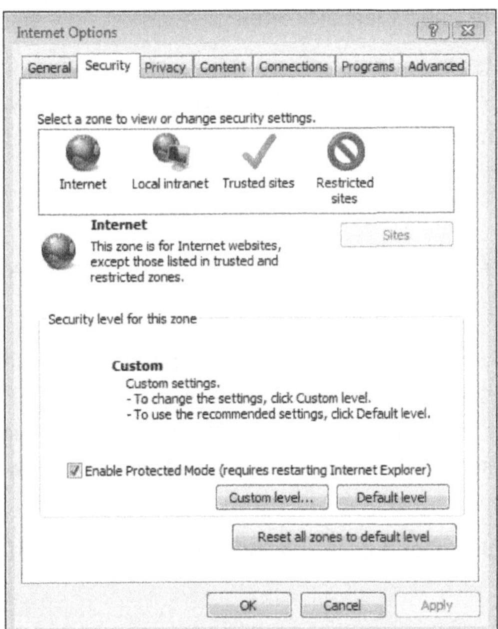

FIGURE 3-3 Web content zones in Internet Explorer

By altering the security settings, you can change how Internet Explorer passes your logon information to various websites, such as your Microsoft Dynamics CRM website.

Turning off automatic logon in the Local intranet zone

1. In the Security tab, click Local intranet, and then click Custom level.
2. In the Security Settings dialog box, scroll down until you see the User Authentication section, and then select Prompt for user name and password.

When you disable automatic logon, Internet Explorer does not automatically pass your user credentials to Microsoft Dynamics CRM (or any other website on your local intranet). Instead, it prompts you to enter your user name and password when you browse to the Microsoft Dynamics CRM server. This prompt gives you the opportunity to enter any user credentials that you want, including user credentials from a different domain. As an administrator, you may want to log on as a different user during your setup and configuration phase to confirm that your security settings are correct.

In addition to disabling automatic logon, you may want to add Microsoft Dynamics CRM as a trusted site in Internet Explorer or list it as part of your intranet zone. The steps and benefits of either are almost identical; you use the following steps to add Microsoft Dynamics CRM as a trusted site.

Adding a trusted site to Internet Explorer

1. In the Security tab, click Trusted sites, and then click Sites.
2. In the Trusted sites dialog box, enter the address of your Microsoft Dynamics CRM server (include the *http://* portion of the address), and then click Add. You may need to clear the Require server verification check box if your Microsoft Dynamics CRM deployment does not use *https://*.
3. Click OK.

Adding a trusted site to Internet Explorer accomplishes two things in regard to Microsoft Dynamics CRM:

- Internet Explorer will automatically pass your user credentials to the website and attempt to log you on. You may want to set this up for your Microsoft Dynamics CRM users who are not located on your local intranet (such as offsite or remote users) so that they do not have to enter a user name and password each time they browse to Microsoft Dynamics CRM.
- The Internet Explorer Pop-up Blocker allows pop-up windows for any website listed in your Trusted sites zone.

Caution Intranet sites and trusted sites in Internet Explorer become quite powerful, so you must use caution when deciding which sites you will trust. For example, the default security settings for trusted sites in Internet Explorer automatically install signed Microsoft ActiveX controls on your computer.

Microsoft Dynamics CRM and Pop-up Blockers

Many users utilize a pop-up blocker add-in for Internet Explorer in an attempt to limit the number of pop-up advertisements they see when browsing the Internet. Unfortunately, some of these pop-up blockers may also block some of the web browser windows that Microsoft Dynamics CRM uses. Consequently, you'll probably need to let your users know how to configure their pop-up blockers to allow pop-up windows from the Microsoft Dynamics CRM application.

Internet Explorer 8 includes a pop-up blocker, but the default setting allows sites in the Local intranet and Trusted sites zones to open pop-up windows. If Internet Explorer does not recognize Microsoft Dynamics CRM as an intranet site, or if you don't want to add it as a trusted site, you can configure the pop-up blocker to allow pop-up windows from the Microsoft Dynamics CRM website. (On the Tools menu, point to Pop-Up Blocker, and then click Pop-up Blocker Settings to enter the Microsoft Dynamics CRM address.)

Some pop-up blockers do not allow you to enter a trusted address manually like the Internet Explorer pop-up blocker does. Therefore, you have to browse to the website you want to allow, and then click some sort of Allow Pop-ups button.

Here's another trick related to pop-up windows: You can reference the same Microsoft Dynamics CRM website by using several different techniques. For example, you could access Microsoft Dynamics CRM by using any of the following:

- Computer (NetBIOS) name (Example: *http://crm*)
- Internet Protocol (IP) address (Example: *http://127.0.0.1*)
- Fully qualified domain name (Example: *http://crm.domain.local*)
- A new entry in your Hosts file (add by editing C:\WINDOWS\system32\drivers\etc\hosts)

Although all of these URLs take you to the same Microsoft Dynamics CRM server, Internet Explorer 8 treats each of these as different websites. Therefore, you could configure different security settings in Internet Explorer for each of these URLs. For example, you can browse to the NetBIOS name by using Integrated Windows authentication to log on as yourself, but you could configure Internet Explorer to prompt for a logon when you browse to the IP address to impersonate a user.

Claims-Based Authentication

Although many users will access Microsoft Dynamics CRM over a local intranet connection using Integrated Windows authentication, Microsoft Dynamics CRM also offers customers the option of deploying Microsoft Dynamics CRM as an Internet-facing deployment (often abbreviated as *IFD*). In an IFD scenario, customers could browse over the Internet to a custom URL address such as *http://crm.yourdomainname.com* to access your Microsoft Dynamics CRM system. Using this access method, users do not need to create a virtual private network (VPN) connection to your network. They could use any type of standard Internet connection to access their data remotely. If you want to set up an IFD deployment, Microsoft Dynamics CRM 2011 requires federated services that support claims-based authentication. Most companies will use Active Directory Federation Services 2.0 (AD FS 2.0) for their federation services.

More Info Microsoft Windows Server introduced a claims-based access platform where it added support for the WS-Trust, WS-Federation, and SAML 2.0 protocols. Microsoft Dynamics CRM 2011 discontinues the Microsoft Dynamics CRM 4.0 forms-based authentication design for IFD and it uses the new claims-based option instead. After claims is properly enabled in your environment, you still need to go through the CRM IFD setup steps to make your CRM application accessible outside of your network. For more information on setting up claims-based authentication for Microsoft Dynamics CRM, please refer to the Microsoft Dynamics CRM Implementation Guide at *http://www.microsoft.com/downloads*.

When users browse to the external IFD URL that you configure, users see a logon screen like the one shown in Figure 3-4.

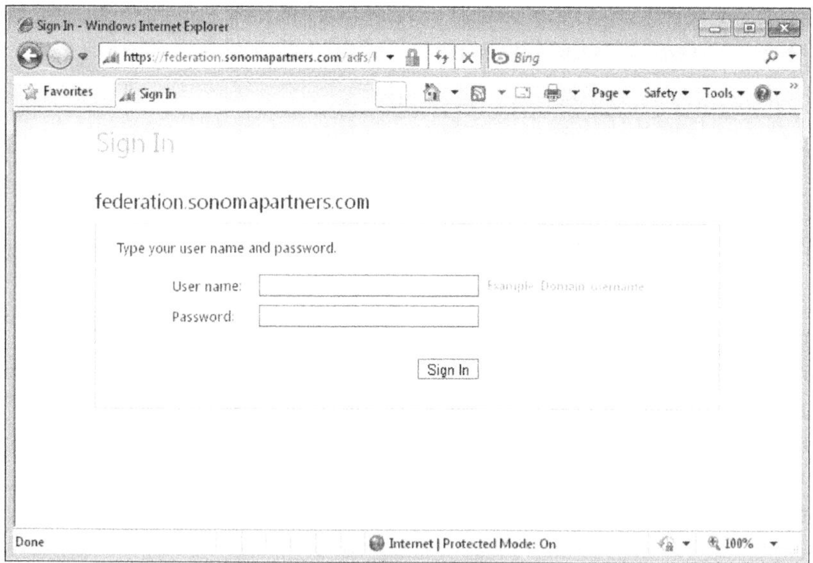

FIGURE 3-4 Internet-facing deployment logon screen

At the logon screen, the user can enter his or her Active Directory user name and password into the specified form fields. After users log on to Microsoft Dynamics CRM by using the web form, the system will behave in a nearly identical way as when users connect to the system over the local intranet using Integrated Windows authentication. However, some parts of the system, such as the dynamic worksheets in Microsoft Office Excel, will not work correctly unless the user also has Microsoft Dynamics CRM for Outlook installed on the computer.

Important When accessing Microsoft Dynamics CRM through forms-based authentication, some portions of the software such as dynamic worksheets will require that the user install the Microsoft Dynamics CRM for Outlook.

The Microsoft Dynamics CRM Implementation Guide explains how to set up and configure claims-based authentication and IFD, so we won't repeat that material here.

Windows Live ID

As we previously stated, only Microsoft Dynamics CRM Online customers will use Windows Live ID to authenticate when they log on to their system. Microsoft offers Windows Live ID as a single sign-on service that businesses and consumers can use throughout various Internet websites. By allowing people to use a single logon and password, Windows Live ID simplifies the end-user experience regarding authentication.

More Info Microsoft previously referred to Windows Live ID as the Microsoft Passport Network. Windows Live ID works with MSN Messenger, MSN Hotmail, MSN Music, and many other websites.

When users browse to *http://crm.dynamics.com* and log on, they are prompted to enter their Windows Live ID credentials, as shown in Figure 3-5.

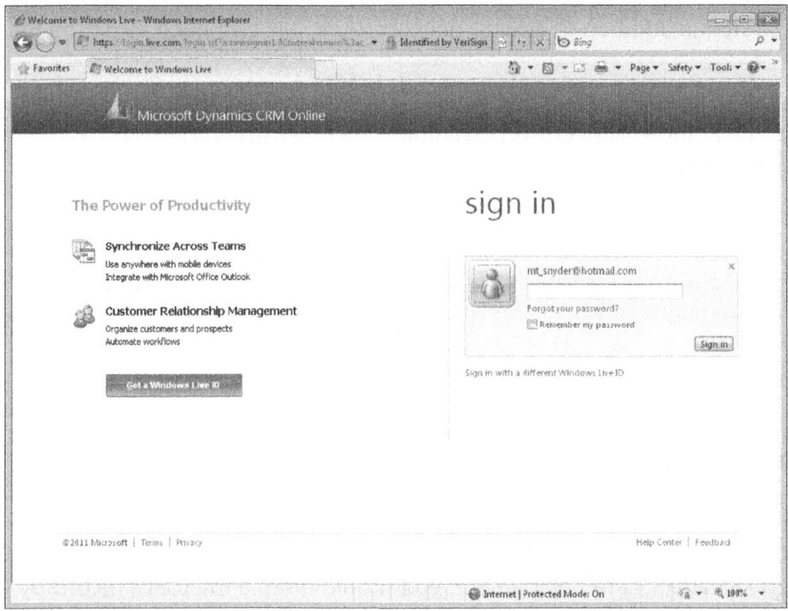

FIGURE 3-5 Entering Windows Live ID credentials on Microsoft Dynamics CRM Online

Please note that when you invite a user to your Microsoft Dynamics CRM Online organization, you must use the email address of that user's Windows Live ID account.

Managing Users

A user is someone with access to Microsoft Dynamics CRM who typically works for your organization. To manage users in Microsoft Dynamics CRM, browse to Administration in the Settings area, and click Users. For each user, you must complete the following security-related tasks:

- Assign one or more security roles to the user.
- Assign the user to one business unit.
- Assign the user to one or more teams.
- Assign a Client Access License type.

The combination of these four settings determines a user's access to information in Microsoft Dynamics CRM.

Note Although most of your users will be employees of your organization, you can create user accounts for trusted third-party vendors or suppliers if you want to grant them access to your system. Obviously, you should carefully structure the business units and security roles to make sure that third-party users don't see information that you don't want them to view.

As an administrator, in addition to adding new users you will also need to do the following:

- Disable old users and reassign their records to different users.
- Monitor the number of Microsoft Dynamics CRM licenses you're using to make sure you are compliant.

Tip If you change a user's business unit, Microsoft Dynamics CRM removes all of that user's security roles because roles can vary by business unit. In such a situation, remember to assign the user security roles again; otherwise, he or she won't be able to log on to Microsoft Dynamics CRM.

Reassigning User Records

As part of the usual course of business, employees will leave your organization and you'll need to adjust their user record in the system accordingly. When a user stops working with your Microsoft Dynamics CRM deployment, you should disable the user's record by clicking the Disable button located in the ribbon. When you disable the user, she can no longer log on to your Microsoft Dynamics CRM system. However, disabling a user will not change her record ownership because disabled users can still own records.

Note To maintain data integrity, Microsoft Dynamics CRM does not allow you to delete users.

After disabling the user, you will also probably want to reassign his or her records to a different user in the system. By doing so, you can make sure that a different user will address any open activities or follow-ups that the previous user didn't complete yet. We recommend that you reassign the records using one of two methods:

- Bulk reassign
- Manually reassigning active records

Bulk Reassign

If you open a user record in Microsoft Dynamics CRM, you will see the Reassign Records button in the ribbon. When you click the Reassign Records button, the dialog box shown in Figure 3-6 appears.

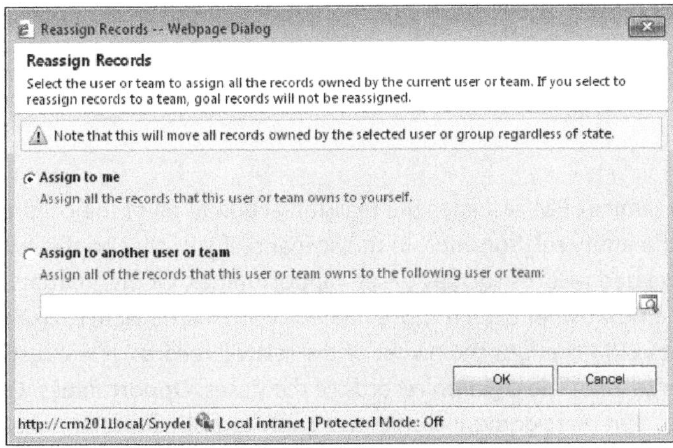

FIGURE 3-6 Reassign Bulk Records dialog box

When you select a different user and click OK, Microsoft Dynamics CRM reassigns all of the records from the old user to the new user you specified. Although this provides a quick and easy method to reassign records, it moves all of the old user's records regardless of their state. This typically does not accomplish what most customers want because it changes the owner of inactive records such as completed activities, qualified leads, won opportunities, and so on. This caused some confusion for one of our customers because it changed the data that appeared in the commission and sales activity reports! In addition, the bulk reassign can confuse users looking at the activity history for a particular account because the owner of the old inactive activities changes from the previous user to the new user.

Note Reassigning records only changes the owner of a record. It does not change the user who created or modified the record; that information stays intact.

In light of these constraints, we consider the Reassign Bulk Records option something of a brute force tool that you should use only in limited circumstances.

Manually Reassign Active Records

Although no one likes to see the word *manual* appear in any task description, we strongly encourage you to reassign the records manually from the old user to a new user instead of using the Reassign Bulk Records tool. By doing so, you maintain the history of the data linked to the previous user. At first this may appear easy to accomplish because you can simply select the active records for the various entities and assign them to a new owner. For example, you could select just the open leads, cases, and opportunities and assign them to a new owner. However, Microsoft Dynamics CRM maintains entity relationships between records so that actions taken against a parent record cascade down to its children records. For example, when you change the owner of an opportunity record, Microsoft Dynamics CRM automatically changes the owner of the activities related to that opportunity based on the relationship configuration.

More Info We explain entity relationships and cascading actions in detail later in Chapter 9, "Entity Relationships."

By default, Microsoft Dynamics CRM cascades the reassign action to all of the children records in almost all of the entity relationships. In this scenario, if you change the owner of an Account, all of its related records such as Cases, Opportunities, Quotes, Orders, and so on will also receive the new owner even if those related records are inactive. Likewise, when Microsoft Dynamics CRM changes the owner of the related records, it will cascade that reassignment action to all of the children records of the Cases, Opportunities, Quotes, Orders, and so on. Again, that reassignment would also apply to both active and inactive records, which most customers would not want to happen.

To avoid this scenario, we recommend that you change the default entity relationship behaviors before you start reassigning records. You should configure the cascading behavior from Cascade All to Cascade Active so that it takes action only against active children records, as shown in Figure 3-7 for the Account to Task entity relationship.

Unfortunately, you can't change this entity relationship behavior for the entire system in one place. You need to configure the relationships manually for each of the various entity relationships.

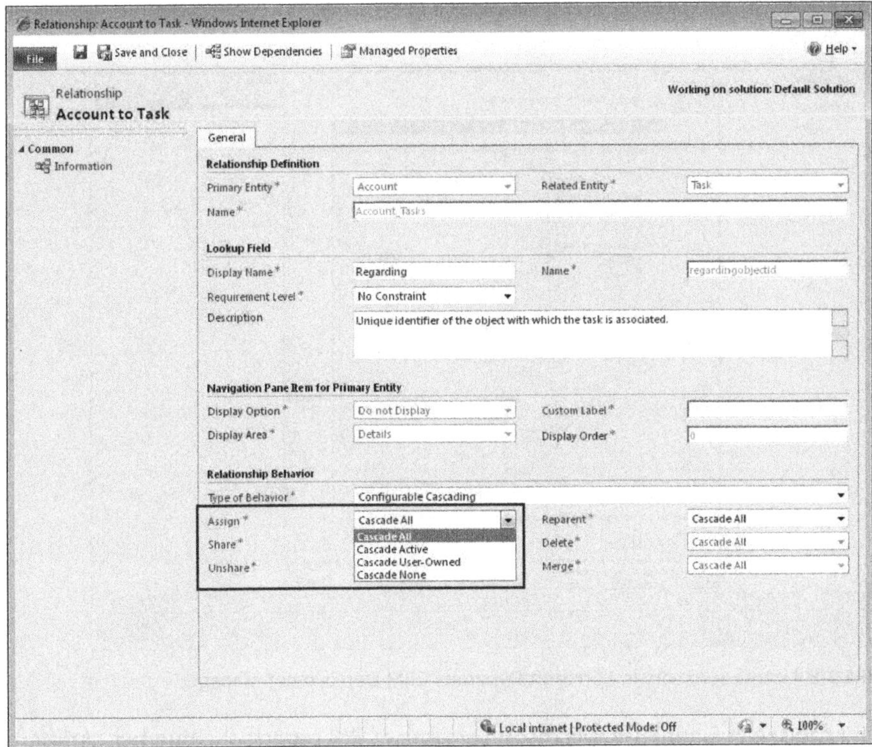

FIGURE 3-7 Changing the default relationship behavior between entities before reassigning records

Monitoring License Usage for Compliance

With the on-premise version of Microsoft Dynamics CRM, you need to keep track of the number of active Microsoft Dynamics CRM licenses your company uses to ensure that you do not use more licenses than you should. As we mentioned earlier, Microsoft Dynamics CRM licensing trusts customers to monitor their own usage because the software lets customers add as many servers and users as they want (regardless of how many they actually purchased). Therefore, the administrator needs to monitor license usage on a consistent basis to ensure compliance.

Note Microsoft Dynamics CRM Online licensing differs from on-premise licensing because it uses a hard enforcement on the number of user licenses. If you try to add more users than you have licenses for, the system will send you an error message and reject the action.

If you want to view a summary of your current active licenses, start the Microsoft Dynamics CRM Deployment Manager on the Microsoft Dynamics CRM web server, right-click the Microsoft Dynamics CRM link in the left column, and select Properties. The Microsoft Dynamics CRM Properties dialog box opens. Click the License tab (shown in Figure 3-8).

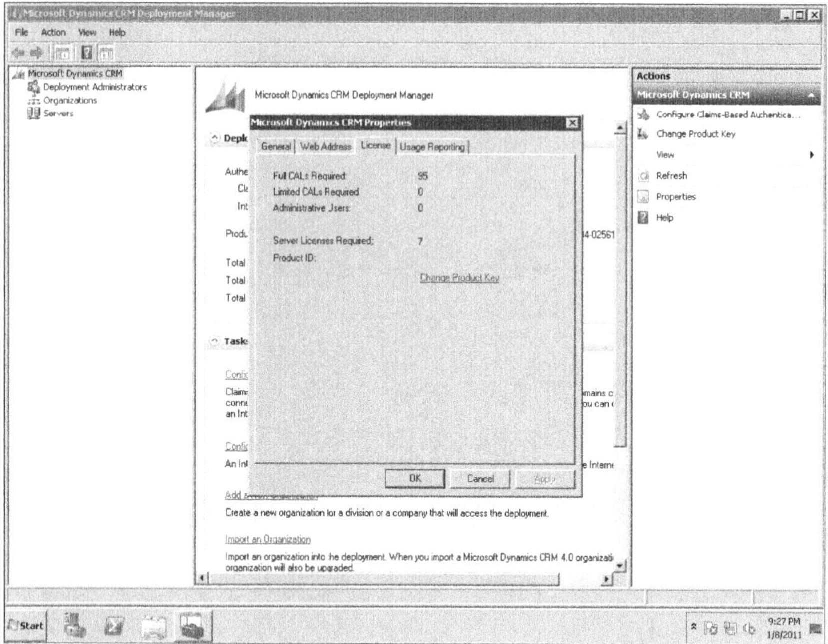

FIGURE 3-8 License summary in Microsoft Dynamics CRM Deployment Manager

As you can see in Figure 3-8, Microsoft Dynamics CRM reports the number of different users for each of the different license types: Full, Limited, and Administrative. It also shows how many server licenses should be owned. You must purchase the corresponding number of licenses to match the number of Full and Limited users in your system, but you do not need to purchase user licenses for administrative users.

Microsoft Dynamics CRM allows you to set up multiple organizations in a single Microsoft Dynamics CRM deployment, and this license summary will display the total number of users across all of the organizations. Unfortunately, you cannot run this license summary tool for a single organization, so if you need this information detailed by organization, you must log on manually to each organization and perform a query to determine the number of active users in each category.

Measuring End User Usage

The license summary shows you how many enabled Microsoft Dynamics CRM users your system contains. However, just because you enable a user to access Microsoft Dynamics CRM, that doesn't mean that user is actively using the system! Because Microsoft Dynamics CRM licensing is based on a named user model (not a concurrent user model), you're paying a license fee for each user you enable. To maximize your software investment you should make sure that the enabled users actively use Microsoft Dynamics CRM.

Unfortunately, Microsoft Dynamics CRM doesn't include any pre-built tools or utilities to provide you with end-user usage reporting. You can create your own custom reports based on data fields such as created on, modified on, and possibly the audit data. Unfortunately, relying just on this data to provide you with usage data might not tell you the complete story because auditing might not be enabled for all entities and all data fields. In addition you should be careful about enabling audit for *everything* because that might negatively impact your system performance.

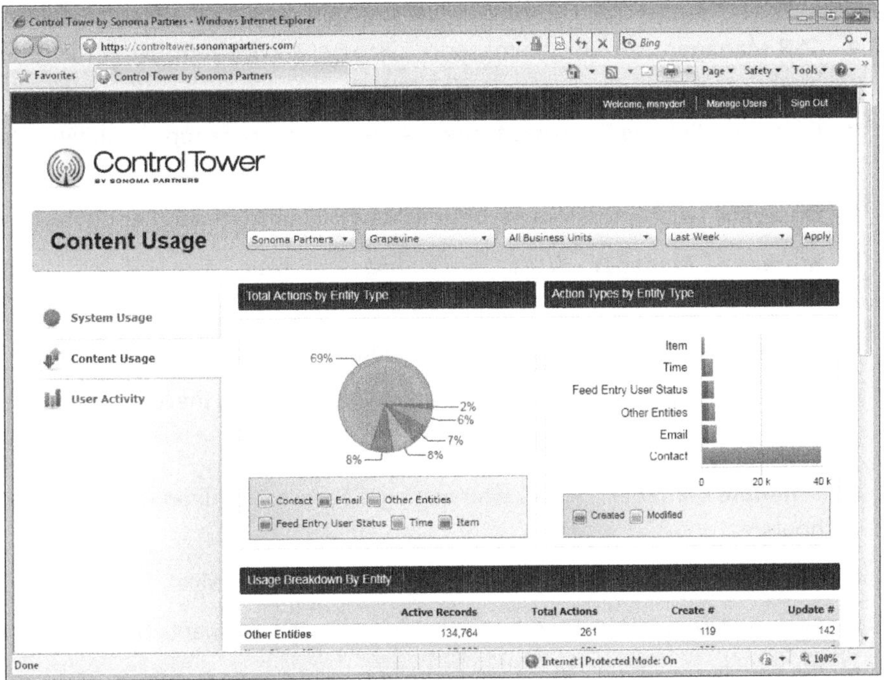

To help provide our Microsoft Dynamics CRM customers with detailed usage information, our firm Sonoma Partners created a proprietary cloud-based solution named Control Tower that helps customers answer these questions:

- Are people using your CRM system?
- How are people using your CRM system?
- How is a specific user interacting with your CRM system?

The Control Tower application takes nightly snapshots of the data and provides web-based reports from an Azure-hosted website. By offloading the reporting to a different server and not requiring auditing to be enabled for all entities, Control Tower provides a quick and efficient end-user reporting tool. For more information about Control Tower, visit *http://www.sonomapartners.com*.

Security Roles and Business Units

As we explained earlier, Microsoft Dynamics CRM uses a combination of role-based security and object-based security to determine what users can see and do in the deployment. Instead of configuring security for each user one record at a time, you assign security settings and permissions to a security role, and then you assign one or more security roles to a user. Microsoft Dynamics CRM includes the following 14 predefined security roles:

- **CEO-Business Manager** A user who manages the organization at the corporate business level
- **CSR Manager** A user who manages customer service activities at the local or team level
- **Customer Service Representative** A customer service representative (CSR) at any level
- **Delegate** A user that can perform actions on behalf of another user
- **Marketing Manager** A user who manages marketing activities at the local or team level
- **Marketing Professional** A user engaged in marketing activities at any level
- **Sales Manager** A user who manages sales activities at the local or team level
- **Salesperson** A salesperson at any level
- **Schedule Manager** A user who manages services, required resources, and working hours
- **Scheduler** A user who schedules appointments for services
- **System Administrator** A user who defines and implements the process at any level
- **System Customizer** A user who customizes Microsoft Dynamics CRM records, attributes, relationships, and forms
- **Vice President of Marketing** A user who manages marketing activities at the business unit level
- **Vice President of Sales** A user who manages the organization at the business unit level

These default security roles include predefined rights and permissions typically associated with these roles so that you can save time by using them as the starting point for your deployment. You can edit any of the default security roles, except for System Administrator, to fit the needs of your business.

When you assign multiple security roles to a user, Microsoft Dynamics CRM combines the user rights so that the user can perform the highest-level activity associated with any of her roles. In other words, if you assign two security roles that have conflicting security rights,

Microsoft Dynamics CRM grants the user the least-restrictive permission of the two. Security roles combine together to grant users all of the permissions for all of their assigned security roles. If one of a user's security roles grants a permission, that user *always* possesses that permission, even if you assign him another security role that conflicts with the original permission. For example, consider a fictional Vice President of Sales named Connie Watson. Figure 3-9 shows that Connie has two security roles assigned to her: Salesperson and Vice President of Marketing.

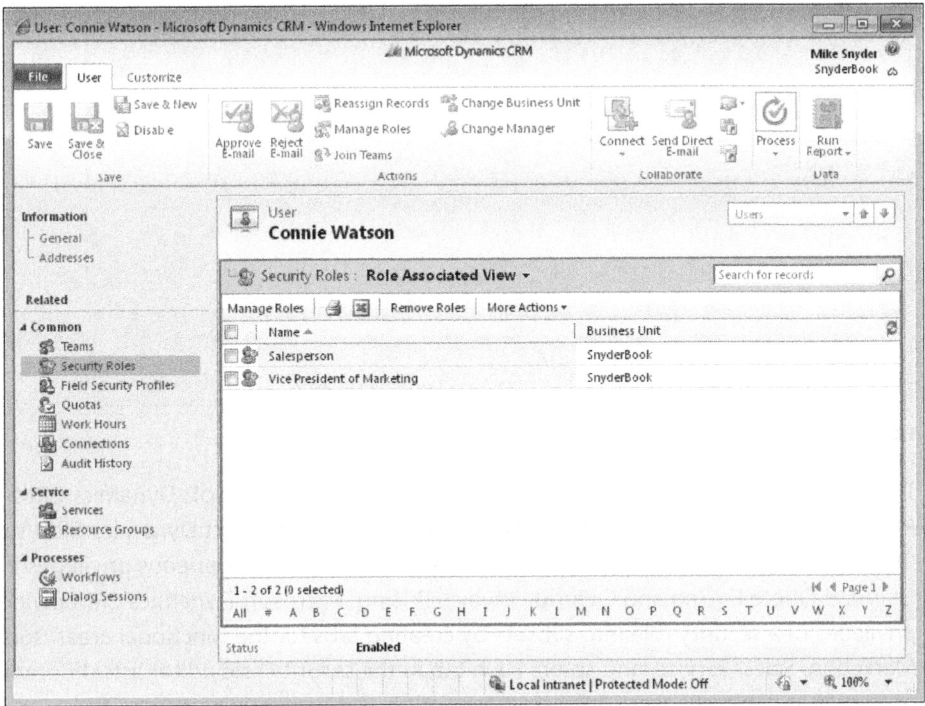

FIGURE 3-9 Multiple security roles assigned to a user

In the Microsoft Dynamics CRM default security roles, a user with only the Salesperson security role cannot create new announcements, but the Vice President of Marketing security role can. Because Microsoft Dynamics CRM grants the least-restrictive permission across all of a user's roles, Connie is able to create announcements in this example because she is also assigned the Vice President of Marketing security role.

Security Role Definitions

Before we explain how to modify security roles, we quickly cover the terminology related to security roles. To view and manage the settings for a security role, browse to Administration in the Settings area and click Security Roles. Double-click one of the roles listed in the grid. Figure 3-10 shows the Salesperson default security role settings.

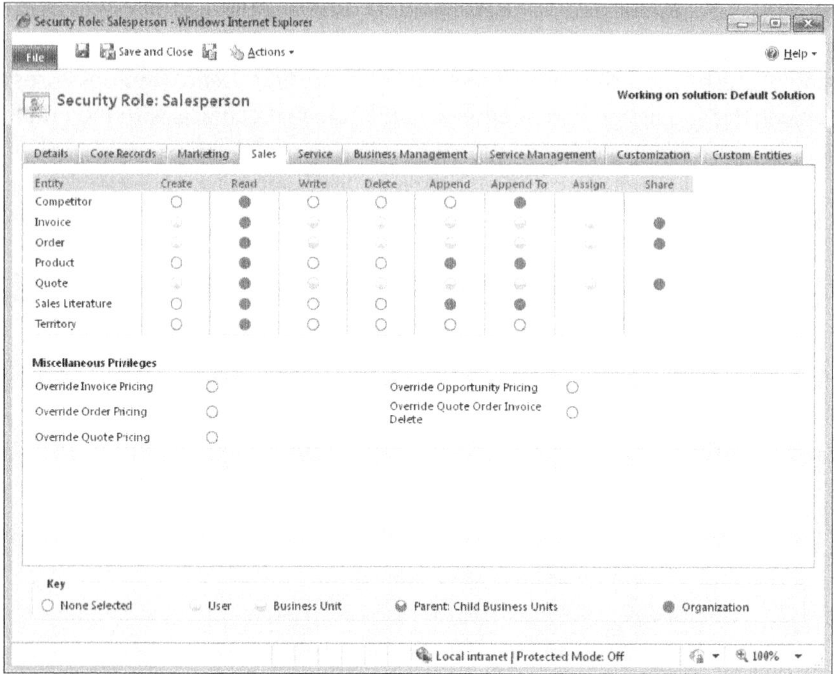

FIGURE 3-10 Salesperson security role settings

The columns in the top table represent entity privileges in Microsoft Dynamics CRM. *Privileges* give a user permission to perform an action in Microsoft Dynamics CRM such as Create, Read, or Write. The bottom section lists additional miscellaneous privileges including Override Quote Pricing and Override Invoice Pricing. Microsoft Dynamics CRM divides the privileges of a security role into subsets by creating tabs for the functional areas, such as Marketing, Sales, Service, and so on. Each tab in the security role editor lists different entity privileges and miscellaneous privileges for entities in Microsoft Dynamics CRM.

The colored circles in the security role settings define the access level for that privilege. *Access levels* determine how deep or high in the organizational business unit hierarchy the user can perform the specified privilege. For example, you could configure access levels for a security role so that a user could delete any record owned by someone in her business unit but only read records owned by users in different business units.

Important The actions that privileges grant to users (such as Create and Delete) do not vary by access level. For example, the Read privilege for the User access level offers the same action (functionality) as the Read privilege for the Organization access level. However, the different access levels determine on which records in Microsoft Dynamics CRM the user can execute the privilege.

In the following subsections, we explore configuring access levels for a security role in more detail.

Access Levels

As you can see in the key (located at the bottom of Figure 3-10), Microsoft Dynamics CRM offers five access levels:

- **None Selected** Always denies the privilege to the users assigned to the role.
- **User** Grants the privilege for records that the user or team owns, in addition to records explicitly shared with the user and records shared with a team to which the user belongs. We explain sharing records later in this chapter.
- **Business Unit** Grants the privilege for records with ownership in the user's business unit.
- **Parent: Child Business Units** Grants the privilege for records with ownership in the user's business unit, in addition to records with ownership in a child business unit of the user's business unit.
- **Organization** Grants the privilege for all records in the organization, regardless of the business unit hierarchical level to which the object or user belongs.

Note The User, Business Unit, and Parent: Child Business Units access levels do not apply to some privileges, such as Bulk Edit and Print (found in the Business Management tab under Miscellaneous Privileges), because the concept of user ownership or business units doesn't apply to those privileges. No user or business unit owns Bulk Edit or Print because they're just actions. Therefore, these types of privileges offer only two access levels: None Selected and Organization. In these scenarios, you can think of None Selected as "No" and Organization as "Yes" in regard to whether the user possesses that privilege.

Consider an example scenario to understand access levels in a real-world context. Figure 3-11 shows five business units, six users, and six Contact records.

We examine the impact of configuring different access levels for a single privilege (Contact Read) in the context of a fictional user named Gail Erickson. Gail belongs to the Service business unit, which is a child of the Adventure Works Cycle business unit and is also a parent of the Central Region business unit. Each of the Contacts shown is owned by the user record to which it is linked. Table 3-1 shows which Contact records Gail could read for each of the five possible access level configurations.

TABLE 3-1 Read Privileges for Gail Erickson by Access Level

Read privilege access level for the Contact entity	Bob Gage	Twanna Evans	Cathan Cook	Alice Ciccu	David Jones	Allison Brown
None	No	No	No	No	No	No
User	No	No	Yes	No	No	No
Business Unit	No	No	Yes	Yes	No	No
Parent: Child Business Units	No	No	Yes	Yes	Yes	Yes
Organization	Yes	Yes	Yes	Yes	Yes	Yes

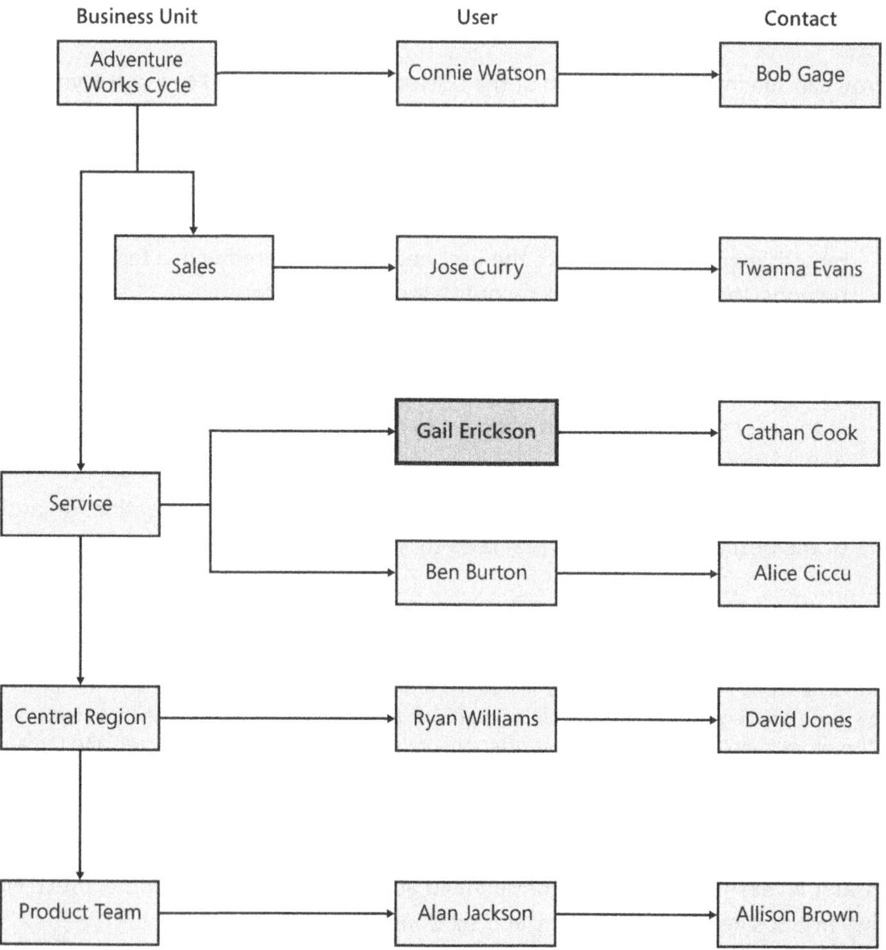

FIGURE 3-11 Access levels example

For the Business Unit access level, Microsoft Dynamics CRM grants Gail the Read privilege for the Alice Ciccu contact because Ben Burton owns that record and he belongs to the same business unit as Gail. For the Parent: Child Business Units access level, Microsoft Dynamics CRM grants Gail the Read privilege for the David Jones and Allison Brown records because the Central Region and Product Team business units are children of the Service business unit that Gail belongs to, and both the David Jones and Allison Brown records are owned by users that belong to these child business units.

As this example illustrates, configuring access levels for a security role requires that you understand and consider the following parameters:

- The organization and business unit hierarchy
- Record ownership and the business unit that the record owner belongs to
- The business unit of the logged-in user

Important Microsoft Dynamics CRM treats records owned by teams the same as if a user in the team's business unit owned it. For example, if team ABC from the Sales business unit owned the Twanna Evans record, the security system would function the same as the user Jose Curry owning the Twanna Evans record.

Table 3-2 summarizes how Microsoft Dynamics CRM grants and denies privileges based on these parameters.

TABLE 3-2 Privileges Granted Based on Access Level and Record Ownerships

Privilege access level	Record owned by user	Record owned by different user in same business unit	Record owned by user in any child business unit	Record owned by user in any nonchild business unit
None	Deny	Deny	Deny	Deny
User	Grant	Deny	Deny	Deny
Business Unit	Grant	Grant	Deny	Deny
Parent: Child Business Units	Grant	Grant	Grant	Deny
Organization	Grant	Grant	Grant	Grant

By now you should have a good understanding of how Microsoft Dynamics CRM determines whether to grant security privileges to users based on access levels. Now we discuss what each of the privileges means and the actions that they allow users to perform in the system.

Privileges

Privileges define what users can view and do in Microsoft Dynamics CRM, and you bundle privileges together in a security role definition. Some of the privileges describe actions that users can take against entity records such as delete or create, and other privileges define features in Microsoft Dynamics CRM such as Mail Merge and Export to Excel. In this section, we explore the following topics:

- Entity privileges
- Miscellaneous privileges
- Privilege impact on application navigation

Entity Privileges

As Figure 3-10 showed earlier, privileges such as Create, Read, and Write apply to the entities in Microsoft Dynamics CRM. For each entity type and privilege, you can configure a different access level. The following list describes the actions that each privilege allows:

- **Create** Permits the user to add a new record
- **Read** Permits the user to view a record

- **Write** Permits the user to edit an existing record
- **Delete** Permits the user to delete a record
- **Append** Permits the user to attach another entity to, or associate another entity with, a parent record
- **Append To** Permits the user to attach other entities to, or associate other entities with, the record
- **Assign** Permits the user to change a record's owner to a different user
- **Share** Permits the user to share a record with another user or team

More Info Not all of the entity privileges apply to all of the entities in Microsoft Dynamics CRM. For example, the Share privilege does not apply to any of the entities in the Service Management tab. The Enable/Disable privilege applies only to the Business Unit and User entities.

The Append and Append To actions behave a little differently from the other privileges because you must configure them on two different entities for them to work correctly. To understand the Append and Append To actions better, consider the analogy of attaching a sticky note to a wall. To configure the sticky note concept using Microsoft Dynamics CRM security privileges, you need to assign Append privileges to the sticky note and then configure Append To privileges to the wall. Translating that concept to Microsoft Dynamics CRM entities if you want to attach (or append) a Contact (the sticky note) to an Account (the wall), the user would need Append privileges for the Contact and Append To privileges for the Account record.

In Microsoft Dynamics CRM, you can also configure entity privileges for any custom entities that you create in your deployment. You can configure all five access levels for each custom entity for all of the entity privileges.

More Info If you're wondering what the Web Wizard entities are, they refer to web pages Microsoft Dynamics CRM Online users see during sign up. They are only for Microsoft Dynamics CRM internal use—any changes you make will not have any impact.

Troubleshooting Entity Privilege Errors

Sometimes when you're adjusting Microsoft Dynamics CRM security roles, you may later get an error message telling you that the user does not have permission to complete an action. You may think to yourself, "What in the world is this talking about?" After you review the security roles, you wonder which privilege could *possibly* be missing that would result in this error.

Many times you will need to grant a user a security privilege that would not be obvious to you by simply looking at the security role configuration screens. For example, would you guess that you need the Append To Order privilege before you can create an Appointment record?

If you find yourself getting stuck trying to track down the appropriate privileges that a user needs to perform an action, we recommend that you refer to the Microsoft Dynamics CRM software development kit (SDK) because it contains documentation regarding the various privileges users need to complete certain actions. You can find this information in the "Privileges by Message" section of the SDK. For example, you'll see something like this for the privileges needed to create an appointment:

- prvAppendActivity
- prvAppendToAccount
- prvAppendToActivity
- prvAppendToContact
- prvAppendToContract
- prvAppendToIncident
- prvAppendToInvoice
- prvAppendToLead
- prvAppendToOpportunity
- prvAppendToOrder
- prvAppendToQuote
- prvAppendToService
- prvCreateActivity
- prvReadActivity
- prvShareActivity

Although at first this list appears a little cryptic, you can use this information as a starting point to determine which privileges the user will need in a security role to perform the desired action. Unfortunately, in Microsoft Dynamics CRM 4.0 we did find a few instances for which the SDK documentation did not list *all* of the necessary privileges. In those instances, we recommend you enable system tracing for the server. The trace should capture the exact privilege identifier, which you can use to look up the missing privilege. Because this approach requires server and database administration rights it won't work with Microsoft Dynamics CRM Online. Therefore, you would need to rely on a more tedious trial-and-error method to toggle off and on the other privileges in the security role to figure out what the user needs.

Miscellaneous Privileges

In addition to entity privileges, Microsoft Dynamics CRM includes additional miscellaneous privileges in each tab of the security role editor. The privilege name often provides enough information about what the privilege covers, but sometimes the description can leave you guessing. This is especially true for miscellaneous privileges that relate to areas of the application that you may not use often. In the following list, we provide a little more description about each of the miscellaneous privileges and, in some cases, where to find the related feature.

- **Add Reporting Services Reports** Permits the user to upload an existing Reporting Services report file to Microsoft Dynamics CRM. Reporting Services files are in the RDL format. This privilege differs from the Create privilege of the Report entity, which refers to creating a new report by using the Report Wizard or by adding another file type (such as an Excel file or PDF report).
- **Delete Audit Partitions** Permits the user to delete an audit partition. Microsoft Dynamics CRM creates audit partitions for each three-month period.
- **Publish Duplicate Detection Rules** Permits the user to publish duplicate detection rules configured in the data management section.
- **Publish Mail Merge Templates to Organization** Permits the user to make mail merge templates available to the entire organization. Individually owned mail merge templates follow the standard Microsoft Dynamics CRM security model.
- **View Audit History** Permits the user to access the Audit History located on an individual record.
- **View Audit Summary** Permits the user to access the Audit Summary View located in the Auditing area of Settings.
- **Bulk Delete** Permits the user to use the Bulk Deletion Wizard.
- **Manage User Synchronization Filters** Provides the ability for a user to modify a different user's synchronization and offline filters in Microsoft Dynamics CRM for Outlook. Please note there is no user interface to do this—it must be accomplished through custom programming.
- **Publish E-mail Templates** Permits the user to make a personal email template available to the organization. Users can access this feature by browsing to Templates in the Settings section, and opening a personal E-mail template by double-clicking it. Then the user can click Make Template Available to Organization in the ribbon.
- **Publish Reports** Allows a user to make a report available (or viewable) to the entire organization. For Reporting Services reports, this privilege will also allow the user to publish the report to the Reporting Services web server for external use.

- **View Audit Partitions** Allows a user to view the audit log partitions.
- **Configure Internet Marketing module** Permits a user to configure the Internet marketing module that can be set up as an external web page that captures inbound leads.
- **Use Internet Marketing module** Permits a user to access the Internet marketing module data, but not set it up or configure it.
- **Create Quick Campaign** Permits the user to create a single activity and distribute it to multiple records by using a marketing quick campaign. The user also needs to have the correct security configuration to create the quick campaign activities.
- **Override Quote Pricing** Permits the user to override the calculated price of a quote (based on products added to the quote) and manually enter new quote pricing. Users can access the Override Price button when they're editing a Quote Product attached to a Quote.
- **Override Invoice Pricing** Permits the user to override the system-generated price of an invoice and manually enter new invoice pricing. Users can access the Override Price button when they're editing an Invoice Product attached to an Invoice.
- **Override Order Pricing** Permits the user to override the system-generated price of an order and manually enter new order pricing. Users can access the Override Price button when they're editing an Order Product attached to an Order.
- **Override Opportunity Pricing** Permits the user to override the system-generated price of an opportunity and manually enter new opportunity pricing. Users can access the Override Price button when they're editing an Opportunity Product attached to an Opportunity.
- **Override Quote Order Invoice Delete** Permits the user to delete inactive Quotes, Orders, and Invoices.
- **Publish Articles** Permits the user to publish unapproved Knowledge Base articles. Users access the Approve (publish) button on the grid toolbar of the Unapproved Article Queue located in the Knowledge Base area.
- **Act on Behalf of Another User** Provides delegation capabilities to a user.
- **Assign Manager for a User** Allows a user to change the manager of an existing user.
- **Bulk Edit** Permits the user to edit multiple records at the same time. Users with this privilege can access the feature from an entity's grid toolbar. This feature does not apply to all entities.
- **Enable or Disable Business Unit** Permits the user to enable or disable business units.

- **Export to Excel** Permits the user to export the grid data to Microsoft Office Excel. Users with this privilege access the Export to Excel feature from the grid toolbar.
- **Go Offline** Permits a user with Microsoft Dynamics CRM for Outlook with Offline Access installed to work in an offline mode. Working offline creates a local copy of the database on the laptop. Because the user can remove the laptop (with the offline data) from work premises, the offline option raises a potential security question that you must consider.
- **Mail Merge** Permits the user to create mail merge items such as letters, email messages, envelopes, and labels. This privilege refers to creating mail merge items using Microsoft Dynamics CRM for Outlook.
- **Override Created on or Created by for Records during Data Import** Permits the user to include new values for the Created on and Created by fields while using the Data Import Wizard. This would be helpful when you're migrating data from an old system into Microsoft Dynamics CRM and you want to preserve the original values. Without this privilege, all imported records imported by a user will be stamped with that user's information for Created by and Created on.
- **Print** Permits the user to create a printer-friendly display of a grid. Users with this privilege can access this feature by clicking the Print button on the grid toolbar. You cannot vary this privilege by entity type.
- **Reparent Business unit** Just as it sounds, permits the user to reparent a business unit.
- **Reparent User** Again just as it sounds, permits the user to reparent a different user.
- **Send Invitation** Permits a user to send an email invitation to an employee to join the organization. This privilege applies only to Microsoft Dynamics CRM Online deployments.
- **Update Business Closures** Permits the user to modify business working hours and closure information. Users access the Business Closures information in the Settings area.
- **Approve E-mail Addresses for Users or Queues** Permits the user to approve valid email addresses for users and queues. This additional security step prevents a user from fraudulently gaining access to a mailbox he or she should not be able to access.
- **Assign Territory to User** Permits the user to add or remove users from a sales territory. Users access the Sales Territories information in the Business Administration section of the Settings area.
- **CRM Address Book** Permits a user of the Microsoft Dynamics CRM clients for Outlook to select CRM records from his or her address book in Outlook.

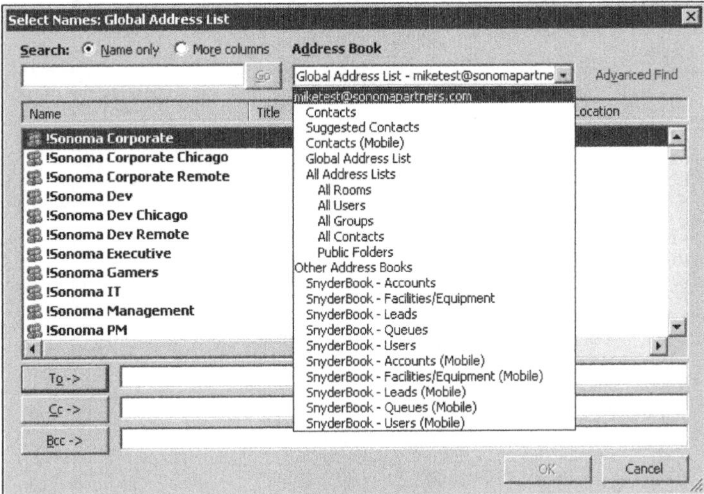

- **Enable or Disable User** Permits the user to enable or disable users.
- **Go Mobile** Permits the user to access the Microsoft Dynamics CRM Mobile Express user interface.
- **Language Settings** Permits the user to access the language settings for the organization, including installing new language packs.
- **Merge** Permits the user to merge two records into a single record. Users with this privilege can access the Merge feature from the grid toolbar.
- **Perform In-sync Rollups on Goals** Permits the user to roll up goal data on demand, instead of waiting for the next scheduled update period.
- **Read License Info** Permits the user to access information about the Microsoft Dynamics CRM license information via the Application Programming Interface. No user interface is associated with this privilege.
- **Reparent Team** Permits the user to reparent a team.
- **Send E-mail as Another User** Permits the user to select a different user or queue for the From address of an email message sent with the Microsoft Dynamics CRM Send Direct E-mail feature. The Send Direct E-mail button appears on grids only if the user has the following security privileges:
    - Read and Append privileges on the Activity entity
    - Append To privileges for the entity to which the user is sending direct email (such as Contact or Account)
    - Read privileges on the E-mail Template entity

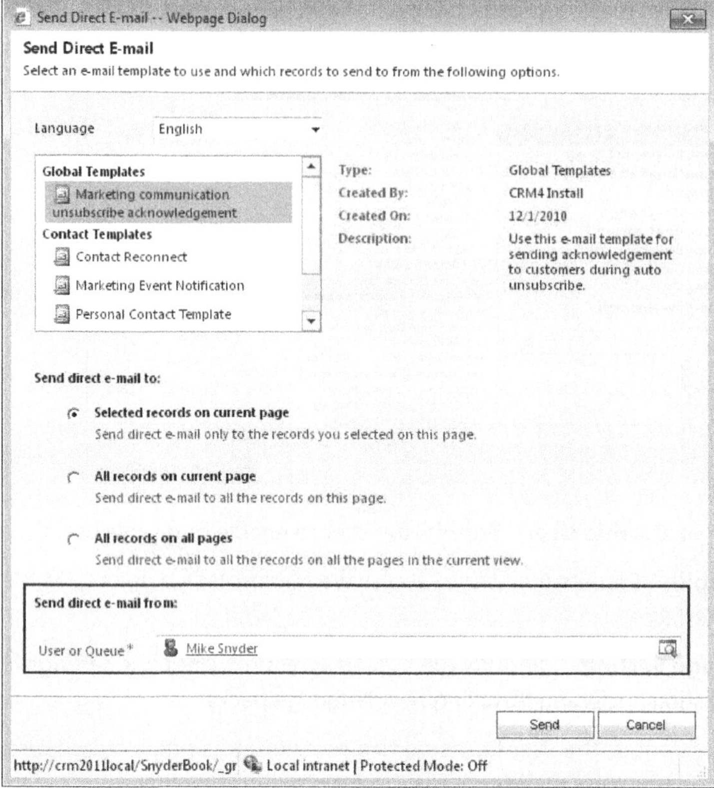

- **Sync to Outlook** Permits a user of Microsoft Dynamics CRM for Outlook to synchronize Microsoft Dynamics CRM data such as Contacts, Tasks, and Appointments to his or her Outlook file.
- **Web Mail Merge** Same as the Mail Merge privilege, but permits the user to access the mail merge functionality in the web interface without using Microsoft Dynamics CRM for Outlook.
- **Browse Availability** Permits the user to view the Service Calendar located in the Service area.
- **Delete Own Calendar** Permits users to delete the service calendar related to their work hours.
- **Search Availability** Permits the user to search for available times when scheduling a Service activity.
- **Create Own Calendar** Permits users to create new work hours for themselves.
- **Read Own Calendar** Allows users to see their own work hours and calendar.
- **Write Own Calendar** Allows users to modify their work hours and the associated calendar.

- **Execute Workflow Job** In addition to proper permissions to the System Job entity, users need this privilege to execute manual workflow rules or automatic workflow rules.
- **Import Customizations** Permits the user to import a configuration file into Microsoft Dynamics CRM.
- **Modify Customization Constraints** This privilege does not impact the system; Microsoft refactored this feature but did not remove the privilege.
- **Export Customizations** Permits the user to export system customizations from Microsoft Dynamics CRM to a configuration file.
- **Publish Customizations** Permits the user to publish customizations applied to an entity.
- **ISV Extensions** This privilege exists for backward compatibility with Microsoft Dynamics CRM 4.0. During the upgrade process, Microsoft Dynamics CRM converts custom 4.0 controls to ribbon buttons in Microsoft Dynamics CRM 2011 and then uses this privilege to determine which ribbon buttons users should see in the upgraded environment.

If you're still not sure what a specific privilege does or whether it will do what you want, you can easily test a privilege by simply selecting the access level for a security role, saving the role, and then logging on to Microsoft Dynamics CRM as a user with only that security role. Remember that if your personal account has a System Administrator role, you have Organization access level rights for all privileges, so don't log on as a System Administrator to test security privileges. Testing security privileges is a good example of when you may want to impersonate a different user when you log on to Microsoft Dynamics CRM. We explained earlier in the chapter how you can modify your Internet Explorer security settings so that Microsoft Dynamics CRM prompts you to enter a user name and password instead of using Integrated Windows authentication.

Note Miscellaneous privileges don't apply to custom entities that you create.

Privilege Impact on Application Navigation

Microsoft Dynamics CRM includes more than 100 entities and thousands of features in the Sales, Marketing, and Customer Service areas. However, very few organizations will use *all* of the entities that Microsoft Dynamics CRM offers to track and manage their customer data. Consequently, users commonly request to see only the areas of the application that their organization actually uses. For example, if your organization doesn't use the Sales Literature or Invoices entities, your users won't want to see these entities as they navigate through the user interface.

Although it would be technically possible to use the site map to remove some areas of the navigation (Sales Literature and Invoices, in this example), the better solution is to modify user security roles and privileges, which also changes the user interface.

Important You should modify security roles—instead of modifying the site map—to hide areas of Microsoft Dynamics CRM that your organization does not use. By modifying security roles, you also can change the display of the entity navigation pane, which is an area of the user interface that you cannot edit by using the site map. Chapter 12, "Solution: Client Extensions (Ribbon and SiteMap)," explains the site map in more detail and discusses when you should modify it.

If you modify a security role and set the access level of the Read privilege for an entity to None Selected, Microsoft Dynamics CRM automatically removes that entity from the user interface for users with that security role, including the menu bar, the application navigation pane, and the entity record. Most of the 14 default security roles include an Organization access level for the Read privilege on all of the entities, so users will see all of the entities in the application navigation. Therefore, we recommend that you change the Read privilege access level to None Selected for any entity that you're not using in your deployment. By doing so, you create a streamlined user interface that can help new users learn the system more quickly and that lets existing users navigate more efficiently.

Tip To see the updated application navigation after you modify a security role, you may have to refresh your web browser window or restart Outlook.

Figure 3-12 shows the Account record for a user with the default Customer Service Representative security role assigned. Because that role includes the Read privilege for most of the entities, the user can see all of the links in the entity navigation pane, such as Quotes, Orders, Invoices, Marketing Lists, and Campaigns.

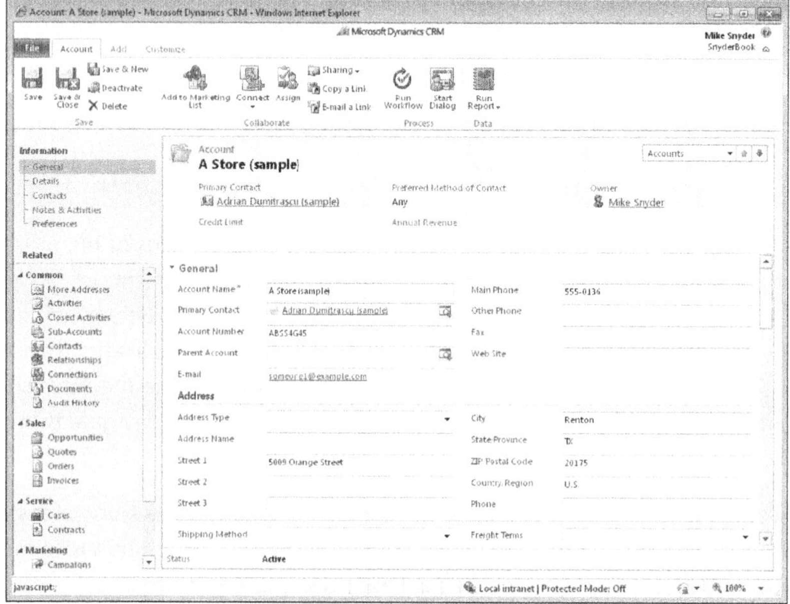

FIGURE 3-12 Account record as seen by a user with the default Customer Service Representative security role

In reality, most customer service representatives don't need to see all of this information on an Account record. Instead, assume that you want your customer service representatives to see only the information shown in the Details and Service groups. By modifying their security roles and setting the Read privilege to None Selected for the entities that you want to hide, the revised Account form can appear like the one shown in Figure 3-13.

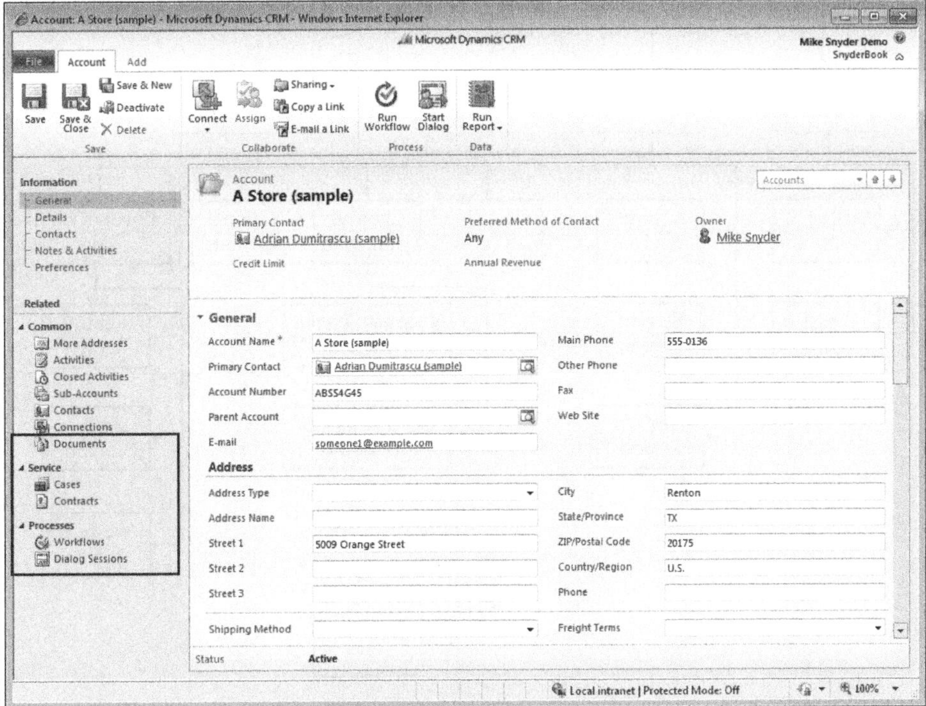

FIGURE 3-13 Account record as seen by a user with a revised Customer Service Representative security role

You can see that we removed the Sales and Marketing links from the navigation pane by modifying the security role. This provides a much cleaner user interface, which your users will appreciate. Likewise, you could also revise the Salesperson security role so that salespeople see only entities that they need to perform their jobs.

Security Role Inheritance

If your deployment includes multiple business units, you must understand how Microsoft Dynamics CRM inherits security roles in the business unit hierarchy. When you create a new security role in a business unit, Microsoft Dynamics CRM creates an instance (copy) of that security role for every business unit that is a child of the business unit for which you created the new security role. If you try to edit the security role in one of the child business units, you will see a warning message stating, "Inherited roles cannot be modified or updated." You can edit only the parent security role, and then Microsoft Dynamics CRM automatically copies your changes to all of the security roles in the child business units. Consider the organization hierarchy of the sample organization Adventure Works Cycle, as shown in Figure 3-14.

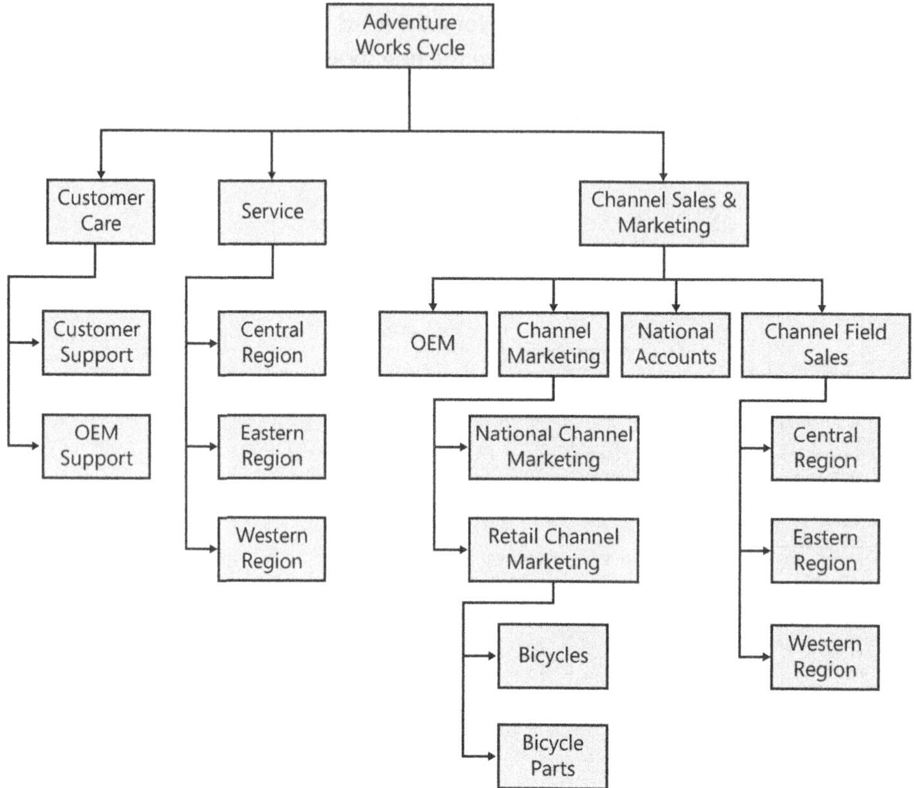

FIGURE 3-14 Organizational structure for the sample company Adventure Works Cycle

If you create a new security role called Director assigned to the Customer Care business unit, Microsoft Dynamics CRM automatically creates noneditable copies of the Director security role in the Customer Support and OEM Support business units because they are children of the Customer Care business unit. Any changes you make to the Director security role are automatically propagated to all of the Director security roles in the child business units. When you view the security roles for one of the other business units, such as Service or OEM, you do not see the Director security role listed because the Service and OEM business units are not children of the Customer Care business unit.

Tip When you create a new security role, Microsoft Dynamics CRM assigns the security role to the root business unit by default, so make sure that you remember to change the role's business unit by using the business unit lookup if you want to create a role in a nonroot business unit.

Every user belongs to only one business unit, and you can assign users security roles only from the business unit to which they belong. Therefore, in this example, you could not assign the Director security role to users who belong to any business unit other than Customer Care, Customer Support, and OEM Support. You can view all of the security roles for a single business unit by using the business unit view filter drop-down list to select a specific business unit.

Because Microsoft Dynamics CRM inherits security roles to children business units, you cannot make the privileges of a security role be different for each business unit. However, you can create a varying number of security roles for each business unit in your deployment. The ability to create unique security roles for each business unit gives you great flexibility to create and configure security roles to meet your organization's needs.

Field Level Security

So far we reviewed security role and configuration settings from an entity perspective, but what if there are sensitive data fields on the entity record that you want to secure? We refer to managing the securing of a single field as *field level security*. Some examples of data fields that you want to secure might include:

- A contact's social security or credit card numbers
- An account's sales numbers
- A lead's ranking or priority

In the contact example, it might be OK if a user had the ability to edit or view all of the contact's information *except* for the social security number. However by giving a user a security role with the edit privilege to the contact entity, that user could edit *all* of the contact fields. Fortunately, Microsoft Dynamics CRM 2011 includes a new field level security feature that allows you to configure security permissions down to an individual field level. Figure 3-15 shows how Microsoft Dynamics CRM could lock down the social security field so that certain users could not view or edit the data in the field. You can also see that Microsoft Dynamics CRM includes a key icon to indicate to users that the field is secured.

Tip Microsoft Dynamics CRM always displays the masked out characters on the form in a secured field if a user does not have access. This is true even if that data field does not contain any data.

Field level security extends beyond the record form to cover *all* aspects of the Microsoft Dynamics CRM, including the advanced find feature, the audit history, Microsoft Dynamics CRM for Outlook with Offline Access and the programming API. Therefore, if a user does not have access to a specific field, Microsoft Dynamics CRM will honor that restriction everywhere in the system. The field security model even allows users to *share* secured fields on a record with other users that might not have access to the secured field (assuming the sharer has the appropriate sharing security settings to do so).

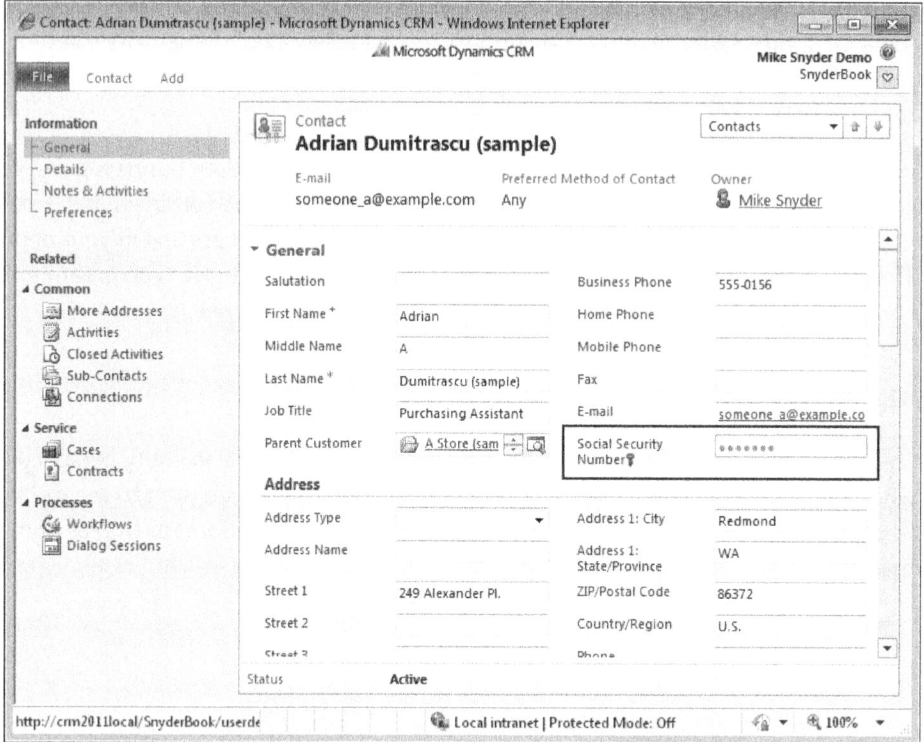

FIGURE 3-15 Field level security activated on the social security number field

Setting up field level security takes a few simple steps:

- Enable field security for the data field you want to secure.
- Create a field security profile and assign to users/teams.
- Edit field level permissions with the field security profile.

Enabling Field Security

By default none of the Microsoft Dynamics CRM data fields have field level security enabled. To enable field level security for a specific field, you must select the Enable button for Field Security on the field editor (Figure 3-16). Chapter 6, "Entity: Fields and Option Sets," covers how to use the entity and field editor in detail.

Unfortunately, you can only enable field security for custom fields that you add to the system. You cannot turn on field security for the default system fields created in the initial Microsoft Dynamics CRM installation. Some of the default fields that you might want to enable field security for (but cannot) include contact birth date, contact home phone, contact mobile phone, and so on. Of course you could create new custom fields to track this data and then secure it. However, if you used custom data fields, the information would not synchronize to a user's Outlook file, so you must consider the trade-off benefits between securing those fields versus having the ability to synchronize phone numbers into Outlook.

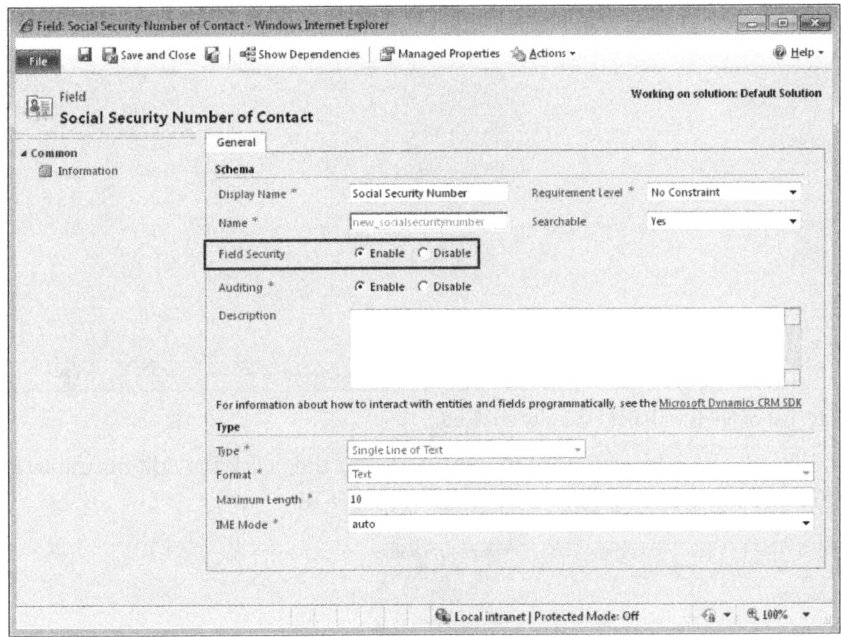

FIGURE 3-16 Enabling field level security for a field

When you enable field security, no user can access that field until you explicitly give him or her permission. However, users with the System Administrator security role will always have full access to all secured fields in Microsoft Dynamics CRM.

Field Security Profiles

Like security roles, field security profiles offer a way for administrators to group together a set of security settings. Obviously the field security profiles apply to field security settings. To manage the field security profiles, click the Settings button, click Administration, and then click Field Security Profiles. By default Microsoft Dynamics CRM includes a system administrator field security profile.

When you create new profiles, try to create them in functional groups to help reduce the amount of maintenance work required. To create a new profile, click the New button in the grid and a new form will open. After you name it, click Save. Now you can add the users and teams that this field security profile should apply to.

Now click the Field Permissions link in the left-hand navigation to start editing the field level permissions. You will see a list of all the data fields in the system with field security enabled (Figure 3-17).

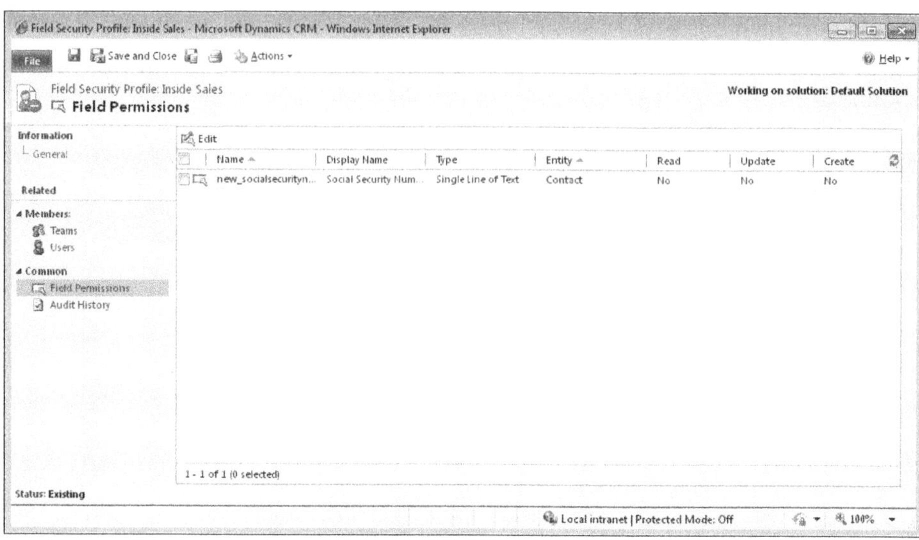

FIGURE 3-17 List of fields with field security enabled

Select which secured fields you want to work with and then click the Edit button to launch the Edit Field Security dialog box, as shown in Figure 3-18.

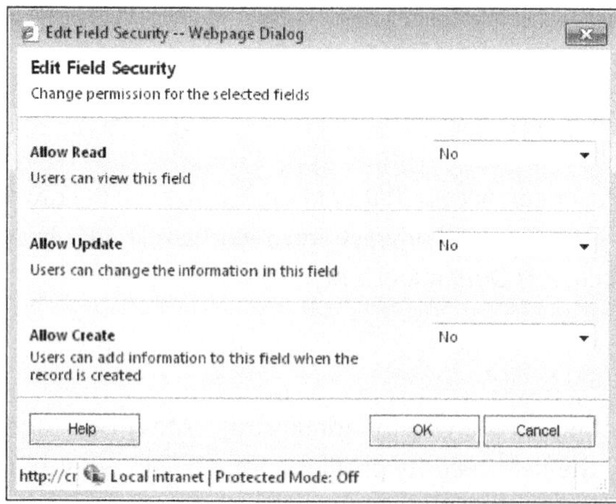

FIGURE 3-18 Edit read, update, and create permissions for a secured field

By changing these values to Yes, users or teams with this field security profile assigned to them will now be able to perform reads, updates, or creates on the secured fields. The Allow Create option is interesting because this allows the user to enter data in this field while creating a record, but when the record is created the field is secured and the user can no longer access it.

In summary, field level security is a powerful new feature in Microsoft Dynamics CRM 2011 that allows administrators to set up a very detailed and flexible security model to meet most organization's needs.

Sharing Records

Despite the numerous security options and configuration choices already discussed, you will probably encounter scenarios in which users need to share and collaborate on records that the business unit hierarchy does not support. Consider a fictional company called Coho Vineyard & Winery (the root business unit) that has two children business units named Vineyard and Winery. Coho Vineyard & Winery CEO Laura Owen (user assigned to root business unit) owns the Woodgrove Bank account. However, the security roles for Gretchen Rivas (assigned to Vineyard business unit) and Heidi Steen (assigned to Winery business unit) do not have the Write privilege for the Account entity. The CEO decides that she wants Gretchen and Heidi to work on a special project related to Woodgrove Bank for which they will need to edit the record. However, Laura doesn't want them to edit any other Account records that she owns other than Woodgrove Bank. This type of security configuration is not possible using the security configurations covered so far. If Laura gives Gretchen and Heidi privileges to edit Account records for the Organization, they would be able to edit *any* Account, not just the Woodgrove Bank record. Fortunately, Microsoft Dynamics CRM allows users to share records to accommodate exactly this type of collaboration scenario. *Sharing* records allows a user to grant privileges for a specific record so that other users can work with the shared record, even though they would not usually have the necessary privileges to do so.

To share records, users must have a security role assigned the appropriate Share privilege. To set up a share such as the one described in the Woodgrove Bank example, open the entity record and click Sharing on the Actions menu of the entity menu bar. In the Share dialog box, select the users with whom you want to share this record by clicking Add User/Team. Use the Lookup tool to find the records that you want, and then click OK. Microsoft Dynamics CRM adds the users to the page, as shown in Figure 3-19.

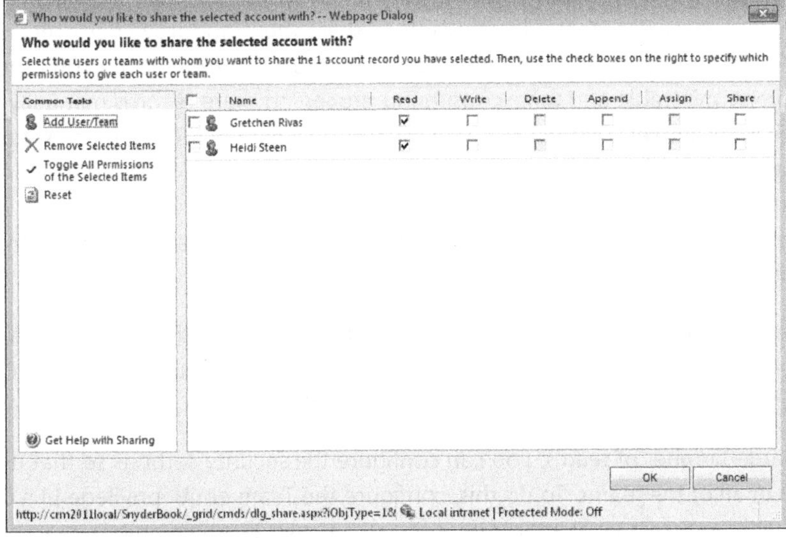

FIGURE 3-19 Sharing records with users

Next, specify which privileges you want to share with these users. In the Woodgrove Bank example, Laura Owen can select the Read and Write privileges so that Gretchen and Heidi can edit this record. Note that the Delete and Assign privilege check boxes are unavailable because Laura doesn't have those privileges for this record, and therefore cannot share them with any other user.

More Info Users can't share a privilege if they do not possess the privilege themselves. For example, a user cannot share Delete privileges for a record if she does not have the Delete privilege for that record.

With this share in place, Gretchen and Heidi can now read and write just the Woodgrove Bank Account record. Of course, you can revoke a share at any time by simply opening the record and clearing the check boxes of the privileges that you want to revoke.

Tip In addition to sharing records through the user interface, you can also programmatically share records using the application programming interface. Therefore you could set up automation to share records with specific users or teams when certain conditions are met. However, take care not to create too many automated shares because the user interface doesn't contain a tool to help you quickly identify a group of records with sharing permissions (though you can examine one record at a time). For example, it would be difficult to answer the question "Which of the existing accounts in the system have shares set up on them?" Therefore, creating too many shares might become a maintenance headache down the road.

Sharing with Teams

In the Coho Vineyard & Winery example, it is easy to set up the share because you need to select only two users. But what if Laura wants to share the Woodgrove Bank record with 100 users? What if she wants to share five different records with those same 100 users? It would be a pretty miserable and time-consuming process to share records manually one user at a time in these examples. Fortunately, with Microsoft Dynamics CRM you can set up and configure teams of users to expedite the sharing process. By sharing a record with a team instead of with individual users, you do not have to select user records manually for each share that you create. Rather, you simply select the team that you want to share with, and all of the users in that team participate in the share.

You can create and modify teams by browsing to Administration in the Settings area, and then clicking Teams. When you create a team, you specify the business unit that the team belongs to, and then you simply add members to the team.

If you use a large number of teams, you can configure the security settings so that users see only a subset of all of the teams. To do this, configure the Team entity privilege in a user's security role with an access level appropriate for each team's business unit. For example, if you create a team that belongs to the root business unit but you grant a security role only with a User access level for the team privilege, users with that security role won't see that root business unit team in the user interface unless they personally created that team. By using this type of configuration, you can restrict the teams that each user is allowed to view (and share records with) in case you want to hide specific teams (such as executive or financial teams).

Sharing Secured Fields

In addition to sharing entire records between users, you can also shared secured fields, assuming the sharing user has access to the secured fields. To share secured fields, click the Sharing button in the ribbon and then select Share Secured Fields (Figure 3-20).

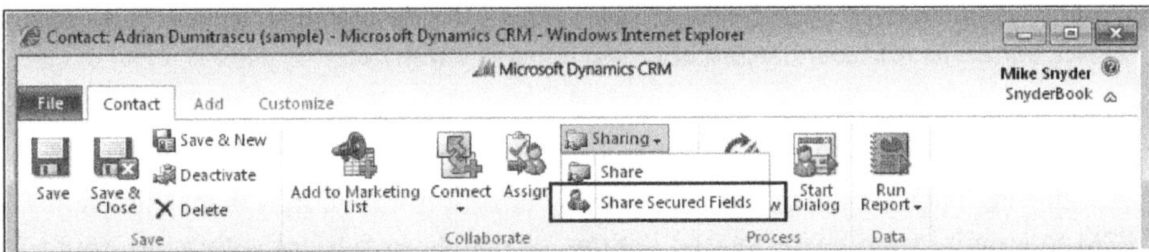

FIGURE 3-20 Sharing secured fields

After you click this button, Microsoft Dynamics CRM will launch a sharing dialog box (as seen in Figure 3-21) where the sharer can select which secured fields and permissions he or she wants to share. Just like record level sharing, you can shared secured fields with specific users or teams.

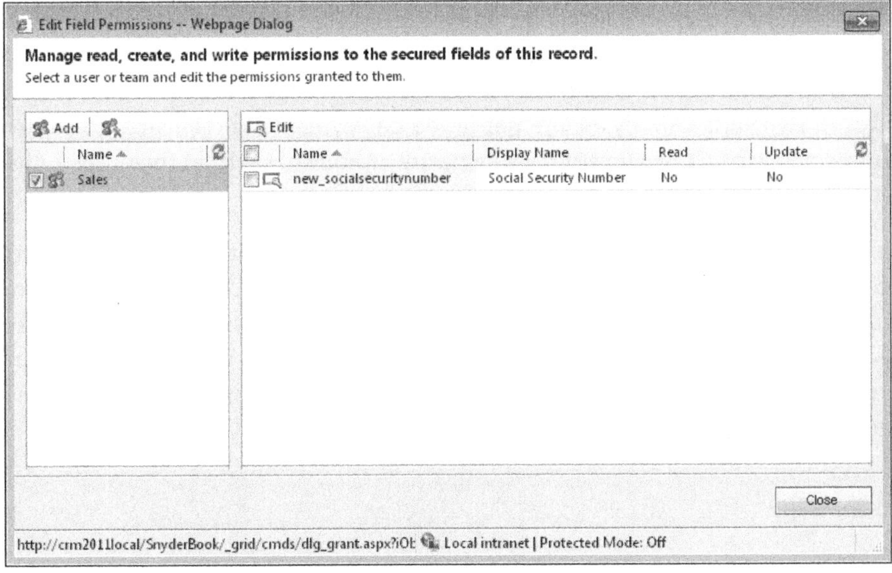

FIGURE 3-21 Sharing secured fields

Sharing and Inheritance

When you share a record with a team or user, child entities of the shared record inherit the same sharing settings as the parent record. In the Woodgrove Bank example, Gretchen and Heidi can edit the Account record and its related entities, such as Tasks, Phone Calls, and Notes, because they inherit the same share as their parent record. A record with inherited sharing privileges can also have its own sets of sharing privileges. and Microsoft Dynamics CRM maintains two different sets of sharing privileges for the record.

More Info For shared records (directly shared or inherited), users receive only the shared privileges for the entity if they have at least a User access level for that entity. For example, if Heidi has an access level of None Selected for the Activity entity, she is not able to view activities related to Woodgrove Bank even if someone shares Read privileges with her for that Account record. Likewise, she needs to have at least a User access level for the Account entity to view the Woodgrove Bank account record after Laura shares it with her.

You can configure how Microsoft Dynamics CRM shares related records by editing the relationship behavior between two entities. For example, you may want Microsoft Dynamics CRM to inherit sharing with related entities such as Tasks but not with a different related entity such as Activities.

Summary

Microsoft Dynamics CRM includes a powerful and highly configurable security model that you can use to configure and restrict information access according to your business needs. The on-premise version of Microsoft Dynamics CRM uses Active Directory to manage user accounts and passwords. On-premise users accessing Microsoft Dynamics CRM by the local intranet authenticate with Integrated Windows authentication, whereas users accessing Microsoft Dynamics CRM by an Internet-facing deployment use claims-based authentication. All users of Microsoft Dynamics CRM Online use Windows Live ID as their user authentication method.

By combining role-based and object-based security settings with your organization's business unit structure, in Microsoft Dynamics CRM you can accommodate very complex security and information access needs. Field level security allows administrators to secure specific data fields, providing even more control over access to sensitive information. Microsoft Dynamics CRM also supports project-based and collaborative work by enabling users to share records with teams and individual users.

Chapter 4

Data and Document Management

In this chapter:

One of the primary goals of most CRM systems is to make users more productive and efficient with their time. In today's world of knowledge workers, most employees spend a lot of time each day interacting with data and documents. Therefore, it makes sense that any CRM system should provide excellent data and document management tools. In this chapter, we'll review the key capabilities in Microsoft Dynamics CRM related to:

- Data Management
- Document Management

Data Management

A CRM system can provide your organization lots of great benefits, but poor data quality in your database can eliminate many of the best benefits. Many times you'll hear the expression "garbage in, garbage out" when organizations talk about data in their CRM system. If you don't do a good job of keeping your database up to date, you shouldn't expect great analytics, insightful reporting, or improved efficiency from your system.

Fortunately, Microsoft Dynamics CRM includes several features to help you load, update, and cleanse your data on a regular basis:

- Import Data Wizard
- Data Enrichment
- Duplicate Detection
- Bulk Record Deletion

Import Data Wizard

Very rarely does a company deploy Microsoft Dynamics CRM without any existing customer data. Even if you don't already have a software system with customer names, addresses, and so on, you probably have a bunch of customer data in various Excel and Outlook files. Consequently, there's almost always a data import process to go along with each Microsoft Dynamics CRM deployment. After the initial setup and data import, you will find that at times you want to bulk load additional data into Microsoft Dynamics CRM. The Import Data Wizard feature in Microsoft Dynamics CRM provides excellent bulk data capabilities to minimize the time you need to manually enter data into Microsoft Dynamics CRM. With this wizard, you can import hundreds or thousands of records in just a few clicks. In addition to importing core record types such as leads, contacts, and accounts, you can also use the Import Data Wizard to import other record types, including any custom record types.

Examples of bulk data imports might include:

- A list of leads, contacts, or accounts purchased from a third party.
- A list of contacts obtained from a conference recently attended by the sales staff.
- A file full of business contacts brought by an employee who has just joined the company.

One of the key benefits of the Import Data Wizard is that it's easy enough for most end users to learn. However, it also contains some powerful tools that allow system administrators to perform more complex data imports. You can even use the Import Data Wizard to dynamically create new data fields and custom entities on the fly, assuming that you have the proper security credentials.

For the most part, the Import Data Wizard always follows the same basic process:

1. Prepare the import files.
2. Import the file and map the records.
3. View the results and correct failures.

Prepare the Import Files

Obviously, before you can import anything, you need to gather the data into electronic files. The import files should meet the following criteria:

- The source data files must be in one of the following formats:
    - XML Spreadsheet 2003 (.xml)
    - Comma-separated values (.csv)
    - Text (.txt)
    - Compressed files (.zip)

- Include a column for each business-required field on the entity into which you are importing the data.
- You need one import file for each type of entity that you want to import. For example, if you want to import leads, accounts, and contacts, you need three files. Note that you can import multiple source files in one process by combining them into a single .zip file.
- Each import file must be 8 megabytes (MB) or smaller in file size. If you zip multiple files together, the total (including attachments) must not exceed 32 MB.
- If you want to import multiple source files that link records together (such as linking opportunities to accounts), each source file must contain at least one common column containing a unique ID or value that can be used to link the records.

Tip If you combine multiple source files in a single .zip file, all of the source files must be of the same file type. You cannot combine different file types such as .csv and .xml into a single .zip file for the Import Data Wizard.

Fortunately, Microsoft Dynamics CRM allows you to create templates for your import that you can download from the system. You can access the import templates one of two ways:

- On the application ribbon, click the Import Data button and select Download Template for Import.
- In the Settings area, click Data Management and then click Templates for Data Import.

When you download an import template, Microsoft Dynamics CRM outputs an XML file with all of the columns for the entity you selected. Starting with the import template provided by Microsoft Dynamics CRM (instead of starting from scratch to create your data file) provides several benefits, including:

- All possible data fields for the entity are included.
- All of the column headers are named and labeled correctly. This helps later because the Import Data Wizard will automatically map the fields.
- Required data field names are bolded in the top row.
- Hovering your cursor over a cell in Excel provides you with additional information about the data that should go in the field, such as its data type, maximum and minimum values, or maximum length.
- For option sets, the template displays a list of the possible values for the field. If you try to enter a value that is not included in the option set, you receive an error message. Please note that even though users cannot manually enter valid option set data into a cell, they could accidentally populate a cell with invalid option set values by dragging values through multiple cells where Excel auto-fills the values.

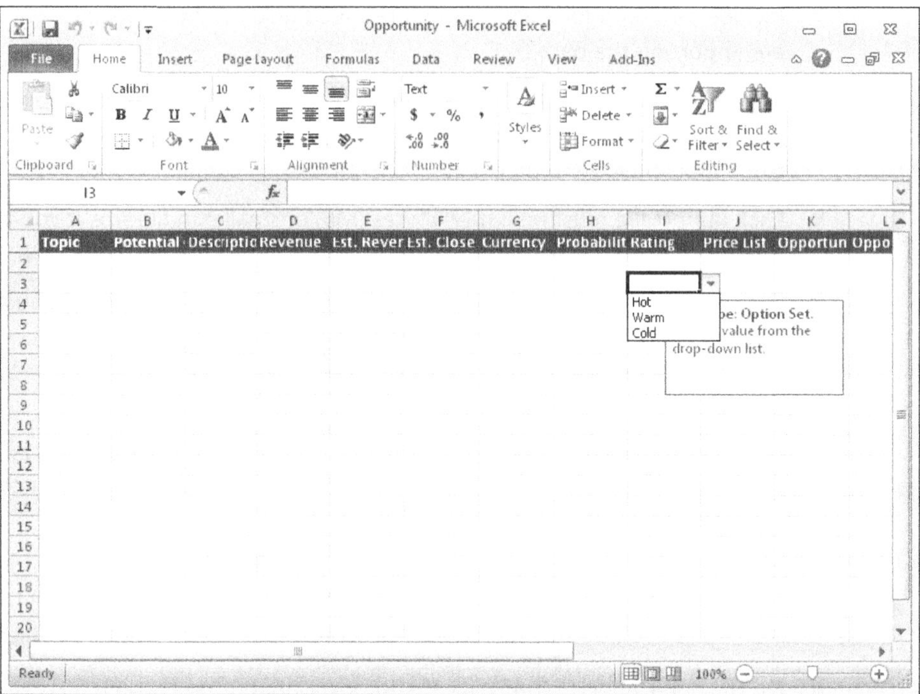

For these reasons, we strongly encourage you to download import templates from Microsoft Dynamics CRM as your first step when importing data, although this is not a requirement.

Tip If you receive an error message that states "The file is corrupt and cannot be opened" when you try to open the file, first make sure that you save the import template to your local computer before opening it. If that does not work, you might need to disable Protected View for files originating from the Internet. To disable this, open Microsoft Excel 2010, click File, click Options, and then click Trust Center and Trust Center Settings. Clear the Enable Protected View for files originating from the Internet check box and click OK.

Import the File and Map the Records

With your source data files complete, you're ready to import the data into Microsoft Dynamics CRM. To access the Import Data Wizard, click the Import Data button in the ribbon, or click the File tab, and then select Import Data from the Tools menu. The Import Data Wizard opens and you start by selecting your source file. Again, you can import multiple files at one time by zipping them together first and selecting the .zip file as your source. Microsoft Dynamics CRM then reviews the file you uploaded and provides a verification screen. If you used CSV source files, you also need to specify your delimiter settings at this time. If any of your records use the delimiter (such as commas included in number fields), you need to add quotation marks or a single quotation mark as the data delimiter.

On the next screen, the Import Data Wizard provides a list of the source data files it will import. If you uploaded multiple files zipped together, you'll see the complete list of files contained in the .zip file.

After you verify the source import files, you need to choose a data map to use during the import process. Microsoft Dynamics CRM uses data maps as the basis for translating how a source field converts into a related destination field. Consider the following example: you have a file of contacts you would like to import into Microsoft Dynamics CRM. Within your source file is a column called First, which contains the first name of a contact. In Microsoft Dynamics CRM, the related field is named First Name. To import the data in the source file, you need to map the First field in the source file to the First Name field in Microsoft Dynamics CRM.

Microsoft Dynamics CRM includes the following options for mapping data in the Import Data Wizard:

- **Default (Automatic Mapping)** Microsoft Dynamics CRM automatically creates the data maps during the import process. This option is only available if you carefully name the source file column headers to match the field display names. Remember, downloading a data import template from Microsoft Dynamics CRM provides a quick way to get the correct headers in your source file.
- **SampleDataMap** Microsoft Dynamics CRM automatically creates a data map when you install the sample data. You will probably never use this map—it's designed for use with the sample data utility.
- **Salesforce.com Full Data Export** This pre-built data map imports data from a full export .zip file extracted from Salesforce.com Enterprise, Unlimited, or Professional editions.
- **Salesforce.com Report Export** This pre-built data map imports report files exported from Salesforce.com. Use this option if you don't have the full data export option in Salesforce.com.
- **Outlook Business Contact Manager 2010** This pre-built data map imports data from Microsoft Outlook Business Contact Manger 2010.

Microsoft Dynamics CRM includes multiple data maps out of the box, shown in Figure 4-1.

Tip Whenever possible, start by downloading the data import templates because they will almost always map the data automatically, which saves you a lot of time and headaches.

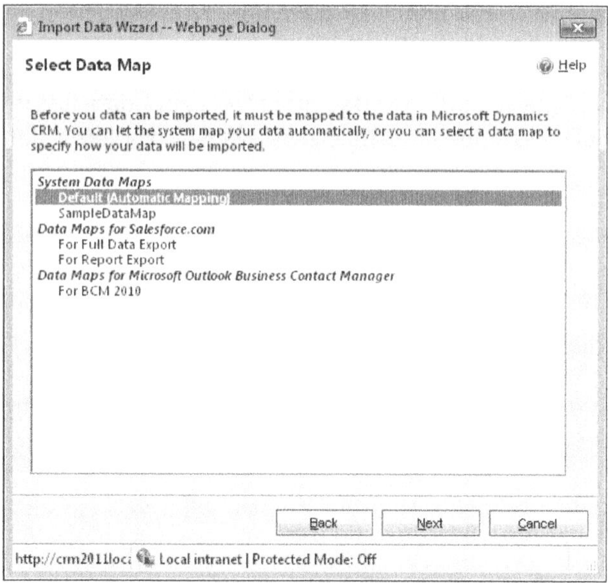

FIGURE 4-1 Default data maps included in Microsoft Dynamics CRM

After you select a data map, the Import Data Wizard tries to match the record types of the import files to correct entities in Microsoft Dynamics CRM. If you named your import file with the same name as the destination entity, the import will match the source file to the correct entity automatically. For example, if your source file contains account records, name it account.xml and the import process will know the source file contains account records. If one of the import file names doesn't match an existing entity, the Map Record Types dialog box will present one of three options:

- Map the source file to an existing entity by selecting the entity name in a picklist.
- Choose the Ignore option in the picklist to skip the file in the import process.
- Select the Create New option in the picklist to create a custom entity in Microsoft Dynamics CRM on the fly for the data import, assuming you have the appropriate security privileges.

Figure 4-2 shows an import with a source data file named Project.xml. Because Project is not one of the Microsoft Dynamics CRM entities, it did not map automatically, as indicated by the yellow icon. For this example, let's assume we want to create a custom entity called Project into which we will import the data.

After you select Create New, you need to enter the name and primary field of the new custom entity, as shown in Figure 4-2. Chapter 10, "Entity Customization: Custom Entities and Custom Activities," explains how to create custom entities in more detail, but for the purposes of our import process, you can just accept the default primary field value of Name.

You also need to enter a plural name for the entity. We used Projects for our example, as shown in Figure 4-3.

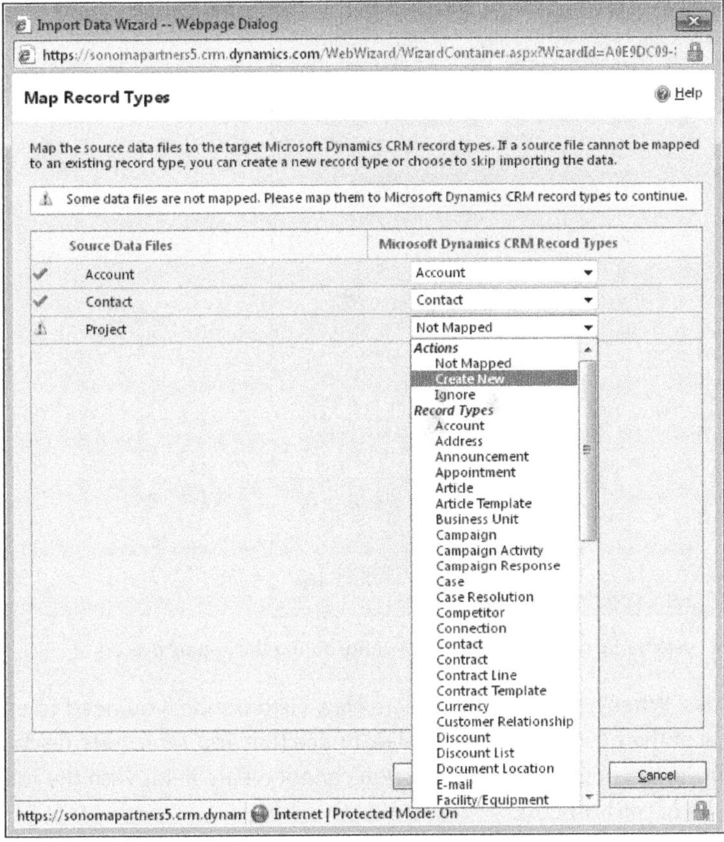

FIGURE 4-2 Mapping source data files to Microsoft Dynamics CRM record types

After you finish mapping each of the source data files to an entity in Microsoft Dynamics CRM, proceed to the next step of the Import Data Wizard, where you will map fields. In the Map Fields dialog box, the import displays a green check mark next to the entities where the field mappings are complete and ready for import. If you used an import template downloaded from the system as your starting point, you probably won't need to map any fields because that would be handled as part of the automatic mapping. Entities with a yellow yield icon indicate that you must complete the field mapping. In our example with the project data that will be imported into our new Project entity, we'll need to address each field of the custom entity in the mapping process. Again, you have the option to ignore the field, create a new field, or map it to one of the two default fields (Created On and Owner) created by the Import Data Wizard. We will create new fields for everything except for the Owner field in the source file, which we will map to the Microsoft Dynamics CRM Owner field.

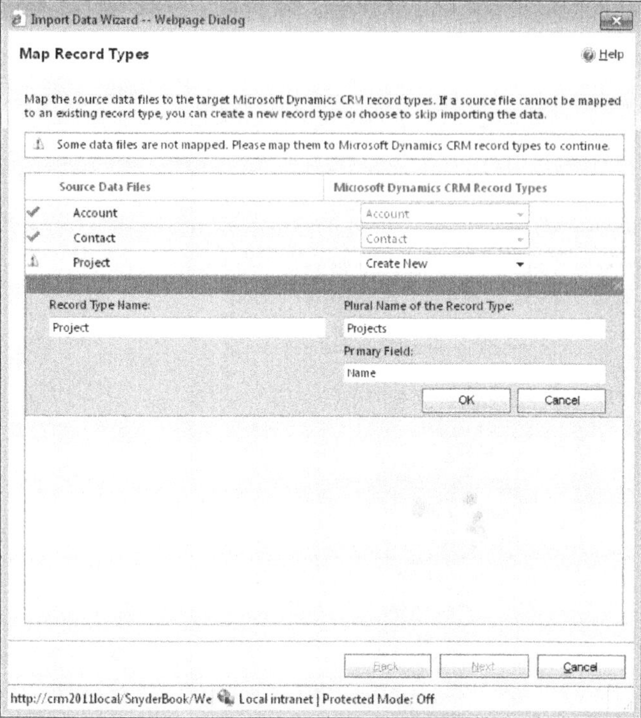

FIGURE 4-3 Creating a custom Microsoft Dynamics CRM entity during the import process

Creating New Fields When you select the Create New Field option, you need to enter the name and data type of the new field. In Figure 4-4, notice that you can create fields with most data types during the import process, but you cannot create fields with the following data types during the import process:

- Lookup
- Floating point number
- Currency
- Multiple lines of text

You might also notice that when you create fields you cannot adjust some of the additional parameters regarding the data type, such as maximum length, maximum and minimum values, and precision. After you complete the import process and the entity is created, you can adjust these settings using the standard entity customization process.

In our example with the custom Project entity, the limitations on data types we can use in our new fields force us to ignore the following columns:

- **Budget** Currency data type
- **Description** Multiple lines of text data type
- **Customer** Lookup field that we want to map to the Account entity

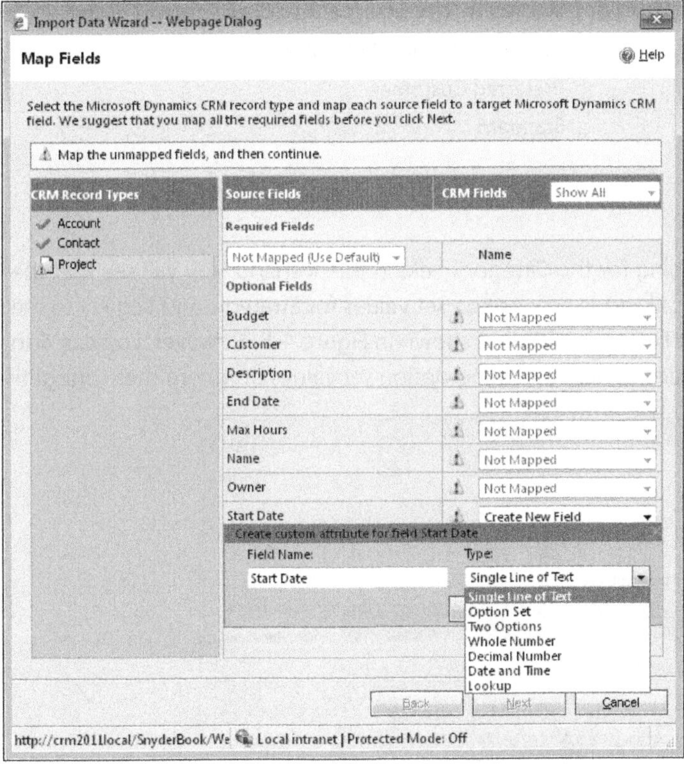

FIGURE 4-4 Selecting data types for a field created during the import process

Tip If your source file contains a field with one of the data types that you cannot use when creating fields during the import process, you could create the custom entity *first* (with all data fields necessary) before importing the data. Alternatively, you can create the custom entity during the import process and exclude a few data fields, and then go back to add those missing fields later. Unfortunately, you would then need to perform another import or update to update the data in the new fields. This seems like more work to us, so we'd recommend the first option of creating the custom entity before starting the import.

Tip You can use this field mapping dialog box to specify one of the data fields as a Required Field by selecting it in the Required Field picklist.

Option Set Mapping When you're importing data into option sets (formerly known as picklists), you might need to further adjust your data map because the source values need to match the option set values in Microsoft Dynamics CRM. If the Import Data Wizard finds option set values that don't exist in Microsoft Dynamics CRM, it assumes you want to automatically create new option set values to match the source file. Table 4-1 shows an example of importing option set data into the Category field on the Account entity with a source data file that contains account category values that do not exist in Microsoft Dynamics CRM.

TABLE 4-1 Different Option Set Values in the Source and Destination Fields

Source Data Values	Category Option Set Values
Preferred Customer	Preferred Customer
Standard	Standard
Strategic	
Legacy	

If you look at the mapping for the Category field in this scenario, you will see that the Import Data Wizard automatically adds new option set values for Strategic and Legacy to the Category option set in Microsoft Dynamics CRM, as shown in Figure 4-5. However, you can also choose to map the source picklist values to existing option set values or ignore them altogether.

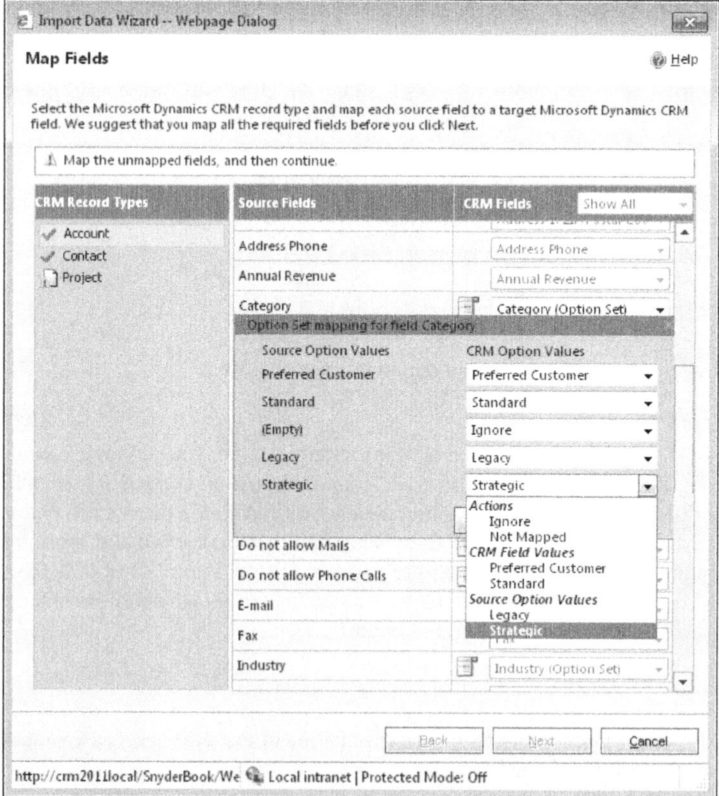

FIGURE 4-5 Creating new picklist values during the import process

Important The Import Data Wizard automatically creates new picklist and option set values in Microsoft Dynamics CRM to match new values in the source data. You will not receive a prompt or warning when this occurs, so make sure your source data contains the values you want. If you're using an XML Spreadsheet 2003 as your source data format, you won't have to worry about the Import Data Wizard creating new option set values because you cannot enter new values in the spreadsheet—it validates data against the existing Microsoft Dynamics CRM values.

Lookup Mapping Similar to option set mapping, importing source data that contains lookup fields might require additional attention when mapping fields. Lookup fields that are typically included in data imports include the Owner, Parent Account, and Primary Contact fields on the Account entity. In these cases, you want to link an imported record to another Microsoft Dynamics CRM record, such as linking an opportunity to an account or owner to a contact. You can map imported records to data already in Microsoft Dynamics CRM, or you can map them to records that are part of the same import process (such as in the same imported .zip file).

When you view the field mapping for a lookup field included in your source data file, you can specify the lookup reference for that field. Figure 4-6 shows how you can specify the reference for the Owner field. Because either a team or user can own a record, you need to specify which fields in the Team and User entities the Import Data Wizard should reference when identifying a match for the source data record in Microsoft Dynamics CRM.

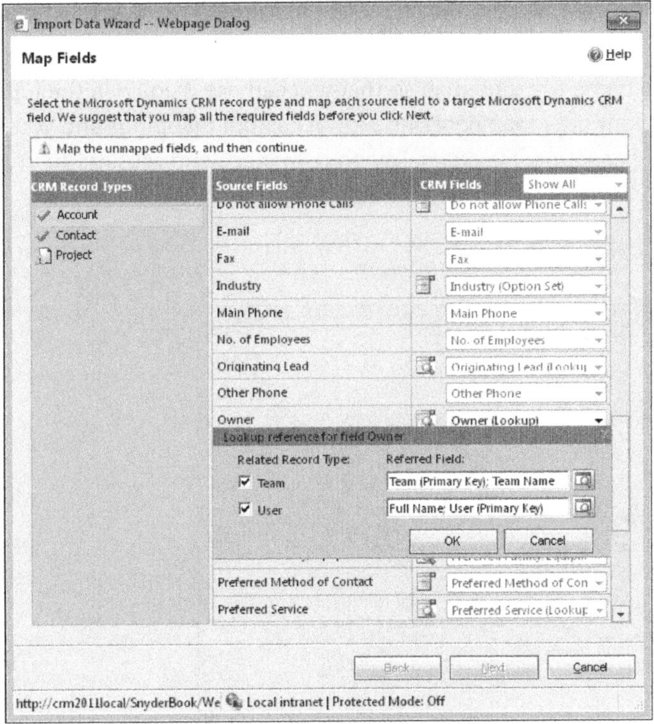

FIGURE 4-6 Configuring the reference fields for lookups

Most of the time, you will probably map the source data to the name field of the reference entity. In other words, if you want to import an account owned by a user named Mike Snyder, you would configure the lookup mapping on the Owner field to match the Full Name field on the User entity. Note that you have some flexibility in deciding which fields to map. For example, you could use another field such as email address to perform this lookup mapping. If you used the E-mail Address field on the User entity for your mapping, your source file would need to have the users' email addresses in the Owner column, instead of their full names. To ensure the best possible mapping results in an import process, you should configure the field lookup mappings on data fields that contain unique values, such as email address, social security number, or other identifier.

Completing the Import You can make a few additional settings in the Import Data Wizard before completing the import process.

First, you can choose whether you want the import process to allow duplicates. If you choose not to import duplicates, the Import Data Wizard will not prompt you to resolve duplicates during the import. Instead, it will not import the duplicate record and will create a log of unimported records for you to resolve later. The option to exclude or import duplicates only appears for entities with duplicate detection enabled.

Next, you need to specify which user should own the imported records if the imported records do not have any owner specified in the data map.

Finally, you can choose to name the data map so that you can use it again in the future. This can save you time if your data map contains a lot of custom mappings and you're likely to import data from a similar source file again. Saving data maps and reusing them also comes in handy when you're testing a data migration.

These options are shown in Figure 4-7.

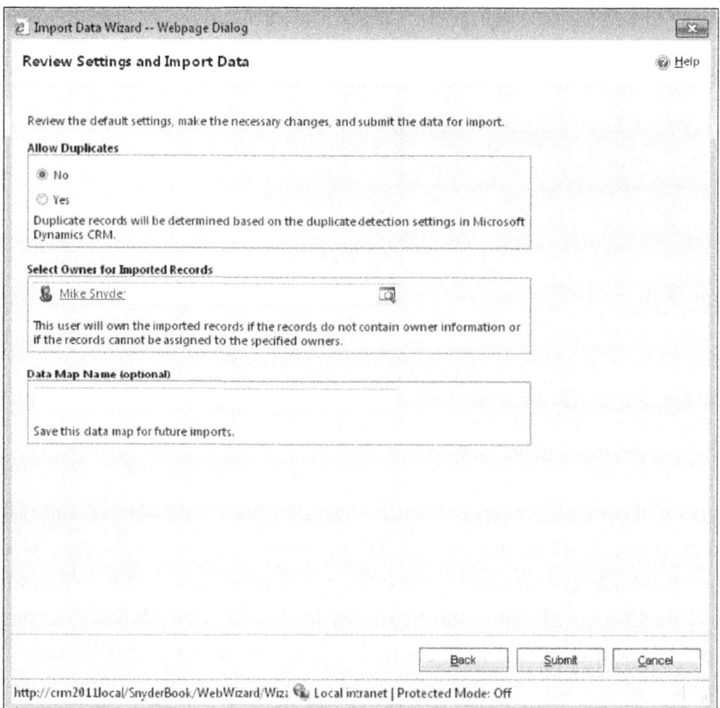

FIGURE 4-7 Final Import Data Wizard settings before completing the import process

Tip In addition to importing data records through the Import Data Wizard, you can also use the tool to import Notes and Attachments into Microsoft Dynamics CRM. Please note that importing notes and attachments is a little more involved process, so plan accordingly.

Reviewing the Import Status

After you submit the import, the process runs in the background until all of the records are imported or logged as errors. You can continue to use Microsoft Dynamics CRM during this time. The duration of the process depends on the size of the import file, but it might take just a few minutes for a small file.

After the process completes, you should review the results of the import to ensure that all records have been imported as expected and, if necessary, troubleshoot import-related errors. Microsoft Dynamics CRM lets you easily obtain this information without leaving the web interface.

You can view the status of an import in the Imports view, which is available in the Workplace area. Each import is displayed as a separate record in the Imports grid, and if you double-click a record you can view the details of that import job. The import record shows important information, such as the user who submitted the import, the date and time the import was submitted, and the import file name and file size. Additionally, you can view the records that were created during the import process and examine the errors for records that were not imported.

The ability to view failures for each import allows you to easily identify issues with your import file so that you can update it and re-import the records that did not get created during the import process. To assist with your import troubleshooting, you can also download a comma-separated value file of these failed records, including all of their original source data, by clicking the Export Error Rows button on the grid toolbar.

Even though the Import Data Wizard provides a straightforward interface, you should not expect to get perfect data imports each time! After you review the failed records and adjust the data maps or source files, you should resubmit your import. However, you will also probably want to "undo" the previously completed import so that you don't import the same data twice. Fortunately, Microsoft Dynamics CRM makes it very easy for you to delete all of the records associated with a particular data import.

When you browse to the list of imports and open an import job, you can click the Delete button in the ribbon and choose to delete the records associated with that import, as shown in Figure 4-8.

You can choose to delete all of the imported records associated with the .zip file (helpful if the .zip file contained multiple source data files), or you can choose to just delete the data from one of the source files contained in the .zip file. After you delete the imported data, you can rerun your import process with the corrected mappings and source files, and most likely you won't receive any failures. Of course, if you do, you can repeat this process.

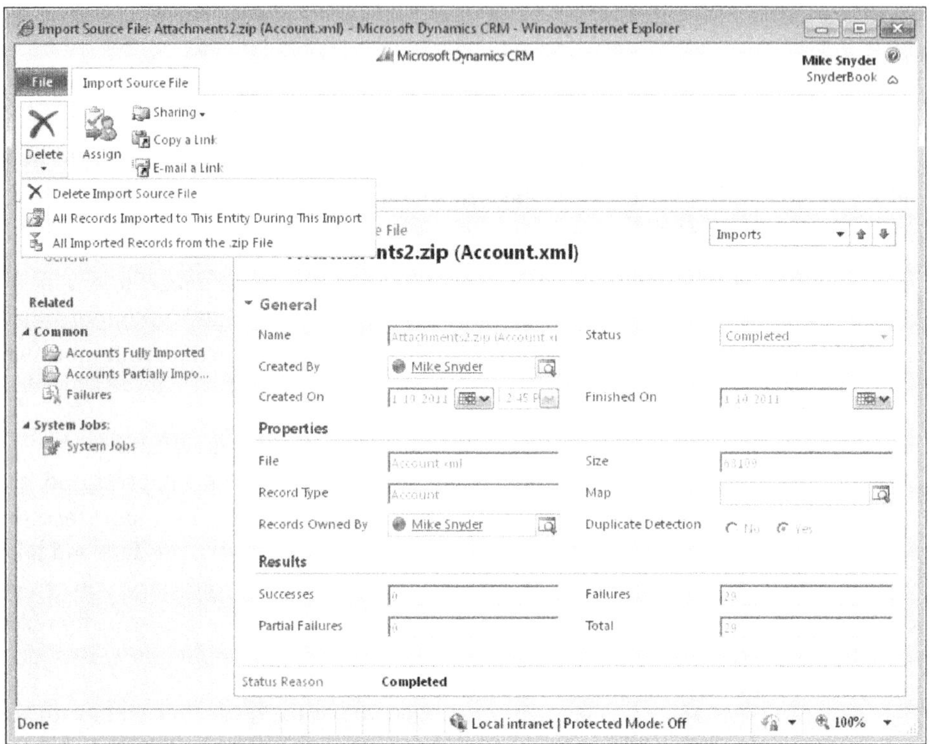

FIGURE 4-8 Deleting all records associated with an import job

Data Enrichment

As you can see, the Import Data Wizard allows you to easily create records in bulk by using a simple, intuitive wizard. In addition to creating data with this wizard, you might want to update data in bulk through a similar interface. Sometimes you might need to update multiple records, but make different updates to different records.

Consider a scenario where your sales staff has a weekly meeting in which they review a list of opportunities with their manager. Each salesperson edits a list of opportunities every week, updating the ratings, close dates, and revenue values associated with these opportunities. If a salesperson has a large list of opportunities, he might prefer to make these updates in Microsoft Office Excel instead of editing each record individually in Microsoft Dynamics CRM. The *data enrichment* capabilities in Microsoft Dynamics CRM allow users to do so.

Suppose you are one of these sales users. To use the data enrichment feature, you must first export your opportunity list to Microsoft Office Excel. Do this by clicking the Export to Excel button in the application ribbon. A dialog box opens, from which you can select the export type. The data enrichment feature only works with static worksheets, so select one of the static worksheet options. After doing so, you can select the option at the bottom of the dialog box to enable re-importing, as shown in Figure 4-9.

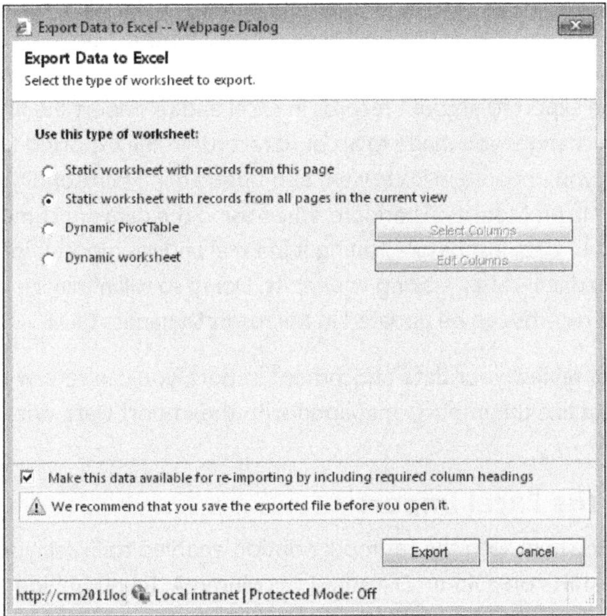

FIGURE 4-9 Enabling data enrichment while exporting to Excel

After clicking the Export button in the dialog box, you should download and save the file, then open the file in Excel and begin updating the data. Just like the data import templates, the exported Excel file includes tips on each column about the data type. Each option set displays a list of the possible values from Microsoft Dynamics CRM, and you cannot create new values in option set fields in the spreadsheet. All other functionality works as usual in Microsoft Office Excel. After you complete your updates in Excel, you can re-import the file into Microsoft Dynamics CRM.

Tip In addition to editing the existing records, you can add new records to Microsoft Dynamics CRM by simply adding rows in your Excel spreadsheet.

To re-import the file, click the Import Data button in the application ribbon, select your file, and step through the instructions to complete the import. Microsoft Dynamics CRM recognizes the import file as an update to existing records and performs the update in the background.

Please note that data enrichment only updates the records that changed in the Excel file. For example, let's assume that you exported 100 records, updated two of them, and then re-imported the file. Microsoft Dynamics CRM would only update the two records you modified and ignore the other 98 rows. This is ideal from an audit history perspective because only two audit records are created instead of 100.

The data enrichment feature also ignores updates made to records that are updated since the original static worksheet was exported. For example, assume you exported a static worksheet of accounts on Monday. On Tuesday, another user modifies several accounts in Microsoft Dynamics CRM, including some of the account records you exported on Monday. Without knowing this, on Wednesday, you modify the exported account records in Excel and re-import the file into Microsoft Dynamics CRM. Any changes you made to account records in the exported file are ignored if the account records you updated in Excel were also updated in Microsoft Dynamics CRM after you exported the data on Monday. Therefore, when using the data enrichment feature, make sure to export your data just before editing it in Excel and re-import it into Microsoft Dynamics CRM immediately after making your edits. Doing so will minimize the window in which the exported records can be updated in Microsoft Dynamics CRM.

If you need to troubleshoot or review your data enrichment import, you can review the details in the Imports view, just like the imports managed with the Import Data Wizard.

Hidden Columns in the Excel Import

After exporting a static worksheet with the re-import option enabled to Excel, you might notice the Excel file starts on column D instead of column A. If you unhide columns A, B, and C in Excel, you will see the following columns:

- Entity ID – The globally unique identifier (GUID) of the record
- Checksum
- Modified On

The ID is the unique ID of the record and the Modified On column has the date and timestamp of when the record was exported. The Checksum column is an internal code that Microsoft Dynamics CRM uses to determine whether the record has been edited since it was exported. You cannot edit any of these columns because the Excel sheet is protected, but you should know that Microsoft Dynamics CRM uses them when re-importing records. If necessary you can disable the Excel sheet protection in Excel 2010 by clicking File in the Ribbon and then clicking Info. Under Permissions, click the Unprotect links to disable the worksheet protection.

Column A includes the GUID for a record, and you can use this GUID to link imported records in your source file. You might want to use this technique when you have a large number of records with common values that might fail during an import because the lookup values aren't unique. The GUID is a 32-digit hexadecimal number in the query string.

Duplicate Detection

After loading data into your system, of course you want to make sure the database remains free of too many duplicate records. Fortunately, Microsoft Dynamics CRM includes duplicate detection functionality to help you maintain the integrity of your data. Duplicate detection consists of three main areas:

- Duplication detection settings
- Duplicate detection rules
- Duplicate detection jobs

You access almost all of the duplicate detection configuration in the Data Management section located in the Settings area.

Duplication Detection Settings

You can enable duplicate detection for your organization and determine when Microsoft Dynamics CRM should perform the duplicate checks. The three options to configure these settings are:

- When a record is created or updated
- When Microsoft Dynamics CRM for Outlook goes from offline to online
- During a data import

You can choose to enable duplicate detection for some or all of these settings, but you cannot selectively apply these settings to specific entities. For example, if you enable duplicate detection when a record is created or updated, Microsoft Dynamics CRM applies that setting to *all* entities.

Duplicate Detection Rules

Because every organization defines duplicates differently, Microsoft Dynamics CRM lets you configure duplicate detection rules specific to your business needs. After you define and publish a duplicate detection rule, Microsoft Dynamics CRM creates a *matchcode* for every record created or updated in the previous five minutes. This matchcode process runs continually in the background every five minutes, even for inactive records. Microsoft Dynamics CRM uses matchcodes behind the scenes to look for duplicate records based on your duplicate detection settings. Figure 4-10 shows a sample duplicate detection rule for the Contact entity.

In this example, Microsoft Dynamics CRM identifies a duplicate if all of the following conditions are met:

- The first three characters of the first name match.
- The first five characters of the last name match.
- All of the characters in the state/province field match.

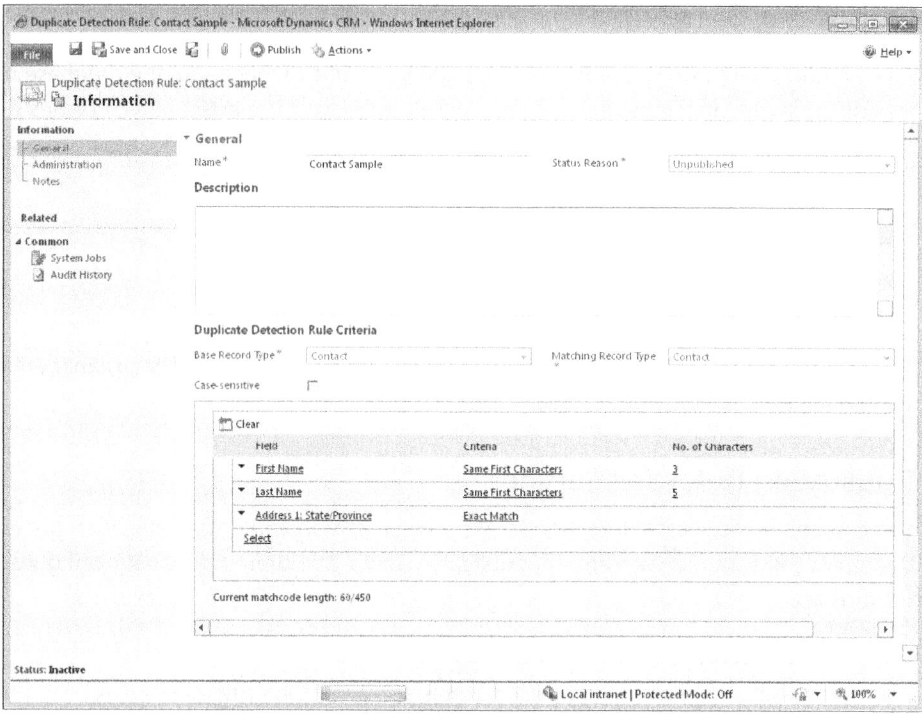

FIGURE 4-10 Duplicate detection rule configured for the Contact entity

Unlike the Advanced Find tool, you cannot configure OR conditions in a duplicate detection rule, but can you set up multiple rules for a single entity. In addition, you can configure your rule to search across two entities (such as Contact to Lead) and can specify whether the checks should be case-sensitive. Finally, you need to consider that each attribute you add to your duplicate detection rule adds to the matchcode length, because Microsoft Dynamics CRM enforces a maximum matchcode length of 450 characters. Each change to the rule updates the current matchcode length displayed in the bottom of the page so that you can monitor where you stand in relation to the maximum. When you're finished configuring the rule, publish it by clicking the Publish button on the toolbar.

Then, when a user tries to enter a record that Microsoft Dynamics CRM identifies as a duplicate, the user will see a dialog box like the one shown in Figure 4-11.

From here, the user can choose to save the record or cancel the create/update operation. Unfortunately, there is no way to merge the new or updated record into one of the duplicates identified by Microsoft Dynamics CRM.

Important Because the matchcode process runs every five minutes, if you rapidly create or update records that qualify as duplicates before the matchcodes can update, Microsoft Dynamics CRM will not immediately recognize those records as duplicates. To find these duplicates, you should use the duplicate job process that we explain in the next section.

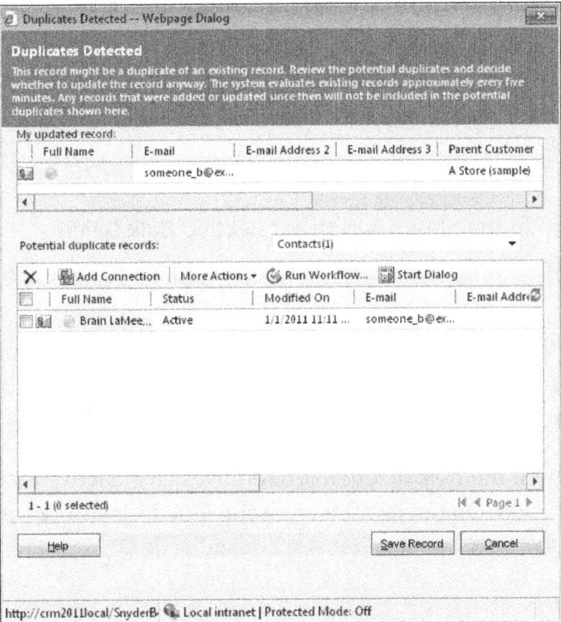

FIGURE 4-11 Duplicates Detected dialog box

You may wonder if you can permanently dismiss this duplicate warning if you know for a fact that the record you updated is not a duplicate, even though it meets the duplicate detection rules. Unfortunately, you cannot permanently dismiss a duplicate check for a record, so you will see this dialog box each time you update the record. In this scenario, we recommend that you modify your duplicate detection rule to avoid the situation.

Duplicate Jobs

In addition to the duplicate detection settings, you can also configure Microsoft Dynamics CRM to perform a duplicate detection job at a scheduled interval to look for potential duplicates. To create a duplicate detection job, navigate to the Data Management section in the Settings area and click Duplicate Detection Jobs. Next, click the New button on the grid toolbar, and Microsoft Dynamics CRM displays a Select Records page with an interface similar to Advanced Find. For each duplicate detection job, you can use this Advanced Find interface to create a subset of records on which to perform the duplicate check. You can also schedule the duplicate detection job to run at a scheduled interval, such as every 7, 30, 90, 180, or 365 days. After Microsoft Dynamics CRM completes the duplicate detection job, you can open the job record and click View Duplicates in the navigation pane to resolve any duplicates found during the job.

Bulk Record Deletion

From time to time, you might need to delete multiple records from your Microsoft Dynamics CRM database. Of course, you can use the delete functionality to perform this action from views, but you can only delete one page of records at a time. If you need to delete 500 or more records, this might be a time-consuming process. In addition, you might want to set up an automated process where you delete old records from your database at a scheduled interval to keep the file size down. The bulk record deletion functionality is a good way to resolve these scenarios.

You can start a bulk deletion job in one of two ways:

- By clicking the Delete button in the ribbon and then selecting Bulk Delete
- By clicking the Bulk Record Deletion link located in the Data Management section of the Settings area

In either approach, the Bulk Deletion Wizard appears, allowing you to define the search criteria for the records you want to delete. You can specify your own criteria in this dialog box, or you can select one of your saved views.

Figure 4-12 shows an example where the bulk deletion job removes any inactive record modified on or before January 1, 2009. On the last screen of the Bulk Deletion Wizard, you can configure additional options, such as:

- Naming the bulk delete job
- Specifying a specific start time (typically run in the off-hours, when other users aren't on the system)
- Specifying a recurrence pattern where the bulk delete process repeats every 7, 30, 90, 180, or 365 days
- Selecting users to receive email notifications when the bulk delete process completes

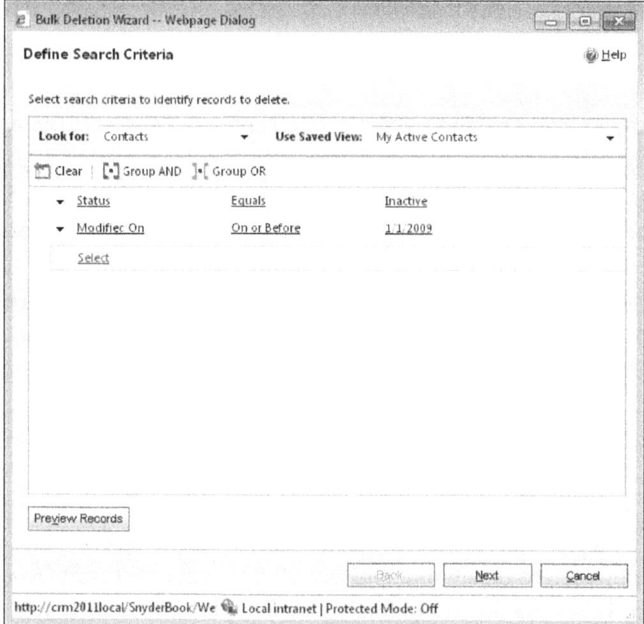

FIGURE 4-12 Defining search criteria for a bulk deletion job

The options are shown in Figure 4-13.

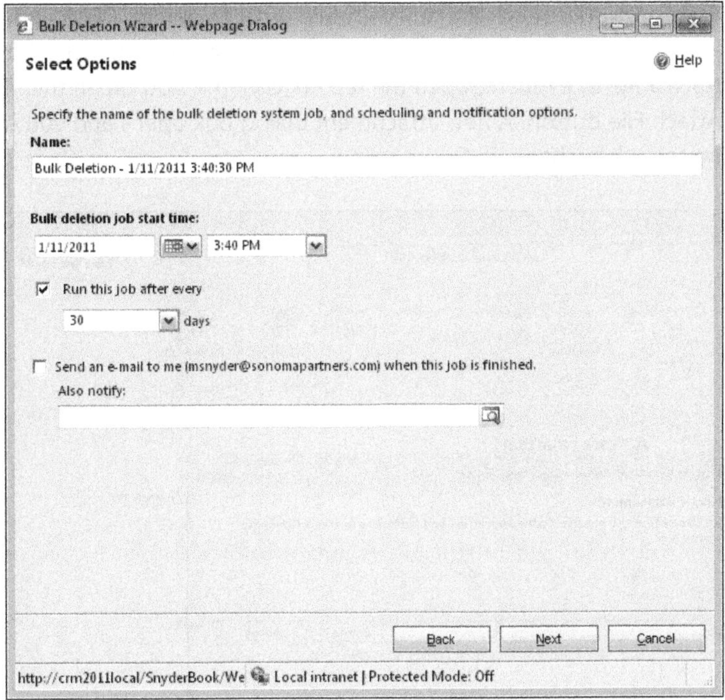

FIGURE 4-13 Configuring bulk deletion job options

Important The bulk delete feature provides a quick and easy way to remove unwanted data from your Microsoft Dynamics CRM. However, use it with extreme caution. Data deleted from Microsoft Dynamics CRM cannot be recovered without an external backup process!

Document Management

Microsoft Dynamics CRM provides a great database for tracking data about sales, marketing, and customer service. However, a lot of your customer data lives in other types of files too, such as Excel, Word, and PowerPoint. Of course, your users would love to have quick and easy access to their key documents in Microsoft Dynamics CRM, and fortunately the document management features in the software make this possible.

The two primary document management options in Microsoft Dynamics CRM are:

- File attachments
- SharePoint document integration

File Attachments

The file attachment option works out of the box with Microsoft Dynamics CRM, and it works equally well in both Microsoft Dynamics CRM Online and on-premises or partner-hosted deployments. To attach a file to a record, open the record, click the Add tab in the ribbon, and then click the Attach File button. A new attachment dialog box opens and you can select a file to attach to the record, as shown in Figure 4-14.

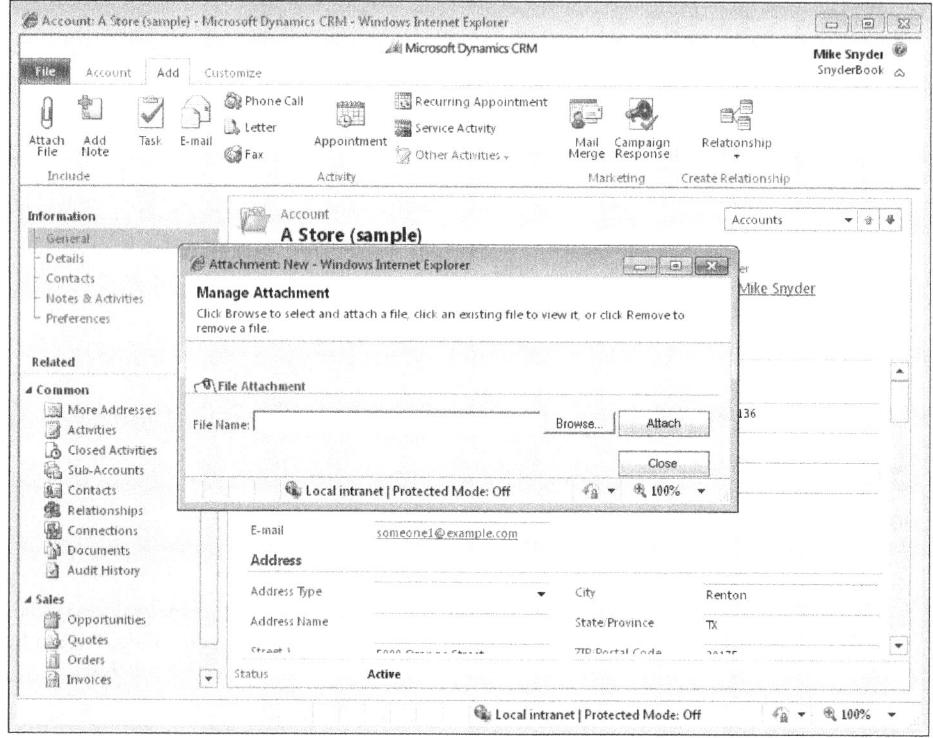

FIGURE 4-14 Attaching a file to an account

After you finish attaching the file, you can view the file under the Notes section of a record. If you right-click the attachment, you can access a few menu options, such as opening or deleting the file, as shown in Figure 4-15.

This file attachment feature works well for basic document management needs, but it does not provide a great experience for a document that will go through many revisions. If you download this file, make some edits to it, and then attach it back to the same account, Microsoft Dynamics CRM treats the revised file as a brand-new attachment. Therefore, you would see two different files attached to the record. Most users would not enjoy this experience, so we recommend that you use the file attachment option for files that don't need any revisions, such as signed contracts.

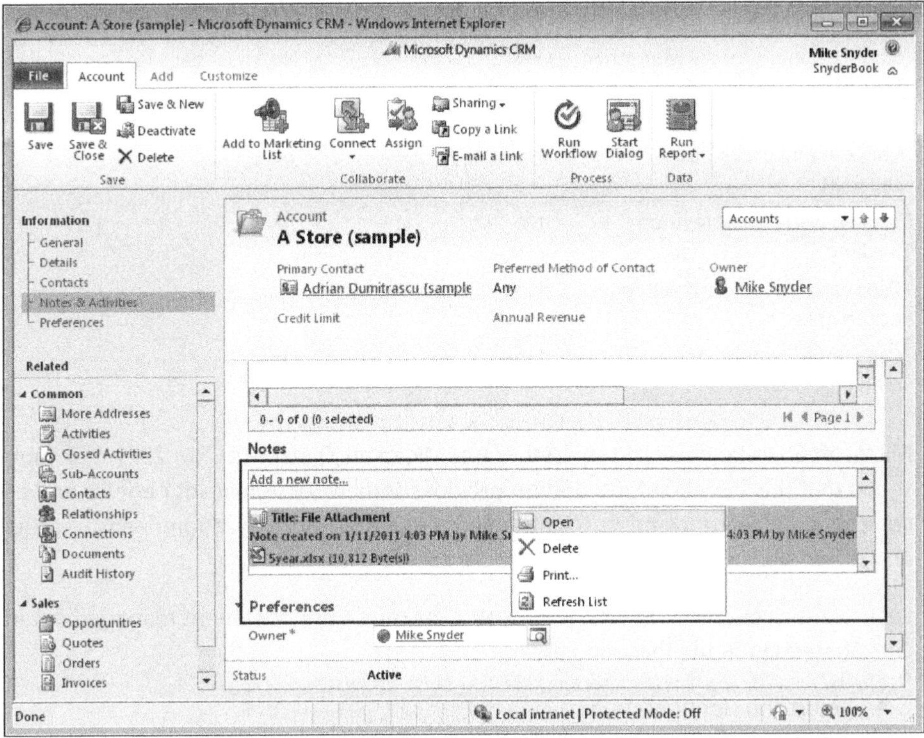

FIGURE 4-15 Accessing the actions menu on a file attachment

SharePoint Document Integration

For organizations with more complex document management needs, the integration between Microsoft Dynamics CRM and Microsoft SharePoint offers great additional features and benefits. Table 4-2 compares the differences between using file attachments and the SharePoint integration for your document management needs in Microsoft Dynamics CRM.

TABLE 4-2 Document Management Features in Microsoft Dynamics CRM

	File Attachments	SharePoint Integration
Additional software required	No	Yes, Microsoft Office SharePoint Server
Stores documents in Microsoft Dynamics CRM database	Yes	No
Can take documents offline with Microsoft Dynamics CRM for Outlook with Offline Access	Yes	No
Uses Microsoft Dynamics CRM security roles and settings	Yes	No, SharePoint security settings must be configured separately

	File Attachments	SharePoint Integration
Single backup process with other Microsoft Dynamics CRM data for documents	Yes	No, must back up SharePoint data in addition to Microsoft Dynamics CRM backups
Check in and check out capabilities	No	Yes
Version history and revision tracking	No	Yes
Can search for content within documents	No	Yes
Can configure alerts for modifications	No	Yes

Microsoft SharePoint is not required to use Microsoft Dynamics CRM 2011, but Table 4-2 shows that the SharePoint integration provides some very significant benefits and capabilities compared to file attachments. The trade-off is that your organization needs to acquire and set up Microsoft Office SharePoint Server.

Let's take a deeper look at how Microsoft Dynamics CRM document management integrates with SharePoint in the following areas:

- Setup and Configuration
- User Interface

Setup and Configuration

At the time this book went to press, Microsoft Dynamics CRM supported the following versions of SharePoint:

- Microsoft SharePoint 2010 (all editions)
- Microsoft Office SharePoint Server (MOSS) 2007

Microsoft Dynamics CRM 2011 List Component for Microsoft SharePoint Server 2010

Although Microsoft Dynamics CRM supports Microsoft SharePoint 2010 and Microsoft Office SharePoint Server 2007, SharePoint 2010 offers additional features by also installing the Microsoft Dynamics CRM 2011 List Component for Microsoft SharePoint Server 2010. With this list component installed, you get the following benefits:

- The document management interface in Microsoft Dynamics CRM will mirror the rest of the application by displaying a grid of documents.
- You can configure Microsoft Dynamics CRM and SharePoint to automatically create folders for your documents.

Without this list component, Microsoft Dynamics CRM displays SharePoint documents in an inline frame (IFrame), which works fine but doesn't match the look and feel of Microsoft Dynamics CRM. We will show an example of the list component later in this chapter.

We won't go through the entire process of setting up the SharePoint integration because the Microsoft Dynamics CRM Implementation Guide covers this process in detail. However, we want to highlight a few key configuration parameters. You can access the Document Management configuration options by clicking the Document Management link in the Settings area of Microsoft Dynamics CRM.

Next, click the Document Management Settings link. A dialog box opens and you can select the entities for which you want to enable document management, as shown in Figure 4-16.

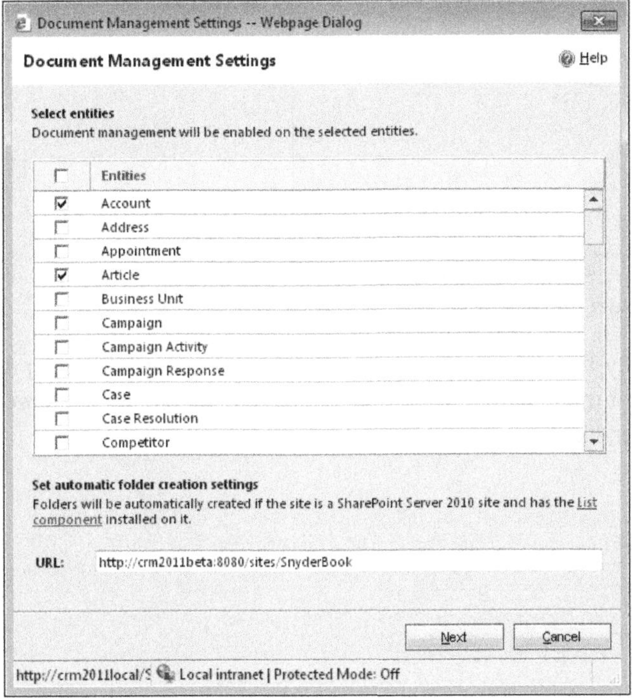

FIGURE 4-16 Enabling entities for SharePoint document management

After you select the entities you want to enable, the next screen in the dialog box allows you to configure the folder structure by either the Account or the Contact entity, as shown in Figure 4-17.

Tip You can specify an entity-based folder structure for only the Account or only the Contact entity. These two folder structure options will work well for most organizations deploying Microsoft Dynamics CRM. However, if your organization does not rely on the Account and Contact entity, you might not want to structure your folders by entity.

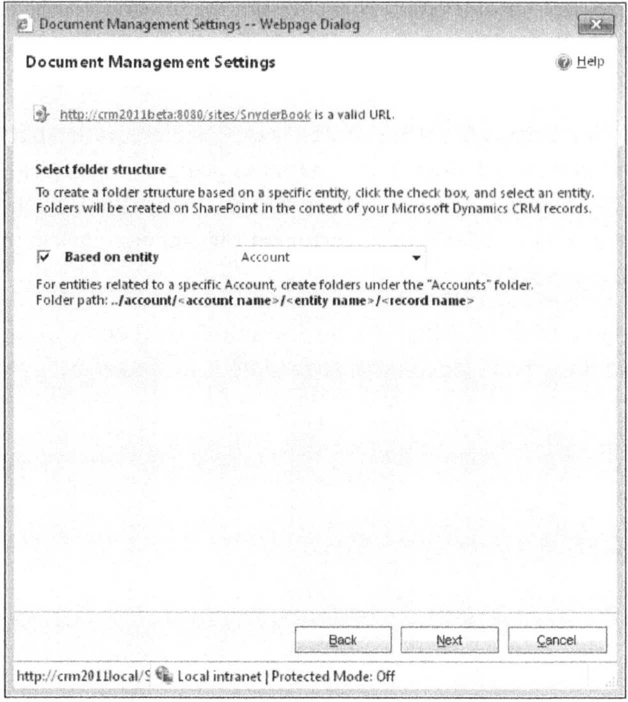

FIGURE 4-17 Configuring the folder structure by entity

If you don't enable the entity-based folder structure, SharePoint creates folders for every entity enabled for document management and then creates sub-folders for each record underneath the entity folder, like this:

- Account folder
    - Account X folder
    - Account Y folder
    - Account Z folder
- Contact folder
    - Contact A folder (related to Account X)
    - Contact B folder (related to Account Y)
    - Contact C folder (related to Account Z)
- Opportunity folder
    - Opportunity D folder (related to Account X)
    - Opportunity E folder (related to Account Y)
    - Opportunity F folder (related to Account Z)

However, if you enable an entity-based folder structure for the Account entity, SharePoint creates folders following this structure:

- Account folder
    - Account X folder
        - Opportunity D folder (related to Account X)
        - Contact A folder (related to Account X)
    - Account Y folder
        - Opportunity E folder (related to Account Y)
        - Contact B folder (related to Account Y)
    - Account Z folder
        - Opportunity F folder (related to Account Z)
        - Contact C folder (related to Account Z)

Either folder structure will work, and the Microsoft Dynamics CRM user interface will appear the same regardless of which option you select, so the choice depends on your preference. If your users will browse to the SharePoint folders directly (instead of always accessing the documents in the Microsoft Dynamics CRM user interface), an account- or contact-based folder structure might make the SharePoint folders easier to navigate. However, setting up SharePoint security and locking down the files and folders might be complicated under this model.

Tip You can configure multiple SharePoint sites with your Microsoft Dynamics CRM system, but you need to specify one site as the default for automatic folder creation.

User Interface

If you open a record for an entity that has document management enabled, you will see a Documents link in the left navigation pane on the record. When you click that link, Microsoft Dynamics CRM prompts you to automatically create a document folder for the record. Assuming that you click OK, it creates a folder. Each record can have multiple document locations, so each time you click the Add Location button Microsoft Dynamics CRM prompts you to create an additional document location.

Important The automatic folder creation prompt only appears if you have the Microsoft Dynamics CRM 2011 List Component installed on Microsoft SharePoint Server 2010.

With the folder created, you can add files to the record. To add one or more files, click the Add button on the grid toolbar and follow the screens to select and upload your files. After you add a few files, you'll see them listed, as shown in Figure 4-18.

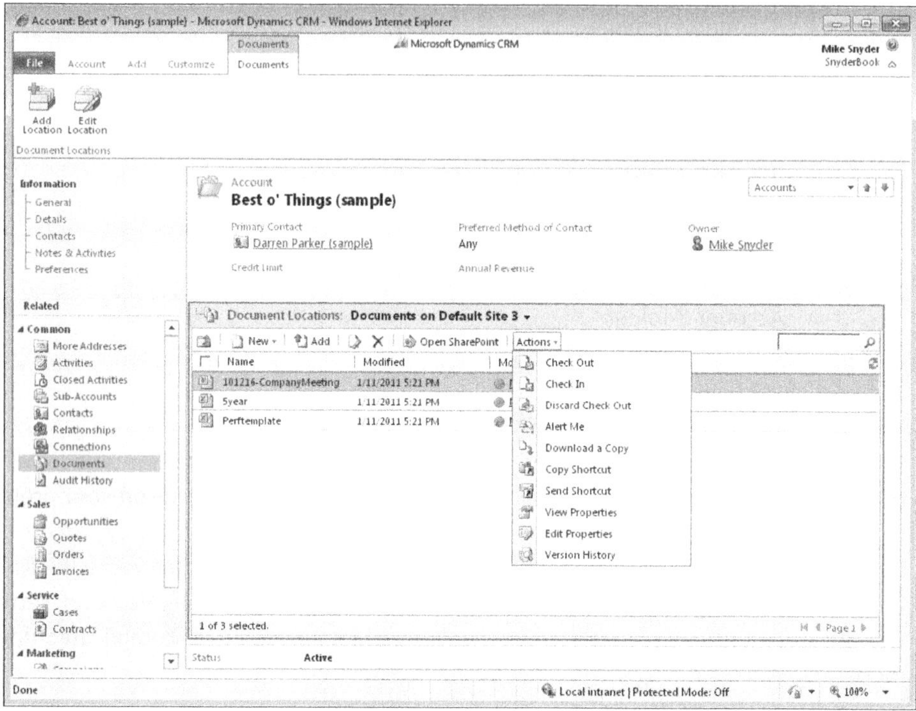

FIGURE 4-18 Accessing SharePoint functionality in the Microsoft Dynamics CRM user interface

We want to highlight a few very significant features in Figure 4-18:

- The user interface and the document list styling matches the rest of the Microsoft Dynamics CRM system, even though all of the data comes from SharePoint.
- Under the Actions menu, you can access SharePoint document functionality to check in, check out, configure alerts, view the version history, and more.
- You can edit or delete the document by clicking those buttons on the toolbar.
- You can click the Open SharePoint button to launch an Internet Explorer window that navigates directly to the SharePoint folder that stores these documents.

As you can see, setting up SharePoint document integration with Microsoft Dynamics CRM provides the user with the best of both worlds because they can access their SharePoint documents directly from the record related to those documents.

In the example we just covered, we created a SharePoint folder to store documents. What if we want to link an existing SharePoint document folder (possibly on an entirely different SharePoint site) to the record? Microsoft Dynamics CRM allows you to do so by supporting multiple document locations for each record. To do this, click the Add Location button in the ribbon. Microsoft Dynamics CRM launches the Add Document Location dialog box shown in Figure 4-19.

Add Document Location -- Webpage Dialog

Add Document Location

Create a new SharePoint folder or add an existing SharePoint folder as a document location in Microsoft Dynamics CRM.

Name: Location 2

Document Location: Specify the URL of an existing SharePoint folder

Tip: Copy the URL of the existing SharePoint folder here to associate the folder with this Microsoft Dynamics CRM record.

Create a new folder

Parent Site or Location: Default Site

Folder Name: Best o' Things (sample)

Save Cancel

http://crm2011local/SnyderBook/too Local intranet | Protected Mode: Off

FIGURE 4-19 Adding a SharePoint document location

From here, you can enter the URL of an existing SharePoint document library and click Save. After setting up the second document location, you can now quickly toggle between the two locations by selecting them in the drop-down list, as shown in Figure 4-20.

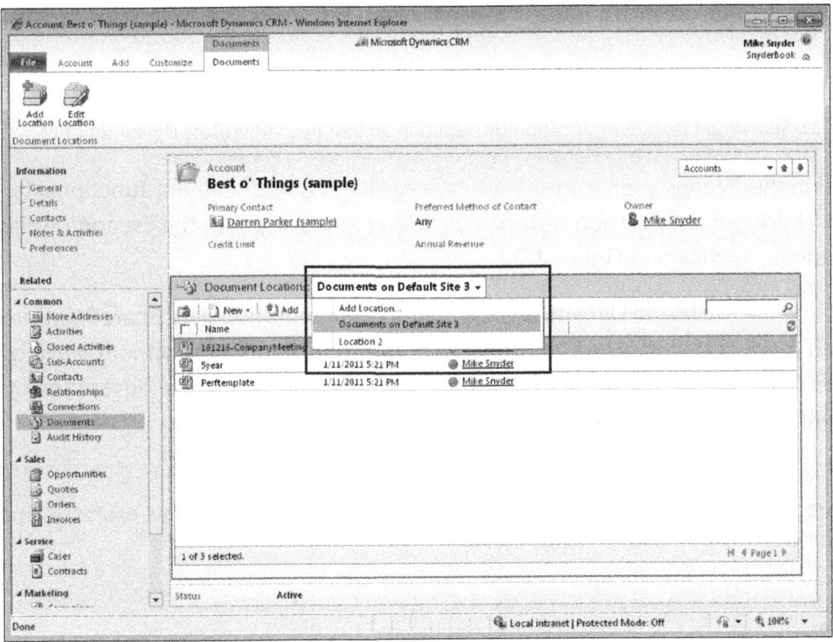

FIGURE 4-20 Toggling between SharePoint document locations

As we mentioned previously, you will only see the Microsoft Dynamics CRM grid style if the SharePoint 2010 site has the Microsoft Dynamics CRM 2011 List Component installed. If you add a document location from a SharePoint 2007 site or a SharePoint 2010 site that does not have the list component installed, the interface shows an IFrame around the SharePoint site, as shown in Figure 4-21.

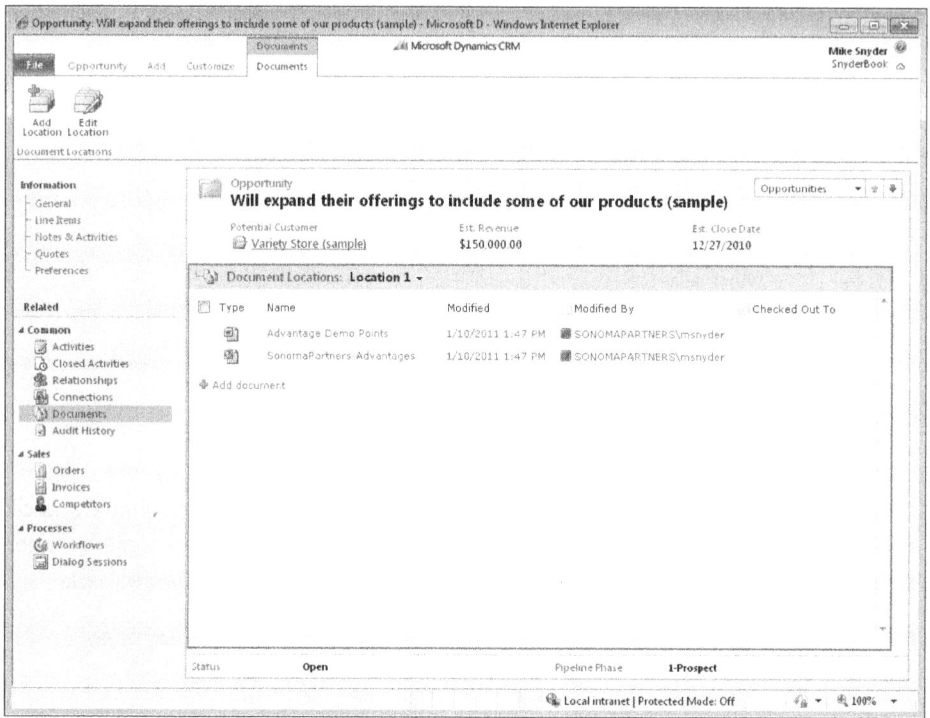

FIGURE 4-21 SharePoint document location displayed in an IFrame in Microsoft Dynamics CRM

Even within this IFrame, users can still access key SharePoint document functionality, such as check in, check out, and version history, by clicking a document in the list and displaying the context menu, as shown in Figure 4-22.

In summary, the Microsoft Dynamics CRM document integration with SharePoint provides users with quick and easy access to documents stored in SharePoint without leaving the Microsoft Dynamics CRM interface. In addition, organizations can take advantage of SharePoint's robust document management functionality.

Important The documents stored in SharePoint do not go offline with Microsoft Dynamics CRM for Outlook with Offline Access users.

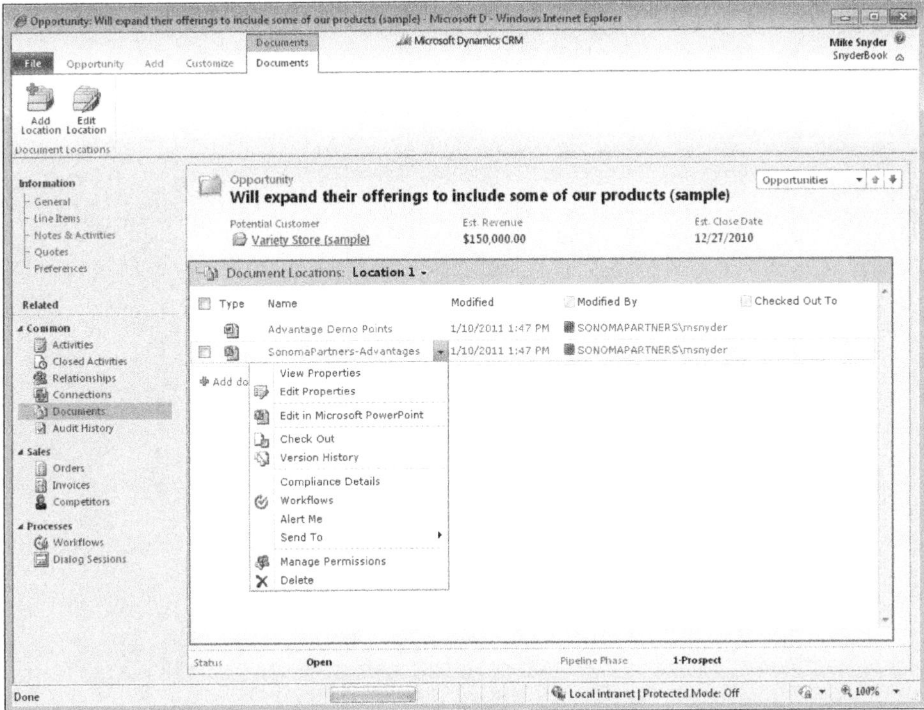

FIGURE 4-22 Accessing additional SharePoint actions in the IFrame

Summary

Microsoft Dynamics CRM offers powerful data and document management tools. The Import Data Wizard provides a user-friendly tool to add data in bulk, whereas the data enrichment capabilities allow you to easily update and modify existing data in Microsoft Dynamics CRM. In addition, the Import Data Wizard provides administrators the ability to modify the database structure on the fly based on the imported data. Although Microsoft Dynamics CRM includes a file attachment feature, most organizations will enjoy the more robust document management features available by using the integration with Microsoft Office SharePoint Server. The document management integration with SharePoint allows you to work with files related to your CRM records in the Microsoft Dynamics CRM user interface.

Part II
Solutions

Chapter 5

Solutions Overview and Concepts

In this chapter:

With almost every deployment of Microsoft Dynamics CRM we've encountered has some level of customization, from minor form and field changes to full-scale, custom application development. So it's a safe bet that you'll need to customize your system, too. Assume your company is considering Microsoft Dynamics CRM and you've installed the trial version of the software. As soon as you show the company executives the user interface and they see one of the default forms (such as the Account form shown in Figure 5-1), their first responses will likely be, "That's not the information we track about our customers. We would never use the Shipping Method and Freight Term fields, and where do we enter the SIC code and the number of employees for each customer? Also, we don't call our customers accounts; we refer to them as companies."

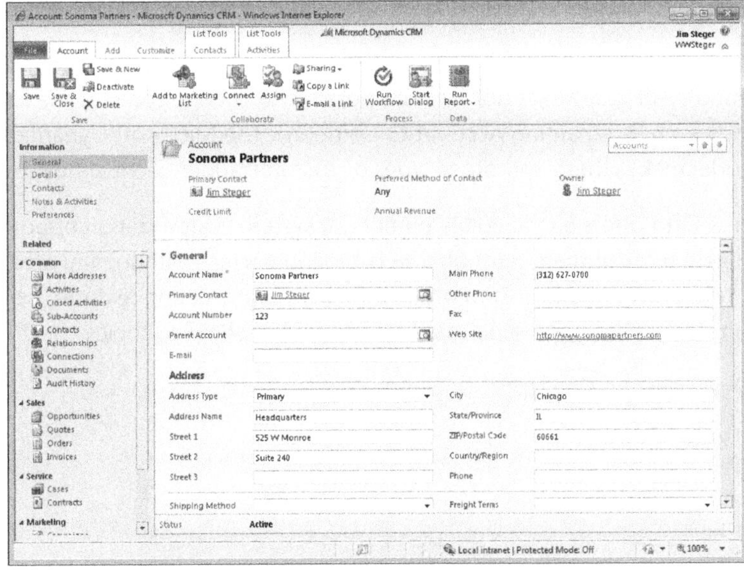

FIGURE 5-1 Default Account form

See? It took only one meeting for your users to start demanding customizations to the Microsoft Dynamics CRM system to better match their business needs. However, in just a few minutes and without a single line of programming code, you can customize Microsoft Dynamics CRM to accommodate their requests, similar to the result shown in Figure 5-2.

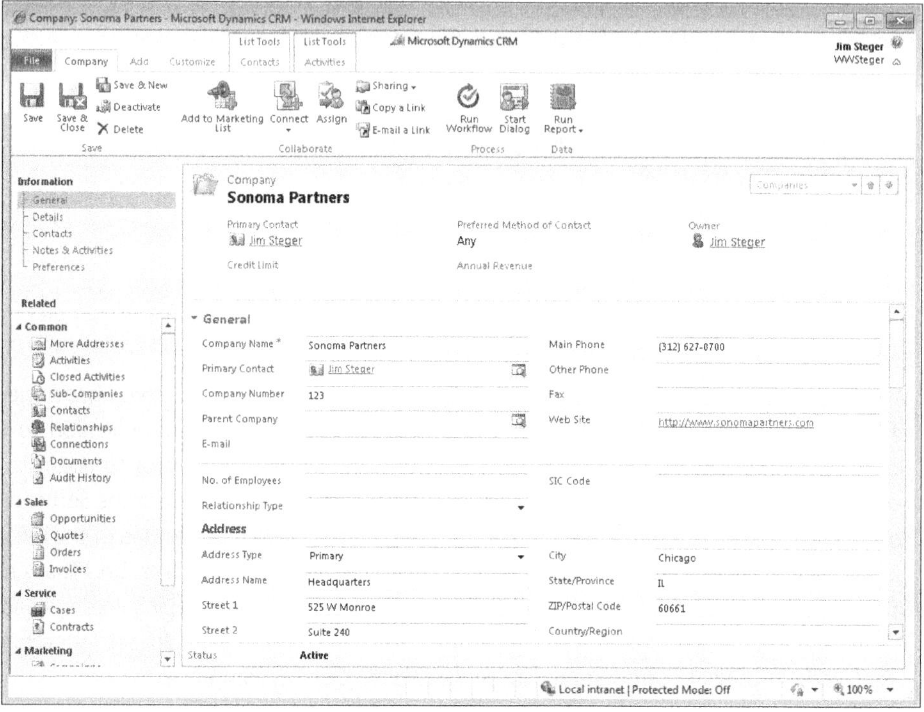

FIGURE 5-2 Account form revised with new fields and renamed Company

Implementing this type of customization in other CRM vendors' applications might take weeks of coding and testing. It might not even be possible to change some of the key system terminology such as renaming Account to Company. The Microsoft Dynamics CRM customization model makes these and other types of customizations seem almost trivial.

Microsoft Dynamics CRM offers an incredible number of system customization opportunities, and you can complete most of them through a web-based interface without any programming expertise. In fact, Microsoft Dynamics CRM offers so many customization features, we had to break the customization section into separate chapters on the following topics:

- Solutions Overview and Concepts
- Fields and Option Sets
- Forms
- Views and Charts
- Entity Relationships

- Custom Entities and Activities
- Web Resources
- Client Extensions (Site Map and Ribbon)

In this chapter, we review solutions and other customization concepts related to Microsoft Dynamics CRM.

Microsoft Dynamics CRM Customizations

Throughout this section, we'll discuss the key components of the customization model in Microsoft Dynamics CRM. These components are grouped as *solutions* in Microsoft Dynamics CRM. Solutions are containers of customization components and metadata that are used to create or update functionality in Microsoft Dynamics CRM. Each solution has a *publisher*, defined as the owner of the solution.

Customization Concepts

Microsoft Dynamics CRM can be used by any company, regardless of industry or size. Because no two businesses use the same processes or track the same customer data, Microsoft Dynamics CRM is designed for easy customization by using a metadata-driven product architecture.

Metadata is defined as data about data. When users look up a customer or prospect, Microsoft Dynamics CRM retrieves the record data from the metadata, which in turn retrieves information from the underlying system data. Microsoft Dynamics CRM stores its underlying system data in a relational database using Microsoft SQL Server. Figure 5-3 illustrates a highly simplified representation of this metadata-driven concept.

FIGURE 5-3 Metadata product architecture

Of course, your users will never know that Microsoft Dynamics CRM uses a metadata architecture, but it's important that you know about it for several reasons:

- The metadata makes heavy use of web services and XML data formats, so you see terminology related to those technologies in the Microsoft Dynamics CRM documentation and in this book (such as *entity* and *field*).
- With the metadata-driven architecture in Microsoft Dynamics CRM, you can quickly and easily make customizations that would be extremely difficult or perhaps impossible to implement in other CRM systems.

- Microsoft Dynamics CRM automatically manages the extremely complex details of the metadata on your behalf. If you attempt to make changes directly to the underlying system data in Microsoft SQL Server, you run the risk of damaging the metadata and creating irreversible errors in your system.

To ensure the metadata and its underlying SQL data always remain well structured, Microsoft Dynamics CRM offers two ways to customize your system. The first method is a web-based interface specifically designed for you to manage metadata changes. The second method allows you to use the Microsoft Dynamics CRM software development kit (SDK) to programmatically alter the metadata. Both of these tools work in the predefined framework of Microsoft Dynamics CRM to update the metadata and its underlying SQL data correctly.

Note You can download the Microsoft Dynamics CRM SDK at *http://www.microsoft.com/downloads/en/details.aspx?FamilyID=420f0f05-c226-4194-b7e1-f23ceaa83b69* for more information regarding the programmatic capabilities of Microsoft Dynamics CRM.

In addition to helping you protect your software investment, using the Microsoft Dynamics CRM administration tools for your customizations includes the following additional benefits:

- The web-based administration tools provide a simple and easy-to-understand interface.
- Microsoft technical support can assist you with any changes that you make using the customization tools.
- Your customizations should upgrade smoothly to future releases and updates of Microsoft Dynamics CRM.
- You can install third-party software add-ons for Microsoft Dynamics CRM.
- You can package and distribute your solutions to other Microsoft Dynamics CRM deployments.

New in Microsoft Dynamics CRM 2011, solutions provide a more granular framework in which system administrators and programmers can develop custom applications. To use solutions and make customization changes to the application, you must have the appropriate security privileges.

Security and Permissions

Users who have the System Administrator security role can perform all functions in the system, including the customizations described in this chapter. However, you might want to let certain users customize the system without granting them System Administrator rights. Fortunately, in Microsoft Dynamics CRM, you can configure security roles to specify who can perform different levels of customization. Microsoft Dynamics CRM includes two default security roles associated with system customization privileges: System Administrator and System Customizer. Figure 5-4 shows the default security settings for the System Customizer role.

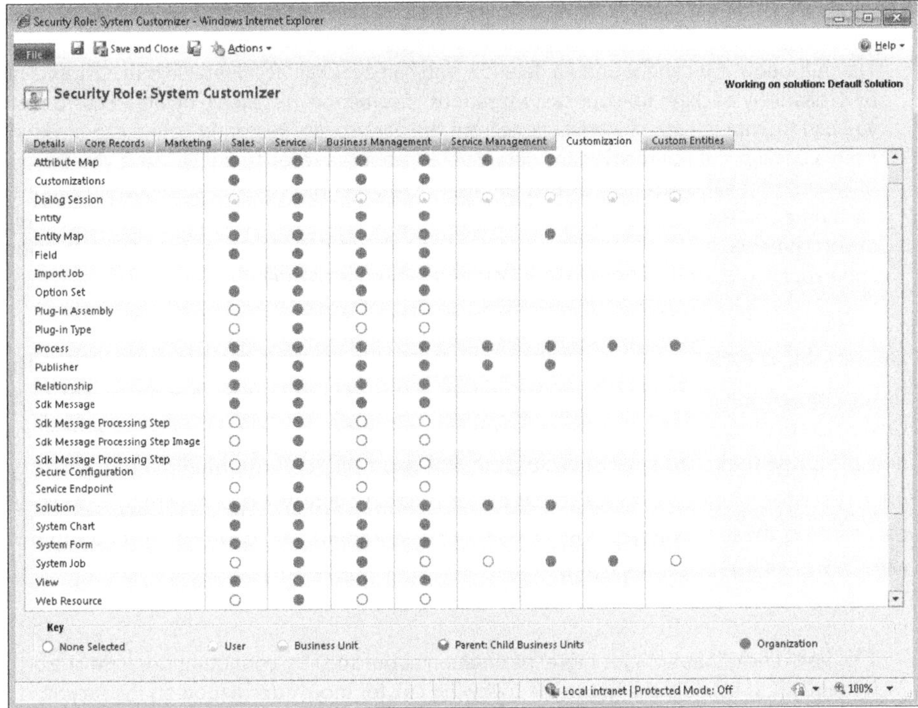

FIGURE 5-4 Default security settings for the System Customizer role

In this screen shot, notice that you can refine the customization rights on a more detailed level than just specifying "yes" or "no." For example, you might allow some of your users to create fields but not allow the same users to create entities. You can also remove delete permissions related to entity customization. If the person performing your customizations is new to Microsoft Dynamics CRM, we strongly recommend that you modify the default System Customizer role to remove all of the delete permissions and do not assign the user to the System Administrator role.

Caution As you will learn later in the chapter, you can now import solutions that include plug-in and workflow assemblies. As you can see in Figure 5-4, the System Customizer does not allow the create or write privileges for the Sdk Message and Processing Steps. You can create a modified security role to allow for this or ensure that your user importing solutions with assemblies has the System Administrator role.

Microsoft Dynamics CRM is very forgiving in regard to mistakes made when you're modifying customizations, but you can't recover a deleted customization. If you spend 40 hours customizing an entity and someone accidentally deletes it, your work is gone forever if you didn't create a backup of your customizations or database. To change the security settings of the System Customizer role, click the appropriate option and save the security role, as you learned in Chapter 3, "Managing Security and Information Access."

Tip Although you cannot undo a deletion, you can avoid an accidental loss of customizations by proactively backing up your customizations. If someone mistakenly deletes a customization, you can re-import your customizations from the backup file. Restoring your customizations from a backup will not recover any data deleted from the records, but will save you the time of having to reconstruct the customizations. We suggest you back up your customizations after each time you successfully publish them. To create a backup of your customizations, simply export the default solution and save the file to a safe location. We explain publishing, importing, and exporting customizations in more detail later in this chapter.

Later in this chapter, we review importing, exporting, publishing, and a few other aspects of the new solutions model. All users assigned the default System Administrator or System Customizer role can perform these actions. In addition, you can toggle these privileges on and off individually for each security role. For example, you might allow one security role to import customizations but not to export or publish customizations. Mostly, you should plan on granting these privileges only to users who will need to customize and configure your Microsoft Dynamics CRM system.

Tip Reference Chapter 3 for more information about security configurations in Microsoft Dynamics CRM. Additionally, use the following link for more information on the security privileges in Microsoft Dynamics CRM: *http://rc.crm.dynamics.com/rc/2011/en-us/on-prem/5.0/help/source_sec_cust.htm.*

You can see the benefits of the Microsoft Dynamics CRM metadata architecture and using the customization tools that Microsoft Dynamics CRM provides. To understand how to use solutions to customize Microsoft Dynamics CRM, we'll delve deeper into their functionality and components.

Solution Framework Overview

Solutions are packages of customizations and metadata that allow system administrators and software developers to create, transport, and maintain business applications or functionality that run on the Microsoft Dynamics CRM framework.

Microsoft Dynamics CRM installs a default solution with each organization. The default solution works identically to the customizations concept of previous versions of Microsoft Dynamics CRM and contains a reference to all components in the system (including components installed by managed solutions).

Note You'll learn more about managed solutions later in the chapter.

If you have the appropriate permissions, you can access the default solution by navigating to the Settings area and then clicking Customizations. On the Customization screen, click Customize the System to open the default solution. The default solution is shown in Figure 5-5.

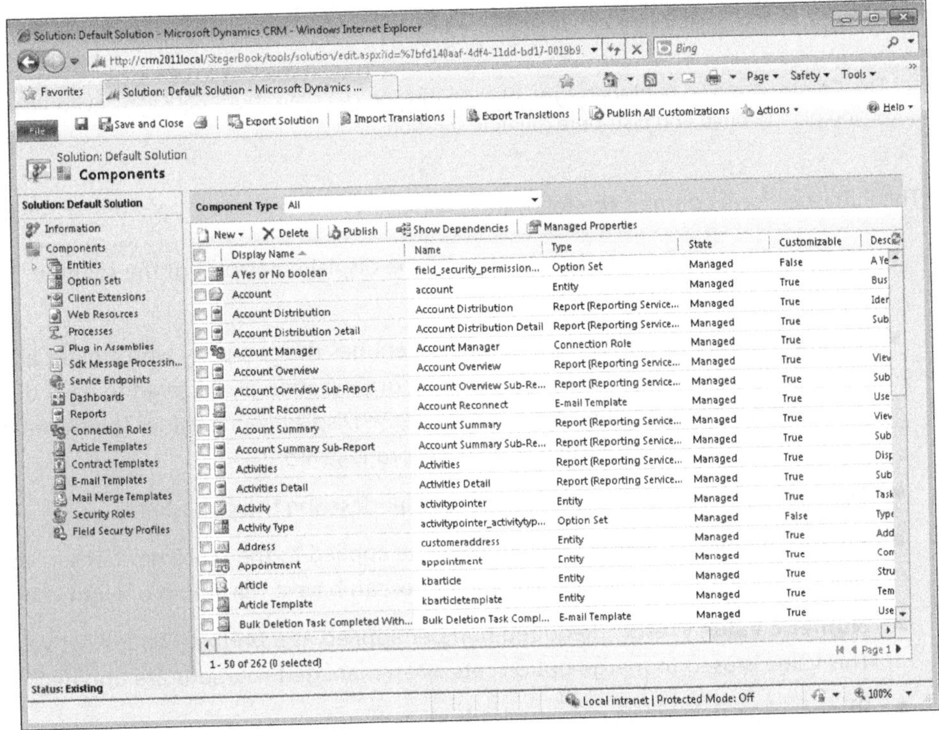

FIGURE 5-5 Default solution

Important You do not need to create solutions to customize Microsoft Dynamics CRM. Instead, you can just customize the default solution.

Unlike previous versions of the software, Microsoft Dynamics CRM 2011 packages customizations into solutions, providing improved control over the development, packaging, and distribution of customizations (including using a managed solution). You can create your own solutions or customize the default solution, depending on the complexity of your business requirements.

Every solution—including the default solution—references a publisher and has a few configurable properties. Let's review them.

Publisher

Each solution has a publisher that defines its owner or creator. You can access the list of publishers from the Customizations link in the Settings area.

Microsoft Dynamics CRM creates a default publisher when an organization is created. The default publisher can be associated to solutions you don't expect to export. If you plan on deploying any changes to other environments, such as a staging or production environment, we recommend creating your own publisher.

Tip Create your own publisher if you plan on moving customizations between environments or you plan to build and distribute multiple solutions.

The Publisher form contains the following properties:

- **Display Name** Required name that will be displayed as part of the solution. Typically this is your company name.
- **Name** Unique name for the publisher; identifies the company who creates and owns the solution. No two publishers on a given organization are allowed to have the same Name value, although they can have the same Display Name value. The Name field cannot be changed after the publisher record is saved.
- **Description** Notes or comments to further describe the publisher.
- **Prefix** Required, unique prefix that will be applied to the customizations in your solution, such as entities or fields. The prefix can have a maximum of eight characters.
- **Numeric Value Prefix** Required number applied as a prefix to option set values. This value is used to merge option sets when managed solutions are updated.
- **Phone** The publishing company's phone number.
- **E-mail** The publishing company's email address.
- **Web Site** The publishing company's website.
- **Address Fields** The publishing company's address information.
- **Marketplace** If you install a signed solution downloaded from the Microsoft Dynamics CRM Marketplace, this section automatically displays the solution publisher information from the marketplace. The Marketplace solution file will have a .cab extension.

More Info The publisher contact details are optional on the form, but if you decide to publish your solution to the Microsoft Dynamics CRM Marketplace, you will need to enter this information for the publisher to pass the Microsoft Platform Ready (MPR) test.

As you'll see later in the chapter, Microsoft Dynamics CRM uses the publisher's unique name value when binding the components to a solution. For instance, the solution import uses the publisher's unique name to grant or deny actions for managed solutions.

Solution Properties

You access the Solutions view from the Settings area. You won't see the default solution in this view because it can only be accessed from the ribbon or from the Customizations link in the Settings area. However, you can create custom solutions, import an existing solution, or download and import a solution from the Microsoft Dynamics CRM Marketplace from the Solutions view.

Let's review the key properties on the Solution form, as shown in Figure 5-6.

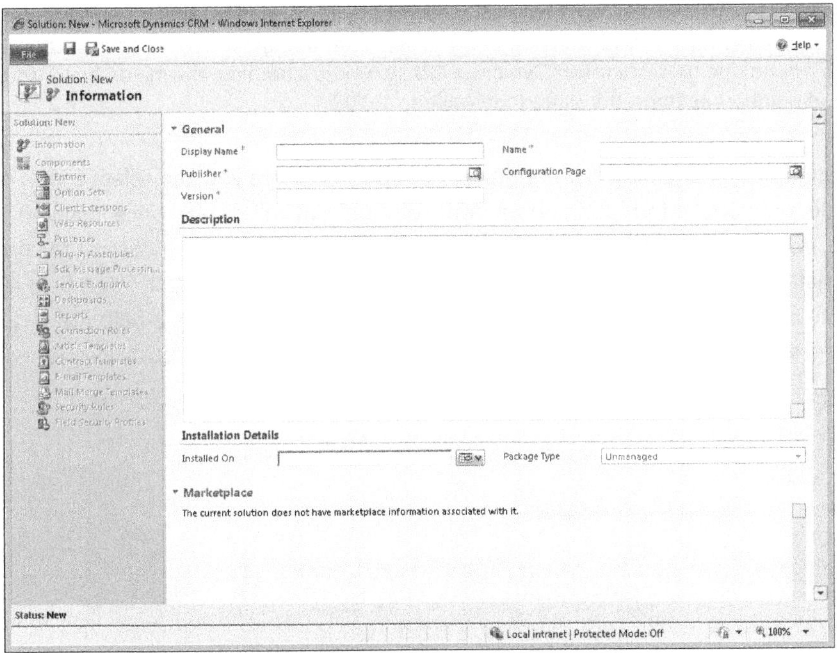

FIGURE 5-6 New Solution form

Solutions have the following properties:

- **Display Name** Required name that will be displayed to the user. This can be your product name for a managed solution or a descriptive name (such as "Site Map Updates") for development solutions.
- **Name** Unique name for the solution. No two solutions are allowed to have the same unique name in an organization. The Name field cannot be changed after the solution is saved.
- **Publisher** The publisher associated with the solution. If no custom publisher exists, use the organization's default publisher.

- **Configuration Page** Use this field to associate a web resource component that can be used to configure or further the solution.
- **Version** Use this field to track the version number of the solution.
- **Description** Notes or comments further describing the solution.
- **Marketplace** If the solution was downloaded and installed from the Microsoft Dynamics CRM Marketplace, you will see additional information about the solution and publisher in this section. The Marketplace solution file will have a .cab extension.

You must manually enter and manage the version number. The value is typically entered in the standard major.minor[.build[.revision]] format (i.e., 1.0.0.0). Microsoft Dynamics CRM does not provide any functionality to auto-increment this value.

Tip When entering a new version number, you can enter a single whole number (such as 1) and tab out of the field. Microsoft Dynamics CRM will auto-complete the minor, build, and revision numbers as zeros, translating the value to 1.0.0.0.

The Configuration Page field is an optional lookup field where you can select a web resource to include additional information about your solution that will display once installed. For instance, you could use this field to include an installation help page, a control to configure sample data, adding licensing information, and so on. The Configuration Page field allows you to include additional configuration steps in your solution, or associate a help file, if desired. Figure 5-7 shows an example of a Silverlight configuration page for a custom solution.

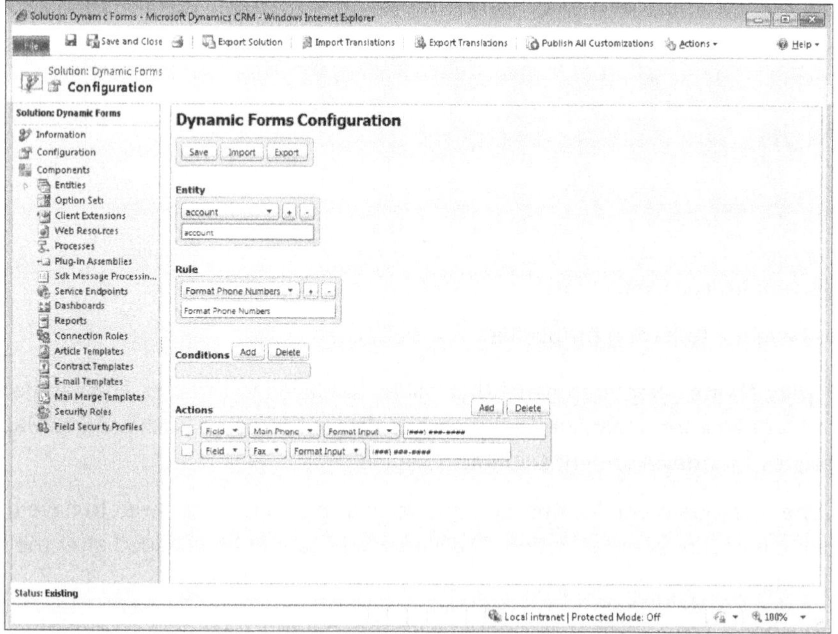

FIGURE 5-7 Sample configuration page

More Info A Configuration link appears in the solution's left navigation pane after you select a valid value for the Configuration Page field.

Let's walk through a quick example of creating a solution.

Creating a solution

1. Navigate to the Settings area, click Solutions, and then click the New icon in the Solutions grid. The New Solution form appears.
2. In the New Solution form, set the following properties:
   a. Display Name: **SiteMap Development**
   b. Name: **SiteMapDevelopment**
   c. Publisher: Select the default publisher for your installation.
   d. Version: **1.0.0.0**
   e. Description: **Used for modifications to the default sitemap.**

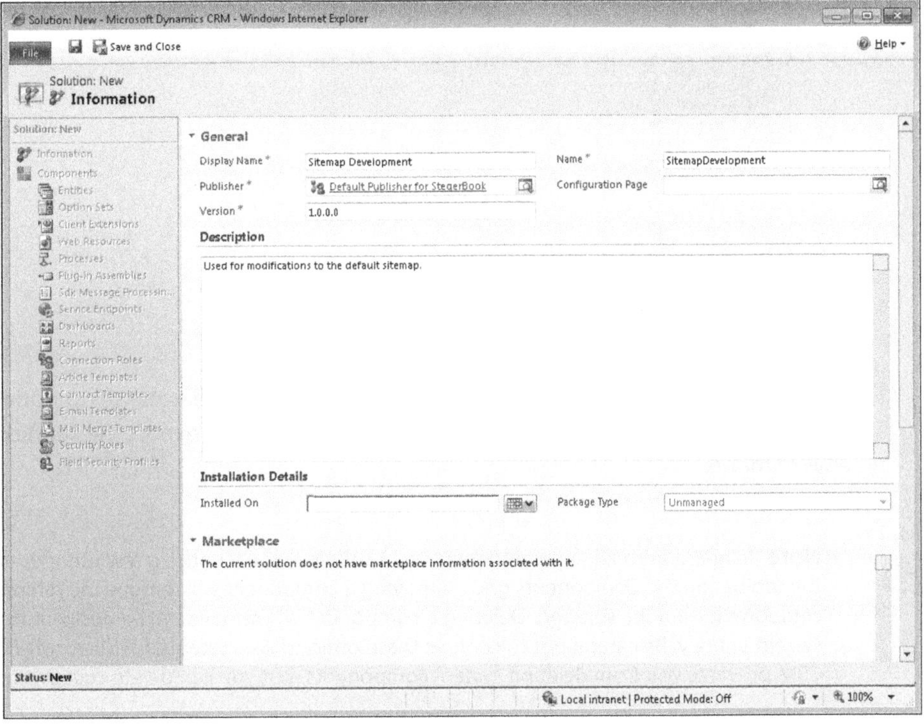

3. Click Save.
4. In the Solutions grid, click Add Existing and select Site Map.

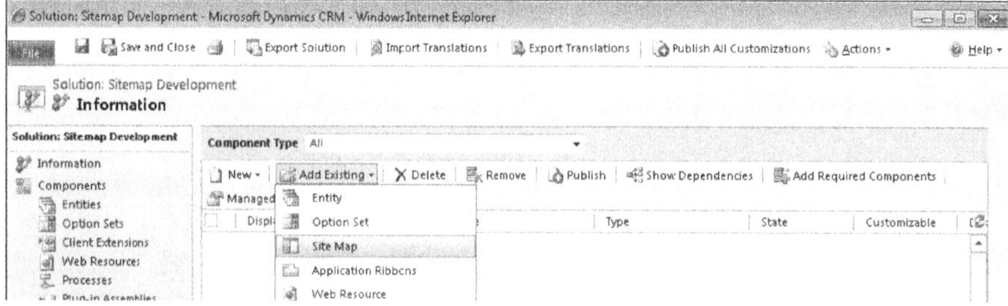

5. Click Save and Close.

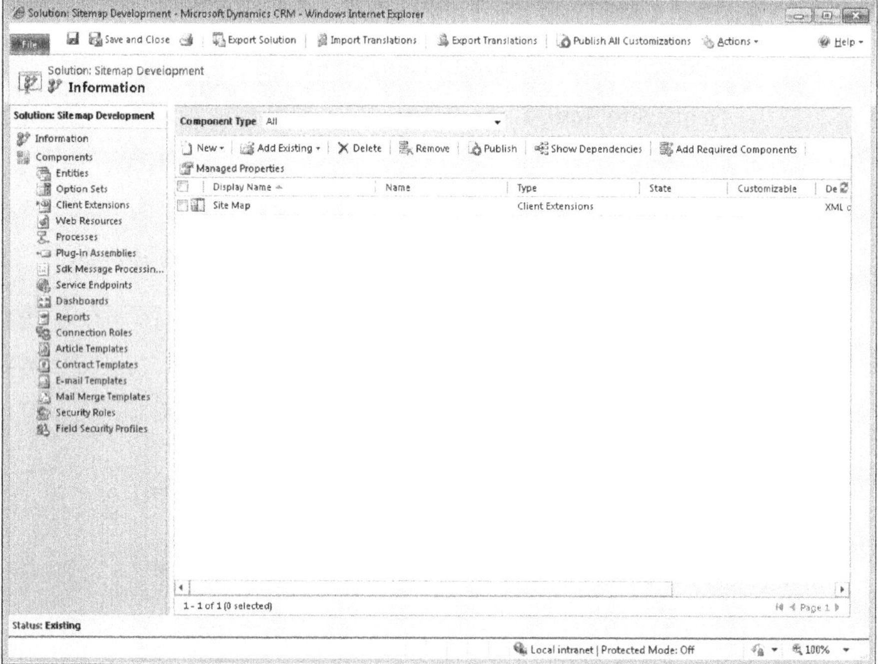

That's it! You have created your first solution. You can use this solution to update the site map in your Microsoft Dynamics CRM system and import or export the solution between environments.

Note In addition to adding components to a solution, you'll notice a few other options in the toolbar on the Components grid. Removing a component will remove the reference of the component from the solution. Deleting a component will remove the component from the system entirely. Be careful not to confuse these options! As a safeguard, Microsoft Dynamics CRM prevents you from deleting system components, but you can delete custom components.

More Info Chapter 12, "Solutions: Client Extensions," covers customizing the site map in more detail.

Solution Components

After you create a solution, you can add or create components to associate to it. Components are the heart of the new solution model, allowing you to group entities, web resources, and other customizations by a function, feature, or other category. This makes it easier for you to locate and manage changes to your customizations, and package them for distribution to other Microsoft Dynamics CRM environments.

A solution can contain one or many of the following components:

- Entity and Entity Components (Fields, forms, charts, views, entity ribbon definitions)
- Option sets (Global drop-down lists shared across entities)
- Client Extensions (Site map and application ribbon)
- Web Resources (Custom pages, images, script, or other files referenced in the application)
- Processes Workflow and dialogs
- Plug-ins and Workflow Assemblies
- Reports and Dashboards
- Remaining Components
  - Service Endpoints
  - Connection Roles
  - Article, Contract, E-mail, and Mail Merge Templates
  - Security Roles
  - Field Security Profiles
- System Settings

Each of these component types has different capabilities and functionality in Microsoft Dynamics CRM. Further, you can select existing components from a Microsoft Dynamics CRM organization or create your own. As a consequence of the variety and complexity each component presents, we'll review each component type. We've got a lot to say about some of the more complex components, so you'll learn more about them in subsequent chapters.

Entity and Entity Components

If you have worked with relational databases such as Microsoft Office Access or SQL Server, you understand the meaning of the terms *table* and *column*. In Microsoft Dynamics CRM's metadata-driven, XML-based terminology, these concepts translate to *entity* and *field*, as shown in Table 5-1.

TABLE 5-1 Terminology Comparison

Relational database terminology	Microsoft Dynamics CRM terminology
Table	Entity
Column	Field

Microsoft Dynamics CRM stores data in entities such as Accounts, Contacts, Leads, and Opportunities. The data related to an entity, such as a phone number for a contact, is a field of the entity.

Entities

When you install Microsoft Dynamics CRM, it creates more than 100 *system entities* (also known as *default entities* or *default system entities*), and of course you will want to customize many of them. The type of customizations Microsoft Dynamics CRM allows you to make on system entities is determined during installation. For some system entities, you can perform only limited customizations, for other system entities you cannot perform any customizations at all. In addition to system and customizable entities, you can create entirely new entities, known as *custom entities*, in Microsoft Dynamics CRM. In summary, the three types of entities are:

- **System** Microsoft Dynamics CRM uses more than 100 non-customizable system entities (such as Privilege, License, and Calendar) to manage the internal operations of the software. You cannot edit the settings of any of these entities, add new fields, or delete these entities from the system.
- **Customizable** Microsoft Dynamics CRM includes more than 50 customizable system entities. Account, Contact, and User are a few examples. These entities give you extensive customization capabilities, from adding fields to changing the form layout. You also can rename customizable entities. However, you cannot delete any of the customizable system entities.
- **Custom** You can create, modify, and delete custom entities. Further, you can now create custom activity entities. We explain using custom entities and custom activities in detail in Chapter 10, "Entity Customization: Custom Entities and Activities."

Important Microsoft Dynamics CRM allows for managed solutions to define properties of its components that can prevent certain actions (such as deleting a specific custom entity). We'll discuss this aspect later in the chapter.

To view all of the entities in your system using the default solution, go to the Customizations section in the Settings area and click Customize the System. Under Components, click Entities to view a list of every entity in the default solution.

Tip The terminology used in the Entity grid's view selector can be confusing. The Customizable Entities view displays both customizable system entities and custom entities. In addition, sometimes Microsoft Dynamics CRM refers to customizable entities as system entities because they were created during the installation process. For example, if you try to delete a customizable entity such as Account, the error message says, "System entities cannot be deleted."

You can customize the following data for custom and customizable entities:

- Forms
- Views
- Charts
- Fields
- Relationships
- Messages

Forms, Views, and Charts

A form provides the user interface for displaying an entity's fields in the application. A new feature in Microsoft Dynamics CRM 2011 supports multiple forms to be associated with an entity, as well as a mobile form.

Similar to forms, views are configured by Microsoft Dynamics CRM system administrators to display multiple records in a grid, based on common filter criteria. Microsoft Dynamics CRM 2011 even allows you to copy existing views using the new Save As feature.

Another new feature in Microsoft Dynamics CRM 2011 allows you to create and modify charts that are associated with an entity. These charts are natively displayed to the right of an entity view or in a dashboard.

More Info In Chapter 7, "Entity Customization: Forms," we discuss form customizations in detail. Please review Chapter 8 for more information about view and chart customizations.

Fields

Every entity possesses one or more fields that store its associated data points. Microsoft Dynamics CRM uses two types of fields:

- **System** As with system entities, Microsoft Dynamics CRM uses system fields to manage the internal workings of the software. To avoid any irrecoverable damage to your system, Microsoft Dynamics CRM prevents you from deleting system fields. However, you can modify some system field properties, such as the requirement level (such as Business Required, Business Recommended, or No Constraint).

- **Custom** As with custom entities, Microsoft Dynamics CRM includes the ability to add custom fields. You can add or delete custom fields on both customizable entities and custom entities, but you cannot add custom fields to system entities.

Tip As we will discuss later, the component's Managed Properties functionality dictates the customizations allowed for a given entity.

Table 5-2 summarizes the customizations that you can perform on each type of entity.

TABLE 5-2 Customizations Allowed by Entity Type

Entity type	System (non-customizable)	Customizable (system created)	Custom
Forms			
Add custom form	n/a	Yes	Yes
Modify form	n/a	Yes	Yes
Delete form	n/a	Yes, but limited to custom forms	Yes
Views			
Add custom views	n/a	Yes	Yes
Modify views	n/a	Yes	Yes
Delete custom views	n/a	Yes	Yes
System Fields			
Add system fields	No	No	No
Modify system fields	No	Yes, but limited	Yes, but limited
Delete system fields	No	No	No
Custom Fields			
Add custom fields	No	Yes	Yes
Modify custom fields	No	Yes	Yes
Delete custom fields	No	Yes	Yes
Messages			
Add messages	No	No	n/a
Modify messages	No	Yes	n/a
Delete messages	No	No	n/a

More Info Messages are customizable errors and other alerts displayed in the user interface for native entities. We'll discuss messages in greater detail later in this chapter.

More Info Please review Chapter 6, "Entity Customization: Fields and Option Sets," for more information about customizing fields.

Relationships

One of the aspects that makes Microsoft Dynamics CRM such a powerful development framework is the ability to create custom relationships between entities. These relationships can be one-to-many (1:N), many-to-one (N:1), or many-to-many (N:N). You can also define custom mappings between entities.

More Info Chapter 9, "Entity Customization: Relationships," walks you through the details of creating and managing entity relationships.

Messages

For each native entity, Microsoft Dynamics CRM includes several *system messages* that appear throughout the system, such as errors and alerts. When you rename an entity, we recommend you update its system messages to make them consistent with the new name. If you do not update the system messages, a user might see an error message regarding a "contact" even though you renamed the Contact entity to Client. You can view an entity's system messages from the Messages link on the Entity form, as shown in Figure 5-8.

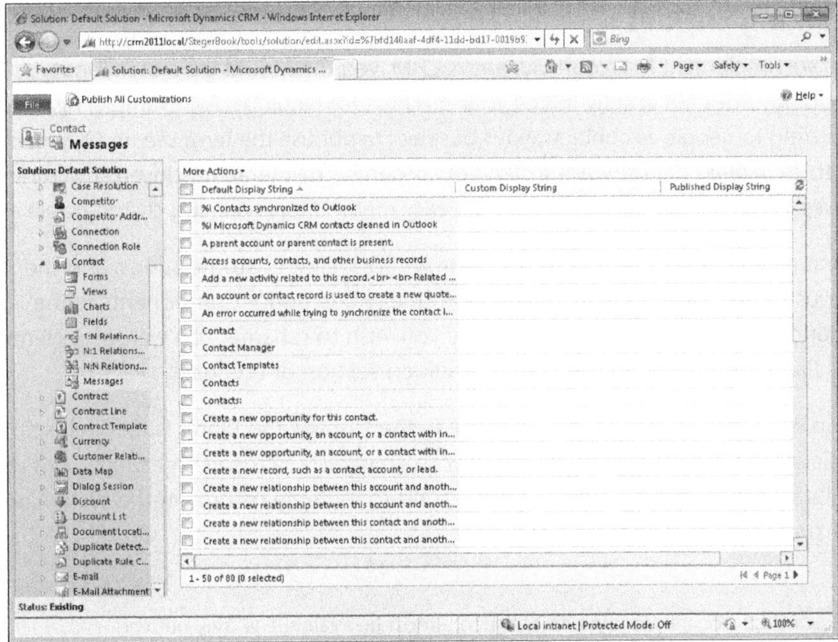

FIGURE 5-8 System messages for the Contact entity

To edit a system message, double-click it in the Messages view and enter an updated message in the Custom Display String field. You can also add more descriptive information about the system message to help users.

You should note four important things about editing system messages:

- You cannot include hyperlinks in the Custom Display String field.
- Some system messages contain data placeholders, such as numbers in braces ({0}) or symbols and letters (%i). You should not remove or edit these data placeholders because Microsoft Dynamics CRM populates them with dynamic data when displaying the system message.
- Several entities use a large number of system messages. For example, the Account and Contact entities each include 80 messages. In addition, the same message might be used in several locations throughout the system. Therefore, rely on your best judgment when updating messages.
- The links included in the left navigation pane of every form are updated from the entity's form definition in Microsoft Dynamics CRM 2011. For example, if you decide to rename the Account entity as Company, you might also want to rename the Sub-Accounts link in the entity navigation pane as Sub-Companies.

If you rename entities, carefully review and edit *all* of the system messages so that the new entity name is consistent throughout the user interface.

Renaming Entities

When you implement Microsoft Dynamics CRM, you might find the system entity terminology does not exactly match your business terminology. For example, instead of referring to people as contacts, your business might use the term *clients*. Or you might refer to *companies* or *businesses* instead of accounts. The metadata-driven structure of Microsoft Dynamics CRM offers you an easy method for renaming customizable entities.

To rename an entity, navigate to the Settings area, click Customizations, and then click Customize the System. Expand the Entities node under Components in the left navigation pane and then click the entity you wish to rename. You will see a Name field and a Plural Name field in the Entity Definition section of the form.

On this form, simply enter the new name in the Display and Plural Name fields, click Save, and then click Publish to see your changes. Microsoft Dynamics CRM uses the plural version of the name when referring to multiple records in the system, so make sure that you complete this field.

Important You can rename an entity to almost any value. The only naming recommendation is that you should not use the name of another entity in the system. This might seem obvious as it would cause some confusion to your users. Microsoft Dynamics CRM contains many system entities such as Site, Organization, and Unit, but you might forget that these entity names already exist in Microsoft Dynamics CRM because they're not customizable entities.

After you rename the entity, you should also manually update the additional sections of Microsoft Dynamics CRM that reference the entity name so that the user interface remains consistent with the new name you assigned to the entity. The following additional updates are recommended when renaming an entity:

- Rename the entity view names. For example, change Active Contacts to Active Clients.
- Update form labels that reference the old entity name. For example, on the Account form, change Primary Contact field to Primary Client.
- Update the form's Navigation labels.
- Change system messages as appropriate.
- Modify any reports that reference the entity name. Modifying reports is explained in Chapter 13, "Reports and Dashboards."

After making these changes, remember to publish all of the entities you customized. Figure 5-9 shows how renaming the Contact entity as Client correctly updates the application navigation pane. We also renamed the My Active Contacts default view as My Active Clients to remain consistent with the new entity name.

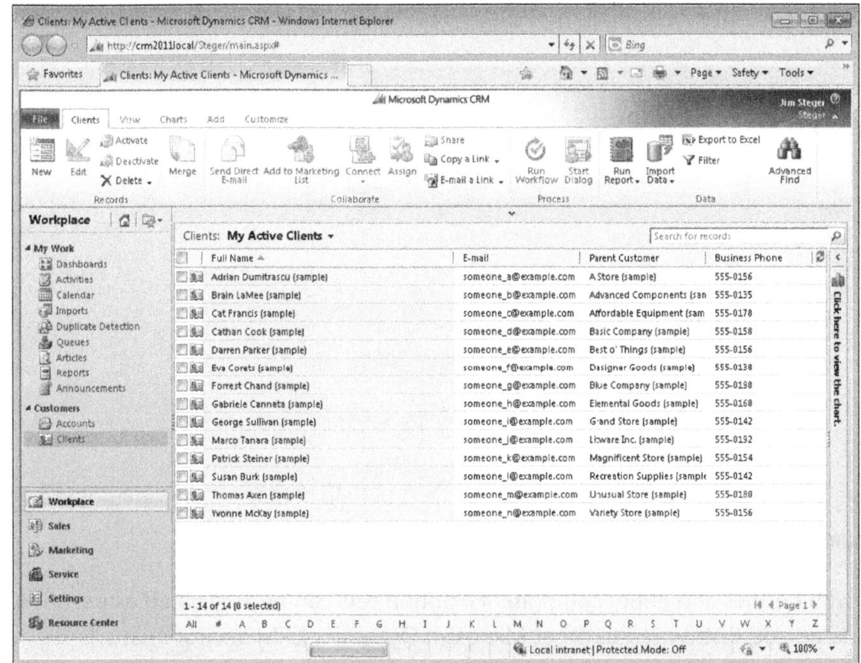

FIGURE 5-9 Contact entity renamed as Client

You can use this technique to rename any of the customizable entities, including activity type entities such as Task, Phone Call, Letter, and Appointment.

Global Option Sets

An option set is list of data that includes a series of names and associated values stored as metadata within the application and displayed as a drop-down list in the user interface. Microsoft Dynamics CRM 2011 introduces the concept of global option sets that can be used multiple times on an entity or shared across multiple entities. This additional functionality not only frees you from having to create the same option set multiple times for different entities—which can become very tedious for longer option sets—but also greatly reduces the issues that can arise when mapping option sets from one entity to another. Figure 5-10 shows the Connection Role Category option set created by Microsoft Dynamics CRM when an organization is created.

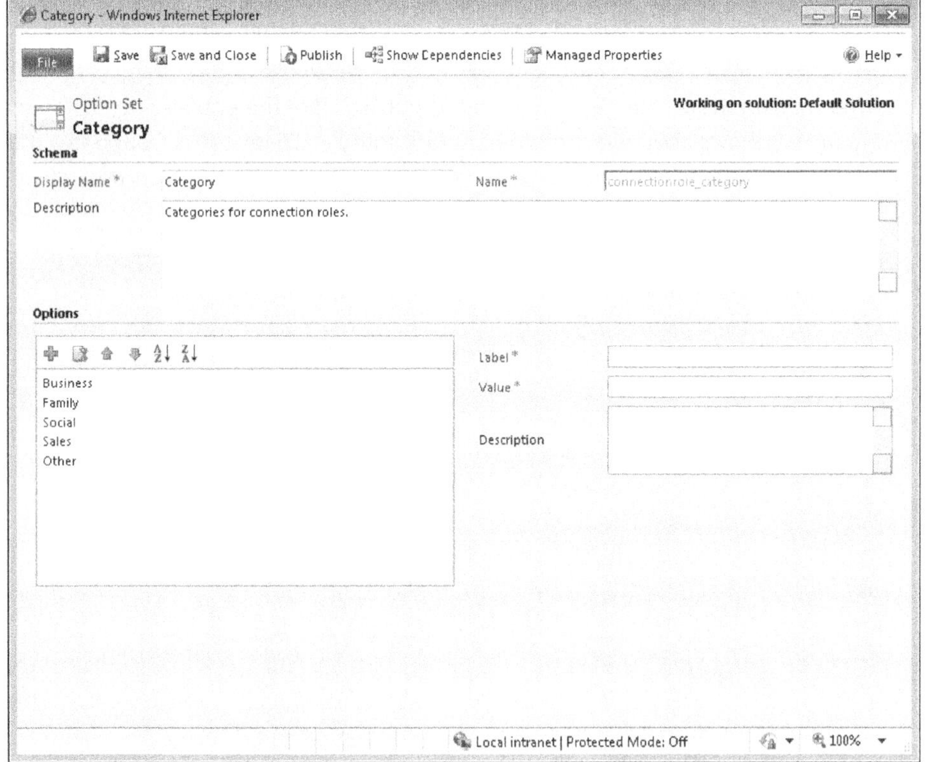

FIGURE 5-10 Option set example

As with entities and entity components, option sets can be associated as part of a solution package and distributed to other Microsoft Dynamics CRM environments.

More Info Learn more about option sets in Chapter 6.

Client Extensions (Site Map and Ribbon)

Microsoft Dynamics CRM enables system administrators and programmers to extend the application's user interface. The site map and application ribbon are stored as XML files, making them customizable. And, unlike the other solution components available for customization, the site map and ribbon controls can only be customized by using an external editor, such as Visual Studio.

Note Microsoft Dynamics CRM 2011 uses the ribbon in place of the ISV.Config feature from previous versions of the software.

The site map controls the application areas and links in the left navigation pane of the main application window, as shown in Figure 5-11.

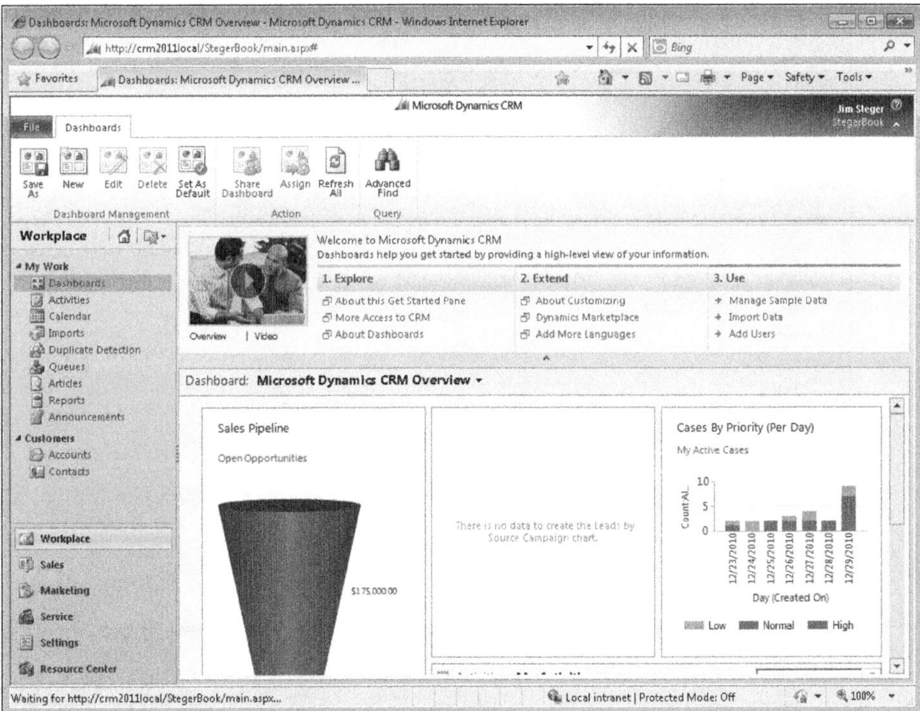

FIGURE 5-11 Application areas controlled by the site map

The ribbon definition is stored in three places, depending on which ribbon you wish to update. For updating the main application window's ribbon, you must update the Application Ribbons definition in a custom solution. For the ribbon associated with the entity grid, you update the ribbon in the entity. For form ribbons, you update the ribbon definition associated to a specific entity's form.

Microsoft Dynamics CRM only allows you to update the application ribbon by adding it to a custom solution. Using the site map solution we created earlier, we'll now add the application ribbon component to our custom solution.

Adding the Application Ribbons component to a solution

1. Navigate to the Settings area and click Solutions.

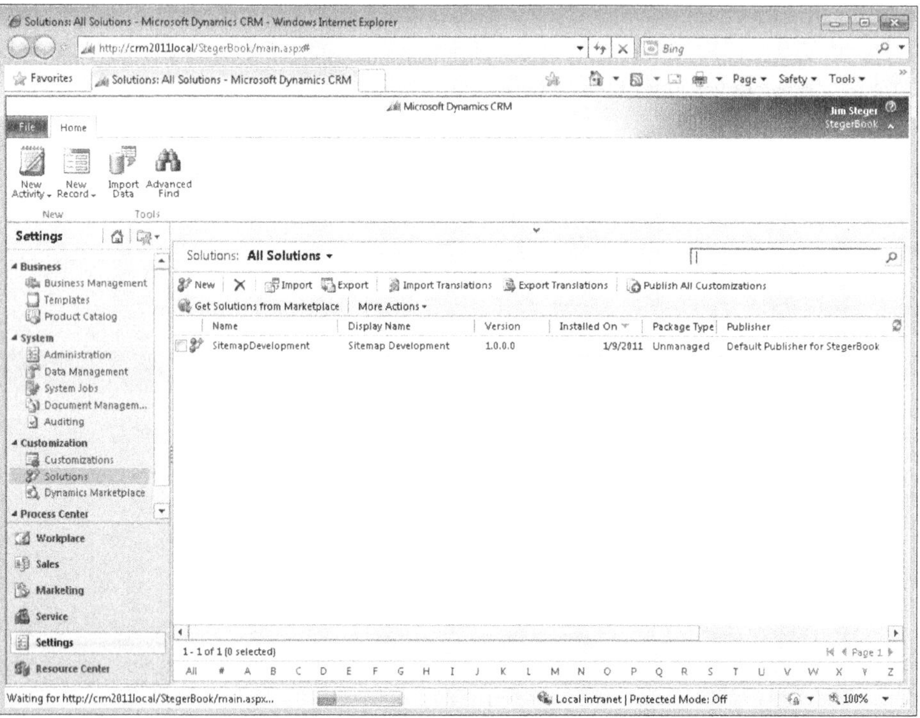

2. Double-click the Site Map Development solution you created earlier. If this solution doesn't exist, create a blank solution.

3. In the Solutions grid, click Add Existing and select Application Ribbons.

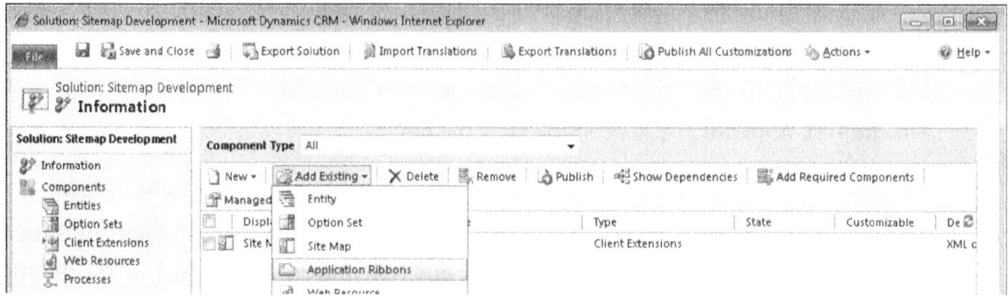

4. Microsoft Dynamics CRM adds the Application Ribbons component to the solution components grid. Click Save and Close.

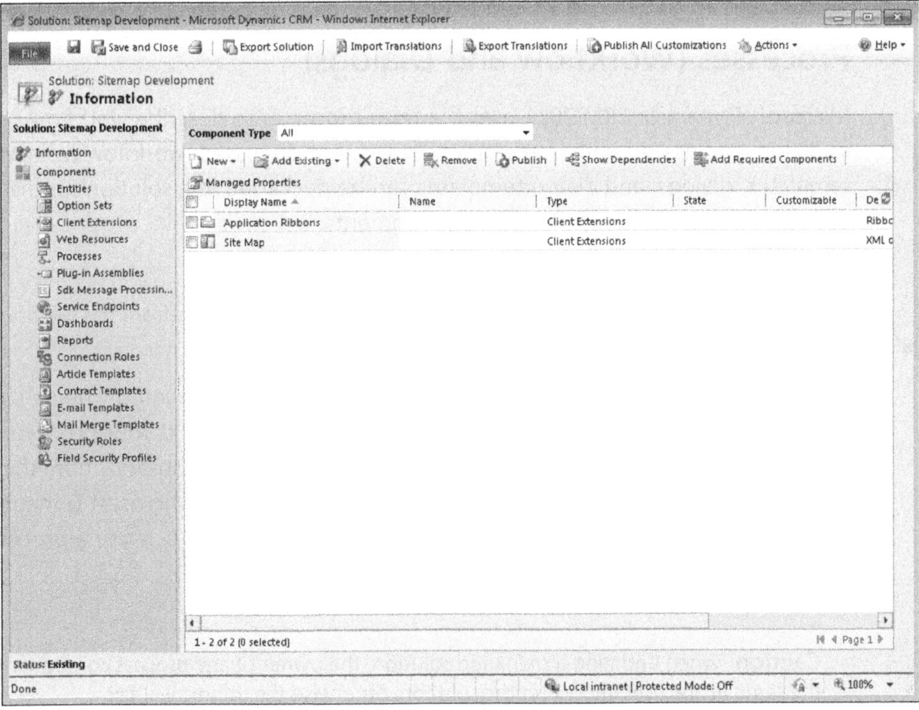

From here, you'll need to export the solution, manually update the resulting XML file for the application ribbon, and import the updated solution into Microsoft Dynamics CRM to view your changes.

More Info We discuss exporting and importing solutions later in this chapter; more information about updating the site map and ribbon is in Chapter 12, "Solutions: Client Extensions."

Web Resources

Web resources describe files stored in the Microsoft Dynamics CRM database that you can retrieve by using a unique URL address. As such, web resources allow you to significantly extend the appearance and functionality of Microsoft Dynamics CRM. Web resources can be HTML pages, Silverlight controls, script files, or image files.

The ability to store these client files directly in the Microsoft Dynamics CRM application creates all sorts of development and extensibility options without adding the overhead of configuring, managing, and deploying files to custom websites.

More Info Learn more about web resources in Chapter 11, "Solutions: Web Resources."

Processes (Workflow and Dialogs)

Microsoft Dynamics CRM 2011 uses the term *processes* to describe workflow rules as well as dialog routines. As with every other component discussed, workflow rules, workflow templates, dialogs, and dialog templates can be packaged in a solution for distribution between Microsoft Dynamics CRM environments.

Tip You can activate or deactivate workflow and dialog processes from the solution page.

Not all workflow and dialog processes can be immediately activated when a solution is imported into a new Microsoft Dynamics CRM organization. If your processes have dependencies or references that must be updated in the new organization, they must be updated with valid data before the process can be activated. Microsoft Dynamics CRM displays a warning about these dependencies when you try to activate a process that requires data updates.

Caution When updating a managed solution, the owner of any process components has to be the same as the user importing the solution, otherwise the import will fail.

More Info Chapter 14, "Workflow Processes," reviews the details of using workflow in your application.

Plug-ins and Workflow Assemblies

In addition to the web-based configuration and customization tools discussed so far, Microsoft Dynamics CRM provides a programming interface that you can use to create *even more* complex and sophisticated customizations. Information about accessing the Microsoft Dynamics CRM programming interface is published in a document called the *Microsoft Dynamics CRM Software Development Kit* (SDK). To create customizations and integrations with the information in the SDK, you must be comfortable developing web-based applications using tools such as Microsoft Visual Studio.

Plug-ins provide a server-based mechanism to run custom logic or spawn custom processes before and after Microsoft Dynamics CRM executes a request against the platform layer in either a synchronous or asynchronous fashion. Workflow assemblies can be executed in an asynchronous fashion in conjunction with workflow rules.

The programming aspects of plug-ins or workflow assemblies are beyond the scope of this book. Please refer to the Microsoft Dynamics CRM SDK for more information about these topics.

Caution Workflow assemblies currently only apply to on-premise deployments of Microsoft Dynamics CRM.

Microsoft Dynamics CRM splits plug-in components into two groups within a solution, called *Plug-in Assemblies* and *Sdk Message Processing Steps*, as shown in Figure 5-12.

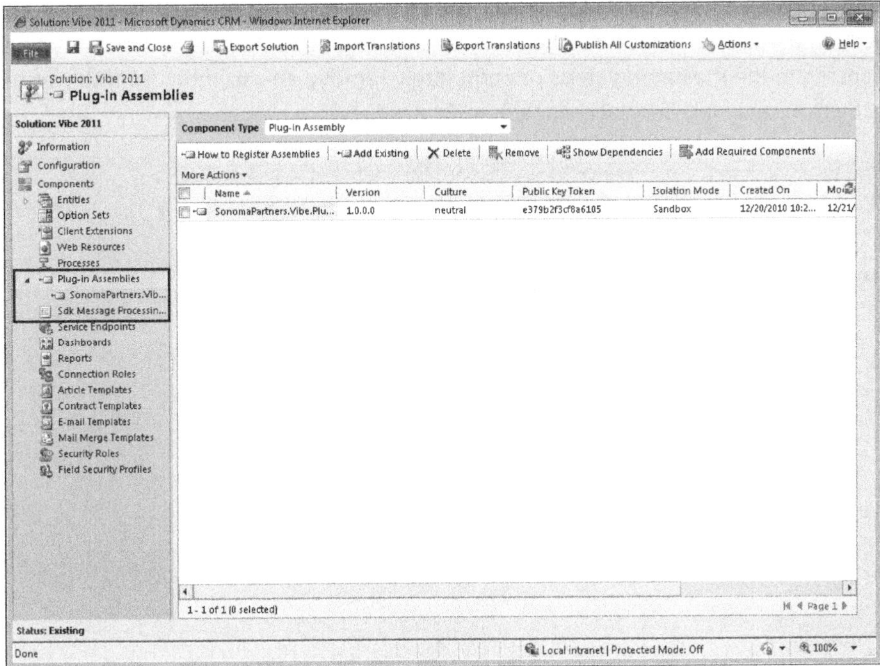

FIGURE 5-12 Assembly links on the Solution form

If you drill into an assembly, the solution grid will show the registered plug-in classes, as shown in Figure 5-13.

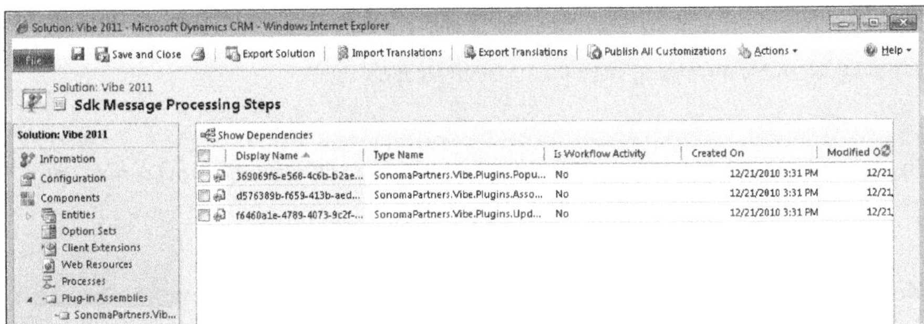

FIGURE 5-13 Registered assembly methods for a custom solution

The solution user interface does not allow you to add a new plug-in or workflow assembly. To install a plug-in or workflow assembly, you must use separate tools provided by the Microsoft Dynamics CRM SDK, the same as in previous versions of the software.

Important To install full trust assemblies, you must be a Deployment Administrator. If you are installing the assemblies into the partial trust sandbox, you need to be a Microsoft Dynamics CRM System administrator (or have a security role with the equivalent privileges for SDK message and processing steps).

However, Microsoft Dynamics CRM 2011 displays the installed files and configured steps directly in the user interface. Further, system administrators now have the ability to activate or deactivate the messaging steps or completely remove an assembly from the system directly from the web interface, as seen in Figure 5-14.

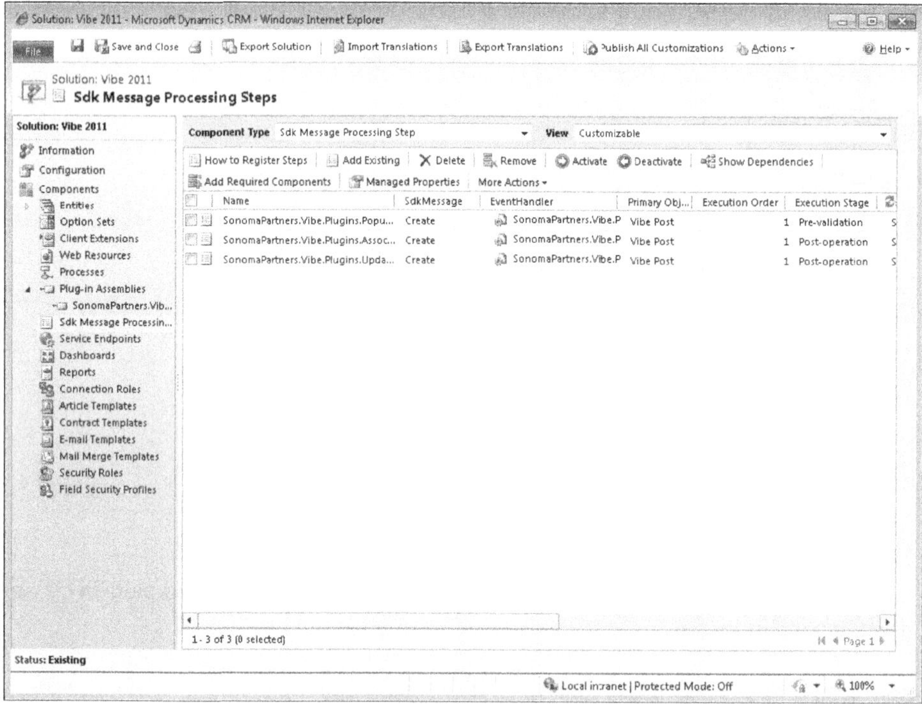

FIGURE 5-14 Assembly messaging steps for a custom solution

Tip You can also use Advanced Find to further filter the Sdk message processing steps.

More Info Please refer to the Microsoft Dynamics CRM SDK for more information about this topic.

Reports and Dashboards

You can create your own reports and associate them to a solution package. As with other components, the addition of reports to the solution package makes the process of moving reports from one organization to another much easier than it was in previous versions of Microsoft Dynamics CRM, especially for organizations with a large number of custom reports.

The default solution lists all reports deployed to the organization, and you must open each report file to edit any properties specific to a report. You can also delete reports, including both custom reports and the default reports created by Microsoft Dynamics CRM.

Similar to charts and views, dashboards can be configured by a user or a system administrator to aggregate or visualize Microsoft Dynamics CRM data. And again, like the other components, dashboards can be included in a solution for easy distribution to other systems.

You can set the default system dashboard as well as create a copy of an existing dashboard using the Save As button located on the grid toolbar. You can also delete any of the default or custom dashboards.

Caution You must ensure that all dependent components of your dashboard are included in your solution or exist on the destination system for your dashboard to work correctly.

More Info Please review Chapter 13 for more information about reports and dashboards.

Remaining Components

The remaining components available for solution packaging are:

- Service Endpoints
- Connection Roles
- Article, Contract, E-mail, and Contract Templates
- Security Roles
- Field Security Profiles
- System Settings
  - Auto-numbering
  - Calendar

- ❑ Customization
- ❑ E-mail Tracking
- ❑ General
- ❑ Marketing
- ❑ Outlook Synchronization
- ❑ Relationship Roles
- ❑ ISV Config

Service endpoints are Windows Azure AppFabric Service Bus endpoints that you can register to your solution so that they're available in your application customizations.

More Info Please refer to *http://msdn.microsoft.com/en-us/library/gg309340.aspx* for more information regarding the Windows Azure AppFabric Service Bus endpoints.

Connection roles, templates, security roles, and field security profiles can each be configured and deployed from one system to another by using the solution packaging.

Note Relationship roles are deprecated in Microsoft Dynamics CRM 2011. The ISV Config has been replaced with the Microsoft Dynamics CRM ribbon and is available for backward compatibility.

The system settings mentioned are configured for an organization and do not appear in the Solution form. System settings are not solution aware: They can be packaged and transported with your solution, but cannot be rolled back as part of the deletion of a managed solution once installed.

More Info The templates available in Microsoft Dynamics CRM are described in Chapter 2, "Setup and Common Tasks." Chapter 3, "Managing Security and Information Access," discusses security roles and field security profiles.

Excluded Components

Microsoft Dynamics CRM solutions include a large variety of components used for extending and enhancing the application. However, a few common items cannot be packaged in solutions, requiring you to manage and deploy them manually or through a custom-built installer instead. The following components are not included in solution packaging:

- Server-executed web files such as .aspx and .asmx files

- Data such as users, business units, accounts, products, or data in custom entities
- Duplicate detection rules
- Plug-ins' secure configuration strings

Solution Details

You now have an understanding of solution basics, including publishers and solution components. Solutions have additional functionality that you need to understand to properly design your Microsoft Dynamics CRM customizations. In this section, we'll discuss the following topics:

- Publishing Customizations
- Understanding Solution Package Types
- Managing Component Properties
- Exporting and Importing Solution Packages

Publishing Customizations

When you perform customizations on solution components, such as entities and web resources, your users will not immediately see your changes. Rather, you decide when you want to *publish* the customizations so that users can see them. The ability to decide when you want to publish customizations allows you to work on a set of customizations and then make all of your changes available to users at the same time. Microsoft Dynamics CRM conveniently provides several ways for you to publish your customizations:

- A single component at a time
- Multiple components at the same time
- All publishable components at one time
- Upon a managed solution import

Microsoft Dynamics CRM makes publishing customizations a very simple process.

Note When you create a component, Microsoft Dynamics CRM automatically publishes it. You need to explicitly publish when you update the component.

Publishing Process

When you publish a solution component, Microsoft Dynamics CRM makes the changes to those components available to all users. When you publish an entity, Microsoft Dynamics CRM also publishes all of the changes related to the entity, including the fields, field properties, form, views, and relationships. The publishing process also updates the SDK messages, filtered views, and all other aspects of the platform.

Note For relationships, you must select both sides of the relationship when you publish to see the relationship changes updated.

Let's walk through the steps necessary to publish changes made to a few entities.

Publishing customizations for select entities

1. Navigate to the Settings area, click Customizations, and then click Customize the System to open the default solution.
2. Click Entities in the left navigation pane.
3. In the Entities view, select the entities to which you have made changes and now want to publish, such as Account and Contact.
4. Click the Publish button on the grid toolbar. A message appears, indicating that your customizations are being published.

When the message disappears and you have regained control of the browser, all of the customizations on the selected entities will be visible to all users. You can also publish customizations for a single component by clicking Publish on the component form toolbar.

Real World Microsoft Dynamics CRM is a web application running on Microsoft Internet Information Services (IIS). Publishing solution components requires an update to the Microsoft Dynamics CRM metadata. Therefore, some users might experience glitches if they try to access Microsoft Dynamics CRM in the middle of the publishing process. If possible, try to publish your customizations in the off-hours to impact the fewest number of users.

In addition to publishing select components, you can also publish all components in the system at one time.

Publishing customizations for all components

1. Navigate to the Settings area, click Customizations, and then click Customize the System to open the default solution.
2. On the grid toolbar of the default solution, click Publish All Customizations.

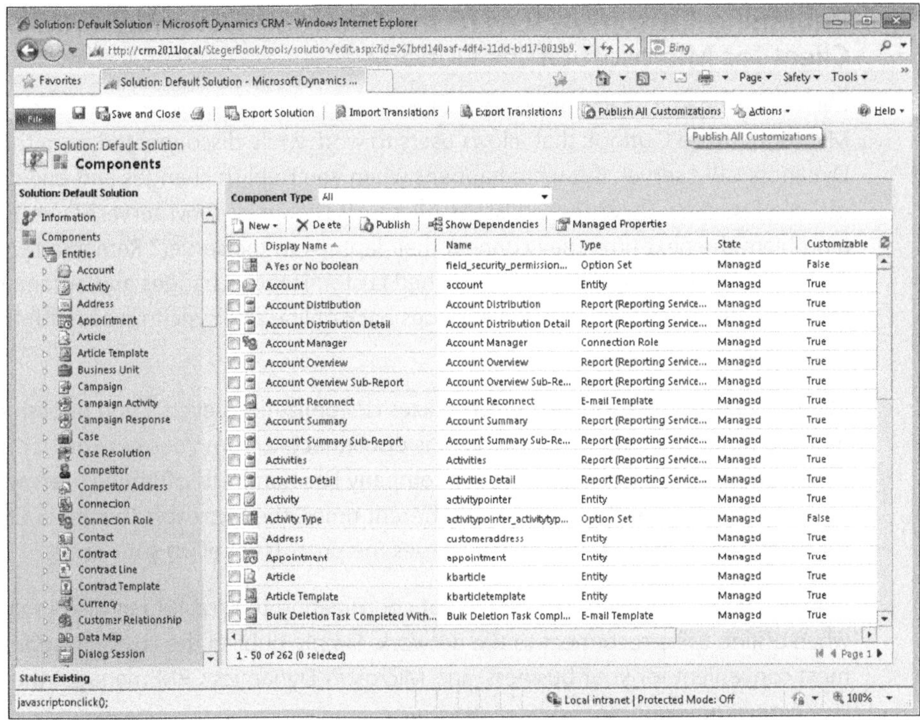

3. A message will appear, indicating that your customizations are being published.

Another important factor to consider before publishing all customizations is whether other system customizers have made customizations that they don't want to publish yet. When you publish all customizations, you might unknowingly publish someone else's changes before that person has finished and tested the changes. This type of situation can create system errors or confuse users. To be safe, we encourage you to publish only the components that you change. You can't "unpublish" customizations, so make sure you're ready before you publish any changes!

Real World Although you can publish changes whenever you want and as often as you want in Microsoft Dynamics CRM, frequent changes to the system might cause confusion for your users. We recommend that you create a business process in which you queue and publish customizations on a schedule that makes sense for your business, such as weekly, biweekly, or monthly. You can also help users understand the changes that you published to the system by creating an announcement in Microsoft Dynamics CRM. Announcements appear in the Workplace area; you can use them to provide highlights of the changes in the system.

Publishing Customizations to the Microsoft Dynamics CRM Offline Client for Microsoft Office Outlook

Microsoft Dynamics CRM offers an offline version of the Microsoft Dynamics CRM client for Microsoft Office Outlook that allows users to work while disconnected from the Microsoft Dynamics CRM server. But what happens when you publish changes and one or more of your offline users are not connected to the Microsoft Dynamics CRM server? Does this cause a problem the next time they connect their laptops to the server? Remarkably, Microsoft Dynamics CRM queues all of the published customization changes and automatically deploys them to offline users when the client goes back online and synchronizes with the Microsoft Dynamics CRM server.

Microsoft Dynamics CRM also synchronizes customizations even if you publish changes multiple times while the Outlook client is disconnected from your network for an extended period of time. Even if your company has hundreds of offline users who connect and disconnect from the network at different times, the Microsoft Dynamics CRM synchronization engine smoothly manages the process for all of your users.

In effect, you don't need to worry about coordinating the publishing of your customizations when offline users reconnect to the network. Simply publish the customizations at a time most convenient for your business, and Microsoft Dynamics CRM manages the complicated synchronization work for you.

Reviewing Solution Packages Types

The real power of solutions is their ability to be packaged and distributed to another Microsoft Dynamics CRM deployment easily and efficiently. Solutions can be packaged as *managed* or *unmanaged.* You need to fully understand the capabilities and limitations that each package type presents, as this determines how Microsoft Dynamics CRM processes the solution components.

Unmanaged

All solutions are initially created as unmanaged. In an unmanaged solution, the components you add or create are stored only as references in the solution. For example, a custom entity you create in a custom, unmanaged solution will also appear in the default solution. The component does not exist within the unmanaged solution; it is merely referenced there as an associated component that should be included when the solution is imported or exported.

Further, this means multiple unmanaged solutions can have a reference to the same component, and any changes made to that component will impact the other solutions that contain the component, regardless of which solution was used to make the changes. Those changes also will be included when any solution that references the component is exported.

For instance, let's assume you have two unmanaged solutions that both include the Account entity as a component. As shown in Figure 5-15, each solution includes a reference to the Account entity in the unmanaged customizations layer. That layer in turn points to the core system metadata because Account is a system entity.

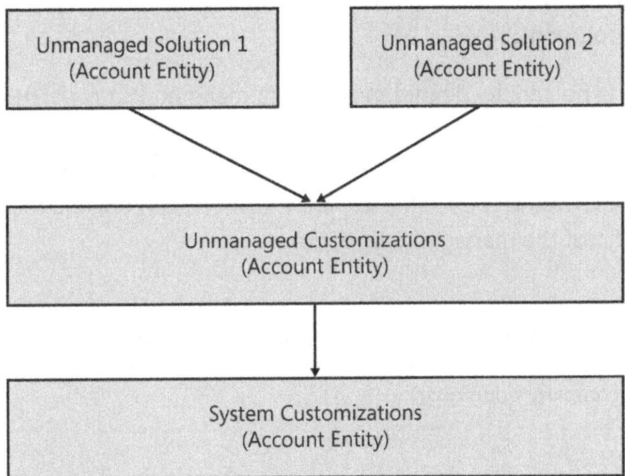

FIGURE 5-15 Unmanaged solutions updating the Account entity

If you make a change to the Account entity, such as moving the addresses on the form, those changes will be seen in both unmanaged solutions, as well as any other solution that includes the Account entity in its components.

> **Important** Unmanaged solution components merely reference the underlying unmanaged component layer. Deleting an unmanaged solution will only delete the solution container; the components will remain in the system.

Therefore, one of the caveats of an unmanaged solution is that you cannot automatically delete components by simply deleting the solution. To fully remove a custom component, you must manually delete it from the solution or use the Microsoft Dynamics CRM SDK.

We'll discuss importing and exporting solutions later in the chapter, but it is important to know that when you import an unmanaged solution into another Microsoft Dynamics CRM 2011 organization, it always overwrites the included components. This functionality is identical to previous versions of Microsoft Dynamics CRM.

> **Tip** Although you can use the default solution for your changes, we recommend you create unmanaged solution packages when making changes. This allows you to better isolate and manage your changes.

Managed

As you have learned, unmanaged solutions behave identically to previous versions of Microsoft Dynamics CRM in terms of sharing customization of a single component across the entire systems and handling conflicts between Microsoft Dynamics CRM environments. To provide publishers greater control of their distributed solutions, Microsoft Dynamics CRM 2011 also includes managed solutions.

When a managed solution is exported, its definition is locked, meaning its properties and components cannot be added or removed when the solution is imported into another Microsoft Dynamics CRM organization. As you'll learn in the next section, some components of a managed solution can be customized, but those customizations can only be made from an unmanaged solution on top of the managed component.

Caution The default solution cannot be exported as a managed solution, so if you want to distribute your solution as managed, you will need your own solution and we strongly recommend using your own company's publisher.

For example, let's go back to changes made on the Account entity. As a system entity, the Account entity could be included in several unmanaged solutions, as well as having form or view customizations specific to a couple of managed solutions. A system administrator can make additional, unmanaged changes to the Account entity from one of the unmanaged solutions or the default solution. All changes are tracked as customizations in the hierarchy shown in Figure 5-16 based on the type of component being altered.

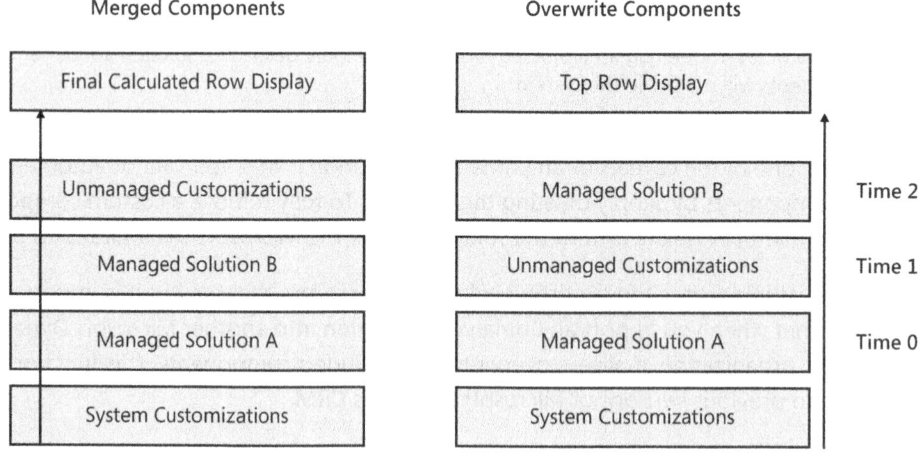

FIGURE 5-16 Hierarchy of merged and overwrite customizations, including managed solutions and unmanaged component customizations

This hierarchy shows how the final, calculated Account entity displayed to the user will be based on the system customizations, then each managed solution, and finally any unmanaged customizations. Each component will either merge or overwrite the previous layer on conflict resolution based on the chart in Figure 5-16. For merged components, the order of install of managed solutions, followed by the active unmanaged layer, will determine the final calculated display. For override components, Microsoft Dynamics CRM creates a stack of changes based on the update order of the solution or component. We'll discuss the topic of conflict resolution later in the chapter.

This layered approach to solutions allows administrators and publishers to build multiple managed solutions, which they can then customize in a controlled way.

Figure 5-16 also highlights the importance of installing managed solutions in the order you want those solutions to appear to users. For example, assume you have the following two solutions with the following component updates as detailed in Table 5-3.

TABLE 5-3 Solution Definitions

Solution	Account Component Changes
Managed Solution A	Form: Rename E-mail field to E-mail Address Form: Rename Main Phone field to Phone View: Changed name Active Accounts to Open Accounts
Managed Solution B	Form: Rename Main Phone field to Business Phone View: Added Account Number column to Active Accounts view, but doesn't change the view name.

With no changes to the unmanaged layer, what do you expect to see on the Account form, assuming you installed Managed Solution A, and then installed Managed Solution B? Did you answer that E-mail would be E-mail Address and Main Phone would be Business Phone? If so, you would be right, as you can see in Figure 5-17.

Based on the layering shown in Figure 5-16, you should expect to see the changes included in last imported solution (Managed Solution B) to display in the user interface. So it makes sense that Business Phone would display instead of the Phone label from Managed Solution A. But why does the label change of E-Mail Address from Managed Solution A still show, as opposed to the default value from Managed Solution B? We'll cover exporting and importing solutions shortly, but to clarify this example, when the solution file is exported from Microsoft Dynamics CRM, only the *differences* from the base system the solution are included in the exported solution file. Therefore, Managed Solution B had only one change on the Account form: the Business Phone label.

So what about the Active Accounts view? As you would expect, when we install Managed Solution A, the view updates to Open Accounts. However, when we then install Managed Solution B, we will see that the view is named Active Accounts and the Account Number field is now displaying. Table 5-4 describes the sequence Microsoft Dynamics CRM 2011 used for Active Accounts view.

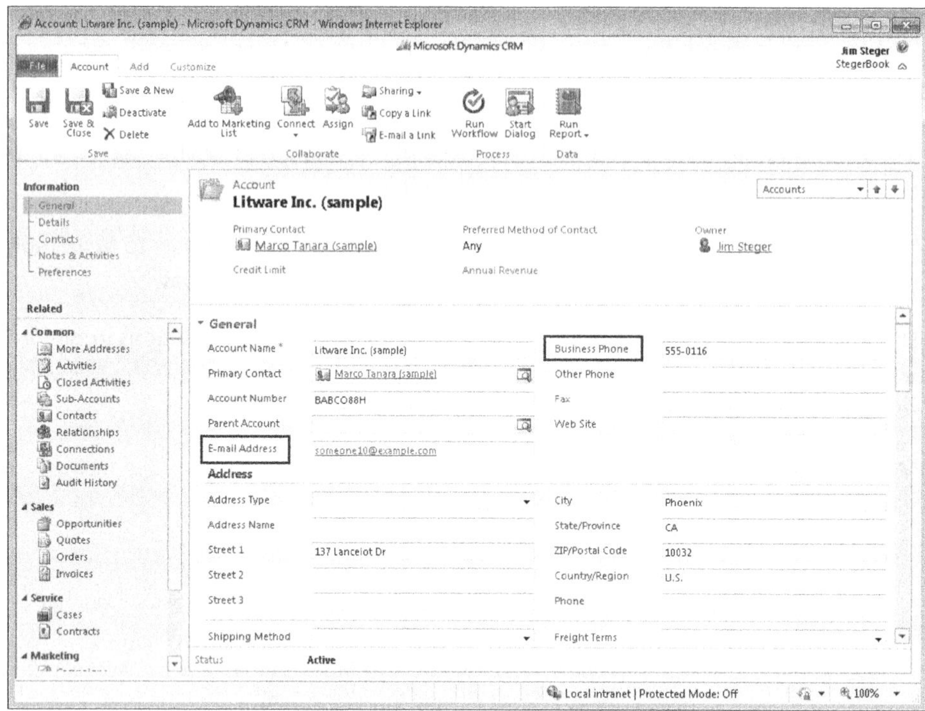

FIGURE 5-17 Multiple managed solutions impact on the Account form

TABLE 5-4 Solution Install Sequence for the View Component

Time	Change	Result
T1	Install Managed Solution A	View name changes to Open Accounts
T2	Install Managed Solution B	View name changes to Active Accounts View displays Account Number column

Because views are not a merged component, the view definition is completely overwritten with each layered change, meaning the last updated change will win. So even though Managed Solution B did not alter the view name, the entire view definition from Managed Solution A was overwritten. We'll review solution conflict resolution in more depth shortly.

Another key benefit of managed solutions is that they can be uninstalled, along with its components from a Microsoft Dynamics CRM organization. To uninstall a managed solution, system administrators simply need to delete the solution. Microsoft Dynamics CRM removes the solution and its components and rolls back any changes to existing components (such as system entities) included in the solution. When deleting a managed solution, you should also be aware of the following considerations:

- Microsoft Dynamics CRM will not remove any managed components shared between multiple managed solutions from the same publisher.
- Any system settings imported with the solution will *not* be rolled back when a solution is deleted.
- It's possible to make unmanaged customizations that touch or are dependent components used by the managed solution. For dependent components, Microsoft Dynamics CRM will prevent you from deleting the managed solution until the dependency is removed. An example would be creating a workflow process based on a custom entity or field of the managed solution. For customizations such as changing a label on a view, the solution will be removed, but those changes will remain in the system and need to be manually cleaned up. You'll see an example of this later in the chapter.

Updating Managed Solutions

When you publish changes to a managed solution, those changes are deployed to the corresponding solution customization layer, which allows the system to maintain any customizations made after the solution was first imported. For example, if you've downloaded a managed solution from the Microsoft Dynamics CRM Marketplace and the solution publisher releases an update for the solution, Microsoft Dynamics CRM will automatically detect that the solution is installed when you import the update, and you will be prompted to confirm they want to install the solution update. Users can maintain their customizations or overwrite any changes with the managed solution's updates. Figure 5-18 shows an example.

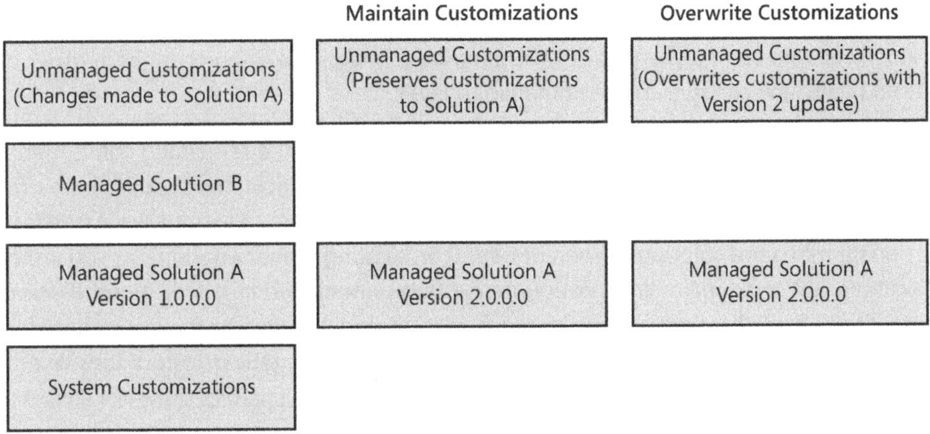

FIGURE 5-18 Solution update options and impact to system

Note To update a managed solution in your system, the updated solution file must include the identical publisher name for Microsoft Dynamics CRM to match the update to the original version.

Conflict Resolution

As demonstrated in the preceding examples, when two or more solutions perform changes on the same component, Microsoft Dynamics CRM resolves the conflict using the following rules:

- Merge the changes
- Give preference to the top row of updated stack (typically the most recent change)

Merging Changes When determining which customizations to display, Microsoft Dynamics CRM attempts to merge the following components:

- Forms
- Ribbons
- Site Map
- Option Sets

Microsoft Dynamics CRM starts with the system or baseline solution, and then continues with each managed solution in the order they were created, and finally adds any additional, unmanaged customizations. At each step, the system merges the changes and users see the result at run time. Microsoft Dynamics CRM always attempts to merge these components, regardless of the option selected when importing an update to a managed solution. For any conflicts, Microsoft Dynamics CRM applies the managed solution changes in order of install and finally any changes to the unmanaged layer.

Top Row Displays This strategy applies to conflicts with the remaining components that do not support merging. In these cases, the "top row" is calculated based on the order of update, with the last update being what is displayed. Where this isn't always true is when you update managed solutions. When updating an existing managed solution, you are prompted with an option to maintain or overwrite existing unmanaged customizations. If you choose to maintain, then the changes to non-merged components made to the last updated layer will be preserved and the top row will still include the unmanaged customizations layer and not the contents of the managed solution update. Microsoft Dynamics CRM will always attempt to merge changes for merged components.

Let's review a more complicated scenario based on our two managed solutions from Table 5-3. Consider the following sequence and the results to the system shown in Table 5-5.

TABLE 5-5 System Impact from Multiple Customization Changes

Time	Change	Result
T1	Install Managed Solution A	View name displays Open Accounts Form Phone Number label is Phone Form E-mail label is E-mail Address
T2	Install Managed Solution B	View name displays Active Accounts, Account Number included in view Form Phone Number label is Business Phone Form E-mail label is E-mail Address
T3	User changes the Active Accounts view name to Active Clients in Unmanaged Solution	View name displays Active Clients View displays Account Number column Form Phone Number label is Business Phone Form E-mail label is E-mail Address
T4	Reinstall Managed Solution A and maintain customizations	No changes from T3! View name displays Active Clients View displays Account Number column Form Phone Number label is Business Phone Form E-mail label is E-mail Address
T5	Reinstall Managed Solution A and overwrite customizations	View name displays Open Accounts View does not display Account Number column No form changes from T4 Form Phone Number label is Business Phone Form E-mail label is E-mail Address
T6	Uninstall Managed Solution A	View name displays Open Accounts View does not display Account Number column Form Phone Number label is Business Phone Form E-mail label is E-mail

When you uninstall Managed Solution A, all the components from the solution are indeed removed. The form returns to the last merged update in the stack without Managed Solution A, which occurred at step T2. The Active Accounts view will still reflect the changes made by Managed Solution A because when you update the same override component label (the view name in this case) with another change (the change was made by Managed Solution B in T2 for this example), the change is reflected in the unmanaged customizations layer. Consequently, Microsoft Dynamics CRM will not be able to fully remove this change when the managed solution is deleted.

Caution Security roles and Field Level Security profiles are always overwritten in the customization sequence, even if you select the Maintains Customizations option. You'll learn more about this option in the "Exporting and Importing Solution Packages" section.

Managing Component Properties

You've learned that you can customize most solution components, and you'll learn how to do so in the following chapters. However, at times certain behaviors of a component might need to be restricted to facilitate maintenance of the component or prevent changes that might result in irrecoverable damage to the system. For example, allowing users to delete key components on the system would cause your solution to break.

Managed properties of components provide more granular control over how a component can be modified after the managed solution is installed. Most custom components include at least one managed property, which are typically true or false fields indicating whether a feature can be customized. Figure 5-19 shows the managed properties of an entity.

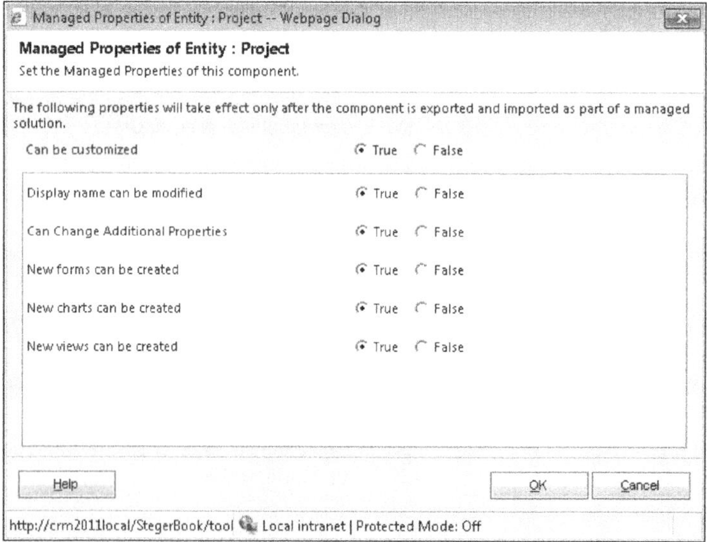

FIGURE 5-19 Managed properties for an entity

To update a component's managed properties, click the Managed Properties button in the solution's component view or click Managed Properties from the component's toolbar.

Note Only custom unmanaged components have managed properties. If the custom component was installed from a managed solution, you cannot change the managed properties.

When a managed solution is imported into a Microsoft Dynamics CRM organization, the system enforces the managed properties for each component. Additionally, Microsoft Dynamics CRM prevents users from changing any managed properties.

Important The only time Microsoft Dynamics CRM allows the value of the managed property to be updated is when the solution is imported. During the import process, the system matches the solution publisher on the package with the solution publisher on the target system. If they match, Microsoft Dynamics CRM imports any changes to the managed properties. However, after a customization is allowed, Microsoft Dynamics CRM will not update the managed property to make it more restrictive. For example, if a component is allowed to be customized, and an administrator customizes that component before importing an update to the managed solution, that component cannot be restricted from customizations by the solution update.

Although managed properties provide an effective mechanism to prevent users from changing or breaking your solution, they are not intended to manage the following:

- Licensing or Digital Rights Management
- Encryption

Microsoft Dynamics CRM does not provide built-in digital rights management or licensing capabilities. Further, solution packages are not encrypted, nor are the metadata in the Microsoft Dynamics CRM database. You need to provide your own licensing mechanisms or intellectual property protection as needed.

Dependency Tracking

For solutions to work properly, Microsoft Dynamics CRM must properly track dependencies across components. Every core operation (such as create, update, and delete) on a component automatically calculates its dependencies to other components in the system. The dependency information is used to maintain the integrity of the system and prevent operations that might cause irrecoverable damage. Some key concepts of dependency tracking are the following:

- Microsoft Dynamics CRM prevents the deletion of a component if another component in the system depends on it.
- When you export a solution, Microsoft Dynamics CRM will warn you if any dependent components are missing.

Note Some of the warnings that are displayed during the export process can be safely ignored, especially if the warning is for a component that will definitely be in the target system, such as the System User entity. You will have to decide whether the solution needs the required components before exporting the solution package.

- Microsoft Dynamics CRM will prevent you from importing a solution if all required components are not contained in the solution or don't exist in the target system.

- Dependencies work across components using their unique identifiers (unique name or GUID) and do not depend or reference the solution's version information.
- The dependency framework also checks the state of the component (managed or unmanaged). For instance, let's say you install a managed solution with the entity called Project. You then create a new unmanaged solution and create a workflow rule that depends on the Project entity. When you export that workflow solution and try to import in a brand-new organization, Microsoft Dynamics CRM checks to see that the Project entity exists *and* is in the managed state; otherwise, it will fail the import.

Dependencies between customizations were not always made apparent in previous versions of Microsoft Dynamics CRM, so being able to check dependencies and add required components for any solution are helpful features in Microsoft Dynamics CRM 2011. To check dependencies of a component, click the Show Dependencies button in the component's toolbar. Microsoft Dynamics CRM calculates and displays the dependencies associated to the component. For example, Figure 5-20 shows the default dependencies on the Case entity.

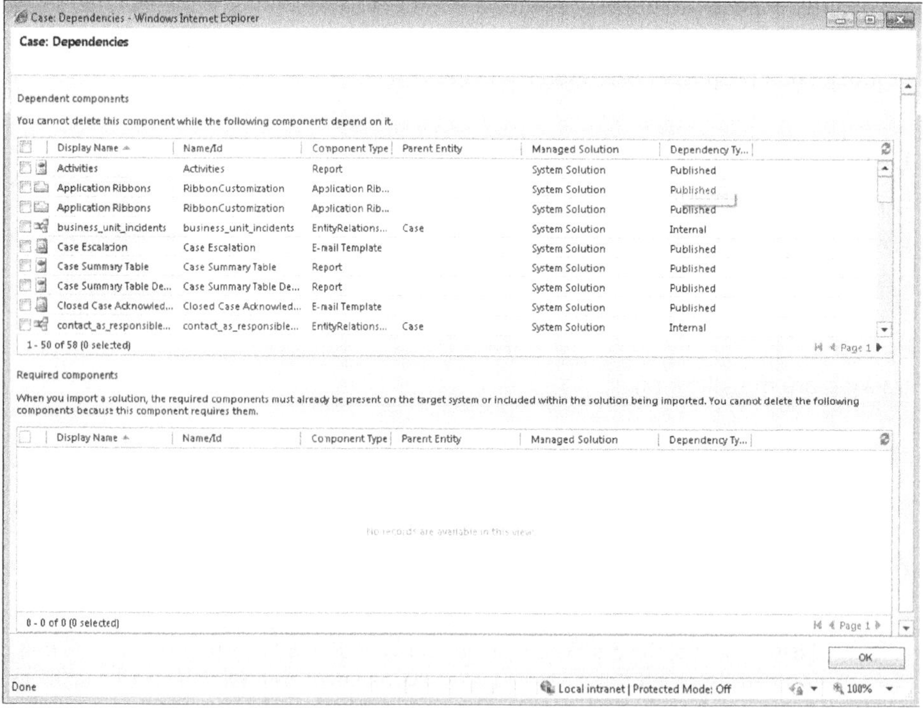

FIGURE 5-20 Default Case entity dependencies

When you add an existing component to a solution, Microsoft Dynamics CRM asks if you also want to include any of the component's dependencies, as shown in Figure 5-21.

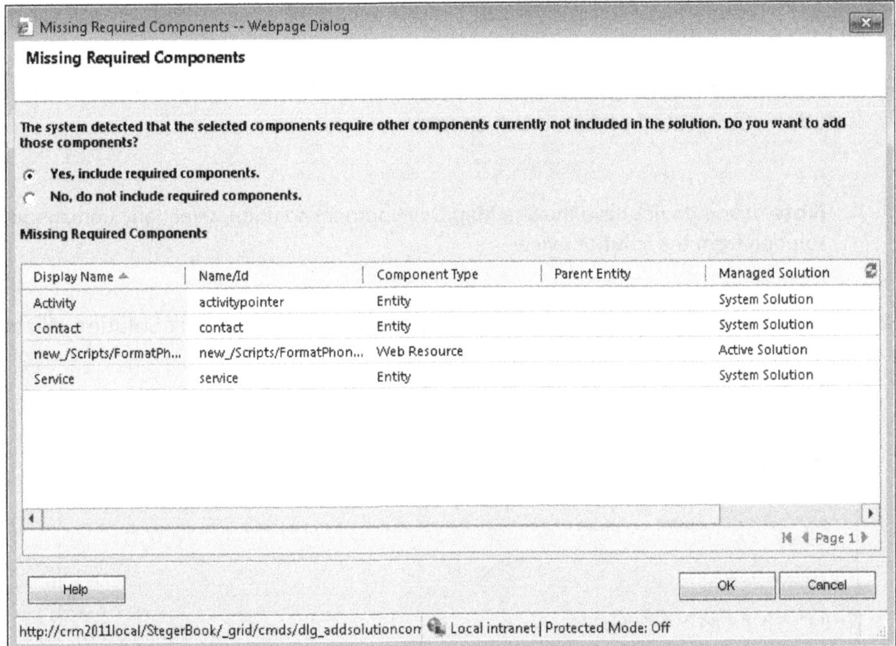

FIGURE 5-21 Required, dependent components for the Account entity

You can also add required components after the fact with the Add Required Components button in the component grid toolbar.

Exporting and Importing Solution Packages

With all of the customization options available in Microsoft Dynamics CRM, you could invest anywhere from 30 minutes to several thousand hours customizing the software. Fortunately, with Microsoft Dynamics CRM, you can export some or all of your customizations, and then import them into a different Microsoft Dynamics CRM system. The import and export features save you valuable time because you won't have to repeat your customization work between development and production environments. You can also export your customizations to make sure you always have a backup copy.

Let's walk through the export and import processes.

Exporting Solutions

First, we'll step through the export process, which includes a helpful wizard to guide you through each step.

Exporting a solution

1. Navigate to the Settings area, click Solutions, and then click the Site Map Development solution you created earlier in the chapter.

Note If you do not have the Site Map Development solution, select any unmanaged solution from the Solutions view.

2. In the solutions grid toolbar, click the Export button. The Export Solution Wizard appears.

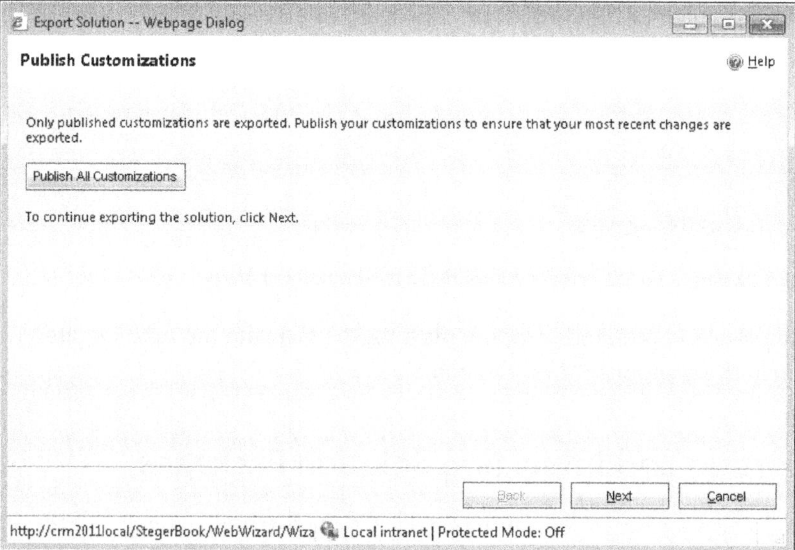

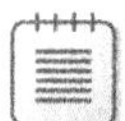

Note You can also click the Export button directly from the Solution form.

3. The first step of the wizard allows you to publish the components in your solution to ensure that you have the latest updates. In this example, we'll assume the solution was previously published, so click Next.
4. The next step allows you to include some of the system settings as part of your exported solution. Click Next to leave the system settings in the target system intact.

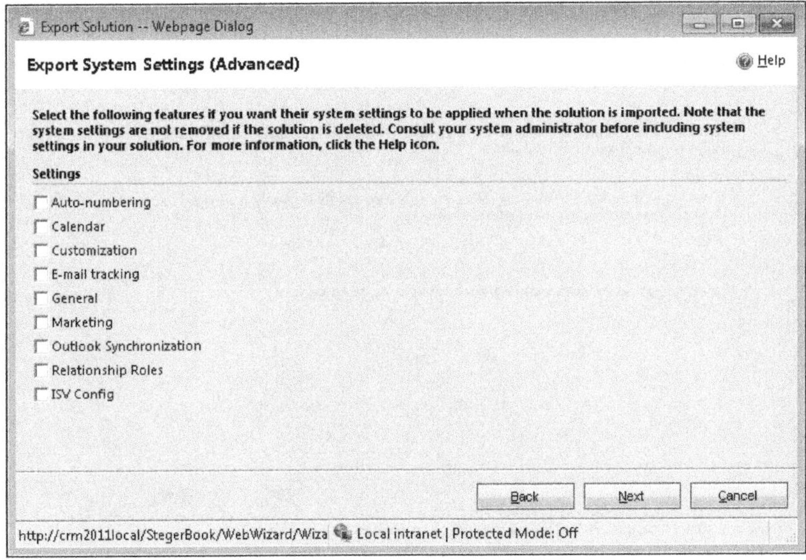

Note If your solution is missing any required components, you will be presented with the Missing Required Components page after the Export System Settings page.

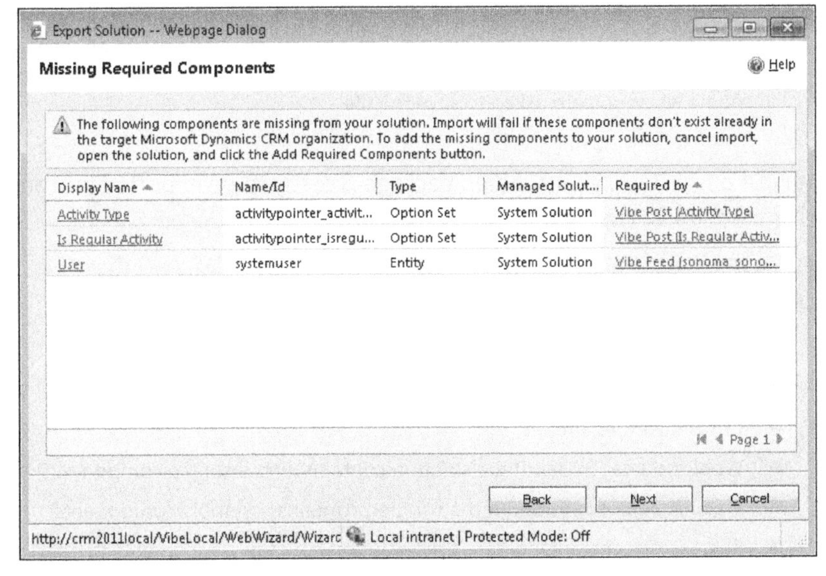

5. In the next step, you have the opportunity to select the package type. Select Unmanaged and click Export.

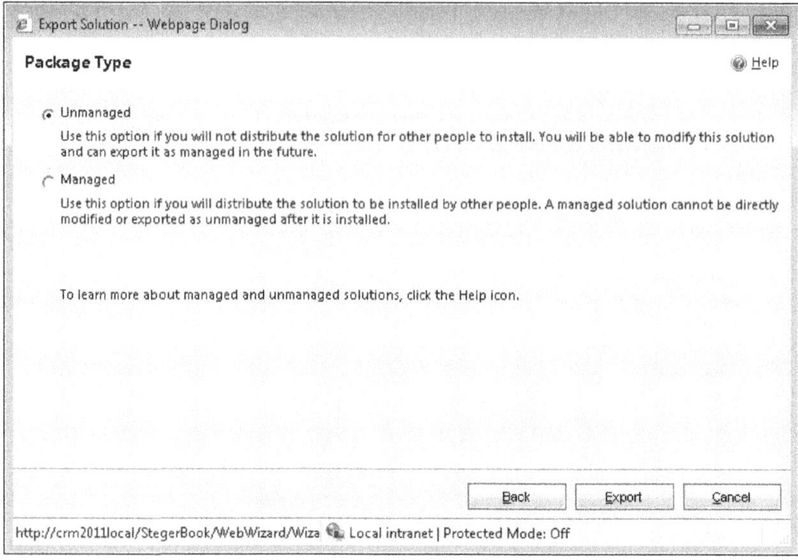

6. Microsoft Dynamics CRM prompts you to save a compressed .zip file. Click Save, choose a location on your computer's hard drive, and click Save again.

Note Microsoft Dynamics CRM automatically names the .zip file using the convention [*Solution Name*]_[*Version*]_[*Package Type*].zip. [*Package Type*] will be managed if you select a managed solution or blank if you select an unmanaged solution. You can change this name when you are asked to save the file.

With just a few steps, your solution package is ready to be imported into another Microsoft Dynamics CRM 2011 system.

Note The solution's .zip file will contain the following files and folder:

- [Content_Types].xml
- Solution.xml
- Customizations.xml
- WebResources folder (if the solution contains web resource components)
- PluginAssemblies folder (if the solution contains assembly components)
- SolutionAttachments folder (if the solution contains attachments to email template components)
- Workflows folder (if the solution contains processes)
- Reports folder (if the solution contains custom reports)

Warning Do not add other files to a compressed (.zip) file that contains customizations and settings exported from Microsoft Dynamics CRM. Doing so might cause the import process to fail.

Some user information may be exported when exporting workflows, such as the domain logon, Forms Authentication user name, or Windows Live unique user identifier (PUID) values.

Importing Solutions

Microsoft Dynamics CRM 2011 will accept only valid .zip or .cab files. Solutions downloaded from the marketplace may have a .cab extension. The .cab file essentially wraps the Marketplace information around the standard Microsoft Dynamics CRM 2011 solution .zip file.

Now that you've exported a valid solution .zip file, the next step is to import it into another organization. Importing the solution will have a significant impact to the final calculated row and ultimately the display and functionality of the system, depending the following:

- Is the solution unmanaged or managed?
- If managed, is the solution new or an update?
- If an update, did you select to maintain or overwrite the customizations?

Table 5-6 summarizes the results based on the possible combination of answers to these questions.

TABLE 5-6 Import Results

Import Situation	Merge Components Result	Non-Merge Components Result
Unmanaged Solution	Attempts to merge based on hierarchy of Figure 5-16	Overwrites
Managed Solution – First Install	Attempts to merge based on hierarchy of Figure 5-16	Overwrites
Managed Solution – Update – Maintain Customizations	Attempts to merge based on hierarchy of Figure 5-16	Ignores solution update
Managed Solution – Update – Overwrite Customizations	Attempts to merge based on hierarchy of Figure 5-16	Overwrites

Caution Do not import a managed solution back to the same Microsoft Dynamics CRM organization from which you created the solution; otherwise, you will lose your original unmanaged solution package and won't be able to make changes to it without a backup copy!

Importing an unmanaged solution

1. Navigate to the Settings area and click Solutions.
2. In the solutions grid toolbar, click the Import button to launch the Import Solution Wizard.
3. Click Browse, select the solution file created during the previous export exercise, and then click Next.

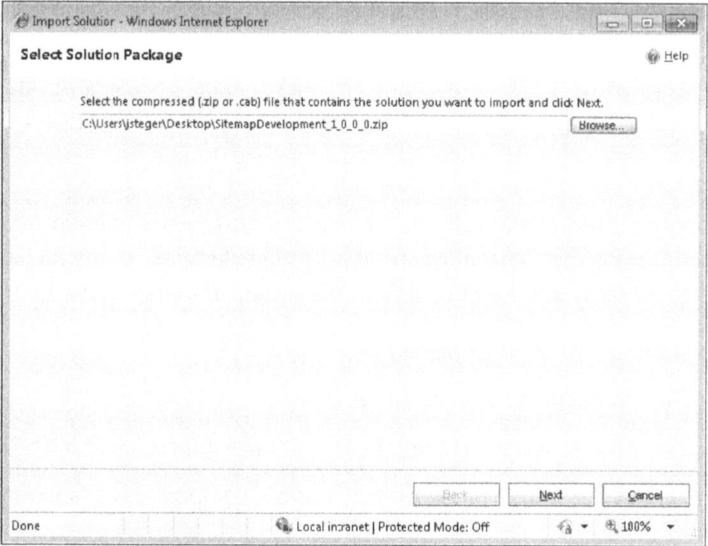

4. The Solution Information page displays information about the solution, including displaying the full package details if you click the View solution package details button. Click Next to move to the next step—you're already familiar with the files in the solution.

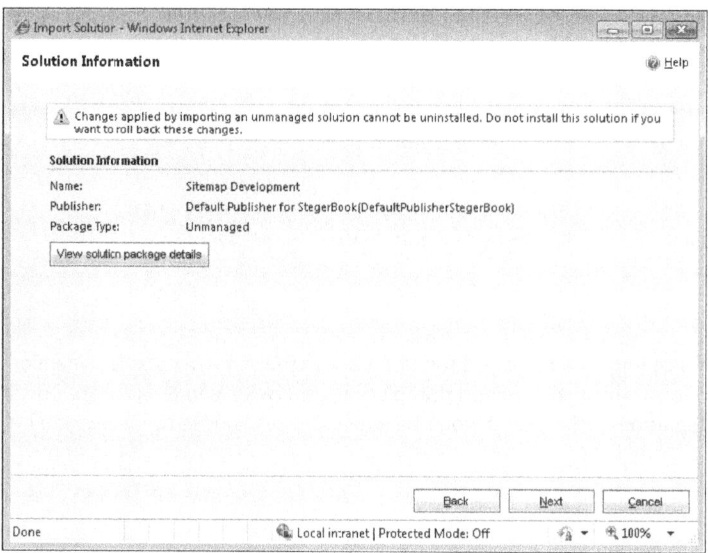

5. The next page allows you to include any system settings included in the solution file. Click Next because you did not include any system settings when exporting the solution in the previous exercise.

   If you are updating an existing managed solution, you will be prompted with the choice to maintain or overwrite any unmanaged customizations made to the managed solution components.

   Further, if your solution contains any processes or plug-in or workflow assembly processing steps, you will also have the opportunity to have the import activate those processes.

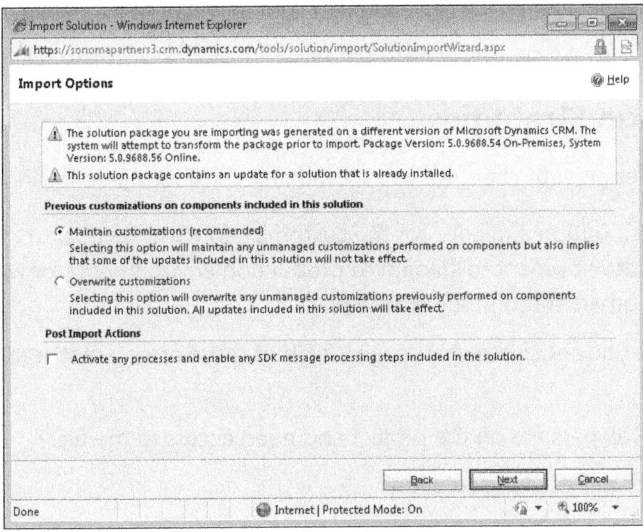

6. In the next step, Microsoft Dynamics CRM displays the import status and all imported files. You'll also see any errors or warnings with the import process, if one occurred. Finally, you have the opportunity to publish directly from this page for some solutions. Click Close.

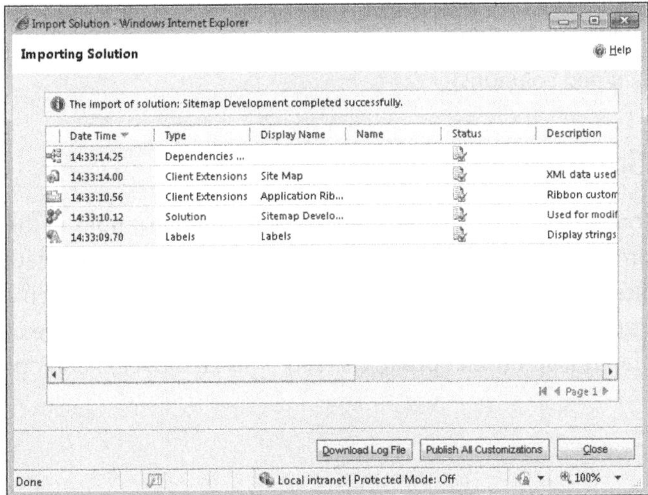

Tip The Download Log File button allows you to download detailed import information regarding the import. You can then save these text files for reference or to examine any errors that occurred during import.

Solution Considerations

Now that you have a general overview, we want to conclude by briefly discussing some strategies for designing your solutions. Given that every situation is unique, we hope some of these ideas help you design a successful solution for your application.

Solution Design Strategies

As you prepare to design your changes, you should first consider the following questions:

- What is the distribution audience for the customizations? Is the goal to move your solution from development to staging to production environments, or will the solution be offered by others through the Marketplace?
- What areas do you anticipate changing? Which of those areas are shared system components?
- How many developers are on the project and need access to the files?
- Do you need to uninstall the solution?

In general, we recommend you start with the easiest path for your design and increase the complexity only if necessary. We'll review the following strategies, starting with the simplest approach before getting into more complex scenarios:

- Unmanaged solution
- Independent managed solutions
- Dependent managed solutions

Unmanaged Solution

As we have shown throughout this chapter, you can click Customizations in the Settings area and then click Customize the System to make immediate changes to the default solution in Microsoft Dynamics CRM. This approach is analogous to the customization approach used in previous versions of the software. You could also create one or more unmanaged solutions to make changes, and this approach is recommended over changing the default solution.

The unmanaged solution approach works well for single organizations making minor to moderate changes to Microsoft Dynamics CRM. Unmanaged solutions will also be your primary development option and are more effective for transporting solutions (and publishers) between environments.

Tip You can and should change the prefix of the default solution.

Pros

- The biggest advantage here is simplicity. Any changes are made to the base unmanaged customization layer and you avoid the complexity of managed solutions.
- More predictability in the resulting display because you have only the unmanaged layer on top of the baseline system.

Cons

- You don't have the ability to easily roll back or remove changes.
- It's not easy to segment development work using the default solution, although you could mitigate this by creating separate unmanaged solutions for development.
- Version control is challenging.
- You cannot protect changes with component managed properties.

Independent Managed Solutions

For more complex customization requirements, you could create one or more individual managed solutions that contain all of your customized components. These solutions could be exported as managed solutions so that they'd offer the benefit of granular component control and the ability to remove the solution from the target system. The key to this strategy is that all of the solutions work independently of each other; development would not share any components between the solutions. The solutions can use common components (such as the Site Map or Account entities), but the functionality of each custom managed solution doesn't depend on any another one.

Figure 5-22 shows an example of the independent managed solution approach. In this example, a managed expense solution updates the Account entity and includes several custom components. A second managed solution is used to develop a custom social application and includes its own unique components. The result to the target system is a clean merge of those independent components, allowing users on the destination system to leverage both sets of functionality. Further, this approach allows either application to be distributed independently of the other.

Unmanaged Customizations
(Includes both Expense Solution and Soical Solution)

Managed Social Solution
(Includes multiple unique web resources, four custom entities specific to solution)

Managed Expense Solution
(Includes customized Account, multiple web resources, custom project, and expense entity)

System Customizations

FIGURE 5-22 Multiple independent managed solutions example

This type of solution works best for larger organizations looking to provide more structure around their Microsoft Dynamics CRM deployment process and also horizontal-product, independent software vendors (ISVs). Remember to always use the same publisher if you develope multiple solutions.

Pros

- You can easily remove the solution.
- You can more easily maintain the version and update the solution.
- You can allow customizations to be made on top of the changes in your solution.
- There's less overhead, management, testing, and complexity than a dependent solution.
- You can install and update functionality granularly.

Cons

- You need one organization for each managed solution to properly develop and create the independent managed solution files.

Note In theory you could share an organization because the solutions are independent. However, in practice, most solutions will at a minimum update the site map or a ribbon control. Because of this overlap, those independent solutions cannot be exported independently, so you should plan on having a separate organization database for each managed solution.

- This approach adds more complexity as managed solutions introduce component merging for any overlapping components in the destination system.
- If you have multiple managed solutions, you will have duplicate effort between solutions that might use similar functionality.
- It can be difficult to move to a shared or dependent approach later.

Dependent Managed Solutions

Creating a series of dependent managed solutions is the most complex design strategy and should be used for larger ISVs and more complex Microsoft Dynamics CRM deployments. Dependent solutions can be as simple as sharing a component (such as a web resource or a custom license entity), or as complex as a library or module solution with which you build subsequent solutions. For instance, if you wish to reuse a similar entity component (such as a common license entity) between two solutions, you could develop each solution as an independent solution (each on their own organization), with each solution containing a copy of the license entity.

Important If you choose the lightweight dependency approach, you must export and import any shared entities as unmanaged between development environments, rather than creating them independently in each environment. You can use an unmanaged solution (typically referred to as a *transport solution*) to move the shared customizations between environments. This ensures that each instance of Microsoft Dynamics CRM has the same GUID for some of the entity's references in the metadata. Assuming that you use the same publisher, this will allow you to install each solution to a common target system without collision.

A more complicated version to this strategy would be to build common or overlapping components into base managed solutions, and subsequent solutions are then built on top of that base. For instance, consider creating a common library of files and customizations. You could export that library as a managed solution, and then import it into your development organization. You would then build your next layer of customizations from that initial base.

In Figure 5-23, your time solution builds upon the base expense application. This means that if you want a user to use your time solution, that user must first install the expense application.

This strategy is most applicable to larger, more complex ISV scenarios as well as system integrators who have common reusable intellectual property. Although you can use a common base, this approach should be used cautiously because it brings additional challenges.

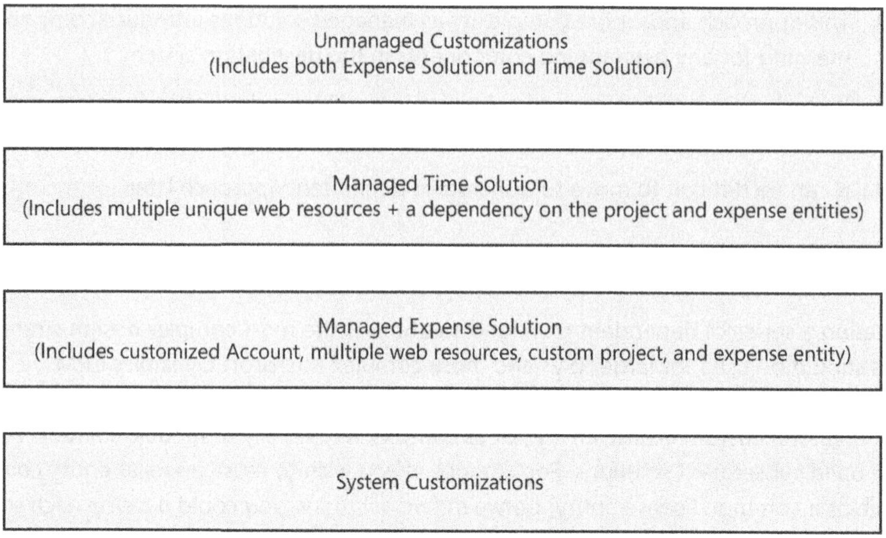

Unmanaged Customizations (Includes both Expense Solution and Time Solution)
Managed Time Solution (Includes multiple unique web resources + a dependency on the project and expense entities)
Managed Expense Solution (Includes customized Account, multiple web resources, custom project, and expense entity)
System Customizations

FIGURE 5-23 Multiple dependent managed solutions example

Pros

- You can more easily track the version and update the base solution, and then apply the update to all solutions that reference the base.
- You duplicate less effort as you create common functionality in the base solution shared across additional solutions.
- You can partition development efforts and responsibilities more easily.

Cons

- You need one organization for each managed solution to properly develop and create the solution files, and you need to ensure that each subsequent environment has the base solution installed.
- You cannot easily remove the base solution because you have other solutions dependent on it.
- This approach adds more complexity as managed solutions introduce component merging for overlapping components in the destination system.
- You have more testing complexity because you need to test each dependent component and their subsequent interaction with the base solution.
- You must install multiple solutions in the correct order for each solution to work properly.
- Depending on the number of features in the base solution, you might end up installing more functionality than needed for the required solution to work properly.

Additional Considerations

We'll leave you with the following additional thoughts and tips when working with solutions:

- You should create a separate organization for each planned managed solution because most solutions will at a minimum share the site map. These organizations should be considered your development environments and contain the unmanaged solution code.
- You should have a test organization to verify the managed solutions before placing them on your production system.
- Regardless of the solution strategy you employ, test the approach with a small subset of both merging and overwrite components to ensure that you understand the interaction and impact.
- Be sure to back up the unmanaged solution file or the organization database for every managed solution in case you need to revert or restore any lost work.
- When building dependent solutions, consider using a separate form or creating separate tabs or sections on the form for each solution. Although Microsoft Dynamics CRM merges changes made to the form, you can't always be sure how it will merge the field layouts within a section. By using a separate form for each solution—or at minimum a separate tab or section on the form—you can better control the layout.
- Do not include the site map or application ribbon in multiple unmanaged developer solutions. Instead, consider creating a separate unmanaged solution for site map and application ribbon customizations. This allows developers to only work on that solution and avoid overwriting each other's changes when they import their specific development solution.
- Use the Microsoft Dynamics CRM SDK and create automated build processes for your solution files.
- Create a publisher and set a default prefix even if you are only using unmanaged solutions. Remember that all managed components are controlled by the publisher through the solution container. By using the same publisher, you allow yourself options with reorganizing and updating your managed components.
- When using multiple solutions with a shared publisher, create the publisher first and then use it in all the solutions in different organizations.
- Only include dependent components in your solution if you are confident they do not exist on your target environment(s).
- Use version numbers for your solutions and be sure to update them every time you change the solutions components.
- Consider using the Configuration page for any post-install steps or configuration, or additional help documentation for your solution applications.

- Consider using the Get Started pane for additional user interface opportunities beyond the help file for your custom applications.
- If you import a managed solution to a target system that has an unmanaged set of the same components, Microsoft Dynamics CRM tries to pull those unmanaged components into the managed solution on the target environment, based on the solution publisher and prefix. This functionality is ideal for upgrade scenarios. Review the Microsoft Dynamics CRM SDK for more information.
- Microsoft Dynamics CRM has a file size limit for your solution .zip or .cab files (8 MB for on-premises and around 28 MB for CRM Online). Although your system administrator can raise the 8 MB limit for on-premises deployments, you need to split any solution files larger than the limits into smaller solution packages.
- Microsoft Dynamics CRM supports the export and import of language translations. When you export translations for a given solution, Microsoft Dynamics CRM will produce the translations and languages in an Excel file. You can then import that Excel file back into Microsoft Dynamics CRM and easily have your labels update for multiple languages!

Summary

In this chapter, we explained the concepts, terminology, and processes related to customizing entities. Microsoft Dynamics CRM stores data as entities, and each entity possesses multiple fields that define its characteristics. The software uses three different types of entities: system customizable, system non-customizable, and custom. Every entity consists of multiple fields, and Microsoft Dynamics CRM supports two different types of fields: system and custom. Only users with the correct security rights, such as users with the System Administrator or System Customizer security roles, can perform customizations. After you complete your updates, you publish them so that they take effect in the system. If you need to copy your customizations from one system to another, you can export your customizations as either a managed or unmanaged solution file that can be imported into another Microsoft Dynamics CRM system. In Microsoft Dynamics CRM, you also can easily rename the default system entities using terminology that better fits your business.

This chapter also explored the additional functionality and components available for solution packaging, transport, and installation. Unmanaged solution components are simply references to the underlying controls. When you export and subsequently import a solution as managed, you have the ability to more granularly control and version your solution, as well as completely delete it from the target system.

Chapter 6

Entity: Fields and Option Sets

In this chapter:

Now that we have discussed how to build a solution to fit your company's needs, the components of those solutions, and the ability move that solution from one environment to another, let's dig into the details of each component, starting with the fields that you will create or customize to meet the needs of your business. Entities, as previously discussed, are really just tables within your CRM application. Within those entities, fields can be added to form columns where data can be captured and stored.

Whether you are starting with a Microsoft Dynamics CRM implementation that was highly customized by a Dynamics Partner or another individual in the organization or if you are starting with the out-of-the-box application, you will continue to need to add additional fields to capture information about your business. In a typical scenario, an executive within the organization wants to start receiving a new report, but your current CRM implementation does not capture all of the information required for the structure she is requesting. People often think that adding a few additional fields to an application is too difficult, so they start to track those details in a spreadsheet or another tool. Slowly that spreadsheet expands to also track information already stored in Dynamics CRM. Suddenly the reports that management receives from the individuals using this spreadsheet do not match the data they are getting from your CRM application, and hours are spent reconciling those two systems.

Fortunately that is no longer an issue with Microsoft Dynamics CRM! New fields can be added quickly and easily in literally minutes. In addition, testing of those changes is minimal.

Fields

Fields, also known as attributes in previous versions of Microsoft Dynamics CRM, can also be thought of as columns in a table. For example, the Account entity has fields to store data such as address, city, state, and phone number.

Every entity possesses multiple fields that store data about the entity. Microsoft Dynamics CRM has both custom and system fields; within system fields, there are customizable and non-customizable attributes.

- **Custom** Microsoft Dynamics CRM includes the ability to add entirely new custom fields. You can add or delete custom fields on both custom entities and customizable entities.
- **Customizable** Microsoft Dynamics CRM uses system fields to manage the internal workings of the software. To ensure that the software always works correctly, Microsoft Dynamics CRM prevents you from deleting customizable fields. However, you can modify some properties of customizable fields. For example, you can specify the label and display name for customizable fields.
- **Non-Customizable** Non-customizable fields also are used to manage the internal workings of the software; however, they are not exposed to the end user. None of the properties of these fields can be updated. Non-customizable fields are easy to identify in the field view of an entity because the Customizable column equals False.

Note that the SQL Server database that Microsoft Dynamics CRM uses limits the number of custom fields that you can add to an entity. Most users won't run into a problem with this database limit, but you should recognize that it exists. Microsoft Dynamics CRM also supports deletion of custom fields so that you can delete fields if necessary.

Calculating the Maximum Number of Fields

Adding a new custom field in Microsoft Dynamics CRM adds a column in the SQL Server database. When you add many custom fields to an entity, you might want to consider the number of bytes any single row uses. Although you won't encounter any row byte limits, you want to stay below the 8,060-byte threshold for database performance reasons. We explain here how to calculate the number of bytes in case you're curious.

Microsoft Dynamics CRM stores system fields in the *base* tables (for example, AccountBase). All custom fields are stored in a SQL Server table separate from the system fields so that you can use almost all of the 8,060 bytes available for adding custom fields (for example, AccountExtensionBase). Microsoft Dynamics CRM automatically adds one cross-reference column to link the custom fields to the correct entity.

The maximum number of bytes per row (which provides a guide for calculating the suggested maximum number of custom fields for an entity in Microsoft Dynamics CRM) depends on the data types of the fields in your table. Table 6-1 lists the data types and the number of bytes each data type consumes.

TABLE 6-1 Bytes Required per Data Type

Data type	Bytes required
two options	Up to 1
date and time	8 (stored as two 4-byte integers)
option set	4
whole number	4

Data type	Bytes required
floating point number	8
decimal number	13
currency	8
single line of text (n)	*n* × 2 (where *n* is the length of the *nvarchar* field)
multiple lines of text (n)	*n* × 2
Lookup	16

Obviously, the *single line of text* and *multiple lines of text* fields take up the most space, so exercise caution when adding these to your CRM data. For example, if you were to add 25 custom *single line of text* fields with a length of 100 characters each, you would be using 5,000 bytes (25 × 100 × 2) of the 8,060 bytes available (62 percent). If you add 25 custom *two option* fields, you use only 25 bytes (25 × 1) of the 8,060 available (0.3 percent).

Microsoft Dynamics CRM also does not enforce the row byte limit at the column level. Therefore, you can add two custom *multiple line of text* fields, each with a length of 4,000 characters. This would calculate out to 16,000 bytes total ((4,000 × 2) + (4,000 × 2)), which obviously violates the 8,060-byte SQL Server–recommended maximum. Microsoft Dynamics CRM allows this because SQL Server enforces the byte limit for each individual row (record), not for the entire table. Therefore, if you added a record and populated the two *multiple lines of text* fields with 4,000 characters each, SQL Server 2008 would automatically manage the 8,060-byte overflow for you and you wouldn't receive an error message. However, we recommend that you try to prevent this scenario from occurring frequently because it might negatively affect database performance.

Note With two option fields, known as bit fields in SQL, you may be wondering what we mean when we say that this data type takes "up to 1 byte." In actuality, for every eight bit fields in the database, 1 byte in SQL is consumed. However, if you have just one bit field, it will also consume 1 byte.

The final limit to be aware of is that views within SQL Server 2008 have a physical limit of 1,024 columns. This is important when CRM creates filtered views, which it does for each entity. When designing entities it is important to know that filtered views create joins to all of the associated entities to flatten out the data for each entity. For each *date and time*, *currency*, *lookup*, *two option*, and *multiple option* field, CRM adds two columns to the filtered view. So, for example, if you create an entity with 500 option sets, which is 2,000 bytes and well within the 8,060 bytes available, the total number of columns created in the filtered view is 1,000 columns. In addition, the filtered view includes all of the native columns. So, the view will fail to create and cause an error.

Before you start customizing fields, let's review the terminology and concepts related to fields.

Field Properties

Every field has multiple properties that further define how the field behaves in Microsoft Dynamics CRM. Figure 6-1 shows the field editor and the properties of the field.

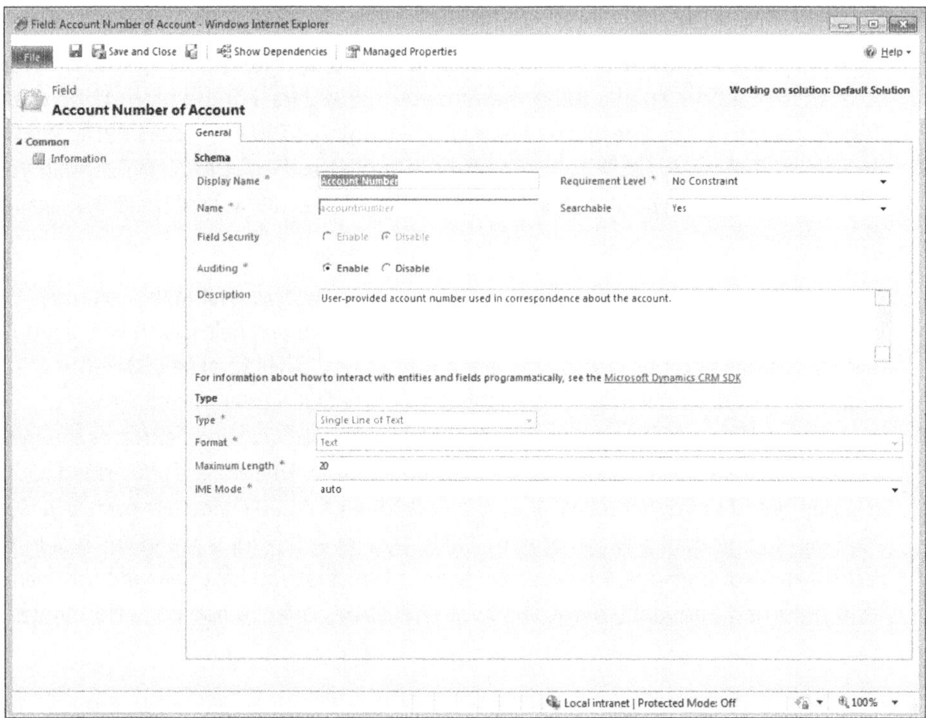

FIGURE 6-1 Field properties for a single field

The following field properties apply to every field:

- **Display Name** Sets the text that users see throughout Microsoft Dynamics CRM, such as on the forms, views, and in Advanced Find. The name entered in this property will be the default label on the form, but you can change the label so that a different indicator is displayed on the form than what the user sees throughout the application, such as within Advanced Find.
- **Name** Displays the metadata schema name. The schema name also correlates to the column name in the underlying SQL Server database. The name of all custom fields added will start with the prefix of the publisher.
- **Field Security** Indicates whether field security can be applied to this field. Keep in mind that field security cannot be applied to customizable fields.

- **Auditing** Indicates whether changes to this field will be tracked when auditing is turned on for the entity.
- **Requirement Level** Dictates the type of data validation that Microsoft Dynamics CRM enforces when users enter or update data on a form (Business Required, Business Recommended, or No Constraint).
- **Searchable** Specifies whether this field will appear in the list of fields for which users can search using an Advanced Find.
- **Description** Describes the field. Your end users do not see this text, but system customizers do.
- **Type** Specifies the data type of the field. See the data type section that follows for a full list of available types.

Tip When you create a new custom field, you might be tempted to skip the Description field because it's optional. However, we strongly encourage you to invest an extra 20 to 30 seconds to enter a description with the purpose of this new field. This can save you time down the road when you (or someone who takes over the project from you) look at the field and wonder, "Why did we add this field?" As a bare minimum we suggest that you enter your name and the date that you created the field.

Depending on the data type of the field, some fields include additional properties. Table 6-2 outlines the additional field properties and the data types to which they apply.

TABLE 6-2 Data Type–Specific Field Properties

Field property	Applies to these data types
Format	*single line of text, whole number,* and *date and time*
Maximum Length	*single line of text* and *multiple lines of text*
Use Existing Option Set	*option set*
Options	*option set* and *two options*
Default Value	*option set* and *two options*
Minimum Value	*whole number, floating point number, decimal number,* and *currency*
Maximum Value	*whole number, floating point number, decimal number,* and *currency*
Precision	*floating point number, decimal number,* and *currency*
Target Record Type	*lookup*
Relationship Name	*lookup*
IME Mode	*single line of text, whole number, floating point number, decimal number, currency, multiple lines of text,* and *date and time*

Next, we review each of these data types in detail to understand how they work in Microsoft Dynamics CRM.

Data Types

In Microsoft Dynamics CRM 2011, many of the data types have been relabeled so that you no longer need to be familiar with relational databases to understand the intended use of each type. The data types indicate how to use each option. For example, users will not have the ability to enter **abc** into a field with a *whole number* data type. In addition, the data type determines what operations you can perform throughout the application. For example, what conditions you can evaluate in Advanced Find.

Microsoft Dynamics CRM allows you to create fields using the following 10 data types to store data:

- ***Single Line of Text*** Stores text and numeric data between 1 and 4,000 characters in length in one field.
- ***Option Set*** Allows you to specify a predefined list of values for the field. Users see a drop-down list on the form.
- ***Two Options*** Stores data as one of two values, 0 or 1. In Microsoft Dynamics CRM, you can relabel the 0 and 1 values so that users see Yes and No, True and False, and so on. Many people use the words *Boolean* or *bit* when referring to this data type.
- ***Whole Number*** Allows you to store only whole numbers, such as –2, –1, 0, 1, 2, and so on. Values can range from –2,147,483,648 to 2,147,483,647.
- ***Floating Point Number*** Stores approximate numeric values with a variable number of decimals, such as 1.3333 or 3.14. Values can range from –100,000,000,000.00000 to 100,000,000,000.00000.
- ***Decimal Number*** Stores exact numeric values with decimals such as 1.5. Values can range from –100,000,000,000.00000 to 100,000,000,000.00000.
- ***Currency*** Stores currency amounts. You will have the ability to set the exact precision of currency fields or select Pricing Decimal Precision or Currency Precision. The Setup program of Microsoft Dynamics CRM sets the default value in the Pricing Decimal Precision to 2. The Currency Precision option will display the amount stored in the field in the correct precision for the currency selected on the record. Values can range from –922,337,203,685,477.0000 to 922,337,203,685,477.0000.
- ***Multiple Lines of Text*** Stores text and numeric data between 1 and 1,048,576 characters in length in one field.
- ***Date and Time*** Stores date and time data.
- ***lookup*** System data type that Stores information about related records.

In addition to these data types, Microsoft Dynamics CRM also uses the following system data types in the default fields that are created with each entity:

- ***Status Reason*** System data type that Stores status information about an entity.
- ***Status*** System data type that Stores state information about an entity.

- ***Primary Key*** System data type that Stores cross-reference information.
- ***Owner*** System data type that Stores the entity's owner.
- ***Time Stamp*** Tracks the version number of each entity.

Microsoft Dynamics CRM automatically creates and manages the system data types, so you really don't have to worry about them too much. However, you should know that they exist because you will see fields with system data types listed on every entity.

Tip Although both floats and decimals store real numbers, SQL Server stores float data as approximations, whereas decimals are stored exactly as specified. Your users might not notice any difference between the *float* and *decimal* data types because both types can display values in the Microsoft Dynamics CRM user interface with configurable precision such as 1.25 or 5.786. Therefore, you may wonder which data type to use. Naturally, the answer will depend on what you want to do with the data. One possible guideline you can use is the following: Use a *decimal* data type when you require queries with sums across a large set of numbers or when performing comparisons in which you use the equal (=) or not equal (<>) operators. Consider using a *float* when you need to store fractions or numeric values you will be comparing with the greater than (>) or less than (<) operators. If you're really not sure how the data will be used, we recommend that you use a *float* data type.

More Info For those familiar with previous versions of Dynamics CRM, the first thing you may have noticed when reviewing the list of data types is that many of them have changed. Table 6-3 compares the data types in previous versions of CRM with those in Dynamics CRM 2011.

TABLE 6-3 Data Type by Dynamics CRM Version Comparison

Dynamics CRM 2011 Data Type	Dynamic CRM Previous Version Data Type
single line of text	*nvarchar*
option set	*picklist*
two options	*bit*
whole number	*int*
floating point number	*float*
decimal number	*decimal*
currency	*money*
multiple lines of text	*ntext*
date and time	*datetime*
lookup	*lookup*
status reason	*status*
status	*state*
primary key	*primarykey*
owner	*owner*

We discuss the different data types in more detail later in this chapter when we explain how to add custom fields to an entity.

Requirement Levels

For every field, Microsoft Dynamics CRM defines a *requirement level*. The requirement level dictates the type of data validation that Microsoft Dynamics CRM should enforce when users enter or update data on a form. In addition to enforcing data validation, Microsoft Dynamics CRM automatically adds a label indicator to provide users with a visual cue regarding the requirement level of the field. Table 6-4 explains the three requirement levels and color coding.

TABLE 6-4 Requirement Levels

Requirement level	Description	Field label indicator on form
Business Required	Requires users to enter a value for this field. If they leave it blank, the system prompts them when they try to save.	Red asterisk
Business Recommended	Provides a visual cue to users that your business recommends completion of this field. Users can save the record with no data if necessary. Saving a record with no data in a Business Recommended field does not prompt or warn the user.	Blue plus sign
No Constraint	Indicates to users that no constraint exists on the data field.	No indicator

If you specify a field as Business Required, you cannot remove it from the entity form. Likewise, you should not set a field as Business Required if it isn't displayed on the form.

Modifying, Adding, and Deleting Fields

After you've reviewed the entities and you understand their fields, you're ready to start making some changes. Field customizations fall into one of three categories:

- Modifying fields
- Adding custom fields
- Deleting fields

Modifying Fields

The simplest type of field customization you can perform is to modify an existing field. When you modify fields, you actually modify the properties of the field. You make changes to the field properties in the field editor, as shown in Figure 6-2.

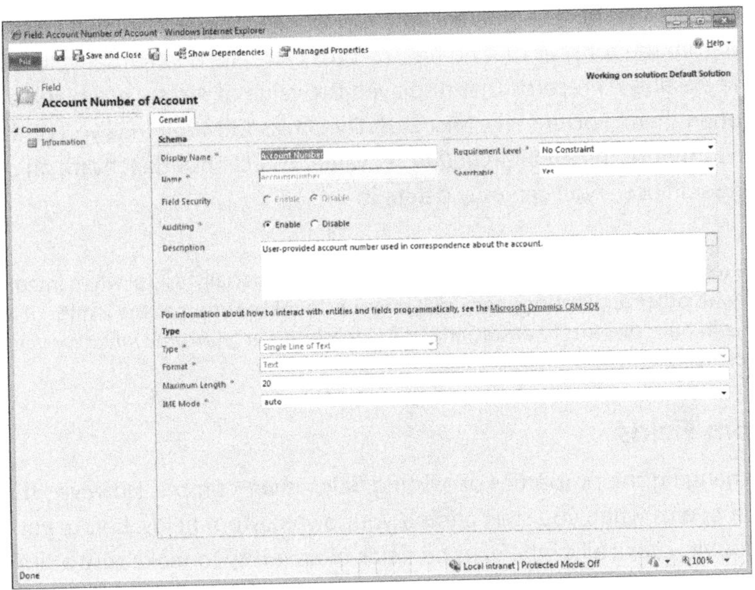

FIGURE 6-2 Field editor for *Account Number* field

To change any one of the field properties, simply follow these steps.

Modifying a field property

1. Navigate to the Settings area, click Customizations, and then click Customize the System. The default solution opens. Expand the entity that you want to customize, and then click Fields.
2. Double-click the field that you want to modify. The field editor appears.
3. Update a value, and then click Save.
4. An "Updating Field" message appears. When the message disappears, your change is complete.

As we explained earlier, Your users will not see the changes you make until you publish your customizations.

Although Figure 6-2 might not clearly show it, Microsoft Dynamics CRM disables or makes unavailable some of the attribute property fields. As you probably expect, the unavailable property fields indicate that you cannot edit the field properties. You can never edit the schema name or data type for an existing field. You are also not able to enable field security on customizable fields. Finally, in some cases, Microsoft Dynamics CRM prevents you from editing field properties on the customizable entities. Of course, these few restrictions help ensure that the software always works correctly and that your system will upgrade smoothly to future releases of Microsoft Dynamics CRM.

When you're modifying a field, take extra care when deleting the *option set* values of existing fields because you might permanently lose access to the data in the user interface. Consider a set of 75 records that use a custom option set. The option set contains three options: A,

B, and C (with 25 records each). If you delete *option set* value A, Microsoft Dynamics CRM deletes that value from the form so that no new records can select *option set* value A. Unfortunately, the existing 25 records that displayed the value of A display a blank *option set* value when you open them. Fortunately, Microsoft Dynamics CRM reminds you of this data deletion when you attempt to delete an *option set* value. You cannot deactivate an *option set* value if it's no longer in use—you can only delete it.

Tip You can increase the length of a field if necessary. This is especially useful when integrating Dynamics CRM with other applications because you want to make sure that the length of all text fields is the same in both systems to ensure that data does not get truncated when moving from one database to the other.

Adding Custom Fields

As you can see, changing the properties of existing fields is very simple. However, the real customization fun begins when you start adding your own custom fields. Before you add a custom field, double-check all of the existing fields of an entity to make sure a similar field doesn't already exist. When you're ready to add a custom field, follow these steps.

Adding a custom field

1. Navigate to the Settings area, click Customizations, and then click Customize the System. The default solution opens. Expand the entity that you want to customize, and then click Fields.
2. After the field list has loaded, click New on the view toolbar.
3. The following form appears for you to complete.

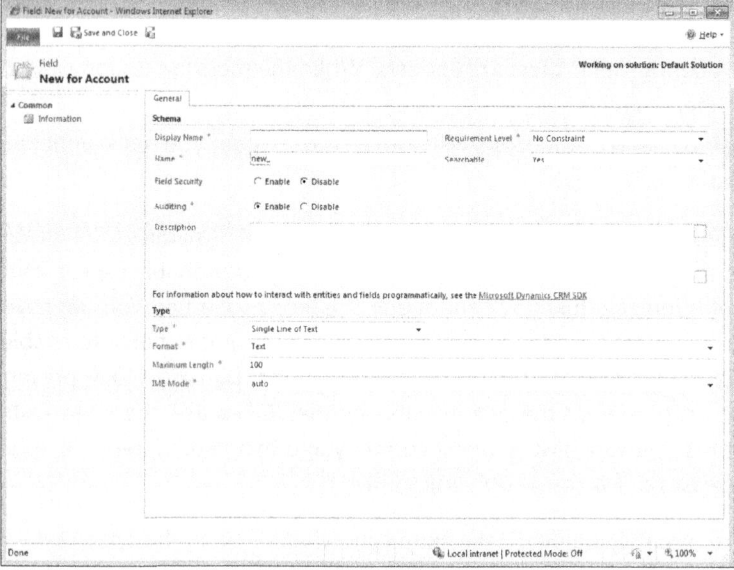

4. Populate the required values and select Save.

To create a custom field, you must enter the following field properties:

- Display name
- Schema name
- Requirement level
- Auditing
- Searchable (optional)
- Description (optional)
- Type
- Format (on applicable data types)
- Precision (on applicable data types)
- Minimum Length (on applicable data types)
- Maximum Length (on applicable data types)
- IME Mode (on applicable data types)
- Target Record Type (on applicable data types)
- Relationship Name (on applicable data types)

We defined each of these properties earlier in this chapter, but now we cover the schema name and type in more detail.

Schema Name

The schema name represents the name of the field in the metadata. Every custom field includes a prefix value in the schema name (such as *new_customfield*) depending on the publisher creating the field. Microsoft Dynamics CRM creates the Default Publisher with the *new_* default schema prefix. When you create a custom field, notice that the schema prefix field is read-only and you can't edit it when you're creating a field.

Important Each publisher should have a unique prefix so that it is easy to determine where custom entities and fields are created from. You can change the schema prefix by navigating to Customizations in the Settings section. Then click Publishers and select the Publisher to edit the prefix for tab. The prefix must contain between two and eight alphanumeric characters, and it cannot start with *mscrm*.

When you enter text in the display name field and you change focus on the field (by pressing the Tab key or clicking elsewhere on the page), Microsoft Dynamics CRM automatically fills in the rest of the schema name after the prefix. Because the schema name can consist of alphanumeric and underscore characters only, Microsoft Dynamics CRM removes any inappropriate characters. When you are creating a schema name, keep the following in mind:

- Your users will never see the schema name.
- You cannot change the schema name after you create the field.
- Schema names must be unique within a single entity.
- Any advanced customizations you create, such as the SDK code, scripting, and reports, will reference the schema name instead of the display name, so try to be consistent with casing (such as all lowercase, all Pascal case, or all camel case). Also, save your developers some keystrokes by keeping the name just long enough to describe its function but not so long that it takes forever to type.

Type

When creating new fields, you can choose from one of 10 data types, some of which you can use to specify further how Microsoft Dynamics CRM should format the data. Table 6-5 summarizes the data types and data formatting options available for custom fields.

TABLE 6-5 Data Types and Formats for Custom Fields

Field data type	Format	Description
single line of text	E-mail	Displays text as a clickable mailto: hyperlink.
	Text	Displays text on one line. You can specify a maximum length.
	Text Area	Displays a multiline text box with scrollbars.
	URL	Displays text as a hyperlink. Microsoft Dynamics CRM automatically adds *http://* to whatever the user enters.
	Ticker Symbol	Displays text as a live hyperlink that starts a stock quote request on *http://moneycentral.msn.com*.
option set	Option List	Additional information about option sets is detailed later in this chapter.
two options	Bit	Displays two possible options on the form. You can change No and Yes to new values such as False and True, and you can specify the order in which the values appear. You can also specify the default value. On the form editor, you can determine whether you want the text to appear with two radio buttons, a check box, or a list (or drop-down).
whole number	None	Whole numbers only (1, 2, 3, and so on). You can also set a minimum and maximum range for this value.
	Duration	Displays a picklist with 23 predefined *duration* values ranging from one minute to three days.
	Time zone	Displays a picklist from which users can select one of 75 different time zones from around the world.
	Language	By default, English is available in this list with a database value of 1033. Additional languages will be added as language packs are installed.

Field data type	Format	Description
floating point number	Float	Used to store numeric values with a configurable precision (such as 1.23 or 3.145) up to five digits. You can also specify a minimum and maximum range.
decimal number	Decimal	Used to store numeric values with a configurable precision (such as 1.23 or 3.145) up to 10 digits. You can also specify a minimum and maximum range.
currency	Money	Used to store currency amounts. You can specify the precision and a minimum and maximum range.
multiple lines of text	Text	Displays a multi-line text box with scrollbars. You can specify a maximum length.
date and time	Date only	Date default formatted as month, date, and year. A calendar control automatically appears on the form. Although only the date is displayed, a time stamp is still stored in the database.
	Date and Time	Date default formatted as month, date, year along with hours and minutes. A calendar control and time selection drop-down list automatically appear on the form.

Figure 6-3 shows a mockup of how each of these data types appears to users on the entity form. As you can see, each data type saves and displays information differently, so it's important that you select the appropriate data type for your custom fields.

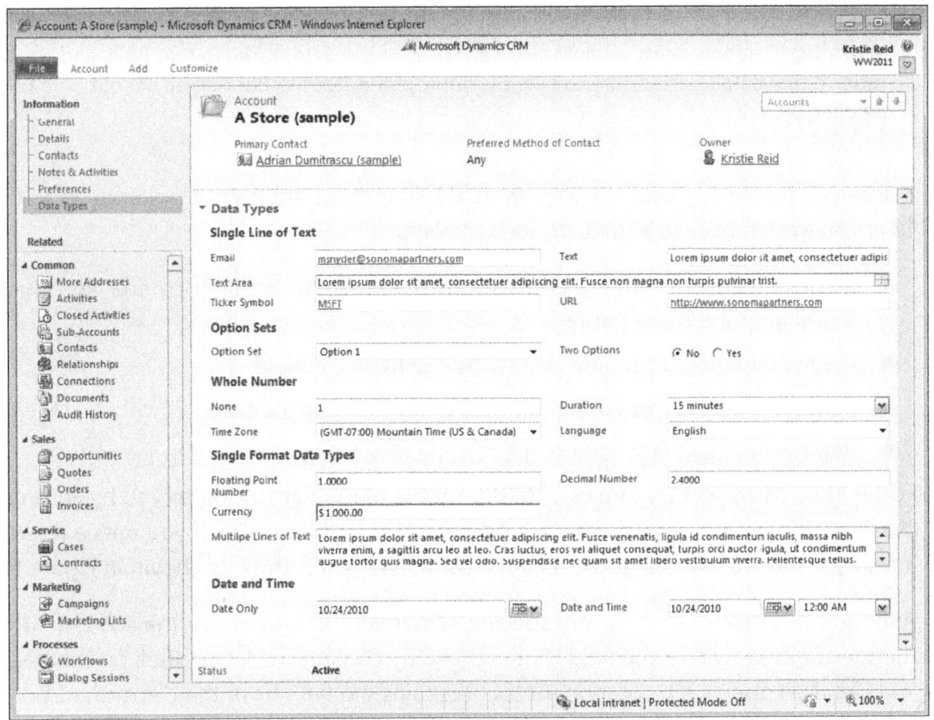

FIGURE 6-3 How different data types and formats appear on an entity form

More Info Both the *single line of text* and *multiple lines of text* data types store text and numeric data, and both data types format the data on the form by using a text area, so how should you decide which data type to use? For fields with a length greater than eight characters, the *single line of text* data type consumes more bytes in SQL Server. However, data stored using the *single line of text* data type provides better performance than does data stored using *multiple lines of text*. Therefore, a good rule of thumb is to use the *single line of text* data type fields with up to 100 characters, and use *multiple lines of text* for fields with more than 100 characters.

Field Icons

When you view a list of fields for an entity, you can quickly distinguish the fields that you created (custom) from the system fields (customizable) by looking at the icon in the far-left column. Microsoft Dynamics CRM displays an icon for custom fields that is different from the one used for customizable fields.

Deleting Fields

Because it's easy to add custom fields, you might find yourself getting a little overzealous and adding more fields than you need or want. Of course, you could simply remove any unused fields from an entity's form, but they will still appear in Advanced Find, SDK, database, filtered views, and so on. If these extra fields bother you and you decide to delete old or unused custom fields, you'll find the process very simple.

Warning Deleting a custom field also deletes all of the data stored in that field, and you cannot retrieve that data later. Be sure to take the appropriate steps to back up all of your data before deleting a field.

Before you delete any fields, make sure that you remove any existing references to that field. To remove references to a field, do the following:

- Remove the field from the entity's form, views, including filter criteria, and charts, and then publish the entity.
- Remove the field from any reports that contain the field.
- Remove the field from any processes that reference the field.
- Remove the field from any script or code references.

Fortunately, Microsoft Dynamics CRM does most of the hard work for you by automatically checking all the forms, views, charts, and processes in the system. If you miss a reference to a field you want to delete, you'll see an error message like the one shown in Figure 6-4.

Although this message is not very specific, Dynamics CRM gives you the ability to drill into the specific areas where the field is referenced by clicking the Details link on this page. You can then open each component that contains the field from the Dependent Components Detected list by double-clicking the item, as shown in Figure 6-5.

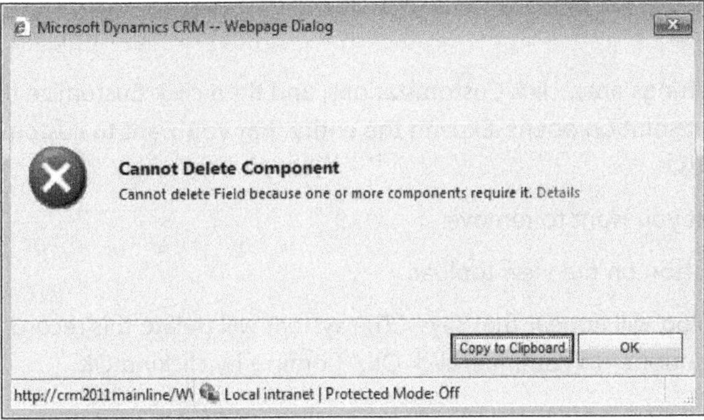

FIGURE 6-4 Error message shown when attempting to delete a referenced field

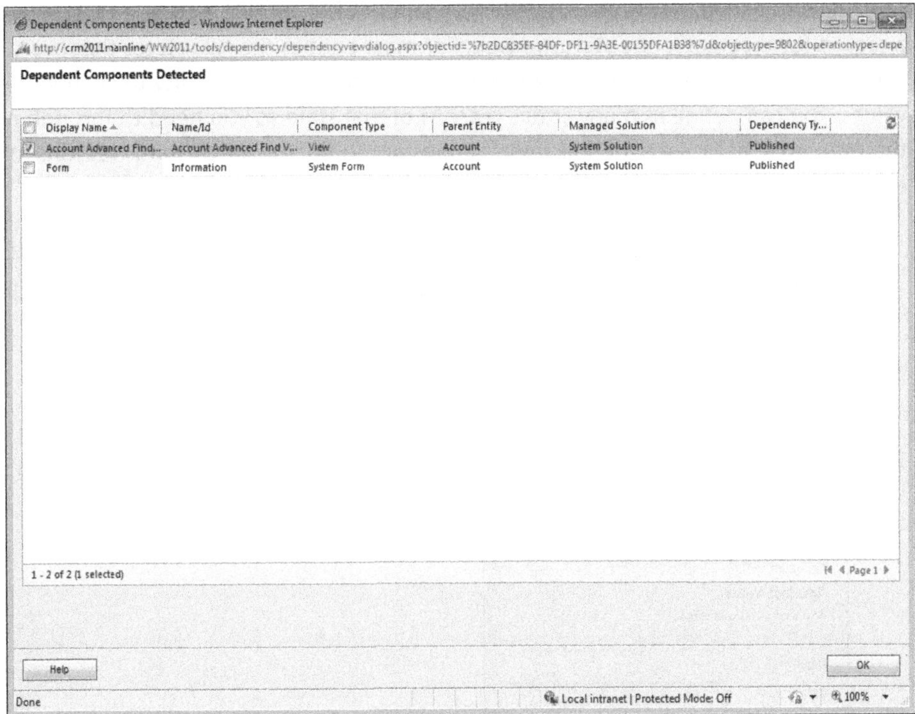

FIGURE 6-5 Dependent Components Detected list

Even though Microsoft Dynamics CRM checks the forms, views, charts, and processes for references to deleted fields, you must scrub the reports and code yourself to remove any references to the deleted field.

After you're certain that you have removed all references to the field and published the entity, you can delete the field by following these steps.

Deleting a custom field

1. Navigate to the Settings area, click Customizations, and then click Customize the System. The default solution opens. Expand the entity that you want to customize, and then click Fields.
2. Select the field that you want to remove.
3. Click the Delete button on the view toolbar.
4. A confirmation dialog will appear that says, "The system will delete this record. This action cannot be undone. To continue, click OK." Confirm by clicking OK.

Status and Status Reason Fields

As explained earlier, most records within Dynamics CRM contain a state, or status, and a reason for that state, or a status reason. For most entities the two states that every record can be in are Active and Inactive. Although you do not have the ability to change these values, you can define as many status reasons of that state as you need to through modifying the *statuscode* field. Take the following actions to modify the list of status reasons for most entities:

1. Navigate to the Settings area, click Customizations, and then click Customize the System. The default solution opens. Expand the appropriate entity, and then click Fields.
2. Double-click the *statuscode* field. The field editor appears.
3. Select the Status that you want to modify or add the Status Reason for.
4. If you want to edit an existing reason from the list, either double-click that value or highlight that option and click the Edit button. If you want to add a new value, click the Add button and enter the appropriate Label in the Add List Value dialog box.

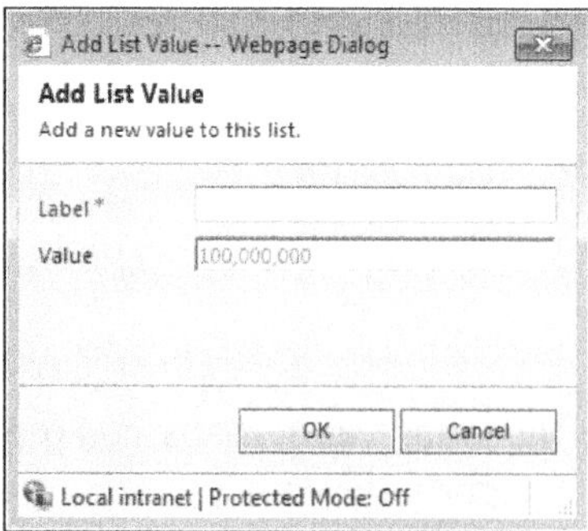

5. Set the appropriate default value.

Figure 6-6 shows the Status Reason field of the Contact entity. In this example, the native Active status reason was changed to Prospect and a new status reason of Member was added, both for the status of Active.

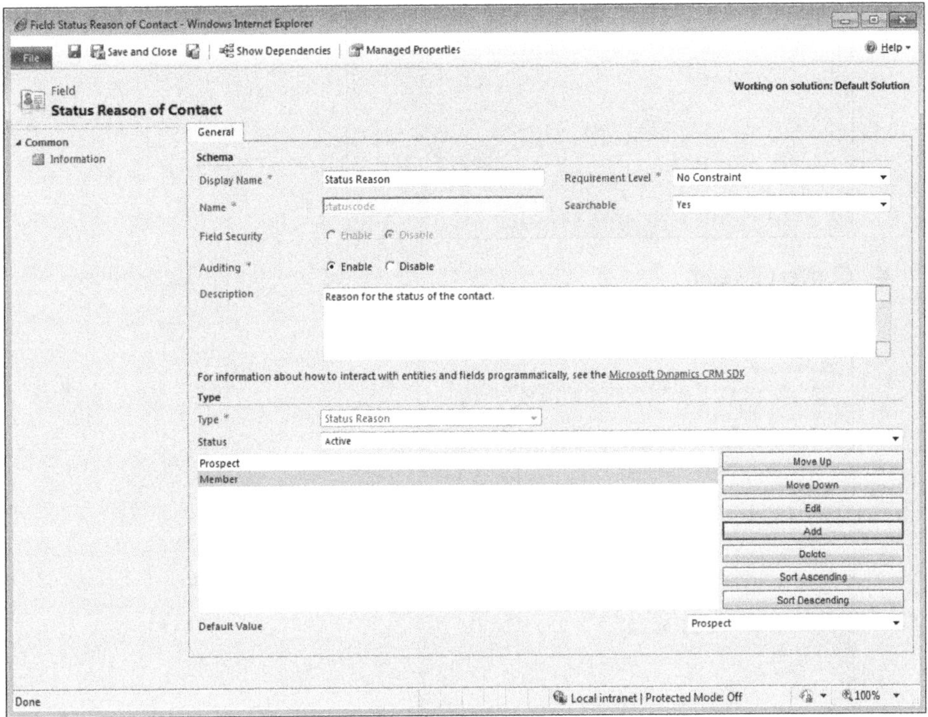

FIGURE 6-6 Updated Status Reason Of Contact

Note Certain entities have a status other than Active and Inactive. In addition, for some entities the status is tied to other functionality, which does not make editing the status reason list possible.

The next section identifies areas throughout the application where the status reason affects functionality within native dialogs. For all of the following examples, Dynamics CRM gives you the flexibility to add new and modify existing Status Reasons. However, you cannot modify the Statuses of those records.

Fields and Closing Dialog Boxes

Closing dialog boxes present a special case you need to consider when you're customizing entity fields. A *closing dialog box* is a dialog box that appears when a user takes one of the following actions:

- Close an activity, such as Phone Call

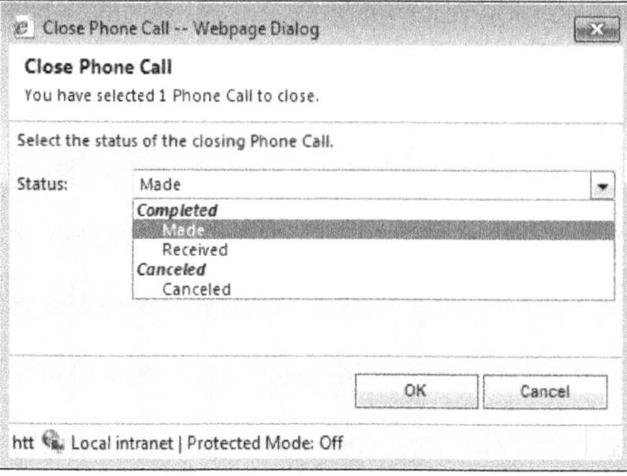

- Convert a Lead

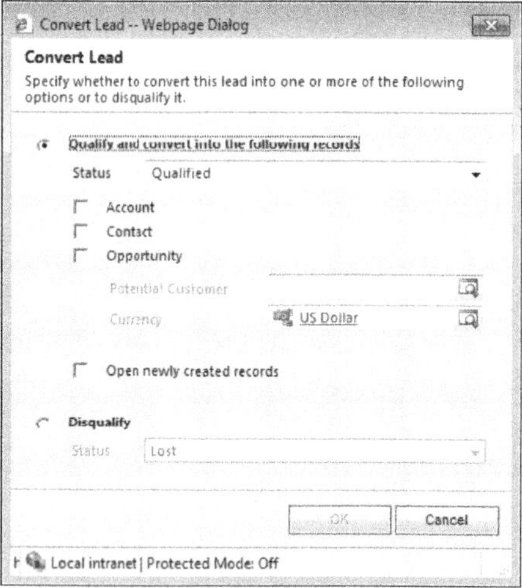

- Close an Opportunity

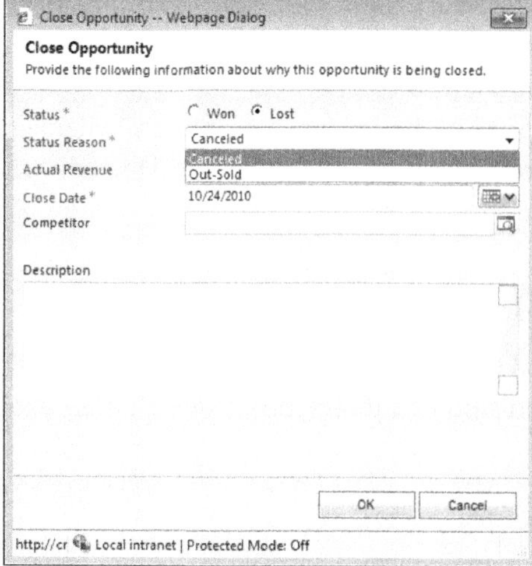

- Resolve a Case

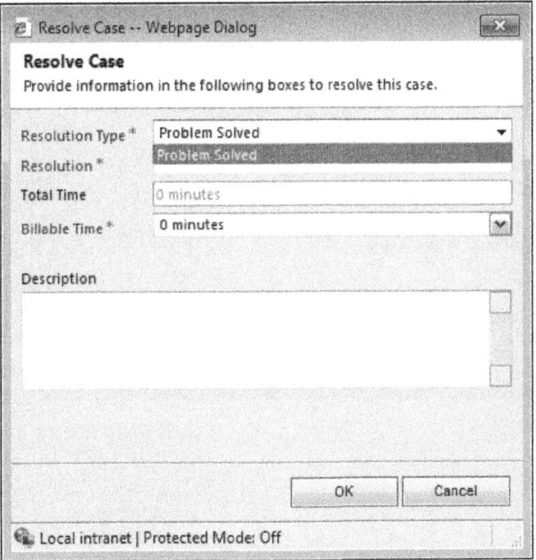

When a user initiates one of these actions, a closing dialog box prompts the user to specify how she wants to close the entity. It might not be obvious where you should customize the closing dialog box *status reason* values because these closing dialog boxes aren't entity forms, but they do display fields of the entity. To edit the closing dialog box *status reason* values, you must modify the *statuscode* field (Status Reason display name) of the entity you're closing. We'll quickly show you how to edit the closing dialog box values for the Phone Call entity, and then you will know how to apply the same concept and process to the other closing dialog boxes referenced in the preceding list.

Important For entities that users can close in Microsoft Dynamics CRM (such as Phone Calls and Letters), the *statuscode* field behaves a little differently from a standard *Option Set* field. In these examples, you can specify different values for each *statecode* value (Status Reason display name) where most option sets contain only one range of values. You can specify different *statuscode* picklist values for each of the three *statecode* values: Open, Completed, and Canceled.

Editing the Phone Call Closing Dialog Box Values

When you close activities such as Tasks and Phone Calls, a closing dialog box appears in which the user determines whether to mark the activity Completed or Canceled. The following procedure explains how to customize those values.

1. Navigate to the Settings area, click Customizations, and then click Customize the System. The default solution opens. Expand the Phone Call entity, and then click Fields.
2. Double-click the *statuscode* field. The field editor appears.

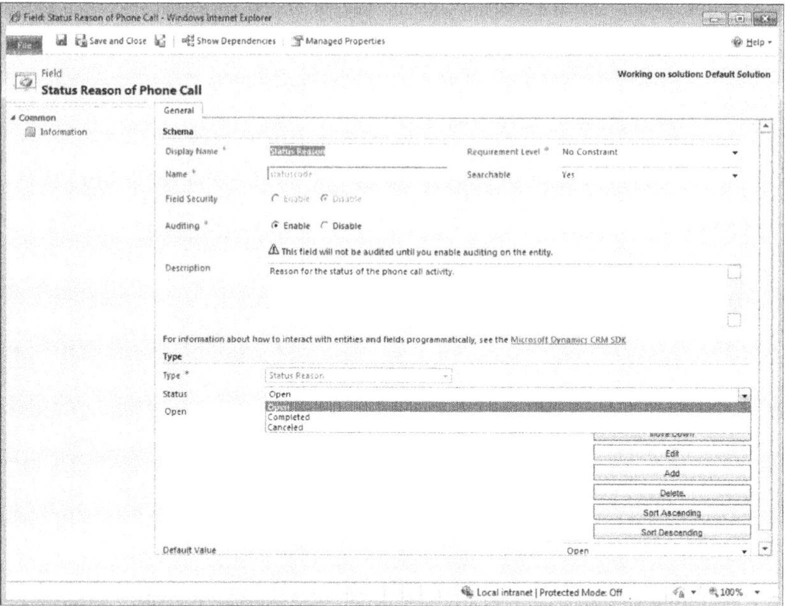

3. In the Status drop-down list, select Completed. The picklist values change from the Open value (Open) to the Completed values (Made, Received).
4. Click Add, and then type **Left Message** in the Label field. Click OK.
5. In the Status drop-down list, click Canceled. Then, click Add, and type **Wrong Number** in the Label field. Click OK. You will see that the Wrong Number picklist value is added under the Canceled value.

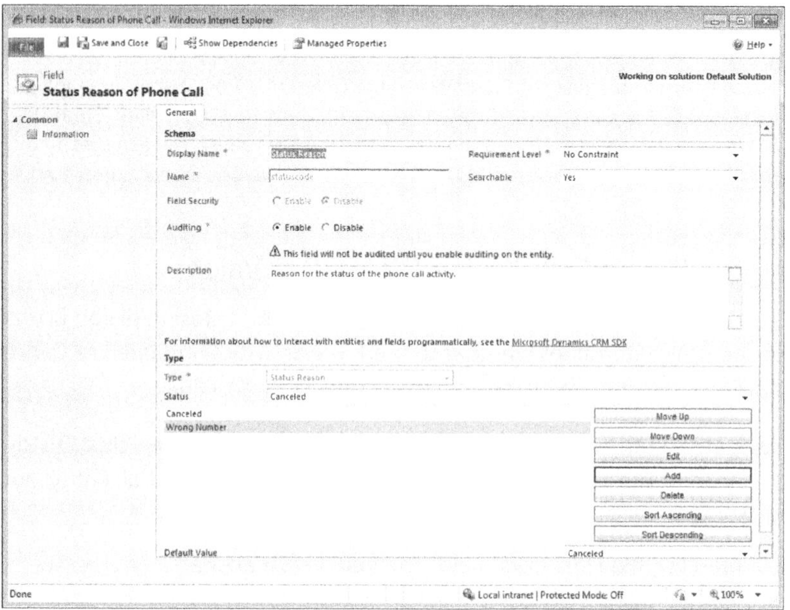

6. Click Save and Close on the field editor toolbar.
7. Select the Phone Call entity and then click Publish.
8. Now when your users close a Phone Call activity, they will see the following closing dialog box that incorporates your new customizations.

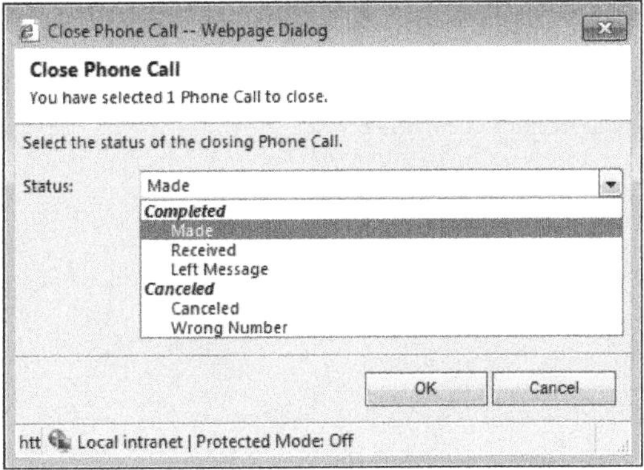

Important If users click the Mark Complete button on the toolbar, they will not see the closing dialog box. In this case, Microsoft Dynamics CRM uses the value that you specify as the default value of the Completed state. Because most users will probably click the Mark Complete button, make sure you choose the default value that you want.

Noneditable Status Reasons

Microsoft Dynamics CRM includes some entities with closing dialog boxes that behave differently from the ones just discussed, limiting your ability to customize them. For example, the campaign response displays a dialog box to convert records that appear similar to the examples we just covered, but you cannot modify the Close Response values by modifying the Status Reasons.

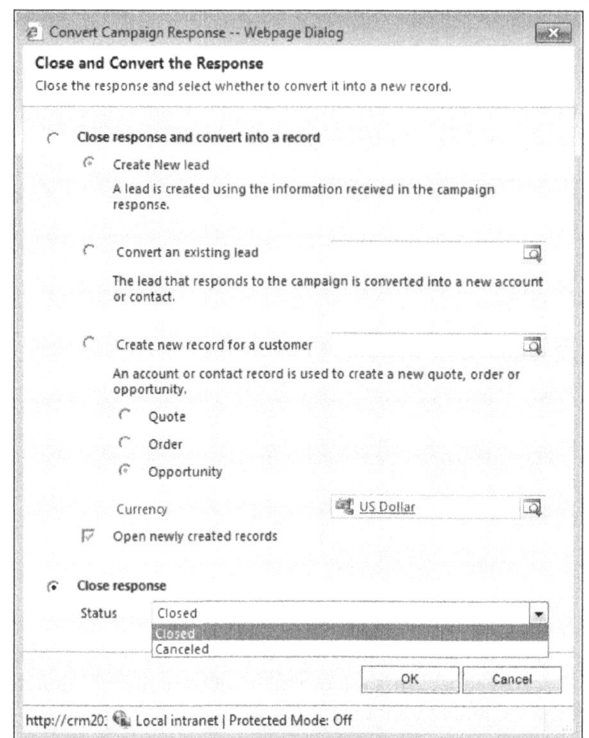

In addition, even though you can modify the status reasons for phone calls and letters, you cannot modify the status reasons for the Task, E-mail, and Appointment entities.

Option Sets

New to Microsoft Dynamics CRM 2011 is the concept of option sets that can be shared across multiple entities. This additional functionality not only prevents you from having to create the same Option Set multiple times for different entities—which can become very tedious for longer Option Sets—but also greatly reduces the issues that can arise when mapping Option Sets from one entity to another.

You can create shared Option Sets while creating a field in a specific entity or prior to use.

Let's take an example where you want to replace the native State fields on the Lead, Account, and Contact forms with a drop-down list rather than a text field. You will then map that new field on the Lead, Account, and Contact entities. The following procedure walks you through how to create an Option Set and then add a field with those values to the Account entity.

1. Navigate to the Settings area, click Customizations, and then click Customize the System. The default solution opens. Select Option Sets.
2. Click the New button on the grid toolbar to open a new Option Set window.
3. Enter **State** in the Display Name, type in a Description, and create all of the state abbreviations as the Values for this Option Set.

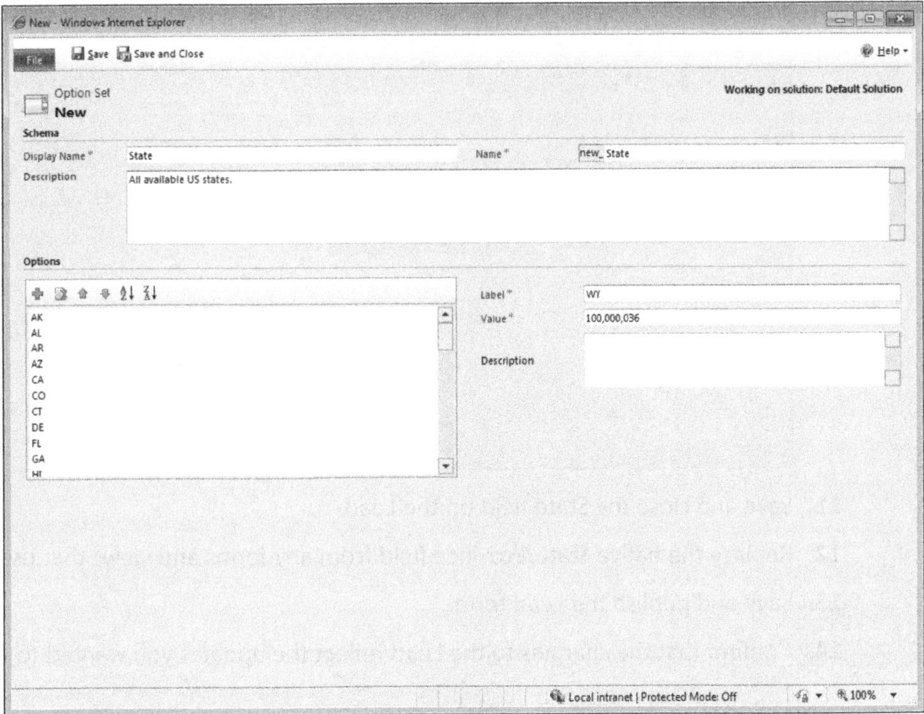

4. Save and close the Option Set. Return to the solution.
5. Expand the Entities list and the Lead entity.
6. Select Fields from the Lead and click New on the fields view.
7. Enter **State** in the Display Name, type a Description, and choose Option Set as the data type.
8. Select Yes in the Use Existing Option Set radio button.
9. Choose the newly created State from the list of available Option Sets. Notice that you also have the ability to edit or create new Option Sets from this area.

10. Set a default value if appropriate.

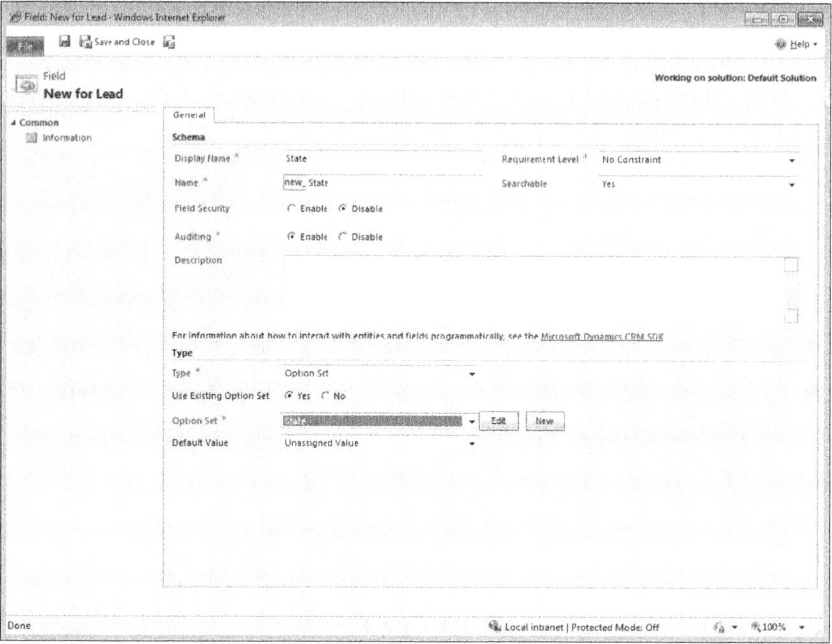

11. Save and close the State field on the Lead.
12. Replace the native State/Province field from any forms and views that used that field.
13. Save and publish the Lead form.
14. Confirm that the changes to the Lead reflect the updates you wanted to make.

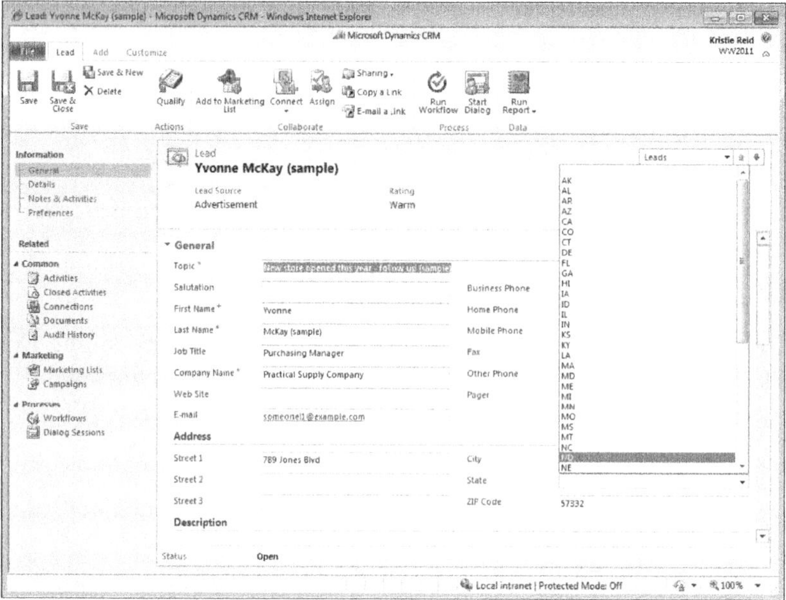

15. Repeat steps 5 through 14 on the Account and Contact entities.

16. Return to the Lead entity in the solutions area and select 1:N Relationships from the left navigation.

17. Double-click the Lead To Account relationship that has the schema name *account_originating_lead*.

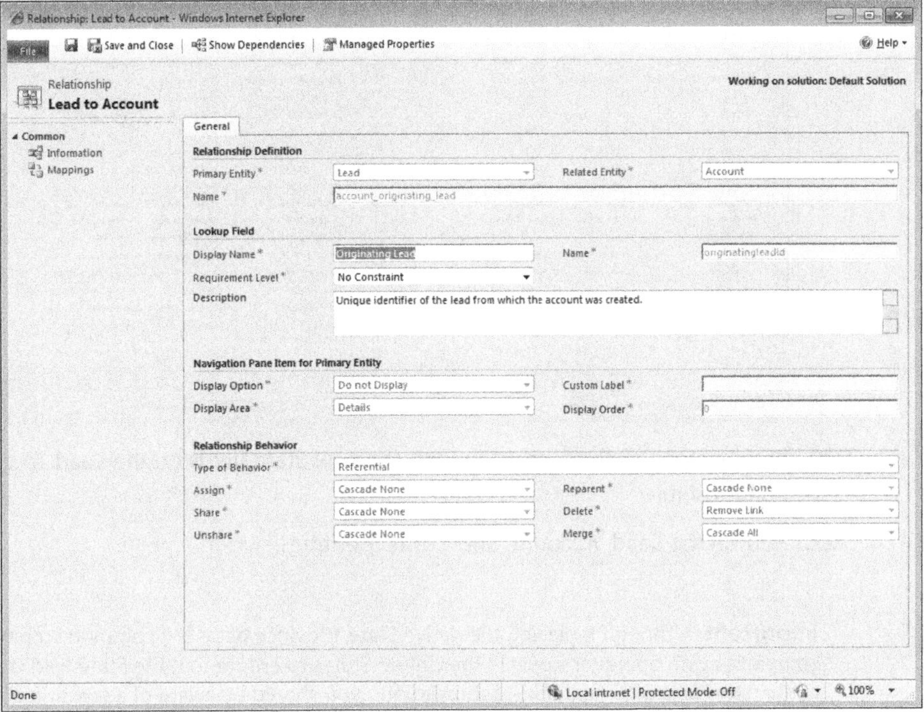

18. Select Mappings from the left navigation. When the list of existing mappings loads, click New on the view menu bar.

19. Add a mapping between on the newly created state fields from the Lead To The Account entity and click OK.

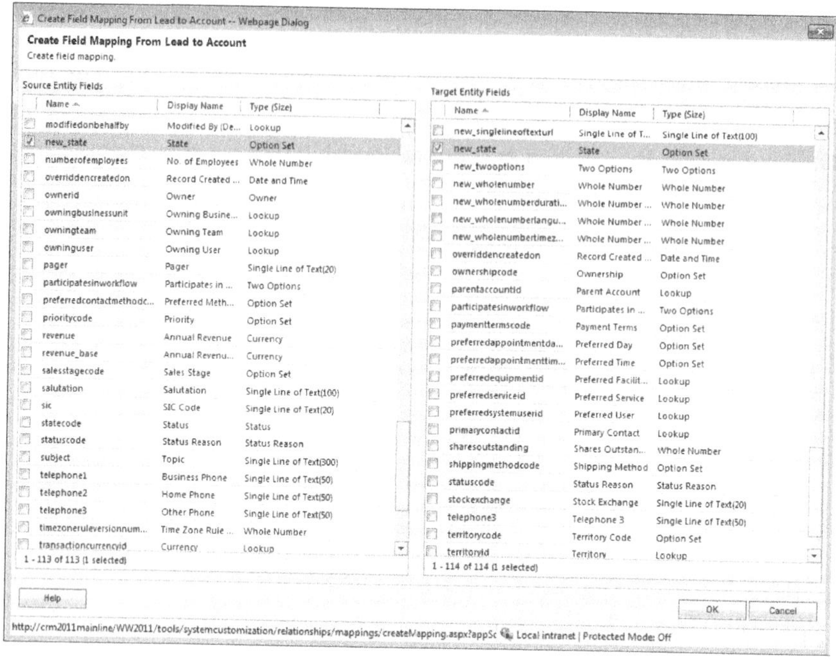

20. Repeat steps 16 through 19 to map the new State fields on the Lead To Contact relationship.

21. Publish the Lead, Account, and Contact entities.

Important Although replacing the native State/Province fields is a common scenario for companies with operations only in the United States to ensure that the State field is populated consistently and with valid State abbreviations, you should be aware of a few side effects of this change.

First, mappings exist between the native Status/Province fields throughout the application. As you may have already concluded from the example above, Leads also have a State/Province field that automatically populates the Account and Contact records created when a lead record is converted. In addition, the native State/Province form on the Contact entity maps to the State/Province field on Contacts in Outlook when the records sync between CRM and Outlook. You need to write a plug-in to keep the native and the custom State fields in sync so that users do not lose the ability to enter that information into one system and have it reflected correctly in the other.

To maintain consistency throughout your Dynamics CRM application, you should also update the State/Province field in all areas where a state is available on the form or view. The following entities include address information out of the box:

- Account
- Address
- Business Unit
- Competitor

- Competitor Address
- Contact
- Contract
- Internal Address
- Invoice
- Invoice Product
- Lead
- Lead Address
- Order
- Order Product
- Publisher
- Quote
- Quote Product
- Site
- User

Finally, if your Dynamics CRM application has been implemented for some time, you will need to migrate all of the data in the native State/Province field to the new custom field developed. This could be challenging because up to this point, users have had the ability to type freely into the native field where they may be using the full state name or some form of abbreviation that may not necessarily match the correct state abbreviations. In addition, you want to confirm with users that none of their personal views or templates rely on the native State/Province data field.

Summary

In this chapter, we explained the concepts, terminology, and processes related to modifying, adding, and deleting fields. Every entity consists of multiple fields, and Microsoft Dynamics CRM supports two different types of fields: custom and system. In addition, this chapter also explored the details related to entity fields. Each entity field consists of common properties (such as display name and schema name) in addition to properties unique to the data type of the field.

This chapter then went into additional detail about the *Option Set* data type. More specifically, we looked at an example of using a common Option Set across multiple entities. This functionality, new to Microsoft Dynamics CRM 2011, greatly reduces the effort required to maintain long Option Sets that are shared across more than one entity. In addition, when mapping fields between entities that have the same Option Set values, you have the ability to use the same Option Set and thereby eliminate the issue of field values not being carried over from one record to another correctly.

Chapter 7
Entity Customization: Forms

In this chapter:

As we've already highlighted, Microsoft Dynamics CRM is a flexible framework that allows you to customize the application to fit your unique business scenarios. One of the main ways the application achieves this flexibility is through the form design tool. The beauty of the customizations available in the system is that you can achieve a screen design specific to your business without hours of coding to accomplish the format you want. Configuration tools are available for both the main pages that are displayed in the web and Outlook clients as well as mobile pages that are accessed on mobile devices. In this chapter we will discuss the components of each form, how to customize those forms, and how to use multiple forms when appropriate.

Form Components

When you open a record, Microsoft Dynamics CRM displays the form for that record's entity. The various areas of each form, including the body, header, footer, and navigation pane, are shown in Figure 7-1.

Body

The body of the form contains all of the information that will be displayed or editable for each record in Microsoft Dynamics CRM. Fields, sub-grids of related entities, web resources, and IFrames are examples of content typically included in the body of a form. Users can scroll through the information on the form or they can quickly access different areas by using the tabs found in the left navigation pane. Tabs provide a great way to organize data fields into logical groupings. Figure 7-2 shows the ability to jump to the Details tab simply by clicking the Details link in the left navigation pane.

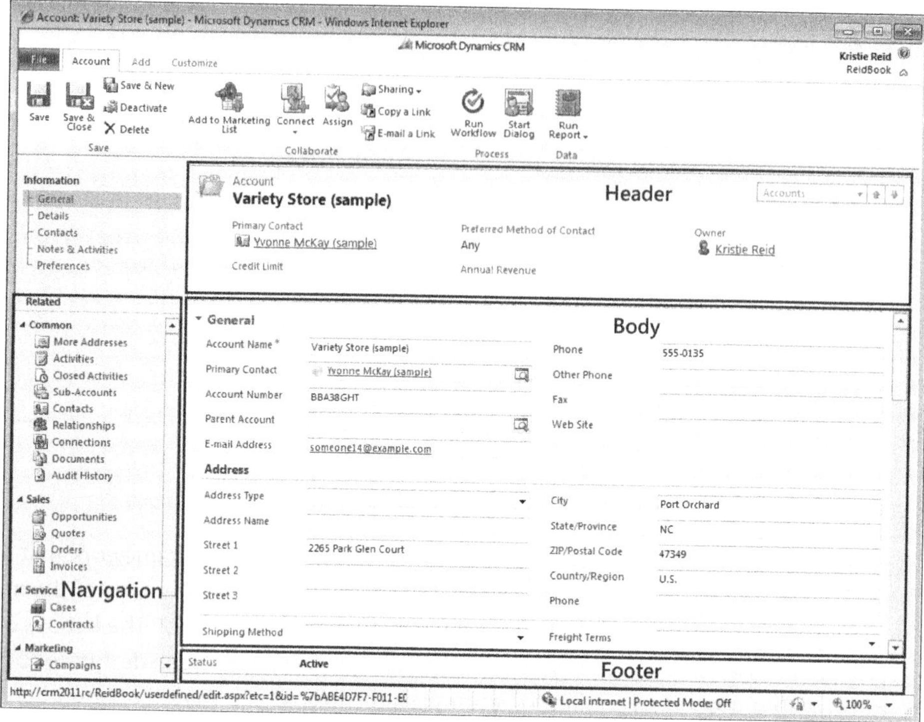

FIGURE 7-1 Form areas

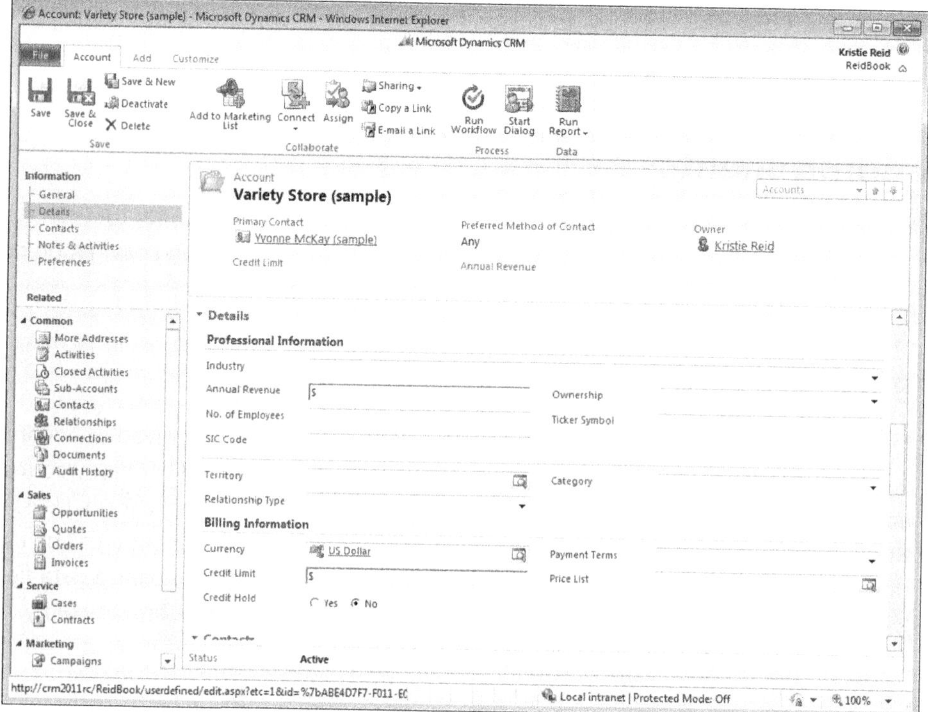

FIGURE 7-2 Navigation using tabs

Header

The header of the form is visible at all times and typically contains just a few read-only fields that users need when working with a record. This differs from the body of the form, in which users can scroll through the available information. In addition, the body is replaced by views or other pages when a link in the navigation pane is selected; however, the header remains available, as shown in Figure 7-3.

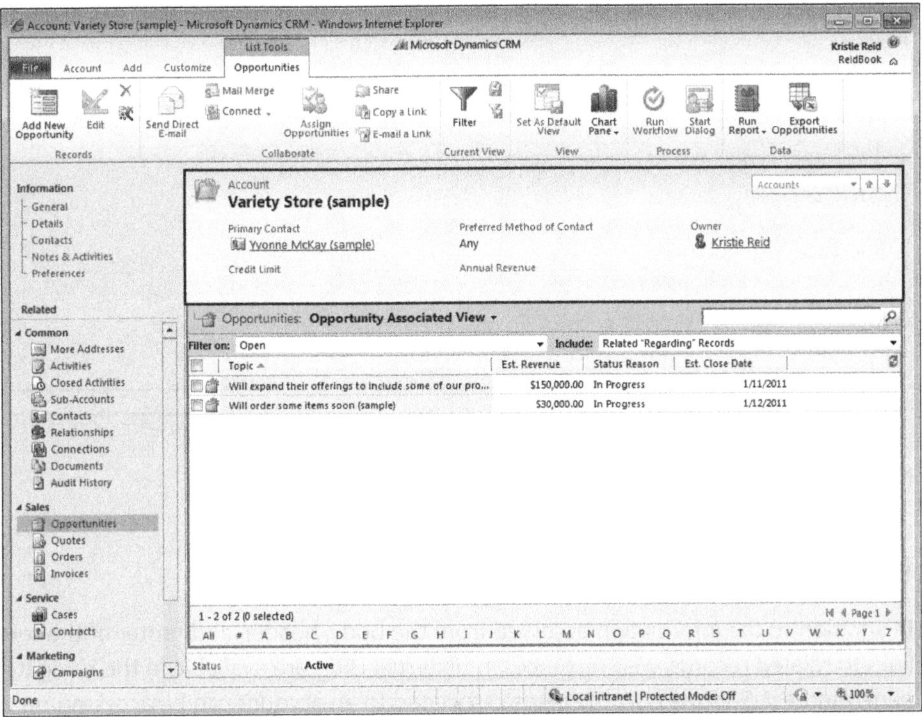

FIGURE 7-3 Form header

Notice that the upper-right corner of the header also contains a view selector. From this view selector, you can change the view from which you opened the record and use the up and down arrows next to the view to scroll through the previous and next records in the selected view. This saves you time when navigating through records because you do not have to close and open a window for each record.

Footer

Similar to the header, the information displayed in the footer is also always shown on the form, but at the bottom of the page, as shown in Figure 7-4.

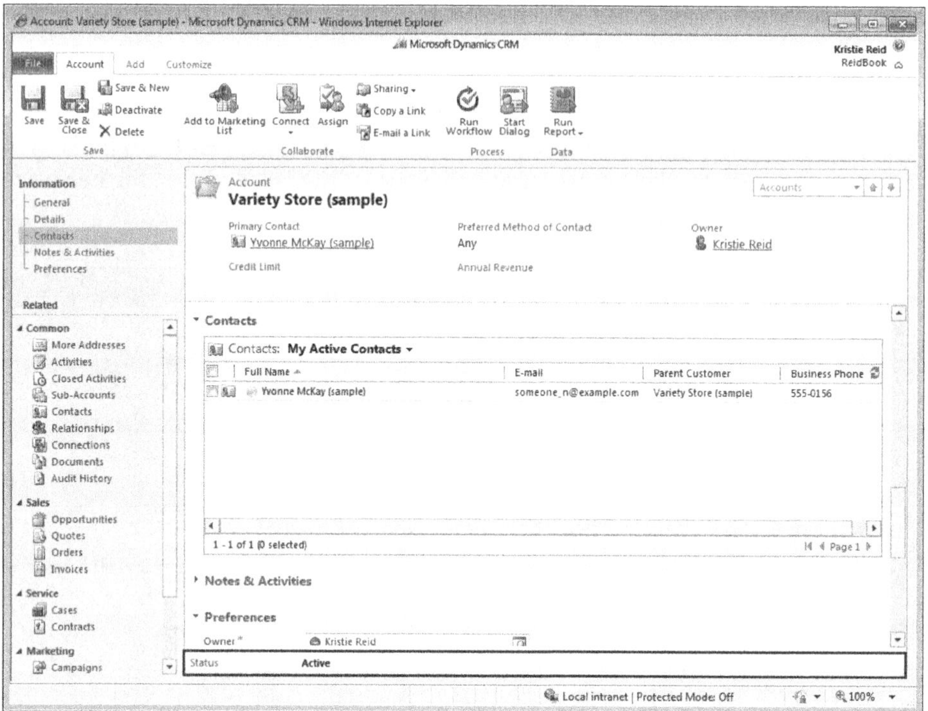

FIGURE 7-4 Form footer

Navigation

In addition to the information accessed from the body, header, and footer of the form, links to related records, web resources, or external URLs are available in the navigation pane. Figure 7-5 shows how the cases associated to an account can be accessed on the Account form.

Note As you can imagine, an entity's mobile form is much simpler than the web and Outlook client form. In mobile forms, you can view the body of the form and links to the related entities. The intent of this simplicity is to provide users with the information that they need quickly and succinctly.

Now that we have identified the components on a form, let's look at how to change those areas in a form to meet your business needs. We will review customizations to both types of forms: main and mobile.

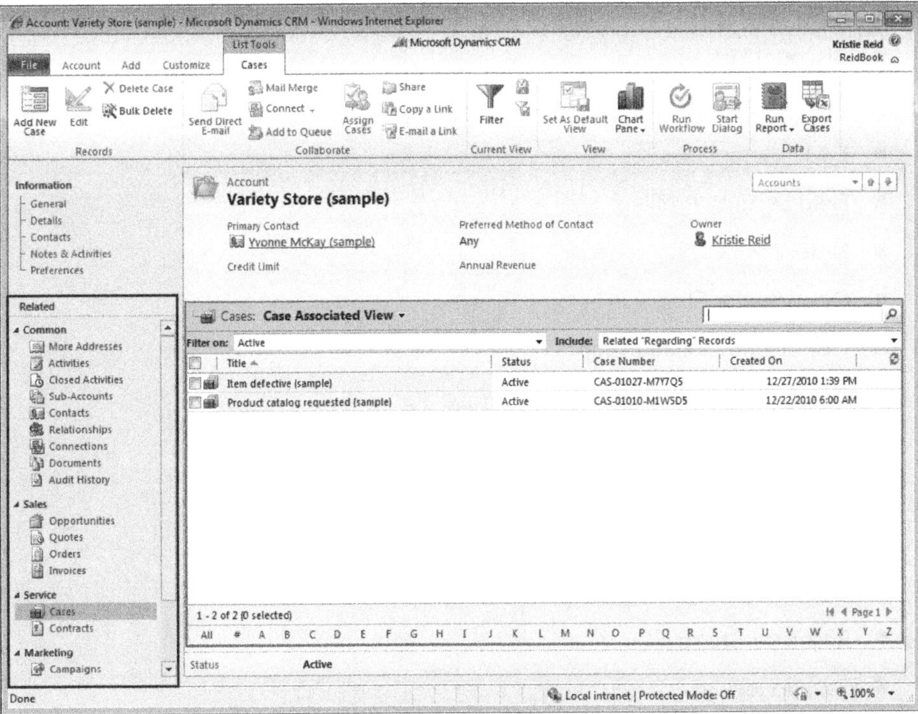

FIGURE 7-5 Form navigation

Form Customizations

Most of the system entities in Microsoft Dynamics CRM have at least one form that can be customized, but some of the non-customizable system entities, such as Activity and Organization, don't use a form because users don't view or update these records directly. Further, the following customizable system entities include forms that cannot be customized:

- Article Template
- Case Resolution
- Connection Roles
- Contract Template
- Customer Relationship
- Data Map

- Dialog Session
- Discount List
- E-Mail Attachment
- E-Mail Template
- Field Security Profile
- Note
- Opportunity Close
- Opportunity Relationship
- Order Close
- Process
- Publisher
- Quick Campaign
- Quote Close
- Resource Group
- Saved View
- Security Role
- Service
- Site
- Solution
- Unit (mobile form only)
- Unit Group
- View

Note It is important to know that some entities do not have a mobile form, such as Solution. These are typically entities used for system administrator functions, so they do not need to be accessed on mobile devices. For entities that have mobile forms, you need to enable the Mobile Express property on the Entity form and publish the entity to make the mobile form available to users.

Even with these constraints, there are still quite a few system entities in Microsoft Dynamics CRM that have customizable forms, and remember, you can create custom entities and customize their forms as well.

To access an entity's form, navigate to the Settings area, click Customizations, and then click Customize the System to open the default solution. In the navigation pane, expand the

Entities list, expand the entity you want to edit, and then click Forms. The available forms for the entity appear, and you can select the one you want to customize.

Tip You can also get to an entity's form editor directly from the Customize tab in that entity's ribbon. This can save you a lot of time when making quick updates to forms because you do not need to navigate back to the Settings area each time you want to make changes.

You will notice that most entities have two default forms. Both will be named Information but one will have a form type of Main and the other will have a form type of Mobile. As the names indicate, the main form will be what users will see when they log into the web or Outlook clients. The mobile form will be displayed when they log into Mobile Express. The steps used to customize these forms are very different, so we will explore them separately.

Main Form Customizations

When designing the main forms that appear in the web and Outlook interfaces, you have the ability to customize all of the form components we discussed: body, header, footer, and navigation. Within these components you can add fields and relationships to other entities. In addition, you can add controls, such as sub-grids, IFrames, and several others. In this section, we'll discuss how you can customize each of these areas on a form. We will also review the Field Explorer, which you will use heavily when customizing the body, header, and footer of forms. Keep in mind that controls can also be added to forms, but we will discuss these form enhancement types in more detail in later in this chapter.

Body

Within the body of the form, you have the flexibility to set up tabs, sections, and controls.

Tabs Tabs allow you to organize the fields for an entity into logical groups that can be used for navigating within a form. Microsoft Dynamics CRM enables you to quickly jump between tabs on a form using links in the navigation pane. After you determine the tabs you want to include on a form, you can design the layout of each tab, which can contain one or two columns and as many sections as you want. Each section can then contain up to four columns, so technically your form can have up to eight columns.

Important When designing your forms, it's important to consider the typical screen resolution of your users' computers. For example, if you attempt to use a two-column tab with four column sections, some fields will be cut off in a 1024 × 768 screen resolution, and you'll have to scroll left and right to see the fields.

To create a tab on a form, follow these steps:

1. Navigate to Settings area, click Customizations, and then click Customize the System. The default solution opens.
2. Expand the Entities list, select the entity you want to customize, and then click Forms.
3. Open the form you want to edit.
4. On the form ribbon, click the Insert tab.
5. Click the One Column or Two Column button in the Tab section of the ribbon. The new tab appears on your form.

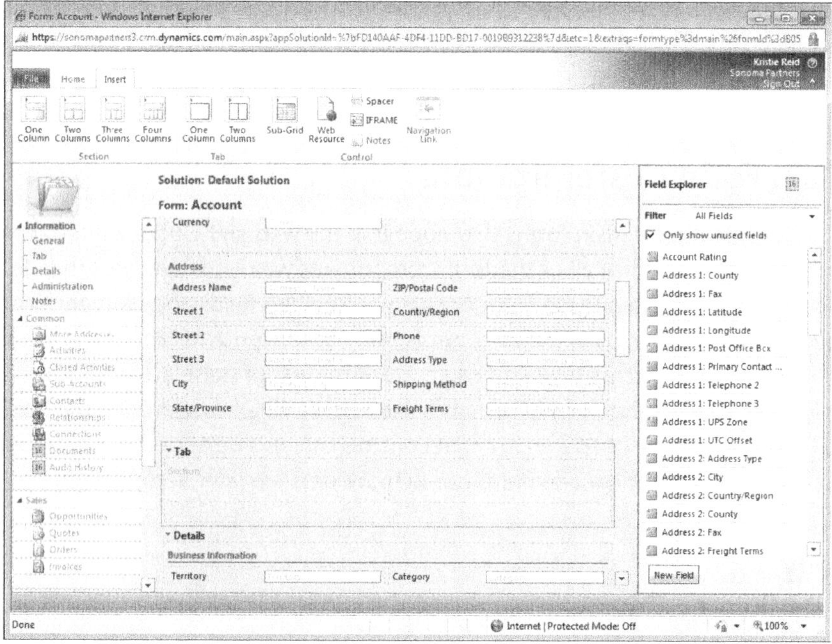

Tabs have the following properties:

- **Name** Unique name for the tab.
- **Label** Display name of the tab that will appear on the form. You can also opt to hide the label so that it's not displayed on the form and select whether you want the tab expanded or collapsed when the form is first opened.
- **Visibility** Field for toggling whether the tab is displayed or hidden on the form.
- **Layout** Tabs can have a one- or two-column layout, which can be changed at any time. You can also specify the width of each column when the two-column option is selected.
- **Events** You can associate events and functions to a tab. We'll cover this advanced functionality in Chapter 11, "Solutions: Web Resources," and Chapter 12, "Solutions: Client Extensions."

To edit the properties of a tab, double-click the tab in the form editor, or select the tab and click the Change Properties button in the Home tab in the ribbon. The Tab Properties dialog box is shown in Figure 7-6.

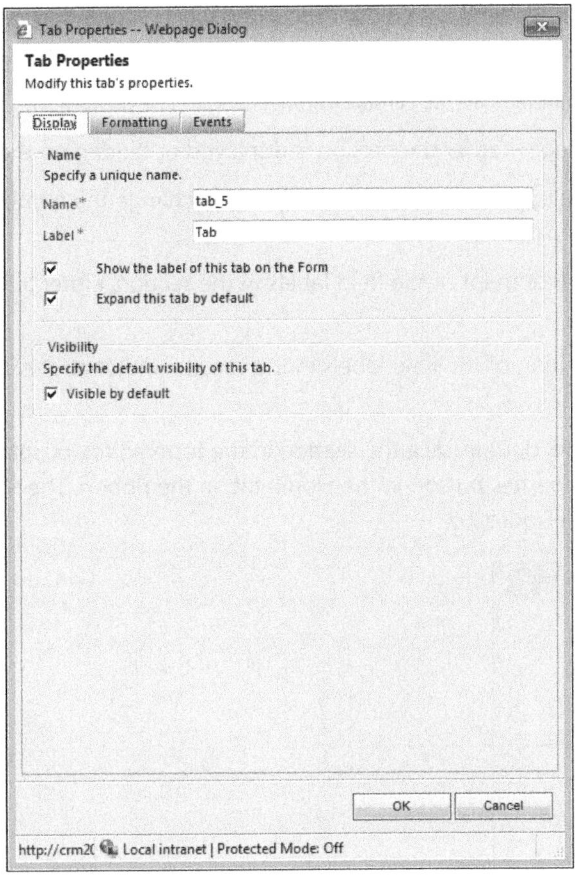

FIGURE 7-6 Tab Properties dialog box

To remove a tab, click the tab to select it and click the Remove button on the Home tab in the ribbon.

Sections In each tab, you can group information in sections. In Figure 7-2, Professional Information and Billing Information are sections on the Details tab.

A default section is created in each column when you add a tab to a form. The steps to create a section are similar to those used to create a tab. In the form editor, select the tab to which you want to add the section, click the Insert tab in the ribbon, and then click the button with the number of columns you want in your section in the ribbon's Section area.

Sections have the following properties:

- **Name** Unique name for the section.
- **Label** Display name of the section that will appear on the form. You can also opt to hide the label so that it's not displayed on the form and select whether you want a dividing line to appear under the label.
- **Width** Width of the field label area, specified in pixels.
- **Visibility** Field for toggling whether the section is displayed or hidden on the form.
- **Layout** Sections can have up to four columns, and you can change the number of columns in a section at any time.
- **Field Label Alignment** Alignment of the field labels in the section, either left, right, or center.
- **Field Label Position** Position of the field labels in the section, either above or on the left side of the fields.

To edit the properties of a section, double-click the section in the form editor, or select the section and click the Change Properties button in the Home tab in the ribbon. The Section Properties dialog box is shown in Figure 7-7.

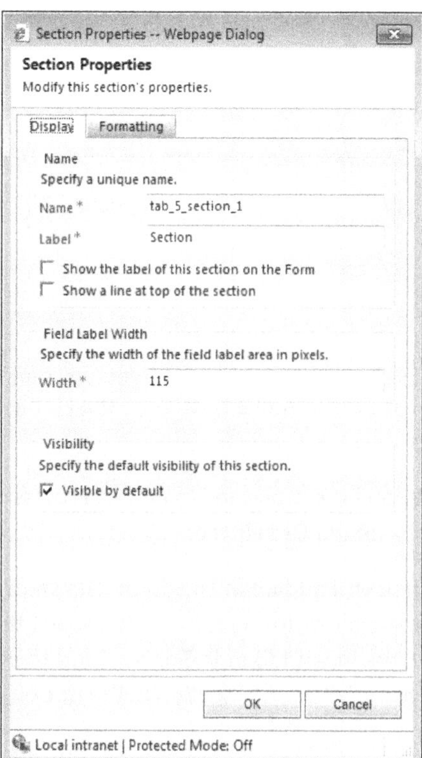

FIGURE 7-7 Section Properties dialog box

To remove a section, select the section and click the Remove button on the Home tab in the ribbon.

Important When designing your tabs and sections, pay close attention to the order of the fields in each section. You can use the Tab key to advance from one field to the next on the form. Microsoft Dynamics CRM moves the cursor from field to field down the column of a section, and then it moves to the top of the next column, working from left to right. When you reach the last field in a section, pressing the Tab key advances you to the upper-left field of the next section, either below or to the right of the section you are leaving. Consider this tab ordering when adding fields to a section so that sequential fields appear vertically.

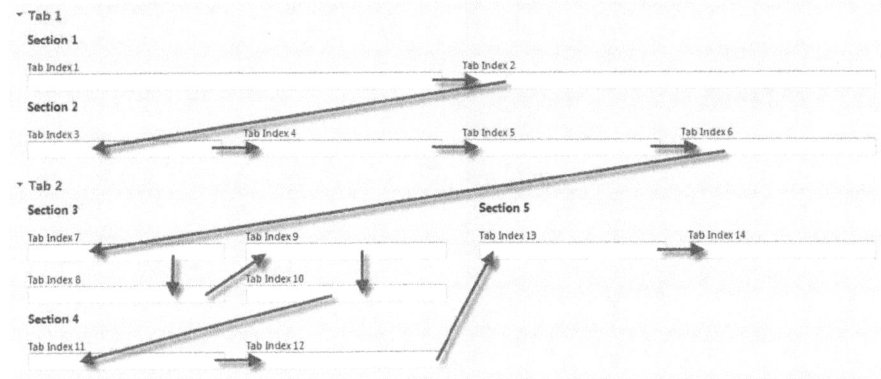

By clicking the Shift and Tab keys simultaneously, you can move back to the previous field on a form. These keyboard shortcuts allow you to enter data in forms faster, without requiring several mouse clicks.

Header

The form's header can display any field from the entity, including lookups, which will appear as hyperlinks so that you can quickly open the associated record. Although you cannot remove the header from a form, you can remove all of the fields in the header to reduce the amount of space the header consumes. To edit the header, click the Header button in the Select area of the ribbon's Home tab.

Headers have the following properties:

- **Width** Width of the field label area, specified in pixels.
- **Layout** The header can have up to four columns, and you can change the number of columns in the header at any time.
- **Field Label Alignment** Alignment of the field labels in the header, either left, right, or center.
- **Field Label Position** Position of the field labels in the header, either above or on the left side of the fields.

To edit the header properties, double-click the header in the form editor, or select the header and click the Change Properties button in the Home tab in the ribbon. The Header Properties dialog box is shown in Figure 7-8.

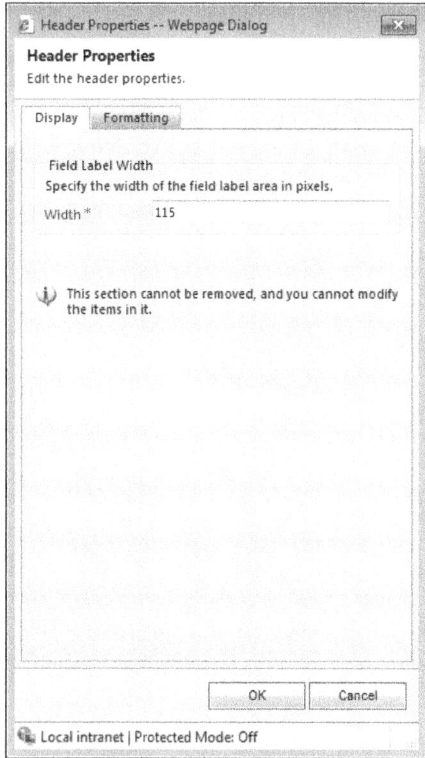

FIGURE 7-8 Header Properties dialog box

Footer

Footers work exactly like headers in that they can contain fields from the form's entity, cannot be removed, and can include the same types of controls. To edit the footer, click the Footer button in the Select area of the ribbon's Home tab and use the same steps described in the Header section.

Field Explorer

The Field Explorer is used to add fields to a form's body, header, and footer, as shown in Figure 7-9. In addition, you can create fields in the Field Explorer without having to navigate to the entity's Fields view by clicking the New Field button.

To add fields to the body, header, or footer of a form, click a section in the form editor or in the Select area of the ribbon's Home tab, and then drag a field from the Field Explorer list to the section.

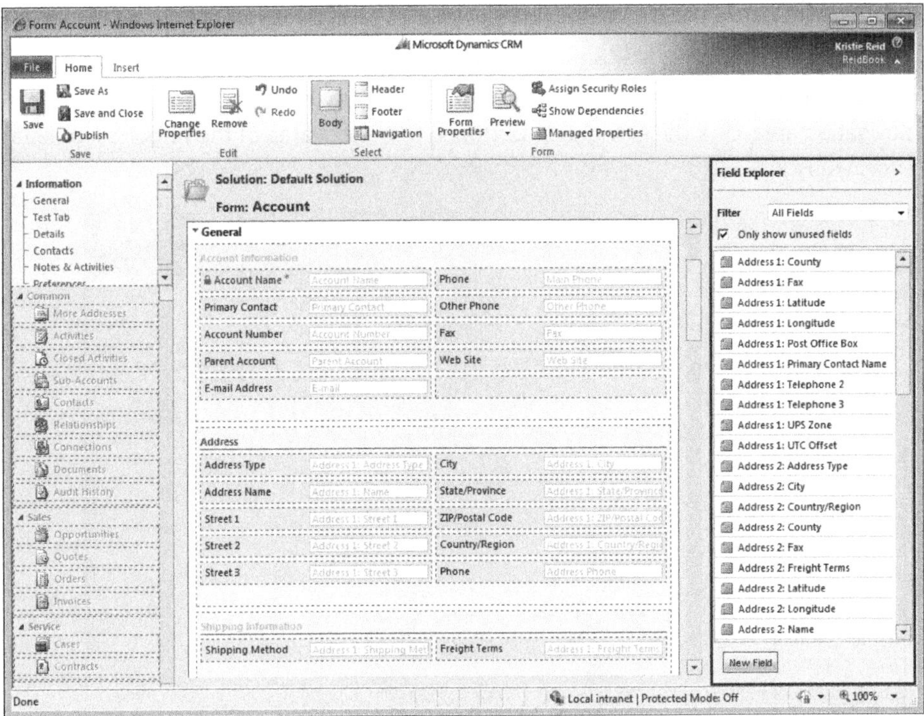

FIGURE 7-9 Field Explorer

Important After you add a tab, section, or field to a form, you can use the mouse to drag and drop the item to the desired position on the form. You can also use the arrow keys on your keyboard to perform the same actions. Select the tab, section, or field you want to move, and use the arrow keys to move the item to the appropriate area of the form.

In the Field Explorer, you also have the ability to select All Fields or Custom Fields from the Filter drop-down list. Selecting Custom Fields will narrow the list of fields that displays. Further, the fields list excludes the fields already on the form by default. If you need to add the same field multiple times on the form, the entire list of fields displays when you clear the *Only show unused fields* check box in the Field Explorer.

Note You might be wondering what happens to the values entered in an instance of a field that is displayed multiple times on a form. This would definitely be cause for concern if users were allowed to enter different values in each instance of the field. Fortunately, Microsoft Dynamics CRM prevents this scenario. When a field appears multiple times on a form, Microsoft Dynamics CRM updates all instances of the field with the value entered as soon as the user clicks out of the field.

Navigation

Unlike previous versions of the software, Microsoft Dynamics CRM 2011 allows you to change the items in the left navigation pane of an entity by using the form editor. To edit the navigation area, click the Navigation button in the Select area of the ribbon's Home tab, as shown in Figure 7-10.

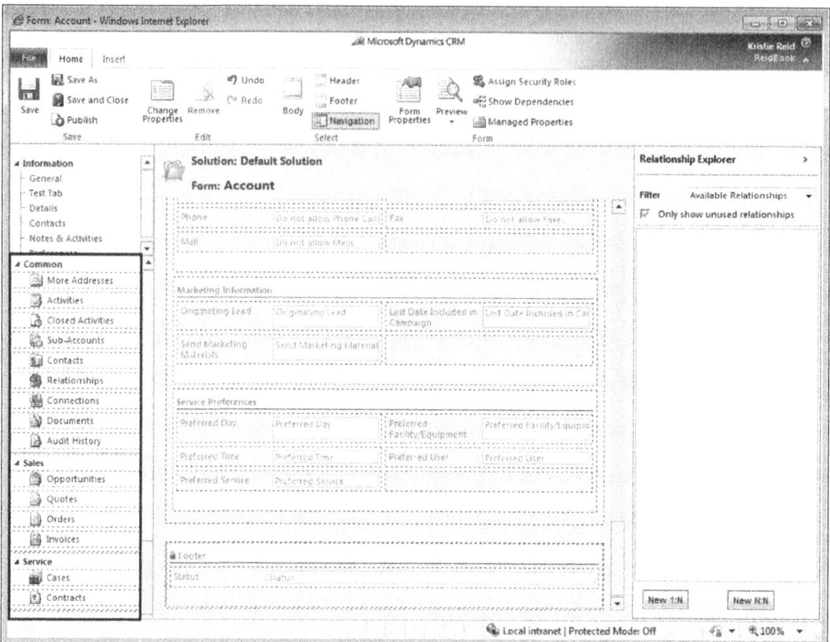

FIGURE 7-10 Form navigation

The navigation pane comprises of groups, relationships, and navigation links.

Groups A *group* is a collection of links under a shared heading. You can edit a group's name by double-clicking the group in the form editor or selecting the group and then clicking the Change Properties button in the ribbon's Home tab. The Group Name dialog box is shown in Figure 7-11.

FIGURE 7-11 Group Name dialog box

Relationships *Relationships* are links to the associated views of related entities accessed in a form's navigation pane. The default links included for each entity only appear for those users who have security rights to the related entity. However, you can remove relationship links for all users in the form editor. To do this, click the link and then click the Remove button in the ribbon's Home tab. When you remove a link to a related entity, you'll notice the relationship appears in the Relationship Explorer, so you can re-add it to the navigation pane later if necessary. Figure 7-12 shows the form editor after the More Addresses relationship is removed from the Account form.

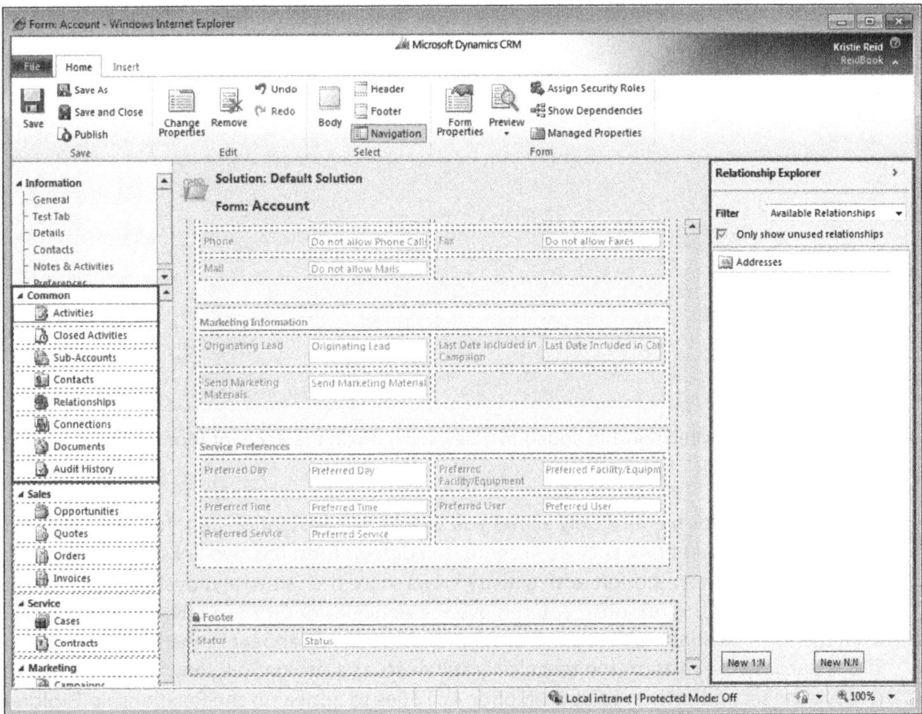

FIGURE 7-12 Account form with the Addresses relationship removed

In the Relationship Explorer, you also have the ability to create new 1:N and N:N relationships. This saves you time by allowing you to add relationships from the form editor, rather than navigating to the appropriate relationship view for the entity.

To add a relationship to the navigation, select the relationship and drag it back to the desired position in the navigation pane, as shown in Figure 7-13.

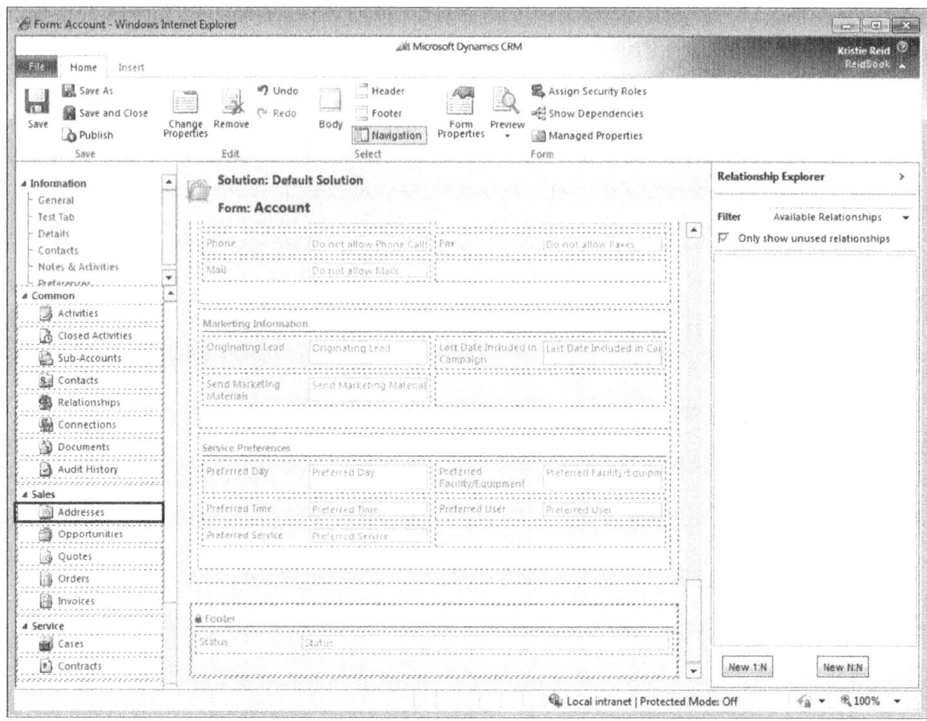

FIGURE 7-13 Addresses relationship added to a new location on the Account form

Important The form editor only allows you to add one navigation item for each relationship. However, on some entities, such as Account, the default form has two links for activities in the navigation pane, even though both activity views share the same relationship with the Activity Pointer entity. For this reason, if you remove the Activities or Closed Activities relationship link from the form navigation, the Activities relationship will not appear in the Relationship Explorer. This is because the relationship technically still exists as a navigation item. You also need to remove the second activity relationship for Activities to appear in the Relationship Explorer. Further, when you add the Activities relationship back to the navigation, only one relationship can be re-added, so be careful when removing the activity views from a form's navigation! Until the form editor is saved and closed, you can use the Undo button in the ribbon to undo this action. If the form is saved without these links and those links are needed at a later time, you must edit the form xml to retrieve them.

Navigation Links In addition to related entities, you can also add other navigation links to an entity's form, including web resources and external URLs. We'll discuss these options in more detail in the "Form Controls" section later in this chapter.

Mobile Form Customizations

When designing mobile forms, keep in mind the size of the screen that most users will see on their mobile devices. For example, it probably does not make sense to display all of the fields available on the Account form. Rather, you should display only the critical information that remote users need when they do not have access to the web or Outlook clients.

With this constraint in mind, Microsoft designed Mobile Express, a simple format of displaying fields in a single column to ensure the best user experience on most web-enabled mobile devices. Although there is no form editor for mobile forms, you can configure which fields are included on the form and reorder them. To edit a mobile form, navigate to the Form view of the appropriate entity and double-click the mobile form, as shown in Figure 7-14.

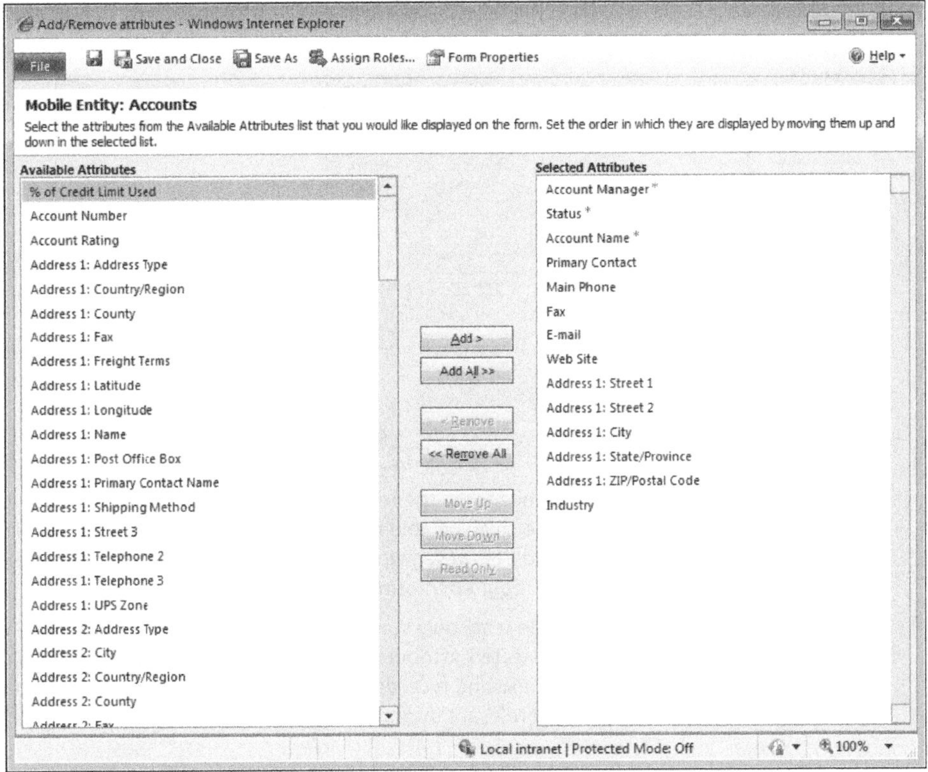

FIGURE 7-14 Mobile Entity field editor

To add a field to the mobile form, double-click the field in the Available Attributes list or highlight the field and click the Add button. You can use the Add, Add All, Remove, and Remove All buttons to change the fields that are displayed on the form.

After adding the fields you want to display to the Selected Attributes list, use the Move Up and Move Down buttons to change the order the fields appear in on the form. Remember, the mobile form simply lists each of the selected fields in a single column. You can also make a field read-only on the form by selecting the field and clicking the Read Only button. To make a read-only field editable, select the field and click the Read Only button again.

Note Fields that you mark as read-only on a mobile form appear in gray text with an icon indicating read-only status.

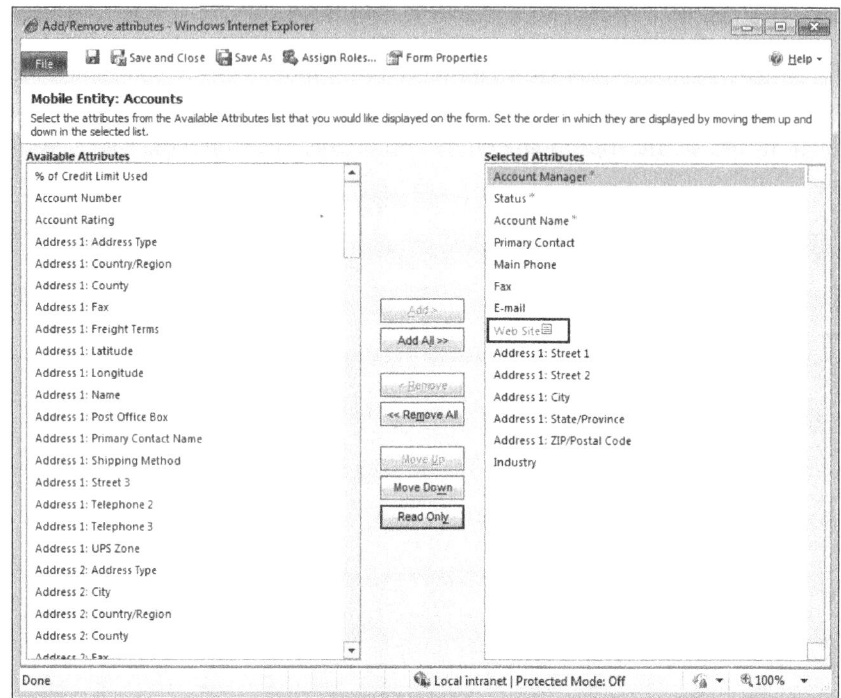

When a record is created from a mobile form, the read-only fields will not appear on the form, even if they are required. Further, users will be able to edit and save record without entering values in the required, read-only fields. However, when a user opens the record in the web or Outlook client, he must enter the required information before he can save the record.

Although required fields can be made read-only so that they do not display on the create form, they cannot be removed from the Selected Attributes list. Also, only fields that contain values will be displayed on the mobile form for existing records. These restrictions ensure the best mobile experience possible by only showing relevant information.

Form Actions

This section covers the following form actions:

- Modify Form Properties
- Preview a Form
- Assign Security Roles
- Show Dependencies
- Configure Managed Properties

As you have already seen, the way you configure main forms is different than how you customize the mobile form. The form actions available for each form type are also different. For the main forms, you can access all of these actions from the Home tab in the form ribbon. Mobile forms only have the Assign Roles and Form Properties options, which are accessible from the Add/Remove attribute dialog box. Assigning roles to mobile forms works like the main forms. You can only update the Form Name and Description on the form properties for mobile forms, which is very different than the main form as we discuss in this section.

Modify Form Properties

Form properties are broken into the following groups, which we'll review in the sections that follow:

- Events
- Display
- Parameters
- Non-Event Dependencies

The Form Properties dialog box is shown in Figure 7-15.

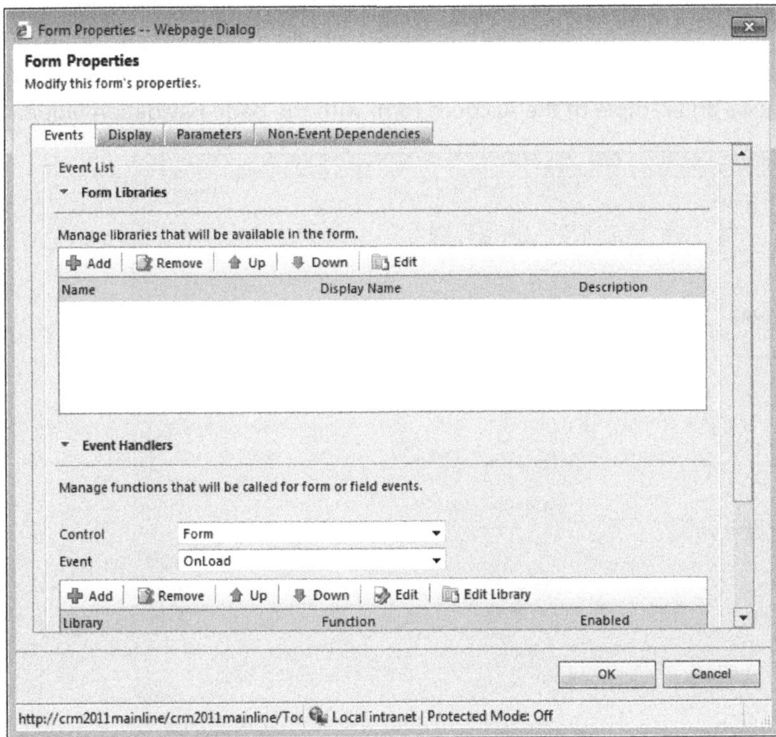

FIGURE 7-15 Form Properties dialog box

Events

Events allow you to add custom scripts to a form that runs on the client when key events occur on the form. Table 7-1 shows the form events and the related control for each.

TABLE 7-1 Form Event Types and Controls

Event	Control	Description
OnLoad	Form	Fires on the initial load of the form
OnSave	Form	Fires when the form is saved
TabStateChange	Tab	Occurs when a tab is expanded or collapsed
OnChange	Field	Triggered when a user changes the value of a field

Custom scripts must be created as web resources and then managed in a form's Form Libraries list. The Event Handlers allow you to specify how and when the code in the script will be executed—including whether the event that triggers the code is at the form, tab, or field level. When an event is assigned to a form, tab, or field, Microsoft Dynamics CRM creates a dependency on the script, which prevents you and other system customizers from accidentally removing a script-dependent control from the form.

Display

Forms have only a few display options. You can change the name and description of the form that appear in the Form views, which is important when managing multiple forms for an entity. You also can specify whether you want the navigation pane to appear on the form. Figure 7-16 shows an example of the Account form with the page navigation hidden.

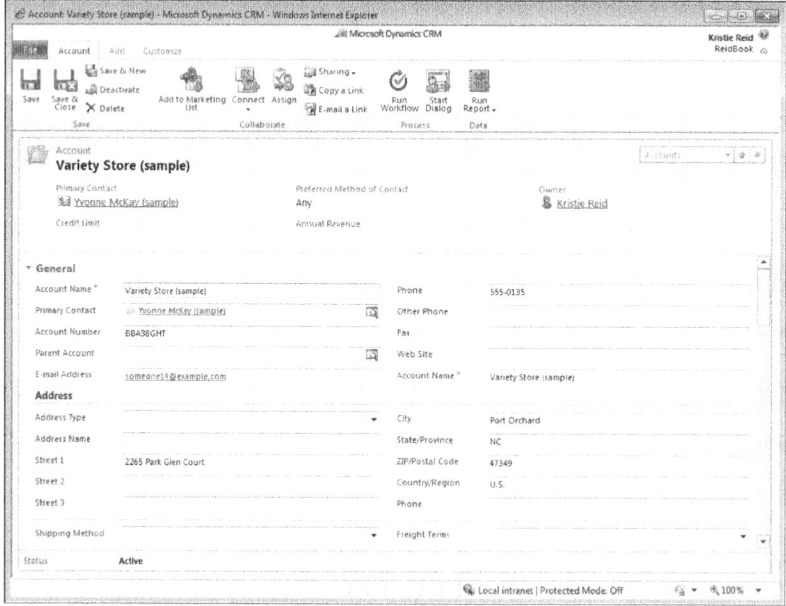

FIGURE 7-16 Account form with the navigation pane hidden

Parameters

Parameters are query string variables that can be used to pass details about the record in scripts and event handlers on the form to pass data to the form. You can create and modify a form's parameters from the Parameters tab in the Form Properties dialog box. Figure 7-17 shows a parameter on the Account form used to pass the credit check information being passed from an external application about the account into a custom field.

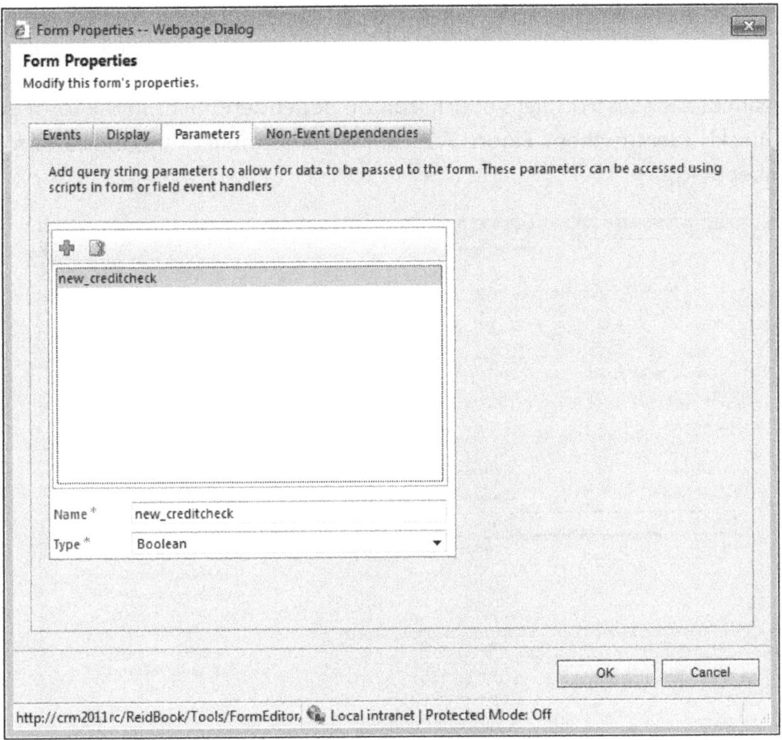

FIGURE 7-17 Parameters list in the Form Properties dialog box

Non-Event Dependencies

In addition to event-based scripts, you can add external scripts to a form. Because the external scripts are not based on one of the form events in Table 7-1, Microsoft Dynamics CRM does not automatically create dependencies on the fields required by the script, as it does for event-based scripts. Therefore, you should manually identify the dependent fields for external scripts. This is done on the Non-Event Dependencies tab in the Form Properties dialog box.

As mentioned earlier, if you or another system customizer tries to remove a field from a form that has dependencies, Microsoft Dynamics CRM prevents the field from being removed. Instead, the error message shown in Figure 7-18 is displayed.

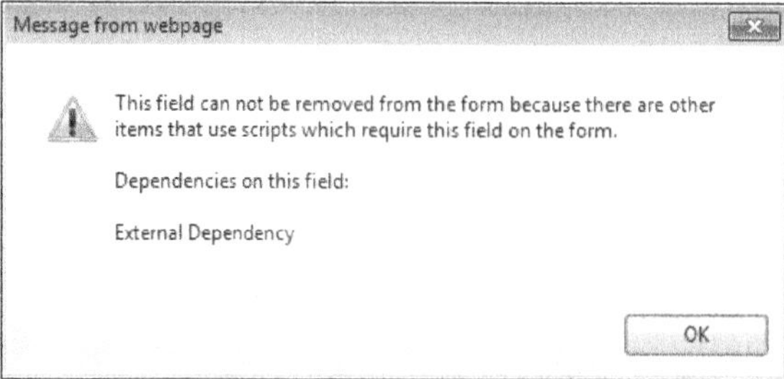

FIGURE 7-18 Error message displayed when a user tries to remove a dependent field from a form

Microsoft Dynamics CRM also displays a lock icon on dependent fields in the form editor so that you can quickly identify them. Figure 7-19 shows an example of this indicator for the Account Number field.

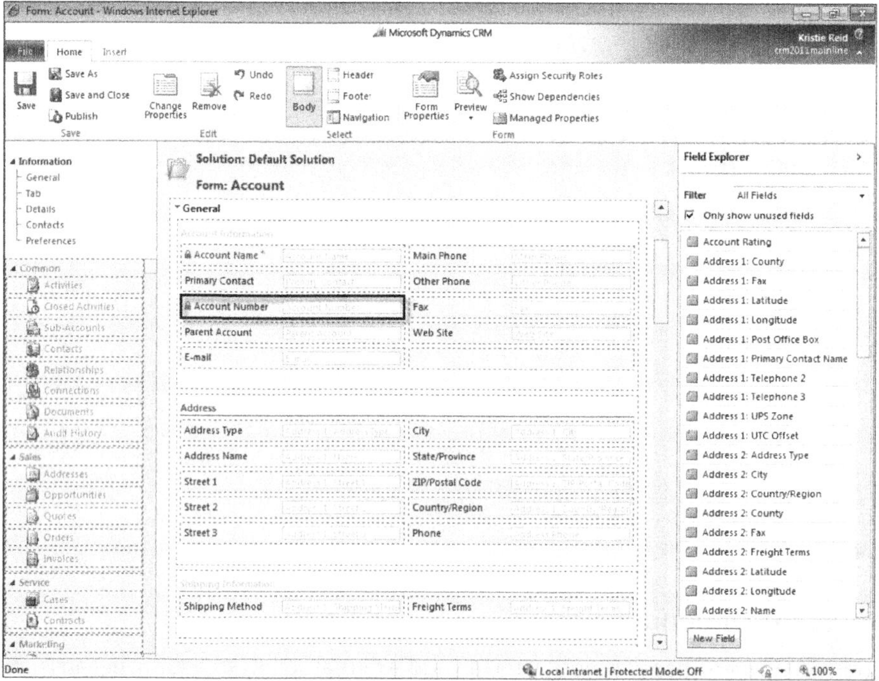

FIGURE 7-19 Locked icon on the Account Number field in the form editor

Tip Microsoft Dynamics CRM doesn't require you to specify dependent fields, but taking the extra time to complete this step can save you a headache later.

The properties of mobile forms only include the ability to update the name and description, as shown in Figure 7-20. You can access these properties from the Form Properties button in the mobile form editor.

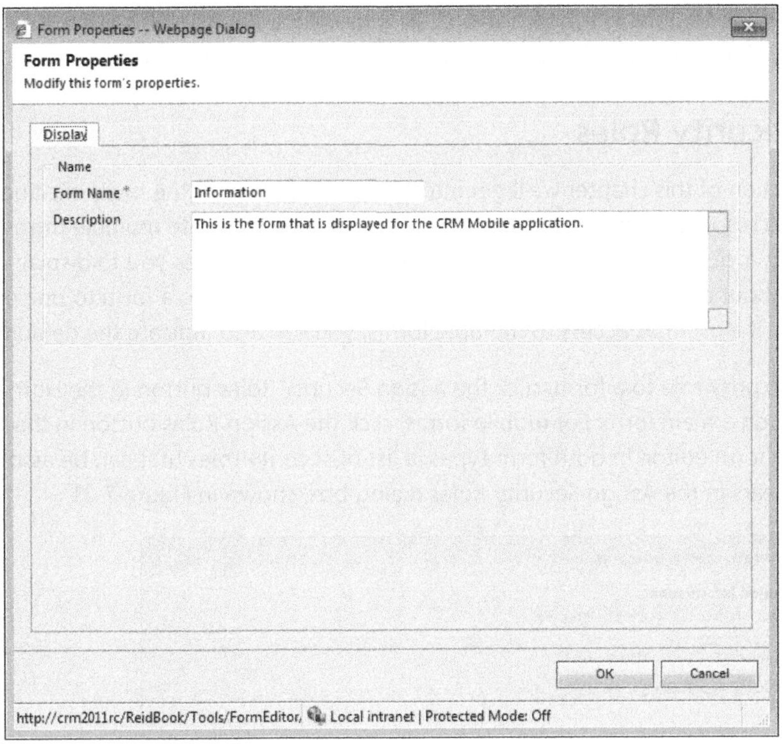

FIGURE 7-20 Mobile form properties

Preview a Form

When you've made changes to a form, you can preview the form to verify that the layout, fields, and labels are correct before publishing your changes. Microsoft Dynamics CRM offers the following types of form previews:

- **Create Form** Simulates how the form will appear and behave when users create a record for the entity
- **Update Form** Simulates how the form will appear and behave when users edit an existing record for the entity
- **Read-Only Form** Shows how the form will appear to users who do not have permissions to edit a record

The form preview feature does more than just show you the form layout—you can also test any custom scripts that you added to the form events listed in Table 7-1.

Obviously, being able to test and debug your event scripts using the preview tool can save you time. When you start the form preview, Microsoft Dynamics CRM fires the *onLoad* event. However, you cannot create a record in preview mode, so you need to use the Simulate Form

Save button in the toolbar to trigger the *onSave* form event. You can also fire the *onChange* field event by changing the field value and then clicking out of the field.

Assign Security Roles

In the last section of this chapter we'll get into the details of one of the more exciting features in Microsoft Dynamics CRM 2011, which allows you to create multiple forms for a single entity, including mobile forms. This powerful feature enables you to display different information about a record to different groups of users by assigning a form to one or more security roles. If a user has access to multiple forms, you can also indicate the default form.

To assign a security role to a form, click the Assign Security Roles button in the Home tab of the ribbon on a main form. For mobile forms, click the Assign Roles button in the toolbar of the mobile form editor. In both form types, a list of security roles that can be associated to the form appears in the Assign Security Roles dialog box, shown in Figure 7-21.

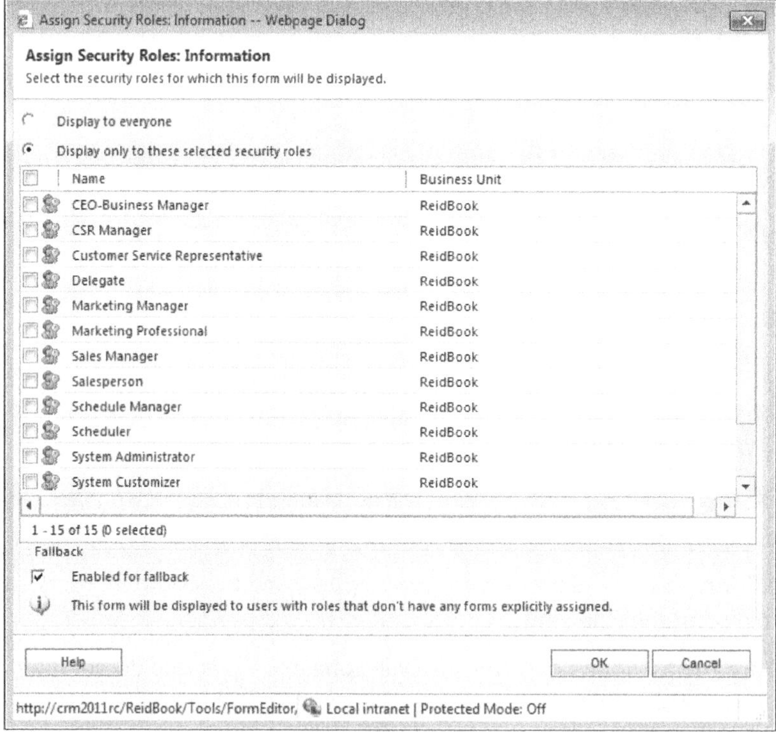

FIGURE 7-21 Assign Security Roles dialog box

In this dialog box, you can choose to display the form to everyone or select specific security roles that will have access to the form. In addition, you can indicate whether the form should be the default form or the fallback form, for users who do not have a form assigned to their security role. This option will only be enabled if more than one form of the same form type has been created.

> **Note** When security roles are copied, the permissions to forms are not replicated on the new role. Therefore, each time you create a security role, you need to add the role to the forms users with the role will need to access. Fortunately, Microsoft Dynamics CRM requires at least one form be enabled as the fallback, so as long as the security role contains permission to an entity, users with the role will be able to see the fallback form.

If a security role is assigned to multiple forms for the same entity, you need to make sure the form order is set appropriately, so the correct form appears when users with the role open a record. We will get into how this is handled later in this chapter.

Show Dependencies

As discussed in Chapter 5, "Solutions Overview and Concepts," Microsoft Dynamics CRM tracks dependencies to ensure that components used by other areas in the application are not deleted. You can view a form's dependencies by clicking the Show Dependencies button in the Home tab in the ribbon. The Form Dependencies dialog box displays the components dependent on the form as well as the required components on which the form depends, as shown in Figure 7-22.

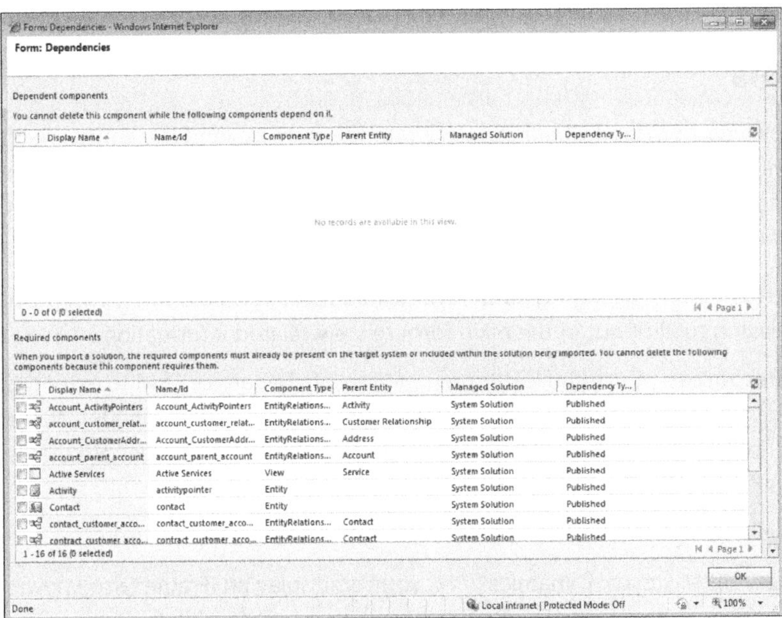

FIGURE 7-22 Form Dependencies dialog box

Configure Managed Properties

As you learned in Chapter 5 the *managed properties* of a solution or component allow you to control the customization of the item when it's installed in another Microsoft Dynamics CRM organization. Forms can also be managed, meaning you can prevent others from changing the layout, fields, and other form properties when the associated entity is imported into another organization. To mark the form as managed, click the Managed Properties button in the Home tab of the form ribbon and select whether the form should be customizable, as shown in Figure 7-23.

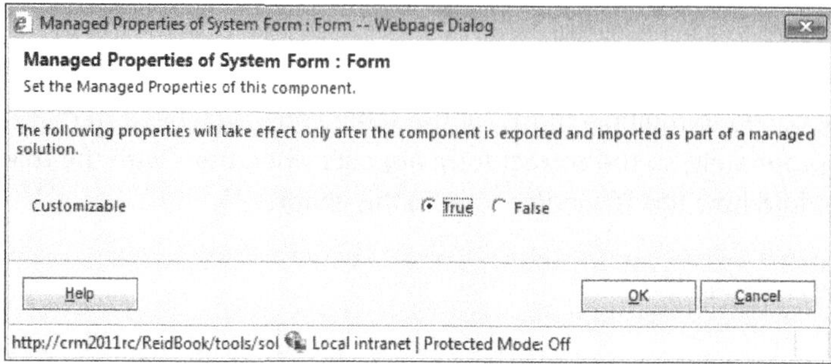

FIGURE 7-23 Managed Properties of System Form dialog box

When the Customizable field in a form's managed properties is set to False, users working in an environment where a managed solution including this form has been installed will not be able to change the form.

Form Controls

Controls allow you to extend what is displayed on the form beyond the entity's fields. By using controls, you can display anything from related records to other websites or data from other applications, all within the familiar user interface of Microsoft Dynamics CRM. The types of controls you can add to forms include:

- **Sub-grids** Grids displaying data from related records on the form. This prevents users from having to click out of the main form to view related information.
- **Web Resources** Custom files stored in Microsoft Dynamics CRM to extend the appearance and functionality of Microsoft Dynamics CRM, including HTML files, JavaScript, static images, and Silverlight applications. Web resources are discussed in detail in Chapter 11.
- **Spacers** Blank spaces used when designing the layout of forms.
- **IFrames** In Microsoft Dynamics CRM, you can display an IFrame (also known as an inline frame) on a form. Think of an IFrame as a "window" in the form that you can use to display a different web page inside the window frame. We explain IFrames in more detail and give examples later in this chapter.
- **Notes** List of the notes related to the record on the form. This option is only available if a Notes control does not already exist on the form.
- **Navigation Link** Links available in the navigation pane, including web resources and external URLs. This option is only available when you are editing the navigation area.

Not all of these controls can be used in all of the form sections. Table 7-2 shows the different control types and where within the user interface you are able to add the control.

TABLE 7-2 Form Event Types and Controls

Control	Body	Header	Footer	Navigation
Sub-grid	X			
Web Resource	X	X	X	
Spacer	X	X	X	
IFrame	X	X	X	
Notes	X			
Navigation Link				X

Let's look in more detail at how to use each control type. You can access the controls from the Insert tab of the form ribbon, as shown in Figure 7-24.

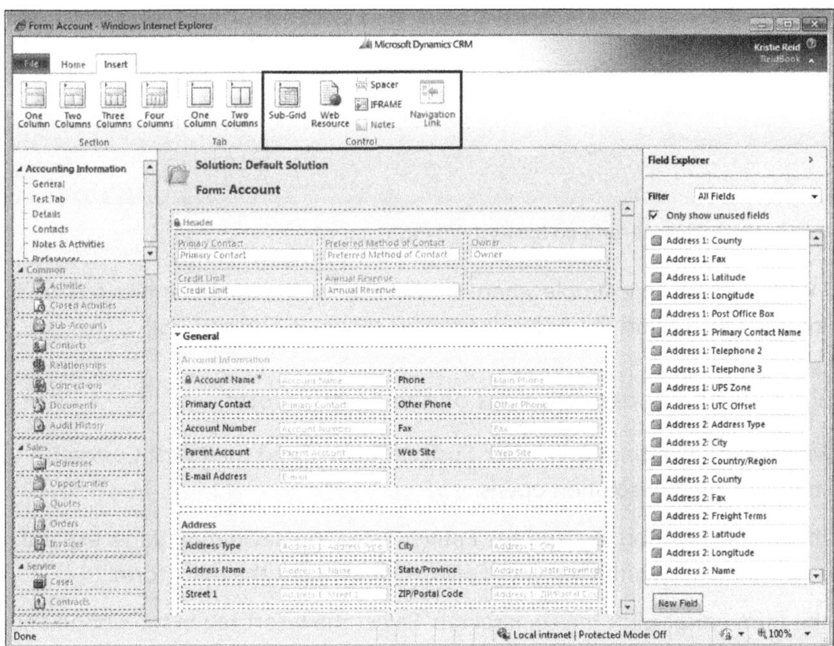

FIGURE 7-24 Form controls in the ribbon

Sub-grids

A *sub-grid* displays a view of related records or charts for the record type or related record types directly on a form. This allows users to see additional information about the record they are on without having to click in the navigation area, therefore leaving the information they were viewing on the form. In addition to the convenience of the display, users can also take action on records within that sub-grid directly from the ribbon on the form, as shown in Figure 7-25.

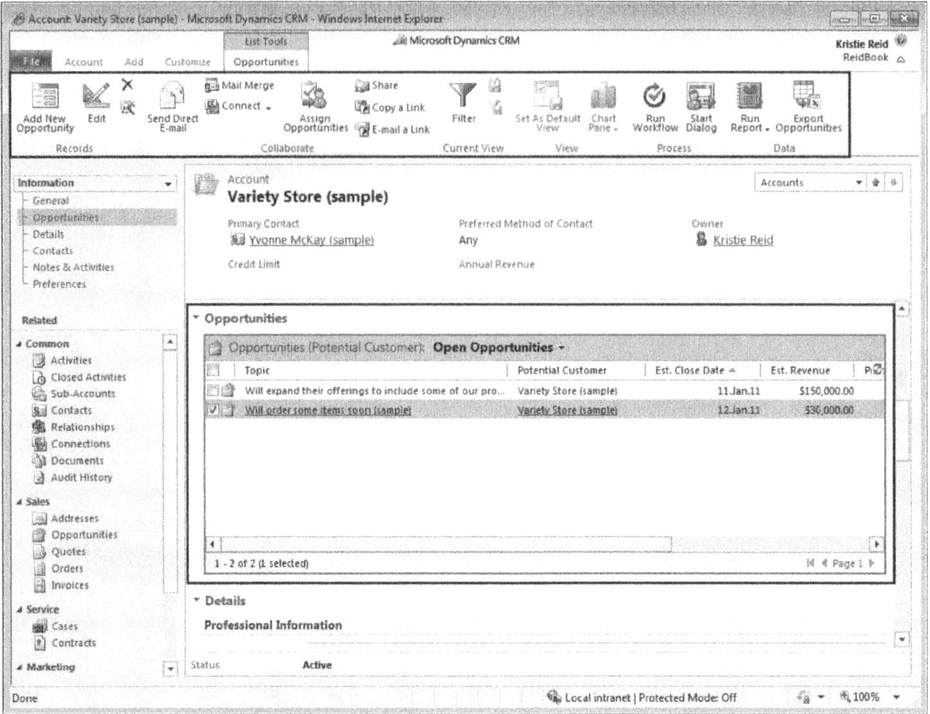

FIGURE 7-25 Opportunities sub-grid on the Account form

Let's first walk through an example where we will display the opportunities related to an account in a sub-grid on the Account form, as shown in Figure 7-25.

Creating a sub-grid of opportunities on the Account form

1. Navigate to the Settings area, click Customizations, and then click Customize the System. The default solution opens.
2. In the default solution, expand the Entities list in the navigation pane, expand the Account entity, and then click Forms. Double-click the main form.
3. In the form editor, click the General tab. Select the Insert tab in the ribbon and click the One Column button in the Tab section to add a new tab directly under the General tab.
4. Double-click the new tab and enter **Opportunities** in the Label field. Click OK.
5. With the tab still selected, click the Sub-Grid button in the Control section of the ribbon.
6. Enter **OpenOpportunities** in the Name field. In the Data Source area, select Opportunities (Potential Customer) as the entity, and then select Open Opportunities as the Default View. Click OK.

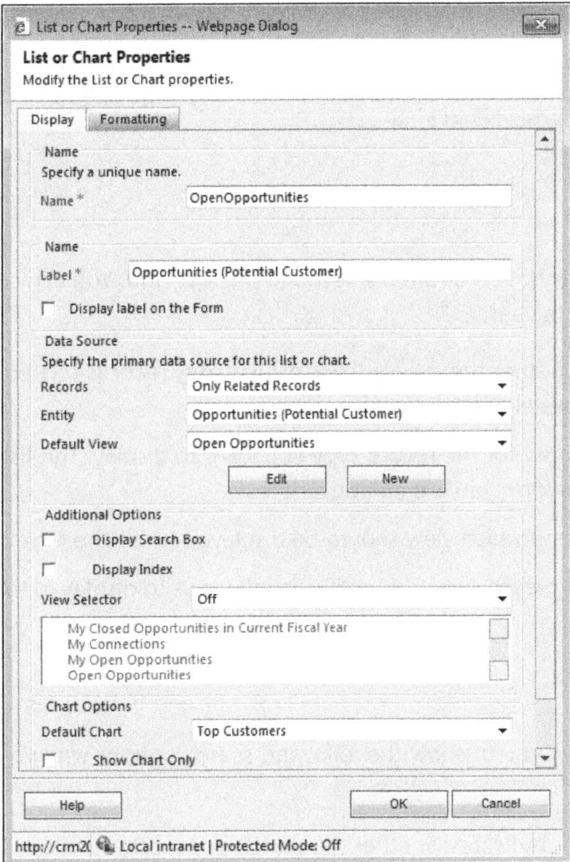

7. In the Home tab of the ribbon, click Save and then click Publish.

Your sub-grid now appears on the Account form. Let's review the properties you can configure for the sub-grid.

Name

Each sub-grid must have a unique name. The name must start with an alphabetic character and cannot contain spaces or special characters, with the exception of underscores.

Label

In addition to a unique name, you must provide a label for each sub-grid. You also have the option of hiding the label on the form.

The label will display automatically on the form when the View Selector in the Additional Options area is changed to Show All Views or Show Selected Views.

Note Sub-grid labels don't work exactly as you might expect. The label only appears on the form when the View Selector in the Additional Options area is changed to Show All Views or Show Selected Views. If the View Selector is not enabled for the sub-grid, the label only appears in the form editor, not in the published form.

Data Source

The *data source* defines which records are displayed in the sub-grid. You can configure the following details for the data source:

- **Records** Indicate whether the sub-grid will display only records related to the record or all records from the selected entity.
- **Entity** Select the entity for the record type you want to display. This list will include all entities related to the form you are editing.
- **Default View** Indicate which view should be displayed when the form is opened.

You also have the ability to create views and edit existing views to display in the sub-grid.

Additional Options

The additional options allow you to show the following search options with your sub-grid:

- **Display Search Box** Indicates whether the search box located in the upper-right corner of the view will be displayed. The search box allows you to quickly find records using text searches. This option will not be available if you select the Show Chart Only option in the Chart Options area.
- **Display Index** Indicates whether the index located at the bottom of the view will be displayed. The index bar allows you to find records by the first letter of the primary sort column. This option will not be available if you select the Show Chart Only option in the Chart Options area.
- **View Selector** Indicates whether the view selector located next to the view label will be displayed. The view selector allows you to switch the view displayed in the sub-grid. You have the option to turn the view selector off, show all views associated with the entity selected as the data source, or only show views selected in the list of available views.

The configurable search options in a sub-grid are shown in Figure 7-26.

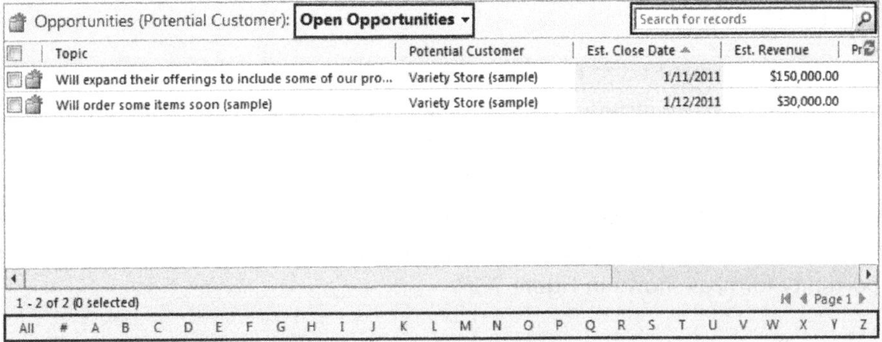

FIGURE 7-26 Additional search options in the Opportunities sub-grid

Chart Options

You can also display a chart in the sub-grid, assuming one exists for the related entity selected in the data source. You can configure the following options when displaying a chart in a sub-grid:

- **Default Chart** Identifies the default chart that will be displayed when the form is opened. You can select from any of the charts created for the entity selected in the data source.
- **Show Chart Only** Indicates whether the sub-grid area will display only the chart, or the data grid and the chart. This option only appears if charts have been created for the entity selected in the data source.
- **Display Chart Selection** Indicates whether users will be able to change the chart displayed in the sub-grid.

Layout

Similar to tabs and sections, you can configure the layout of the sub-grid to specify the number of columns it will span.

Row Layout

You can also specify the number of rows the sub-grid will span. You can automatically expand the rows to use the available space. If you select this option, the form will override the number of rows you specify and expand depending on the number of records in the view. This option is not available if the Show Chart Only option is selected in the Chart Options area.

Web Resources

Web resources can be used to extend the appearance and functionality of Microsoft Dynamics CRM and can include HTML files, JavaScript, static images, and Silverlight applications. We discuss the details of web resources in Chapter 11. Without getting into specifics about web resources, let's walk through a simple example of how to add a web resource to a form. In the following example, we'll add a diagram of the sales process to the header of the Opportunity form. The sales process image appears in the header of the Opportunity form, as shown in Figure 7-27.

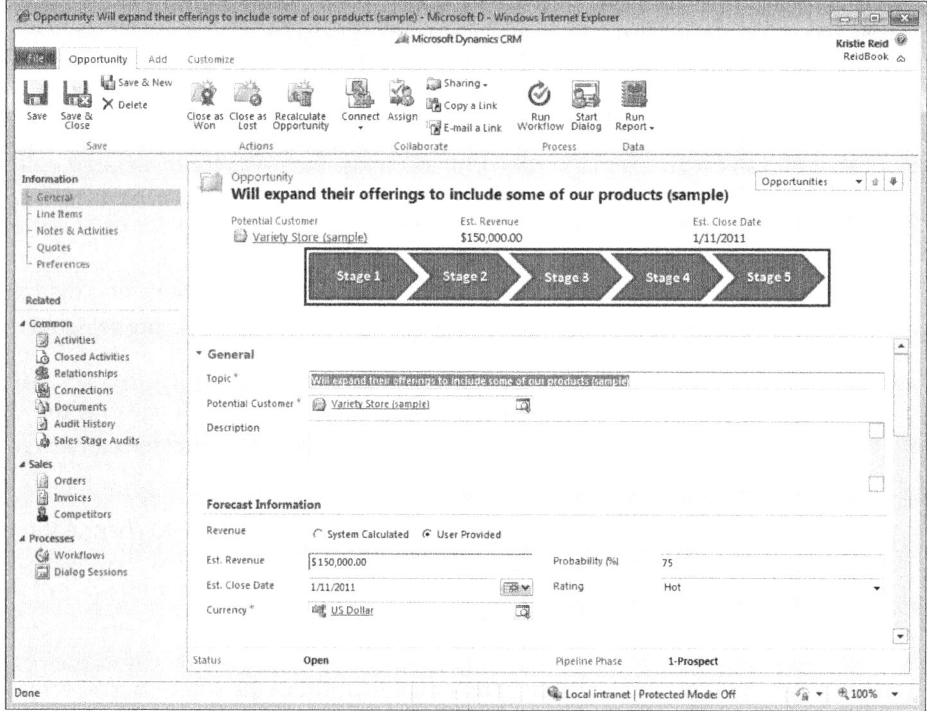

FIGURE 7-27 Web resource image added to the Opportunity form header

Adding a graphic web resource to the Opportunity header

1. Navigate to the Settings area, click Customizations, and then click Customize the System. The default solution opens.
2. In the default solution, expand the Entities list, expand the Opportunity entity, and then click Forms. Open the main form.
3. On the main form, click the Header button in the ribbon. Click the Insert tab on the ribbon and click the Web Resource button.

4. Click the web resource lookup and select New on the Look Up Record dialog box. Type **Opp_Process** in the Name field, type **Opportunity Process** in the Display Name, and type **Diagram of the opportunity process** in the Description fields.
5. Select the type of the image file in the Type drop-down list. Select the file location by using the Browse button and navigating to where the image is.
6. Double-click the image file or select the file and click Open. Save and close the Web Resource dialog box. Select OK on the Look Up Record dialog box.
7. Enter **OpportunityProcess** in the Name field of the Add Web Resource dialog box and type **Opportunity Process** as the label. Click the Formatting tab and update the Number of Rows to **2**. Change the Size option to Original Image Size (the original size of our image is 572 × 51 pixels). Click OK.

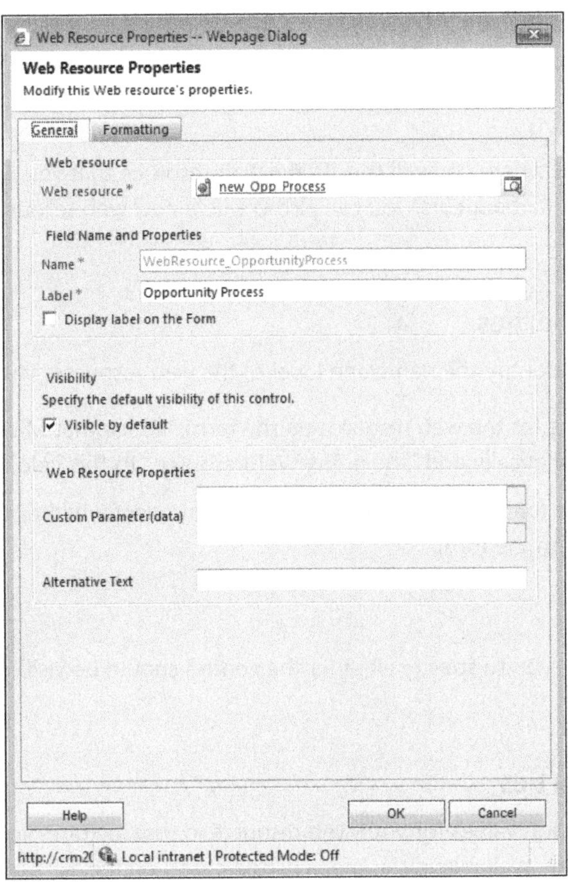

8. In the Home tab of the ribbon, click Save and then click Publish.

Similar to sub-grids, you can configure a number of options to ensure that your web resources display as you want them to on your form, including:

- Web Resource
- Field Name and Properties
- Visibility
- Properties
- Layout and Row Layout
- Scrolling
- Border
- Image Appearance
- Dependencies

Web Resource

The web resource lookup is where you will specify the web resource that you want to use on the form. From the lookup that appears, you can also create a new web resource as you are customizing the form.

Field Name and Properties

This section allows you to identify the name and label of the web resource. More specifically:

- **Name** Unique name for the web resource on the form. Notice that Microsoft Dynamics CRM automatically adds the prefix WebResource_ to this field.
- **Label** Display name for the web resource. You also can select whether the label should be displayed on the form.

Visibility

The visibility section allows you to specify whether the control should be visible by default on the form.

Web Resource Properties

You can provide configuration values for your web resource in the Custom Parameter (data) area. Notice that the options available in this area change based on the type of web resource you are using in the control. Figure 7-28 shows custom parameters from the Account entity that will be passed to an HTML web resource.

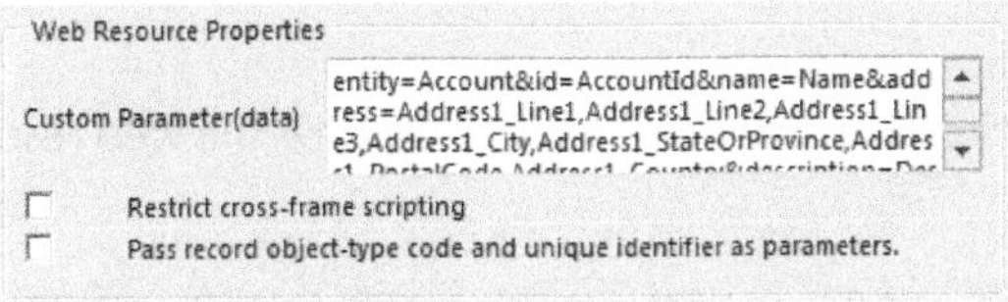

Web Resource Properties

Custom Parameter(data) entity=Account&id=AccountId&name=Name&address=Address1_Line1,Address1_Line2,Address1_Line3,Address1_City,Address1_StateOrProvince,Addres

Restrict cross-frame scripting

Pass record object-type code and unique identifier as parameters.

FIGURE 7-28 Custom parameters for the Account entity

You can restrict cross-frame scripting and the pass record's object-type code and unique identifiers as parameters when using an HTML web resource. We get into more details about cross-frame scripting and passing object-type codes when we discuss IFrames later in this chapter.

Layout and Row Layout

Similar to the sub-grid control, you can configure the number of columns a web resource control spans. The number of columns will be limited to the number of columns specified as the layout of the tab, header, or footer in which you are adding the web resource.

You can also specify the number of rows the web resource will span, just as with the sub-grid control.

Scrolling

You can configure the scrolling type for each web resource. *Scrolling* refers to adding a scroll bar to the web resource so that users can move the page up and down in the web resource. The three scrolling options are:

- **As Necessary** Microsoft Dynamics CRM automatically determines whether it needs to add scroll bars. If the content in the web resource takes more vertical (or horizontal) space than the web resource offers, Microsoft Dynamics CRM adds scroll bars.
- **Always** Microsoft Dynamics CRM always includes horizontal and vertical scroll bars.
- **Never** Microsoft Dynamics CRM never includes horizontal and vertical scroll bars.

We recommend that you leave the default option, As Necessary, selected. This option will not display with all web resource types.

Border

You can display a small, one-pixel-wide, gray border around the web resource. This border exactly matches the style of the border that surrounds each of the fields on the form. This option will not display with all web resource types.

Image Appearance

The image appearance provides additional options for configuring how the web resource displays on the form, including:

- **Vertical alignment** Select top, middle, or bottom.
- **Horizontal alignment** Select right, center, or left.
- **Size** Choose to use available area (stretch to fit), use available area (lock aspect ratio), original image size, and specific size. If you select specific size, you will have the option to enter the width and height in pixels. This option will not display with all web resource types.

Dependencies

If you use scripts in your web resource that reference fields on the form, you can specify those fields in the Dependencies tab. This prevents you from accidentally removing dependent fields from the form. This tab will not display with all web resource types.

Spacers

Spacers provide better control over the layout of your form. For example, if you have a section with two columns and three rows and you want the first row of the second column to be blank, you could use a spacer to ensure that nothing appears in that area. Adding spacers is handled similarly to how you add fields, but from the control area of the ribbon rather than from the Field Explorer.

Notes

The notes control is available on all customizable forms for entities that have Notes enabled, which must be done when the entity is created. For additional information on creating custom entities, see Chapter 10, "Entity Customization: Custom Entities and Activities." You can add only one notes control to each form. To do this, simply drag and drop the notes component into any tab in the body of the form.

IFrame

IFrames open a number customization and integration options. Conceptually, an IFrame creates a window within a web page that displays a second web page. IFrames can display any web page, whether it is hosted on your Microsoft Dynamics CRM server or elsewhere. An example of an IFrame that displays a map website on the Account form is shown in Figure 7-29.

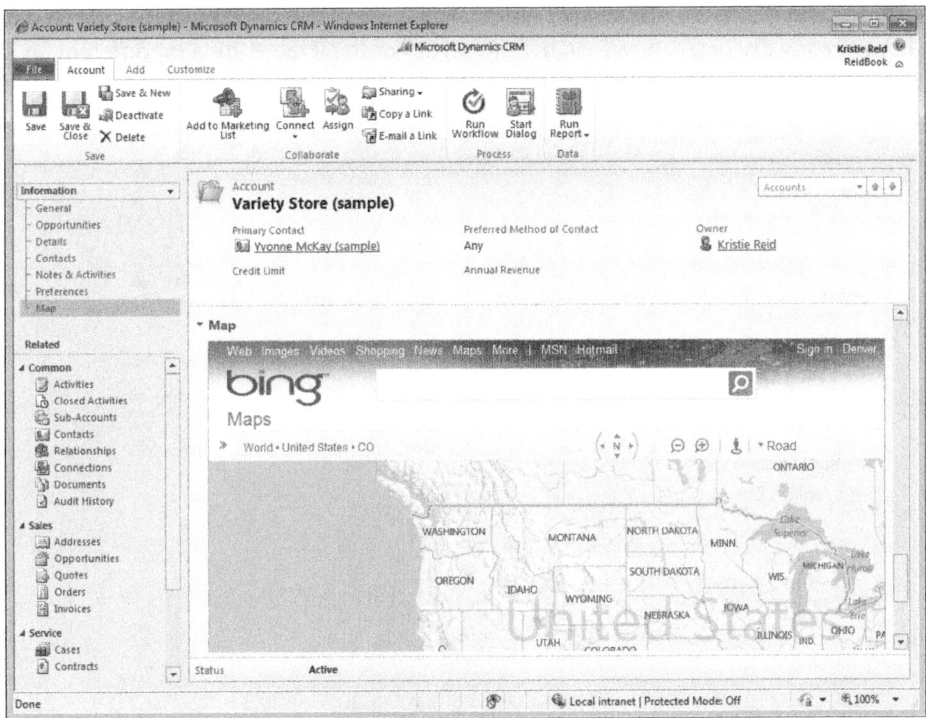

FIGURE 7-29 IFrame on the Account form that references Bing Maps

Although this is a very simple example, the key concept is that you can display non–Microsoft Dynamics CRM content *within the context of a record's form* by using an IFrame. Potential uses for an IFrame on a form include:

- Displaying external websites
- Displaying your own custom web pages
- Displaying other websites on your intranet

The most important feature of the IFrame capability is that Microsoft Dynamics CRM can automatically append the IFrame URL with additional information from Microsoft Dynamics CRM, such as the record type, GUID, organization name, and language preference. By taking advantage of the additional dynamic information in the URL, you can display web content in the IFrame that is unique to the record you are looking at, instead of displaying a generic resource.

Tip Each IFrame references a URL. Typically, this is a website, but URLs can also be used to reference images, documents, and other files in your network or on the Internet. You can also specify protocols other than Hypertext Transfer Protocol (HTTP), such as Secure HTTP (HTTPS) or File Transfer Protocol (FTP).

The steps to create an IFrame are similar to the sub-grid and web resource controls that we have already discussed; however, the properties of the IFrame are a bit different, as shown in Figure 7-30.

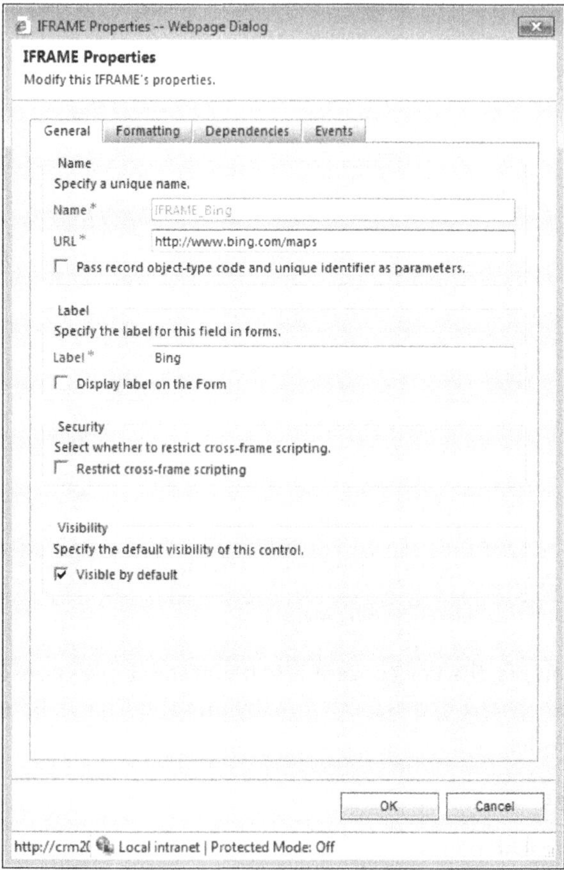

FIGURE 7-30 IFrame Properties dialog box

Name

As with other controls, you must specify a name and label for the IFrame. In addition to these values, you also need to enter the URL.

- **Name** Notice that Microsoft Dynamics CRM automatically prefixes the value *IFrame_* to your IFrame's name. Unlike the attribute schema prefix that you can configure, you cannot alter this value. After you create an IFrame, you cannot change its name.
- **URL** In the URL field, enter the address of the web page or resource that you want to reference in the IFrame. You can specify a full URL (including the *http://*) or a relative URL.

- **Parameters** You also have the option to pass record object-type code and unique identifier as parameters. When this option is selected, Microsoft Dynamics CRM appends query string parameters to the IFrame URL. Table 7-3 shows how an IFrame URL would appear for a sample record with and without parameters.

Tip You can view the full URL of an IFrame that you create by right-clicking in the IFrame and clicking Properties.

TABLE 7-3 Passing Parameters to IFrames

Parameters passed?	URL of the resource displayed in the IFrame
No	*http://www.adatum.com/sample.aspx*
Yes	*http://www.adatum.com/sample.aspx?id=%7bABE4D7F7-F011-E011-9C74-5C260AFC36D8%7d&orglcid=1033&orgname=ReidBook&type=1&typename=account&userlcid=1033*

You can see that passing parameters appends the following data to the URL query string:

- ***id*** Displays the globally unique identifier, or GUID, of the current record.
- ***orglcid*** Displays the language code ID for the organization.
- ***orgname*** Displays the organization name.
- ***type*** Every Microsoft Dynamics CRM entity has a corresponding object type code that references entities (for example, 1 = Account, 2 = Contact, and so on).
- ***typename*** Displays the user-friendly entity name.
- ***userlcid*** Displays the language code ID for the user. For example, user language code 1033 stands for U.S. English.

With all of this additional information in the URL query string, you can tell exactly which record the user is looking at, which organization the user belongs to, the user's preferred language, and the organization's default language. From here, you can design your own custom web pages that take advantage of this query string information to render information relevant to the record the user is viewing. We also want to highlight the fact that even though Table 7-3 shows a custom .aspx page, you don't need to create custom web pages using Microsoft technology. The Microsoft Dynamics CRM IFrame can append the parameters to any type of URL, so you can create custom pages using the web development platform of your choice.

Important By passing parameters to IFrames, you can create custom web pages that dynamically update to display data related to the open record. Your custom web page must retrieve data from the additional query string parameters and update the web page display accordingly.

Security

Because IFrames typically display content from other websites, scripts from the other websites could run and perform malicious or unintended behavior in Microsoft Dynamics CRM. By default, Microsoft Dynamics CRM blocks cross-frame scripting. For the most part, you should leave the Restrict cross-frame scripting option selected unless you know that you need to allow cross-frame scripting.

Visibility

The visibility section allows you to specify whether the control should be visible by default on the form.

Layout and Row Layout

You can configure the number of columns and rows the IFrame will span. The column layout will be limited to the number of columns specified in the layout of the tab, header, or footer in which you added the IFrame.

Formatting

Formatting of IFrames is exactly like the formatting options available in web resources, including scrolling and border.

Dependencies

Dependencies also match the functionality of web resources and can be added to ensure that you do not accidentally remove fields that the IFrame is dependent on from the form.

Events

Events on IFrames act similarly to those on fields, which you can read more about in Chapter 11. The main difference is that the event option available on IFrames is the *OnReadyStateComplete* event. This event fires when the IFrame content has finished loading.

Navigation Links

Navigation links appear in the navigation area. In addition to relationships which we've already covered, navigation links can also display web resources or external URLs. You would want to use a navigation link rather than adding a web resource or IFrame to an external website on the form for two reasons. First, using navigation links can increase performance when the form loads. All of the components that are displayed on tabs in a form load when a record is opened, but content in navigation links is only displayed when the link is clicked. In addition, navigation links can be arranged with the other groups in the navigation pane.

Instead of creating an IFrame to show the map website referenced in the previous example, let's use navigation links to link the map content in the Account form. The result is shown in Figure 7-31.

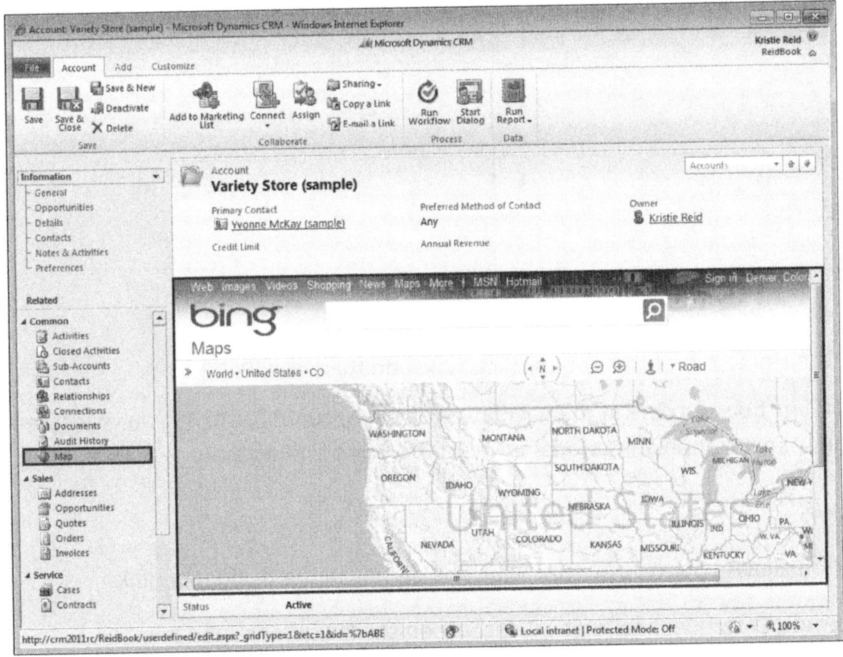

FIGURE 7-31 Navigation link on the Account form

Adding a navigation link

1. Navigate to the Settings area, click Customizations, and then select Customize the System. The default solution opens.
2. In the default solution, expand the Entities list, expand the Account entity, and then click Forms. Open the main form.
3. On the main form, click the Navigation button in the ribbon. Click the Insert tab on the ribbon and then click the Navigation Link button.
4. Type **Map** in the Name field.
5. Click the Icon lookup and select New in the Look Up Record dialog box. Type **Map** in the Name field, type **Map** in the Display Name, and type **Icon for Map navigation link** in the Description fields. Select the type of the image file in the Type drop-down list. Select the file location using the Browse button and navigating to where the image is (the size of our image is 16 × 16 pixels and has a transparent background). Double-click the image file or select the file and click Open. Save and close the Web Resource dialog box. Click OK on the Look Up Record dialog box.

6. In the Specify an existing Web Resource or external URL area of the Navigation Link Properties dialog box, select External URL and type **http://www.bing.com/maps/**. Click OK.

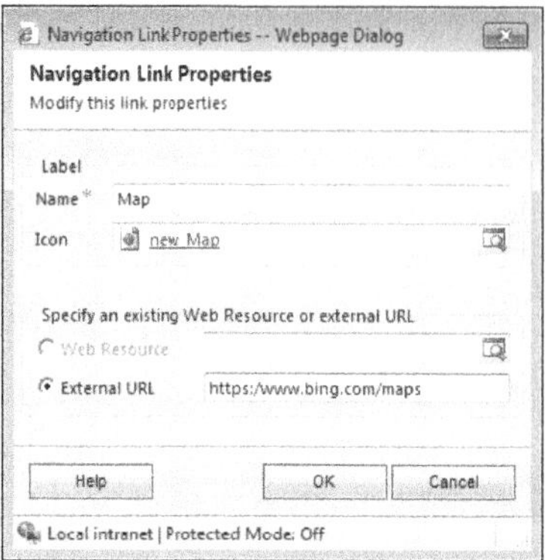

7. In the Home tab of the ribbon, click Save and then click Publish.

The Maps link now appears in the navigation of the Account form. As you've just seen, the properties of navigation links are fairly straightforward and include:

Label

This section allows you to customize what will display in the navigation link.

- **Name** Enter the label that will display on the link.
- **Icon** Select an icon that will display to the left of the label, so that the style of the link matches that of the relationships. As with other images you can use, remember that you must create the image as a web resource to use it in a link.

Specify an Existing Web Resource or External URL

This section allows you to customize what will display in the navigation link.

- **Web Resource** Select a web resource in the lookup.
- **External URL** Enter the external URL you want to load when users select the navigation link. You will need to enter the full URL (for example, **http://www.bing.com/maps/**).

As you can see, you have extensive options to manipulate your forms to meet the needs of your organization. Now let's look at how to use multiple forms to meet the needs of different groups in your user base.

Using Multiple Forms

Not surprisingly, different groups in an organization want to track different things about their customers. Enabling those groups to track the information relevant to their work while maintaining a single data repository for reports can lead to the creation of a lot of fields, all of which need to be entered on a form. The upside to using Microsoft Dynamics CRM is that you have the flexibility to do just that—reducing, if not eliminating, the need for people to store data in other locations. The downside is that having all of those fields on a single form could lead to information overload, a surefire way to hinder user adoption.

Instead of information overload, imagine being able to display only the data that each user group needs on a form. Microsoft Dynamics CRM 2011 introduces the support of multiple forms for each entity. This concept is available both through the main interface as well as on mobile devices.

> **Important** Notice that we have not mentioned security to data in this discussion. It is important to keep in mind that even though a user is not able to see a field on a form, she might still have permissions to see the data in that field through views, including those created through Advanced Find, and reports. If you need to restrict users from seeing data, you can use Field Level Security, which is covered in Chapter 3, "Managing Security and Information Access."

In this section, we will cover three components that you should be aware of when designing multiple forms:

- Creating multiple forms
- Ordering forms
- Viewing entities with forms

The fourth and final critical design element is applying security roles to each form, which we covered earlier in this chapter.

Creating Multiple Forms

You have two options to create a form. You can create a form from scratch or you can copy an existing form using the Save As button on the form ribbon. Let's walk through each of these options.

Creating a new Account form

1. Navigate to the Settings area, click Customizations, and then click Customize the System. The default solution opens.
2. In the default solution, expand the Entities list, expand the Account entity, and then click Forms.
3. Click the New button in the grid toolbar and select Main as the form type.
4. Click the Form Properties button in the ribbon and enter a name and description in the Form Properties dialog box.
5. After you have made the appropriate changes, save and publish the form.

You will notice that the new form that you create will be an exact copy, including any components you have added, of the default form for that entity. If the form you are creating should more closely match a custom form that you have created for that entity, you also can make a copy of the form. This functionality can save a lot of time when creating a number of forms that closely resemble each other.

Copying an existing Account form

1. Navigate to the Settings area, click Customizations, and then click Customize the System. The default solution opens.
2. In the default solution, expand the Entities list, expand the Account entity, and then click Forms.
3. Open the form you want to copy, and then click the Save As button in the ribbon. Enter the name and description of the new form.
4. After you have made the appropriate changes, save and publish the form.

Note Although all fields and components of the form will be replicated, the security roles assigned to those forms will not carry over to the new form, regardless of which approach you used to create it. When a form is first created, only the native System Administrator and System Customizer security roles have permissions to view the form.

One other thing to keep in mind is that once a separate form is created, all additional changes made to either form are completely separate. So, let's say that you create a copy of the main form called Information and label the new form Accounting Information. Later you create a new Navigation Link on the Information form. If you also want to see that new link on the Accounting form, you would have to reproduce your steps on the Accounting Information form separately from the Information form.

You can also delete forms as long as they are in the unmanaged state. You cannot delete system forms.

Tip If there is a system form that you do not want users to see, you can simply remove all security roles from that form. Keep in mind that you must have another form of the same type indicated as the fallback for this to work correctly.

Ordering Forms

When you create multiple forms for the same entity, you need to assign each version of the form to the appropriate group of users. The primary way to do this is by assigning the security roles to each form. Keep in mind that at least one form will be designated as the fallback for users who have a security role that is not assigned to a form. Microsoft Dynamics CRM relies on the form order to handle situations in which a user has permission to view multiple forms. Let's step through an example of form ordering to demonstrate how Microsoft Dynamics CRM addresses this situation.

Setting the form order

1. Navigate to the Settings area, click Customizations, and then click Customize the System. The default solution opens.
2. In the default solution, expand the Entities list, expand the Account entity, and then click Forms.
3. Click the Form Order button in the Forms view. Select the form set that you want to order, either main or mobile.
4. Use the arrow buttons in the Form Order dialog box to sort the forms, and then click OK.

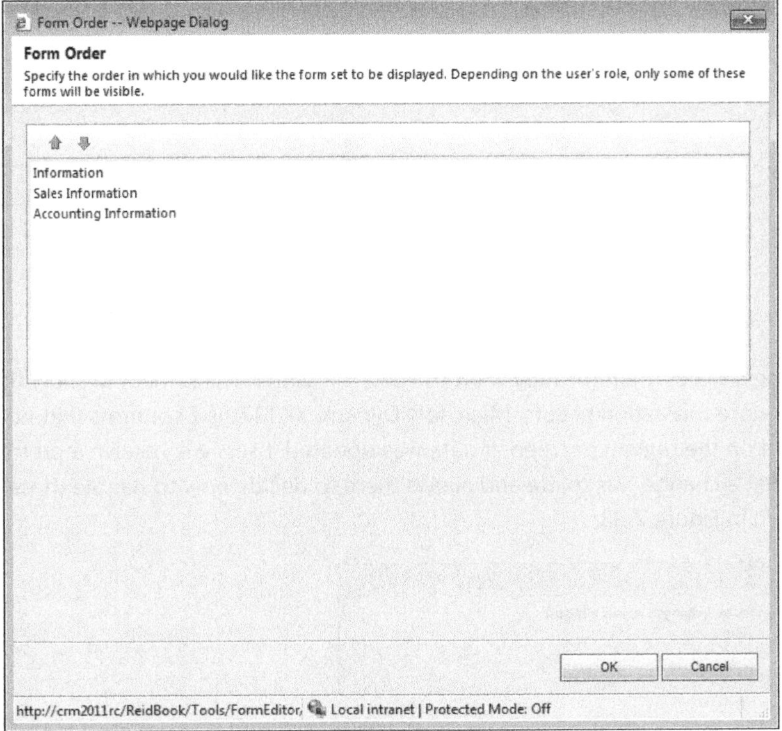

Important When using the form order function, users will see the first form that they have access to. In the example above, this would be the Information form, as indicated in the form order list. This rule will hold true until the user switches their preferred form, which we will review in the next section. After they select a different form, their selection becomes their default form associated to that entity.

Viewing Entities with Multiple Forms

Users who have permission to see multiple forms may view each of the forms by selecting the form they want to view directly above the tab navigation, as shown in Figure 7-32.

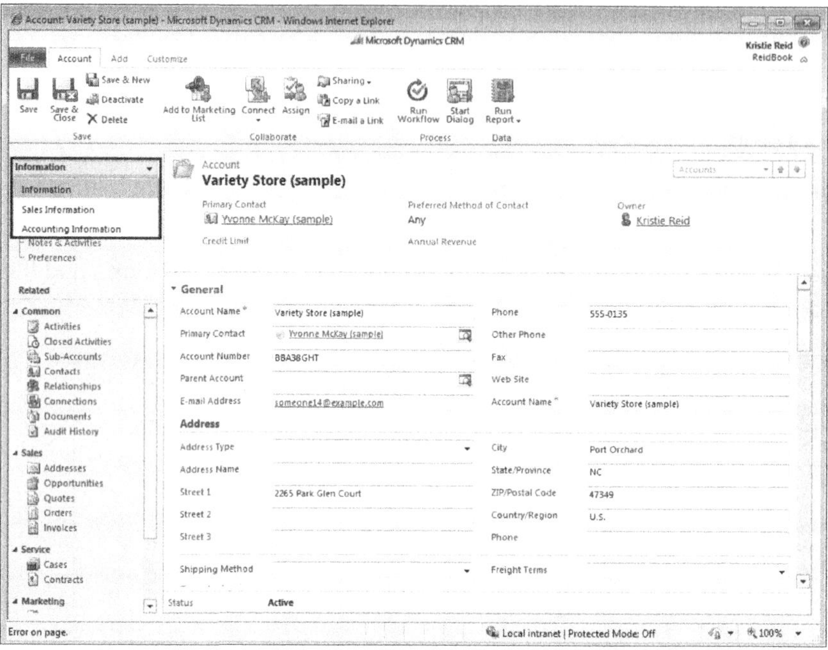

FIGURE 7-32 Multiple form selection

After users select the form they want to view, the screen will refresh to show the selected form. Before this action occurs, Microsoft Dynamics CRM first confirms that no data was updated on the previous screen. If data was updated, users will receive a prompt that notifies them that a change was made and allows them to decide how to handle those changes, as shown in Figure 7-33.

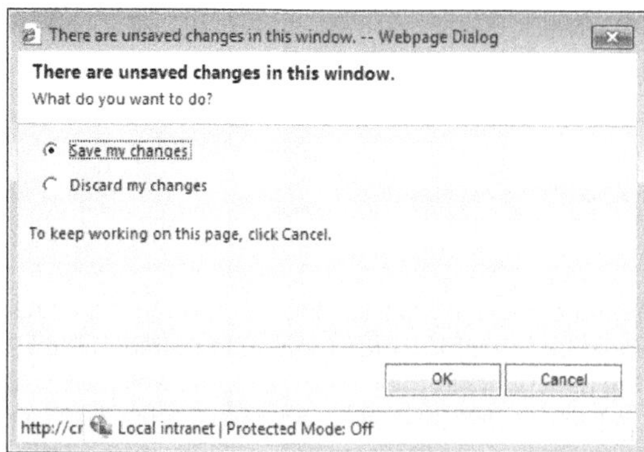

FIGURE 7-33 Unsaved changes notification

Note Mobile Express users do not have the ability to view multiple forms. If users' security roles give them permission to see multiple mobile forms, only the form listed first in the form order will display.

Summary

In this chapter, you learned more about entity customization, specifically around forms. We reviewed how to customize main forms, which are accessed through the web or Outlook clients, along with mobile forms. Within the main form types, each customizable entity form has a body, header, footer, and navigation pane that you can modify. Within the mobile forms, we discussed how to limit the display to only those fields that are critical to your mobile users. Finally, we reviewed how to create and use multiple forms and assign security roles to those forms, all to provide additional enhancements to the user experience.

Chapter 8

Entity Customization: Views and Charts

In this chapter:

In this chapter, we continue our journey with entity customizations and give a detailed explanation of views and charts.

Customizing Views

Microsoft Dynamics CRM uses views to display multiple records at one time. You can customize almost all of the views used in Microsoft Dynamics CRM to display only the data you want your users to see. You also can create your own custom views to display different data sets. First, we define the various components of a view, as shown in Figure 8-1:

- **Quick Find** Users can enter search terms and click Find to search within the view.
- **View Selector** This list shows all of the predefined views available to the user.
- **Grid** The grid displays the records for the view in rows and columns.
- **Ribbon** With the ribbon, users can perform additional actions on the records in the grid. Users can select more than one record at a time to perform these grid toolbar actions, such as assigning records or exporting data to Microsoft Office Excel.
- **Columns** Each view consists of one or more data columns. Users can click the column header to sort the view's records in ascending order (A to Z). Clicking the column header a second time sorts the records in descending order (from Z to A).
- **Index** Users can click a letter to quickly filter the records shown in the view. The index filter will work on the column currently selected in the view for sorting.

More Info People frequently use the term *grid* interchangeably with the term *view* in regard to Microsoft Dynamics CRM.

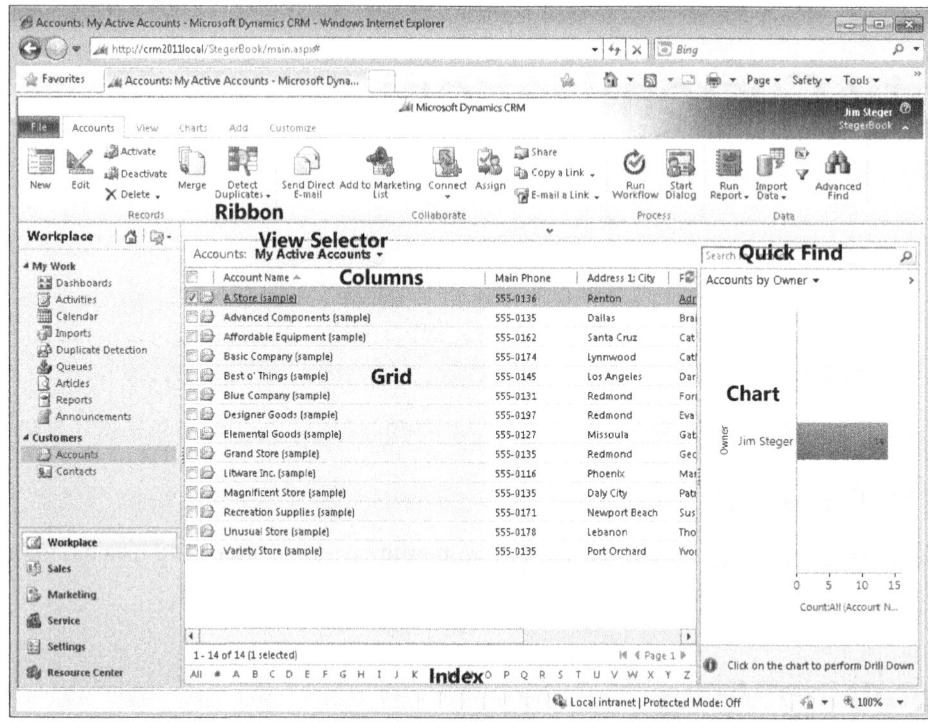

FIGURE 8-1 View components

Tip Users can sort by multiple columns at the same time by holding down the Shift key when clicking a column header. Further, users can now filter data within the columns by clicking the filter icon located in the Data group on the ribbon.

To customize views, navigate to the Customizations section of Microsoft Dynamics CRM and click Customize the System. Then find and expand the entity that you want to modify, and click Views in the tree view as shown in Figure 8-2.

If you work with the default solution, you can more quickly customize the system views by clicking the Customize tab on the grid's ribbon and then clicking System Views. This opens the default solution and immediately takes you to the same screen shown in Figure 8-2. The Customize tab only appears if you have customization privileges in Microsoft Dynamics CRM, such as the System Administrator or System Customizer security roles.

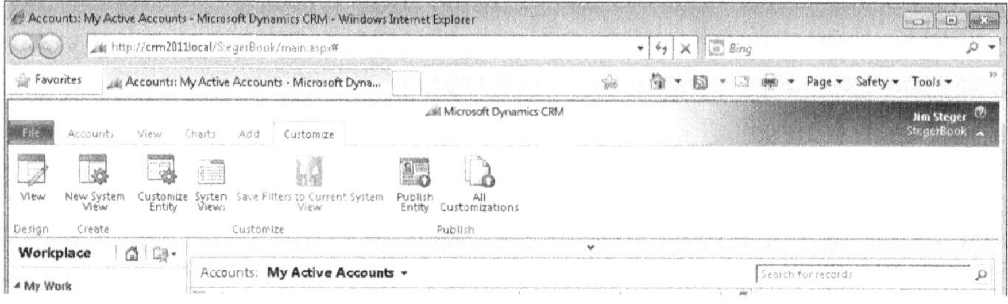

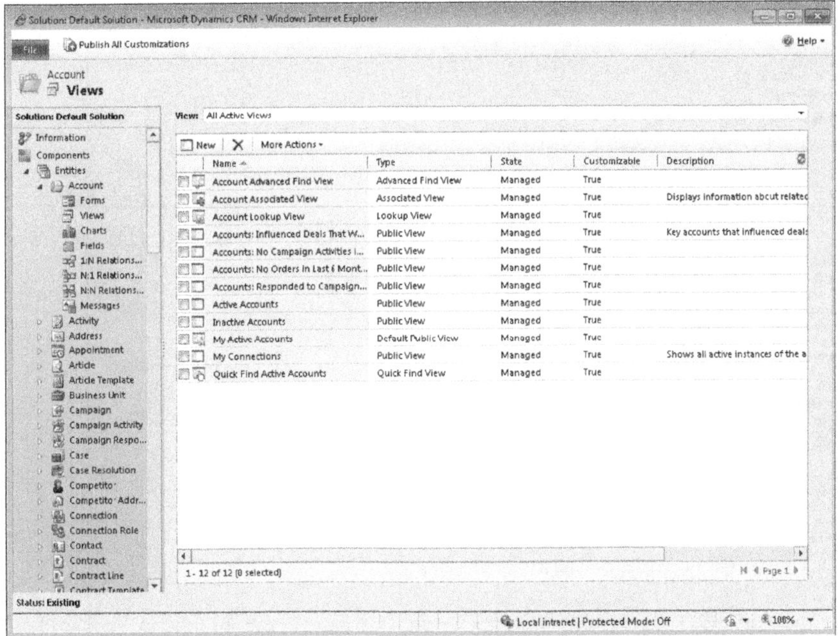

FIGURE 8-2 Customizing system views

View Types

Microsoft Dynamics CRM uses three types of views:

- Public Views
- System-Defined Views
- Saved Views

Saved Views are different from the other two views because you do not manage them in the Customization section of Microsoft Dynamics CRM. Rather, you use the Advanced Find tools to create, modify, and delete Saved Views.

Public Views

Any Microsoft Dynamics CRM user can access the Public Views for an entity. All of the Public Views appear in the View Selector for each entity. You can also specify a Default Public View for each entity. The Default Public View loads the first time a user browses to an entity area. Therefore, if you want to create a new view for accounts that every user will see the first time he or she browses to the Account workspace, create a new view and set it as the Default Public View for the Account entity. You can change the Default Public View in the entity editor by clicking the view that you want to make the default and then clicking Set Default on the More Actions menu, as shown in Figure 8-3.

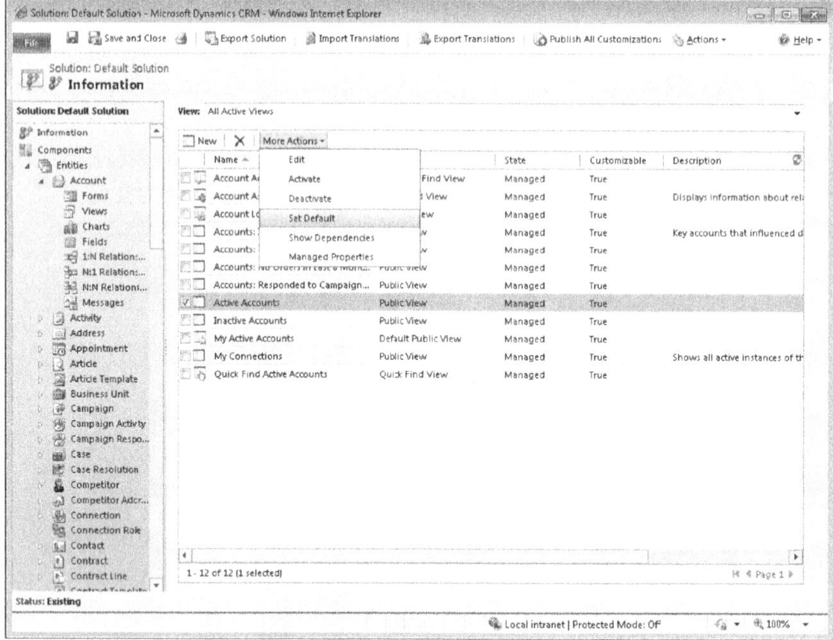

FIGURE 8-3 Setting a different view as the Default Public View

System-Defined Views

In addition to the Default Public View, Microsoft Dynamics CRM includes four other System-Defined Views:

- Associated View
- Advanced Find View
- Lookup View
- Quick Find View

Similar to system entities, Microsoft Dynamics CRM automatically creates these System-Defined Views upon installation of the software. Each serves a unique purpose in the user interface, so the software constrains your ability to modify any System-Defined View. In particular, Microsoft Dynamics CRM implements a few notable customization restrictions with these views:

- Only one of each System-Defined View can exist for an entity.
- You cannot delete any of the System-Defined Views.

Next, we discuss how Microsoft Dynamics CRM uses each of these views and how you can customize them.

Associated View When you look at the records related to an entity, Microsoft Dynamics CRM displays the related active records using the Associated View. For example, when you view the contacts related to an account, Microsoft Dynamics CRM uses the Associated View of the Contact entity to display the records (Figure 8-4). When you look up the sub-accounts of an account, Microsoft Dynamics CRM displays the Associated View of the Account entity.

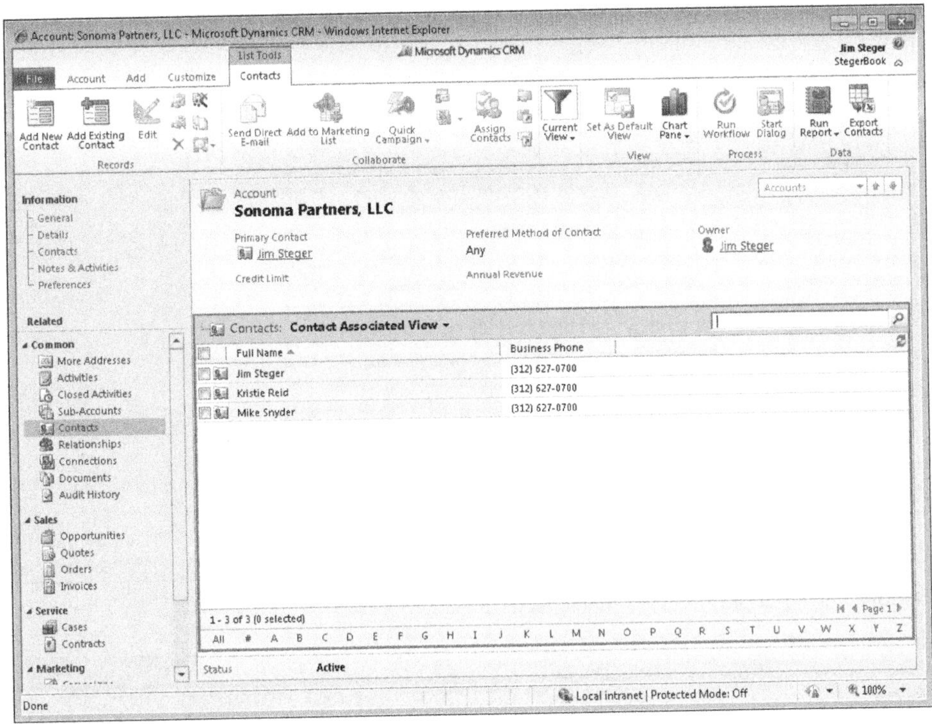

FIGURE 8-4 Contact Associated View as seen on an account record

Therefore, if you want to add a contact's title to the view in Figure 8-4, you would edit the Contact Associated View even though you're actually viewing an account record. Because only one Associated View exists per entity, you cannot display different views based on the related entity. For example, both the Lead and Opportunity entities reference the Activity Associated View. If you change the Activity Associated View, this change appears on both leads *and* opportunities.

> **Tip** Microsoft Dynamics CRM 2011 allows users to select different views from the associated grid. Therefore, you can create custom views that are more relevant to specific associated entities and have users change to that view to see the data most relevant to their roles.

Advanced Find View With the Advanced Find View, you can define the default columns that appear when users use the Advanced Find feature. Figure 8-5 shows the Advanced Find View for the Contact entity.

Note that users can easily edit the columns that appear in the Advanced Find results, as shown in Figure 8-6, but their updates will not change the Advanced Find View for the entity.

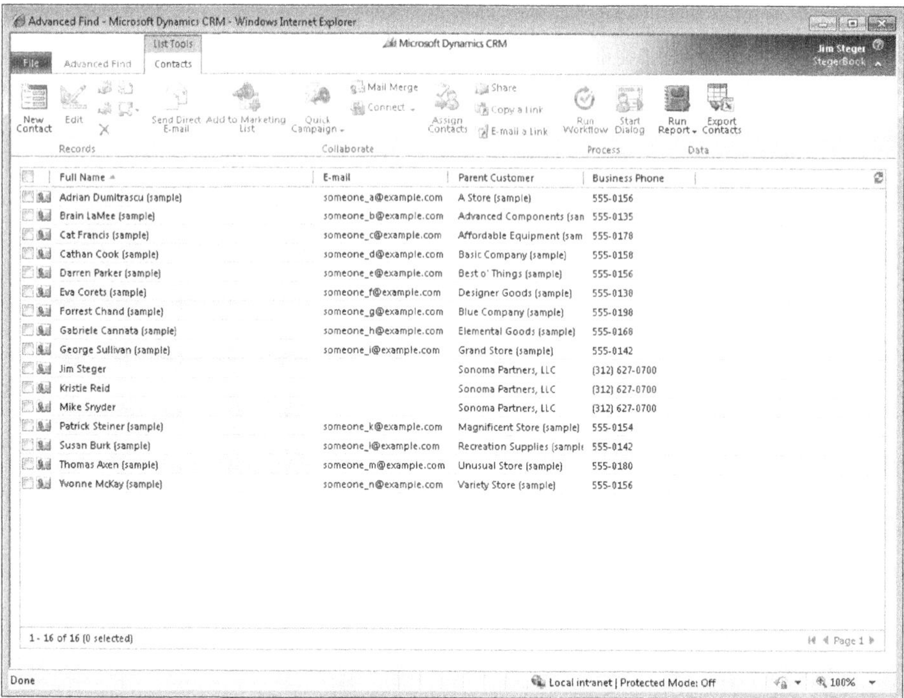

FIGURE 8-5 Advanced Find View for contacts

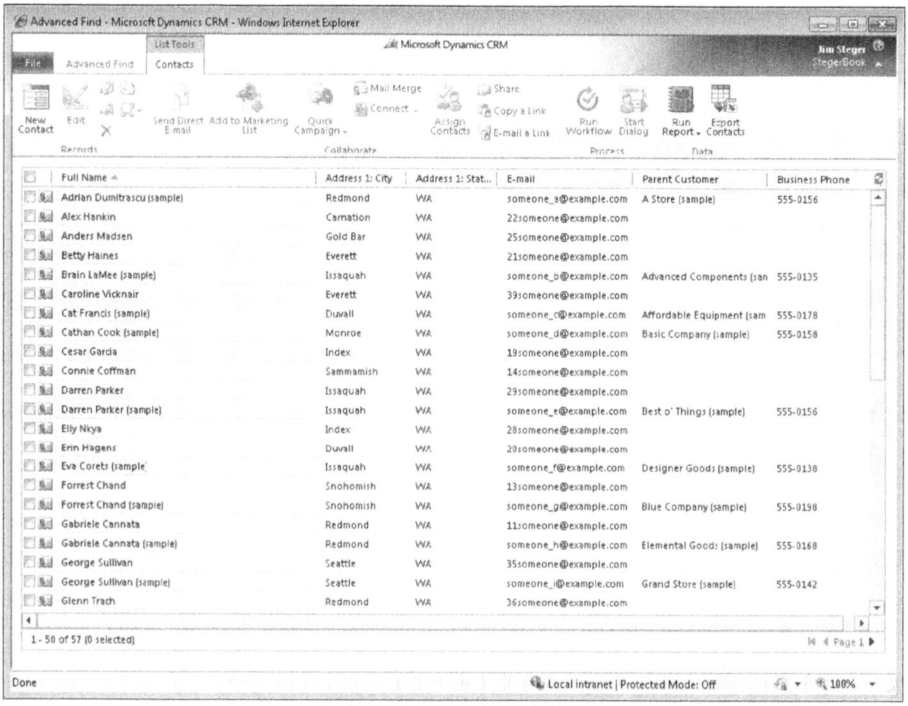

FIGURE 8-6 Advanced Find columns that have been edited by a user

So, every time a user creates a new Advanced Find, the columns from that entity's Advanced Find View are the default results.

Lookup View When users click the magnifying glass icon in a Lookup field, a Look Up Record dialog appears. From this dialog, users can search for a particular record. Figure 8-7 shows the Contact Lookup View that users see when they select a Primary Contact for an account.

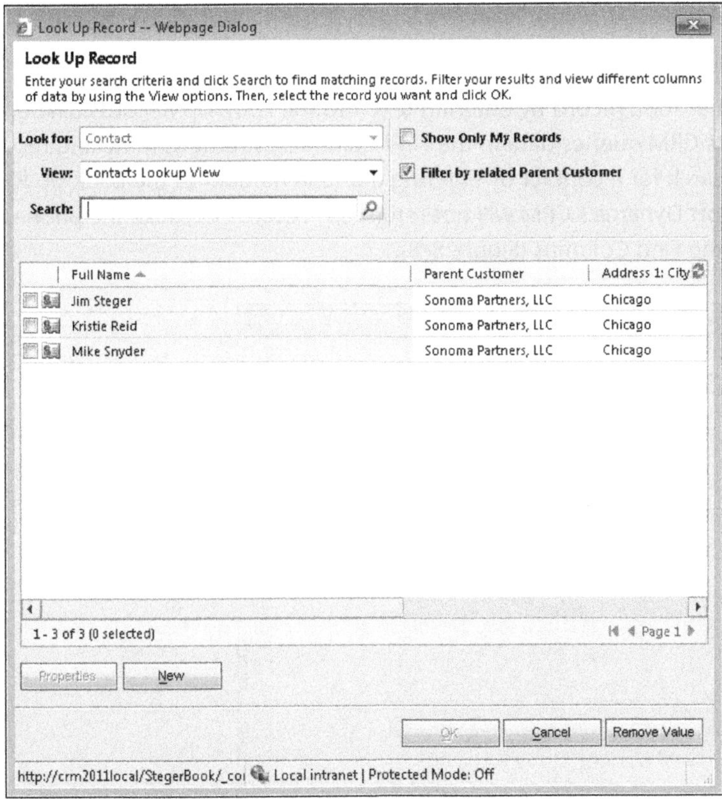

FIGURE 8-7 Contact Lookup View

The Lookup View now contains many more options than previous versions of Microsoft Dynamics CRM. The default view for the lookup is the Lookup View, but users can now change the view to other published views. The Lookup View also offers additional filters depending on the lookup. These filters allow users to quickly find the desired record.

However, the Search option is the primary mechanism that allows users to find records. You can define the columns that appear in the Look Up Records dialog by editing the Lookup View for an entity. In addition to modifying the columns in the view, you can add Find Columns to the view by updating the Quick Find View. Microsoft Dynamics CRM will search for data in all of the Find Columns when users enter search text. For example, the following are the default Find Columns for the Contact entity:

- E-mail
- First Name
- Middle Name
- Last Name
- Full Name
- Parent Customer

When a user searches for a record by entering text into the Look Up Records dialog, Microsoft Dynamics CRM queries data in the Find Columns to retrieve matching records. Therefore, if you search for a contact by entering a phone number in the Look Up Record dialog box, Microsoft Dynamics CRM will not return any records because the phone number field is not one of the Find Columns (Figure 8-8).

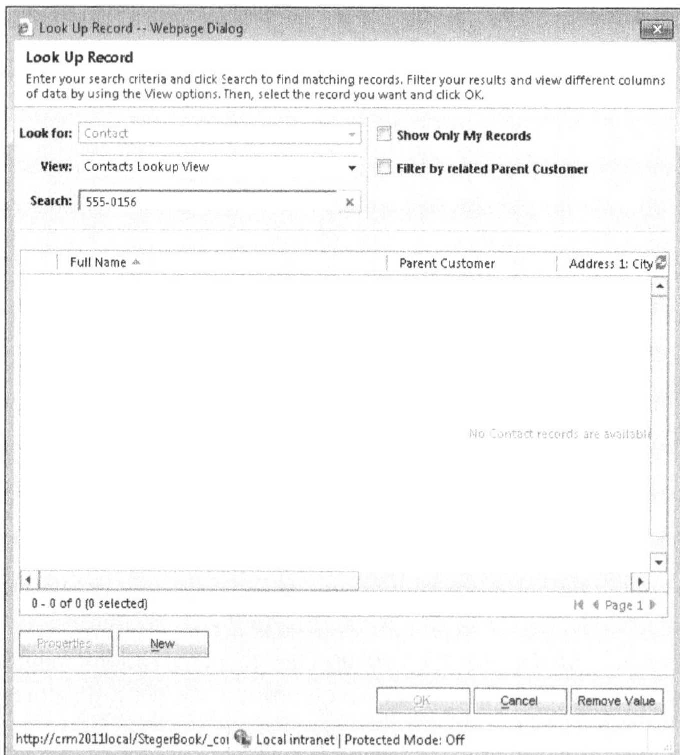

FIGURE 8-8 Results of a phone number search using the default Find Columns

However, if you add the Business Phone field as a Find Column to the Quick Find View on the Contact entity, you can search for customers by entering the customers' phone numbers in a Lookup View. Remember that you need to update Quick Find Active Contacts View to add or remove the columns searched from the Search option, but you might also want to update the Lookup View to display the Business Phone column in the search results. Let's update this view to search the Business Phone field.

Adding the Business Phone Number as a Find Column in the Contact Lookup View

1. Navigate to the Contacts view and click the Customize tab in the ribbon.
2. Click System Views in the ribbon's Customize group.
3. Double-click the Quick Find Active Contacts View, and then click Add Find Columns in the Common Tasks pane. The Add Find Columns dialog opens.
4. In the list of fields for the Contact entity, select the Business Phone check box, and then click OK.
5. Click the Save and Close button on the View Editor toolbar.
6. In the Default Solution window, publish the Contact entity by clicking Publish All Customizations.

The next time a user enters a phone number in the Look Up Record dialog, Microsoft Dynamics CRM will include the Business Phone column in its search for matching records. Figure 8-9 shows the search results.

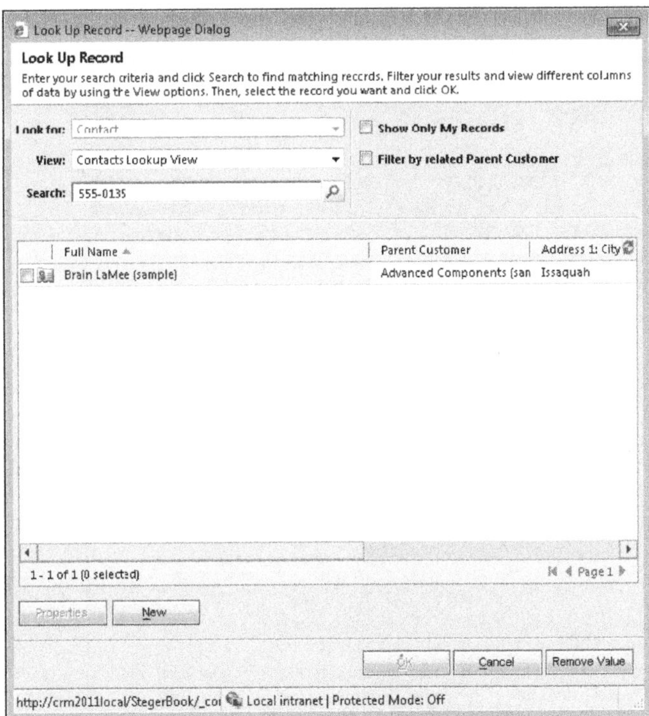

FIGURE 8-9 Contact record returned after adding Business Phone as a Find Column

Caution Use care when adding Find Columns. If your database contains many records, adding additional Find Columns can have a performance impact because those columns might not be indexed in the database. Only include the columns you require.

In addition to phone numbers, you might also want to add a unique customer number (ID) or other custom field as a Find Column to help users find records more quickly.

Important When you enter search values, Microsoft Dynamics CRM searches for the value as is; it does not search for substrings by default. For example, if you search for "555-1212" and the contact's Business Phone field contains "(312) 555-1212", Microsoft Dynamics CRM will not find a match. The software tries to find all records that start with "555-1212", but this record doesn't start with that value. To retrieve the contact in a search result, you need to search for "(312) 555-1212" or "(312)". Obviously, there may be times when you don't know the exact value you're searching for. Therefore, in Microsoft Dynamics CRM you can enter an asterisk (*) as a wildcard character in your Quick Find and Lookup searches. For example, if you do not know the phone number area code, you could search for "*555-1212" and Microsoft Dynamics CRM would find the matching record.

Quick Find View On the main entity pages, users can search for records by using the Quick Find feature. To do this, simply type a search value in the Look For field and click Find. Microsoft Dynamics CRM then searches for matching records and returns the results using the Quick Find View of the entity. Note that the Quick Find View appears as Search Results in the View Selector. Figure 8-10 shows the Quick Find Active Accounts View.

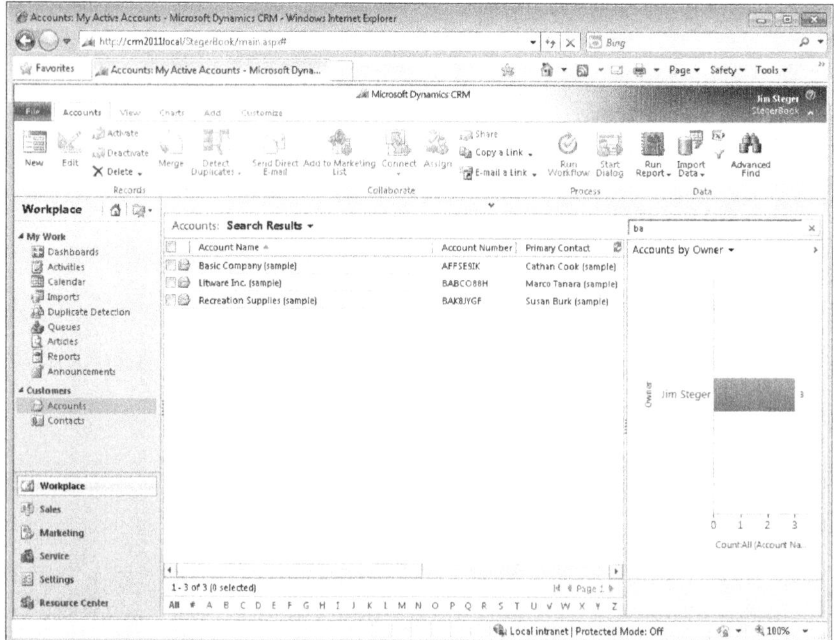

FIGURE 8-10 Account search results using the Quick Find View and a wildcard character

As you learned with the Lookup View, you can customize the Find Columns of the Quick Find View, allowing users to search for records across the specified fields.

Saved Views

Users can create their own saved views a variety of ways, such as by using Advanced Find or grid filters, or even by drilling into a chart.

Remember that you do not manage Saved Views in the Customization section of Microsoft Dynamics CRM. When users create new views, they can save the resulting query as a Saved View. Saved Views have many of the same attributes as the Public and System-Defined Views, but they also have a couple of unique distinctions.

Saved Views are not packaged as part of a solution. Therefore, you cannot easily distribute saved views between environments.

Saved Views also have user ownership. This means that they can be assigned to a specific user, and they will follow the Microsoft Dynamics CRM security rules. The Saved View permission is part of the Security Role configuration, so you can specify which security roles can, for example, read, write, or delete Saved Views. The Saved View ownership and Microsoft Dynamics CRM security role configuration determine which Saved Views each user can access. However, the Public and System-Defined Views exist across the entire system, so that all users can access them. If you create a Saved View that you want to share with everyone, one way to accomplish this is to share the Saved View with a team that every user belongs to or to create it as a Public View in the entity customizations.

Customizing Views

Now that you understand the different view types, we discuss in detail how to customize these views to show the data you want to see. To edit a view, double-click the view name in the Views grid of the entity editor. All of the views use the same editor tool, as shown in Figure 8-11.

The Common Tasks pane in the view editor offers several tools for customizing a view:

- **Directional arrows** Select a column header, and then use these arrows to move it to the left or right in your view.
- **View Properties** Use this tool to change the name of the view. The view's name appears in the View Selector.
- **Edit Filter Criteria** The Edit Filter Criteria tool allows you to create complex criteria that refine the data that each view returns. The Edit Filter Criteria tool uses the same user interface as the Advanced Find feature to create your data query.

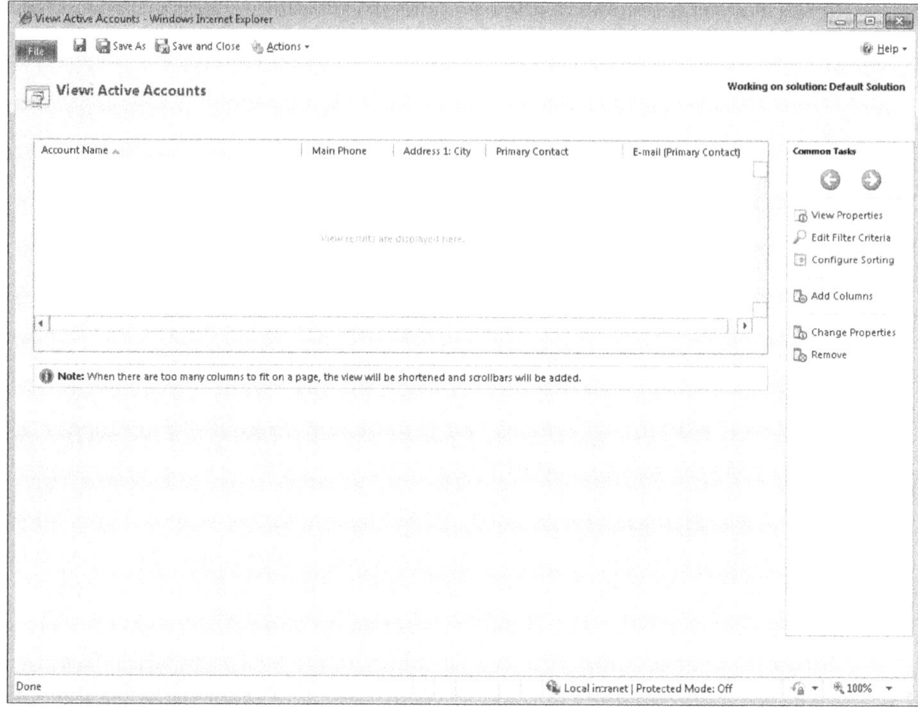

FIGURE 8-11 Active Accounts view editor

- **Configure Sorting** Use this tool to specify the default order in which records are sorted in the view. You can choose to sort by any one column in ascending or descending order. If you closely examine the view editor, you may notice that the default sort order column header has a small arrow that points up (for ascending) or down (for descending). You can add up to two fields to sort. Unfortunately, there is no way to automatically sort more than these two fields, although users can add additional sorting by using the Shift key.

- **Add Columns** Use this feature to add more columns to the view. Microsoft Dynamics CRM also allows you to add fields from related entities to a view. For example, you could choose to display the account relationship type attribute in a contact view. To access the attributes of related entities, select the entity name in the Record Type picklist and Microsoft Dynamics CRM will update the list of fields.

  By default, new columns are added to the right of the view. If you select a column header and then add a View Column, Microsoft Dynamics CRM places the new column to the right of the selected column. This tip can save you some clicks if you have a view with many columns.

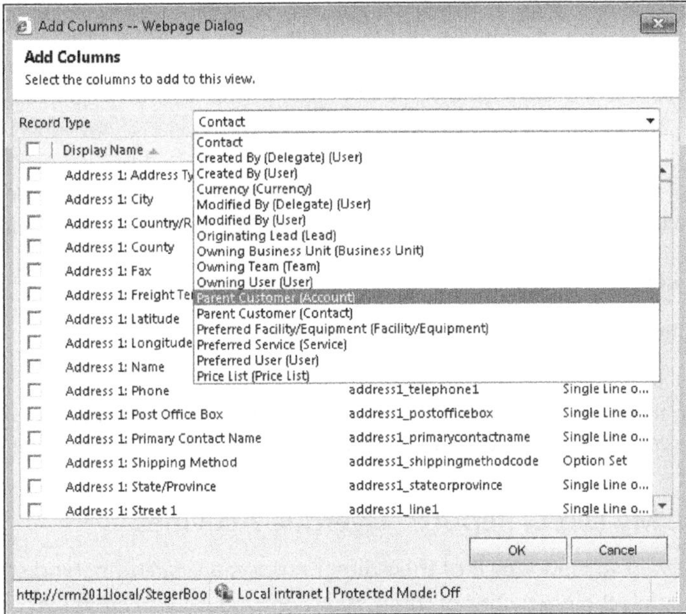

- **Add Find Columns** As discussed previously, with this feature you can specify which columns Microsoft Dynamics CRM should search for matching records. The Add Find Columns feature applies only to the Quick Find view, but the fields selected in the Quick Find view apply to Lookup searches as well.
- **Change Properties** If you want to change the width of a column in the view, select the column header, and then click Change Properties. You can specify the column's width in pixels (abbreviated as *px* in the user interface). For certain types of columns, you can select the Enable Presence For This Column check box if you want to display the Microsoft Lync presence indicator in the view.
- **Remove** Use this option to remove a column from the view.

Tip Even though you can add columns from related entities to a view, you can only configure the default view sorting using attributes from the primary entity.

When you install Microsoft Dynamics CRM, the software creates System-Defined Views for each entity. To make sure the software always functions correctly, Microsoft Dynamics CRM restricts your ability to deactivate or delete these views. However, you have the ability to configure these views, including the filter criteria, default sorting, and columns that appear, just as with any Public or Saved View.

Caution When you add a column to a view, Microsoft Dynamics CRM displays the field name as that column's header. If you add a column from a related entity, Microsoft Dynamics CRM automatically appends the related entity's name in parentheses after the field name in the column header. You cannot customize the column header names in the view editor.

Let's step through the process for creating two sample views to show you how to create custom views, including using the new Save As feature. We'll create two sample views:

- My Direct Reports' Overdue Activities
- Opportunities Opened This Year

Note Creating these samples assumes you have Microsoft Dynamics CRM System Administrator, System Customizer, or a security role with the appropriate permissions to work with views.

Sample View: My Direct Reports' Overdue Activities

Managers often want to view which of their direct reports are falling behind schedule and which are completing their activities on time. We show you how to create an activity view to quickly mine the Microsoft Dynamics CRM database for this information.

Creating an Overdue Activities custom view

1. In the Default Solution window, expand the Entities node, and then expand the Activity node.
2. Click Views from the Activity entity in the navigation pane.
3. Click New on the grid toolbar to create a view.
4. In the View Properties dialog, type the view name **My Direct Reports' Overdue Activities** and then click OK.

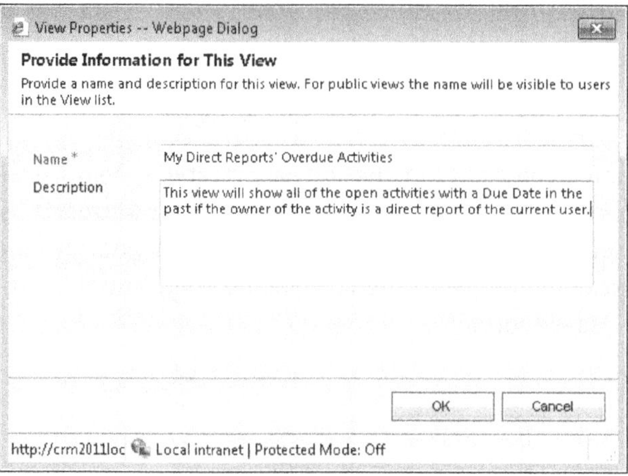

5. Click Edit Filter Criteria in the Common Tasks pane. The Edit Filter Criteria dialog opens.
6. Click the Select link. Under the Fields group of the picklist, select Activity Status. Click Enter Value and then click the ellipsis button (...) that appears.
7. The Select Values dialog opens. Under the Available Values section, select Open, and then click the **>>** button. Click OK to close the Select Values dialog box. With the Activity Status filter set to Open, the view will select only records that have not been completed or canceled.
8. To filter the open Activities to show only those with a Due Date in the past, click the Select link, and then select Due Date, which is listed under the Fields group.
9. Click to the right of the Due Date picklist. Microsoft Dynamics CRM displays a picklist of date operators. However, notice that there is no "in the past" or "overdue" option. If you try to choose "On or Before," Microsoft Dynamics CRM prompts you to enter a specific date. Therefore, if you use "On or Before" and enter a date value, you would have to update the view every day to show overdue activities. You obviously don't want to do this, so use this workaround: Set the Due Date evaluation picklist to Last X Years and type **99** in the Enter Value field. Now Microsoft Dynamics CRM will display all open activities with a Due Date in the last 99 years.

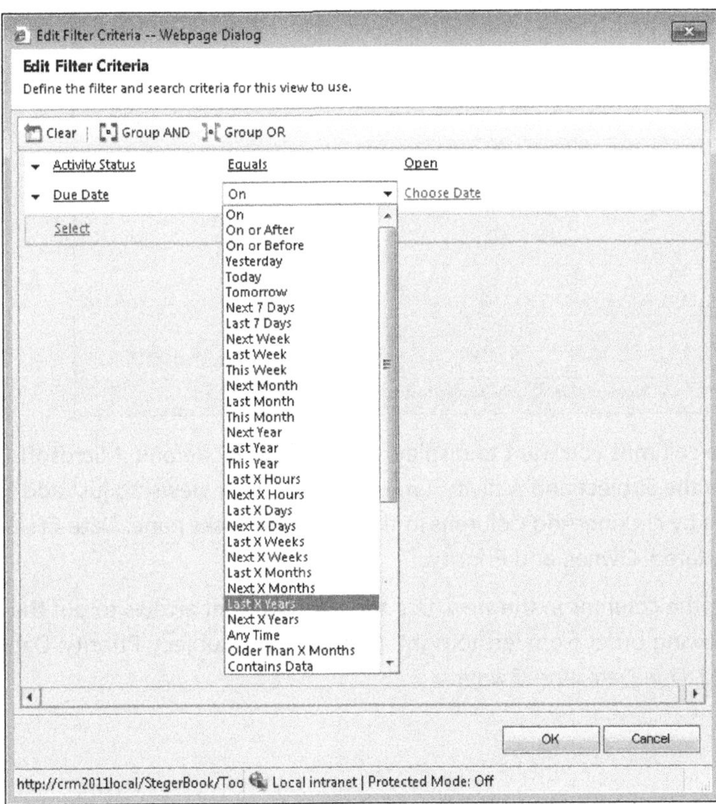

10. So far, the view will return open activities with a Due Date in the last 99 years, but you want to see only the activities assigned to the manager's direct reports. To add this filter, click Select again. In the picklist, scroll down to the Related grouping and choose Owning User (User).
11. Click the Select link that appears under Owning User (User). Under the Fields group, select Manager, leave the default operator value of Equals Current User selected, and click OK to close the Edit Filter Criteria dialog box.

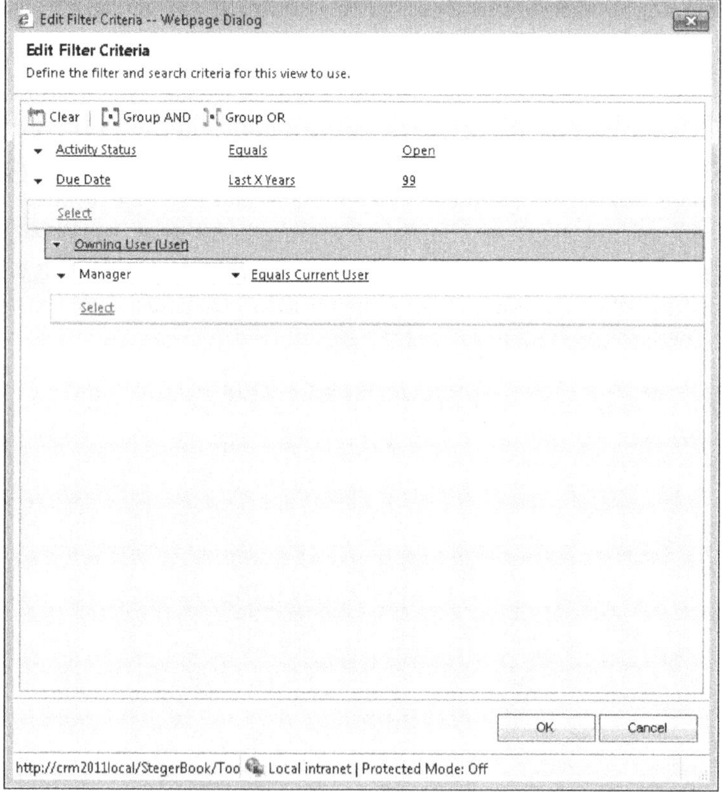

12. Add the columns you want to display in your view. By default, Microsoft Dynamics CRM includes the Subject and Activity Type in new Activity views, so just add the following columns by clicking Add Columns in the Common Tasks pane: Date Created, Due Date, Last Updated, Owner, and Priority.
13. Reorder the columns in the view. Use the left and right arrows to put the columns in the following order from left to right: Activity Type, Subject, Priority, Date Created, Last Updated, Due Date, and Owner.

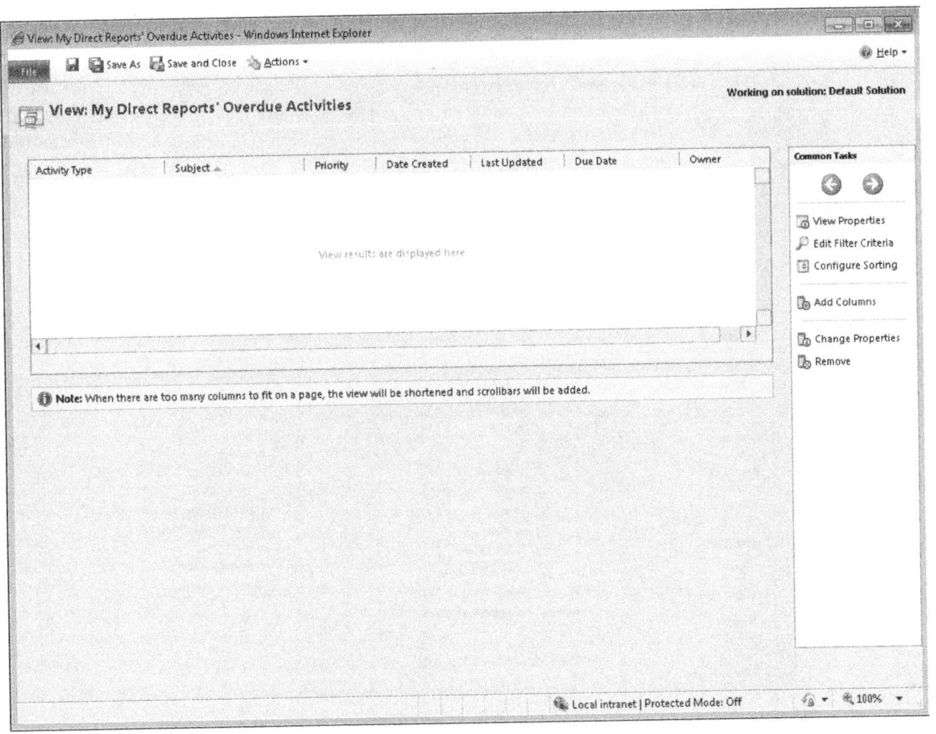

14. When you add a new column, the default column width is 100 pixels (100px). Click Change Properties to change the width of the columns so the width of the Priority column is 75 pixels (75px) and the width of the Due Date column is 125 pixels (125px).
15. Specify the default sort order to show the most overdue activities first by clicking Configure Sorting and selecting Due Date in ascending order. As a secondary sort, select Owner in ascending order. Click OK.
16. Click Save and Close on the view editor toolbar to complete the view customization.
17. In the Default Solutions window, click Publish on the toolbar to publish your new view.
18. A "Publishing customizations…" message appears. When the message disappears, you can use your new view.
19. Browse to the Activities section in the Workplace area and select My Direct Reports' Overdue Activities from the All Activities view selector.

    If you don't see the records you expect, confirm that each user's manager record is set correctly. You can view a user's manager in his or her user record. To view a user's record, go to the Settings area of Microsoft Dynamics CRM, click the Administration link, and then click Users. Double-click the user's name to open the record and set the user's manager by using the Change Manager feature located on the ribbon.

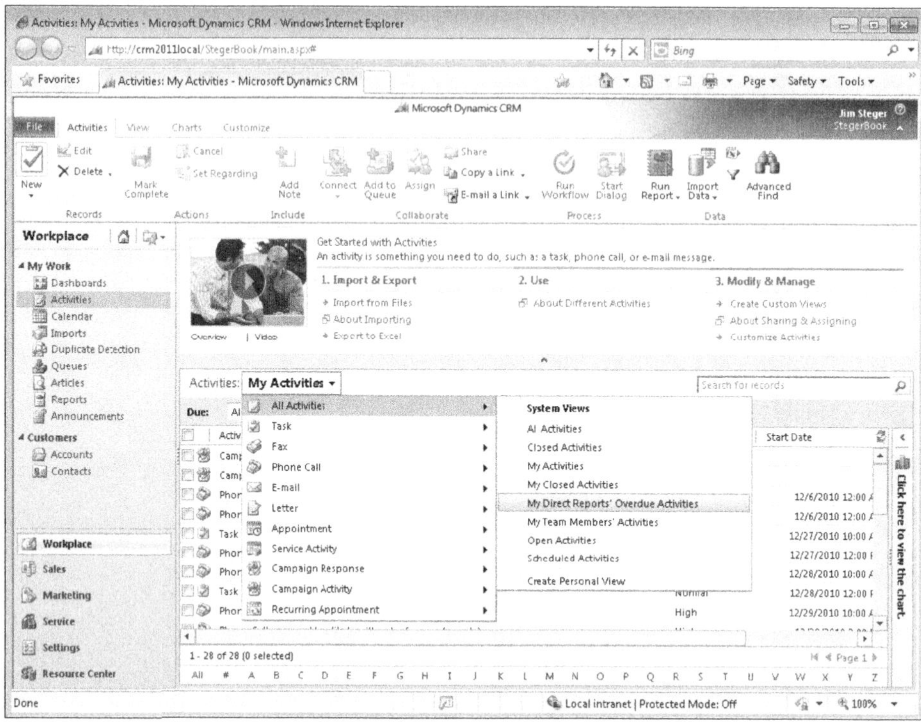

Sample View: Opportunities Opened This Year

Previous versions of Microsoft Dynamics CRM forced you to create each system view from scratch. For each view you had to define the field columns, sort order, and other properties from scratch. With Microsoft Dynamics CRM 2011, you can now copy existing views to create new ones. The copied view will retain all of the columns, sort columns, and filters from the previous view, saving you time when creating very similar views. We'll use this technique to add an opportunity view displaying all of the opportunities from the current year. For this example, we want to use the same columns and sorting as the Opportunities Opened This Week view.

Creating an Opportunities Opened This Year custom view

1. In the Default Solution window, expand the Entities node, and then expand the Opportunity node.
2. Click Views from the Opportunity entity in the navigation pane.
3. Double-click the Opportunities Opened This Week view.
4. From the Opportunities Opened This Week View's toolbar, click Save As.
5. In the View Properties dialog page, enter **Opportunities Opened This Year** for the name of the new view.

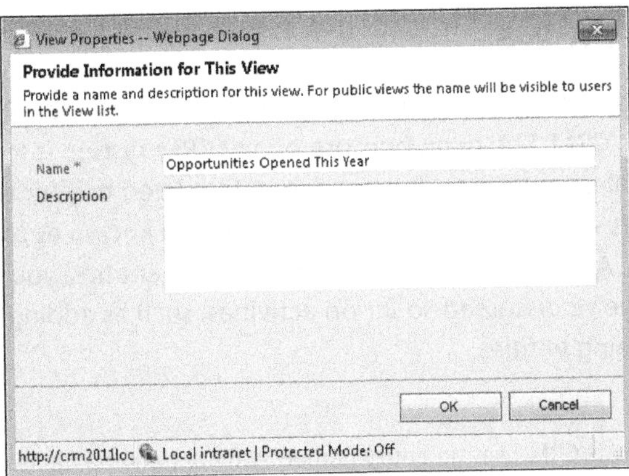

6. Click Edit Filter Criteria in the Common Tasks pane. The Edit Filter Criteria dialog page opens.
7. Change the Created On filter from This Week to This Year.

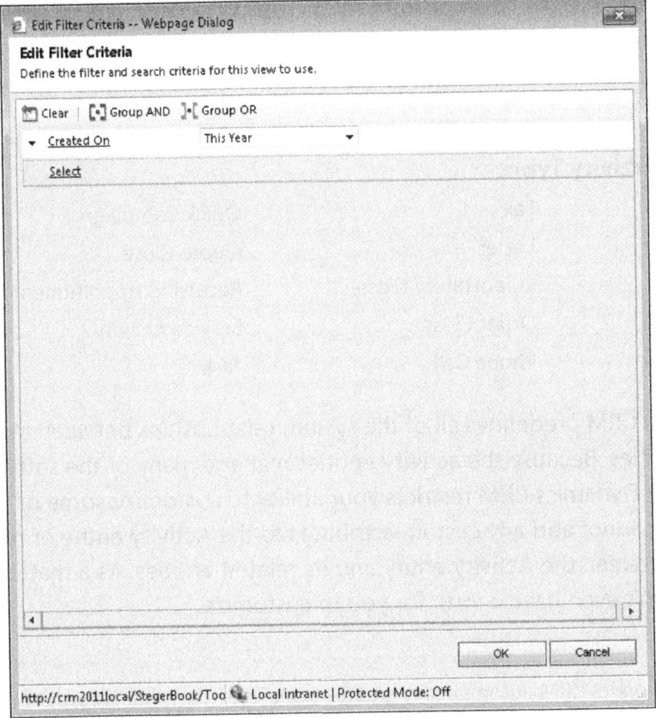

8. Click OK to return to the view editor.
9. Click Save and Close on the view editor toolbar.
10. In the Default Solutions window, click Publish All Customizations on the toolbar to publish your new view.

In just a few steps, you have another system view ready for use.

Customizing Activity Views

Activities are the heart and soul of any customer relationship management (CRM) system, including Microsoft Dynamics CRM. The main purpose of any CRM system is to effectively track and manage all of the sales, service, and marketing data related to your customers, and Microsoft Dynamics CRM stores the vast majority of this data (also known as *touch points*) as activities. As with the Lead, Account, Contact, and Opportunity entities, you can perform many of the customizations we've discussed so far on activities, such as adding fields, customizing views, and renaming entities.

Important Microsoft Dynamics CRM uses an entity named Activity (schema name of *activitypointer*) to act as the parent of other entities such as Appointment, Task, Fax, Phone Call, and E-mail. Microsoft Dynamics CRM also refers to these sub-entities as activities because they're child entities of the parent Activity entity.

However, because activities are so important to Microsoft Dynamics CRM, we want to explicitly cover some activity-specific customizations. The default Microsoft Dynamics CRM installation contains 15 types of activities (child entities of the Activity entity) as shown in Table 8-1.

TABLE 8-1 System Activity Types

Appointment	Fax	Quick Campaign
Campaign Activity	Letter	Quote Close
Campaign Response	Opportunity Close	Recurring Appointment
Case Resolution	Order Close	Service Activity
E-mail	Phone Call	Task

Microsoft Dynamics CRM predefines all of the system relationships between the Activity and its related child entities. Because the activity entities manage many of the software's inner workings, Microsoft Dynamics CRM restricts your ability to customize some of these entities. Consequently, you cannot add any custom attributes to the Activity entity or modify any of the relationships between the Activity entity and its related entities. As a matter of fact, the Activity entity doesn't even have a form for you to customize.

Tip Microsoft Dynamics CRM automatically creates some activities, such as order close and opportunity close when users close those records. You can reference these auto-created activities for reporting or auditing purposes.

Figure 8-12 summarizes the differences between the Activity entity and its child entities.

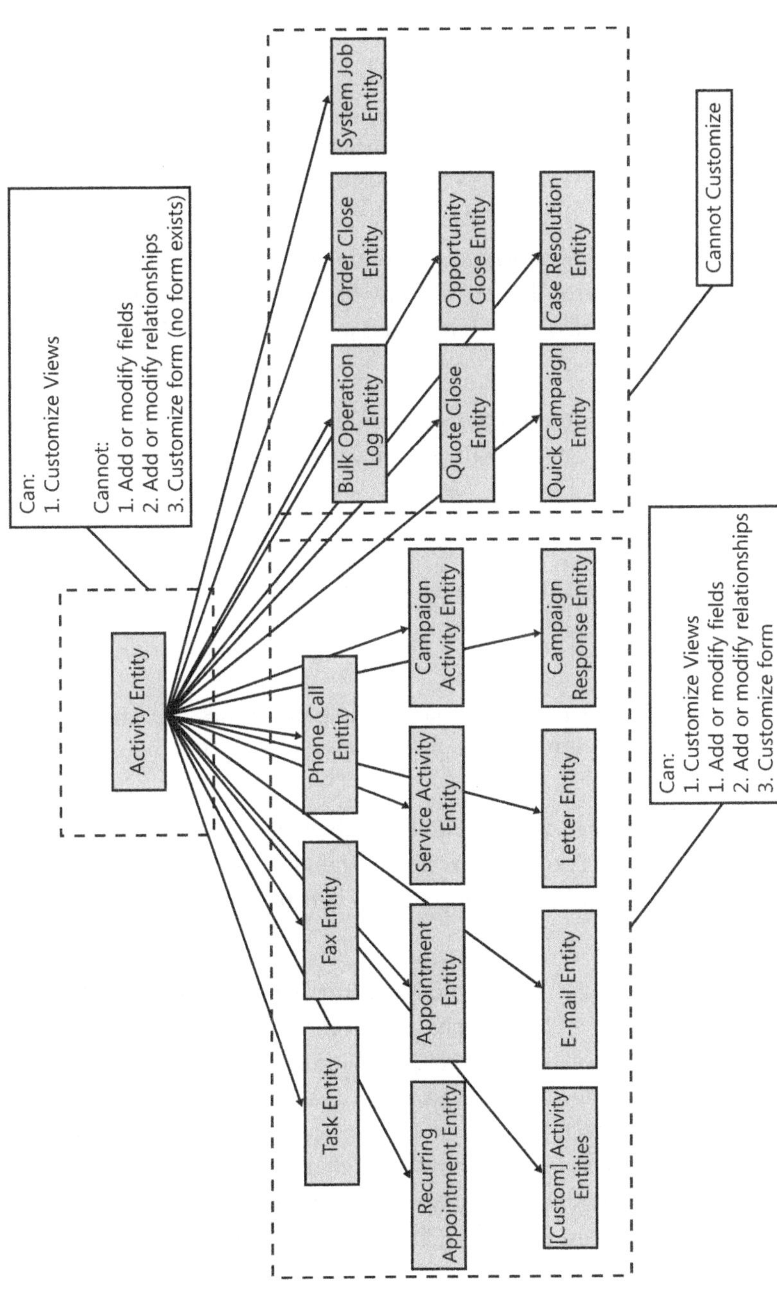

FIGURE 8-12 Differences between the Activity entity and some of its related entities

However, just because Microsoft Dynamics CRM restricts certain customizations of the parent Activity entity, don't make the mistake of thinking that activities cannot be customized. Even though you cannot add fields to the Activity entity, you can add fields to the child entities, such as Task, Phone Call, and Letter.

Important You can add custom fields to the activity sub-entities, such as Task, Phone Call, and Appointment, but you cannot add attributes to the Activity entity. Although you cannot add fields to the Activity entity, you can customize the Activity entity views.

Further, Microsoft Dynamics CRM allows you to create your own custom activity entities. The custom activity entities mirror the functionality of the customizable child activities such as Task or Phone Call. We'll discuss custom activities in more detail in Chapter 10, "Custom Entities and Custom Activities."

You use the same process to customize the views of activities that you use for the other customizable entities, but we want to highlight a few view nuances specific to activities.

Workplace Activities

When users first log on to Microsoft Dynamics CRM, the default start page is the Activities page in the Workplace area.

Tip Each user can specify a different start page by clicking the File menu and then clicking Options. Users can also personalize their own default view for each grid.

From the Activities page, you can quickly filter through all of your activities. In addition to the Quick Find feature that appears on the other pages, the View Selector allows you to filter the view by activity type. The Activities page also allows users to filter records by the Due Date, as shown in Figure 8-13.

The Due Date activity filter is hard-coded into Microsoft Dynamics CRM, so you cannot add your own custom values into the filter options. However, you can modify the data columns that Microsoft Dynamics CRM searches in the Quick Find feature. In addition, you can create new views that appear in the View Selector. However, the View Selector behaves differently on the Activities page from how it behaves on other pages in the system. When you click the View Selector, you will receive a submenu displaying all of the available child activities. You can then select the unique views associated with a specific activity type. From the Activities page, you can immediately access more than 30 different activity views.

When you want to customize the default Activity views or start creating custom views, you need to know that the Activity entity controls the views for the All filter, but the other Activity views are specific to the activity type entities. This is important because the Activity

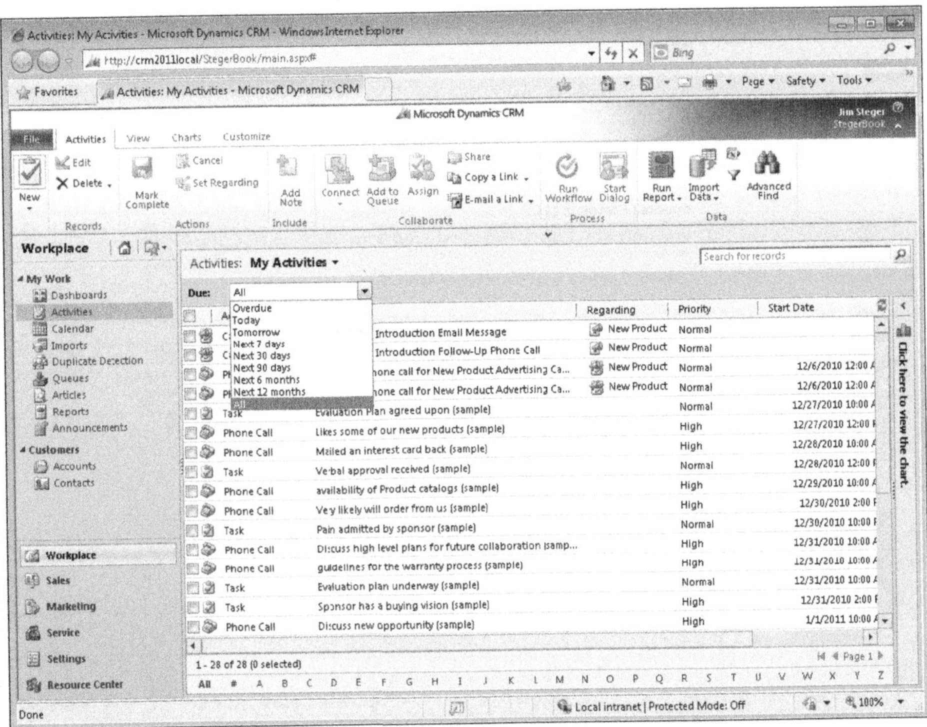

FIGURE 8-13 The Activities page showing the Due Date filter

entity contains only fields that are common to all of the child entities. So, you could not add a child entity-specific field such as Phone Number on the Phone Call entity to any of the views that appear in the All filter. The same constraint applies to the Quick Find feature on the Activities page. You can include Find Columns only from an Activity entity that includes common fields; you cannot include any of the attributes unique to the activity types.

Entity Activity Views

In addition to the Workplace Activity views, two Activity views that contain special features are the Activities and Closed Activities views that appear on any activity-enabled entity. Figure 8-14 shows the Activities views on the Account entity.

Even though both of these views display the activities related to the record, clicking Closed Activities in the navigation pane shows only completed activities. The Activities link displays only open activities. To customize the columns that appear when users click Activities in the navigation pane, you must edit the Open Activity Associated View of the Activity entity. To customize the view that appears when users click Closed Activities in the navigation pane, you must edit the Closed Activity Associated View of the Activity entity. Again, because these views display different types of activities (phone calls, tasks, faxes, and so on), you can display only the columns from the parent Activity entity.

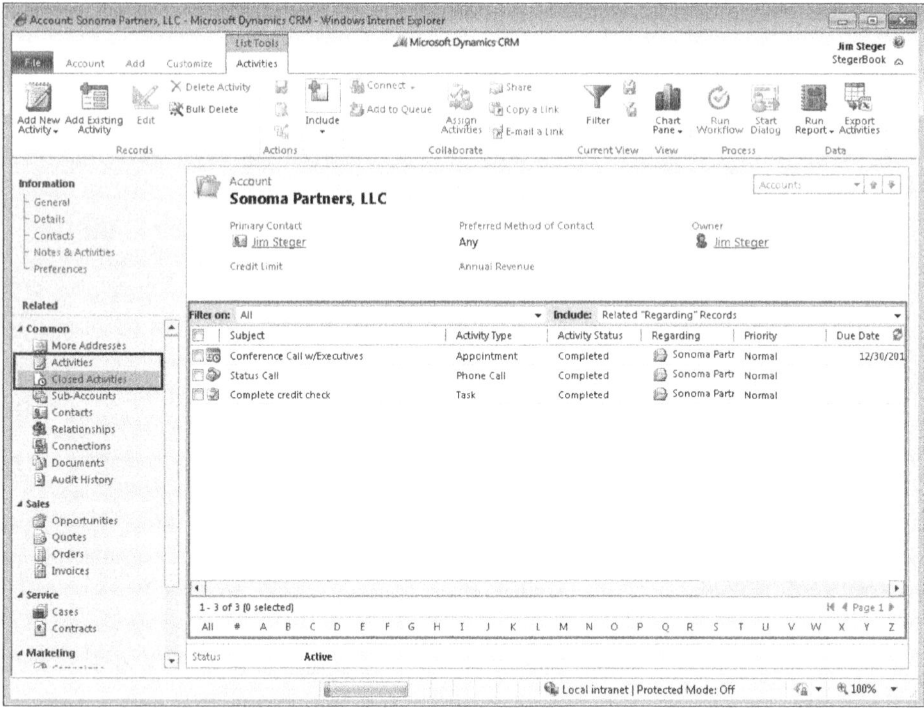

FIGURE 8-14 Activities views on an account record

Customizing Charts

One of the amazing new features of Microsoft Dynamics CRM 2011 is the ability to add inline charts (sometimes referred to as *visualizations*) to grid views. Charts provide several useful features:

- Users can graphically represent their data.
- Because Microsoft Dynamics CRM charts are dynamic, users may drill into the data and save their results.
- Charts can be added to dashboards, so users have a single place to quickly view the data most important to them.
- Users can view aggregate or grouped data from views in charts, such as the total amount of open invoices or total estimated revenue from all open opportunities.

Similar to views, charts can be added by users (personal charts) or by a system administrator (system charts). Figure 8-15 shows a sales pipeline chart for opportunities.

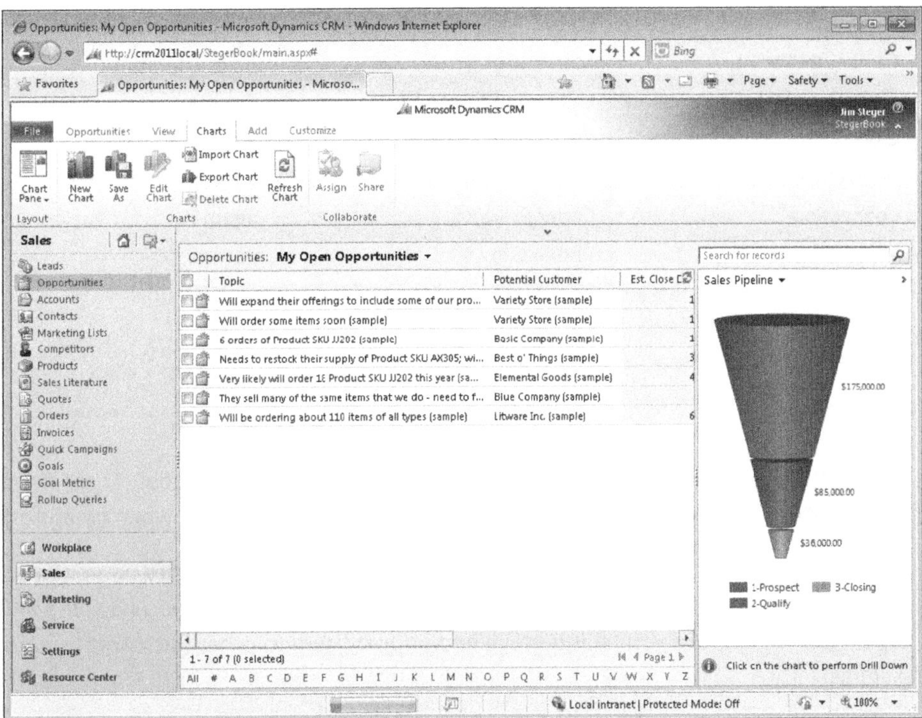

FIGURE 8-15 Opportunity sales pipeline chart

In this section, we'll focus on creating system charts and explain the following:

- Charts Overview
- Chart Properties
- Creating a Chart
- Exporting and Importing Charts

Charts Overview

Charts are defined with an entity and used with that entity's views. Charts can be created for any custom entity as well as for the following system entities included in Microsoft Dynamics CRM. Table 8-2 lists the entities available for charts.

TABLE 8-2 System Entities Available for Chart Use

Account	Goal Metric	Quote
Activity	Invoice	Quote Product
Appointment	Invoice Product	Recurring Appointment
Article	Lead	Report

Campaign	Letter	Rollup Query
Campaign Activity	Marketing List	Sales Literature
Campaign Response	Opportunity	Service
Case	Opportunity Product	Service Activity
Competitor	Order	Task
Connection	Order Product	Team
Contact	Phone Call	Territory
Contract	Price List	Unit Group
E-mail	Product	User
Fax	Queue Item	
Goal	Quick Campaign	

Microsoft Dynamics CRM includes more than 50 charts for these entities. These native charts are available immediately, and you can use these charts as examples when creating your own.

Analogous to views, fields, and forms, you access charts from the entity node of a solution, as shown in Figure 8-16. When creating charts as part of a solution, you have the ability to export them as part of your solution file and import them to other Microsoft Dynamics CRM systems.

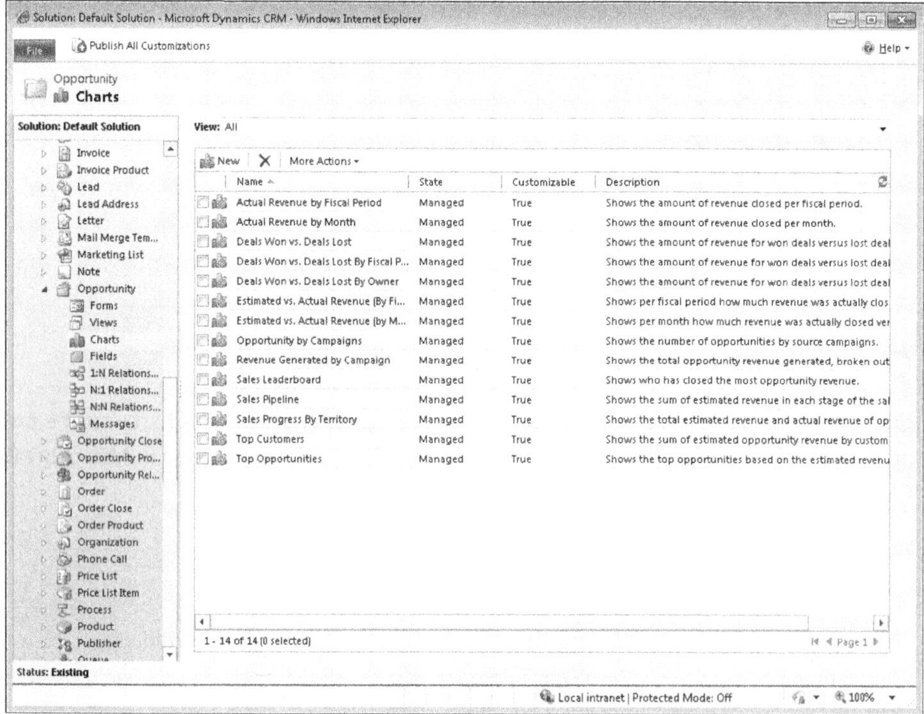

FIGURE 8-16 Accessing charts in a solution

Important The data included in a chart is based on the selected view, and some charts are only useful with certain views. For instance, the Resolved Case Satisfaction chart will only be useful when the Case view shows resolved cases. If this chart is viewed for an open cases view, the chart will load, but the counts will likely be "blank," based on the parameters defined for the chart. Using descriptive names for your charts helps alert users to the purpose of the chart.

Chart Properties

Like views, system administrators can modify charts. Figure 8-17 shows the properties of a chart.

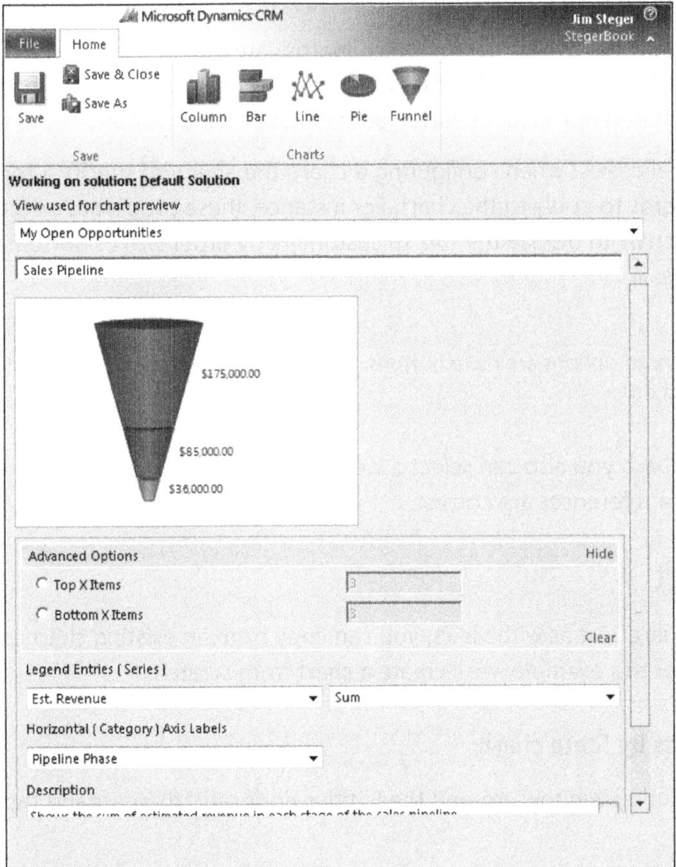

FIGURE 8-17 Chart properties

The properties include:

- Name
- Chart Type (Column, Bar, Line, Pie, Funnel)

- Legend Entries (Series) and grouping (count, sum, and so on)
- Horizontal (Category) Axis Labels
- Description
- Advanced Options
  - Top X Items
  - Bottom X Items

Name and Description are self-explanatory. As a best practice, you should always provide a unique name and description for your chart to clarify the purpose of the chart.

Your chart can be a funnel or a column, bar, line, or pie graph. Users can change these chart types when they view a chart. The chart type choices are located in the chart's ribbon menu.

The axes are defined by the Legend Entries and their appropriate groupings as well as the Horizontal Access Label. For example, in the sales pipeline chart in Figure 8-17, the chart displays the sum of the Estimated Revenue field for each Pipeline Phase on the Opportunity entity.

Two advanced options also exist when configuring a chart: the ability to specify a top or bottom number of records to apply to the chart. For instance, these properties would be useful if you wanted a chart to display the top 10 customers by order size or bottom three performing salespeople.

Tip Because the advanced options are radio buttons, use the Clear link to remove an existing advanced option selection.

Before finalizing your chart, you also can select a view to preview the chart and verify that the formatting and data references are correct.

Creating a Chart

Let's create your first chart. Just as with views, you can copy from an existing chart as a template. However, for this example, we'll create a chart from scratch.

Creating an Accounts By State chart

1. In the Default Solution window, expand the Entities node, and then expand the Account entity.
2. Click Charts under the Account entity in the navigation pane.
3. Click New to launch the New Chart form.
4. Enter **Accounts By State** for the name of the chart.
5. In the Legend Entries (Series) option, choose Account Name from the Select Field list. For the grouping, leave the default Count:All option selected.
6. Choose Address 1: State/Province for the Horizontal (Category) Axis Labels list.

7. In the Description field, enter **Shows the number of accounts by their location.**
8. Leave the default Column chart type in the ribbon.

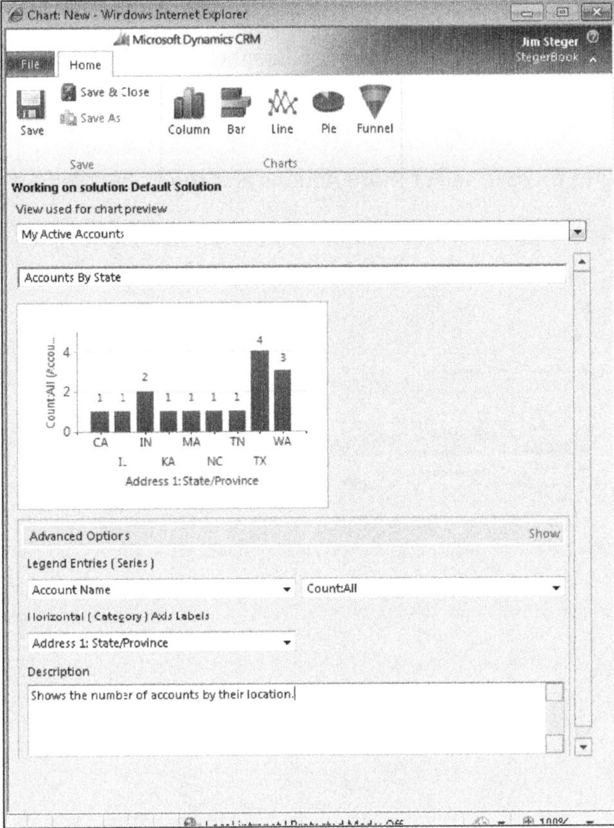

9. Click Save & Close in the chart ribbon.
10. In the Default Solutions window, click Publish All Customizations on the toolbar to publish your new chart.

Your chart is now ready for use and can also be exported as part of a solution file.

Exporting and Importing Charts

Charts are unique among solution components in that they allow you (or users with the correct privileges) to export and import individual charts into the Microsoft Dynamics CRM system. When you export a chart, Microsoft Dynamics CRM creates an XML file that can be imported into another Microsoft Dynamics CRM system without the overhead of a full solution file. You could use the exported chart as a template for other charts, edit the chart with your own styling or custom code, or use this exported file as a backup for a chart, should you or someone else accidentally remove the chart from your system.

Exporting the Accounts By State chart

1. In the Default Solution window, expand the Entities node, and then expand the Account entity.
2. Click Charts under the Account entity in the navigation pane.
3. Select the Accounts By State view you just created in the previous exercise from the grid.
4. From the charts grid toolbar, select More Actions and then select Export Chart.

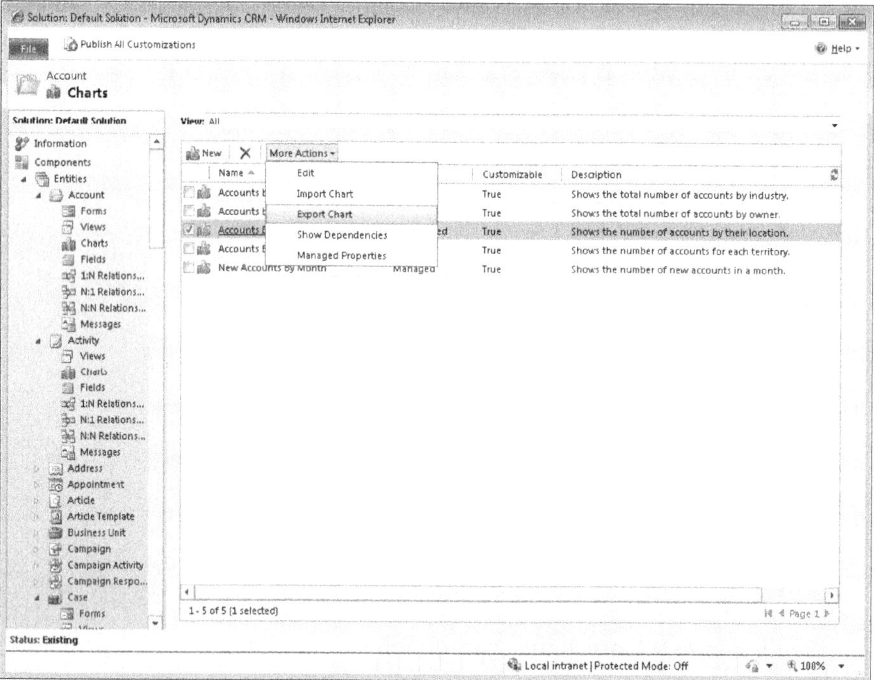

5. Depending on your version of Internet Explorer, the File Download dialog page might appear different from the one shown in Figure 8-12. However it appears, click Save.

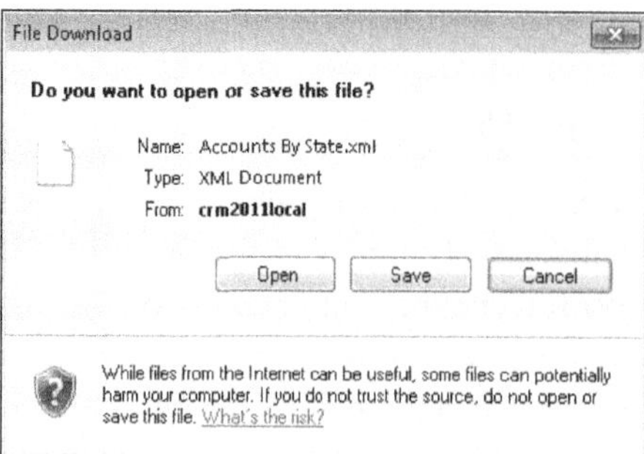

6. Save the file to a location on your computer.

Now that you have a copy of the chart as an XML file, you can go to another system to import it. We will use the default solutions area to import the chart.

Important You can also export and import charts from the entity's ribbon. This is typically how your users will import a chart. Although this approach works fine, the chart would be imported as a personal chart and would not be available for solution export.

Importing the Accounts By State chart

1. In the Default Solution window, expand the Entities node, and then expand the Account entity.
2. Click Charts under the Account entity in the navigation pane.
3. From the grid toolbar, select More Actions and then select Import Chart.

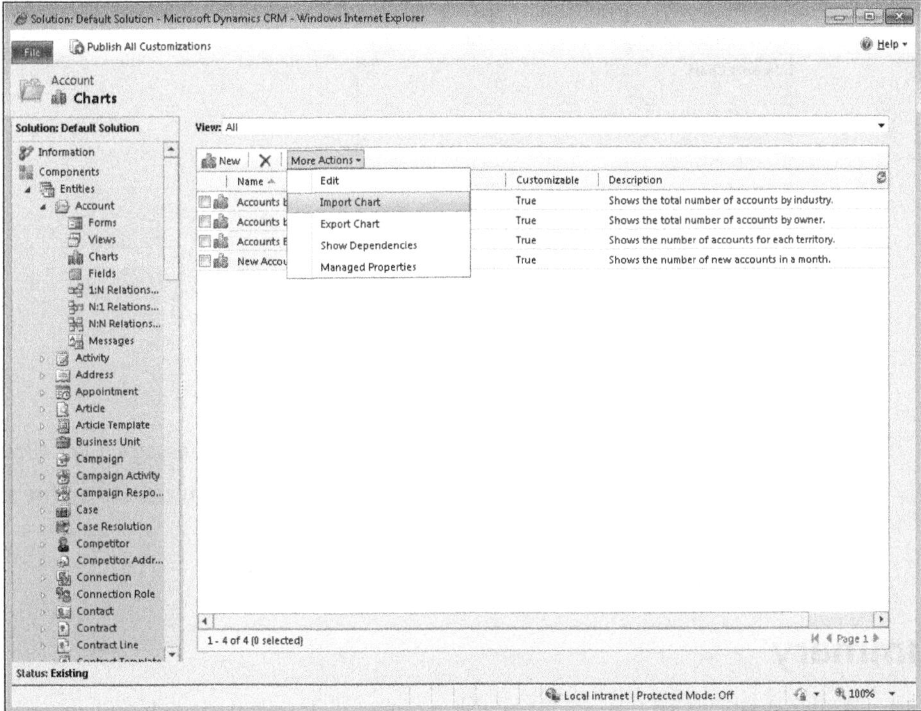

4. The Import Chart dialog appears. Click Browse and select the export file you previously saved.

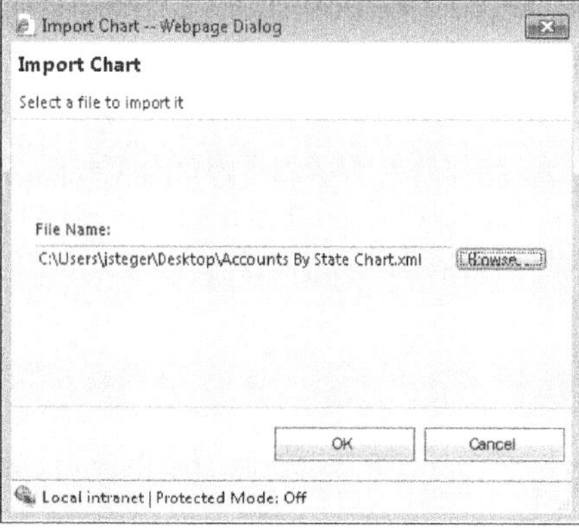

5. Click OK.
6. The next page in the Import Chart dialog appears, allowing you to change the name and description of the chart. Leave the default values and click Import.

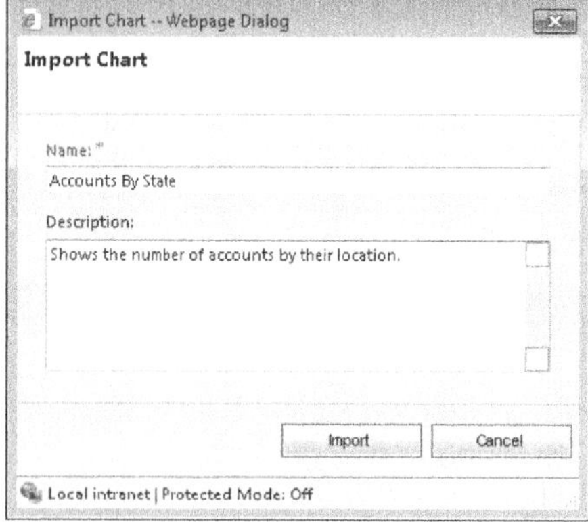

7. The final confirmation page displays with a successful message. Click Close.
8. In the Default Solutions window, click Publish All Customizations on the toolbar to publish your new chart.

Your newly imported chart is now available.

Summary

In this chapter, you learned more about entity customization, with a focus on views and charts. You have the ability to modify many of the public views deployed with Microsoft Dynamics CRM as well as create your own views. You saw what each of the system-defined views does, and how you can customize the views to show only the data that you want to see. And, you learned about some of the nuances related to activity views.

Finally, you had an opportunity to understand and create custom charts that provide rich, graphical representations of your data. You also learned that you can easily export and import the chart definitions between Microsoft Dynamics CRM environments.

Chapter 9

Entity Customization: Relationships

In this chapter:

In earlier chapters, you learned how to customize entities by modifying their fields, forms, and views. In this chapter, we cover all of the details related to entity relationships, including data relationships, relationship behavior, and entity field mapping. When you understand how to create custom entity relationships, you're ready to create custom entities and take full advantage of the Microsoft Dynamics CRM framework.

Understanding Entity Relationships

An *entity relationship* in Microsoft Dynamics CRM defines how two entities interact with each other. A Microsoft Dynamics CRM entity relationship definition includes multiple parameters:

- **Relationship definition** Specifies the nature of the data relationship between two entities (one-to-many, many-to-many, and so on)
- **Relationship field** Specifies the schema name and requirement level
- **Relationship navigation** Determines how the entity relationships should appear in the Microsoft Dynamics CRM user interface
- **Relationship behavior** Specifies the behavior between two entities, and how Microsoft Dynamics CRM uses that behavior to manage data when users take actions against one of the entities in the relationship
- **Entity mapping** Specifies how Microsoft Dynamics CRM maps common fields that two entities share

Microsoft Dynamics CRM includes hundreds of default entity relationships, and you can modify these default relationships or create entirely new entity relationships. You will almost always create at least one relationship between a custom entity and the Microsoft Dynamics CRM default system entities. In reality, you will probably create between 5 and 50 custom entity relationships for each custom entity that you create, depending on the complexity of your data model. Consequently, it's critical that you understand entity relationships before you create any custom entities.

Important You won't need to write a single line of programming code to create custom entities, but you do need a thorough understanding of the different entity relationship types and the custom relationships that Microsoft Dynamics CRM supports.

You can view all of an entity's relationships by using the entity editor in Microsoft Dynamics CRM. Figure 9-1 shows some of the default entity relationships for the Lead entity.

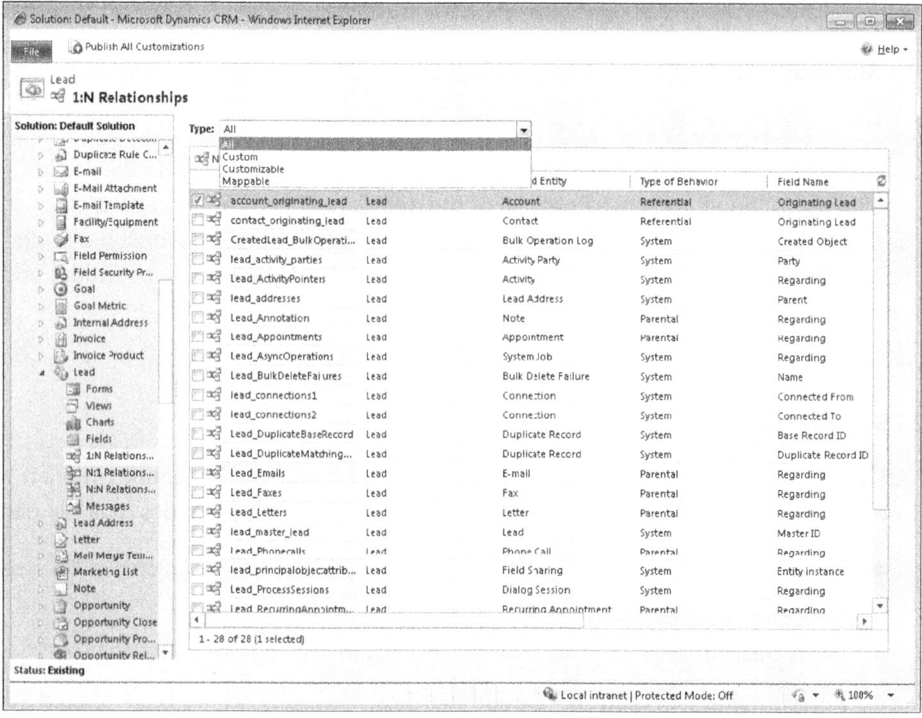

FIGURE 9-1 Default entity relationships for the Lead entity

This grid lists all the Lead entity relationships that Microsoft Dynamics CRM creates by default. To view the details of any one relationship, double-click a record in the grid. For example, double-click the record with the primary entity of Lead and the related entity of Contact, and you'll see the entity relationship editor shown in Figure 9-2.

You can use the relationship editor to view and configure all of the entity relationship parameters. In the next subsections, we review each component of an entity relationship definition, starting with the data relationship.

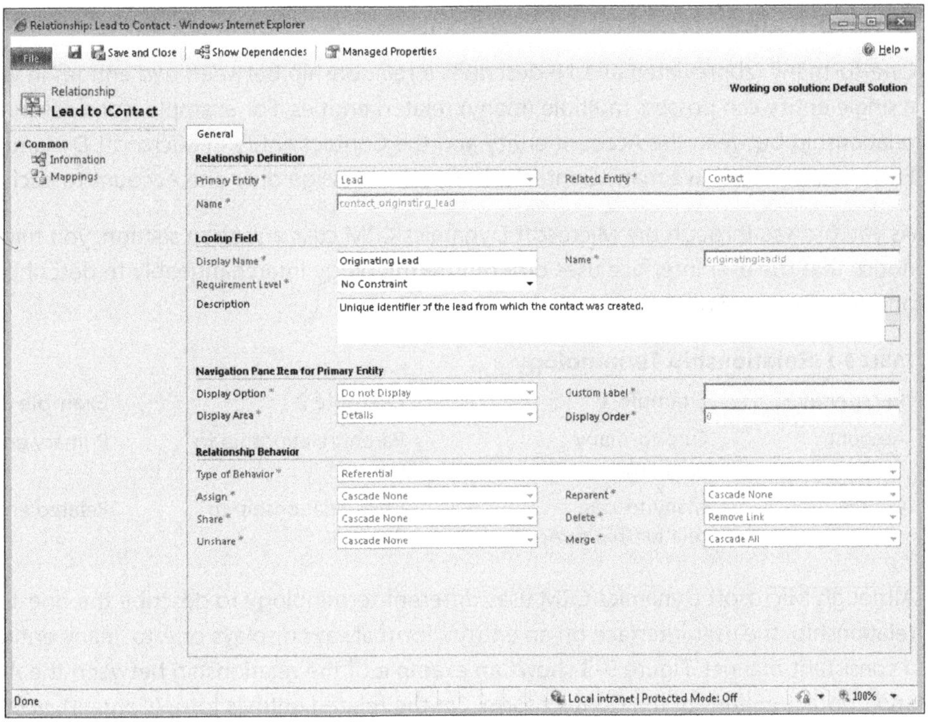

FIGURE 9-2 Relationship editor

Relationship Definition

One purpose of entity relationships is to define the *data relationship* between two entities in the system. Unlike a traditional database, in which you might configure primary and foreign keys to manage data relationships, you use entity relationships in Microsoft Dynamics CRM to manage how data interacts in the system metadata. This metadata design gives you the opportunity to customize and manage the data relationships easily without having to touch the underlying system data (and database keys) in Microsoft SQL Server.

Microsoft Dynamics CRM uses three types of data relationships, which we review in more detail in the following sections:

- One-to-many
- Many-to-one
- Many-to-many

One-to-Many

One-to-many (abbreviated as 1:N) describes a relationship between two entities in which a single entity can possess multiple (many) related entities. For example, consider the relationship between the Account entity and the Contact entity in Microsoft Dynamics CRM. Each Account can have many Contacts, but you can assign only one Account to each Contact.

As you browse through the Microsoft Dynamics CRM customization section, you might notice that the user interface uses different terminology interchangeably to describe the one-to-many data relationship, as shown in Table 9-1.

TABLE 9-1 Relationship Terminology

Perspective	Example 1	Example 2	Example 3
Account	One-to-many relationship to Contact	Parent relationship to Contact	Primary entity
Contact	Many-to-one relationship to Account	Child relationship to Account	Related entity

Although Microsoft Dynamics CRM uses different terminology to describe the one-to-many relationship, the user interface on an entity's form always displays one-to-many entities in a consistent manner. Figure 9-3 shows an example of the relationship between the Account and Contact entities of the Contact form. On the related entity's form (Contact), a *lookup field* labeled Parent Customer appears so that users can select the primary entity (Account).

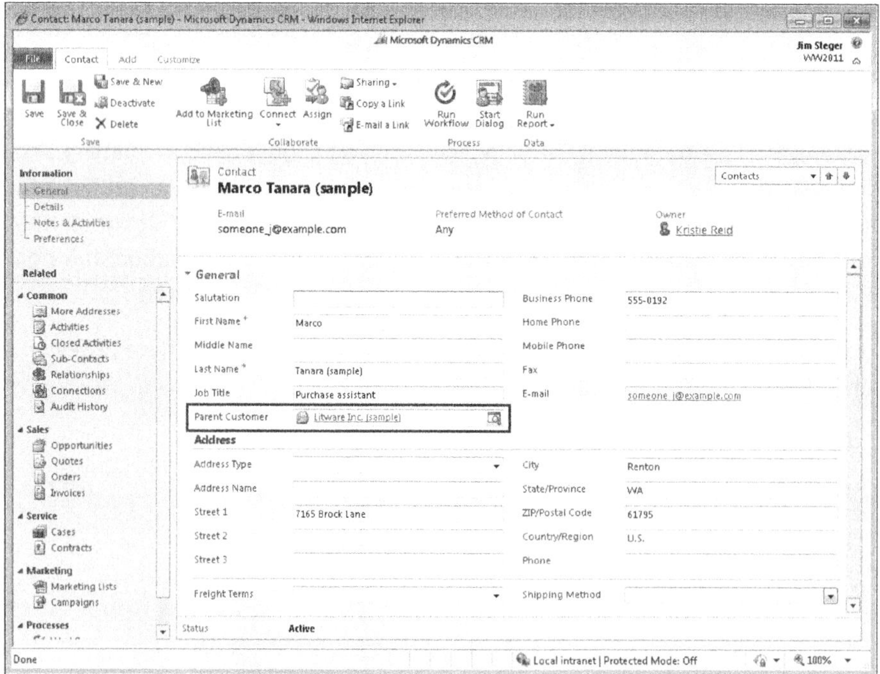

FIGURE 9-3 The primary entity displayed as a lookup on the related entity's form

Conversely, the related entity (Contact) does not appear on the form of the primary entity (Account). Rather, Microsoft Dynamics CRM adds a link in the navigation pane of the primary entity to a page that displays all of the related entities in a grid view, as shown in Figure 9-4.

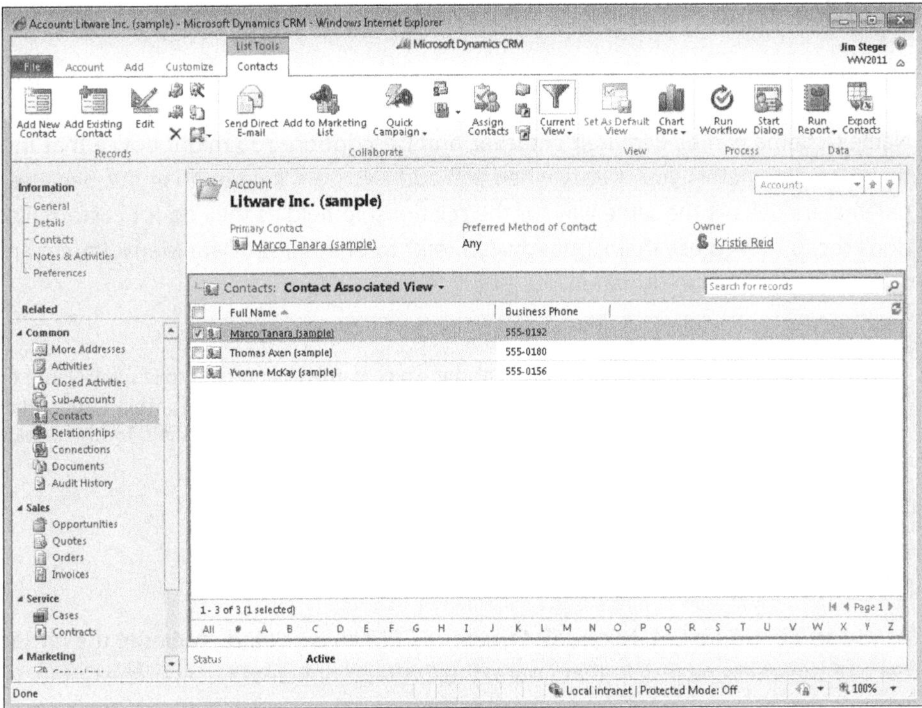

FIGURE 9-4 Related entities in a grid view

Remembering how Microsoft Dynamics CRM displays primary and related entities in the user interface can help eliminate some confusion when you try to decide how to set up your custom entity relationships.

Many-to-One

As you would expect, many-to-one relationships (abbreviated as N:1) behave in the exact opposite manner as do one-to-many relationships. You refer to the relationship type (many-to-one or one-to-many) depending on which entity you're talking about.

Many-to-Many

Many-to-many is the third type of data relationship between entities in Microsoft Dynamics CRM. Consider the relationship between the Marketing List entity and the Marketing List members. You can create many marketing lists in Microsoft Dynamics CRM, and then you can assign multiple members to each list. In addition, you can add members to multiple marketing lists. You can describe this relationship as *many-to-many.* The Microsoft Dynamics CRM user interface always uses grids to display many-to-many relationships between two entities. Therefore, anytime you see a lookup field on a form, you know that a one-to-many relationship exists between the two entities.

Relationship Field

The relationship field applies to one-to-many and many-to-one entity relationships. When you configure the relationship field, you specify the following parameters: Display name, Name (schema name), Requirement level, and Description. You might notice that these are the same parameters you specify when you add a custom field to an entity. Because these parameters behave the same way for the relationship field as they do for custom fields, we don't recap how to use them, but you can refer to Chapter 4, "Data Management and System Jobs," for additional information.

Tip Sometimes you might be confused about which name to enter in the Display Name field. For the most part, enter a name that describes the primary entity's relationship to the related entity. Remember that Microsoft Dynamics CRM uses the Display Name field for the default label on the related entity's form.

Relationship Navigation

As you saw in Figure 9-4, Microsoft Dynamics CRM links related entities in the navigation pane of the entity record. In that figure, the Contacts link displays all of the Contacts related to the Account. Microsoft Dynamics CRM offers you the flexibility of configuring how related entity information appears in the navigation pane. For all types of relationships, you can configure the following, which we look at in more detail in the following sections:

- Display option
- Display area
- Display order

Display Option

You can choose from one of three options:

- **Do Not Display** As you might guess, this option hides the related entity link in the navigation pane of the primary entity.
- **Use Custom Label** When you select this option, the Custom Label field becomes active and you can enter the name that you want to appear in the navigation pane. Even though you can enter up to 50 characters in this field, only the first 17 characters fit in the navigation pane link. However, users can view the entire custom label name in a tooltip by resting the mouse on the navigation pane.

- **Use Plural Name** If you select this option, the plural name of the related entity will appear in the navigation pane. This can cause confusion for your users if multiple relationships exist between two entities; therefore, we recommend that you only use this option if one relationship exists between two entities.

Display Area

With this option, you can specify in which navigation pane group the related entity link will appear. The default navigation pane groups for all entities are Details, Sales, Service, and Marketing.

Tip You cannot add new groups in the entity navigation pane, but you can rename these groups using the site map, as we explain later in this chapter.

Display Order

If you add multiple links to the navigation pane, you may also want to specify in which order the links appear. For example, you might want the most frequently used links at the top and less frequently used links at the bottom. Microsoft Dynamics CRM orders the additional links in the navigation pane from the lowest to the highest value of the display order. Therefore, to reorder the links simply enter new values for the display.

Relationship Behavior

In addition to understanding how Microsoft Dynamics CRM structures the data relationship between entities, you must understand the *relationship behavior* of entity relationships before you can map out your own custom entities and custom relationships. Entity relationships always exhibit one of two behaviors:

- Parental
- Referential

In the case of parental relationship behavior, actions that you take against the primary entity also apply to its related entities. With referential relationship behavior, any actions against the primary entity apply only to that entity, and none of its related entities. In Microsoft Dynamics CRM, only five actions are affected by relationship behaviors:

- Delete
- Assign
- Reparent
- Share
- Unshare

Consequently, if you take any other action against an entity in Microsoft Dynamics CRM (such as running a workflow rule), that action is not affected by the entity's parental or referential relationship behavior.

Tip You might be wondering what the difference is between the Assign action and the Reparent action. When you assign an entity, you change the owner of the record from one user to a different user. When you reparent an entity, you change a record's parent entity by using the lookup tool. Changing the parent account of an Account is an example of reparenting an entity.

It's important to understand the differences between parental and referential behavior because you need to specify relationship behavior anytime you create a relationship between two entities. Usually, you create at least one entity relationship for every custom entity. However, in Microsoft Dynamics CRM you also can modify the default relationship behavior between the default system entities. In the following subsections, we review parental and referential behavior in more detail. We also review a special kind of referential behavior known as Referential, Restrict Delete.

Parental Behavior

If the relationship between entities exhibits parental behavior, actions applied to the parent entity propagate down to all of its child entities. If you delete an Account record (the primary entity) such as the sample record for Coho Vineyard shown in Figure 9-5, Microsoft Dynamics CRM deletes all of that record's related data, including its Activity, Note, custom entity, and Opportunity, because of the parental relationships those entity records have with the Account entity. Likewise, when Microsoft Dynamics CRM deletes the custom entity record and the Opportunity record, it determines whether it should also delete their related entities based on the various relationship behaviors specified.

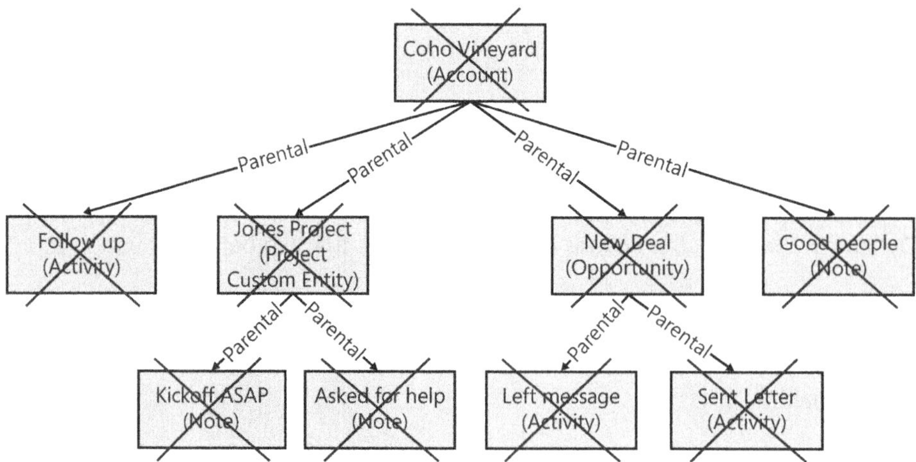

FIGURE 9-5 Parental relationships between entities

In the Coho Vineyard example, Microsoft Dynamics CRM deletes the Notes and Activities related to the custom entity record and the Opportunity because a parental relationship behavior exists between those entities. The software refers to this concept of working down the primary and related entity tree as *cascading*.

More Info All of the default system entities, such as Leads, Accounts, and Contacts, possess a parental relationship with Activities and Notes by default. Therefore, any action you take against the parent entity cascades down to all of its Activities and Notes. For example, if five active and two completed Tasks exist for an Account and you reassign that Account to a new user, all of the Tasks (active and completed) will also be assigned to the new user. Many customers want to reconfigure this default relationship behavior between system entities because they do not want to change the owner of completed Activity records. We explain how to make this change in the section titled "Behavior Configuration Options" later in this chapter.

Referential Behavior

In the case of referential relationships, actions taken against the primary entity do not cascade down to its related entities. To demonstrate referential relationship behavior, we modified the previous example by adding a custom entity B with a referential child relationship to the Project custom entity (see Figure 9-6).

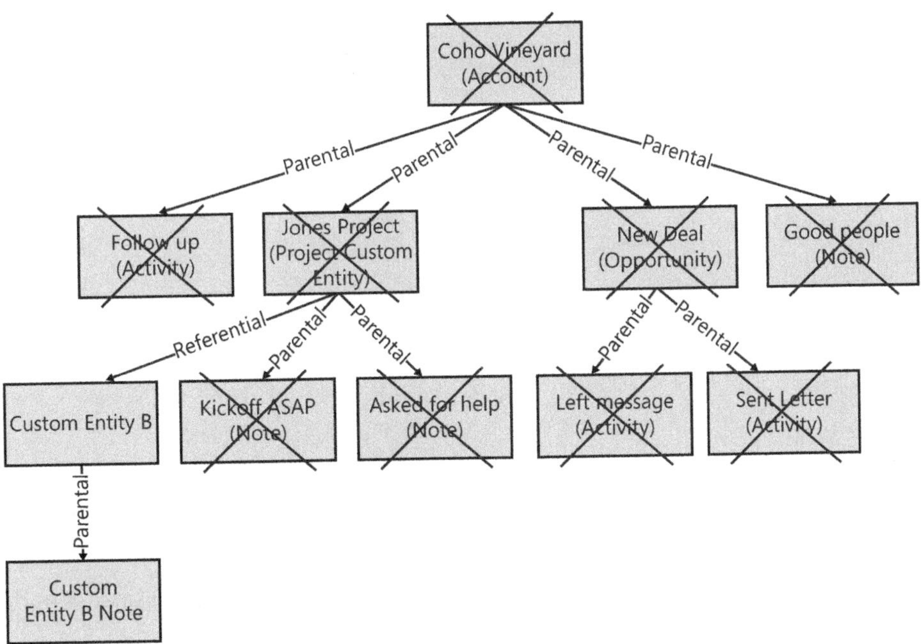

FIGURE 9-6 Referential behavior example

If you delete the Coho Vineyard Account shown in Figure 9-6, Microsoft Dynamics CRM deletes all of the records except custom entity B and its Note. Microsoft Dynamics CRM does not delete custom entity B because that entity has only a referential relationship to the Project custom entity. Microsoft Dynamics CRM deletes the Project custom entity because of the parental relationship behavior to its primary entity Account.

Important Parental relationship behavior applies only to one-to-many and many-to-one entity relationships. All many-to-many relationships exhibit referential behavior.

Behavior Configuration Options

Now that you understand the difference between parental and referential relationship behavior, we examine how you use the relationship editor to configure these relationships in Microsoft Dynamics CRM. Figure 9-7 shows the relationship editor that appears when you create a new one-to-many relationship.

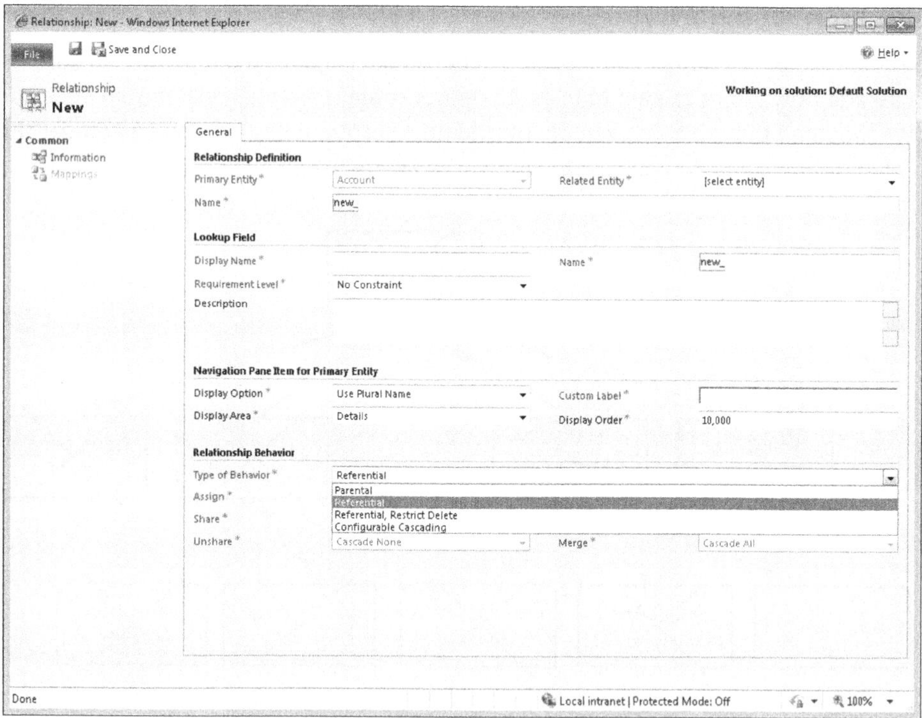

FIGURE 9-7 Entity relationship editor

In the Relationship Behavior section, you can choose from one of four values in the Type Of Behavior list:

- Parental
- Referential

- Referential, Restrict Delete
- Configurable Cascading

Again, entity relationships can exhibit only parental or referential behavior, but Microsoft Dynamics CRM includes four options in this list because they represent different configuration options for how the parental and referential behavior should apply to the various actions.

Selecting Parental or Referential applies that behavior type to the entity relationship for all actions. However the Referential, Restrict Delete option describes a special kind of referential behavior. If you choose Referential, Restrict Delete behavior, Microsoft Dynamics CRM does not allow the user to delete the parent entity if that entity has any related entities. Rather, Microsoft Dynamics CRM displays this error message to the user: "The record cannot be deleted because it is associated with another record." Consequently, Microsoft Dynamics CRM applies referential behavior to all of the other actions *except* the Delete action.

If you choose Configurable Cascading, you can specify different cascading behaviors depending on the action that users take against the parent entity. For example, you can set up parental cascading behavior for Delete actions against the parent, and then assign referential behavior for the assign action. For the Assign, Share, Unshare, and Reparent actions, you can configure one of four cascading rules:

- **Cascade All** Perform the action on the parent entity and all of its child entities; equivalent to parental behavior.
- **Cascade Active** Perform the action on the parent entity and all of its child entities where the status is active or open. You might select this option if you want to maintain a history of which users owned the previously completed Activities (Tasks, Phone Calls, and so on).
- **Cascade User Owned** Perform the action on the parent entity and only those child entities for which the entity owner matches the parent entity owner.
- **Cascade None** Perform the action on the parent entity only; equivalent to referential behavior.

A simple example can illustrate how these cascading rules work in the real world. Figure 9-8 shows an Account with four Tasks (two active, two completed) attached to it.

If you take an action against the Account (the parent entity), such as changing the Account owner from Bill to Fred, the cascading behavior of the relationship between the Account and Task entities determines how Microsoft Dynamics CRM applies the same action (assign) to the children entities. Table 9-2 shows how Microsoft Dynamics CRM would assign the owners of the four tasks for each of the cascading behavior settings.

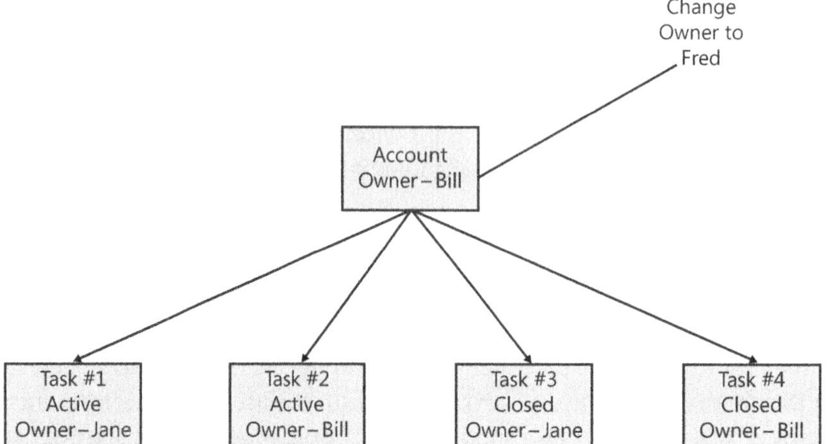

FIGURE 9-8 Account with four Tasks

TABLE 9-2 Ownership Determined by Cascading Behavior

				Final owner			
Type	**Entity**	**Status**	**Original owner**	**Cascade All (parental)**	**Cascade Active**	**Cascade User Owned**	**Cascade None (referential)**
Parent	Account	Active	Bill	Fred	Fred	Fred	Fred
Child	Task 1	Active	Jane	Fred	Fred	Jane	Jane
Child	Task 2	Active	Bill	Fred	Fred	Fred	Bill
Child	Task 3	Closed	Jane	Fred	Jane	Jane	Jane
Child	Task 4	Closed	Bill	Fred	Bill	Fred	Bill

For the Delete action, you can configure one of three behaviors:

- **Cascade All** Delete the parent entity and all of its child entities; equivalent to parental behavior.
- **Remove Link** Delete the link between the parent entity and the child entities, but do not delete the child entities; equivalent to referential behavior.
- **Restrict** Prevent the user from deleting an entity that possesses child entities; equivalent to referential, restrict delete behavior.

Although a Merge option set appears in the Relationship Behavior section, you cannot configure different relationship behaviors for that action. Merge always uses the cascade all (parental) behavior.

Note The merge functionality applies only to the Lead, Contact, and Account entities.

Entity Field Mapping

Entity field mapping is another component of the relationship definition between two entities. Not every relationship between two entities includes an entity mapping, although every relationship must include a data relationship and relationship behavior. By using mapping, you can specify common fields that two entities share. Entity field mapping provides the benefits of saving your users time and reducing data entry errors by automatically *mapping* data from the primary entity to its related entity at the time that Microsoft Dynamics CRM creates a related entity.

For example, if you add a related Contact to an Account, the default entity mapping between these entities automatically populates the address of the Contact with the same address as the Account. Without mappings, the user would have to retype the address information into the Contact even though it's identical to the address of the Account.

Important Microsoft Dynamics CRM maps entity fields only at the time that it creates a related entity. Mapping does not continually keep data synchronized. Therefore, if the address of the Account (primary) record changes, Microsoft Dynamics CRM will not automatically map these changes to the Contact (related) records. This type of synchronization requires additional system customization with custom programming.

Some of the scenarios in which Microsoft Dynamics CRM uses entity field mappings include the following:

- Adding a related entity to a primary entity (clicking New on the contextual ribbon of an associated view)
- Adding an Activity to an entity by using the Add ribbon
- Converting a Lead to an Account, Contact, or Opportunity

To view the entity relationships that include a mapping, open the entity editor and click the Type list in the appropriate relationship list, and then select Mappable. When you open the relationship editor for any mappable relationship, you see a Mappings link in the left navigation pane. Click the Mappings link to display the mapped fields for the relationship. Figure 9-9 shows the field mappings between the Account and Contact entities.

Each mapping consists of a source field and a target field, and you can see that Microsoft Dynamics CRM already mapped fields such as the address information between Account and Contact. Therefore, when you create a related Contact for an Account, Microsoft Dynamics CRM automatically prepopulates the target fields of the Contact with the values from the source entity (Account). Figure 9-10 shows a graphical representation of the Account and Contact mapping.

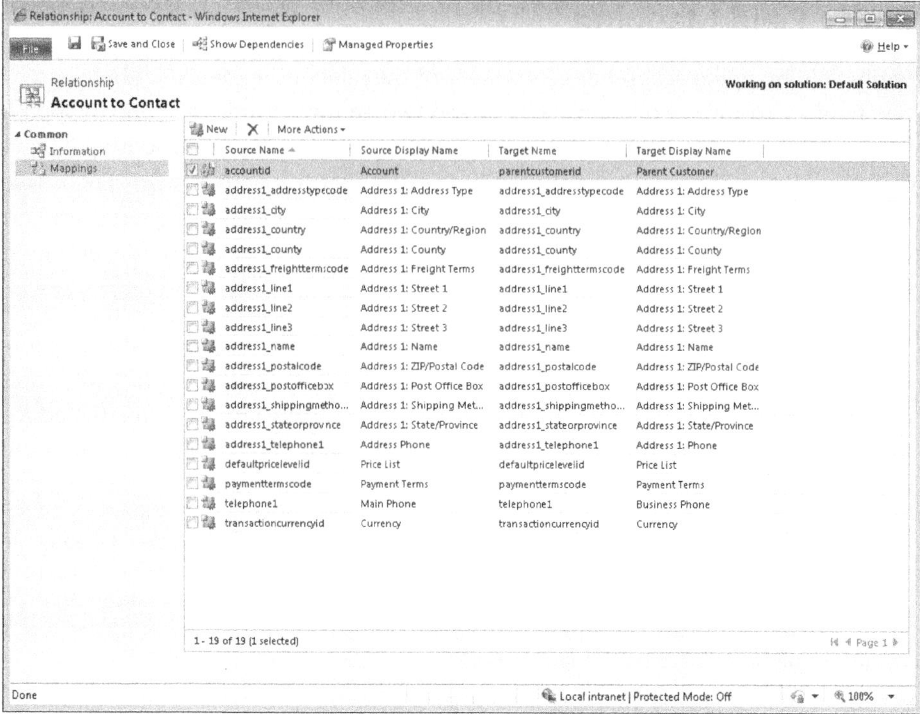

FIGURE 9-9 Field mappings between the Account and Contact entities

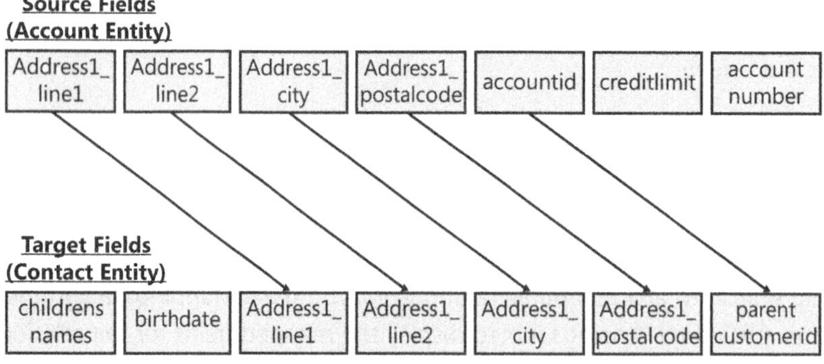

FIGURE 9-10 Mapping fields between the Account and Contact entities

We did not include all of the Account and Contact fields in this figure because of space considerations, but you can see that the Account entity includes fields (such as *accountnumber* and *credit limit*) that do not map to the Contact entity. Likewise, the Contact entity includes fields such as *birthdate* and *childrensnames* that don't apply to the Account entity. The point is, you don't have to map *all* of the fields from one entity to another—only the ones that make sense.

Creating Custom Mappings

Microsoft Dynamics CRM includes thousands of field mappings by default, but at some point you will probably need to create new field mappings or modify the default mappings. Consider an example in which you add a custom option set field with a schema name of *new_customerrating* to the Account and Contact entities (see Figure 9-11). Although both entities use the same schema name of *new_customerrating*, you must still create a mapping between these two fields if you want Microsoft Dynamics CRM to automatically populate the *new_customerrating* field when you create a related Contact from an Account.

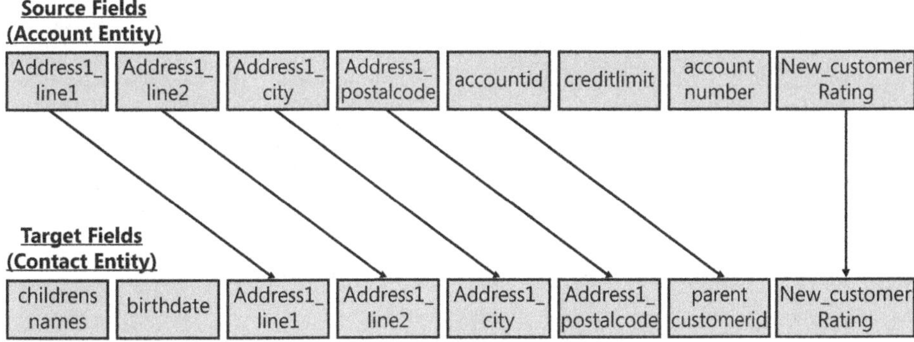

FIGURE 9-11 Mapping custom fields between the Account and Contact entities

To create a custom field mapping between two fields, you must meet the following conditions:

- Both fields must use the same data type.
- The length of the target field must be equal to or greater than the source field.
- You can specify a field as the target value only one time. However, you can map a field from the source entity to multiple target schema names.

Microsoft Dynamics CRM provides two methods for creating mappings. You can manually map fields one at a time, or you can use the Generate Mappings feature to let Microsoft Dynamics CRM automatically generate mappings for you. When you use the Generate Mappings feature, Microsoft Dynamics CRM creates a field map if two fields share a schema name and a data type.

Manually creating a mapping

1. In the Entities section of any solution, expand an entity record and click the type of relationship you want in the navigation pane (such as N:1 Relationships).
2. Double-click the entity relationship for which you want to modify or add a relationship mapping.

3. In the relationship editor window, click Mappings in the navigation pane.
4. To add a new mapping, click New on the grid toolbar. To modify an existing mapping, double-click the mapping you want to modify.

   A dialog box appears with the source entity fields on the left and the target entity fields on the right.

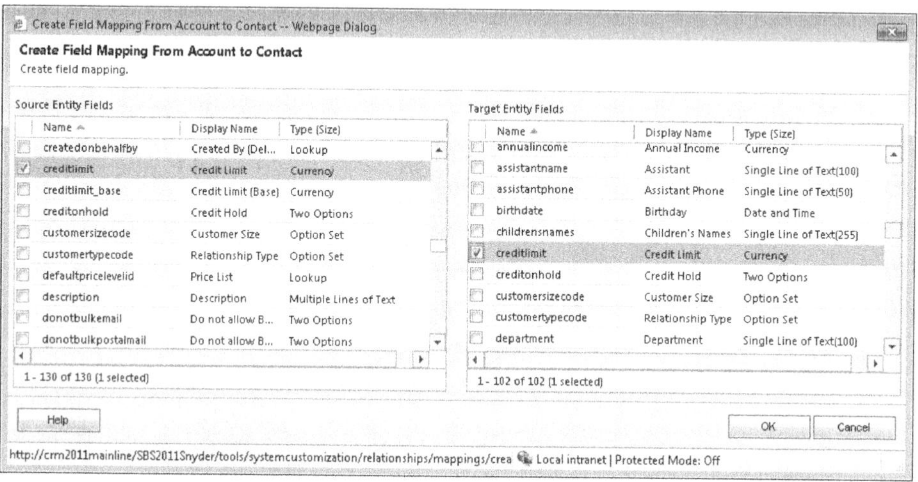

5. Select the source and target fields that you want to map, and then click OK.
6. A "Field Mapping" message appears.
7. Close the relationship editor, and then publish the entities that you customized.

Tip You can map two fields even if they use different schema names.

To use the Generate Mappings feature instead of manual mapping, simply click More Actions on the grid toolbar of the relationship editor, and then click Generate Mappings. Please note that when you generate mappings Microsoft Dynamics CRM removes all of the existing mappings between the entities.

Mapping Option Set Fields

Creating mappings for fields of the *Option Set* data type requires additional steps to ensure that the values map correctly. When you map two option set fields together, you must also make sure that the option set values match up accurately. When a user looks at a drop-down list on a form, Microsoft Dynamics CRM displays the *option set label* to the user. However, when Microsoft Dynamics CRM maps two option set fields together, it uses the *option set value*, not the option set label.

> **Tip** For fields that are equivalent between entities, consider using the new Global Option Set solution component. See Chapter 6, "Entity: Fields and Options Sets," for more details on global option sets.

To illustrate this nuance, we will add a new value to the Industry option set on the Lead entity. Microsoft Dynamics CRM includes a default mapping between the Industry field of Lead to the Industry field of Account. When you convert a Lead and create an Account, Microsoft Dynamics CRM uses this mapping to automatically populate the Account industry with the same value as the Lead industry. If you want to add a new industry to the option set called Software, you must add this value to both the Lead and Account fields to keep the values in sync.

When you click the Add icon (see Figure 9-12), you enter the option set text **Software** in the Label box. The text in the Label box is what the user sees in the drop-down list on the form. However, note that Microsoft Dynamics CRM also uses an integer option set value along with the option set label.

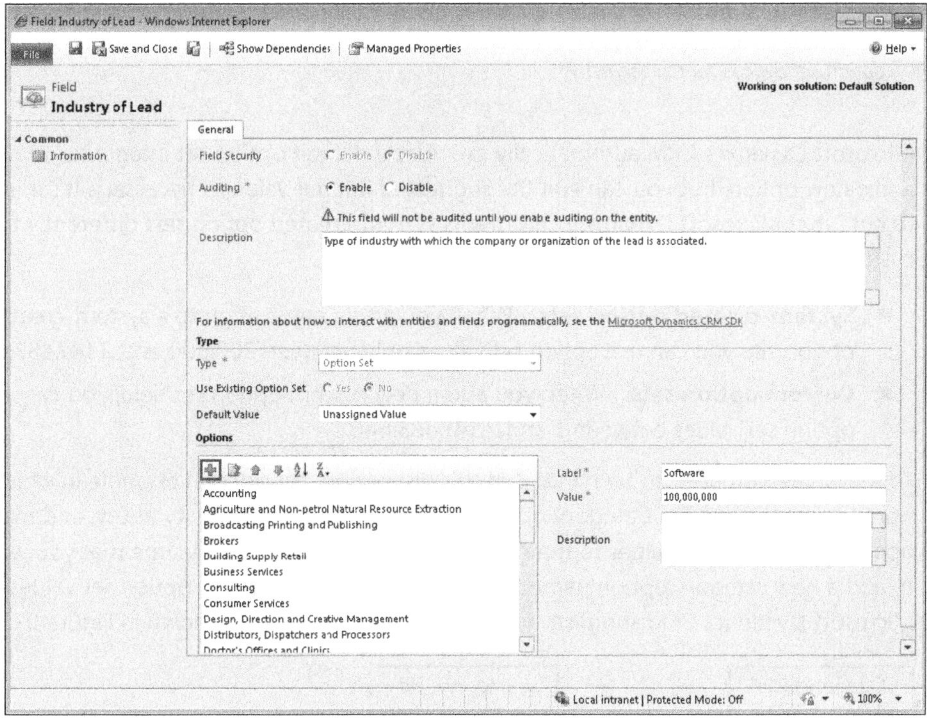

FIGURE 9-12 Adding a new option set value

When Microsoft Dynamics CRM maps the Lead industry to the Account industry, it uses the option set integer value to set the value on the Account. Therefore, Microsoft Dynamics CRM does not care what the label name is of the target option set when it tries to match. Table 9-3 shows some examples of how Microsoft Dynamics CRM will map and display an option set value, depending on the name/value of the target option set.

TABLE 9-3 Option Set Mapping Examples

Source option set value (Lead)	Source option set label (Lead)	Target option set field value (Account)	Target option set field label (Account)	Match?	Resulting option set value (Account Record)	Resulting option set label (Account Record)
1	Consulting	1	Consulting	Yes	1	Consulting
1	Consulting	1	Professional Services	Yes	1	Professional Services
1	Consulting	2	Consulting	No	Blank	Blank
1	Consulting	None	None	No	Blank	Blank

Important Microsoft Dynamics CRM always uses the option set value to determine matches for option set fields. Consequently, *it is critical that you make sure that the integer values of the option set always match correctly.*

Microsoft Dynamics CRM automatically provides a default option set integer value when you add a new option, but you can edit the suggested integer value as necessary. It's important to note that Microsoft Dynamics CRM treats system-created option sets differently from custom option sets that you create:

- **System-created option sets** When you add a new option to a system-created option set, you can use option set values only between 200,000 and 2,147,483,646.
- **Custom option sets** When you add a new custom option set field, you can assign option set values between 1 and 2,147,483,646.

To see where you need to be mindful of this distinction, consider an example in which you want to create a custom Category option set field on the Opportunity entity, and map the opportunity Category values to the Account field Category. Also, assume that you want to add a new category option named VIP. If you accept the default option set values that Microsoft Dynamics CRM suggests, you would have the scenario shown in Figure 9-13.

Category Field Account Entity	Category Field Opportunity Entity
Preferred Customer (value = 1)	Preferred Customer (value = 1)
Standard (value = 2)	Standard (value = 2)
VIP Customer (value = 200,000)	VIP Customer (value = 3)

FIGURE 9-13 Mapping custom option sets to system-created option sets

With this configuration, the Category option set fields would map from the Account to the Opportunity only for Preferred Customers and Standard customers. However, the Category field would not map to the Opportunity record for VIP accounts because the option set values don't match. To correct this, you need to modify manually the VIP option set value on the Opportunity category field to equal 200,000. Remember, you cannot modify the value of the VIP option set option to 3 because Microsoft Dynamics CRM allows you to use only values starting at 1,000,000,000 on system-created option sets.

More Info On system-generated fields, customers who upgraded from Microsoft Dynamics CRM 3.0 to Microsoft Dynamics CRM 4.0 can have custom option set values less than 200,000 because they carried over from the previous version. Likewise, customers who upgraded from Microsoft Dynamics CRM 4.0 might have values between 200,000 and 1,000,000.

This same concept of matching option set values also applies to entities with status reasons and state fields such as Account, Lead, and Opportunity. Please remember to make sure that you match up the values for all of the status reasons for each of the different states between two entities.

Tip Don't worry if you skip integer values in the option set because you deleted an option—just make sure that the values you want to match always use the same integer value.

Creating Custom Relationships

Now that you understand some of the details behind entity relationships, we explore how to create custom relationships in more detail and examine some real-world scenarios. Microsoft Dynamics CRM supports a wide range of custom entity relationships, such as the following:

- **One-to-many and many-to-one** Create primary and related entity relationships between system-to-system, custom-to-custom, and system-to-custom entities.
- **Many-to-many** Create two related entity relationships between entities.
- **Self-referencing** Create a relationship between an entity and itself so that you can have parent:child record support.
- **Multiple references** Create multiple references between the same two entities. For example, you can create multiple references between the Contact and Account entities.
- **System-to-system** Create new relationships between existing Microsoft Dynamics CRM system entities.

Although Microsoft Dynamics CRM supports all of these custom relationships in some shape or form, not all of the entities behave the same way. Consider the following examples of unique entity relationship constraints:

- On the Appointment and Campaign Response entities, you can create custom N:1 relationships, but you cannot create custom 1:N or N:N relationships.

- On the Business Unit and Subject entities, you can create custom 1:N relationships, but you cannot create custom N:1 or N:N relationships.
- You cannot create custom self-referencing relationships on the Business Unit and Subject entities even though they already include those types of relationships.

Microsoft Dynamics CRM includes too many unique entity circumstances to list in their entirety. Consequently, you should *not* assume that you can apply all types of custom entity relationships to all types of entities. Please double-check the entity Customization section to verify what Microsoft Dynamics CRM allows before finalizing an entity relationship design.

To illustrate the benefits of custom relationships, we explore two commonly requested real-world scenarios:

- Adding multiple user references per account
- Creating parent and child cases

Adding Multiple User References per Account

Many customers who deploy Microsoft Dynamics CRM do so because they want to track the various interactions they have with their customers. As more and more people from your company interact with a single customer, managing that interaction becomes more and more complicated. Consequently, many customers want the ability to assign multiple employees to a single account and to designate their individual roles in relation to the account.

By default, each Microsoft Dynamics CRM Account record includes a single owner record. Fortunately, you can use custom relationships to add to the Account entity the additional references you need. Assume that in addition to the account owner, you want to add a salesperson reference and a customer service reference to each Account.

Add additional user references

1. In the Customization section of Microsoft Dynamics CRM, click Customize the System.
2. Click Entities and then click the Account entity to display the Account entity components.
3. Because a single user can have the same role with multiple accounts, you will create a many-to-one (N:1) relationship between the Account and User entities. Click the N:1 Relationships link.
4. Click the New Many-to-1 Relationship button on the grid toolbar.
5. Select User for the Primary entity and type **sales_user_account** in the Name field.
6. For the Display Name, type in **Sales Person**. This is the name that will appear on the form, in the views, and so forth.

7. For Display Option, select the Do Not Display option because you don't want to see the related accounts on the user's record.

8. On the Type Of Behavior drop-down menu, select Referential so that Microsoft Dynamics CRM does not apply the cascading actions such as assign, share, and delete to the user's related accounts when action is taken against the User record.

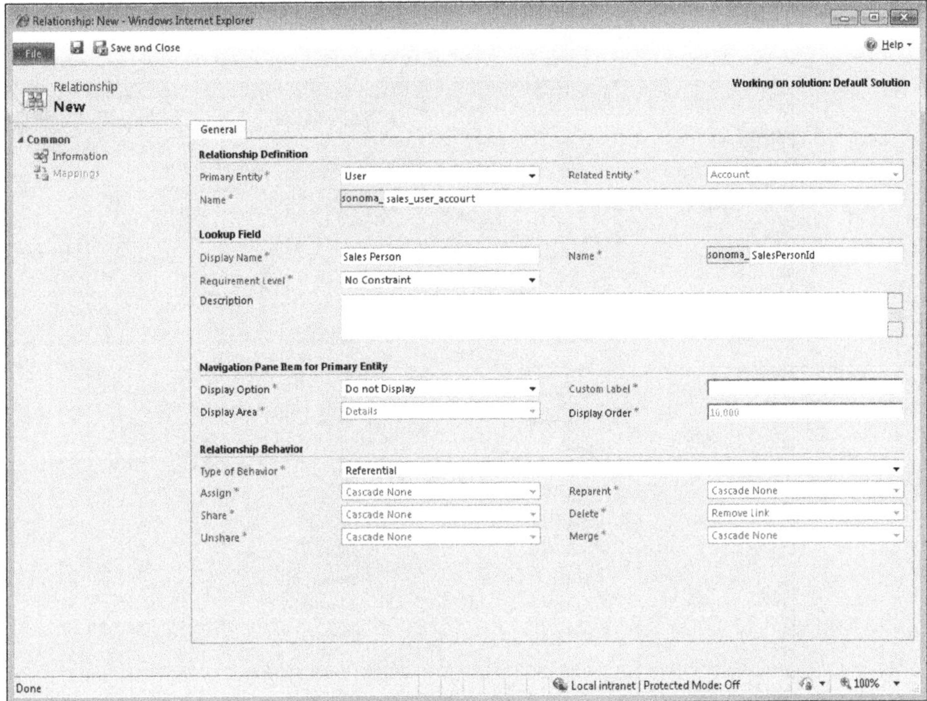

9. Click the Save And Close button. You just created a new custom relationship between the User and Account entities to track which user is the account's salesperson.

   Repeat the process to create the relationship to the account's service manager, as shown in Steps 10-16 below.

10. In the navigation pane, click the N:1 Relationships link.

11. On the grid toolbar, click the New Many-to-1 Relationship button.

12. Select User for the Primary entity, and type **service_user_account** in the Name field.

13. For the Display Name, type in **Service Manager**.

14. For the Display Option, select Do Not Display.

15. For the Type of Behavior, select Referential.

16. Click the Save And Close button.

17. Next, you need to add the new fields to the Account form so that users can select records for each account.

18. In the navigation pane, click Forms, and then double-click the Main form. The form editor opens.

19. In the Field Explorer, change the Filter to Custom Fields and leave the Only show unused fields check box enabled. The Field Explorer will display your two new relationship attributes.

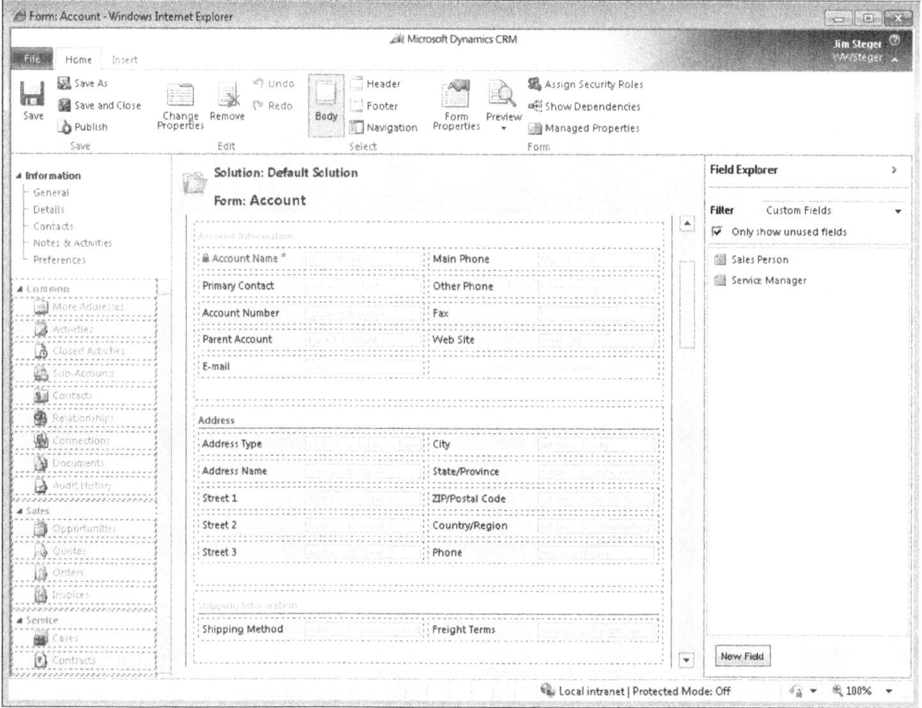

More Info See Chapter 7, "Entity: Forms," for more details on configuring forms.

20. Drag each field onto the form canvas.

21. On the ribbon, click Save, and then click Publish.

Now when you browse to an Account record, you can specify the salesperson and the service manager (using Microsoft Dynamics CRM User records) for each account, as shown in Figure 9-14.

As you learned in Chapter 3, "Managing Security and Information Access," the Microsoft Dynamics CRM security settings are partly determined by each record's owner.

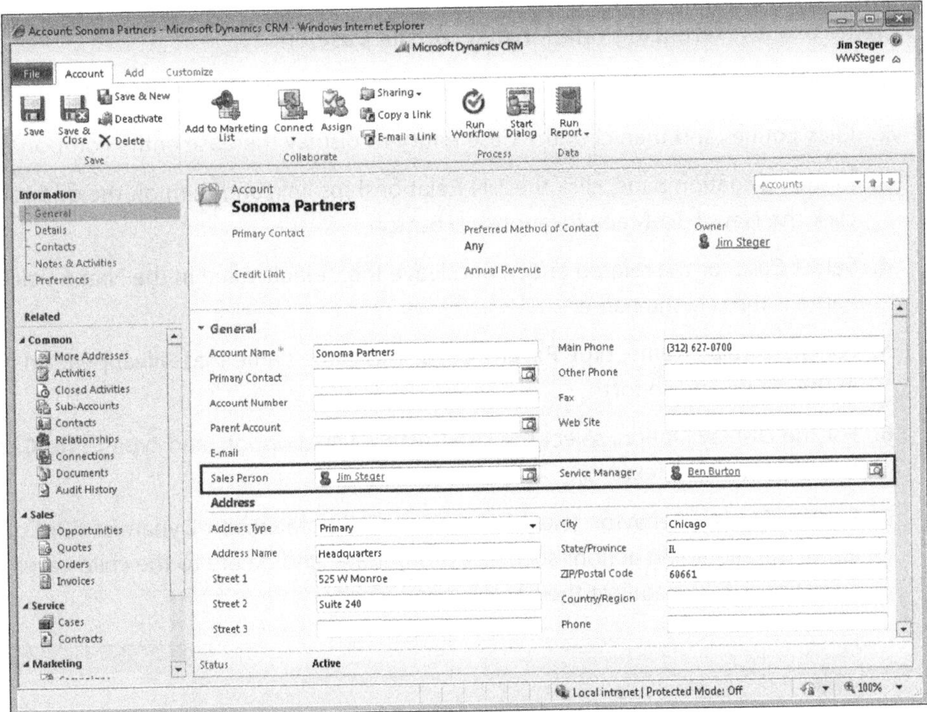

FIGURE 9-14 Additional custom user relationships added to the Account entity

So, even though you added additional users to the Account in this example, Microsoft Dynamics CRM still references the original Owner field to determine the security settings.

Creating Parent and Child Cases

As the previous example shows, adding custom relationships to entities gives you the flexibility to track additional relationship data about how records interact with other entities. You can also use custom relationships to track and manage how records of one entity type interact with records of the same entity type. Microsoft Dynamics CRM 2011 supports these types of self-referencing custom relationships, and we walk through a real-world example of these relationships using the Case entity.

As you know, the Microsoft Dynamics CRM customer service module allows a company to capture data about requests and issues that they want to resolve using a case record. As a company starts to build a database with a large number of cases, they quickly see that many of the cases relate to one another. Consequently, the company might want to create a link between these related cases so that once they resolve a single case, they can quickly apply that same resolution to the related cases. In the following exercise, you use custom relationships to create a parent and child relationship between case records.

Create a self-referencing relationship for the Case entity

1. In the Customization section of Microsoft Dynamics CRM, click Customize the System.
2. Click Entities and then click the Case entity to display the Case entity components.
3. In the navigation pane, click the 1:N Relationships link, and then on the grid toolbar click the New 1-To-Many Relationship button.
4. Select Case for the related entity, and leave the default value in the Name field. This name is the schema name.
5. For the Display Name, type **Parent Case**. This is the name that will appear on the form, in the views, and so forth.
6. For the Display Option, select the Use Custom Label option, and type **Child Cases** into the Custom Label text box.
7. For the Type Of Behavior, select Referential so that Microsoft Dynamics CRM does not apply the cascading actions such as assign, share, and delete to the child cases when an action is taken against the parent case record.

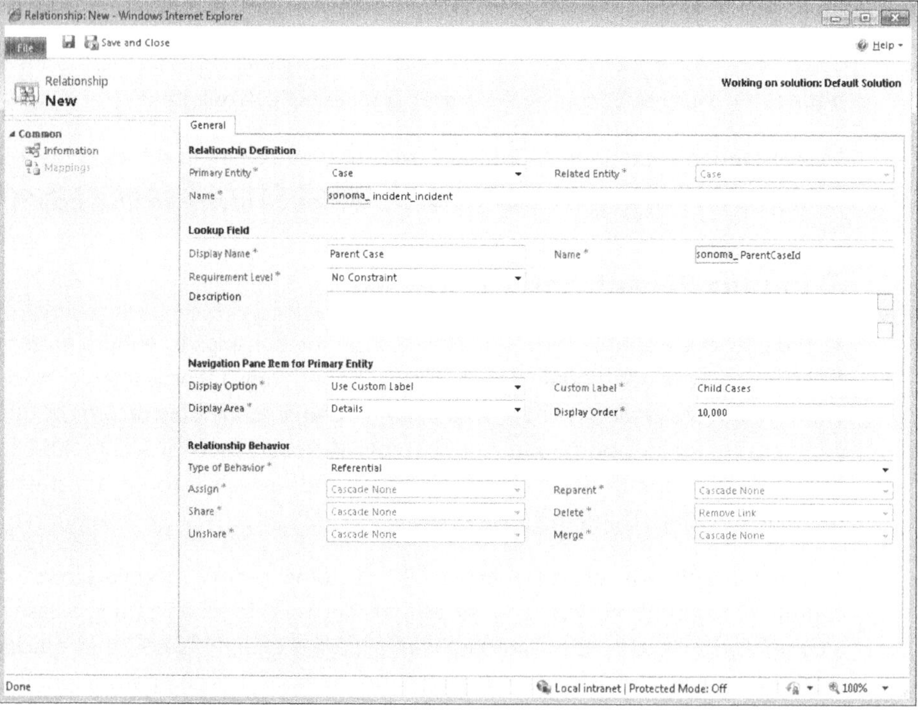

8. Click the Save And Close button.

9. Next, add the new Parent Case field to the case form so that users can select the Parent Case for a record. In the navigation pane, click Forms, and then double-click the Main form. The form editor opens.

10. Find the Parent Case field from the Field Explorer and drag the field onto the form canvas.

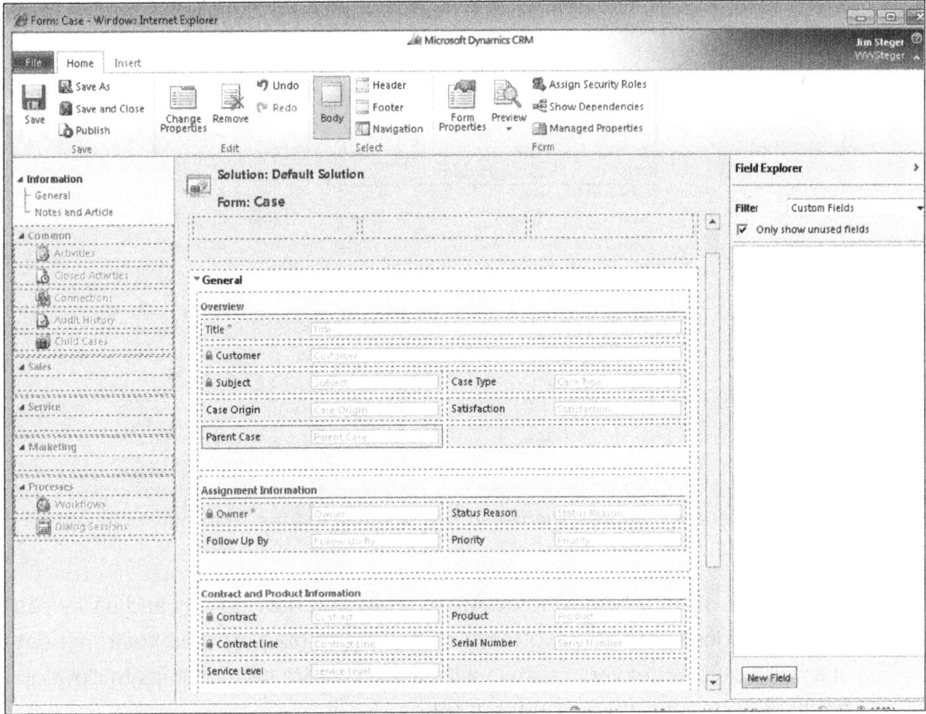

11. On the ribbon, click Save, and then click Publish.

When users work with a case record now, they can track how a single case relates to other cases so that they can manage the list of issues more efficiently. For example, customer service representatives can select a Parent Case for each record using the lookup on the form, and in addition they can click Child Cases in the navigation pane to see a list of child records related to the case (Figure 9-15).

Tip In this example, you set up a referential relationship between the parent and child cases. However, you might want to configure the cascading behavior so that when you reassign the parent case, Microsoft Dynamics CRM automatically assigns all of the child cases to the same case owner.

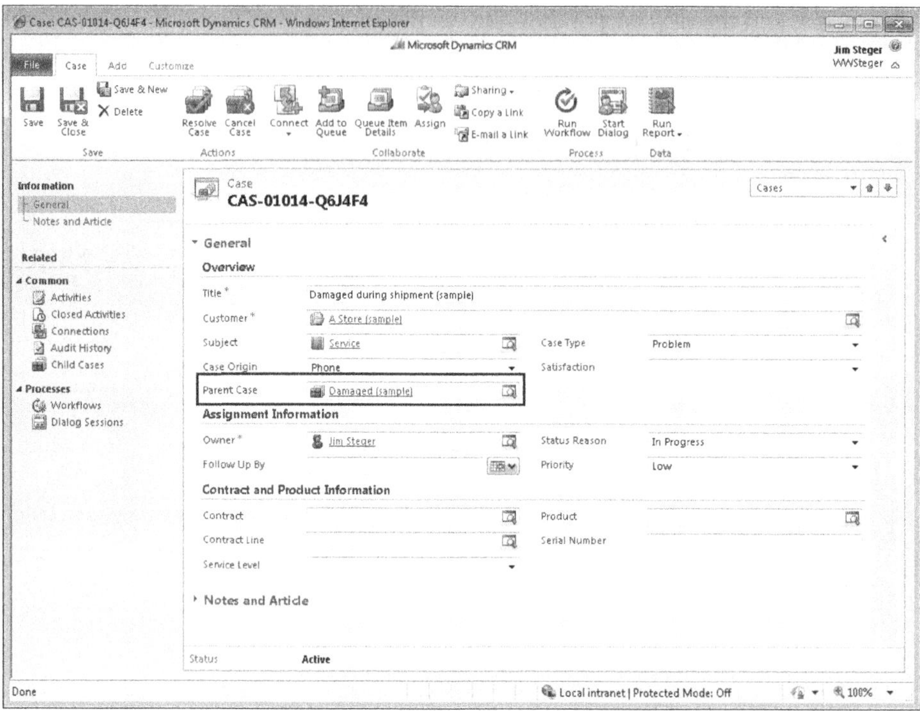

FIGURE 9-15 Adding custom self-referencing relationships to the Case entity to track parent and child case information

These two custom relationship examples show you how quickly and easily you can configure entity relationships in Microsoft Dynamics CRM to manage your customer data. As you can imagine, you can get very creative with these custom relationships to develop a system that perfectly suits your unique business needs.

Summary

Microsoft Dynamics CRM includes many powerful features, but the ability to create custom data relationships through a Web-based administration tool ranks as one of the more important ones. Understanding how Microsoft Dynamics CRM structures entity relationships can help you plan and map your system to ensure that there is a smooth implementation.

Chapter 10

Entity Customization: Custom Entities and Activities

In this chapter:

In the previous chapters, you learned how to customize the default entities in Microsoft Dynamics CRM by modifying their attributes, forms, and views. In Microsoft Dynamics CRM, you also can create entirely new entities to track and manage data in your system. The entities that you create are called *custom entities*. You can also create special custom entities that you denote as activity types so that they function similarly to default activities such as tasks, phone calls, and appointments. Microsoft Dynamics CRM refers to these as *custom activities*.

This chapter will walk you through the steps and configuration settings necessary to create custom entities and custom activities, and highlight some of the tricks we've learned.

Custom Entities

Now that you understand entity relationships and how to create your own custom relationships, we'll explore custom entities. Microsoft Dynamics CRM creates almost 100 customizable entities when you install the software, and you can add an almost unlimited number of custom fields to the customizable entities. However, you will almost certainly want to track business data that does not fit neatly into one of these existing entities. With most other customer relationship management (CRM) applications, tracking new categories of data usually requires a custom application development project to create custom databases and user interface forms that blend into the host CRM application.

In addition to the obvious downsides of using development time and costing money, these customized CRM application projects usually result in less-than-ideal functionality for system administrators and users. Plus, when the host CRM application releases an updated version, the business logic code has to be reprogrammed, the customized databases have to be updated, and the user interface forms have to be revised. Add all these factors and you can understand why CRM customization projects in the past required lots of time, money, and effort.

Tip Many people refer to a Microsoft Dynamics CRM system with a large number of custom entities as an *xRM* system because it is extended CRM. There is no hard definition of what qualifies as an xRM deployment, but it typically refers to using a large number of custom entities beyond the default sales, marketing, and customer service entities.

Custom Entity Benefits

Fortunately, Microsoft Dynamics CRM solves many of the common CRM customization issues related to tracking new categories of data by allowing you to create custom entities. Even more beneficial, Microsoft Dynamics CRM allows you to create custom entities and manage data relationships using the web-based administration interface so that no custom programming is required.

You have almost unlimited options for how you can set up and structure your custom entities. For example, an apartment management company might use custom entities to track its various property locations, leases, and rental applications. A professional services firm can create custom entities to track its customer projects. A magazine publisher might use custom entities to capture data about its magazines and customer subscriptions. As you can see, how you use custom entities depends on the nature of your business and the types of data that you want to capture in Microsoft Dynamics CRM.

When you create a custom entity to store a new category of data, Microsoft Dynamics CRM automatically adds the entity to the metadata and its underlying system data. This means that custom entities behave as "first-class" system entities, sharing almost all of the functionality of the default system entities. Some common benefits of custom entities and the default entities include the following:

- You can customize the custom entity fields, forms, and views with the same web-based administration tools that you use to customize the default entities.
- You can use the Advanced Find feature to create and save queries on custom entities.
- You can add client-side events such as *onChange*, *onLoad*, and *onSave* to the custom entity forms.
- You can import and export custom entities as part of a solution so that you can easily transfer them between different Microsoft Dynamics CRM systems, such as moving from development to staging to production.
- You can access custom entities in the Microsoft Dynamics CRM for Outlook client, including while in offline mode.
- You can add custom relationships and mappings to custom entities, just as you can with the default entities.
- Custom entities fully participate in the Microsoft Dynamics CRM security framework, so you can set privileges such as create, read, and write on an entity-by-entity basis. You can also use field-level security settings on custom entities.

- Developers can programmatically access custom entities through the Microsoft Dynamics CRM software development kit (SDK).
- Microsoft Dynamics CRM supports plug-ins on custom entities.
- You can use the batch edit feature on custom entity records.
- You can configure duplicate detection to check against custom entity records.
- Users can export custom entities to Microsoft Office Excel as a dynamic PivotTable or worksheet.
- You can modify the Microsoft Dynamics CRM application navigation and menu structure to blend custom entities into the user interface seamlessly.

This list illustrates that custom entities behave almost identically to the default entities in Microsoft Dynamics CRM.

Custom Entity Limitations

Despite all of the similarities between custom entities and default entities, a few notable limitations exist for custom entities:

- You cannot merge two custom entity records together.
- The Microsoft Dynamics CRM system entities include a relationship to Customer in which users can select an Account or a Contact. For custom entities, you can specify relationships with the Account and Contact entities, but you cannot create a relationship to the composite customer lookup, in which users can select an Account or a Contact on a single lookup.
- Custom entities don't appear in an entity rollup (showing activities from child entities on the parent entity's record).
- Custom entities cannot have parental relationship behavior with system entities.

As you can see, only a few limitations exist regarding custom entities, so you will probably make heavy use of them in your Microsoft Dynamics CRM deployment. We explain how to configure custom entity relationships and their corresponding limitations next.

Custom Entity Example

To better understand the benefits of custom entities, let's map out a real-world example of creating custom entities and relationships for a fictional property management firm called Litware, Inc.

Litware manages 15 apartment buildings in Chicago, Illinois. The apartment complexes range in size from 25 to 75 apartments per building, including one-bedroom, two-bedroom, and three-bedroom apartments. As part of the rental process, each prospective tenant must complete a rental application and agree to a credit check. After receiving credit approval, all of the tenants sharing an apartment (roommates) sign a lease. Litware uses Microsoft Dynamics CRM to manage its current tenants and track potential tenants.

Based on this description, we created an initial design proposal in which Litware would use the following entities in Microsoft Dynamics CRM:

- **Building** Custom entity with fields such as name and address.
- **Apartment** Custom entity with fields such as number of bedrooms, number of bathrooms, square footage, monthly rent, and floor number.
- **Lease** Custom entity with fields such as monthly rent, start date, end date, and security deposit. Because Litware offers three-bedroom apartments, up to three people can share a single lease.
- **Lease Application** Custom entity with fields such as employment information and previous addresses. Each tenant provides his or her own application.
- **Contact** System entity used to track tenants and applicants.
- **Opportunity** System entity used to track potential rental opportunities.

When you diagram an entity design like this one, you should consider different scenarios because no hard rules exist to let you know whether you should create a custom entity or add attributes to an existing entity. We recommend that you try to map out all of the proposed entities and relationships that you think you'll need in your solution before you start making changes in Microsoft Dynamics CRM. Changing your entity relationships in a modeling tool such as Microsoft Office Visio is much easier and more efficient than making changes in Microsoft Dynamics CRM. Figure 10-1 shows the proposed entity map for Litware.

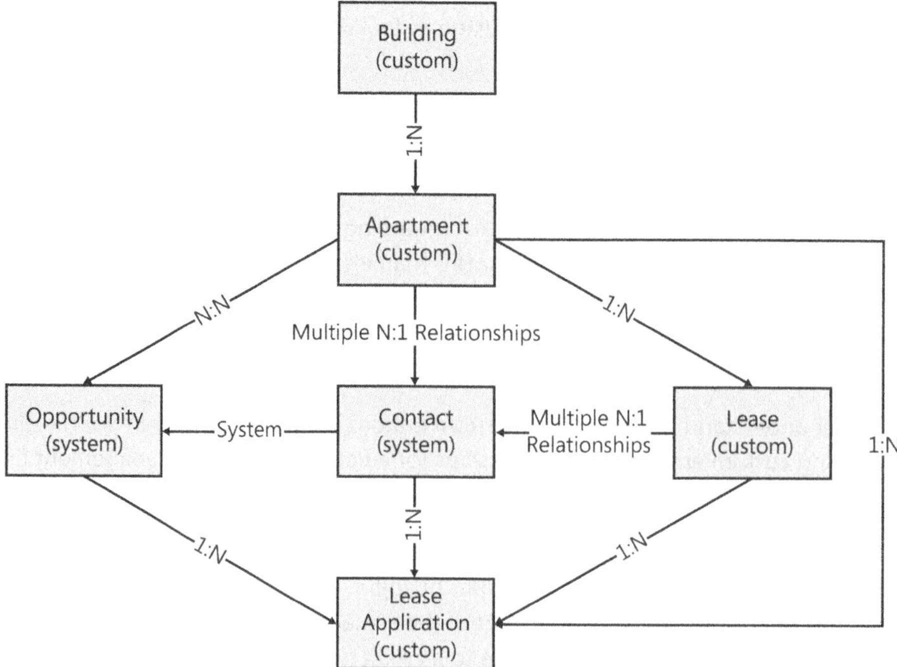

FIGURE 10-1 Proposed entity relationship map for Litware

Based on this initial design, we created visual mockups of the Building, Apartment, Lease, and Lease Application forms, as shown in Figures 10-2 through 10-5.

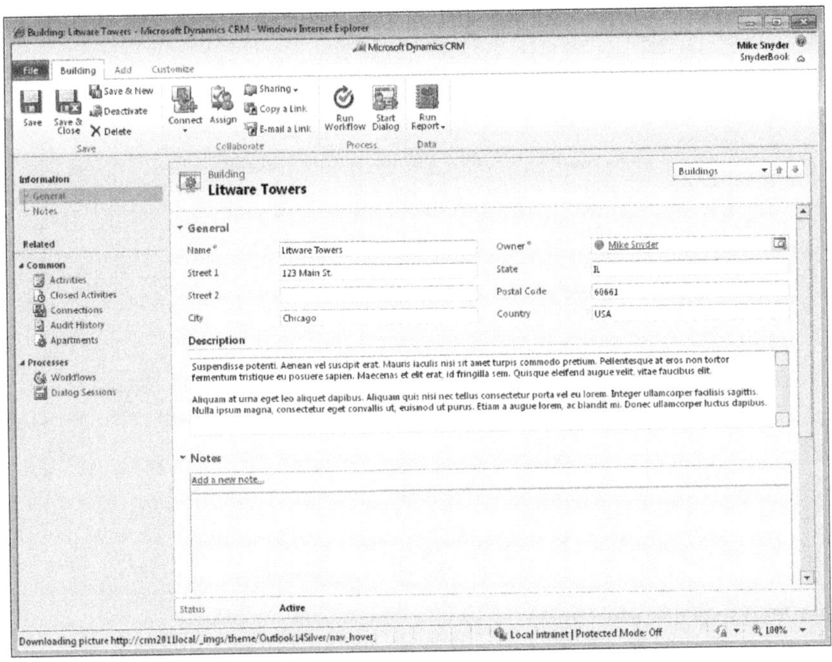

FIGURE 10-2 Mockup of the Building form

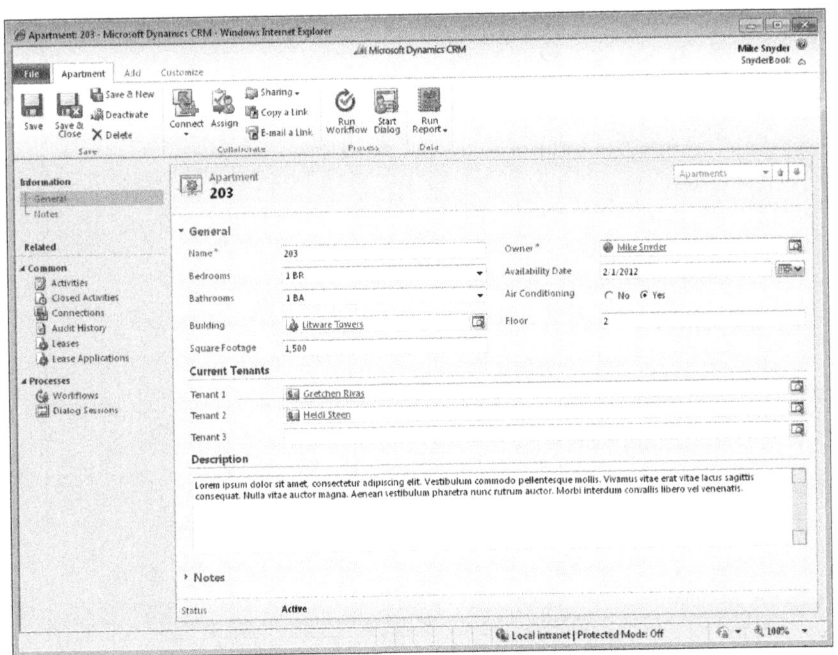

FIGURE 10-3 Mockup of the Apartment form

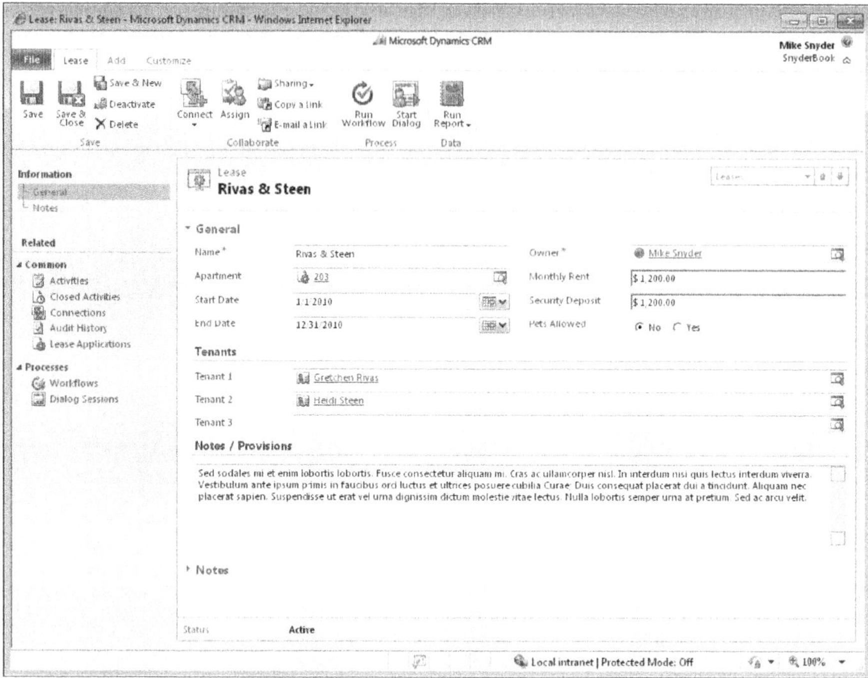

FIGURE 10-4 Mockup of the Lease form

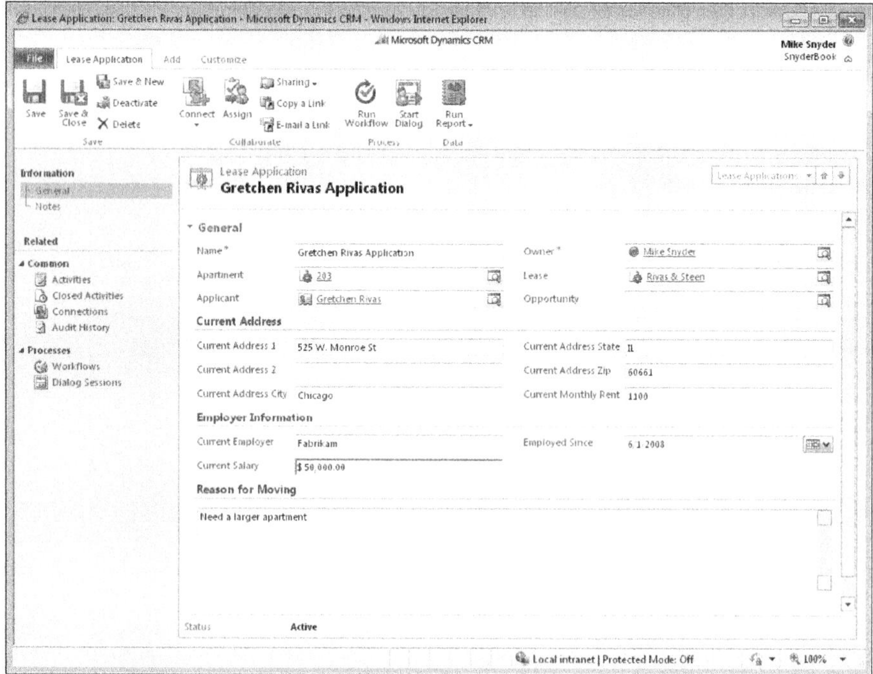

FIGURE 10-5 Mockup of the Lease Application form

You can immediately see how some of the proposed entity relationships manifest in the user interface. For example, the proposed design includes the following benefits:

- You can track multiple tenant records per lease because of the multiple relationships created between Lease and Contact (Tenant 1, Tenant 2, and Tenant 3). This also allows you to track a contact who rented from the company multiple times and consequently has multiple leases on file.
- For any single apartment, you can view all of the related opportunities because of the many-to-many relationship between the Apartment and Opportunity entities. This relationship can show you which apartments a group of tenants might rent in addition to telling you which potential tenants are considering a single apartment.
- The proposed design allows each tenant to complete his or her own lease application independently, yet you can still link tenants together using the Opportunity and Apartment entities.

When Litware reviews the proposed relationship design, the reviewers might decide to make changes to the entity relationships based on their specific business needs. Fortunately, Microsoft Dynamics CRM makes it easy to create custom entities and modify their relationships. We created all of the custom entities, fields, relationships, and forms for this example in less than 20 minutes!

One potential downside of our proposed data model manifests itself when you view a contact record, shown in Figure 10-6.

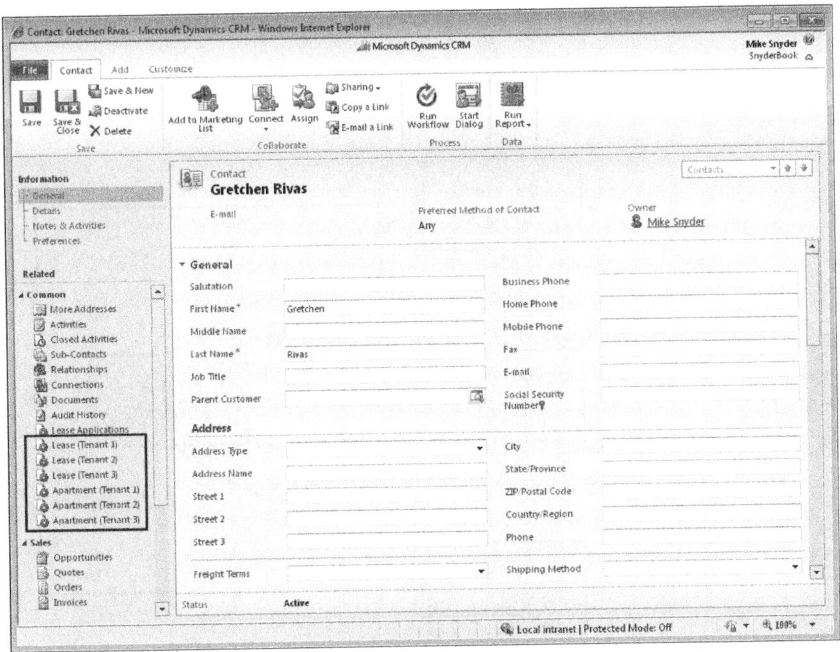

FIGURE 10-6 Multiple relationships between the same two entities

Because we created three N:1 relationships between the Lease and Contact entities (one for each potential tenant), and we also created three N:1 relationships between the Apartment and Contact entities (one for each current tenant), the contact record shows the leases and apartments related to a contact three different times each. If the tenant was listed as Tenant 1 on one lease, but then listed as Tenant 2 on a second lease, those records would be listed under their respective relationships.

From a user perspective, it would be ideal to be able to open a contact and view all of that contact's current and past leases in a single view. Unfortunately, the lease information in our current data model appears in three different places. If the organization decided this data model was not acceptable, we could modify the design.

Figure 10-7 shows a modified data model where we changed the following custom relationships:

- Eliminated multiple custom relationships between the Apartment and Contact entities
- Added a custom N:N (many to many) relationship between the Apartment and Contact entities
- Eliminated multiple custom relationships between the Lease and Contact entities
- Added a custom N:N (many to many) relationship between the Lease and Contact entities

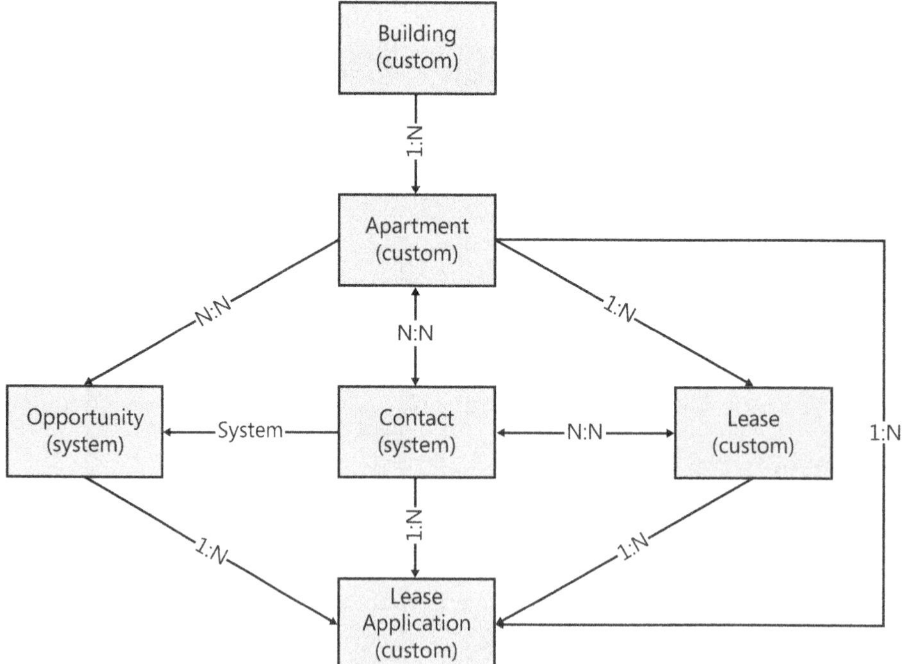

FIGURE 10-7 Modified Litware data model to remove multiple references per entity

These relationships make sense because the tenants can have multiple leases (one for each year), and leases can have multiple contacts (one for each tenant). The revised relationship model also makes sense for apartments and contacts because tenants can have multiple apartments (although usually not at the same time) and each apartment can hold multiple tenants. With this new data model in place, the new Lease and Apartment forms could appear as shown in Figures 10-8 and 10-9.

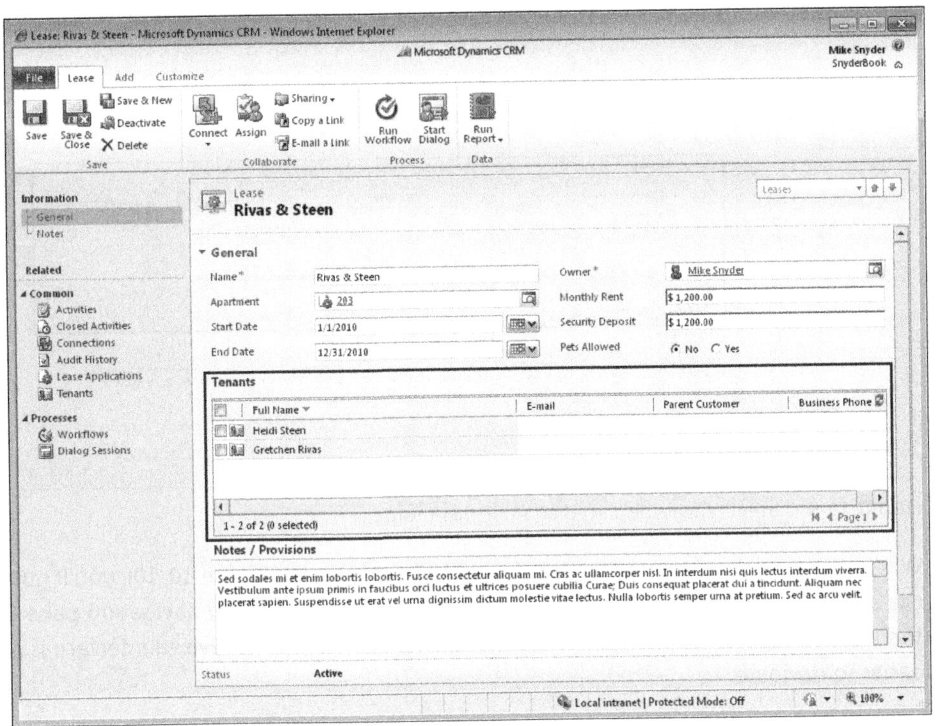

FIGURE 10-8 Tenants displayed on Lease form

In both Figures 10-8 and 10-9, it's important to note that by changing the nature of the custom relationships, the user interface changed as well. Now, instead of displaying multiple lookups in which the user selects each tenant, a sub-grid displays the related tenants on the form.

Tip By default, N:N relationships display as links in the entity navigation pane of both records. However, you can use the form editor to place a sub-grid of those related records directly on the main form, as shown in Figures 10-8 and 10-9. Displaying a sub-grid of related records on the main form saves you a few clicks because you don't have to click the link in the entity navigation pane.

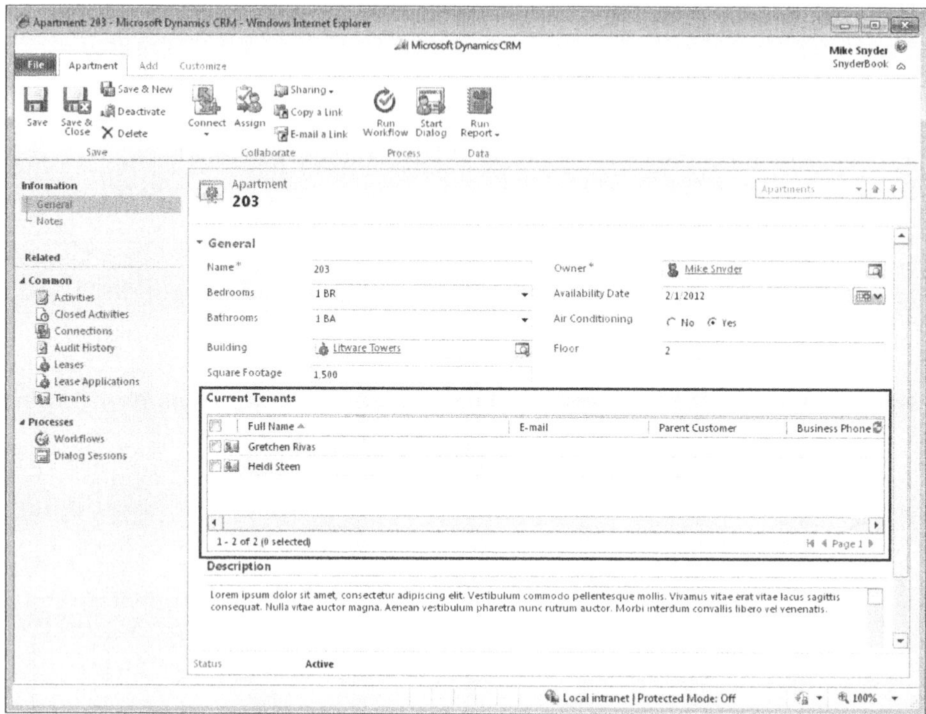

FIGURE 10-9 Current tenants displayed on Apartment form

When you view the Contact form in the revised data model (Figure 10-10), you'll notice that the apartment and leases links only appear once each in the entity navigation pane (versus the three times they appeared in the previous data model). This revised interface is a little bit easier to navigate.

By just looking at the new Apartment, Lease, and Contact forms, you might conclude that Litware should use this revised data model. That might be a good idea, but we want to point out a few drawbacks of the revised design.

One very important limitation to the new data model is that you cannot create Microsoft Dynamics CRM workflow processes that interact with many-to-many relationships. For example, you might have a business process where you want to automatically create a task anytime you add a tenant to an apartment record to get the lease signed. In the original data model (with N:1 relationships between the Contact and Apartment entities), you could very easily trigger a workflow process anytime the Tenant field changes on the apartment record. With the revised N:N data model, you could not create such a workflow process with the web-based workflow editor. However, you could create automated tasks and similar rules using custom programming and the software development kit (SDK).

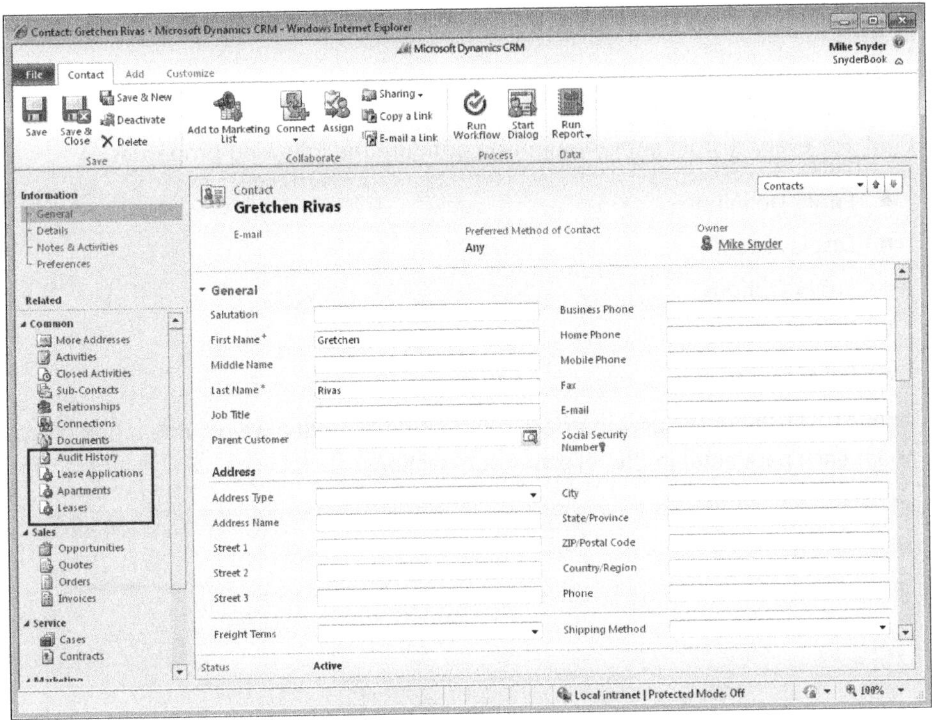

FIGURE 10-10 Apartments and Leases displayed on Contact form

Another drawback you should consider is that the new design requires a few extra clicks (and a new pop-up window) to add tenants to the lease and apartment records. In the previous model with N:1 relationships, users could type directly into the Tenant 1, Tenant 2, and Tenant 3 fields to enter data very quickly. Speed of data entry probably isn't a huge concern in our real estate example because most leases last 12 months. However, other businesses or industries (such as call centers or help desks) could be highly sensitive to speed of data entry and prioritize that benefit over a few extra links in the entity navigation pane.

The key point of this example is that there's no "right answer" for how you design your custom entities. For each possible design, you need to carefully consider the benefits and drawbacks based on your business goals.

Tip When you create a many-to-many relationship directly between two entities, you can't customize that relationship with additional fields. To accomplish this, you have a couple of different choices. One, you can use the Microsoft Dynamics CRM connections feature which provides this type of relationship tracking. Two, you can effectively create a many-to-many relationship between two entities (A and B) by creating an intermediate entity (C), and then creating two custom one-to-many relationships: Create a one-to-many relationship between A and C, and also create a many-to-one relationship between C and B. Consider using this technique when you want to capture additional data (fields) about the many-to-many relationship between the two entities.

Creating a Custom Entity

Now that you understand the concepts, benefits, and limitations related to custom entities, let's go through the steps you will follow to create a custom entity in Microsoft Dynamics CRM. For every custom entity, you must configure the following properties:

- Entity Definition
- Display Areas
- Entity Options
- Primary Field
- Entity Icons

Figure 10-11 shows the user interface for creating an entity; we provide more information about each parameter in the following sub-sections.

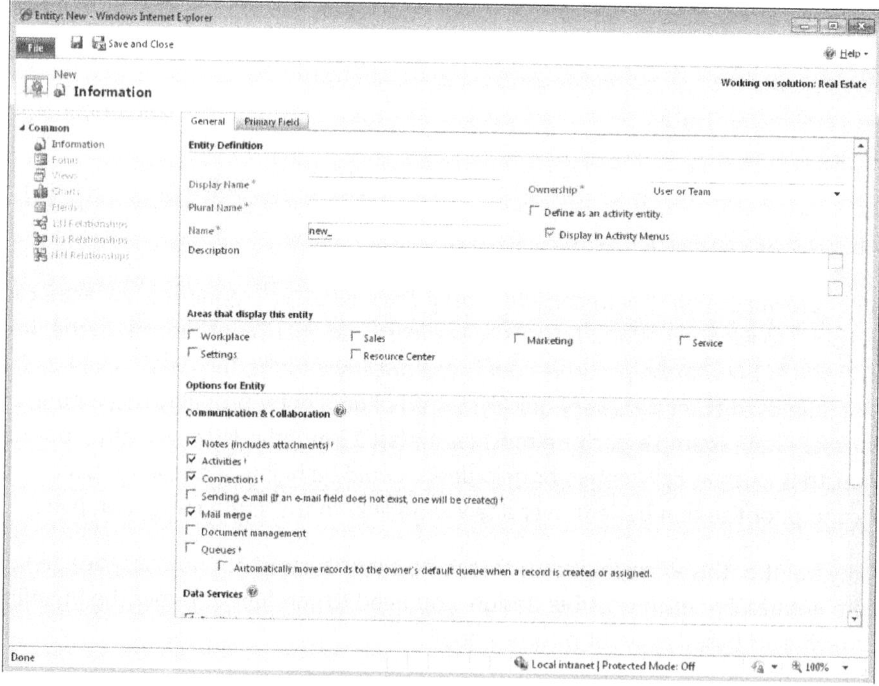

FIGURE 10-11 Creating a custom entity

Entity Definition

In the Entity Definition section, enter basic parameters about the custom entity, including the following:

- Display Name
- Plural Name

- Ownership
- Name
- Activity Entity Designation
- Description (optional)

In Chapter 6, "Entity Customization: Fields and Option Sets," we discussed how the Display Name, Plural Name, Name, and Description parameters work in regard to renaming entities, so you should be familiar with these concepts. Remember that you cannot change the schema name after you create the entity, but you can modify the display name, plural name, and description at any time.

Tip Microsoft Dynamics CRM uses the default schema name prefix *new_* as part of the default solution publisher. You can change the schema prefix to a different value by configuring the schema-name prefix of the solution publisher.

For the ownership parameter, you must specify one of two ownership types:

- User or Team
- Organization

Make the entity ownership decision carefully because you cannot change the ownership type after you create the entity.

Some of the differences between user ownership and organization ownership include the following:

- User- and team-owned entities can be assigned to other users; organization-owned entities cannot.
- User- and team-owned entities can be shared with one or more teams; organization-owned entities cannot.
- User- and team-owned entities provide more flexibility when configuring security than organization-owned entities. When you configure a security role for organization-owned entities, you can specify only None and Organization-level access levels. For user- and team-owned entities, you can specify one of five different access levels: None, User, Business Unit, Parent:Child Business Units, or Organization.

As this list illustrates, making custom entities user- or team-owned provides you with more options and greater configurability. However, user and team ownership requires that you carefully assign each entity to the correct owner and configure the security roles appropriately. If users frequently change business units or job functions, you must update entity ownership accordingly. In such scenarios, the work of maintaining the correct user ownership information might offset the additional configurability benefits.

Display Areas

With Microsoft Dynamics CRM, you can specify where to display the custom entity in the application navigation. The default application areas include Workplace, Sales, Marketing, Service, Settings, and Resource Center. You can choose to display the custom entity in all, some, or none of the areas. When you choose to include a custom entity, Microsoft Dynamics CRM adds a link in the navigation pane and a link in the application ribbon. You can toggle the display settings whenever you want, not only while creating the entity.

Tip You can further customize the user interface and application navigation by using the site map, which we cover in Chapter 12, "Solutions: Client Extensions." By modifying the site map, you can create additional application areas.

Entity Options

In the Options for Entity section of the entity editor, you have the following configuration options:

- **Notes** Enables notes (including file attachments) for the custom entity. After you enable notes, they cannot be disabled.
- **Activities** Enables activities such as tasks, phone calls, letters, and faxes for the custom entity. After you enable activities, they cannot be disabled.
- **Connections** Enables connections for the custom entity. After you enable connections, they cannot be disabled.
- **Sending e-mail** Allows users to use the direct email functionality for the entity.
- **Mail merge** Allows users to run Microsoft Word mail merges against the entity.
- **Document management** Allows you to configure SharePoint document management integration for the entity.
- **Queues** Enables the custom entity for queues, so that users can add these record types to queues. After you enable queues, they cannot be disabled.
- **Duplicate detection** Allows users to configure and use the Microsoft Dynamics CRM duplicate detection functionality on the entity.
- **Auditing** Turns on auditing features for the entity.
- **Mobile Express** Enables the entity for use with Microsoft Dynamics CRM Mobile Express.
- **Reading pane in CRM for Outlook** Provides the option to display the entity records in the Microsoft Dynamics CRM for Outlook reading pane.
- **Offline capability for CRM for Outlook** Allows users to store entity data offline using Microsoft Dynamics CRM for Outlook with Offline Access.

More Info Because some of these settings can't be changed later, you might be tempted always to include them on your custom entities "just to be safe." One thing to remember is that when you include activities on a custom entity, that entity appears as an option in the Regarding field for tasks, phone calls, and so on. If you don't want people to select the custom entity as a regarding value, make sure that you do not include activities.

Tip Even if you decide to include a custom entity for offline capability, the default synchronization settings for Microsoft Dynamics CRM for Microsoft Office Outlook with Offline Access do not include any custom entities. Therefore, users must also manually configure their offline filters to include the custom entity to access that data offline. You can also modify the Microsoft Dynamics CRM security roles to allow only certain users to take data offline.

Primary Field

Every entity, including the default system entities, needs a primary field that Microsoft Dynamics CRM uses to display in the lookup field in related entities. If you reference back to Figure 10-9, the schema field *name* is the primary field of the Building entity, so the name of the building appears in the lookup field of its related apartment record.

Most custom and default entities use a name field as the primary field, but you are not required to do so. However, you will notice that Microsoft Dynamics CRM requires you to create a primary attribute with a data type of *nvarchar* and a format of text. You can set up a maximum length and business requirement level for the primary attribute that makes sense for your business. Many people don't even notice the primary field settings when they create an entity because Microsoft Dynamics CRM displays it on a second tab.

Tip After you create a custom entity, the data fields in the Primary Field tab become read-only, so it appears that you cannot edit the primary field. However, if you navigate to the list of fields for the entity and open the primary field, you can modify the name, searchability, business requirement level, and maximum length in the field editor. Although you can edit some of the primary field's values, you cannot change the primary field of an entity.

Other than the data type and data format requirement, the rules and restrictions for creating a primary field are the same as they are for creating any field for an entity.

Entity Icons

Microsoft Dynamics CRM uses icons in the user interface to represent each of the default system entities. These icons appear in the navigation pane, views, and on the entity's form. In addition to improving the visual aesthetics, these entity icons help users navigate the system by providing graphical indicators about each type of record. By default, Microsoft Dynamics CRM assigns the same icon to all custom entities.

Tip Seeing a Microsoft Dynamics CRM deployment without any custom entity icons typically indicates an amateur or beginner customization. Make sure you update your custom entity icons. Your users will appreciate it!

When you have more than a few custom entities in your system, using the same default icon for all of the custom entities diminishes the aesthetic benefit of icons and might cause confusion with your users. Fortunately, you can upload your own icons for each custom entity. We highly recommend that you use icons for each custom entity in your system. You can upload three types of entity icons for each custom entity:

- **Web application** Image that appears in the grids and navigation pane
- **Microsoft Dynamics CRM client for Microsoft Office Outlook** Image that appears in the Outlook client
- **Icon in entity forms** Image that appears at the top of each entity form

If possible, use files with transparent backgrounds for entity icon files. When the icons appear on dark backgrounds or when Microsoft Dynamics CRM highlights the record, failure to use transparency in your images creates an unpleasant effect.

Most graphics editing programs provide the tools to create these icons to Microsoft Dynamics CRM's specifications. When you have your icon files ready, uploading them to the custom entity is easy.

Updating custom entity icons

1. In the entity editor, click the Update Icons button in the toolbar. The Select New Icons dialog box appears.

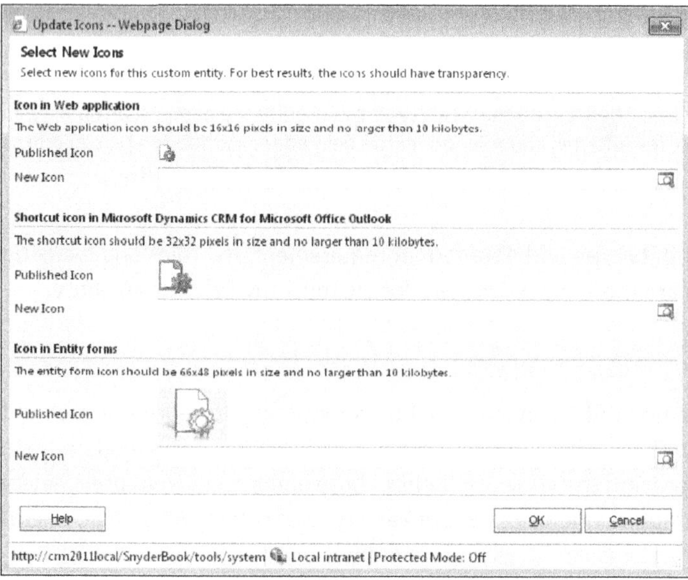

2. For each file type, use the lookup to select an image and then click OK.
   A preview of the icon that you uploaded appears, in addition to the current published icon.
3. Publish the entity so that users can see the new icons.

Important Before you can select an image as an entity icon, you must first add it as a web resource in the solution.

Even though we strongly recommend it, you might not want to take the time to create and upload custom icons. If you're in a rush and if you deployed Microsoft Dynamics CRM on premises, one quick and dirty way to get custom icons is to upload image files you find in the Microsoft Dynamics CRM web folder named _imgs, where you have lots of images to choose from. The Microsoft Dynamics CRM SDK also includes image files that you can use in the resources\images folder. Of course, it is better to create your own custom icons, but reusing the Microsoft Dynamics CRM icons can provide a better user experience than leaving the default custom entity icon.

Deleting a Custom Entity

If you decide that you no longer need to use a custom entity, you can delete it from Microsoft Dynamics CRM. Just like deleting fields, you must remove all existing references to the custom entity in forms and views before Microsoft Dynamics CRM allows you to delete it. To remove references to an entity, do the following:

- Remove references to the entity from the form of any related entities, and then delete any relationships linking to the custom entity.
- Remove the entity from any reports.
- Remove the entity from any script or code references.

Warning Deleting a custom entity also deletes all of the data stored in that entity, and you can never retrieve that data without a database backup in place. Microsoft Dynamics CRM also permanently deletes all of the notes and activities related to that entity. Make sure that you take the appropriate steps to back up all of your data before deleting an entity or field.

Just like when you delete fields, Microsoft Dynamics CRM checks for existing references to custom entities in forms and relationships before it allows you to delete an entity, but you must remove references to deleted entities in reports.

Custom Activities

As you just saw, custom entities provide a lot of customization and design flexibility. One special type of custom entity that you can create is a *custom activity*. You probably already know that the default activity types in Microsoft Dynamics CRM include:

- Task
- E-mail
- Phone Call
- Letter
- Fax
- Appointment
- Service Activity
- Recurring Appointment

Users manage their list of open activities and work through them to completion. Activities can also be part of a queue, so the activities can be shared by a team. The default Microsoft Dynamics CRM activities accommodate different actions that your users might take. Although this list of activities covers most business scenarios, you might find that you want to add your own custom activity to this list. Some common requests for custom activities include:

- Instant message (IM)
- Web chat
- Text message

Beyond this list of potential custom activities that could apply to any organization, you might have other very specific actions within your business or industry that you want to track and manage as an activity in Microsoft Dynamics CRM. Earlier in this chapter, we discussed a fictional real estate company named Litware. Some examples of potential custom activities they might want to create include:

- Open house
- Background check
- Final walkthrough
- Employment verification

To create a custom activity, select the Define as an activity entity check box in the entity editor when you're creating an entity. When you select this check box, Microsoft Dynamics CRM disables most of the other entity options because they do not apply to custom activities, as shown in Figure 10-12. You can also decide whether you want to display the custom activity in the activity menus.

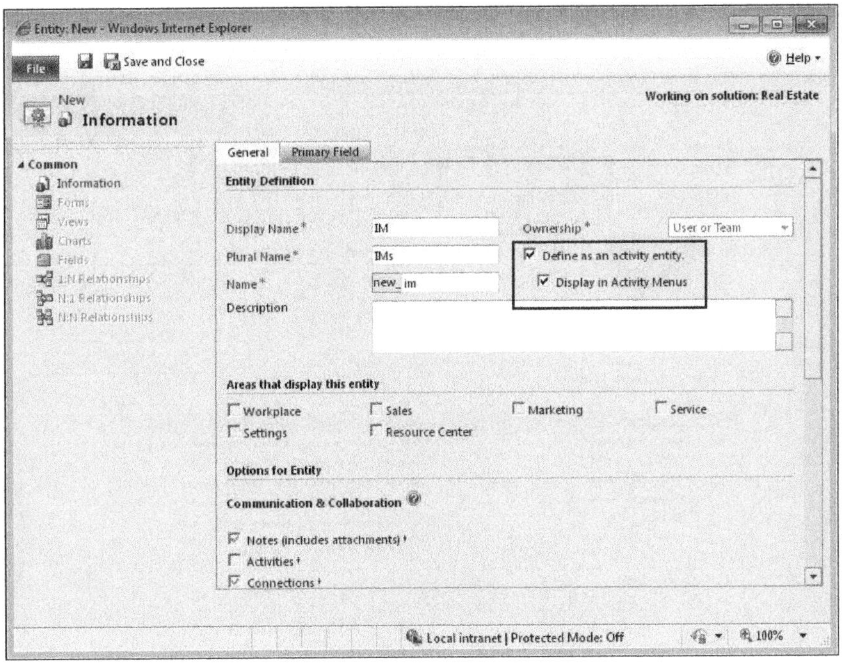

FIGURE 10-12 Defining a custom entity as a custom activity

After you create custom activities (and assuming you choose to display them in the activity menus), the custom activities appear everywhere in the user interface that the default entities appear, as shown in Figures 10-13 and 10-14.

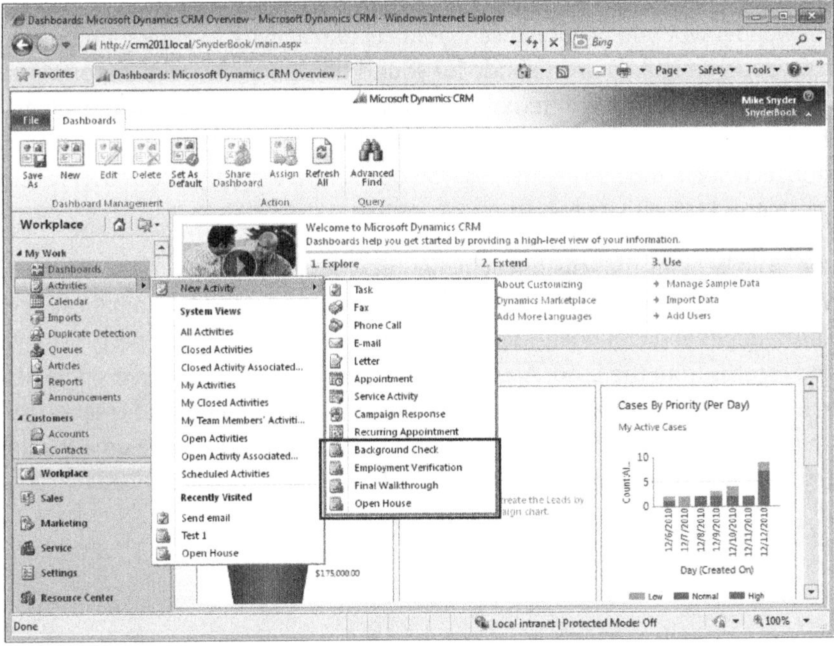

FIGURE 10-13 Custom activities in the activities menu

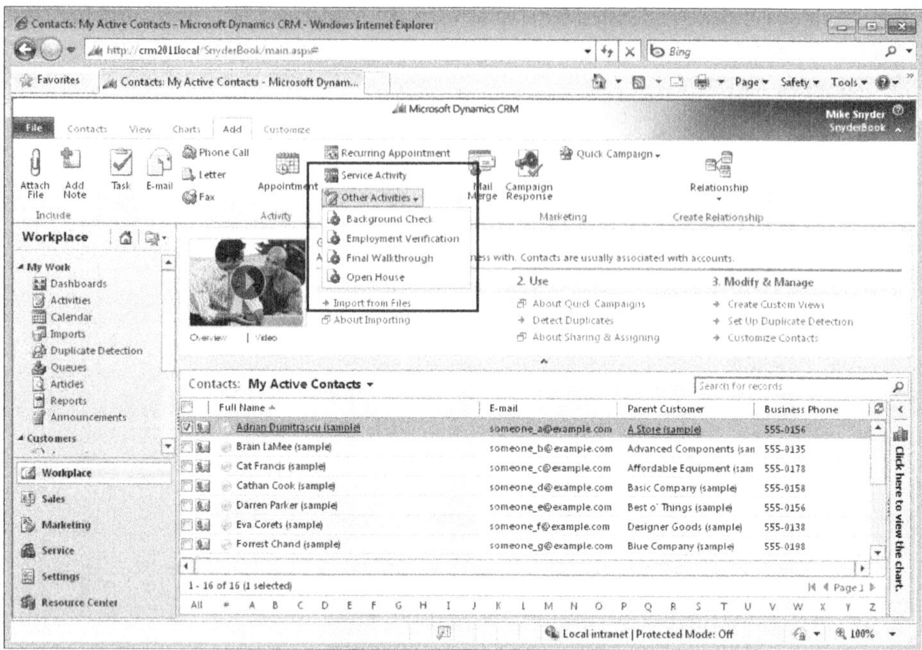

FIGURE 10-14 Custom activities appear in the ribbon under the Other Activities button

Tip Custom activities also appear in the activity menus in Microsoft Dynamics CRM for Outlook. However, you cannot synchronize custom activities into your Outlook task list.

You might wonder why you wouldn't want your custom activity to appear in the activity menus. This option might come in handy for your organization if you're importing the custom activity records from a different system, such as a nightly data load of chats from a web page or SMS messages sent from an external system. By not displaying the chat or SMS custom activity in the activity menus, you don't have to worry about users accidentally creating a chat or SMS activity record.

One of the main benefits that custom activities provides is the ability to use the *party list* fields. When you create a custom activity, Microsoft Dynamics CRM automatically creates Required Attendees and Optional Attendees fields on the entity. These party list fields allow you to add records from the Lead, Account, Contact, and User entities in a single field, as shown in Figure 10-15. Without these party list fields, you would have to create custom relationships to select four different entities. Of course, you're free to rename the Required Attendees and Optional Attendees fields to match your exact business needs.

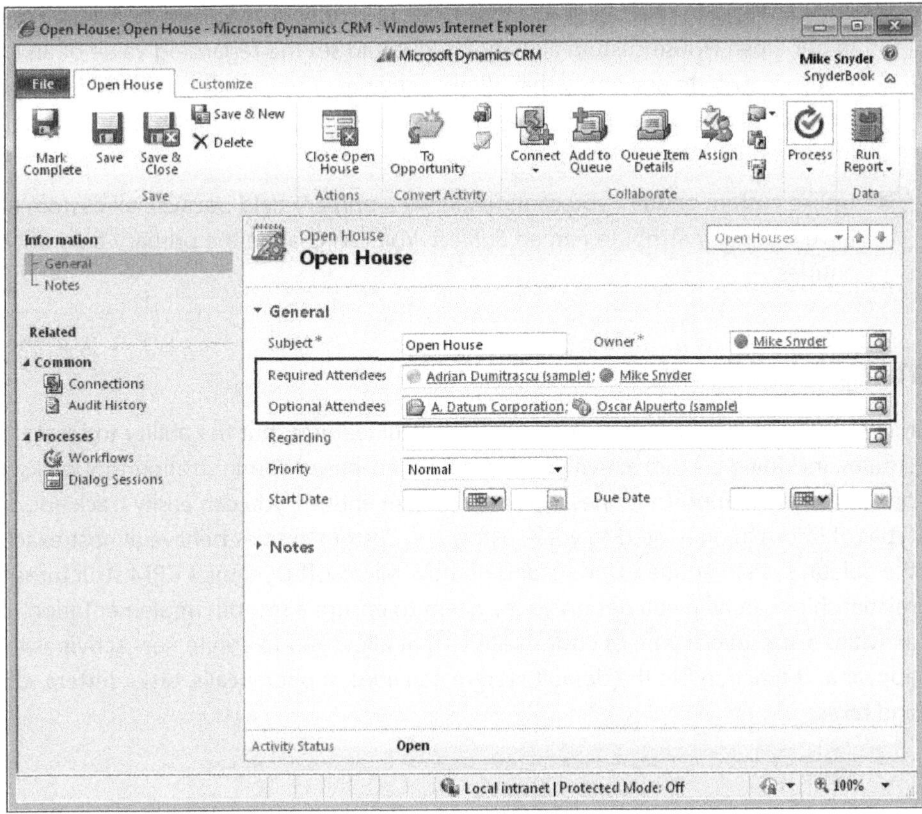

FIGURE 10-15 Custom activity party lists selecting records from different entity types

Even though custom activities provide lots of design flexibility, we want to highlight some of the other constraints you should consider when trying to decide between creating a custom entity versus a custom activity:

- You can't configure different security settings for different custom activities. All security access to activities in Microsoft Dynamics CRM (including the default activities and custom activities) is determined by the Activity entity on the security role editor. Therefore, you can't set up a custom activity and allow only a few users to create it. If a user had access to create any activity, she could create a custom activity. You can set up security on an entity-by-entity basis for custom entities.
- You cannot use custom activities as part of a quick campaign or create campaign activities with them.
- Custom activities cannot synchronize into a user's Outlook tasks the way that phone calls, letters, and tasks do.

- You cannot restrict custom activities to be regarding a specific entity type. For example, in our Open House custom activity, users could set the regarding value of an Open House activity to any entity that allows activities. You cannot configure the Open House custom activity so that users can only set the regarding value to an apartment or building.
- Unlike custom entities, you cannot specify a primary field because all custom activities have a primary attribute named *Subject*. You can change the primary field of custom entities.

Summary

Microsoft Dynamics CRM includes many powerful features, but the ability to create custom entities, including custom activities, through a web-based administration tool ranks as one of the more important ones. By using custom entities, you can easily track additional types of information related to your customers. Custom entities behave almost exactly like the default system entities. Understanding how Microsoft Dynamics CRM structures entity relationships can help you design your system to ensure a smooth implementation. Custom activities are a special type of custom entity that allow you to create new activities that appear and function like the default system activities of phone calls, tasks, letters, emails, and faxes.

Chapter 11

Solutions: Web Resources

In this chapter:

Another new feature in Microsoft Dynamics CRM provides you with the ability to deploy static or browser-processed files, including Silverlight, image files, JavaScript, and HTML web pages. This feature allows you to extend Microsoft Dynamics CRM in just a few installation steps with minimal impact to the deployment. This also means you can now deploy files directly to Microsoft Dynamics CRM Online. This chapter discusses the options for web resources and how to apply them with your own solutions.

Important In the process of describing web resources, we demonstrate using HTML, JavaScript, and Silverlight, but an in-depth examination of these languages and the Microsoft Dynamics CRM SDK are beyond the scope of this book.

Feel free to download the companion content files and use them in conjunction with the examples in this chapter.

Web Resources Overview

The term *web resource* describes files stored in the Microsoft Dynamics CRM database that you can retrieve by using a unique URL. When referenced in Microsoft Dynamics CRM, web resources allow you to extend the appearance and functionality of the application. For instance, Figure 11-1 shows an example of a social application that uses a variety of web resources surfaced through the Microsoft Dynamics CRM site map.

More Info We discuss the Microsoft Dynamics CRM site map in depth in Chapter 12, "Solution: Client Extensions (Ribbon and Map)."

As shown in Figure 11-1, the icon in the left navigation area is an image web resource, whereas the IFrame content is a series of custom, Silverlight web resources hosted within Microsoft Dynamics CRM.

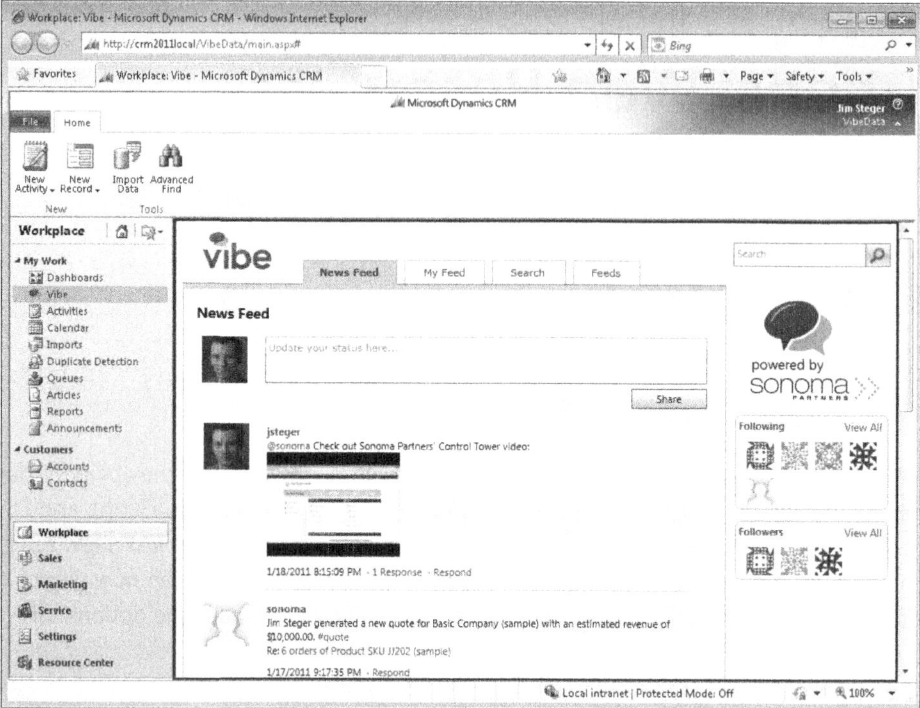

FIGURE 11-1 Example of web resources used in Microsoft Dynamics CRM

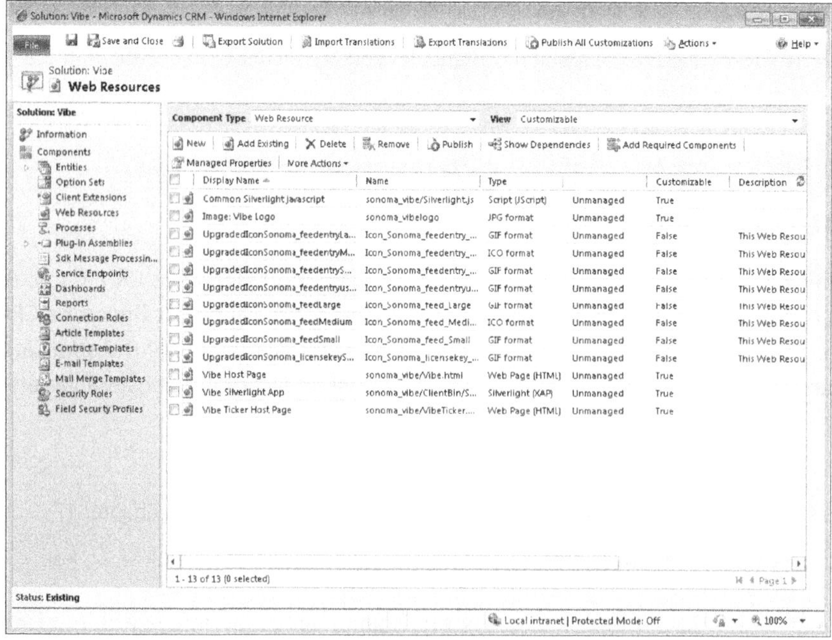

FIGURE 11-2 Example of web resources in a solution

You create web resources in the Settings area of Microsoft Dynamics CRM. Web resources can be added to solutions just like other customization components. Figure 11-2 shows the web resources used for the example in Figure 11-1.

As you can see from Figure 11-2, this particular solution contains a range of possible web resource types, including a Silverlight application, web page, and several images. All of these components belong to the solution and can be transported between Microsoft Dynamics CRM environments. By using HTML, JavaScript, and Silverlight, programmers no longer have to worry about the deployment of their application's associated web files.

Web Resource Properties

Let's examine the properties of a web resource.

When you navigate to the web resources area in a solution in Microsoft Dynamics CRM and click the New button, the New web resource form appears, as shown in Figure 11-3.

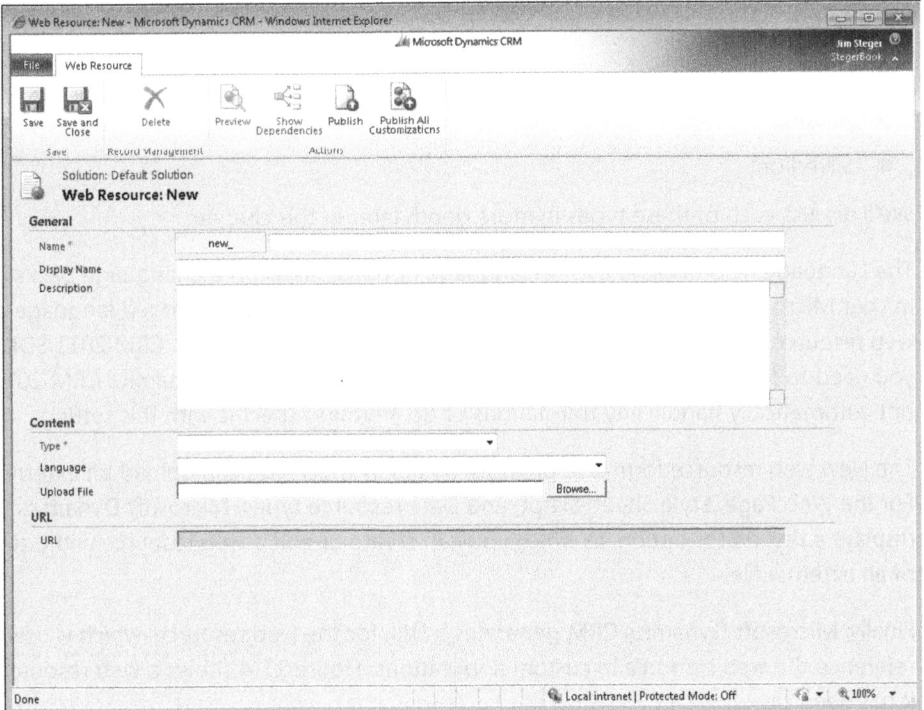

FIGURE 11-3 New web resource form

Each web resource has the following properties:

- Name
- Display Name

- Description
- Type
- Language

The Name field is a unique name you assign to the web resource that will be used as part of its URL in Microsoft Dynamics CRM, which you'll use to reference the web resource in the application. The Display Name provides a more descriptive name for the web resource and should be used to clarify the file's purpose in the solution. The Description field provides additional context around the purpose of the web resource.

The Type property serves as a category for the web resource and determines how the file will be displayed in Microsoft Dynamics CRM, and Web resources are limited to the following types of files:

- Webpage
- Style Sheet
- Script
- Data
- Image
- Silverlight

We'll discuss each of these types in more depth later in this chapter.

The Language field displays a list of language options based on the language packs installed in your Microsoft Dynamics CRM system. This field identifies the intended language of the web resource for reference in the solution or the Microsoft Dynamics CRM 2011 SDK, should you need to find web resources of a specific language. Microsoft Dynamics CRM 2011 does not automatically handle any translations or do anything specific with this setting.

The New web resource form also provides a field in which you can upload an external file. For the Web Page, Style Sheet, Script, and Data resource types, Microsoft Dynamics CRM also displays a text editor option, in which you can create or edit a web resource without the need of an external file.

Finally, Microsoft Dynamics CRM generates a URL for the web resource, which is used to reference the web resource in custom applications. Figure 11-4 shows a web resource after it has been saved.

Clicking the link in the URL field will launch the web resource in a browser. In the example shown in Figure 11-4, we created a simple Hello World web page, shown in Figure 11-5.

When you create web resources, we recommend using a standard naming convention so that programmers can quickly identify each file. A standard naming convention also creates a structured file system so that data is grouped correctly by web analytics tools.

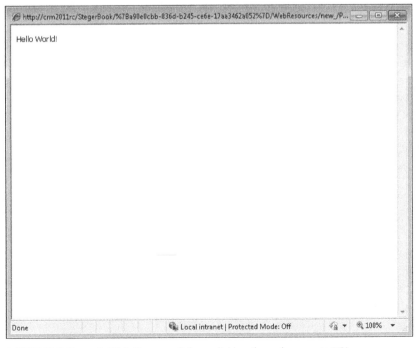

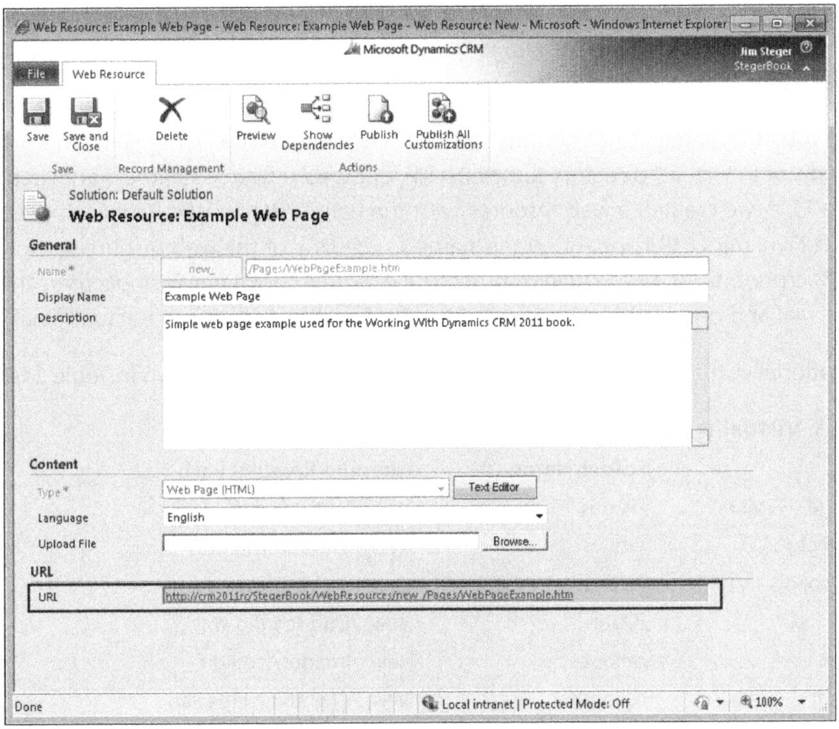

FIGURE 11-4 A saved web resource's URL

FIGURE 11-5 Example Web Page result from clicking the web resource URL

One tip for naming your web resources is to consistently include or exclude the file extension. We prefer to include the file extension in the name, so files are referenced as webpage.htm or master.css.

Also, Microsoft Dynamics CRM permits forward slashes (/) in the Name field. This means you could use a "virtual" directory approach in your web resource's name. For instance, in Figure 11-4, we created a web resource with the name /Pages/WebPageExample.htm. Microsoft Dynamics CRM appended this name to the URL of the web resource as follows: *http://<Microsoft_CRM_URL>/WebResources/new_/Pages/WebPageExample.htm*. This looks like a normal and organized URL path, but the /Pages directory doesn't actually exist!

Some optional virtual folder naming conventions to consider are shown in Table 11-1.

TABLE 11-1 Virtual Folder Naming Convention

File	Folder Name	Example Relative Path
Web Page (HTML)	/Pages	New_/Pages/sample.htm
Style Sheet (CSS)	/Styles	New_/Styles/master.css
Script (Jscript)	/Scripts	New_/Scripts/global.js
Data	/Data	New_/Data/config.xml
Images	/Images	New_/Images/icon.gif
Silverlight	/ClientBin	New_/ClientBin/page.xap

Tip Always include the file extension and /<VirtualFolderName> in your web resource name.

Like other customizations, web resources allow you to manage customization rights on your files. Figure 11-6 shows the Managed Properties dialog box used to lock customization rights on a web resource included in a managed solution. Select the False option in this dialog box to prevent any changes to the file or code in the web resource in the destination Microsoft Dynamics CRM system.

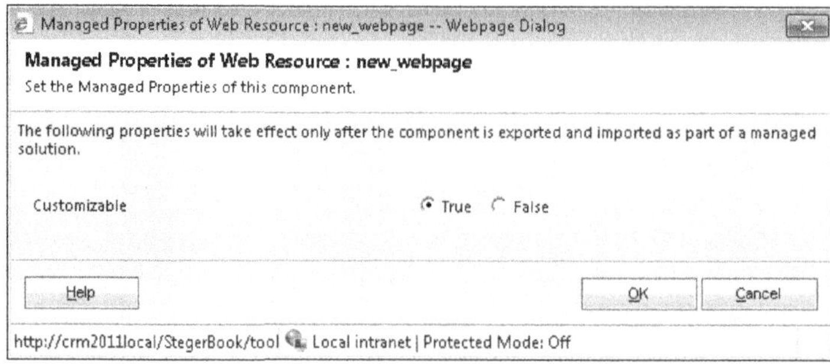

FIGURE 11-6 Web resource Managed Properties dialog box

Referencing Web Resources

Once you provide the name, type, and content for your web resource, you can display the resource in Microsoft Dynamics CRM or in your own applications.

You have two primary means of accessing a web resource. The first is by using the complete URL value shown on the web resource form. For the example in Figure 11-4, that URL is *http://<Microsoft_CRM_URL>/WebResources/new_/Pages/WebPageExample.htm.*

This approach works well when accessing the web resource from another application, such as a custom Web Page or Microsoft SharePoint site.

When referencing a web resource in the Microsoft Dynamics CRM site map, ribbon, or forms (as IFrames), the second method can be employed. This method is called the *$webresource* directive (or token) and uses the following syntax:

```
$webresource:<web resource name>
```

Microsoft Dynamics CRM translates the *$webresource:* reference to the proper server and organization name. To include the Web Page resource from the example in Figure 11-4 in the Microsoft Dynamics CRM site map, we could add the following in the URL attribute in the site map XML:

```
$webresource:new_/Pages/ExampleWebPage.htm
```

Tip Always try to use the *$webresource* directive approach when referencing a web resource from a control that is hosted within Microsoft Dynamics CRM, such as the site map, ribbon, or forms.

The *$webresource* directive allows you to create relative URL references without having to worry about managing the full URL when deploying your solutions to other Microsoft Dynamics CRM systems.

Caution Using the *$webresource* directive in the site map, ribbon, or form IFrame creates a solution dependency to the web resource. You must include the web resource in any exported solution package for the solution to function properly. Solution dependencies are *not* created when web resources reference each other, such as a Web Page resource that references a Style Sheet resource.

Web Resource Constraints

All web resources are either static files or files with code that is processed client-side by the browser. Therefore, the files cannot execute any code or logic on the Microsoft Dynamics CRM server, and ASP.NET files (such as ASPX or ASMX) are not allowed.

Further, web resources are only available by using the Microsoft Dynamics CRM web application security context. As a result, only licensed Microsoft Dynamics CRM users who have the necessary privileges can access them.

You can still extend Microsoft Dynamics CRM with server-side web development; however, those files will not be a part of the Microsoft Dynamics CRM solution package. For on-premise deployments, you need to create a custom website and update your user interface extensions to reference that location. For Microsoft Dynamics CRM Online deployments, you need to deploy your files to a hosted site that is accessible over the web, such as Windows Azure. You are responsible for the hosting and authentication of those files.

More Info Microsoft Dynamics CRM provides capabilities that assist with the integration from Microsoft Dynamics CRM to Windows Azure AppFabric. See the Microsoft Dynamics CRM SDK for further information.

Finally, Microsoft Dynamics CRM does not support some client-side web technologies, such as Flash.

Web Resource Types

Now that you have a general understanding of web resources, let's delve into the specifics. Table 11-2 lists the web resource types, their extensions, and the Microsoft Dynamics CRM metadata type code associated with each type.

TABLE 11-2 Web Resource Types

File	File Extensions	Type Code
Web Page (HTML)	.htm, .html	1
Style Sheet (CSS)	.css	2
Script (JScript)	.js	3
Data (XML)	.xml	4
Image (PNG)	.png	5
Image (JPG)	.jpg	6
Image (GIF)	.gif	7
Silverlight (XAP)	.xap	8
StyleSheet (XSL)	.xsl, .xslt	9
Image (ICO)	.ico	10

Web Page (HTML)

The Web Page (HTML) option allows you to package standard web pages and reference them in Microsoft Dynamics CRM. Common examples are custom help files and application interfaces. Because no server-side code can be executed by web resources, you should verify that all code logic can be executed in a web browser, such as HTML or JavaScript.

In addition to the name and other identifying parameters, Microsoft Dynamics CRM supports an optional query string parameter (called "data") that can be used to pass any value to your web page. The full list of parameters is shown in Table 11-3. For security reasons, including any other parameters will cause your web resources to not load.

TABLE 11-3 Parameters for HTML Web Resources

Parameter	Name	Description
typename	Entity Name	The name of the entity.
type	Entity Type Code	An integer that uniquely identifies the entity in a specific organization.
id	Object GUID	The GUID that represents a record.
orgname	Organization Name	The unique name of the organization.
userlcid	User Language Code	The language code identifier for the current user.
orglcid	Organization Language Code	The language code identifier for the base language of the organization.
data	Optional Data Parameter	An optional value that may be passed.

Important Microsoft Dynamics CRM does not track any programmatic references included in your web resources as solution dependencies. It's up to you to ensure that the required files—such as style sheets and JavaScript files—are included in the solution.

Let's create a web resource. We'll create a web page that provides a visual cue indicating the lead form type so that we can quickly note that we're viewing a lead. We'll do this by showing a simple green line in the header of a lead record.

Creating a simple Web page (HTML) web resource

1. Navigate to the Settings area, click Customizations, and then click Customize the System to launch the default solution.
2. In the default solution, click web resources in the left navigation pane to view the existing web resources.
3. Click New to launch the New web resource form.

4. Set the following properties on the form:
    a. Name: **/Pages/LeadIndication.htm**
    b. Display Name: **Lead Indication**
    c. Description: **Provides a visual indicator to users when they access lead records.**
    d. Type: Web Page (HTML)
    e. Language: English

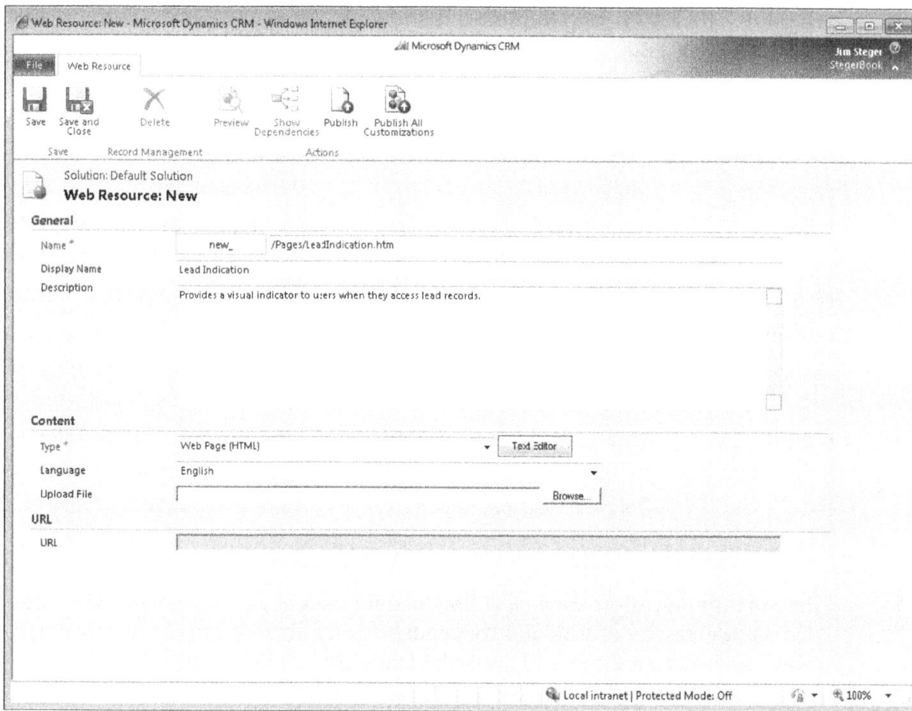

5. Click the Text Editor button. The Edit Content dialog box appears.

Note If you have downloaded the companion content, click the Browse button, select the web resource Files\Pages\LeadIndication.htm file, and skip to Step 8.

6. In the Edit Content dialog box, click the Source tab, enter the code snippet in Listing 11-1, and click back to the Rich Text tab. A thin green bar appears.

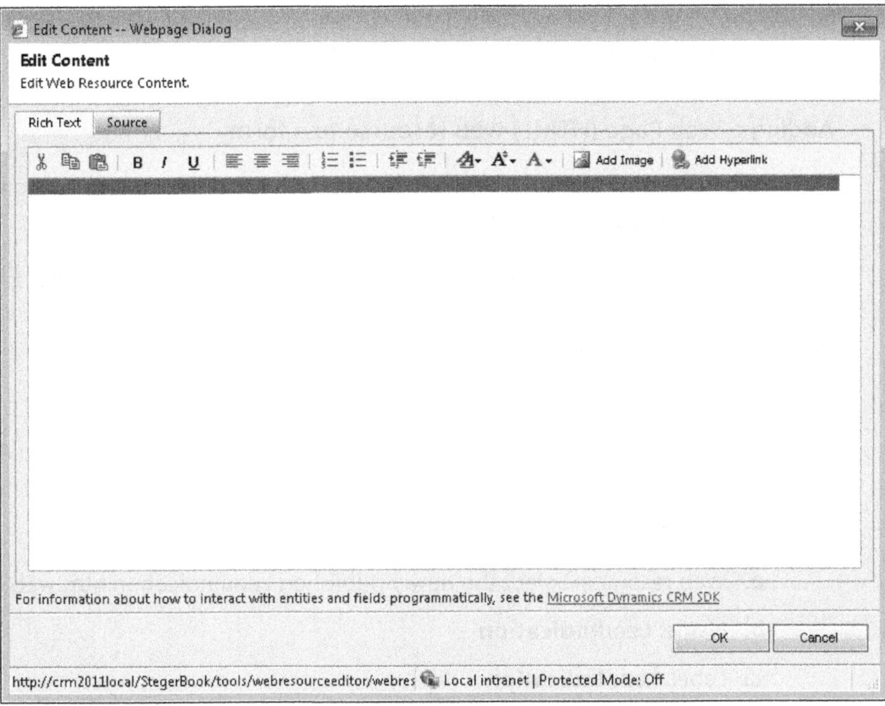

7. Click OK to return to the New web resource form.

Note Microsoft Dynamics CRM automatically saves and publishes the record and returns you to the web resource form when you create a web resource. As a result, the URL field now displays a value. When the web resource is saved for the first time, Microsoft Dynamics CRM automatically publishes the web resource. If you subsequently make any changes to the web resource, you must publish the resource before your changes take effect.

8. In the ribbon, click Save and Close.

LISTING 11-1 LeadIndication.htm

```
<html>
<head>
<title>Lead Indication</title>
<style type="text/css">
body { font-family:Segoe UI; font-size: 11px; margin: 0px;
       background-color:F6F8FA; border:0px; }
div.lead { background-color: Green; width: 100%; height: 2px; padding: 0px }
</style>
</head>
<body>
<div class="lead"></div>
</body>
</html>
```

The web resource has been published, but we need to apply it to the Lead form before we're able to see the change in Microsoft Dynamics CRM.

Adding a Web Page (HTML) web resource to a form

1. Navigate to the Settings area, click Customizations, and then click Customize the System to launch the default solution.
2. In the default solution, expand Entities in the left navigation pane, and then expand the Lead entity node.
3. Click Forms and then double-click the Main Information form.
4. Locate the Select group in the Home ribbon, and then click Header.
5. In the ribbon, click the Insert tab, then click web resource to display the Add Web Resource dialog box.
6. Set the following properties:
    a. Web resource: Select the newly published LeadIndication.htm web resource.
    b. Name: **LeadIndication**
    c. Label: **LeadIndication**
    d. Leave the default values in the remaining fields on the General tab.

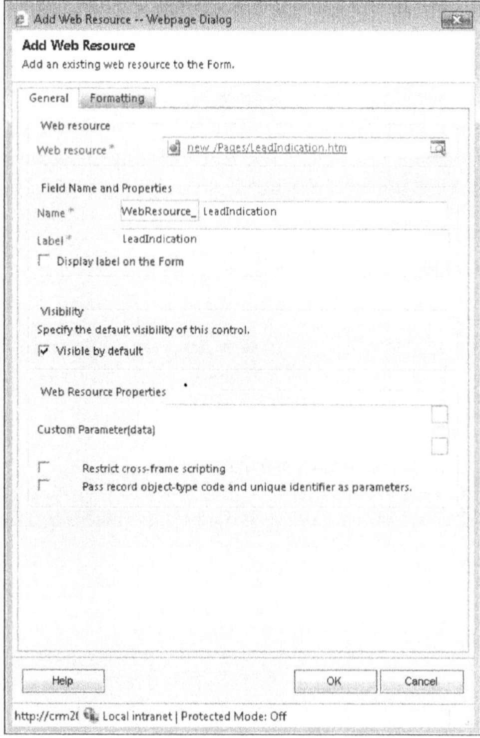

7. Click the Formatting tab and set the following properties:
    a. Layout: Three columns
    b. Number of Rows: **1**
    c. Scrolling: Never
    d. Border: Clear the *Display border* check box. Similar to the scrolling option, removing the border will create the illusion that we are seeing a section on the native Microsoft Dynamics CRM form rather than a custom page.

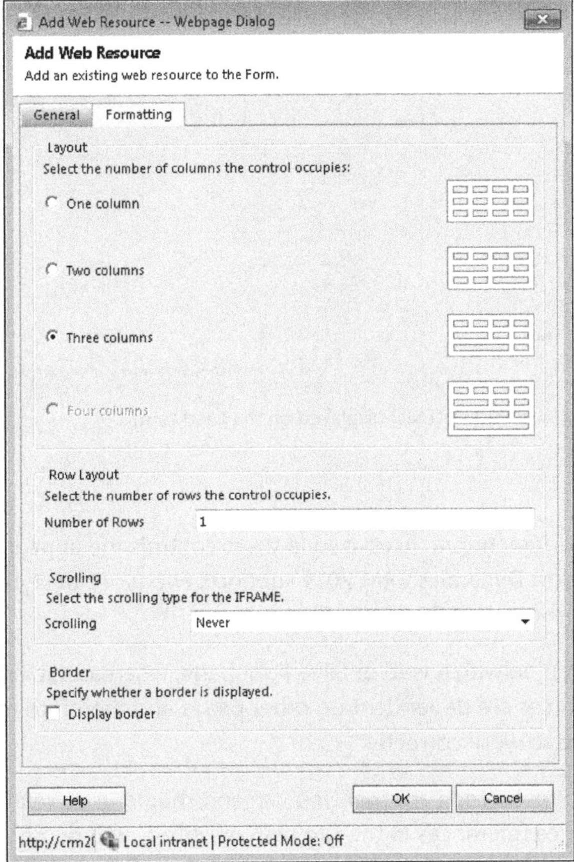

8. Click OK.
9. In the ribbon, click Save, then click Publish.

Figure 11-7 shows the result.

This example demonstrates a simple approach for altering the user interface in a Microsoft Dynamics CRM form. We can extend this example to alter the color of the notification bar based on the lead's rating. We'll step through using a Script web resource to extend our lead notification bar shortly.

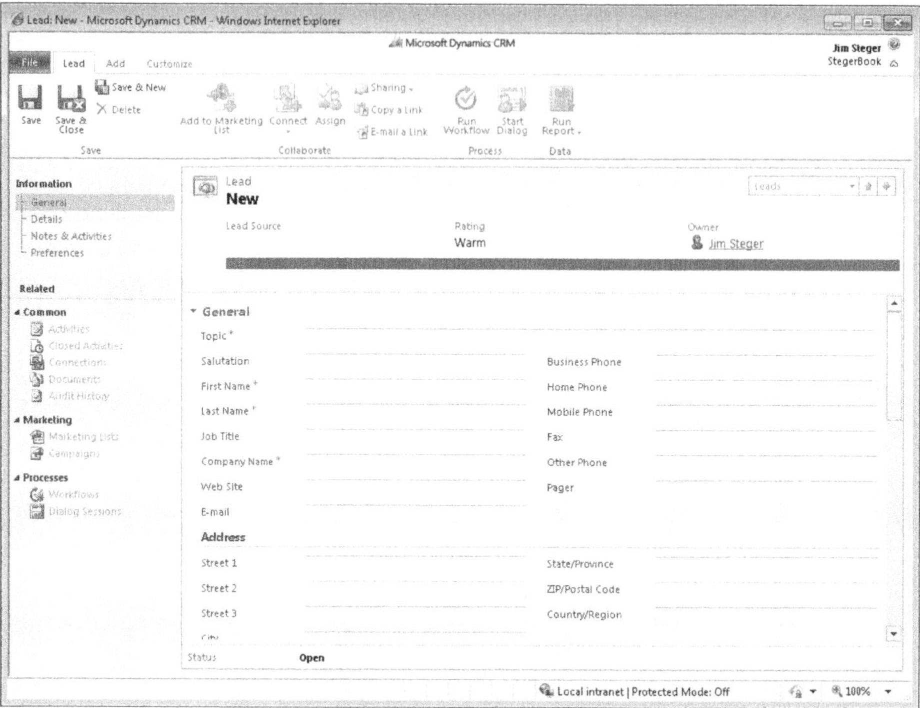

FIGURE 11-7 The web resources Web Page (HTML) displayed on the Lead form

Style Sheet

As with common web development practices, a style sheet controls the appearance of a custom web page. Microsoft Dynamics CRM 2011 supports two types of style sheets that can be uploaded as web resources: CSS and XSL files.

CSS files are used in conjunction with a web or Silverlight page, whereas XSL files transform XML data. These web resources are dependent on other pages and therefore must be referenced in the host page to work correctly.

When referencing one web resource in another, you can and should use a relative path. However, unlike web resource references in the site map or ribbon, you do not need to use the *$webresource* directive when referencing one web resource within each other because Microsoft Dynamics CRM maintains a consistent path between web resources.

For example, let's assume you have a Style Sheet resource called new_/Styles/master.css and you want to apply this style sheet to a Web Page resource. In the Web Page HTML, you would add the following code:

```
<link rel="stylesheet" type="text/css" href="../Styles/styles.css" />
```

Important Solution dependencies are not created when web resources reference each other. You must ensure that all required files are properly packaged in a solution so they are installed correctly in the destination system. We discussed solution dependencies in Chapter 5, "Solution: Overview and Entities."

As with all web resources, Style Sheet resources are only available through the Microsoft Dynamics CRM security context and can only be accessed by an authenticated Microsoft Dynamics CRM user with the appropriate privileges.

Let's update our previous example on the Lead form to use a Style Sheet web resource instead of embedding the styles directly in the HTML. To do this, first we need to create a Style Sheet web resource with the appropriate styles. Then we'll update the Lead Indication Web Page resource created in the previous section to reference our new style sheet.

Creating a Style Sheet web resource

1. Navigate to the Settings area, click Customizations, and then click Customize the System to launch the default solution.
2. In the default solution, click web resources in the left navigation pane to view the web resources.
3. Click New to launch the New web resource form.
4. Set the following properties in the form:
    a. Name: **/Styles/master.css**
    b. Display Name: **Master Style Sheet**
    c. Description: **Master style sheet available for use on Microsoft Dynamics CRM web pages.**
    d. Type: Style Sheet (CSS)
    e. Language: English
5. Click the Text Editor button. The Edit Content dialog box appears.

Note If you have downloaded the companion content, click the Browse button, select the web resource Files\Styles\master.css file, and skip to Step 8.

6. In the Edit Content dialog box, click the Source tab and enter the following:

```
body { font-family:Segoe UI; font-size: 11px; margin: 0px;
       background-color:F6F8FA; border:0px }
```

7. Click OK to return to the web resource form.

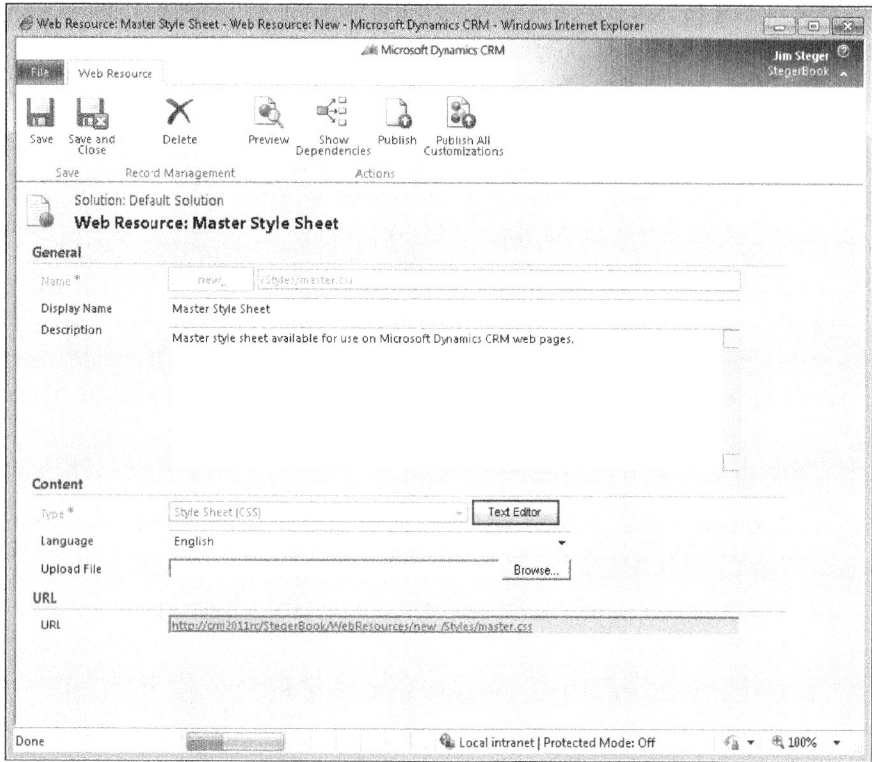

8. In the ribbon, click Save and Close.

Now that the style sheet is ready, we'll update our Web page to reference it. Unlike the previous steps, we need to upload a file for this example instead of using the Text Editor. The Microsoft Dynamics CRM 2011 Text Editor accessed on the web resource form removes all <link> tags from the <head> tag in the Rich Text tab. Because of this glitch, we need to upload Web Page (HTML) files instead of adding them to the Text Editor.

Warning To use a relative style sheet with a Web Page (HTML) web resource, you must use the Upload File option for loading your code. Also, you should never click the Text Editor button for those web resources—doing so will cause your style sheet reference to be removed by Microsoft Dynamics CRM.

Referencing a Style Sheet in a web resource

1. In the default solution's web resources view, double-click the Lead Indication web resource.
2. Download the companion content. Click the Browse button, select the web resource Files\Pages\LeadIndicationWithStyleSheet.htm file, and then click Open.

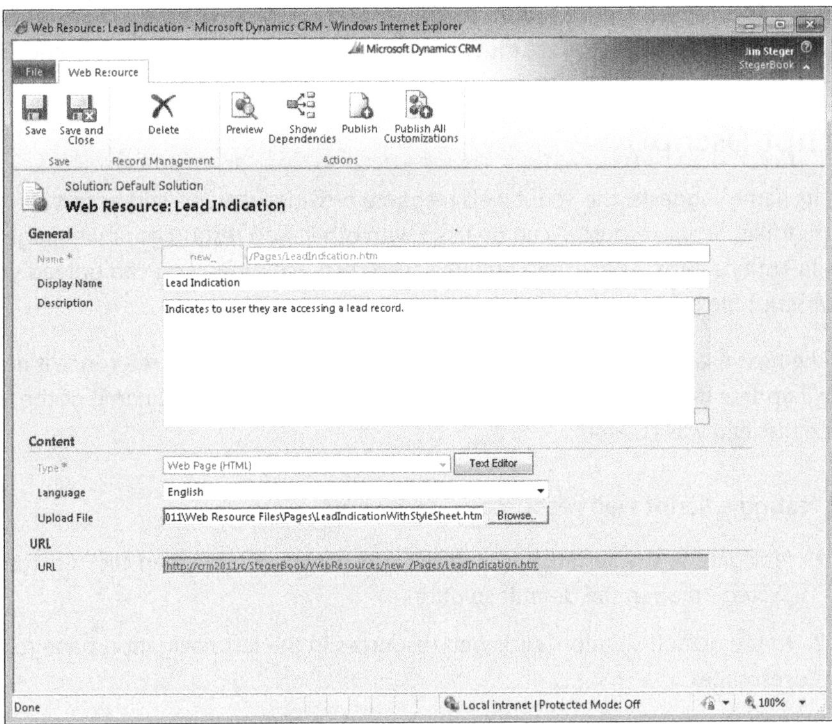

Note If you do not have access to the file, click the link in the URL field and save the existing HTML code to a file on your desktop. Update the code in the <HEAD> tag to the following:

```
<link rel="stylesheet" type="text/css" href="../Styles/master.css" />
<style type="text/css">
div.lead { background-color: Green; width: 100%; height: 2px; padding: 0px }
</style>
```

Save and upload this file.

We are leaving the div.lead style because that is specific to this webpage and not necessarily a generic style. The intent of our master.css file is to keep all of our common styles located in a single file.

3. In the ribbon, click Save and then click Publish.

Important Because we are updating an existing web resource, we need to publish the changes before they take effect.

4. In the ribbon, click Save and Close.

The result on a lead record should be the same. However, we have now established a master style sheet that we can update independently of the webpages that reference it.

Script (Jscript)

As its name suggests, the Script web resource provides storage and access for JavaScript or Jscript files. Script resources can be used with other web resources or webpages, or attached to an entity's form. As with the previous web resource types, you can upload your own JavaScript file or manually type your code in the Text Editor.

In the next example, we'll create a Script web resource and then reference it in the Lead form. We'll update the Topic field on the Lead entity to include the full name of the lead and the date the lead was created.

Creating a Script web resource

1. Navigate to the Settings area, click Customizations, and then click Customize the System to open the default solution.
2. In the default solution, click web resources in the left navigation pane to view the web resources.
3. Click New to launch the New web resource form.
4. Set the following properties in the form:
    a. Name: **/Scripts/lead.js**
    b. Display Name: **Lead Script**
    c. Description: **Script containing Lead specific methods.**
    d. Type: Script (Jscript)
    e. Language: English
5. Click the Text Editor button. The Edit Content dialog box appears.

Note If you have downloaded the companion content, click the Browse button, select the web resource Files\Scripts\lead.js file, and skip to Step 7.

6. In the Edit Content dialog box, click Source and enter the following:

```
function formatTopic() {
	var firstName = Xrm.Page.data.entity.attributes.get("firstname");
	var lastName = Xrm.Page.data.entity.attributes.get("lastname");
	var subject = Xrm.Page.data.entity.attributes.get("subject");
	var createdOn = new Date();
```

```
        var fullName = returnValue(firstName.getValue()) + " " +
                       returnValue(lastName.getValue());
        subject.setValue(fullName + " - " + createdOn.toLocaleString());
}

function returnValue(value) {
        return (value == null) ? "" : value;
}
```

7. Click OK to return to the web resource form.
8. In the ribbon, click Save and Close.

The new Script web resource is automatically published when you save it. Now we need to associate the script with the Lead form and reference it in the *onChange* event of the First Name and Last Name fields.

Referencing the Script (Jscript) web resource on the Lead form

1. Navigate to the Settings area, click Customizations, and then click Customize the System to open the default solution.
2. In the default solution, expand Entities in the left navigation pane and then expand the Lead node.
3. Click Forms and then double-click the Main form.
4. In the ribbon, click Form Properties.

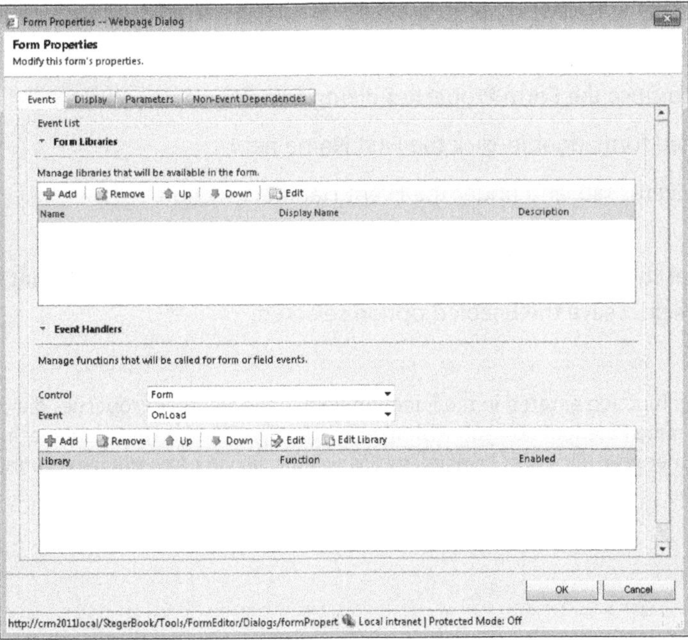

5. In the Form Libraries section, click Add.
6. Select the Lead Script web resource and click OK.

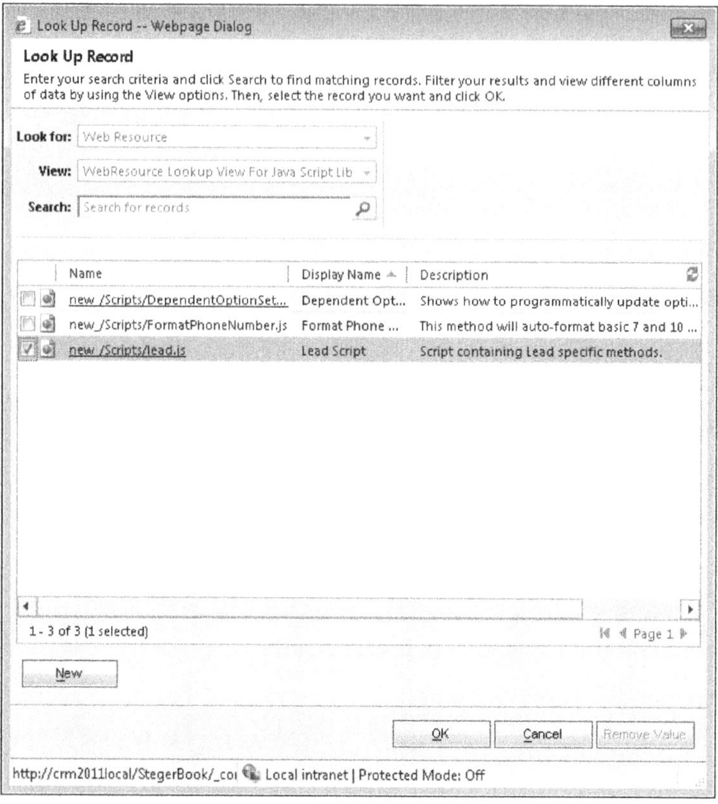

7. Click OK to close the Form Properties dialog box.
8. On the Lead form, double-click the First Name field.
9. Click the Events tab, and under the Event Handlers section, click Add.
10. Ensure that the library shows new_/Scripts/lead.js and then type **formatTopic** in the Function field. Leave the Enabled option selected.

Tip The function entered in the Function field in the Handler Properties dialog box must *exactly* match the function you wish to execute in your Script web resource, including the case. Otherwise, Microsoft Dynamics CRM will display an error when executing the script.

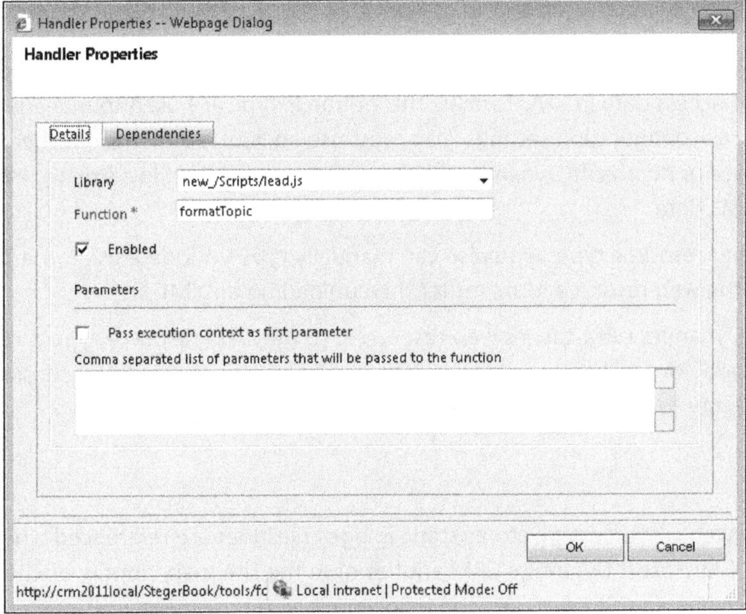

11. Repeat steps 8 through 10 for the Last Name field.
12. In the ribbon, click Save and then click Publish.

Figure 11-8 shows the result of the Topic field once the First Name and Last Name fields have values.

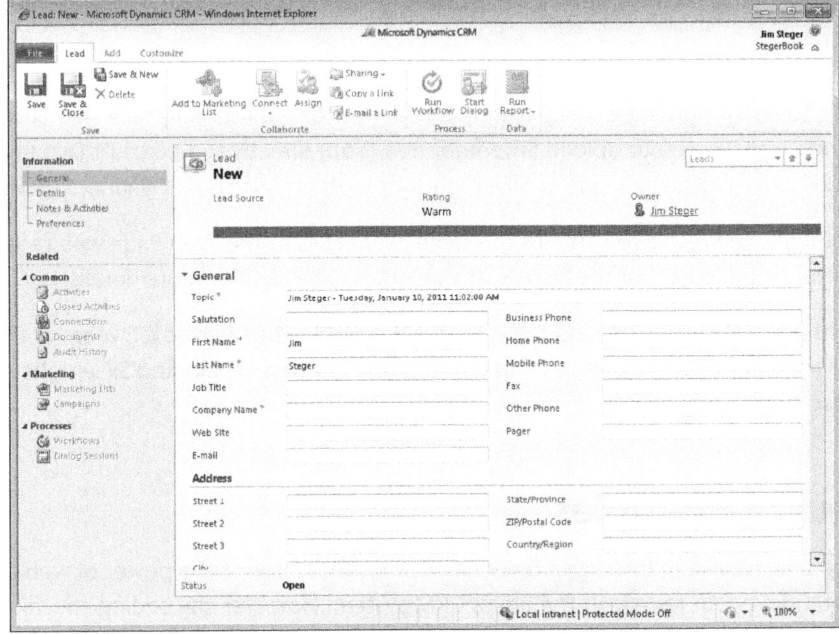

FIGURE 11-8 Topic field on the Lead form, automatically updated with a script

Data (XML)

The Data web resource type (also known as an XML web resource) acts as the primary option to save and access data in XML format. This option is typically used to manage static data fields, such as configuration settings. You must use an .xml file extension when creating your web resource or Microsoft Dynamics CRM won't recognize the file correctly, even if the file contains XML data.

As with other resource types, you also can manually type your data using the Text Editor option on the web resource form, rather than uploading an XML file.

Microsoft Dynamics CRM caches web resources, so the Data resource type is not a good storage model for frequently changing data. For frequent data updates, consider creating a custom entity to store the data instead.

Image

The Image web resource type stores static images files that are referenced when customizing the icons of Microsoft Dynamics CRM entities or in the site map, ribbon, or custom pages. Microsoft Dynamics CRM supports the following image types: .jpg, .gif, .png, and .ico. Unlike previous versions of the software, you must use a web resource to customize the icons of an entity in Microsoft Dynamics CRM 2011.

When referencing an Image web resource in an entity, the site map, or the ribbon, Microsoft Dynamics CRM creates a solution dependency to the web resource. Therefore, you must include the web resource in your solution before importing it into a new environment.

Silverlight (XAP)

Microsoft Silverlight provides a highly interactive, web-based user interface. The Silverlight web resource allows you to upload Silverlight files (.xap) directly to Microsoft Dynamics CRM. Figure 11-1 provided an example of Silverlight displayed in Microsoft Dynamics CRM.

The Silverlight web resource contains the same properties as the Web Page web resource. Please refer to Table 11-3 or the Microsoft Dynamics CRM SDK for more details.

Silverlight development is beyond the scope of this book. The Microsoft Dynamics CRM SDK provides some additional examples and considerations when developing Silverlight controls in Microsoft Dynamics CRM.

Web Resource Examples

In this section, we'll step through a few examples to demonstrate the power of web resources when extending your Microsoft Dynamics CRM system. However, the coding specifics are beyond the scope of this book. Please consult the Microsoft Dynamics CRM SDK or alternate programming resources for more in-depth coverage of the code. Instead, we will focus our attention on applying the code as web resources.

Let's consider the following examples of how web resources can be used:

- Formatting and translating U.S. phone numbers
- Updating a form based on a field value
- Filtering options based on the selection of a field value
- Displaying customer information on an opportunity form

Note We'll walk through examples of web resources in the site map and ribbon in Chapter 12.

Formatting and Translating U.S. Phone Numbers

We often receive the request to translate a telephone number to a common format when helping customers implement Microsoft Dynamics CRM. Although the software does not include this functionality out of the box, a Script web resource can be used to accomplish the requirement. The script included in this section formats any 7- or 10-digit number as 555-1212 or (312) 555-1212. In addition, it translates a phone number entered as letters to their numeric equivalents. For example, if we enter a phone number of 866-555CODE, the script converts the letters in the phone number to (866) 555-2633.

Figure 11-9 shows an example phone number entered by a user.

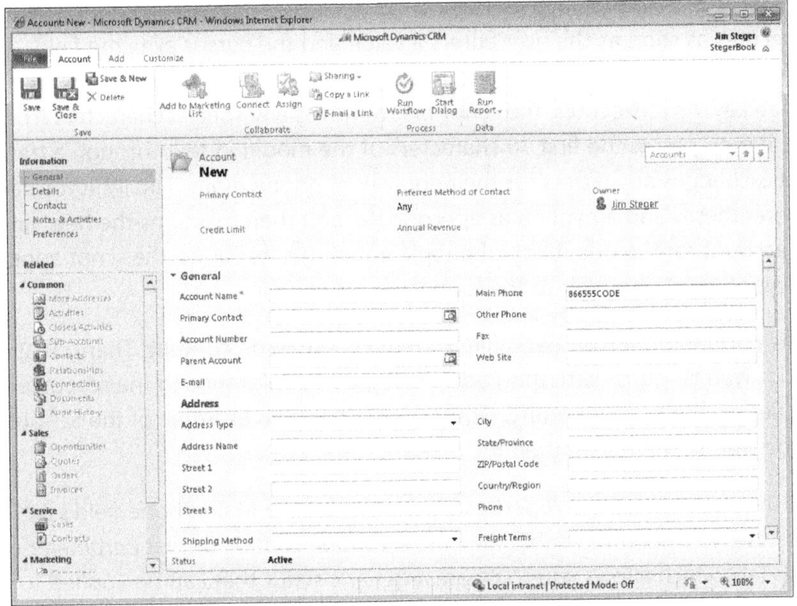

FIGURE 11-9 A phone number on the Account form, as entered by a user

Figure 11-10 shows how the script will translate the entry as soon as the user changes focus from the Main Phone field on the Account form.

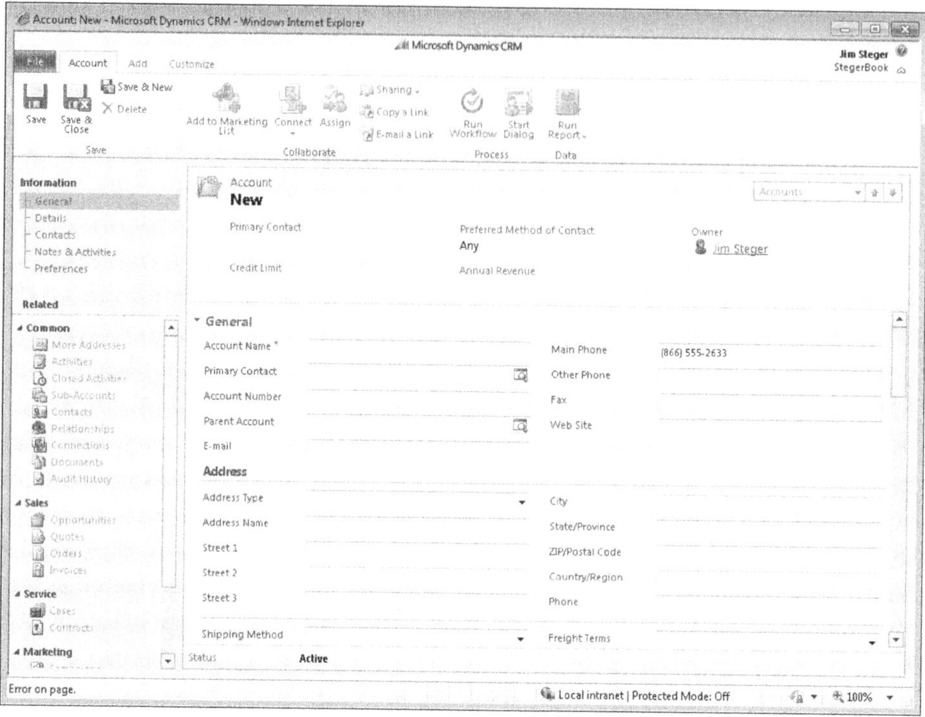

FIGURE 11-10 The formatted phone number, as updated by the script

The script executes as soon as the user enters a value and the cursor exits the field—referred to as *losing focus* or *changing focus*—either because the user clicks elsewhere on the form or presses the Tab key. As it executes, the script first removes any special characters from the entered text. It then passes the first 10 characters of the modified text through a translation function that exchanges any letters for their equivalent phone digits. Finally, it formats the result with parentheses and a hyphen as appropriate, and then reassigns the new value to the field. To account for the possibility of people entering extensions, the script appends any characters beyond the tenth digit to the formatted result.

Download the FormatPhoneNumber.js file from the companion content. Then, create and publish a Script web resource with this code. Finally, add a reference to the resource in the Form Properties on the Account entity. Figure 11-11 shows an example of the Script web resource associated to the Account entity.

Figure 11-12 shows the Handler Properties dialog box for the Main Phone field's *onChange* event. In this case, you need to enable the *Pass execution context as first parameter* option on the Details tab, which allows you to create a generic script that can be applied to any field. Use the same approach with any of the other phone number fields' *onChange* events.

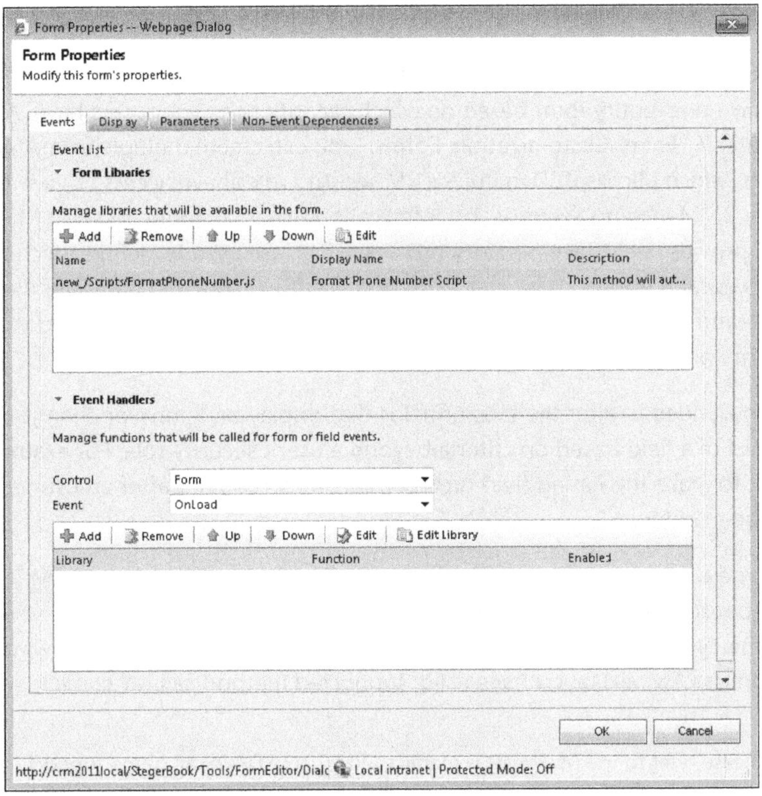

FIGURE 11-11 Associating the FormatPhoneNumber.js script with the Account entity

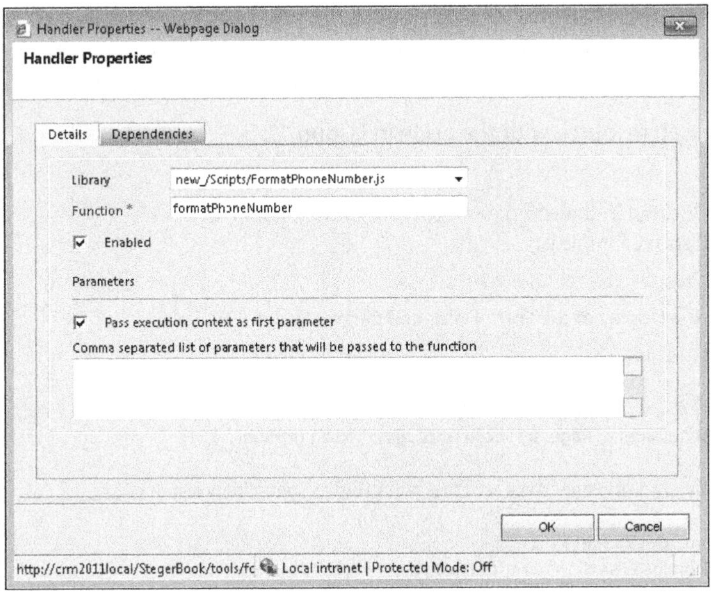

FIGURE 11-12 Associating the *formatPhoneNumber* method to an event handler

Updating a Form Display Based on a Field Value

Microsoft Dynamics CRM 2011 supports role-based forms, meaning you can change the fields that display on an entity form based on which security roles your users have. As you learned in Chapter 7, "Entity Customization: Forms," you can create multiple forms for an entity and assign which Microsoft Dynamics CRM security roles have access to view the form. Further, Chapter 3, "Managing Security and Information Access," taught you that Microsoft Dynamics CRM provides field-level security profiles, which are used to define which fields your users can view and update. However, both of these features have limitations. For instance, both features are limited to Microsoft Dynamics CRM security roles, and the field-level security profiles currently work only for custom fields.

It's likely that you'll need to alter the tabs or fields that display on a form or change the requirement level of a field based on criteria beyond a user's security role. For example, you might want to make the Rating field on an opportunity required after an estimated close date has been entered.

To satisfy this type of requirement, you can leverage the Microsoft Dynamics CRM SDK and a Script web resource. In previous versions of Microsoft Dynamics CRM, you accomplished this type of functionality using unsupported DOM techniques. Now with Microsoft Dynamics CRM 2011, you have valid, supported method calls available!

More Info Please refer to the Microsoft Dynamics CRM 2011 SDK for all of the supported client-side script methods.

The following example demonstrates how to disable the phone number fields if a contact's Phone contact method is set to Do Not Allow. We'll also create a method to hide the Address section on the form if the contact's Mail contact method is set to Do Not Allow.

First, create a Script web resource with the code in Listing 11-2.

Note This code is located in the companion content at web resource Files\Scripts\FormDisplayExample.js.

LISTING 11-2 Toggling the Display of the Form Fields and Section

```
function togglePhoneFields() {
        var telephone1 = Xrm.Page.ui.controls.get("telephone1");
        var telephone2 = Xrm.Page.ui.controls.get("telephone2");
        var mobilePhone = Xrm.Page.ui.controls.get("mobilephone");

        var doNotPhone = Xrm.Page.data.entity.attributes.get("donotphone");

        if (doNotPhone.getValue()) {
                telephone1.setDisabled(true);
```

```
                telephone2.setDisabled(true);
                mobilePhone.setDisabled(true);
        }
        else {
                telephone1.setDisabled(false);
                telephone2.setDisabled(false);
                mobilePhone.setDisabled(false);
        }
}

function toggleAddressSection() {
        var generalTab = Xrm.Page.ui.tabs.get(0);
        var addressSection = generalTab.sections.get("address");

        var doNotPostalMail = Xrm.Page.data.entity.attributes.get("donotpostalmail");

        if (doNotPostalMail.getValue()) {
                addressSection.setVisible(false);
        }
        else {
                addressSection.setVisible(true);
        }
}
```

After the web resource is published, add it to the Contact's Form Library and then add a reference to the *togglePhoneFields* method to the *onChange* event handler of the Phone (donotphone) field, as shown in Figure 11-13.

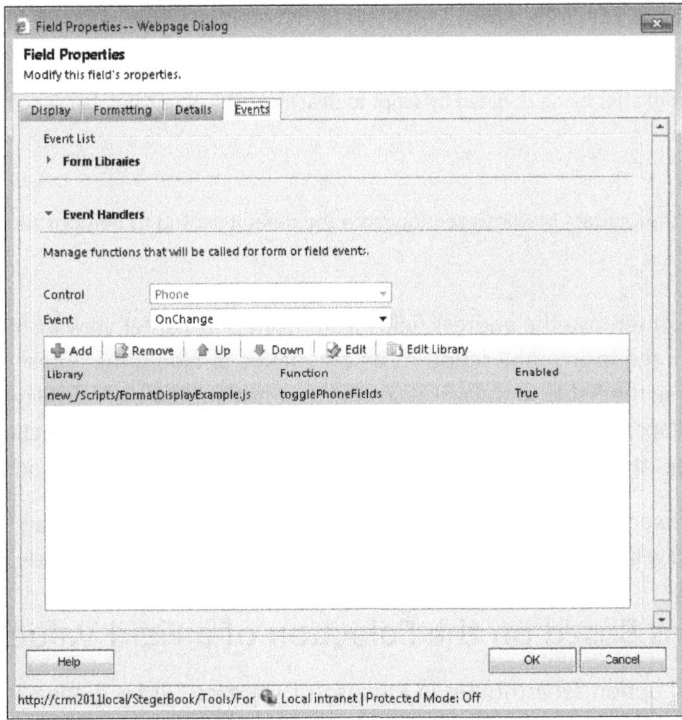

FIGURE 11-13 Associating the *togglePhoneFields* method to the Phone field's event handler

Repeat this process for the Mail (donotpostalmail) field, using the *toggleAddressSection* method instead. Publish the Contact entity so that your changes take effect. If you open a contact and select the Do Not Allow options for the Phone and Mail contact methods, the Business Phone number fields become read-only and the Address section no longer appears, as seen in Figure 11-14.

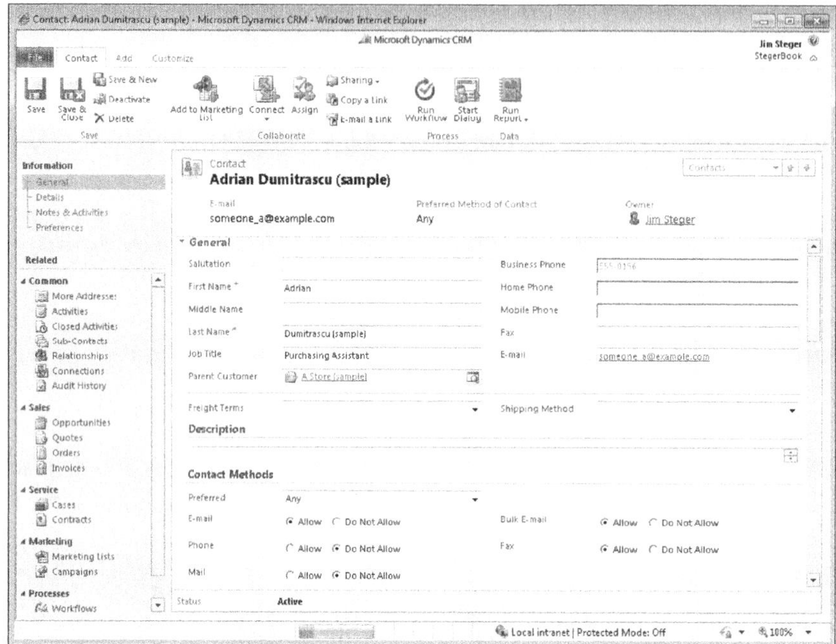

FIGURE 11-14 Contact record after being updated by script to deactivate the phone numbers and hide a section on the form

Note We moved up the Contact Methods section from the default setting to demonstrate this functionality.

Perhaps you'd rather just remove the address fields from front-and-center view instead of removing them from the form in the script. As an alternative to hiding the entire Address section, you can collapse the fields so they're accessible but not immediately displayed. Sections cannot be collapsed, but tabs can. You could move the whole address section to its own tab, and then set the display of the tab to be collapsed in your script instead.

We hope this example demonstrates the powerful flexibility you have with form display, particularly when paired with the power of the Microsoft Dynamics CRM SDK client-side methods.

Filtering Options Based on the Selection of a Field Value

The default behavior of option set attributes in Microsoft Dynamics CRM is that each field operates independently of other values on the form. In reality, you might want to dynamically change the option set values of a record based on other values selected in the record.

For example, if a Shipping Method of Will Call is selected on a contact record, it doesn't make sense to display the FOB (Freight on Board) option in that contact's Freight Terms field.

This example shows how you can dynamically change values of the Freight Terms option set based on the selection of the Shipping Method option set on the Contact entity. When the Shipping Method is set to Will Call, we'll invoke the client-side methods in the Microsoft Dynamics CRM SDK to programmatically remove the FOB option from the Freight Terms option set and automatically set the option to Free of Charge. If the Shipping Method value is updated, our script will programmatically add the FOB option back to the Freight Terms option set.

Tip You can use the code and concepts from this example to extend your company's Microsoft Dynamics CRM deployment to dynamically update different option set values.

Microsoft Dynamics CRM provides a few routines for managing option sets. In this example, we'll use the *Xrm.Page.ui.control.addOption()* and *Xrm.Page.ui.control.removeOption()* routines. We'll also use the *removeOption()* method to remove the FOB option when Will Call is selected. When any other value is selected, we will re-add the FOB option if it has been removed. Figure 11-15 shows the results on the form.

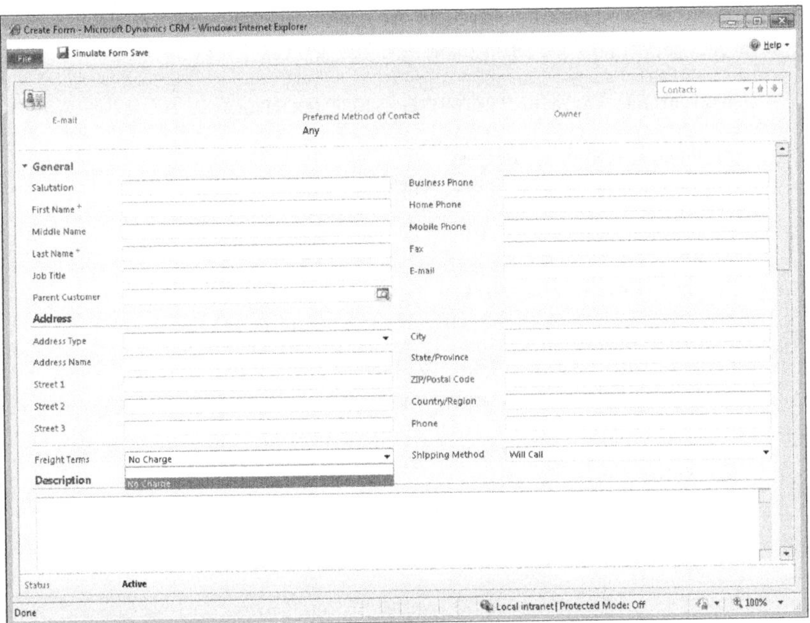

FIGURE 11-15 Form result of the Shipping Method option set script

Important You should not programmatically add options to an option set that do not exist in Microsoft Dynamics CRM. Technically, you can add any name/value option with the *AddOption()* method, but if the value has not been configured in the entity customization, Microsoft Dynamics CRM will not be able to display it correctly on the form.

The script for this example can be found in Listing 11-3.

Note This code is located in the companion content at web resource Files\Scripts\DependentOptionSet.js.

LISTING 11-3 Filtering Options Based on the Selection of a Field Value

```
/*
Description:
This script will remove the FOB option from the Freight Terms option set if the Shipping
Method is Will Call.
*/

function updateFreightTerms() {
        // Set up the option set constants
        // Ensure that these match the codes in CRM
        var SHIPPINGMETHODCODE_WILLCALL = 7;
        var FREIGHTTERMSCODE_FOB = 1;
        var FREIGHTTERMSCODE_NOCHARGE = 2;

        // Gather the field references
        var shipCode = Xrm.Page.data.entity.attributes.get("address1_shippingmethodcode");
        var freightCode = Xrm.Page.data.entity.attributes.get("address1_freighttermscode");
        var freightOptionsControl = Xrm.Page.ui.controls.get("address1_freighttermscode");

        if (shipCode.getValue() == SHIPPINGMETHODCODE_WILLCALL) {
                // Default to No Charge
                freightCode.setValue(FREIGHTTERMSCODE_NOCHARGE);

                // Remove FOB as an option
                freightOptionsControl.removeOption(FREIGHTTERMSCODE_FOB);
        }
        else {
                // Default to blank
                freightCode.setValue(null);

                // First FOB as an option (if it is there) so
                //   we don't add duplicate option
                freightOptionsControl.removeOption(FREIGHTTERMSCODE_FOB);

                //Add back the FOB option
                var fobOption = new Object();
                fobOption.value = FREIGHTTERMSCODE_FOB;
                fobOption.text = "FOB";
                freightOptionsControl.addOption(fobOption, 1);
        }
}

/*
Description:
This script will remove the FOB option if the Shipping Method is Will Call
        and is used for the form's onload event.
*/
function removeFreightTerms() {
        // Set up the option set constants
```

```
        // Ensure that these match the codes in CRM
        var SHIPPINGMETHODCODE_WILLCALL = 7;
        var FREIGHTTERMSCODE_FOB = 1;
        var FREIGHTTERMSCODE_NOCHARGE = 2;

        var shipCode = Xrm.Page.data.entity.attributes.get("address1_shippingmethodcode");
        var freightOptions = Xrm.Page.ui.controls.get("address1_freighttermscode");

        if (shipCode.getValue() == SHIPPINGMETHODCODE_WILLCALL) {
                freightOptions.removeOption(FREIGHTTERMSCODE_FOB);
        }
}
```

After creating the Script web resource, associate the script and methods to the Contact entity and events using the process in the previous two sections. For this example, you should associate the *removeFreightTerms* method to the Contact form's *onLoad* event to address update situations in which Will Call is already selected. Then associate the *updateFreightTerms* method to the Address 1: Shipping Method field's *onChange* event.

Tip When you need to find the value of an option set item, navigate to the entity's Fields page. Double-click the option set field. On the right, you will see the list of options. Double-click an option name, and a dialog box displays the corresponding value, as shown in Figure 11-16.

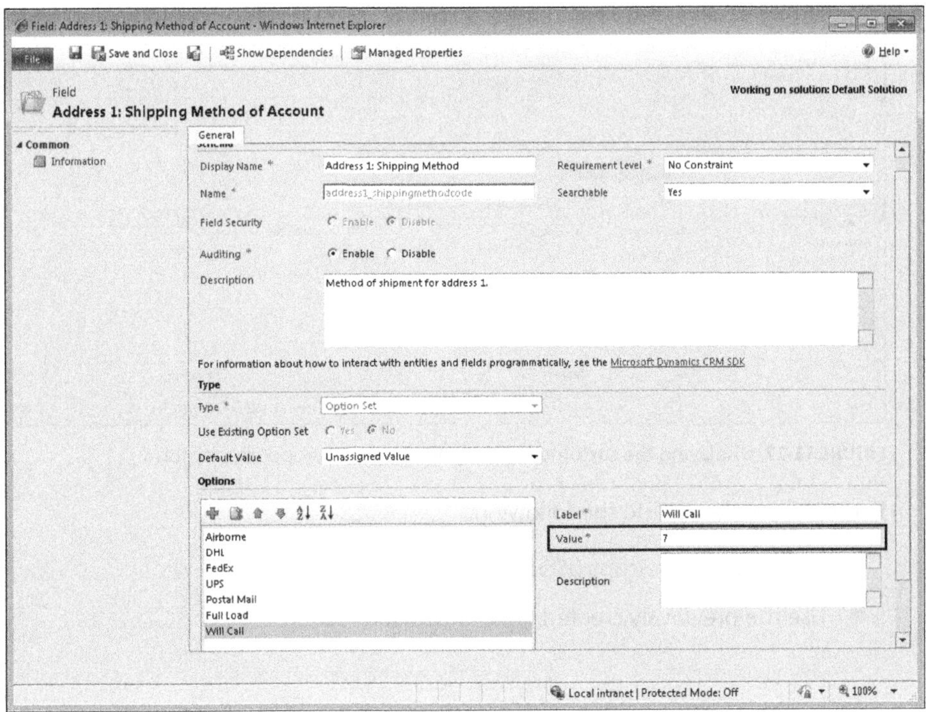

FIGURE 11-16 Retrieving option set values

Displaying Customer Information on an Opportunity Form

The new header area of a form is great for displaying information to the user regardless of where the user is on the form. Microsoft Dynamics CRM 2011 allows you to do display fields, web resources, and IFrames in the header. However, you are unable to display *related* fields in the header or on the form.

One common request we see is to display the customer's phone number directly with the opportunity form. In this example, we'll use a Web Page (HTML) web resource with some JavaScript to accomplish this request. Figure 11-17 shows the results when we are finished.

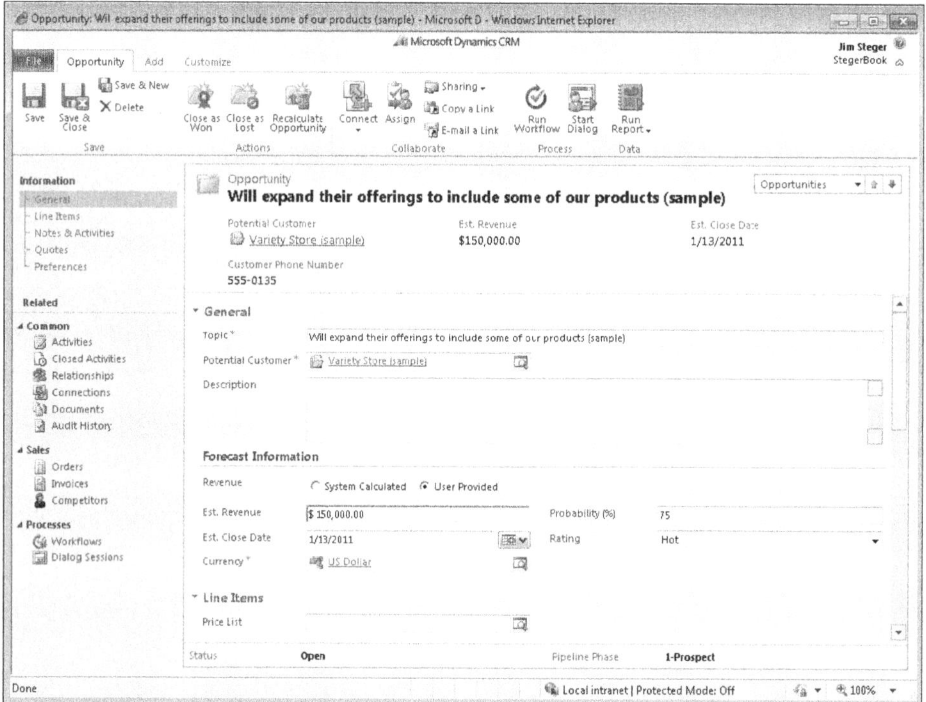

FIGURE 11-17 Displaying the customer's phone number on the opportunity form

For this example we'll do the following:

- Create one new Script (JScript) web resource
- Use the previously created Style Sheet web resource

- Create a new Web Page web resource
- Add the Web Page web resource to the header of the opportunity form

Note For this example, please download the companion content.

Referencing the Script (JScript) web resource on the Lead form

1. Navigate to the Settings area, click Customizations, and then click Customize the System to open the default solution.
2. In the default solution, click the Web Resources link.
3. Click New to create the jQuery web resource. Match the values shown in the following screenshot and then click Browse and select the /Web Resource Files/Scripts/jquery1.4.1.min.js from the companion content. Click Save and Close in ribbon.

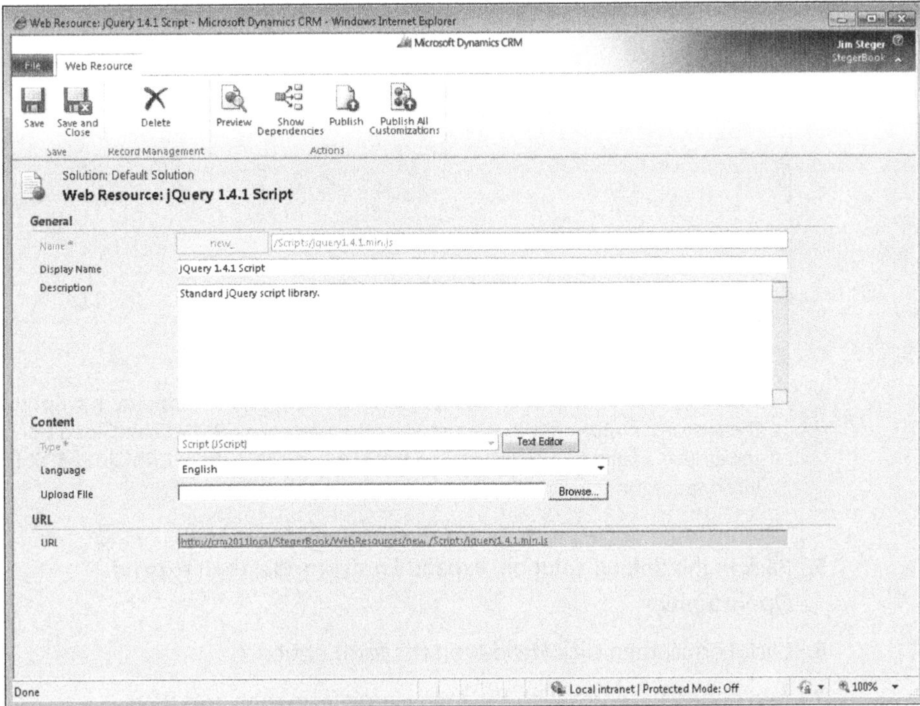

4. Next, we'll create the Web Page web resource. Click New and create a new web resource with the following values. Be sure to click Browse and upload the following file from the companion content: /Web Resource Files/Pages/OpportunityHeader.htm. Click Save and Close.

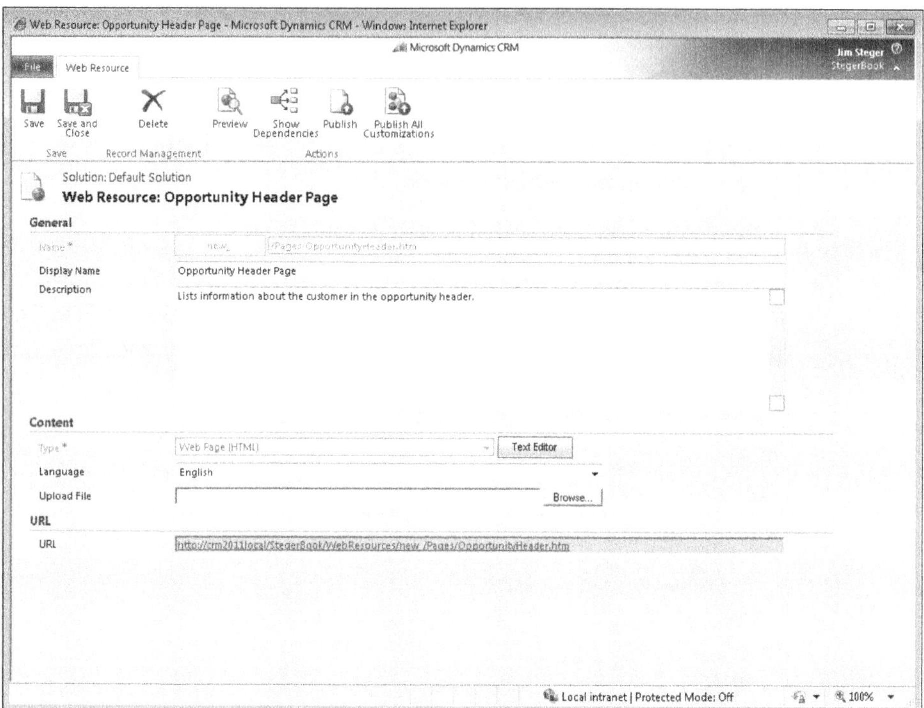

More Info This particular example uses the new OData endpoint in script to retrieve the customer information. We also need to reference CRM's ClientGlobalContext.js.aspx to retrieve a valid CRM context. See the Microsoft Dynamics CRM 2011 SDK for more information on this approach.

5. Back in the default solution, expand Entities node, then expand Opportunity.
6. Click Forms, then click Header on the form ribbon.
7. Add a Web Resource with the following information and then click OK.
8. In the ribbon, click Save and then click Publish, and your new page should be ready for use!

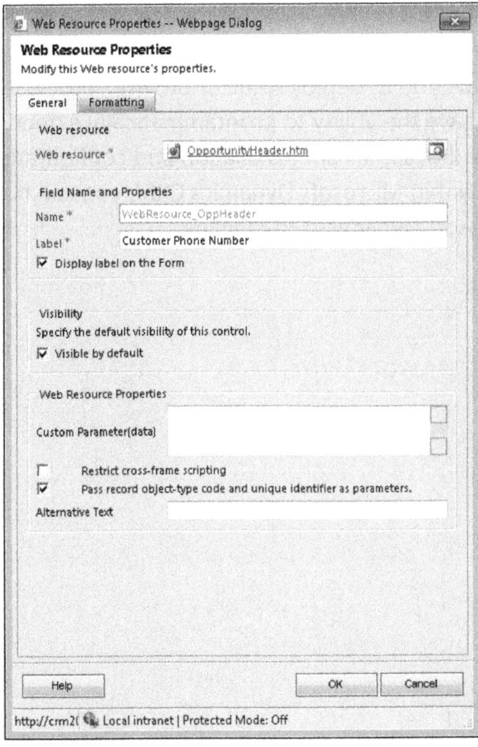
Web Resource Properties -- Webpage Dialog
Web Resource Properties
Modify this Web resource's properties.
General
Formatting
Web resource
Web resource *
OpportunityHeader.htm
Field Name and Properties
Name *
WebResource_OppHeader
Label *
Customer Phone Number
Display label on the Form
Visibility
Specify the default visibility of this control.
Visible by default
Web Resource Properties
Custom Parameter(data)
Restrict cross-frame scripting
Pass record object-type code and unique identifier as parameters.
Alternative Text
Help
OK
Cancel
http://crm2(Local intranet | Protected Mode: Off

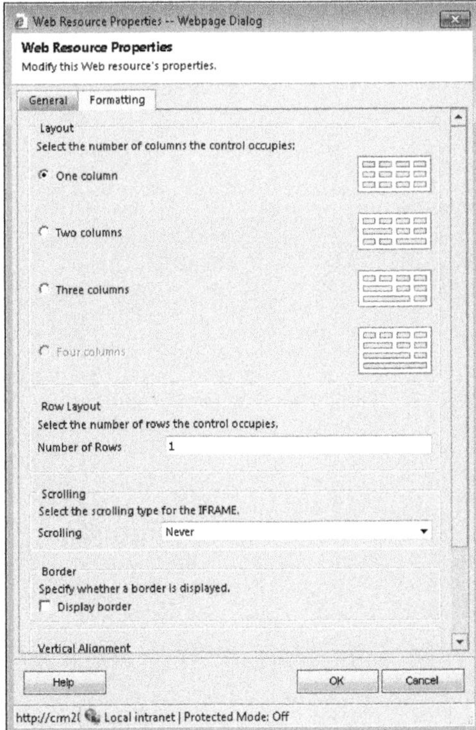
Web Resource Properties -- Webpage Dialog
Web Resource Properties
Modify this Web resource's properties.
General
Formatting
Layout
Select the number of columns the control occupies:
One column
Two columns
Three columns
Four columns
Row Layout
Select the number of rows the control occupies.
Number of Rows
1
Scrolling
Select the scrolling type for the IFRAME.
Scrolling
Never
Border
Specify whether a border is displayed.
Display border
Vertical Alignment
Help
OK
Cancel
http://crm2(Local intranet | Protected Mode: Off

Summary

Microsoft Dynamics CRM 2011 allows you to deploy static or browser-processed files directly to the application. As a result, you have the ability to programmatically extend Microsoft Dynamics CRM without the overhead of significant installation and configuration steps. Further, by deploying files directly within Microsoft Dynamics CRM, you can now extend more complex scenarios with Microsoft Dynamics CRM Online.

Chapter 12
Solutions: Client Extensions

In this chapter:

In previous chapters, you learned how to customize the system by creating and modifying entities, forms, views, relationships. Further, you learned how to extend system functionality with web resources. In this chapter, we demonstrate how to customize the Microsoft Dynamics CRM navigation and ribbon actions.

We'll discuss how you use the Microsoft Dynamics CRM site map to customize and revise the application user interface, as well as introduce the ribbon controls you can use to surface custom functionality.

Understanding the Application Navigation

We've already discussed some of the entity customization features in Microsoft Dynamics CRM, so you should have a good idea of the power and flexibility you have for customizing your system. Depending on your business requirements, chances are you'll find yourself creating several custom entities in your Microsoft Dynamics CRM system. Simple deployments might use just a few custom entities, but a complex deployment might contain over 100 custom entities. Regardless of the level of complexity in your system, you should understand how Microsoft Dynamics CRM displays your custom entities.

By default, Microsoft Dynamics CRM adds custom entities to the user interface and site navigation in the order in which you create them, listing the first custom entity at the top. In addition, Microsoft Dynamics CRM lists the custom entities under the Extensions group in the navigation pane.

Given the robust tools to customize entities, forms, fields, views, charts, and more in the preceding chapters, it probably comes as no surprise that Microsoft Dynamics CRM provides several options for configuring how users access entities and navigate the application. Microsoft Dynamics CRM allows you to customize the following navigation controls:

- Site map
- Entity navigation pane
- Application ribbon
- Entity grid ribbon
- Entity sub-grid ribbon
- Entity form ribbon

As you can see, you have as much flexibility to customize the navigation controls as you do the other areas of the application. Further, Microsoft Dynamics CRM also provides a Personalize Workplace feature that allows users to customize the groups that appear in their Workplace areas. Before we discuss each navigation control, let's review the terminology for the screen region names in Microsoft Dynamics CRM. Figure 12-1 shows the primary application screen regions, Figure 12-2 shows the entity record screen regions, and Figure 12-3 shows the entity record screen with a sub-grid selected.

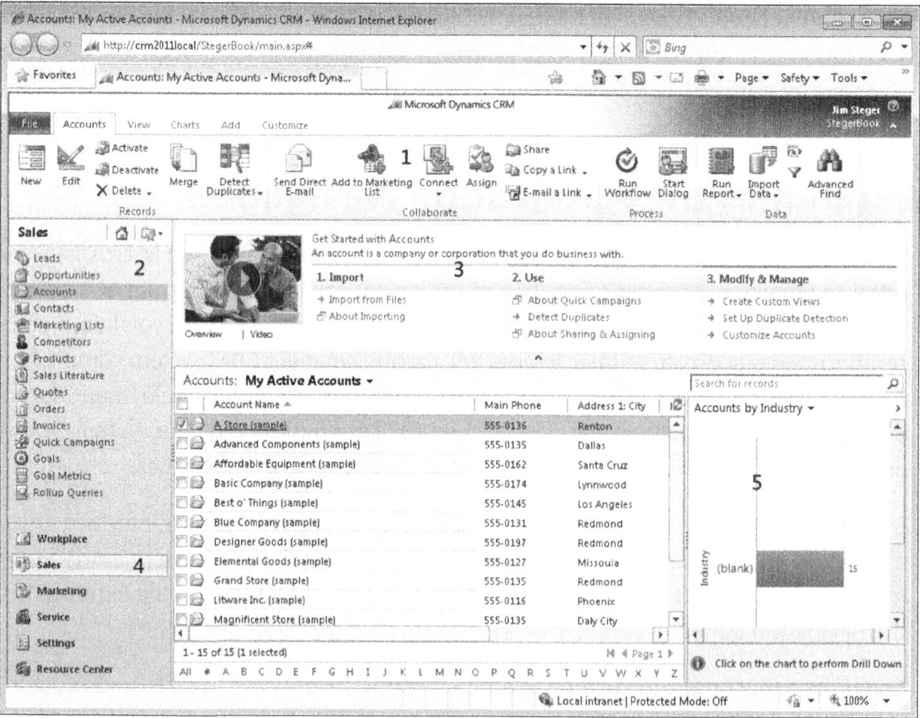

FIGURE 12-1 Screen regions in the Microsoft Dynamics CRM application interface

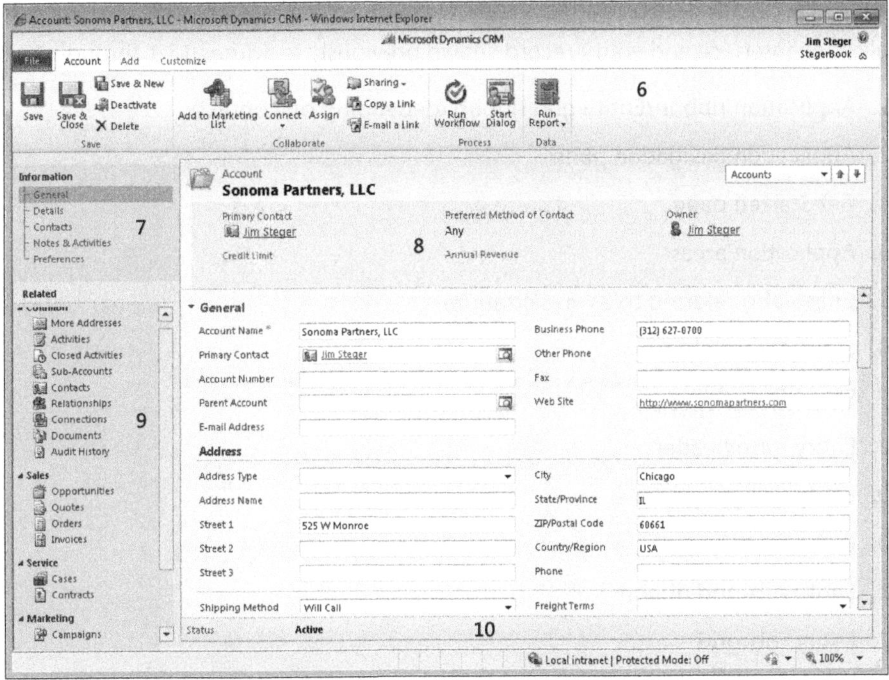

FIGURE 12-2 Screen regions on a Microsoft Dynamics CRM entity record

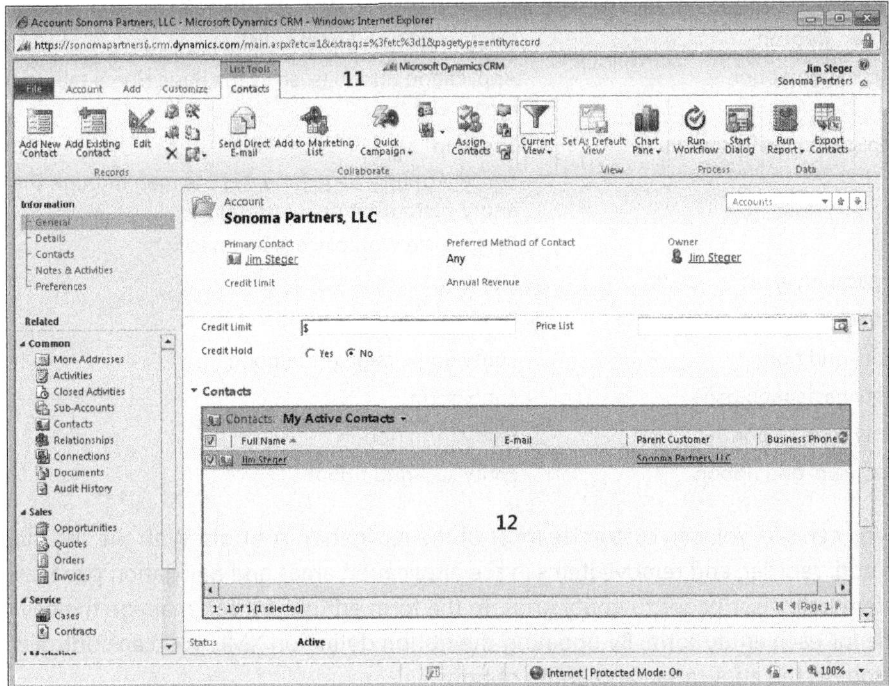

FIGURE 12-3 Screen regions on a Microsoft Dynamics CRM entity record

The following list identifies various screen regions within a Microsoft Dymanics CRM application interface and entity record shown previously in figures 12-1 through 12-3:

1. Application ribbon/Entity grid ribbon (depending on context)
2. Application navigation pane
3. Get Started pane
4. Application areas
5. Chart (also referred to as visualization)
6. Entity form ribbon
7. Entity form tabs
8. Entity form header
9. Entity navigation pane
10. Entity form footer
11. Entity sub-grid ribbon
12. Entity sub-grid

Table 12-1 summarizes the customization areas for each of these screen regions.

TABLE 12-1 Application Navigation Customization Tool Summary

Screen Region	Customization Location(s)
Application ribbon	Application ribbon (such as the Basic Home tab, Jewel menu, etc)
Application navigation pane	Site map Entity property page (updates site map through the entity customization interface) Personalize Workplace (user-specific)
Application areas	Site map
Get Started pane	Site map
Entity grid ribbon	Entity home page grid ribbon
Entity navigation pane	Entity form
Entity form ribbon	Entity form ribbon
Entity sub-grid ribbon	Entity sub-grid ribbon

As you can see, you can customize most of the navigation controls. With the site map, you can add, reorder, and remove items in the application areas and navigation pane, and include custom help visor pages to entity grids. In the form editor, you can manage the navigation pane for each entity form. By updating the ribbon definition XML, you can control the buttons in the application and entity ribbons.

More Info Microsoft Dynamics CRM 2011 still references the ISV.Config file that was used in previous versions of Microsoft Dynamics CRM. The ISV.Config file has been deprecated, so these references are used for backward compatibility, including a legacy setting used to display the service calendar.

Now that you understand the navigation components of Microsoft Dynamics CRM, let's discuss the details of how to modify each.

Modifying the Site Map

By modifying the site map, you can customize the user interface of the application areas and navigation pane as well as the Get Started pane. As discussed earlier, if you add more than a few custom entities to your system, you probably want to modify the site map so that your custom entities appear exactly where you want them. Conceptually, the site map is just XML that is part of the solution's customization components. Unlike form, field, and some of the other customizations in Microsoft Dynamics CRM, you must manually edit the site map with the XML editing tool of your choice. Before we explain how to edit the site map, it will help to further define the screen components in the application areas and navigation pane, as shown in Figure 12-4. The site map references several key terms to describe these areas.

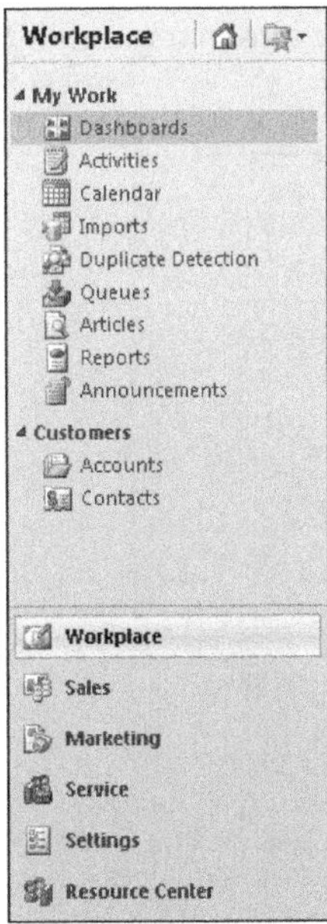

FIGURE 12-4 Screen components of the application areas and navigation pane

By default, Microsoft Dynamics CRM displays six buttons in the applications area: Workplace, Sales, Marketing, Service, Settings, and Resource Center.

When you are working with the site map, Microsoft Dynamics CRM refers to these six buttons as *areas*. When users click an area, Microsoft Dynamics CRM updates the application navigation pane to show the appropriate links for that area. As Figure 12-4 shows, the Workplace area contains two main elements: My Work and Customers.

The site map refers to these elements as *groups*. Microsoft Dynamics CRM formats groups in the web client's application navigation pane with the expand/collapse control. Each group contains additional links that the site map refers to as *subareas*. For example, the My Work group in Figure 12-4 includes nine subareas:

- Dashboards
- Activities
- Calendar
- Imports
- Duplicate Detection
- Queues
- Articles
- Reports
- Announcements

Although the Outlook client uses some of the same screen region names as the web client, it also includes a few unique region names. Figure 12-5 shows the screen regions in the Microsoft Dynamics CRM for Outlook client.

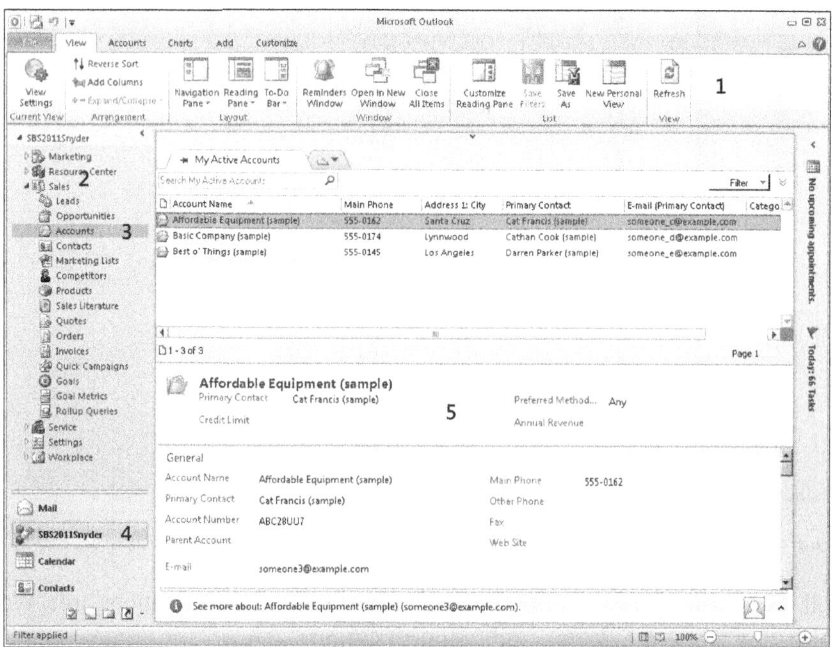

FIGURE 12-5 Screen regions in Microsoft Dynamics CRM for Outlook

The following list identifies the different screen regions in Microsoft Dynamics CRM for Outlook as shown in Figure 12-5:

1. Ribbon
2. Navigation pane - areas
3. Navigation pane - subareas
4. Solution folder
5. Reading pane

You can see that the Outlook client displays areas and subareas in the Outlook navigation just as they are displayed in the web client. However, Outlook alphabetizes the links.

> **Important** Remember that the web and Microsoft Dynamics CRM for Outlook clients share the same site map to configure the application navigation. Therefore, you should always consider how the changes you make in the site map will appear to web and Outlook users.

Editing the Site Map

Now that you understand the terminology used in the Microsoft Dynamics CRM site map, let's modify the site map. As explained earlier, the site map is XML included in a solution's customizations file. To edit it, you must export an unmanaged solution that includes the site map component.

> **Tip** We recommend that you create a solution specifically for site map and application ribbon changes. This solution should not contain any other components other than those used to customize the site map and application ribbon. This will help you avoid collisions when multiple customizers and programmers update the system. As an added bonus, the resulting customizations file will be much smaller and easier to edit with this approach.

In Chapter 5, "Solutions Overview and Concepts," we created a simple solution that contained the site map component. If you haven't already done so, create a custom solution called Site Map Development and add the site map component to it. Export the solution to your computer, unzip the solution file, and then open the customizations.xml file.

You can edit the customizations.xml file by using any text editor, such as Notepad or WordPad, but using an XML-specific editor such as Microsoft Visual Studio makes the editing process much easier because you can expand and collapse each element, as shown in Figure 12-6. You can use Microsoft Internet Explorer to view an .xml file, but you won't be able to edit it there.

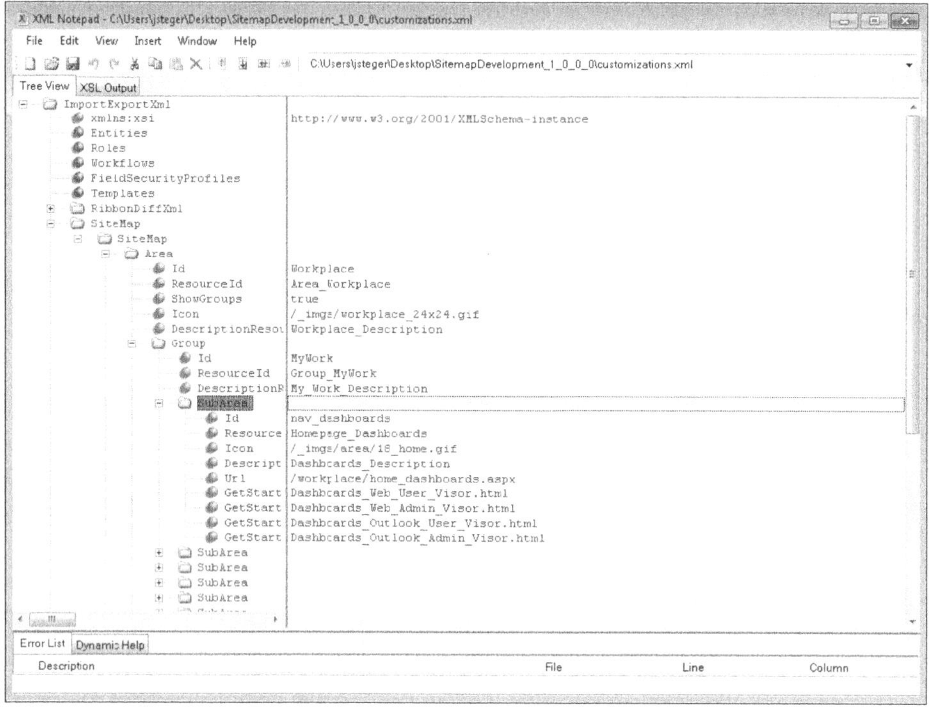

FIGURE 12-6 Viewing the site map section in the customizations.xml using XML Notepad 2007

Tip If you don't have access to Microsoft Visual Studio, we highly recommend that you find another XML editing application. Fortunately, Microsoft offers a free XML editor called XML Notepad 2007. Microsoft designed XML Notepad 2007 as a very lightweight application (less than 2 MB download) for basic editing and manipulation of XML files. With this tool, you can view and edit files such as the Microsoft Dynamics CRM customizations.xml file. Download XML Notepad 2007 at *http://www.microsoft.com/downloads*. Another free option is Visual Web Developer 2010 Express, which can be downloaded from *http://www.microsoft.com/express/Downloads*.

By default, Microsoft Dynamics CRM creates a site map section with the XML structure shown in Figure 12-7.

The components you included in your solution will drive which XML nodes have data. For this section, you should focus only on the *SiteMap* and *Languages* elements in the customizations.xml file. We'll discuss each of the *SiteMap* elements and their attributes in detail in the following subsections.

Important The default site map that you export does not include any of the following elements: *Title*, *Titles*, *Description*, or *Descriptions*. However, you need to use these elements if you add any new areas to the application. Microsoft Dynamics CRM doesn't require these elements for the six default application areas, but they are required for new areas. The *Title*, *Titles*, *Description*, and *Descriptions* elements apply to the *Area*, *Group*, and *SubArea* elements.

```
<ImportExportXml>
  <Entities/>
  <Roles/>
  <Workflows/>
  <FieldSecurityProfiles/>
  <Templates />
  <RibbonDiffXml />
  <SiteMap>
    <SiteMap>
      <Area>
        <Group>
          <SubArea>
            <Privilege/>
          </SubArea>
        </Group>
      </Area>
    </SiteMap>
  </SiteMap>
  <EntityMaps />
  <EntityRelationships />
  <OrganizationSettings />
  <optionsets />
  <Languages>
    <Language/>
  </Languages>
</ImportExportXml>
```

FIGURE 12-7 XML structure of the default site map

Figure 12-8 shows an updated XML element structure of the site map section in the customizations.xml file that includes the *Title*, *Titles*, *Description*, and *Descriptions* elements. Microsoft Dynamics CRM includes these four areas in the site map to support multi-language functionality in each organization.

```
<ImportExportXml>
  <Entities/>
  <Roles/>
  <Workflows/>
  <FieldSecurityProfiles/>
  <Templates />
  <RibbonDiffXml />
  <SiteMap>
    <SiteMap>
      <Area>
        <Titles>
          <Title />
        </Titles>
        <Descriptions>
          <Description />
        </Descriptions>
        <Group>
          <Titles>
            <Title />
          </Titles>
          <Descriptions>
            <Description />
          </Descriptions>
          <SubArea>
            <Titles>
              <Title />
            </Titles>
            <Descriptions>
              <Description />
            </Descriptions>
            <Privilege/>
          </SubArea>
        </Group>
      </Area>
    </SiteMap>
  </SiteMap>
  <EntityMaps />
  <EntityRelationships />
  <OrganizationSettings />
  <optionsets />
  <Languages>
    <Language/>
  </Languages>
</ImportExportXml>
```

FIGURE 12-8 XML element structure of the site map

SiteMap Element

It might seem a little confusing initially, but Microsoft Dynamics CRM uses the name SiteMap as the root node of the *SiteMap* element, as shown in Figure 12-8. Your customizations.xml file can include only one occurrence of the *SiteMap* node under the *SiteMap* element. Table 12-2 lists the only attribute for the *SiteMap* node.

TABLE 12-2 *SiteMap* Attribute

Name	Description	Data type	Required?	Applies to web client?	Applies to Outlook client?
Url	Specifies a URL that Microsoft Dynamics CRM displays in the Microsoft Dynamics CRM for Outlook client when users click the Microsoft Dynamics CRM folder. Valid values: Any valid URL	*String*	No	No	Yes

By using the SiteMap *Url* attribute, you can display the web page of your choice when users click the Microsoft Dynamics CRM folder in the Outlook client. Figure 12-9 shows an example in which we specified the URL *http://sharepoint* to display a Microsoft Office SharePoint Services website.

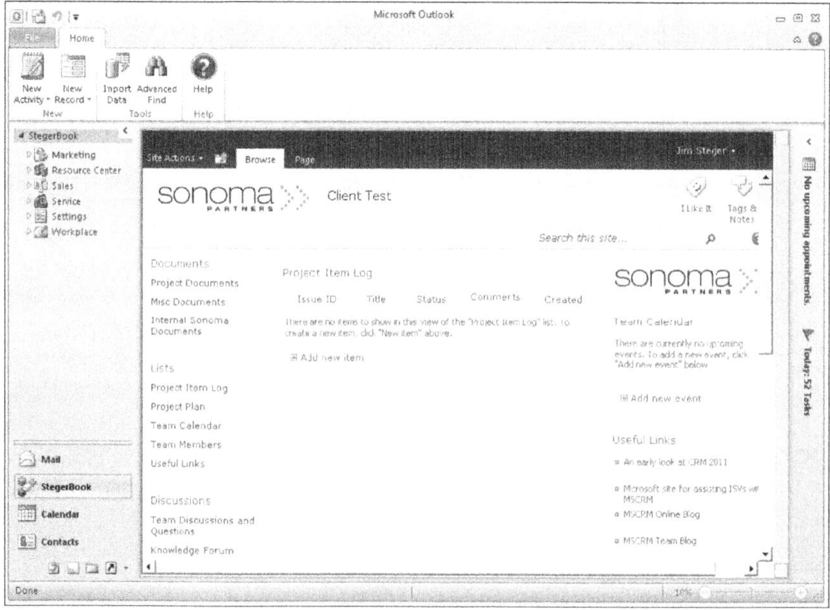

FIGURE 12-9 Using the *Url* attribute of SiteMap to change the default web page in Outlook

To implement the example in Figure 12-8, you can change the *SiteMap* node from the default value.

```
<SiteMap>
```

Add the *Url* attribute to the node so that it looks like the following example.

```
<SiteMap Url="http://sharepoint">
```

In the real world, you might want to display a custom web page such as a dashboard or other intranet site. Note that changing this attribute affects the Outlook client, but it does not affect users who access Microsoft Dynamics CRM through the web client.

Area Elements

The default site map XML includes six *Area* elements with the following labels: Workplace, Sales, Marketing, Service, Settings, and Resource Center. You can modify, reorder, or remove these areas and add new areas by modifying the site map XML. Remember, Microsoft Dynamics CRM displays areas in the lower-left corner of the web client and in the Outlook client folders.

Caution Although technically you can remove the Settings area from the application by removing it from the site map, you might accidentally lock yourself out of the Customizations section by doing so. Therefore, we strongly recommend that you *never* remove the Settings area from the site map. If you do not want users to see this area in the application navigation, you should change their security role settings instead of removing the area from the site map.

Table 12-3 lists the attributes for the *Area* node.

TABLE 12-3 *Area* Attributes

Name	Description	Data type	Required?	Applies to web client?	Applies to Outlook client?
Description	Deprecated. Text that Microsoft Dynamics CRM displays in the Outlook client when users click the parent folder. Use the *Descriptions* element instead.	*string*	No	No	Yes
DescriptionResourceID	For internal use only.	*string*	No	Yes	Yes

Name	Description	Data type	Required?	Applies to web client?	Applies to Outlook client?
Icon	Specifies a URL to an image; allows you to display a different icon for the area.	*string*	No	Yes	Yes
ID	Specifies a unique identifier in ASCII; spaces are not allowed. The following characters are allowed: a–z, A–Z, 0–9, and underscore (_)	*string*	Yes	Yes	Yes
License	Deprecated.	*string*	No	Yes	Yes
ResourceId	For internal use only.	*string*	No	Yes	Yes
ShowGroups	Specifies whether Microsoft Dynamics CRM displays an area's groups in the navigation pane. Valid values: *true* *false*	*boolean*	No	Yes	Yes
Title	Deprecated. Allows you to enter a different text label for the area. Use the *Titles* element instead.	*string*	No	Yes	Yes
Url	Specifies a URL that Microsoft Dynamics CRM displays in the Outlook client when users click the folder that represents the area.	*string*	No	No	Yes

Group Element

In each area of the site map, you can configure the groups that display. Each area can contain multiple groups or none at all. By using groups, you can categorize the subareas in a manner that makes the most sense for your business. The *Group* element in site map XML uses the attributes listed in Table 12-4.

TABLE 12-4 ***Group* Attributes**

Name	Description	Data type	Required?	Applies to web client?	Applies to Outlook client?
Description	Deprecated. Text that Microsoft Dynamics CRM displays in the Outlook client when users click the parent folder. Use the *Descriptions* element instead.	*string*	No	No	Yes
DescriptionResourceID	For internal use only.	*string*	No	Yes	Yes
Icon	Specifies a URL to an image; allows you to display a different icon for the area.	*string*	No	No	Yes
ID	Specifies a unique identifier in ASCII; spaces are not allowed. The following characters are allowed: a–z, A–Z, 0–9, and underscore (_)	*string*	Yes	Yes	Yes
IsProfile	Controls whether this group represents a user-selectable profile for the workplace. Valid values: *true* *false*	*boolean*	No	Yes	No

Name	Description	Data type	Required?	Applies to web client?	Applies to Outlook client?
License	Deprecated.	*string*	No	Yes	Yes
ResourceId	For internal use only.	*string*	No	Yes	Yes
Title	Deprecated. Allows you to enter a different text label for the group. Use the *Titles* element instead.	*string*	No	Yes	Yes
URL	Specifies a URL that Microsoft Dynamics CRM displays in the Outlook clients when users click the folder that represents the group.	*string*	No	No	Yes

Most of these attributes behave in exactly the same way as the *Area* element's attributes, but we want to highlight one attribute unique to the *Group* element: *IsProfile*.

Users can configure their personal options by clicking the File menu and selecting Options. If they click the Workplace tab, Microsoft Dynamics CRM displays the Set Personal Options dialog box, as shown in Figure 12-10.

In this dialog box, a user can select the groups that he wants to see in the Workplace area. Changing the groups displayed affects what that user sees, but does not affect what other users see.

Tip The Microsoft Dynamics CRM user interface uses the phrase *Select Workplace Areas*, but users actually select which workplace *groups* they want to display.

Microsoft Dynamics CRM does not display all of the groups in the Personalize Workplace area; it shows only groups with an *IsProfile* attribute value of *true*. So if you want a particular group in the Workplace area to always appear for all users, set the *IsProfile* attribute of the group to *false* so that Microsoft Dynamics CRM won't allow users to clear the selection of the group in the Personalize Workplace dialog box.

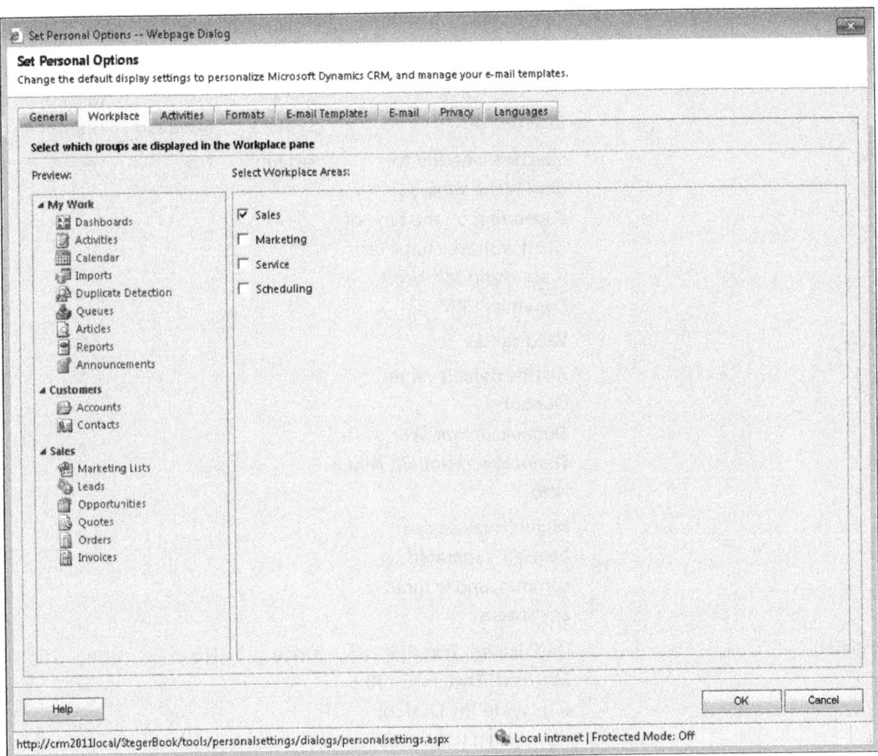

FIGURE 12-10 Set Personal Options dialog box

SubArea Element

Each group element in the site map xml file can contain multiple *SubArea* elements (or no *SubAreas* elements at all). *SubArea* elements possess the attributes shown in Table 12-5.

TABLE 12-5 ***SubArea* Attributes**

Name	Description	Data type	Required?	Applies to web client?	Applies to Outlook client?
AvailableOffline	Specifies whether to display a subarea when the user is offline in Outlook client. Valid values: *true* *false*	*boolean*	No	No	Yes (offline client only)

Name	Description	Data type	Required	Applies to web client?	Applies to Outlook client?
Client	Specifies whether to display the subarea, depending on the type of client with which the user is accessing Microsoft Dynamics CRM. Valid values: *All* (the default value) *Outlook* *OutlookLaptopClient* *OutlookWorkstationClient* *Web* Multiple values can be used, separated by commas, and without any spaces.	*string*	No	Yes	Yes
Description	Deprecated. Text that Microsoft Dynamics CRM displays in the Outlook client when users click the parent folder (group). Use the *Descriptions* element instead.	*string*	No	No	Yes
DescriptionResourceID	For internal use only.	*string*	No	Yes	Yes
Entity	Allows you to enter the schema name of the entity that you want to display when users click the subarea link.	*string*	No	Yes	Yes
GetStartedPanePath	Specifies the path to the Get Started page for this subarea.	*string*	No	Yes	Yes
GetStartedPanePathAdmin	Specifies the path to the Get Started page for this subarea if the user is logged in as a system administrator.	*string*	No	Yes	Yes
GetStartedPanePathAdminOutlook	Specifies the path to the Get Started page for this subarea if the user is logged in as a system administrator and is using the Microsoft Dynamics CRM for Outlook client.	*string*	No	Yes	Yes

Name	Description	Data type	Required	Applies to web client?	Applies to Outlook client?
GetStartedPanePathOutlook	Specifies the path to the Get Started page for this subarea when Microsoft Dynamics CRM for Outlook is in use.	*string*	No	Yes	Yes
Icon	Specifies a URL to an image; allows you to display a different icon for the subarea.	*string*	No	Yes	Yes
ID	Specifies a unique identifier in ASCII, with no spaces. The following characters are allowed: a–z, A–Z, 0–9, and underscore (_)	*string*	Yes	Yes	Yes
License	Deprecated.	*string*	No	Yes	Yes
OutlookShortcutIcon	Specifies the icon to display in the Outlook client.	*string*	No	No	Yes
PassParams	Specifies whether information about the organization and language context are passed to the URL. Valid values: 0 = don't pass parameters [default] 1 = pass parameters	*boolean*	No	Yes	Yes
ResourceId	Used internally to address a localized label to display. The following characters are supported: a–z, A–Z, 0–9, and underscore (_)	*string*	No	Yes	Yes

Name	Description	Data type	Required	Applies to web client?	Applies to Outlook client?
Sku	Specifies the version(s) of Microsoft Dynamics CRM that display this SubArea. Default: All Valid values: All OnPremise Live SPLA Multiple values can be used as long as they are separated by commas and do not contain spaces.	*string*	No	Yes	Yes
Title	Deprecated. Allows you to enter a different text label for the subarea. Use the *Titles* element instead.	*string*	No	Yes	Yes
Url	Specifies a URL that Microsoft Dynamics CRM displays in the Outlook client when users click the folder that represents the subarea; overrides the schema name if you specify both a schema name and a *Url* attribute.	*string*	No	Yes	Yes

Regarding the *Client* attribute, the name values refer to older names of the Microsoft Dynamics CRM for Outlook client, but you can probably figure out what they refer to:

- ***Outlook*** Refers to both the online and offline Outlook clients
- ***OutlookLaptopClient*** Refers to just Microsoft Dynamics CRM for Outlook with Offline Access
- ***OutlookWorkstationClient*** Refers to Microsoft Dynamics CRM for Outlook (no offline access)

Privilege

The last element of the site map XML is the *Privilege* element. Using the *Privilege* element in a *SubArea* element is optional, and you can include multiple *Privilege* elements as needed. By using the *Privilege* element, you can specify security criteria that Microsoft Dynamics CRM evaluates to determine whether to display a subarea to a user.

It's important to note that the *Privilege* element does not override the Microsoft Dynamics CRM security settings for custom and system entities. Therefore, even if you try to assign display (read) rights to a by adding a *Privilege* element for a particular entity in the site map XML, the Microsoft Dynamics CRM security settings would not display the subarea to a user who does not have read permissions to that entity.

If the Microsoft Dynamics CRM security settings always make the final determination on whether to display a subarea to a user, you might wonder why anyone would ever need to use a *Privilege* element. We think the most obvious benefit of the *Privilege* element is that you can use it to configure security display rights for custom web pages that you integrate with Microsoft Dynamics CRM, which you cannot do by using the Microsoft Dynamics CRM security settings.

The *Privilege* element has the attributes listed in Table 12-6.

TABLE 12-6 ***Privilege* Attributes**

Name	Description	Data type	Required?	Applies to web client?	Applies to Outlook client?
Entity	Indicates the schema name of the entity you want to reference for the permissions check.	*string*	Yes	Yes	Yes
Privilege	Specifies the permissions needed to display this subarea. Valid values: A comma-separated list with no spaces, made up of these possible values: *All* *AllowQuickCampaign* *Append* *AppendTo* *Assign* *Create* *Delete* *Read* *Share* *Write* *UseInternetMarketing*	*string*	No	Yes	Yes

The following example uses the *Privilege* element:

```
<SubArea Id="test_subarea" Url="custompage.aspx">
   <Privilege Entity="account" Privilege="Delete, Write"/>
</SubArea>
```

In this example, if a user has delete and write permissions for the Account entity, Microsoft Dynamics CRM displays the subarea in the application navigation pane. Conversely, if you add the custom web page Custompage.aspx to your system and you don't want a particular user to see this page, you can simply use the *Privilege* element in your site map and specify a security permission that you know the user does not have.

Note The *UseInternetMarketing* privilege only applies to Microsoft Dynamics CRM Online. However, you can still use the security privilege in on-premises installations for the purpose of displaying site map subareas.

Importing a Site Map

After you have modified the site map XML, you must save your changes to the customizations.xml file and import the changes into Microsoft Dynamics CRM. Typically, when importing a solution, you use an exported solution file to import changes to a different Microsoft Dynamics CRM organization. However, to edit the site map, you need to unzip the solution package to edit the customizations.xml file. Therefore, you must zip the full exported package with your updated customizations.xml file prior to importing your site map changes back into Microsoft Dynamics CRM.

For a solution that contains only a site map component, you should see the standard solution files of [Content_Types].xml, customizations.xml, and solution.xml.

After you have saved the updated solution .zip file, you can import it back into Microsoft Dynamics CRM.

Working with the Get Started Pane

Microsoft Dynamics CRM provides help content specific to each area of the application above entity grids and dashboards. This content appears in the Get Started pane. By default, Microsoft Dynamics CRM displays help content in the Get Started pane, but you can replace this with any content. Any *SubArea* element that uses the *Entity* attribute to display a grid of entity records in the homepage grid area can be configured to display content in the Get Started pane.

Warning The Get Started Pane cannot be enabled for subarea elements that use the *Url* attribute to display a custom page. Any Get Started attributes in a *SubArea* element that contains a *Url* attribute will be ignored.

You can create HTML or Microsoft Silverlight web resources or provide a website URL to display in the Get Started pane. Further, the Microsoft Dynamics CRM SDK provides templates to mirror the native Get Started pane content. The Get Started pane styles and template can be found in the downloaded Microsoft Dynamics CRM SDK files at \Resources\GetStartedPaneTemplate. Figure 12-11 shows a customized Get Started pane using the styles from the SDK.

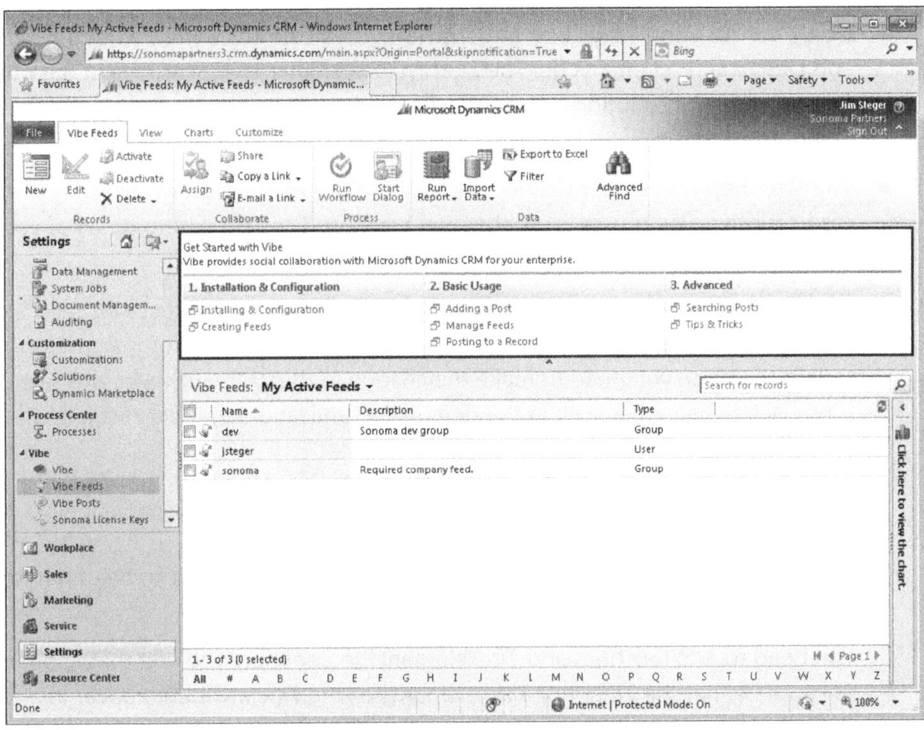

FIGURE 12-11 Custom Get Started pane

Tip If you have only one page for all users and client types, you can specify a value for only the *GetStartedPanePath* attribute and exclude all the other attributes. Microsoft Dynamics CRM will then use this value for all users and clients.

Site Map Tips and Tricks

The following tips and tricks might save you some time when editing the site map section in the customizations.xml file:

- **Isolate the site map** Always create an unmanaged solution dedicated to the site map and application ribbon components. Do not include any other components in the solution. This isolates any changes to the site map to one solution file and makes the resulting customizations.xml much smaller and easier to update.

- **Changing the order of area and group elements in the site map works only in the web client** The Microsoft Dynamics CRM web client displays navigation elements in the order specified in the site map. However, Outlook treats areas and groups as folders and therefore displays them in alphabetical order, not in the order specified in the site map. However, Outlook will display subareas in the order specified in the site map.
- **Don't confuse the *Titles* and *Descriptions*** It's easy to confuse what the *Titles* and *Descriptions* elements do. The *Descriptions* elements appear only in the Microsoft Dynamics CRM for Outlook client; the *Titles* elements appear in both the web and Outlook clients.
- **The site map is case-sensitive** Because the site map uses XML, which is case-sensitive, you must ensure that you have used correct casing for all of your attributes.
- **Watch out for default attributes** When you first open the customization.xml file to edit the name of a group or area (such as Sales), you might look for an area called Sales to find the place you need to make the change in the XML. However, the Sales area is not clearly named as such in the default customizations.xml file. Instead, the *Area* element for sales looks like this:

  ```
  <Area Id="SFA" ResourceId="Area_Sales" Icon="/_imgs/sales_24x24.gif"
   DescriptionResourceId="Sales_Description">
  ```

  It isn't obvious what text you need to change because the word to be updated ("Sales") does not appear anywhere in this element.

  You need to add the *Titles* and *Title* elements to configure the text that appears. Because neither the *Titles* nor *Title* elements or the *Title* attribute appear in any of the default *Area* elements, Microsoft Dynamics CRM uses a behind-the-scenes translation to display the titles of the default entities. So, if you're looking in the site map and you can't find the correct attribute to update in the XML, it's probably a default attribute that you need to add explicitly.
- ***Id* attributes must be unique** Each element requires an *Id* attribute. Remember that it must be unique from all of the other *Id* attributes in the site map.
- **Beware of conditionally required attributes** Earlier in this chapter, we outlined the attributes of each element and identified whether Microsoft Dynamics CRM requires them. In some cases, an attribute might become required depending on the settings of other elements. Microsoft Dynamics CRM usually prompts you with a good description of the error, but you should know that these conditional requirements are possible.
- **Know how to recover from a site map error** Although Microsoft Dynamics CRM validates the customizations.xml file before importing a solution, you might accidentally import a file that causes an error with Microsoft Dynamics CRM.

The good news is that if Microsoft Dynamics CRM detects a problem with your site map customizations, it will apply a default site map for you! Simply fix the problem and try again.

- **Know how to recover when you remove access to solutions import** If you accidentally modify the navigation so that you cannot access the import customizations tool, you obviously can't import a corrected site map solution file! In Microsoft Dynamics CRM, you can access the import customizations tool at: *http://*<crmserver>/ <organizationname>*/tools/solution/import/SolutionImportWizard.aspx.*
- **Refresh site map changes** When you import a new site map, sometimes clicking the Refresh button in Internet Explorer does not update Microsoft Dynamics CRM with your changes. This depends on the type of change you have made. If you don't see the changes you expect, we recommend closing the browser window and opening a new one.
- **Save editing time with consistent attribute ordering** You can put the attributes in any order you want, but putting them in a consistent order will save you time when you edit them later.
- **Create a backup** Always export the latest site map and create a backup copy before making any edits.
- **Add Schema Validation to your XML editor** Most XML editors have the ability to associate a schema to validate your code as you update the XML. The Microsoft Dynamics CRM SDK contains valid schema definitions in the \Schema folder.
- **When you reference web resources in your site map, always use the *$webresource:* directive (you learned this in Chapter 11, "Solutions: Web Resources.")** When you do so, Microsoft Dynamics CRM creates a dependency to the web resource and prevents the resource from being removed as long as it's referenced in the site map.
- **When a web resource is referenced using the *$webresource:* directive, ensure that the web resource exists in the target system or is included in your solution file** Otherwise, your site map will throw an error and be replaced with the default site map.

Entity Display Areas

The entity display areas section of the entity properties is shown in Figure 12-12.

As you learned earlier in this chapter, you can select the areas where you want Microsoft Dynamics CRM to display your custom entities. You select or clear the appropriate areas by using the entity editor in the web client. When you select new areas or remove existing areas by using the entity editor, Microsoft Dynamics CRM automatically edits the site map for you. Because of this nuance, you should *always* export the site map solution before you edit it to make sure that you are working with the latest version.

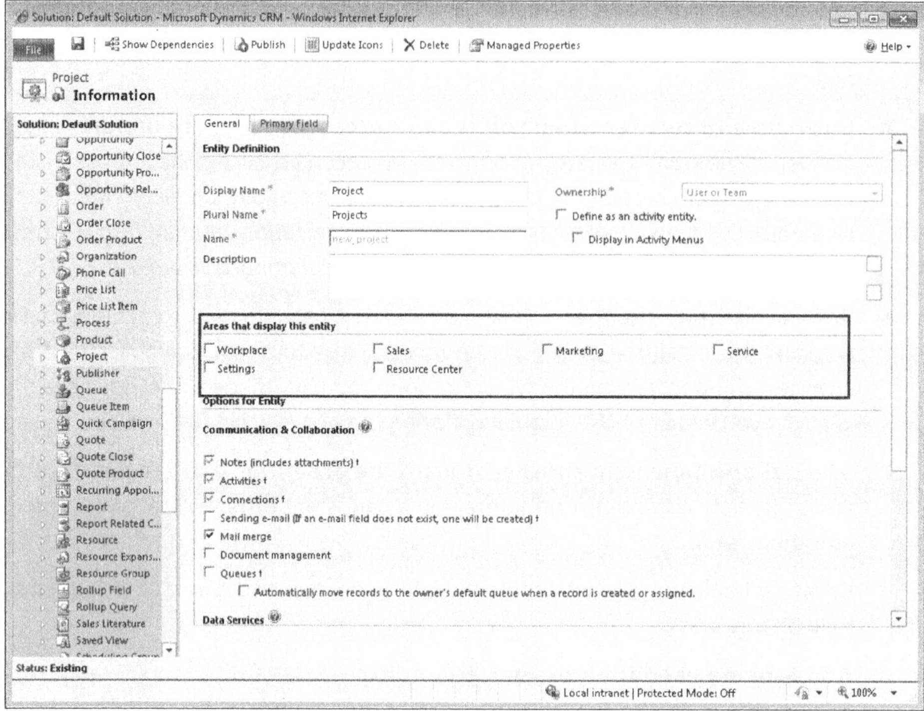

FIGURE 12-12 Selecting the areas that display a link to the entity on the entity's properties page

Conversely, editing the areas of the site map to include different entities and then importing the updated file automatically updates the entity properties in Microsoft Dynamics CRM, meaning the display area check boxes are updated.

Managing Form Navigation

As you learned in Chapter 7, "Entity Customization: Forms," Microsoft Dynamics CRM allows you to create multiple forms for each entity. As such, the form navigation elements are stored directly in the form definition. When you customize an entity's form, you have the ability to add and remove form navigation elements by clicking the Navigation button in the ribbon in the form editor. The form navigation pane is highlighted in Figure 12-13.

In the form editor, you can create, remove, update, and reorder any of the form navigation elements. You can also update the group names while editing the form navigation pane. Because the navigation definition is stored with each form, you will need to make changes to each form that exists for the entity.

More Info Please review Chapter 7 for more information about customizing forms.

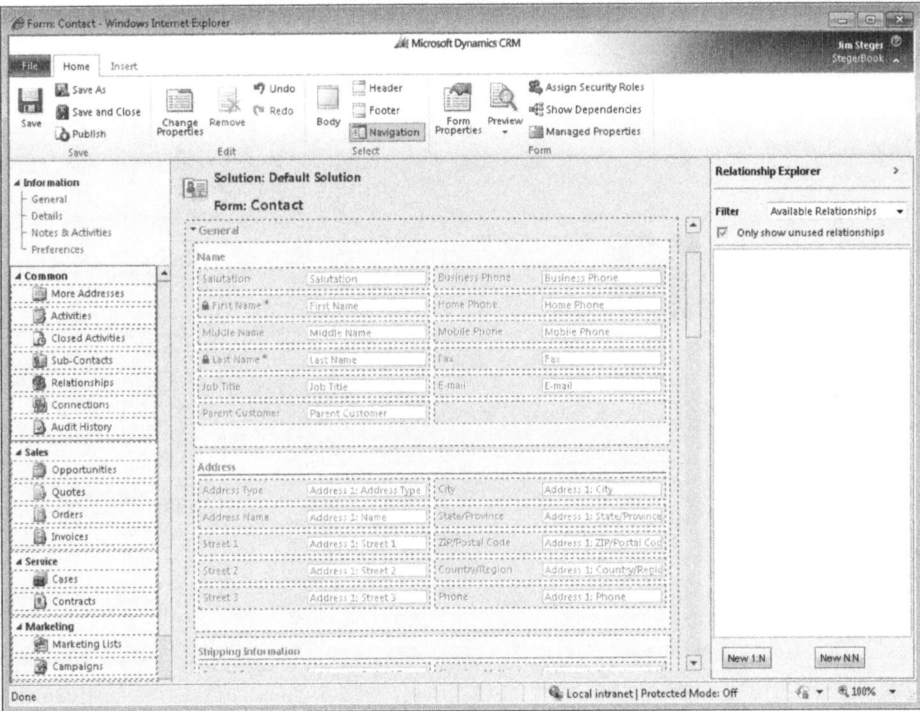

FIGURE 12-13 Form navigation pane

Modifying the Ribbon

The ribbon displays the actions users can take in a graphical and grouped representation. Further, the ribbon is contextual, meaning it displays actions that are relevant to each area of the application as users access them. Figure 12-14 shows the account grid ribbon for the Accounts grid.

A deep examination of ribbon programming is beyond the scope of this book, but we do want to highlight the customization options for it in Microsoft Dynamics CRM. For full details and examples of ribbon functionality, please refer to the Microsoft Dynamics CRM SDK documentation.

Microsoft Dynamics CRM contains default ribbons throughout the application that provide a baseline for customizations to each ribbon. You customize the ribbon by defining how you want it changed from the baseline. Microsoft Dynamics CRM then applies these changes at run time when the ribbon is displayed in the application. Microsoft Dynamics CRM provides *RibbonDiffXml* definitions for all ribbons in the application for you to customize. These elements are applied over the default ribbon definitions provided by Microsoft Dynamics CRM. Figure 12-15 shows the basic ribbon XML structure.

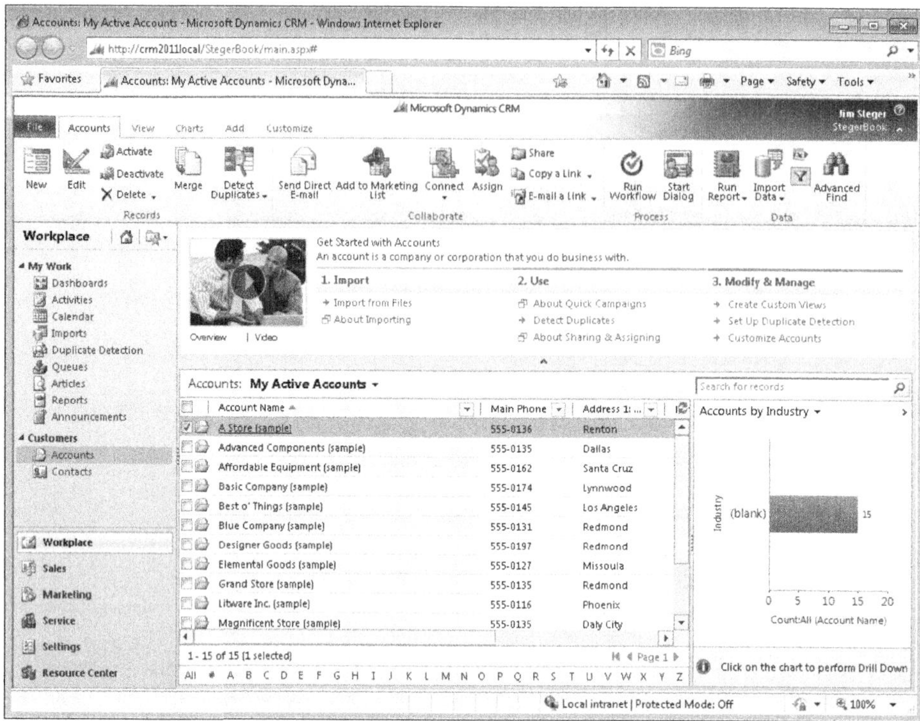

FIGURE 12-14 Accounts grid ribbon

```
<ImportExportXml xmlns:xsi="http://www.w3.org/2001/XMLSchema-instance">
  <Entities></Entities>
  <Roles></Roles>
  <Workflows></Workflows>
  <FieldSecurityProfiles></FieldSecurityProfiles>
  <Templates />
  <RibbonDiffXml>
    <CustomActions />
    <Templates>
      <RibbonTemplates Id="Mscrm.Templates"></RibbonTemplates>
    </Templates>
    <CommandDefinitions />
    <RuleDefinitions>
      <TabDisplayRules />
      <DisplayRules />
      <EnableRules />
    </RuleDefinitions>
    <LocLabels />
  </RibbonDiffXml>
  <EntityMaps />
  <EntityRelationships />
  <OrganizationSettings />
  <optionsets />
  <Languages>
    <Language>1033</Language>
  </Languages>
</ImportExportXml>
```

FIGURE 12-15 Ribbon XML element structure

Important You can export and review the XML defining the baseline ribbon for any area of the application, but you cannot update the baseline ribbon XML directly. You can only apply ribbon XML differences.

To update a ribbon with your changes, you need to reference the definitions of the default ribbons. For example, if you want to hide the Convert Lead button in the Leads ribbon, you need to know the unique identifier of the Convert Button element to remove it. You can find the identifier in the baseline ribbon XML for the Lead entity.

Because you need to reference the definitions to customize the ribbons, it's important that you understand the current ribbon definitions in the system. The Microsoft Dynamics CRM SDK provides a couple of tools to assist you with this exercise. First, you can access the default ribbon definitions in the SDK\SampleCode\CS\Client\Ribbon\ExportRibbonXml\ExportedRibbonXml folder. Figure 12-16 shows a partial sample of the default AccountRibbon.xml file.

```
<RibbonDefinitions>
  <RibbonDefinition>
    <UI>
      <Ribbon>
        <Tabs Id="Mscrm.Tabs">
          <Tab Id="Mscrm.HomepageGrid.account.MainTab" Command="Mscrm.HomepageGrid.account.MainTab" Title="Accounts" Description="Accounts" Sequence="100">
            <Scaling Id="Mscrm.HomepageG">...</Scaling>
            <Groups Id="Mscrm.HomepageGrid.account.MainTab.Groups">
              <Group Id="Mscrm.HomepageGrid.account.MainTab.Management" Command="Mscrm.Enabled" Sequence="10" Title="$Resources:Ribbon.HomepageGrid.MainTab.Man
                <Controls Id="Mscrm.HomepageGrid.account.MainTab.Management.Controls">
                  <Button Id="Mscrm.HomepageGrid.account.NewRecord" ToolTipTitle="$Resources:Ribbon.HomepageGrid.MainTab.New" ToolTipDescription="$Resources(En
                  <Button Id="Mscrm.HomepageGrid.account.Edit" ToolTipTitle="$Resources:Ribbon.HomepageGrid.MainTab.Management.Edit" ToolTipDescription="$Resou
                  <Button Id="Mscrm.HomepageGrid.account.Activate" ToolTipTitle="$Resources:Ribbon.HomepageGrid.account.Record.Status.Activate" ToolTipDescript
                  <Button Id="Mscrm.HomepageGrid.account.Deactivate" ToolTipTitle="$Resources:Ribbon.HomepageGrid.account.Record.Status.Deactivate" ToolTipDesc
                  <SplitButton Id="Mscrm.HomepageGrid.account.DeleteMenu" ToolTipTitle="$Resources:Mscrm_HomepageGrid_Other_MainTab_Management_Delete_ToolTipTi
                    <Menu Id="Mscrm.HomepageGrid.account.DeleteMenu.Menu">
                      <MenuSection Id="Mscrm.HomepageGrid.account.DeleteMenu.MenuSection" Sequence="10" DisplayMode="Menu16">
                        <Controls Id="Mscrm.HomepageGrid.account.DeleteMenu.Controls">
                          <Button Id="Mscrm.HomepageGrid.account.Delete" Command="Mscrm.DeleteSelectedRecord" Sequence="50" ToolTipTitle="$Resources:Mscrm_Home
                          <Button Id="Mscrm.HomepageGrid.account.BulkDelete" Command="Mscrm.HomepageGrid.BulkDelete" Sequence="100" LabelText="$Resources:Ribbo
                        </Controls>
                      </MenuSection>
                    </Menu>
                  </SplitButton>
                  <Button Id="Mscrm.HomepageGrid.account.MergeRecords" ToolTipTitle="$Resources:Ribbon.HomepageGrid.account.Record.Merge.MergeRecords" ToolTipD
                  <FlyoutAnchor Id="Mscrm.HomepageGrid.account.Detect" ToolTipTitle="$Resources:Ribbon.HomepageGrid.account.Record.Dupe.Detect" ToolTipDescript
                    <Menu Id="Mscrm.HomepageGrid.account.Detect.Menu">
                      <MenuSection Id="Mscrm.HomepageGrid.account.Detect.MenuSection" Sequence="10" DisplayMode="Menu16">
                        <Controls Id="Mscrm.HomepageGrid.account.Detect.Controls">
                          <Button Id="Mscrm.HomepageGrid.account.Detect.Selected" Command="Mscrm.HomepageGrid.DetectDupesSelected" Sequence="10" Alt="$Resource
                          <Button Id="Mscrm.HomepageGrid.account.Detect.All" Command="Mscrm.HomepageGrid.DetectDupesAll" Sequence="20" Alt="$Resources:Ribbon.H
                        </Controls>
                      </MenuSection>
                    </Menu>
                  </FlyoutAnchor>
                </Controls>
              </Group>
              <Group Id="Mscrm.HomepageGrid.account.MainTab.Actions" Command="Mscrm.Enabled" Sequence="20" Title="$Resources:Ribbon.HomepageGrid.MainTab.Action
                <Controls Id="Mscrm.HomepageGrid.account.MainTab.Actions.Controls" />
              </Group>
              <Group Id="Mscrm.HomepageGrid.account.MainTab.Collaborate" Command="Mscrm.Enabled" Sequence="30" Title="$Resources:Ribbon.HomepageGrid.MainTab.Co
                <Controls Id="Mscrm.HomepageGrid.account.MainTab.Collaborate.Controls">
                  <Button Id="Mscrm.HomepageGrid.account.SendDirectEmail" Command="Mscrm.AddEmailToSelectedRecord" Sequence="10" ToolTipTitle="$Resources:Ribbo
                  <Button Id="Mscrm.HomepageGrid.account.AddToList" ToolTipTitle="$Resources:Ribbon.HomepageGrid.account.Add.AddToList" ToolTipDescription="$Re
```

FIGURE 12-16 Default Account ribbon XML element structure

The ApplicationRibbon.xml file includes all of the ribbons that are not defined for a specific entity and corresponds to the Application Ribbons component that can be added to solutions. For each entity, you will find an [*entityname*]ribbon.xml file. These are the baseline ribbons that correspond to the *RibbonDiffXml* for each entity. If you want to edit the ribbon for a specific entity, you should locate the ribbon XML file for that entity in the SDK to find the appropriate references.

The default definitions work well if you want to update a ribbon that has not been customized yet. However, if you or another system customizer have made changes to a ribbon, you will want to reference the updated ribbon definition. Fortunately, the SDK provides a sample application at SDK\SampleCode\CS\Client\Ribbon\ExportRibbonXml that allows you to export the latest ribbon definition.

Available Ribbons

As we mentioned earlier, you can customize quite a few ribbons in Microsoft Dynamics CRM, especially when you consider the hundreds of ribbons available for the customizable entities in your system. Several ribbons are specific to each customizable entity, each of which is defined for the following entity controls:

- Form
- Grid
- Sub-Grid

In addition to the entity-specific ribbons, more than a dozen application ribbons display general and administrative actions. Table 12-7 summarizes these application ribbons.

TABLE 12-7 Application Ribbons

Tab	Root Id	Description
Jewel	Mscrm.Jewel.Menu	The blue tab that displays the File menu on the main application and forms
Basic Home	Mscrm.BasicHomeTab	The main ribbon displayed when no other context is available
Web Resource Editor	Mscrm.WebResourceEditTab	Displays when editing web resources in a solution
Form Editor	Mscrm.FormEditorTab	Provides save, edit, select, and view groups of actions for entity forms
Form Editor Insert	Mscrm.FormEditorInsertTab	Provides buttons to insert sections, tabs, and controls in entity forms
Dashboard Homepage	Mscrm.DashboardTab	Displays in the Workplace area when accessing the Dashboards page
Visualization Tools Contextual Group	Mscrm.VisualizationTools	Displays when the New or Edit Chart button is clicked on the Charts tab displayed in the entity grid ribbon
Appointment Book	Mscrm.AptbookTab	Displays when viewing the service calendar in the Service area
Advanced Find	Mscrm.AdvancedFind	Displays in the Advanced Find window
Dashboard Editor	Mscrm.DashboardEditorTab	Displays when editing a dashboard
Documents	Mscrm.DocumentsTab	Displays if SharePoint integration has been enabled for the organization
Chart Editor	Mscrm.VisualizationDesignerTab	Displays when editing a chart from the solutions window
Search Tools Contextual Group	Mscrm.ArticleSearch	Displays when viewing the Article entity

Updating a Ribbon

One of the powerful aspects of the ribbon is the flexibility you have to customize it. As with previous versions of Microsoft Dynamics CRM, you still define the label, icon, and action to take. However, now you also decide where on the ribbon you want the custom action to display and when the action should appear. Finally, you can remove default buttons or override the functionality of a these buttons with custom functionality.

Similar to the site map, you need to export the ribbon definition to make changes. When you do so, Microsoft Dynamics CRM exports only the differences from the baseline ribbon definition as XML. Your initial export will look like the XML shown previously in Figure 12-15. The root element of the ribbon XML is the *RibbonDiffXml* element. Table 12-8 defines the child elements for *RibbonDiffXml*.

TABLE 12-8 *RibbonDiffXml* Child Elements

Element	Description
CustomActions	Actions that can add, replace, or remove items from the ribbon
Templates	Defines the display and scaling for a ribbon group
CommandDefinitions	Commands that can be referenced by ribbon controls
RuleDefinitions	Rules that define the display properties
LocLabels	Contains a collection of localization labels
RibbonNotSupported	Included with the *RibbbonDiffXml* for an entity to indicate that the entity does not support the ribbon

CustomActions

The *CustomActions* element contains two child elements, *CustomAction* and *HideCustomAction*, which you can use to add, override an existing item, or remove an item from the ribbon. For example, if you wanted to remove the ConvertLead button, you would use the following XML:

```
<CustomActions>
 <HideCustomAction Location="Mscrm.HomepageGrid.lead.ConvertLead"
        HideActionId="Sample.Form.HomepageGrid.ConvertLead.HideAction" />
 <HideCustomAction Location="Mscrm.Form.lead.ConvertLead"
        HideActionId="Sample.Form.lead.ConvertLead.HideAction" />
</CustomActions>
```

Note Some buttons for the default actions are also controlled by Microsoft Dynamics CRM security settings. For example, if you want to hide the New account button for a subset of users, you should remove the create privilege on the Account entity from those users as opposed to hiding the New button.

Templates

Templates define how the items in a ribbon group should display and scale as the application user interface changes. The *Templates* element contains a single child element called *RibbonTemplates*. The XML structure resembles the following:

```
<RibbonDiffXml>
  <CustomActions />
  <Templates>
    <RibbonTemplates Id="">
      <GroupTemplate Id="">
        <Layout Title="">
          <OverflowSection/>
          <Section>
            <Row>
              <ControlRef/>
              <OverflowArea/>
              <Strip>
                <ControlRef/>
              </Strip>
            </Row>
          </Section>
        </Layout>
      </GroupTemplate>
    </RibbonTemplates>
  </Templates>
  <CommandDefinitions />
  <RuleDefinitions>
    <TabDisplayRules />
    <DisplayRules />
    <EnableRules />
  </RuleDefinitions>
  <LocLabels />
</RibbonDiffXml>
```

As you can see from the XML structure, you have a lot of flexibility with the design, look, and placement of your ribbon items. However, the simplest ribbon implementation of the templates element would look like this:

```
<Templates>
  <RibbonTemplates Id="Mscrm.Templates"></RibbonTemplates>
</Templates>
```

Review the Microsoft Dynamics CRM SDK for a more in-depth explanation of your template options.

CommandDefinitions

The *CommandDefinitions* element defines a set of rules that control when a ribbon item is displayed and the actions to perform when the item is clicked. The following XML defines the overall structure of the *CommandDefinitions* element:

```
<CommandDefinitions>
  <CommandDefinition>
    <EnableRules>
      <EnableRule/>
    </EnableRules>
```

```
    <DisplayRules>
      <DisplayRule/>
    </DisplayRules>
    <Actions>
      <JavaScriptFunction FunctionName="" Library=""/>
      <Url Address="" PassParams="" WinMode="" WinParams="" />
    </Actions>
  </CommandDefinition>
</CommandDefinitions>
```

The *CommandDefinitions* element displays and enables rules that are referenced in the *RuleDefinitions* element discussed in the next section. The *Actions* element defines the command that should be taken when the button is clicked. As the following code shows, you can specify a JavaScript function or URL:

```
<CommandDefinition
    Id="Sample.all.Developer.Tools.Controls.CustomButton.Command">
  <EnableRules />
  <DisplayRules>
    <DisplayRule
       Id="Sample.all.Developer.Tools.Controls.CustomButton.DisplayRule" />
  </DisplayRules>
  <Actions>
    <JavaScriptFunction
      Library="$webresource:sample_/Scripts/DeveloperTools.js"
      FunctionName="openFormReport" />
  </Actions>
</CommandDefinition>
```

In this example, when the ribbon item is clicked, Microsoft Dynamics CRM executes the *openFormReport* method from a script in a custom web resource. Additionally, the *DisplayRule* element references a rule definition called *Sample.all.Developer.Tools.Controls .CustomButton.DisplayRule*. We'll review the *RuleDefinitions* element next to explain how rules are applied in a ribbon.

RuleDefinitions

The *RuleDefinitions* element defines the actual rules that are referenced from a *CommandDefinition*. The child options under the *RuleDefinitions* element are *TabDisplayRules*, *DisplayRules*, and *EnableRules*. The following code snippet shows the expanded XML:

```
<RuleDefinitions>
  <TabDisplayRules>
    <TabDisplayRule TabCommand="">
      <EntityRule AppliesTo="" Context="" EntityName=""/>
```

```
      <PageRule Address=""/>
    </TabDisplayRule>
  </TabDisplayRules>
  <DisplayRules>
    <DisplayRule Id="">
      <CrmClientTypeRule Type=""/>
      <CrmOfflineAccessStateRule State=""/>
      <CrmOutlookClientTypeRule Type=""/>
      <CrmOutlookClientVersionRule Major=""/>
      <EntityPrivilegeRule PrivilegeDepth="" PrivilegeType=""/>
      <EntityPropertyRule PropertyName="" PropertyValue=""/>
      <EntityRule/>
      <FormEntityContextRule EntityName=""/>
      <FormStateRule State=""/>
      <MiscellaneousPrivilegeRule PrivilegeDepth="" PrivilegeName=""/>
      <OrganizationSettingRule Setting=""/>
      <OrRule/>
      <OutlookRenderTypeRule Type=""/>
      <OutlookVersionRule Version=""/>
      <PageRule Address=""/>
      <ReferencingAttributeRequiredRule/>
      <RelationshipTypeRule AppliesTo=""/>
      <SkuRule Sku=""/>
      <ValueRule Field="" Value=""/>
    </DisplayRule>
  </DisplayRules>
  <EnableRules>
    <EnableRule Id="">
      <CrmClientTypeRule Type=""/>
      <CrmOfflineAccessStateRule State=""/>
      <CrmOutlookClientTypeRule Type=""/>
      <CustomRule Library="" FunctionName=""></CustomRule>
      <EntityRule/>
      <FormStateRule State=""/>
      <OrRule/>
      <OutlookItemTrackingRule AppliesTo="" TrackedInCrm=""/>
      <OutlookVersionRule Version=""/>
      <RecordPrivilegeRule PrivilegeType=""/>
      <SelectionCountRule AppliesTo=""/>
      <PageRule Address=""/>
      <SkuRule Sku=""/>
      <ValueRule Field="" Value=""/>
    </EnableRule>
  </EnableRules>
</RuleDefinitions>
```

In the previous section, our sample code referenced a display rule called *Sample.all.Developer.Tools.Controls.CustomButton.DisplayRule*. We can implement that rule as follows:

```
<RuleDefinitions>
  <TabDisplayRules />
  <DisplayRules>
    <DisplayRule
      Id="Sample.all.Developer.Tools.Controls.CustomButton.DisplayRule">
      <CrmClientTypeRule Type="Web" />
    </DisplayRule>
  </DisplayRules>
  <EnableRules />
</RuleDefinitions>
```

Notice that the *Id* attribute of the *DisplayRule* element is what we used in the *CommandDefinitions DisplayName* element. This rule simply states that our button should only display in the web client and not in the Outlook client.

You have a variety of options for your rule set, so you should be able to find a combination of settings to match almost any requirement.

LocLabels

The *LocLabels* element defines the title and description of your ribbon item. In the *LocLabels* element, you can specify what text should display depending on which language the user has configured.

The *LocLabels* element XML structure follows:

```
<LocLabels>
  <LocLabel Id="">
    <Titles>
      <Title description="" languagecode=""/>
    </Titles>
  </LocLabel>
</LocLabels>
```

You need to define a *LocLabels* element for each ribbon item you add and specify the appropriate language code (1033 is the value for English). In our previous button example, a sample *LocLabels* code would be:

```
<LocLabels>
  <LocLabel Id="Sample.all.Developer.Tools.Controls.CustomButton.Description">
    <Titles>
      <Title languagecode="1033"
             description="View a report on the elements of this form." />
    </Titles>
  </LocLabel>
```

```
    <LocLabel Id="Sample.all.Developer.Tools.Label">
      <Titles>
        <Title languagecode="1033" description="Tools" />
      </Titles>
    </LocLabel>
    <LocLabel Id="Sample.all.Developer.Tools.Controls.CustomButton.Label">
      <Titles>
        <Title languagecode="1033" description="Form Report" />
      </Titles>
    </LocLabel>
  </LocLabels>
```

Ribbon Example

Let's walk through an example of adding a custom button to the contact form ribbon. In this example, we want to duplicate the Phone Call button from the Add tab of the Contact ribbon and move it to the main Contact tab in the ribbon. Figure 12-17 shows the final placement of the new button.

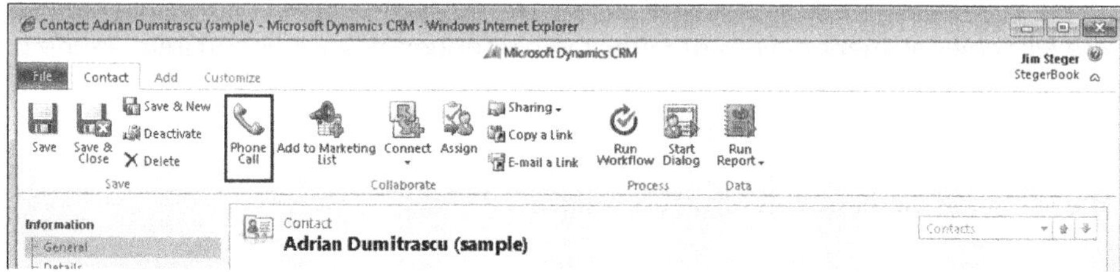

FIGURE 12-17 Adding a Phone Call button to the main Contact tab in the Contact ribbon

By now, you know the basic steps we'll take:

- Create a new blank solution and add the Contact entity component to it.
- Export the solution as an unmanaged solution and save the .zip file to your computer's hard drive.
- Unzip the solution .zip file and then open the customizations.xml file in an XML editor.
- Next, locate the default ContactRibbon.xml file from the Microsoft Dynamics CRM SDK (at SDK\SampleCode\CS\Client\Ribbon\ExportRibbonXml\ExportedRibbonXml). You'll do two searches in this file. The first will be to find the group, template alias, and sequence number for the new button. As Figure 12-17 shows, we want the button to be the first item in the Collaborate group. Using the default ContactRibbon.xml, you'll see that the Add to Marketing List button has the following information:
    - **Group control:** Mscrm.Form.contact.MainTab.Collaborate.Controls._children
    - **Sequence Number:** 5
    - **Template Alias:** o1

- We also want to find and copy the information for the form's Phone Call button. The code snippet should look like the following:

```
<Button Id="Sample.Form.contact.AddPhone"
         Command="Mscrm.AddPhoneToPrimaryRecord"
         Sequence="30"
ToolTipTitle="$Resources:Mscrm_Form_Other_Related_Activities_AddPhone_
ToolTipTitle"
ToolTipDescription="$Resources(EntityDisplayName):Ribbon.Tooltip.AddPhoneCall"
         LabelText="{!EntityDisplayName:phonecall}"
         Alt="{!EntityDisplayName:phonecall}"
         Image16by16="/_imgs/ribbon/AddPhone_16.png"
         Image32by32="/_imgs/ribbon/entity32_4210.png"
         TemplateAlias="c4" />
```

Note There are multiple instances of the Phone Call button, such as the one that exists on the MainTab. Because we are updating the form, we want to copy the details from the form's button definition.

- Now that you know where to place the button and have the button definition, we are ready to update our contact's *RibbonDiffXml*. Listing 12-1 shows the final code.

LISTING 12-1 Adding a Duplicate Phone Call button to the Main Contact Ribbon Tab

```
<RibbonDiffXml>
<CustomActions>
  <CustomAction Id="Sample.contact.form.MainTabPhoneCall.CustomAction"
                Location="Mscrm.Form.contact.MainTab.Collaborate.Controls._children">
    <CommandUIDefinition>
      <Button Id="Sample.Form.contact.AddPhone"
              Command="Mscrm.AddPhoneToPrimaryRecord"
              Sequence="1"
              ToolTipTitle="$Resources:Mscrm_Form_Other_Related_Activities_AddPhone_
ToolTipTitle"
              ToolTipDescription="$Resources(EntityDisplayName):Ribbon.Tooltip.AddPhoneCall"
              LabelText="{!EntityDisplayName:phonecall}"
              Alt="{!EntityDisplayName:phonecall}"
              Image16by16="/_imgs/ribbon/AddPhone_16.png"
              Image32by32="/_imgs/ribbon/entity32_4210.png"
              TemplateAlias="o1" />
    </CommandUIDefinition>
  </CustomAction>
</CustomActions>
<Templates>
  <RibbonTemplates Id="Mscrm.Templates"></RibbonTemplates>
</Templates>
<CommandDefinitions />
<RuleDefinitions>
  <TabDisplayRules />
  <DisplayRules />
```

```
  <EnableRules />
</RuleDefinitions>
<LocLabels />
</RibbonDiffXml>
```

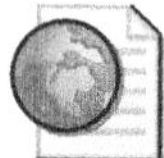

Real World We are referencing existing CRM images to simplify our example. In practice, you would have uploaded your own icons as web resources and would then reference the custom image web resource in your ribbon xml.

Note that we add a *CustomAction* element and create a unique *Id* for it. For the location, we use the control information of the Collaborate group on the main form's ribbon. Next, we add a custom *CommandUIDefinition* element and paste the button information we copied from the default ribbon XML. We make only two changes to the original button. The first is to change the sequence number to a number less than 5 (we want our button to the left of the Add to Marketing List button). The second is to update the button to the group's *TemplateAlias* of o1.

Because of the template architecture of the ribbon, we can reuse Microsoft Dynamics CRM's default commands, template, and localized labels. Therefore, our *RibbonDiffXml* contains only the information in the *CustomAction* and *Button* elements.

The Microsoft Dynamics CRM SDK contains additional examples, and we recommend you review them to understand the details of customizing ribbons in the application. Also be sure to review the default ribbon XML to see how Microsoft Dynamics CRM implements a particular ribbon item.

Ribbon Tips and Tricks

Consider the following tips as you update the Microsoft Dynamics CRM ribbons:

- **Start simple** Until you are comfortable with the ribbon implementation, we recommend you break down your effort. Start first with the placement of the button, and then move to the code it should be executing.
- **Use examples** The Microsoft Dynamics CRM SDK provides numerous examples of common use cases for ribbon customizations. Find the one that is closest to your requirement and start with the example code to make changes in your own system.
- **Review the SDK** The Microsoft Dynamics CRM SDK contains a rich set of content around customizing the ribbon as well as the definitions for the ribbon XML schema.
- **Isolate ribbon customizations** As with site map development, try to maintain your application ribbon's development in an isolated, unmanaged solution. For entity ribbon development, be very conscious of other unmanaged development solutions that may

contain the entity so that you don't accidentally overwrite your ribbon changes with another imported, unmanaged solution.

- **Check your web resources** If your ribbon changes require web resources, ensure that those resources are installed before importing the changed ribbon definition.
- **Use schema validation** Most XML editors have the ability to associate a schema to validate your code as you update the XML. The Microsoft Dynamics CRM SDK contains the CustomizationsSolution.xsd schema definition for use with ribbon editing.
- **Remember that the ribbon XML is case-sensitive** You must use correct casing for all of your attributes in the ribbon XML.
- **Use a consistent naming convention** Create a consistent naming convention for your *Id* attribute. This will make it easier for you and your colleagues to work with the *RibbonDiffXml*. And do not use the Mscrm namespace for your custom Id names. Doing so could overwrite native functionality.

Summary

By using the site map, form, and ribbon tools in Microsoft Dynamics CRM, you can reconfigure almost every area of the application navigation and have it display in both the web and Microsoft Dynamics CRM for Outlook clients. Using the site map allows you to hide or show the entities and links that make the most sense for your users in the main navigation, as well as providing additional help or customized content above the entity grids. By defining your own custom ribbon definitions, you can add, remove, and change any ribbon button or action for your users.

Chapter 13

Reports and Dashboards

In this chapter:

As you already know, CRM systems capture data about interaction with various contacts and organizations, and your database will quickly grow to thousands, or millions, of records. Although it's beneficial to capture these interactions in a database, the real value lies in using and visualizing that data in a simple and easy-to-read format. This data visualization can happen in many ways, but the two methods that we will describe in this chapter are reports and dashboards.

You will quickly find that users have different ideas about reports and dashboards. No matter how you define them, the common elements that all users can probably agree on are that both can contain data and graphical representations of that information. So how do you decide whether you should create a report or a dashboard? Let's start by looking at some of the considerations for how to deliver data to users and explore how to deliver that data in Microsoft Dynamics CRM.

Data Delivery Design

As soon as you roll out the Microsoft Dynamics CRM system to users in your organization, chances are you'll start receiving requests for reports, dashboards, or other aggregated information about the data almost as soon as users finish entering the first few records in the system. Users might know the questions they want answered in such requests, but often, the formatting, design, and calculations behind each number require careful planning. Table 13-1 provides a few guidelines that you should consider when deciding whether to deliver data in a report or dashboard.

TABLE 13-1 Data Delivery Considerations

	Report	Dashboard
Focus of the data	Details of specific records or historical information about groups of records	Current performance indicators or metrics
Use of the data	Referenceable	Actionable
Amount of data to display	Typically detailed data	Concise, visual summaries of information
Frequency	Scheduled, real-time or near real-time	Real-time or near real-time

To give you some context for how these considerations translate to reports and dashboards in Microsoft Dynamics CRM, let's look at an example of each. Figure 13-1 shows the Campaign Performance Report included in Microsoft Dynamics CRM.

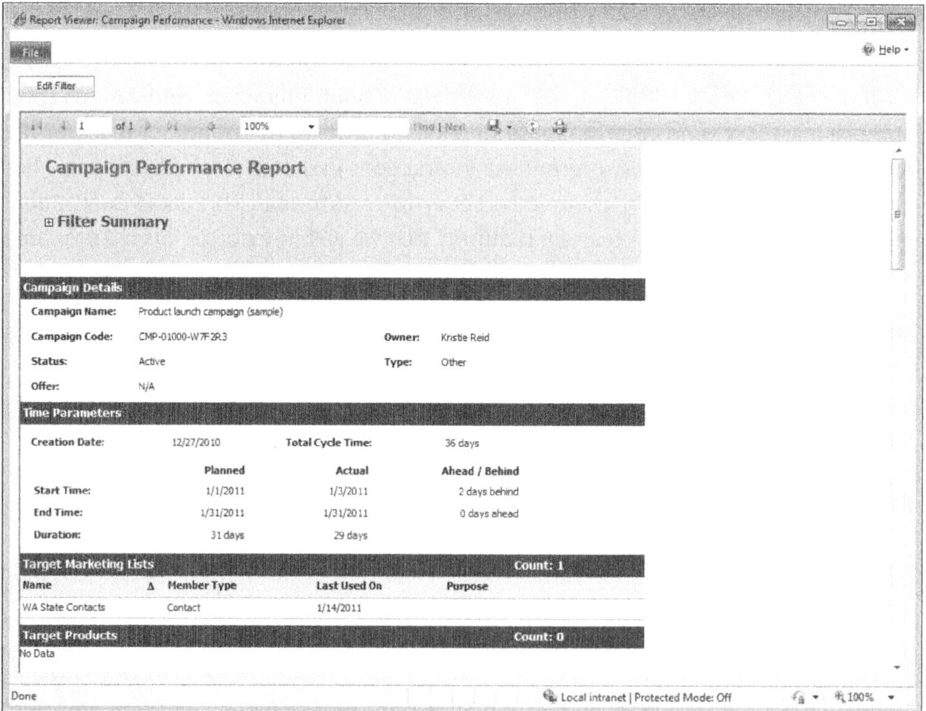

FIGURE 13-1 Campaign Performance Report

When exported as a .pdf file, this report prints to four pages long, even with limited campaign-related data in the system. It includes information about the time frame, products, costs, and revenue generated by the campaign. Fully processing all of this information would take some time and analysis skills.

Next, let's look at the Microsoft Dynamics CRM Overview dashboard that is set as the default home page for all users when you first implement Microsoft Dynamics CRM, as shown in Figure 13-2. Keep in mind that Microsoft SQL Server Reporting Services can deliver the same information and format in this dashboard in a report format, but Microsoft Dynamics CRM makes it easy to create dashboards similar to the one shown in Figure 13-2.

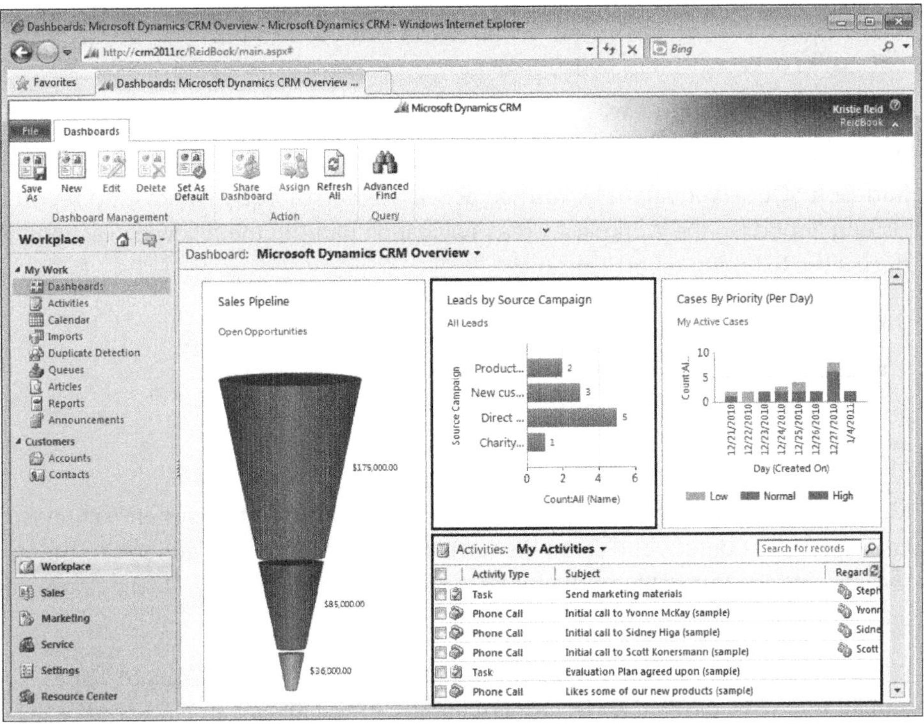

FIGURE 13-2 Microsoft Dynamics CRM Overview dashboard

The first thing that you probably notice is the visual appeal of the charts, which present key data succinctly. Look at the Lead Source by Campaign chart. Rather than showing detailed information about each campaign, as you saw in the Campaign Performance Report, this chart quickly shows which campaign generated the most leads. Further, you can drill into the chart to view the leads that are associated with each source campaign. Also notice the Activities view, which provides easy access to the activities assigned to you.

This example might make dashboards seem like the winning option for presenting data, but it's important to understand both approaches because you'll need both to meet your company's reporting requirements. Let's get into the details of each approach, starting with reports and then moving on to dashboards.

Accessing Reports in Microsoft Dynamics CRM

In Microsoft Dynamics CRM, the term *report* refers to any type of data analysis file, including:

- Microsoft Office Excel, Word, or Access files that can be uploaded to the Microsoft Dynamics CRM server
- Microsoft SQL Server Reporting Services reports
- Links to external web page reports
- Third-party report files

Regardless of the report type, Microsoft Dynamics CRM stores all of the reports in its Microsoft SQL Server database. You can access the Microsoft Dynamics CRM reports by clicking Reports in the Workplace area's navigation pane. In the following sections, we'll discuss the following report concepts:

- Report security
- Reports in the user interface

Report Security

Microsoft Dynamics CRM includes a Report entity, similar to other system entities such as Lead, Account, Contact, and so on. As such, the Report entity also adheres to the standard security settings that apply to all entities, as described in Chapter 3, "Managing Security and Information Access," with a few notable caveats.

Each report in Microsoft Dynamics CRM contains a Viewable By field, with values of *Organization* or *Individual*. If the report's Viewable By value equals *Organization*, all users will be able to run the report, provided that they have a security role that includes at least user-level read privileges on the Report entity. If the Viewable By field is set to *Individual*, access to the report will work like other entities, based on the owner of the report and the privilege level each user has on the Report entity. To create, view, and update reports, users must have the appropriate Report privileges.

Note You can find the Report entity privileges on the Core Records tab on the Security Role form.

In addition to the Report entity, you can also provide the following two report permissions in each security role:

- **Publish Reports** Allows a user to make a report viewable to the entire organization. For Microsoft SQL Server Reporting Services reports, this privilege also allows users to publish the report to the SQL Server Reporting Services web server for external use.
- **Add Reporting Services Reports** Permits the user to upload an existing Microsoft SQL Server Reporting Services report file to Microsoft Dynamics CRM. SQL Server Reporting Services files use the Report Definition Language (RDL) format. This privilege differs from the create privilege of the Report entity, which refers to creating a new report by using the Report Wizard or by adding another file type, such as an Excel file or PDF report.

An additional level of security exists for Microsoft SQL Server Reporting Services reports to protect the data displayed in each report. Provided that a report uses the Microsoft Dynamics CRM filtered views, the report only displays the data that each user should see. This means that even if a user has access to run a report, that user will see only the data she has rights to view, as defined by the user's Microsoft Dynamics CRM security role.

More Info Microsoft Dynamics CRM uses the term *Reporting Services reports* to mean reports in the format of the Report Definition Language (RDL), as opposed to an Excel file or link to another report. Reporting Services reports have additional built-in functionality with Microsoft Dynamics CRM. As you will soon learn, you can create Reporting Services reports through the new Microsoft Dynamics CRM Report Wizard or with a tool such as Microsoft Visual Studio.

Reports in the User Interface

You can run reports in the Microsoft Dynamics CRM user interface from one of three areas:

- Reports view
- Entity ribbon
- Entity form

Reports View

The default Microsoft Dynamics CRM installation creates a subarea called Reports in the My Work group of the Workplace area, as shown in Figure 13-3. In addition to listing all of the available reports, you can use this Reports view to create and manage reports, assuming that you have the appropriate security permissions.

More Info The Reports list grid behaves differently from the other grids in Microsoft Dynamics CRM. Usually, if you double-click a record, you open the form to edit. With reports, double-clicking a record opens the Report Viewer and allows you to run the report. You must click the Edit Report button on the report grid's toolbar to edit the properties of any report.

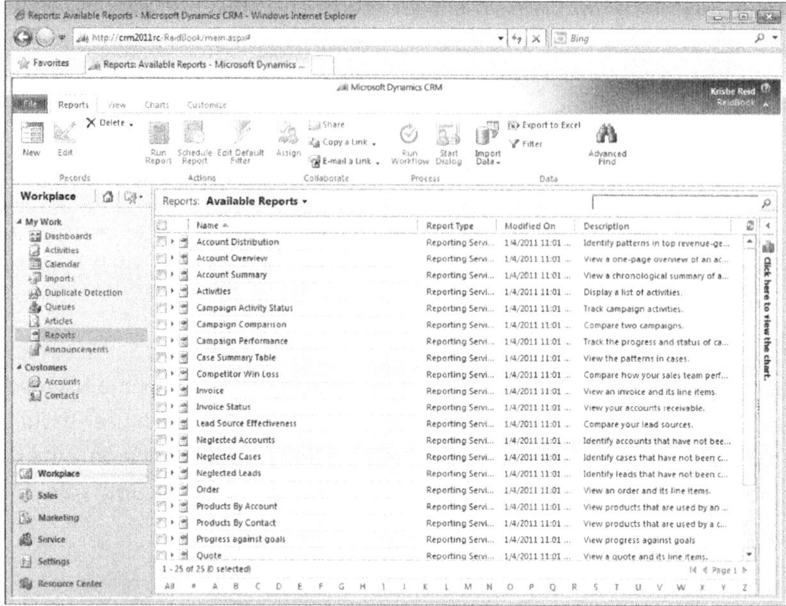

FIGURE 13-3 Reports view in the My Work group

Entity Ribbon

In addition to the Reports view, you can also access reports from the ribbon of an entity's view by clicking the Run Report button, as shown for the Account entity in Figure 13-4. Similarly, you can run the same reports from the Advanced Find results view for a specific entity.

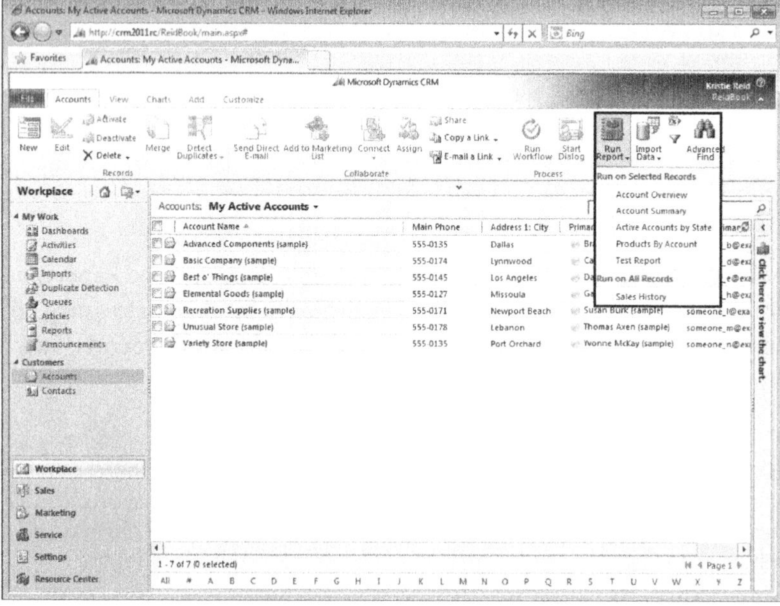

FIGURE 13-4 Accessing reports from an entity's grid ribbon

Figure 13-4 shows reports listed in two groups: Run on Selected Records or Run on All Records. If you run one of the reports listed under Run on Selected Records, Microsoft Dynamics CRM prompts you to select which records to apply to the report based on three options:

- All applicable records
- The selected records
- All records on all pages in the current view

By selecting one of these options, you can filter the records that you want to include in the report results. If you select a report listed under the Run on All Records group, Microsoft Dynamics CRM runs the report independently of the records selected or included in the view.

Important We refer to reports that are run for selected records as *contextual reports* because they run in the context of particular records. To make this option available in a report, you must create the report query using the correct technique. We walk through an example of this later in this chapter.

Entity Form

Similar to running reports from the entity ribbon, you can also run reports directly from the entity's form by clicking the Run Report button in the entity form ribbon, shown on the Account form in Figure 13-5.

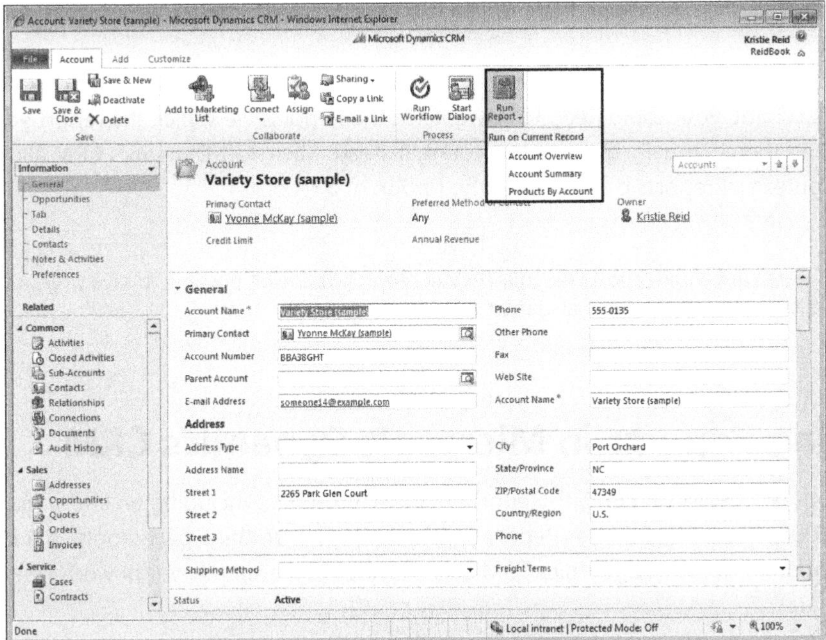

FIGURE 13-5 Accessing reports from the entity form

Unlike running reports from the entity grid ribbon, you can only choose to run a contextual report specific to the open record. Figure 13-6 shows the output if you run the Account Overview report directly from the Variety Store (sample) account record.

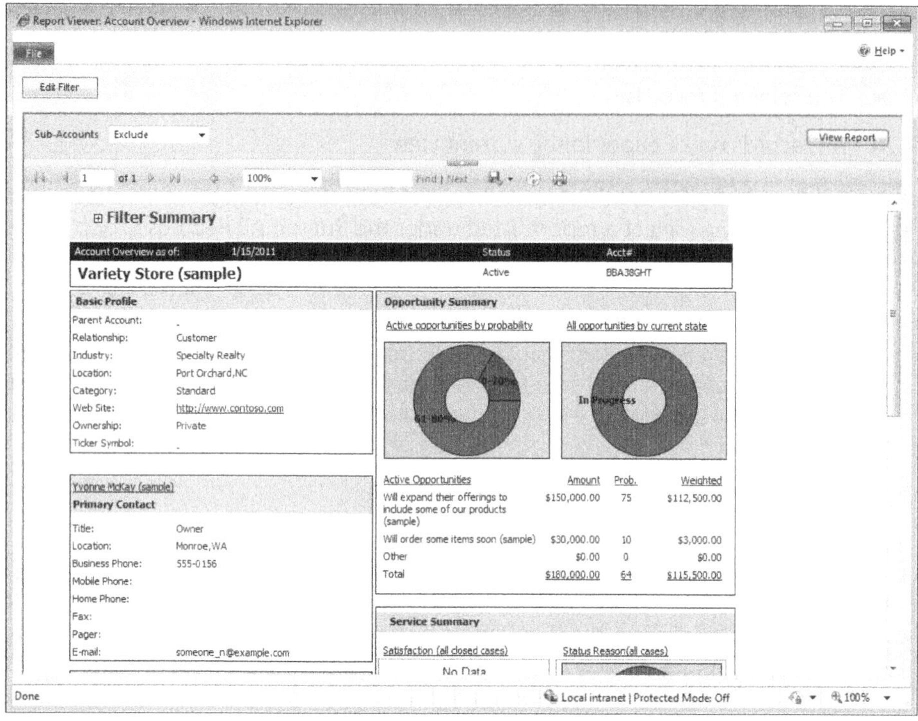

FIGURE 13-6 Account Overview report run for a single record

Without the contextual report feature, if you wanted to run the Account Overview report for a single account, you would need to navigate to the Reports view, pick the report you want to run, and then manually specify an account. Instead, Microsoft Dynamics CRM allows you to run contextual reports directly from the ribbon of a record.

Tip Create contextual reports for your custom reports whenever possible to save your users extra clicks in the application navigation.

Customizing Reports in Microsoft Dynamics CRM

Numerous tools exist for creating Reporting Services reports, including an add-in for Visual Studio 2008, Reporting Services Report Builder, and multiple third-party tools. In addition to these options, Microsoft Dynamics CRM also provides you a simple, yet powerful wizard to create custom reports. The Report Wizard is a great tool for end users who want to run their own ad-hoc reports. However, system administrators will often find that they need a greater ability to customize the reports—beyond what is available in the wizard. Reporting Services gives you that flexibility.

Creating or modifying Reporting Services reports typically requires a more experienced report writer. Therefore, we don't expect to tell you everything you need to know about Reporting Services in this chapter. We do want to demonstrate a few simple examples and highlight some unique areas of Microsoft Dynamics CRM that relate to Reporting Services.

Note The examples that follow assume that you have the Business Intelligence Development Studio add-in for Visual Studio 2008. Because the out-of-the-box reports available with Microsoft Dynamics CRM do not use Fetch XML, you cannot edit them if you are running a CRM Online environment. We do, however, provide an example of creating a new report using Fetch XML later in this chapter.

Editing a Reporting Services Report

Microsoft Dynamics CRM includes approximately 26 Reporting Services reports in the default installation, and those reports include an additional 28 sub-reports. You might find that your business requirements closely match one of those reports. Therefore, you can add custom fields or modify the report of a layout to meet your business needs.

Tip The default Reporting Services reports in Microsoft Dynamics CRM use complex datasets and advanced reporting features. You should edit these reports only if you're extremely comfortable authoring Reporting Services reports. Beginner or intermediate report writers might feel more comfortable creating reports from scratch instead of trying to edit the default Microsoft Dynamics CRM reports.

In the following example, we show you how to modify the Account Overview report. Assume that you want to add the number of employees as a field in the Basic Profile section, and remove the Pager field from the Primary Contact section of the report. Figure 13-7 shows the final report with these changes.

Most of the default Microsoft Dynamics CRM reports use a sub-report to display the report details, and the Account Overview report is no different. Therefore, you need to modify the Account Overview Sub-Report to edit the report layout.

Warning When you update a report, make sure that you save a backup of the original so that you can roll back to the original version if you have any problems.

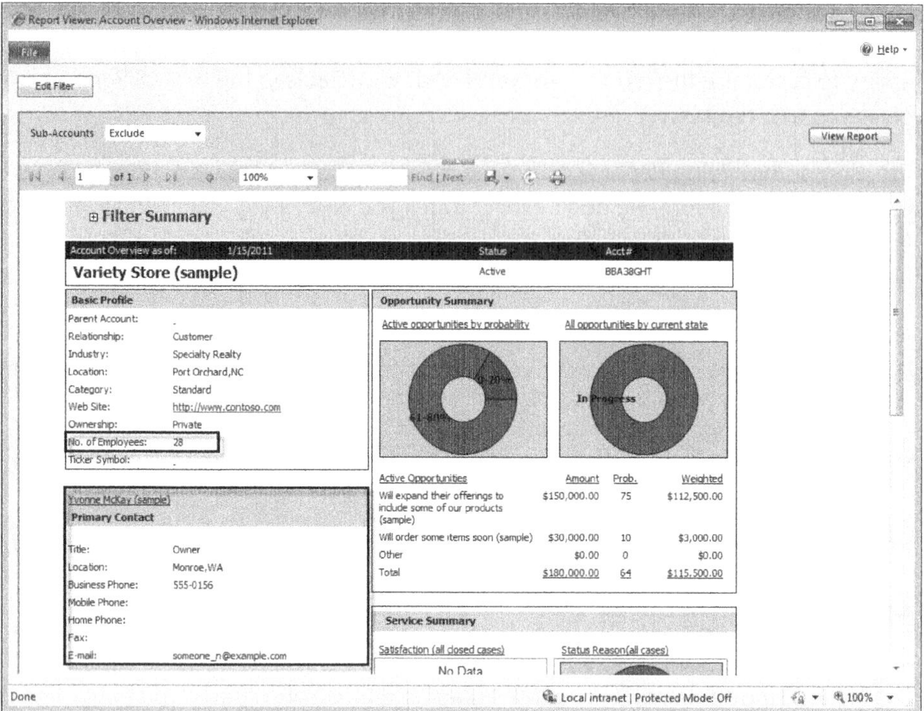

FIGURE 13-7 Modified Account Overview report

Modifying the Account Overview report

1. Navigate to the Workplace area and click Reports in the navigation pane.
2. Change the view to All Reports, Including Sub-Reports so that you can select the Account Overview Sub-Report, and then click Edit in the report ribbon.
3. After the Account Overview Sub-Report dialog box appears, click Actions, and then select Download Report. Save the report to your desktop, making sure that the file you download has an .rdl extension.
4. In Visual Studio 2008, click the File menu, point to New, and then click Project.
5. In the Project Types section, select Business Intelligence Projects, and in the Templates section, select Report Server Project.
6. Give your Visual Studio project the name **WorkingWithDynamicsCRM2011** and click OK. Visual Studio creates a Reporting Services project with two empty folders: Shared Data Sources and Reports.
7. Right-click the Reports folder, point to Add, and then click Add Existing Item.
8. In the Look in list, click Desktop. Select the Account Overview Sub-Report.rdl file, and then click Add.

9. Visual Studio adds the report to your project. Double-click the report to open it in Layout mode.

10. In the Report Data toolbar, select the CRM data source and click the Edit button. When you download reports, sometimes Microsoft Dynamics CRM sets the data source to localhost and the initial catalog to Adventure_Works_Cycle_MSCRM. You will need to change these default values to the correct values for your deployment. The data source should be the name of your Microsoft Dynamics CRM SQL Server. The initial catalog should be the name of the Microsoft Dynamics CRM database. The initial catalog name should appear as *organizationname*_MSCRM, where *organizationname* is the organization name used when Microsoft Dynamics CRM was installed.

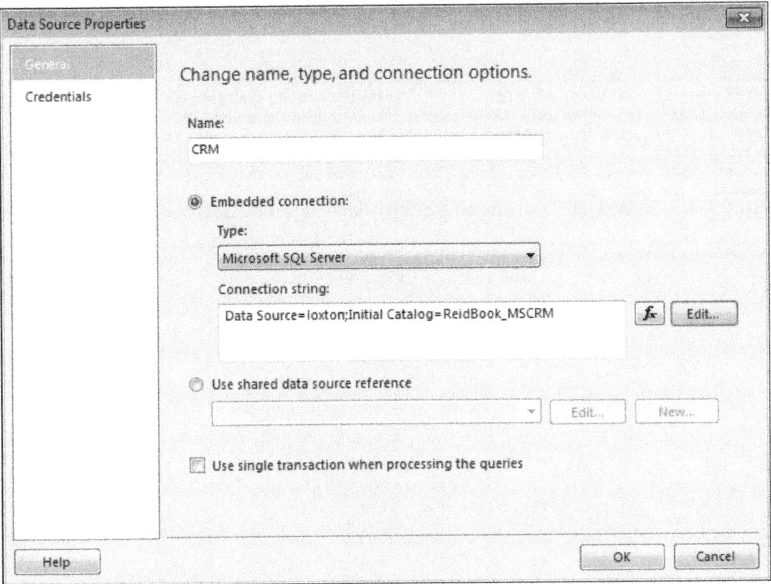

11. After you edit these values, click OK to close the Data Source dialog box. If you click the Preview tab, it should display a blank Account Overview report. If you still receive an error, review your data source settings.

12. Before you can add the No. of Employees field to the report, you must modify the report's dataset so that the report query includes the No. of Employees field in the result set. As we mentioned earlier, most of the default Microsoft Dynamics CRM reports include multiple datasets, so you need to know which dataset to edit. In this example, you want to add the No. of Employees field to the ds_BasicProfile dataset, which is tied to the Basic Profile section in the report. To edit the query, right-click the ds_BasicProfile dataset from the Report Data toolbar and select the Query option. Although you can edit the query from the Dataset Properties dialog box, we prefer to use the Query Designer.

13. To add the No. of Employees field to the query, you need to know the field's schema name, *numberofemployees*. To add this field to the query, add the following text after the SELECT keyword in the query:

```
facct.numberofemployees,
```

This is a complex query that we won't explain in detail; however, *facct* is an alias that the query uses to reference the FilteredAccount database view.

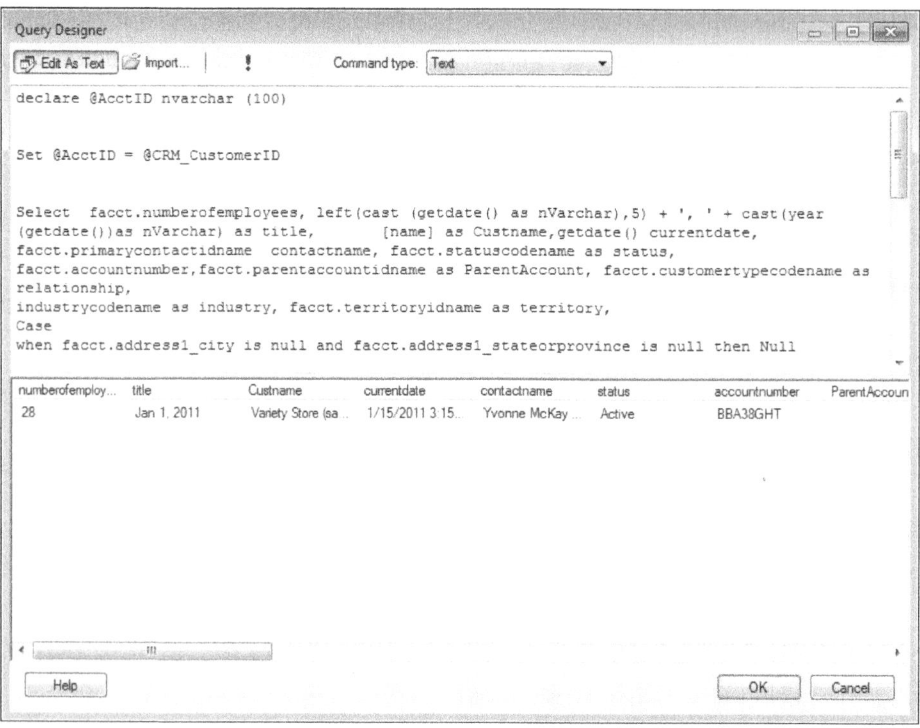

14. You can test the updated query by selecting the red exclamation point in the Query Designer toolbar. You will need to have an account GUID available to enter as the parameter value. One record should be returned with the *numberofemployees* field displayed.

Tip You have several ways to find a record's GUID. The first is to query the database. A simpler way to do this, and one that your users can easily perform if you are helping them troubleshoot an issue, is to review the URL of the record. Figure 13-8 shows the 32-character GUID for the account record toward the end of the URL.

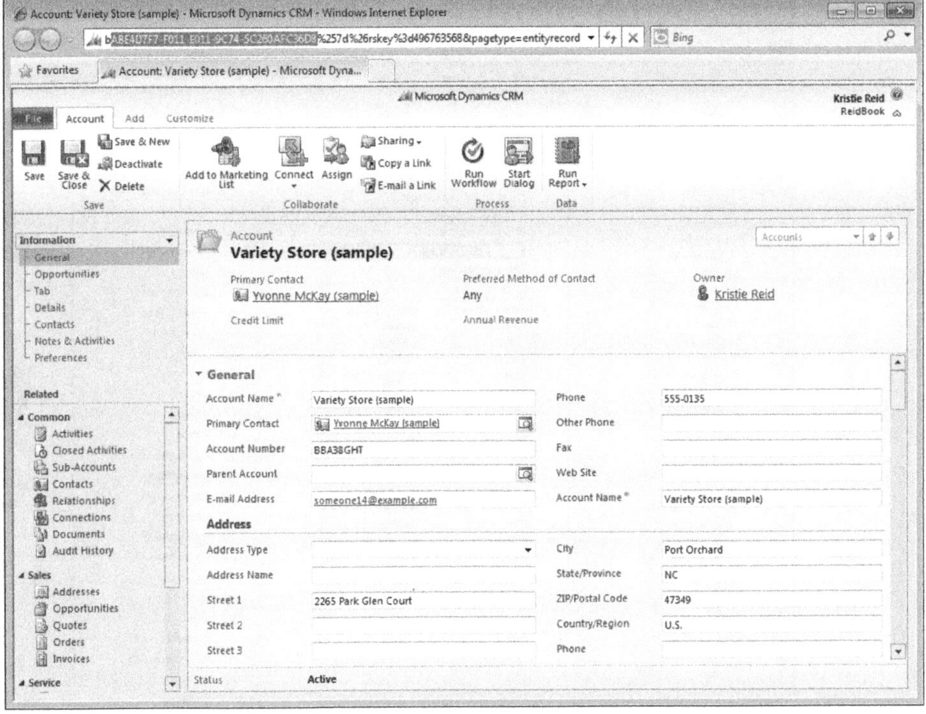

FIGURE 13-8 Finding a record's GUID in the URL

15. After you add the field to the query, click OK. You might be prompted for the @CRM_CustomerID parameter. Click OK. Click the Save button on the Visual Studio 2008 toolbar.

16. Now that the report query results include the No. of Employees field, you can add that field to the report in the Layout section. In the Design tab, click the text box that contains *Ownership*.

17. In the table outline, right-click the icon with the three horizontal lines next to Ownership, and then click Insert Row Below to insert a new row between Ownership and Ticker Symbol.

18. Click the text box under Ownership and type **No. of Employees:**. Click the box to the right of the No. of Employees field, and click the field list icon that displays in the upper-right corner of the field when you rest the mouse over the box. Select numberofemployees.

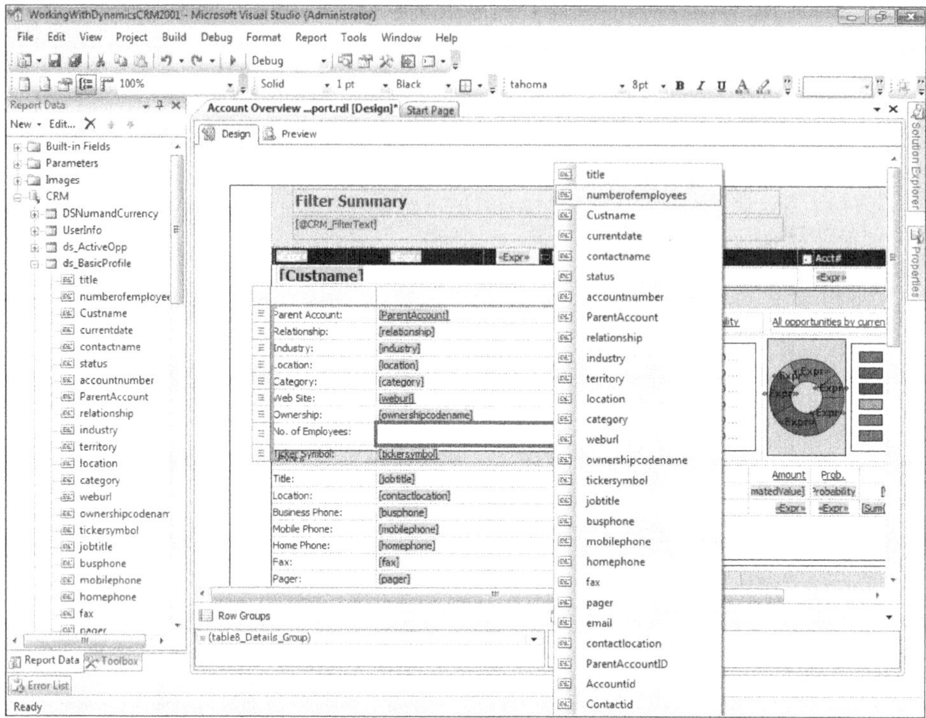

19. Click the [numberofemployees] field and set the TextAlign property to Left and the LineHeight property to .1875in. to remain consistent with the other fields in this column and rows in the table.

20. Right-click the pager field and select Delete Rows. Resize the body of the Primary Contact table and move it down on the page so that it is no longer overlapping the Basic Profile table. Click the Preview tab. You won't see any data because the report needs an account GUID value to run correctly but you will be able to confirm that you do not have any errors. You must upload the report to Microsoft Dynamics CRM to see it work.

21. Save your report by clicking Save All on the File menu.

22. In Microsoft Dynamics CRM Reports, navigate to the Reports view. Select the Account Overview Sub-Report (in the All Reports, Including Sub-Reports view), and click Edit Report.

23. In the Source section, under File Location, click Browse, select the updated Account Overview Sub-Report field, and then click Save and Close. A warning message reminding you that you will overwrite an existing report appears. Click OK to update the existing report.

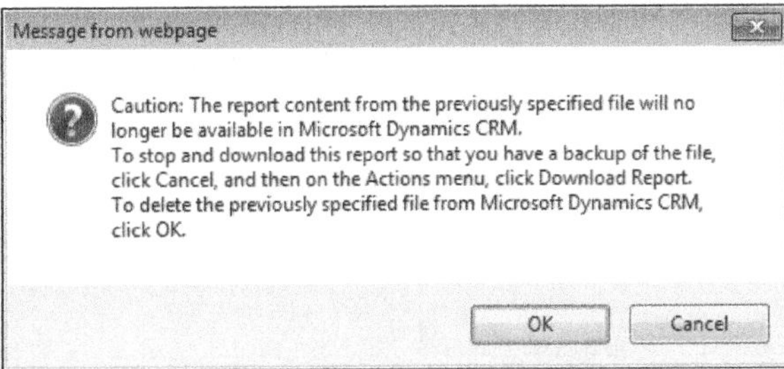

Note Do not select the file you downloaded to your desktop. You must select the updated .rdl file from the directory in which Visual Studio stores your project files.

24. In the reports view, open the Account Overview report, and change the filter to run the report for just one account in your system by setting the Account equal to Variety Store (sample), or any account in your system. Click Run Report. In the report you will see the No. of Employees in the Basic Profile section and the Pager field in the Primary Contact section removed.

As you can see, an inexperienced report author can make simple modifications to add custom fields, make minor formatting changes, and so on despite the default Microsoft Dynamics CRM report complexity. You can imagine how to carry this same concept through to updating the layout of the report to include logos, adding additional fields and charts, or modifying where fields appear in the report layout.

Creating a Reporting Services Report Using Fetch XML

The previous example included details about connecting to an on-premise installation of Microsoft Dynamics CRM. Because the changes required a connection to the SQL server and Microsoft Dynamics CRM database, the example in the previous section is not applicable to organizations using Microsoft Dynamics CRM Online. Although the SQL querying capabilities are not available for Microsoft Dynamics Online organizations, you can still take advantage of the extensive capabilities available in Reporting Services using Fetch XML instead of SQL statements. The following process and example to use Fetch XML can be used in both on premise and online versions of Microsoft Dynamics CRM.

Fetch XML is a proprietary format used to construct queries against the Microsoft Dynamics CRM database. Don't worry; you do not have to learn a programming language to use Fetch XML. Microsoft Dynamics CRM makes creating your Fetch XML statements very easy by allowing you to download the statements directly from an Advanced Find query.

Let's take an example Advanced Find query where you want to display information about your active Opportunities and how many employees are listed from the Potential Customer for the result set. Figure 13-9 shows the details of the query.

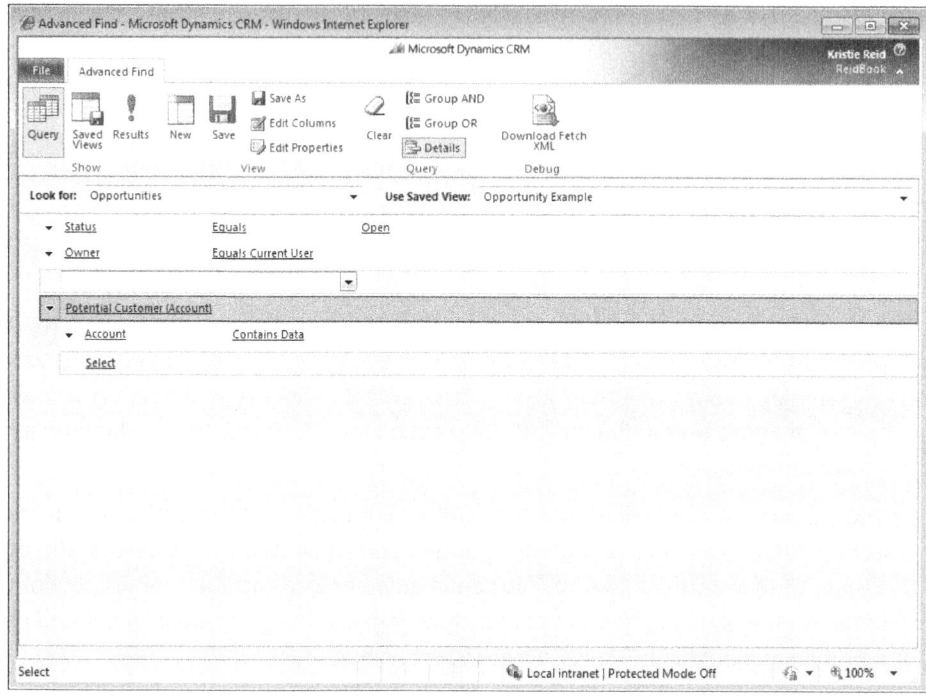

FIGURE 13-9 Advanced Find query example

Note Notice that we have included an additional parameter to only show Opportunities where the Potential Customer is an account record. This is because we want to pull information about the number of employees for the Potential Customer, which only applies to accounts. That field does not exist for a Potential Customer record, which is a contact.

After your query is set up, we want to edit the columns to display the following information:

- Topic
- Est. Revenue
- Est. Close Date
- Potential Customer
- No. of Employees (Potential Customer)

Figure 13-10 shows the results when we run this query.

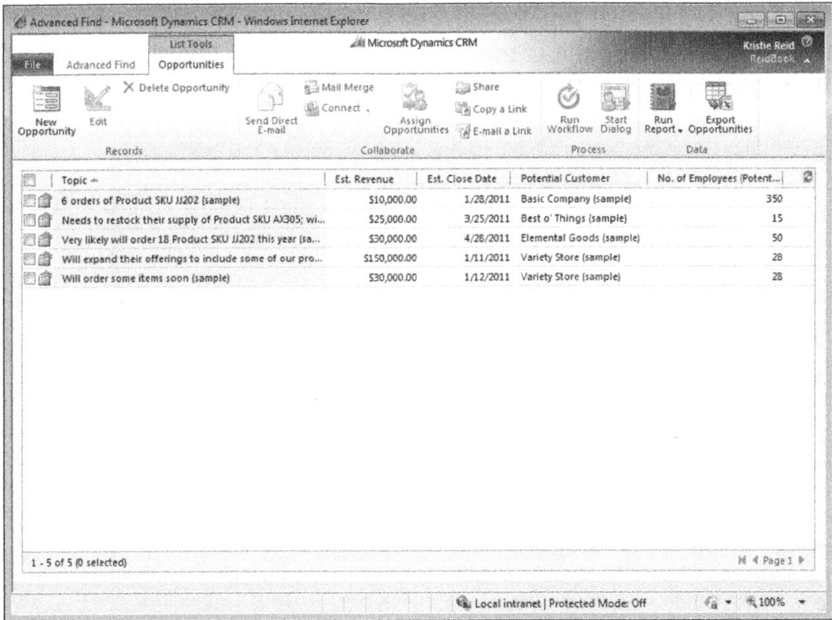

FIGURE 13-10 Advanced Find results

Now that the information needed is displayed, let's take a look at how to export and review the Fetch XML for this example. Microsoft Dynamics CRM provides a button on the Debug area of the Advanced Find ribbon that easily allows you to download the Fetch XML for your query, as shown in Figure 13-11.

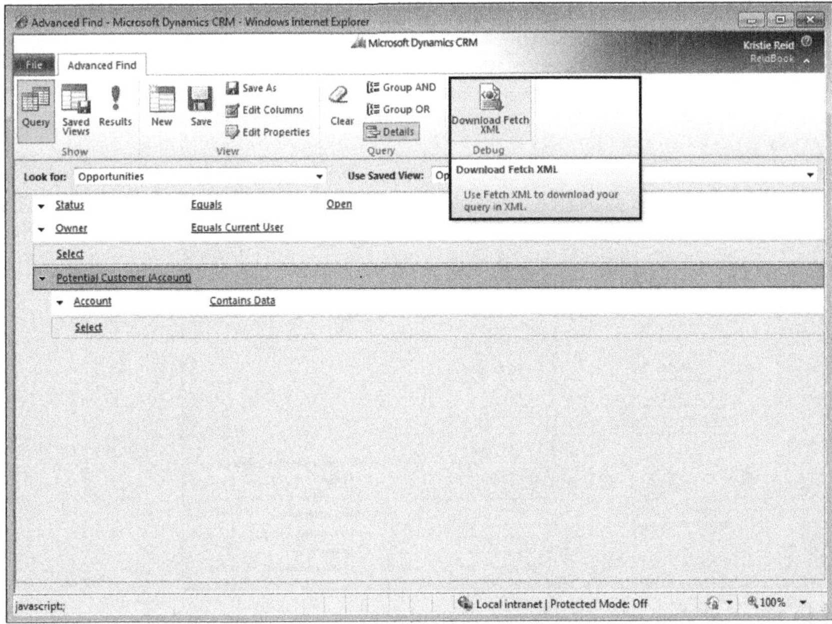

FIGURE 13-11 Download Fetch XML button

You can open the .xml file that you downloaded in Notepad to review the results. To help you better understand the output of the Fetch XML, Figure 13-12 breaks down the XML and highlights the equivalent SQL statement.

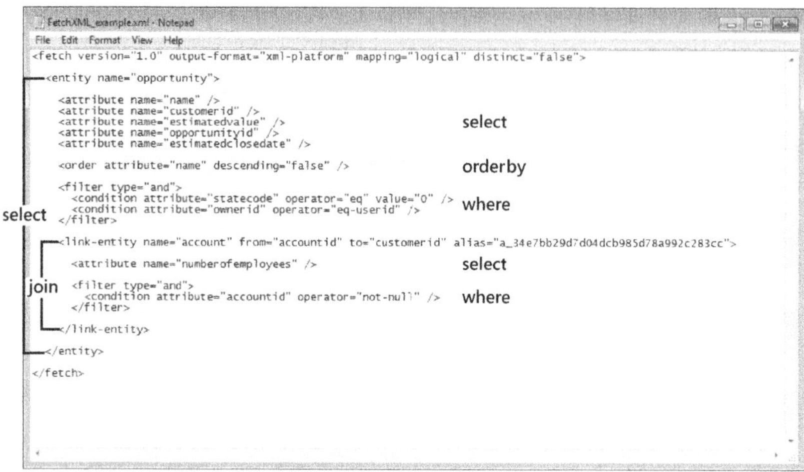

FIGURE 13-12 Fetch XML output compared to SQL syntax

Now let's take what you have learned about Fetch XML and apply the Fetch XML output to a Reporting Services Report.

First, you must install the Microsoft Dynamics CRM Report Authoring Extension. This is available in the Resource Center under Downloads, as shown in Figure 13-13.

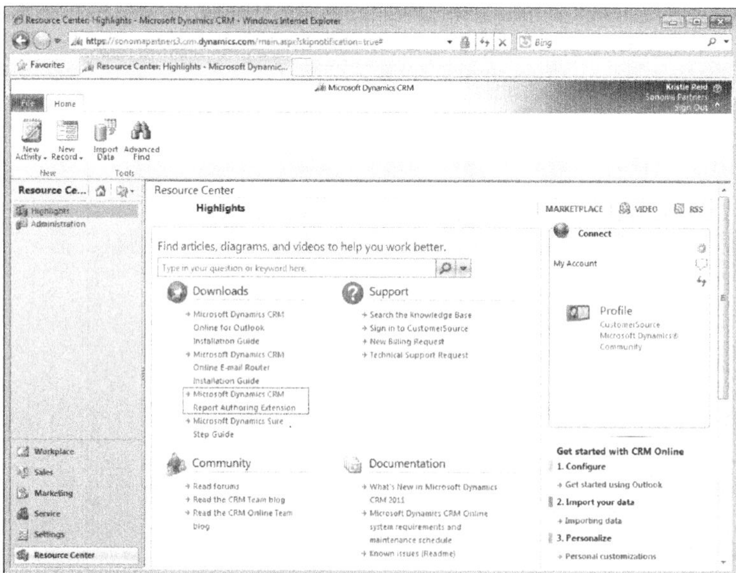

FIGURE 13-13 Microsoft Dynamics CRM Report Authoring Extension link on the Resource Center

When you click the link in the Resource Center, you will be directed to the Microsoft Download Center. After you download and run the CRM2011-Bids-ENU-i386.exe file, you will walk through the Microsoft Dynamics CRM Report Authoring Setup dialog box.

The sample report that we will create lists the activity records for an account. This report will display both open and closed activities for an account on a single page. You will also learn how to use the pre-filtering feature available within Dynamics CRM to contextually filter the records displayed in your report.

Tip Consider creating a template report that you can use when creating new Reporting Services reports. This will help save time and standardize your reports by having an example with the formatting already in place.

Creating a report

1. Open the same reporting project you created in the Account Overview example, right-click the Reports folder, click Add, and then select New Item. Although you can choose to use the Report Wizard, we will start from scratch and select Report from the list of Visual Studio installed templates. Name the report **Account Activities**. Click Add in the Add New Item dialog box.
2. In the Report Data toolbar, click New and select Data Source. Create a new data source with the following properties:
    a. In the Name box, type **CRM**.
    b. In the Type list, select Microsoft Dynamics CRM Fetch.
    c. In the Connection String, type the server URL followed by a semicolon and then the organization unique name as in Figure 13-5.

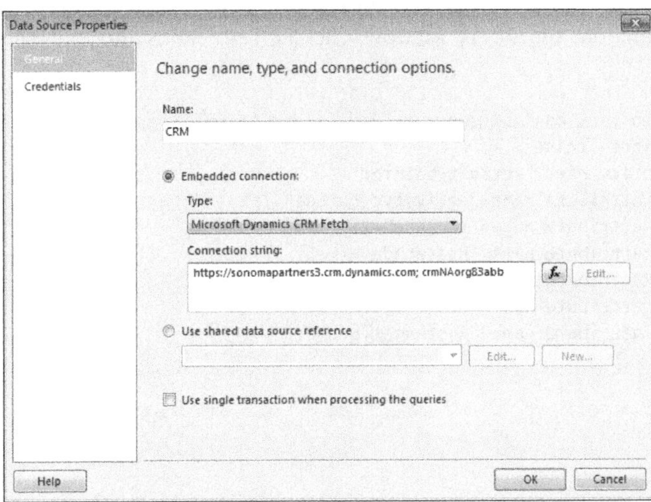

Only the server URL is required unless you have multiple CRM Online environments. The server URL would be the URL to your CRM server (for example, *https://sonomapartners3.crm.dynamics.com*). The optional organization unique name is the Organization Unique Name. To find this, log into your Dynamics CRM Online site, navigate to the Settings area, click Customizations, and click Developer Resources.

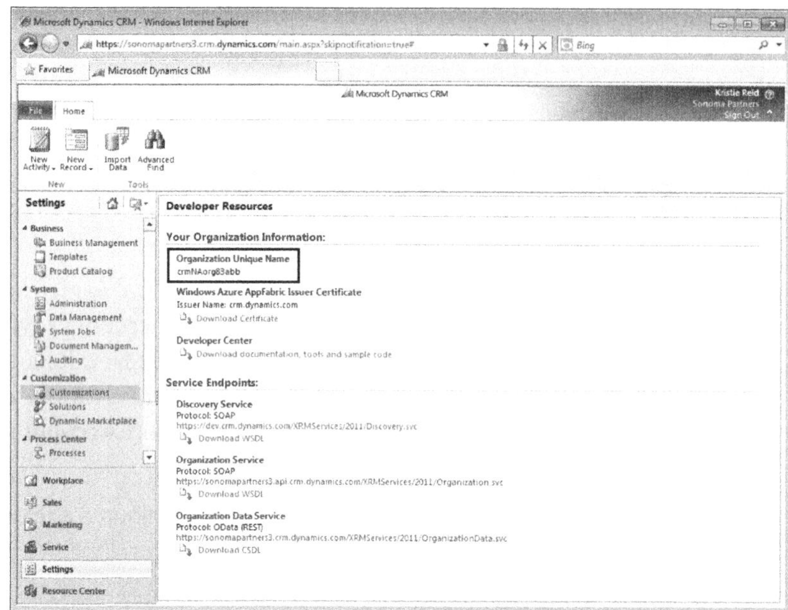

d. On the Credentials tab, select *Use this user name and password* and enter your LiveID information. Click Ok.

3. To create your dataset, click the CRM data source, click New in the Report Data menu, and select Dataset. On the Dataset Properties dialog box, enter the following FetchXML statement into the Query window. Click Refresh Fields and then click OK.

```
<fetch version="1.0" output-format="xml-platform" mapping="logical"
distinct="false">
  <entity name="activitypointer">
    <attribute name="activitytypecode" />
    <attribute name="subject" />
    <attribute name="statecode" />
    <attribute name="modifiedon" />
    <attribute name="activityid" />
    <attribute name="instancetypecode" />
```

```
    <attribute name="regardingobjectid" />
    <attribute name="ownerid" />
    <attribute name="scheduledend" />
    <order attribute="statecode" descending="true" />
    <order attribute="scheduledend" descending="false" />
    <link-entity name="account" from="accountid" to="regardingobjectid"
alias="aa" enableprefiltering = "true">
    </link-entity>
  </entity>
</fetch>
```

4. From the toolbox toolbar, drag and drop a Table onto the report. Return to the Report Data toolbar and add the following fields:
   - *activitytypecode*
   - *subject*
   - *statecode*
   - *modifiedonValue*
   - *scheduledendValue*
   - *ownerid*
5. In the table header, rename the columns:
   - **Activity Type**
   - **Subject**
   - **Status**
   - **Last Updated**
   - **Due Date**
   - **Owner**
6. At this point you will have all of the data that you need to see on the report. Here are some additional formatting options:
   a. In the Report menu option, select Add Page Header. In the Report Data toolbar, right-click Images and select Add Image. Upload a logo and select Open. Drag and drop the logo into the report header. Next, drag and drop a Textbox from the Toolbox to the report header and type **Account Activities**. In the Properties of the text box, update the FontFamily to Calibri, the FontSize to 12pt, and the FontWeight to Bold.
   b. Update the font properties of all of the fields to the FontFamily Calibri. Right-click the *modifiedonValue* field and select Text Box Properties. On the Number tab, select the Date category and select *1/31/2000 as the Type. Click OK. Repeat

the data formatting for the *scheduledendValue* field. Click the icon with the three horizontal lines and select the BackgroundColor property. From the drop-down list, select Expression. Type the following expression:

```
=iif(Fields!statecode.Value = "Open", iif(Fields!scheduledendValue.Value >
today(), "White", "LightGrey"), "White")
```

This expression will highlight rows of activities that are still open but past due or have no due date.

c. Update the font properties of all the column headings to have a BackgroundColor of "Gray", Font Color = "White", FontFamily Calibri, FontWeight to Bold.

d. Click Report in the menu bar and update all of the margins to .5in. Resize your table columns to fit under 7.5 inches, as shown in the ruler. This will ensure that when printing, the width of your report does not spill over onto another page. Figure 13-14 shows the end result after all of these steps.

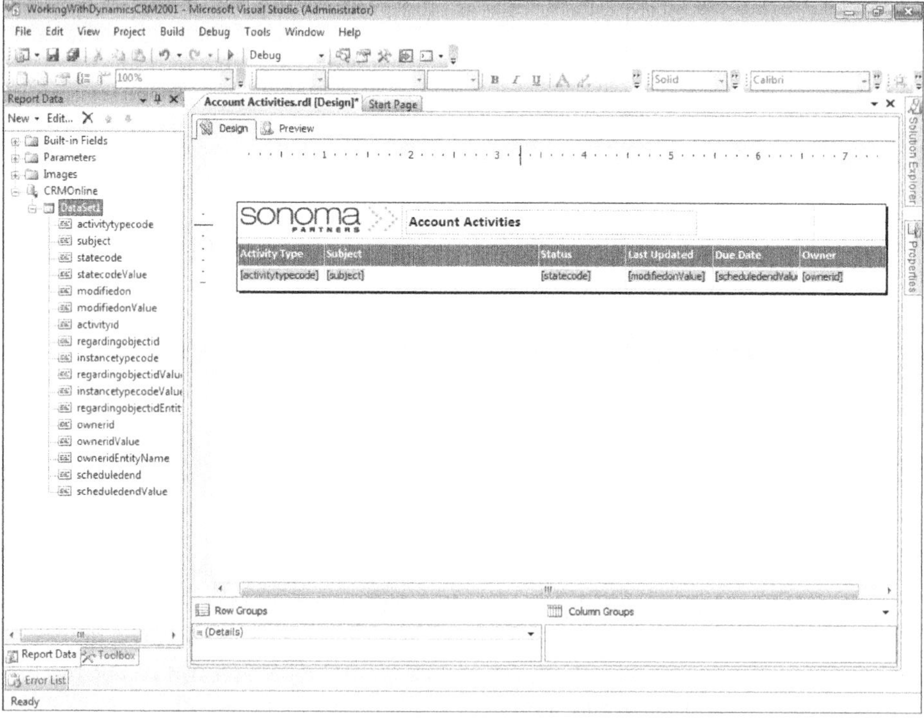

FIGURE 13-14 Microsoft Visual Studio report design results

7. Click the Preview tab and confirm that there are no errors. Click Save All on the File menu to save your report. Now add it to Microsoft Dynamics CRM.

8. In the Microsoft Dynamics CRM Web client, navigate to the Reports list, and click New on the grid toolbar.
9. Select Existing File for the Report Type, and select your new Account Activities.rdl in the File Location field. Enter a description and choose Accounts in the Related Records Type field. For Display In, select all three options: Forms for related record types; Lists for related record types; Reports area.
10. Click Save, and then click Run your new report. The report output looks like the following.

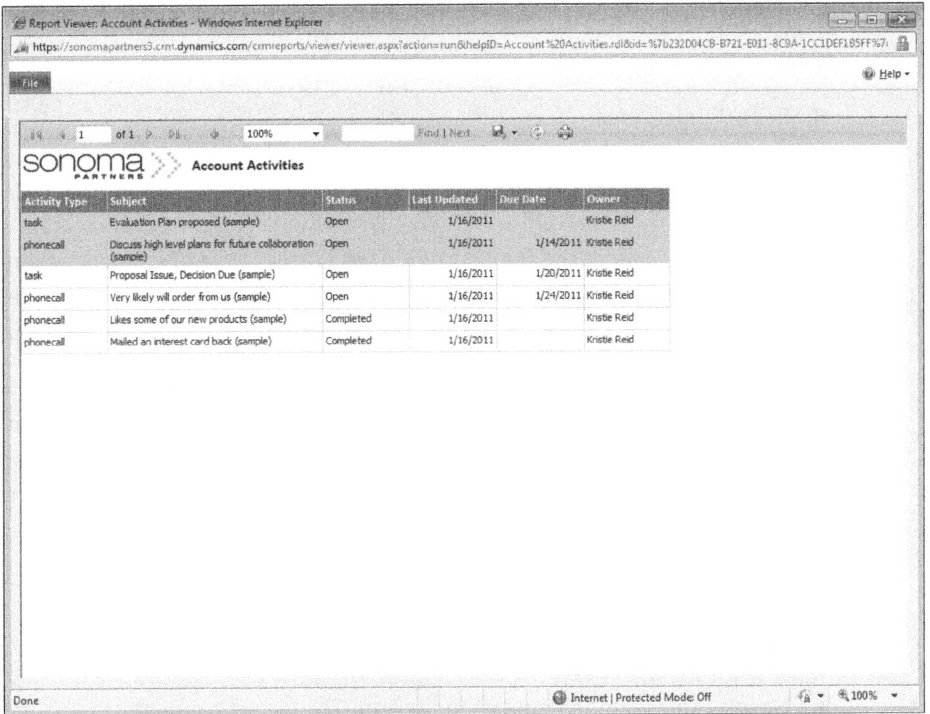

The formatting of this report is obviously not consistent with the formatting of the other reports within your organization. However, we wanted to show some of the benefits of using the Reporting Services toolset, including the ability to add logos and perform conditional formatting, among other things.

Important You should be aware of two additional important considerations when creating reports that will be loaded into the Microsoft Dynamics CRM interface. First, you cannot use a shared data source. Second, if you are used to using SQL queries to write reports, be aware that Fetch XML has some limitations. For example, there are no functions similar to a union in SQL to consolidate data from multiple tables.

Managing Reports with Microsoft Dynamics CRM

You now know how to create and run reports, specifically Reporting Services reports, in Microsoft Dynamics CRM. We now discuss the options you have to manage reports in Microsoft Dynamics CRM, including the following report options:

- Report Records
- Report Actions
- Report Properties
- Schedule Report
- Edit Default Filters
- Report Categories

Report Records

From the Records area of the Report ribbon, you can choose to create a new report or edit an existing one. Both of these options allow you to configure the report properties to set up where you want the report to appear in the user interface. You can alter the following properties when adding or editing a report:

- **Report Type** Includes the following report types: Report Wizard Report, Existing File, and Link to Web Page. The Existing File option allows you to upload a report file to Microsoft Dynamics CRM. The Link to Web Page option stores a link pointing to a web address. The web page address can be either an internal or external URL.
- **File Location** Displays an upload dialog box that appears when you specify a report type of Existing File.
- **Web Page URL** Specifies a web page to use for a report.
- **Name** Displays the name of the report. The report name appears in the Report views, so try to be as descriptive as possible. If you enter the name of an existing report, Microsoft Dynamics CRM will ask if you want to overwrite the existing report file.
- **Description** Allows you to enter more information about what the report does. The description appears in the Reports view.
- **Parent Report** Specifies the parent report for the report's drill-through functionality to work, if the report is a sub-report. The parent report must already exist in Microsoft Dynamics CRM.
- **Categories** Indicates one or more categories to which the report will belong. We explain report categories in more detail later in this chapter.

- **Related Record Types** Allows you to associate the report with system and custom entities. For example, the Account Overview report displays information about an Account record, so you would select account in the Related Record Types field. You must configure this property in conjunction with the Display In property. Adding related record types to a report also determines which entities you can use to edit the pre-filter fields for Reporting Services reports.
- **Display In** Indicates how you want the report to be displayed for those entities. You can select any combination of Reports views, lists for related record types, and forms for related record types. The *Reports area* option displays the report in the Reports view accessed from the Workplace area. The *Lists for related record types* option allows the report to be run from the entity view (grid). The *Forms for related record types* option displays the report as an option from an individual entity's form.

Note The Display In settings apply to all of a report's related record types. For example, you can't display a report on entity A's form and list but only display the report on entity B's list.

- **Owner** As with most records, the owner of the report determines the access permissions.
- **Viewable By** All users in the organization or just an individual owner can run the report, as defined by the user's report security settings.
- **Languages** If your Microsoft Dynamics CRM organization has multiple languages enabled, you need to specify a language. The report will be displayed for all users who have selected that language in their personal options. Select All Languages to make a report available to all users.

Note The Languages option does not change the language displayed in the report output.

In addition to the editable report properties, Microsoft Dynamics CRM displays information about who created the report and the last time a user modified the report. As is the case with all entities, you cannot edit these fields because Microsoft Dynamics CRM automatically populates them.

Report Actions

The report edit form provides some additional actions, if you have the proper security enabled. These actions include standard record options such as Delete Report, Assign,

Sharing, Run Workflow, Start Dialog, Copy a Link, and Email a Link. The following report-specific actions are also available:

- Download Report
- Revert to Personal Report/Make Report Available to Organization
- Publish Report for External Use (not available in Microsoft Dynamics CRM Online)

Download Report

You can download individual report files from the Report view in Microsoft Dynamics CRM. This action saves the report's actual RDL file to your computer so that you can make copies, redistribute, or edit the file.

Revert to Personal Report/Make Report Available to Organization

The Revert to Personal Report and Make Report Available to Organization actions require create and read privileges on the Report entity as well as rights to Publish Reports to Organization. Microsoft Dynamics CRM displays the action based on the value of the *Viewable By* attribute. Table 13-2 shows the options available.

TABLE 13-2 ***Viewable By*** **Actions**

Viewable By **attribute value**	**Action displayed in Microsoft Dynamics CRM**
Individual	Make Report Available to Organization
Organization	Revert to Personal Report

Remember that the data displayed will still be filtered based on the user's record security settings.

Publish Report for External Use

The *Publish Report for External Use* action creates a copy of the report at the root of the organization's folder in Reporting Services. This will more conveniently expose the report to additional features of Reporting Services, such as creating a subscription to email the report on a scheduled basis. We are not able to walk through this particular example in the scope of this book but if you are familiar with scheduling reports using Reporting Services, you will understand how to schedule Microsoft Dynamics CRM reports.

You should be aware that when you publish the report for external use, you make a copy of the report in Reporting Services. Any changes to the original report will need to be republished. Any sub-report will also be published, but the name will be displayed as the Microsoft Dynamics CRM report's globally unique identifier (GUID).

We recommend that you go into the Reporting Services manager and hide any published sub-reports to avoid confusion with your users.

Schedule Report

Running complex reports can drastically reduce the performance of your reporting server. If you install Microsoft Dynamics CRM and Reporting Services on the same server, these complex reports can negatively affect performance for *all* of your Microsoft Dynamics CRM users, including those users not running reports. Therefore, it's ideal for you to install Reporting Services on a dedicated computer separate from Microsoft Dynamics CRM so that you can isolate the reporting demands from standard Microsoft Dynamics CRM usage. Regardless of the Reporting Services configuration, you can use the Microsoft Dynamics CRM Report Scheduling Wizard to reduce the impact of report execution on your Microsoft Dynamics CRM server performance. By using this technique, you can execute a report and cache the results, providing a performance boost at run time when viewing the report, according to a predefined schedule. In addition to caching report results, with this execution setting you also can take a report *snapshot* that freezes the report results as of a specific time, which is useful for quarterly progress reports, monthly quotas, and so on.

Note Microsoft Dynamics CRM Online does not allow scheduled reports.

To use the Report Scheduling Wizard, you need to select the report you want to modify in the Microsoft Dynamics CRM Reports view and click Schedule Report on the report ribbon to start the wizard. We show you an example of how this works.

More Info Microsoft Dynamics CRM actually configures a snapshot of the report in Reporting Services. The options you define in the Report Scheduling Wizard correspond to the options you have in Reporting Services.

Scheduling the Neglected Accounts report to execute monthly

1. Click the Neglected Accounts report in the Reports list.
2. Click the Schedule Report button on the ribbon to open the Report Scheduling Wizard.
3. Choose whether you will schedule the report snapshot manually or per a defined schedule. Each option takes you through different but self-explanatory pages. For this example, select On a schedule, and click Next.
4. Select the frequency with which the report should execute. Each option (once, hourly, daily, weekly, monthly) provides additional unique parameters for you to configure. Select Monthly, and leave the default options. Click Next.

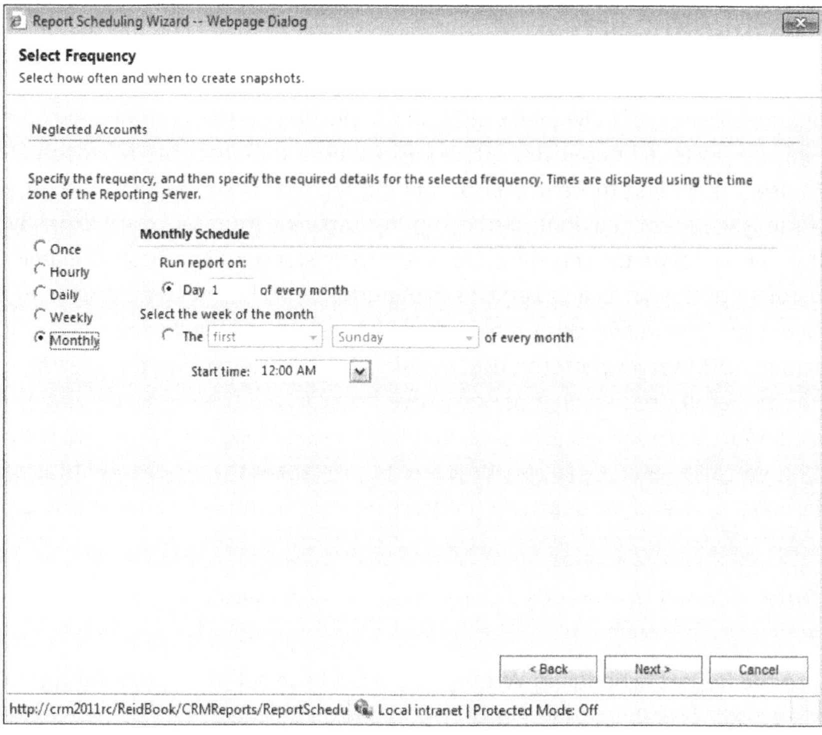

5. Select the start and end dates or indicate that the schedule has no end date. Click Next.

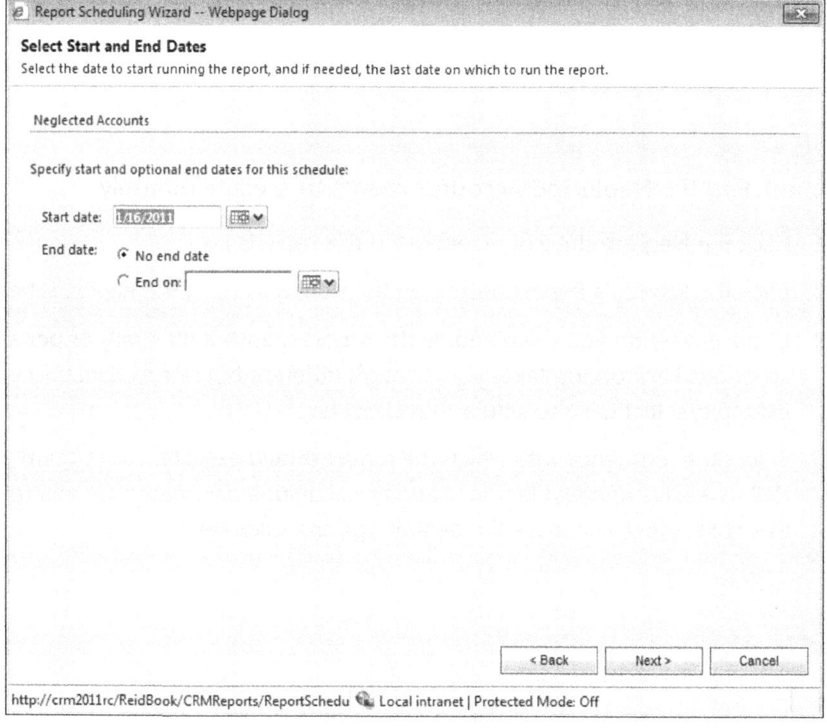

6. In the Define Report Parameters dialog box, you define the report parameters you want to use in your snapshot. This page displays the parameters specific to the report you scheduled. The step also provides an Edit Filter button. Click this button to further refine the filter used for the report snapshot. Keep the defaults, and click Next.

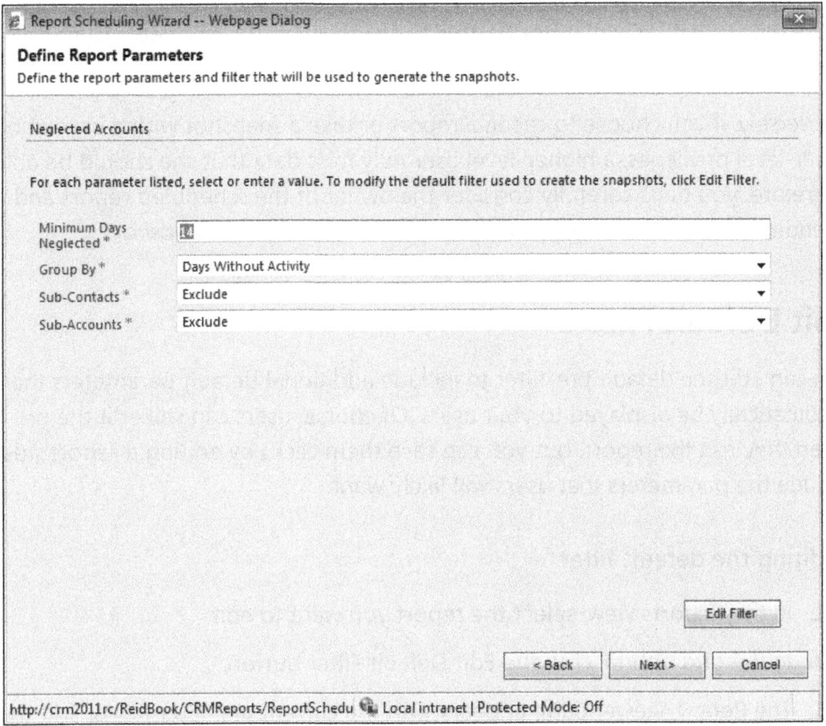

7. On the next page, you can review all of your selections. Pay special attention to the note listed. Only the most recent eight snapshots of your report will be stored. Click Create to complete the report snapshot.

8. After processing the report, the final page appears, letting you know whether your report was properly scheduled or detailing any error the wizard encountered. Click Finish to complete the process.

To edit the snapshot simply click a scheduled snapshot report and select Schedule Report from the actions area of the ribbon. This action will take you through a set of steps similar to the preceding procedure.

The user who created the snapshot becomes the report's owner. The report's *Viewable By* attribute defaults to *Individual*. When you configure report caching or snapshots, the report runs under the context of the report owner.

If you want the report to be viewable by the organization, you must consider the owner of the report and the data that the owner can view. If the report runs in the context of a user with higher privileges (such as a system administrator), every person who views that report will see the same data that the system administrator would see, regardless of the user's individual business unit and security roles. Consequently, a lower-level user may see data in the report that he would not be able to see through the Microsoft Dynamics CRM user interface.

Conversely, if you choose to cache a report or take a snapshot with a user who has lower-level privileges, a higher-level user may miss data that she should be able to view. Therefore, you must carefully consider the owner of the scheduled report and the report's intended audience when you configure report caching and snapshots.

Edit Default Filters

You can edit the default pre-filter to include additional default parameters that will automatically be displayed to your users. Of course, users can still edit the pre-filter on the fly when they run the report, but you can save them clicks by editing a report's default filter to include the parameters that users will likely want.

Editing the default filter

1. In the Reports view, select the report you want to edit.
2. In the grid ribbon, click the Edit Default Filter button.
3. The Report Viewer page appears with the current pre-filter fields. Edit the filter values to fit your needs.
4. Click Save Default Filter.

The next time a user runs this report, he or she will see the update report pre-filter fields.

Note Report pre-filters apply only to Reporting Services reports, so you can edit the default filter only for reports of this type.

Report Categories

By using report categories, you can group similar reports together so that users can filter the Reports view based on these categories, as shown in Figure 13-15.

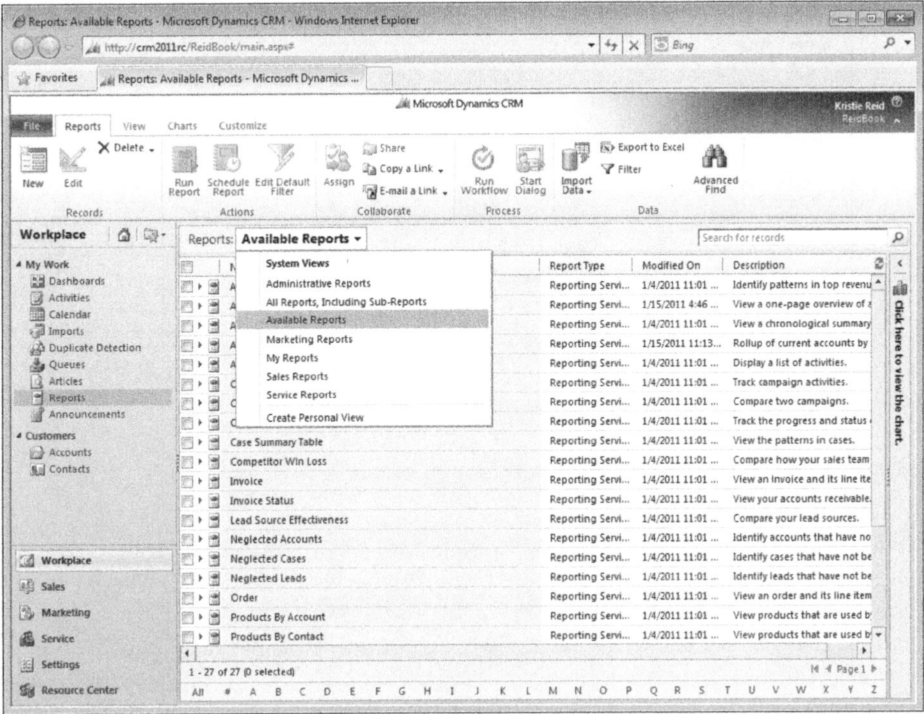

FIGURE 13-15 Filtering reports by report categories

You can assign a report to a single category, or you can assign a report to multiple categories if necessary. Microsoft Dynamics CRM includes four report categories in the default installation:

- Sales Reports
- Service Reports
- Marketing Reports
- Administrative Reports

Of course, you can add, modify, or delete these report categories to fit your business needs. Let's review how to manage report categories.

Managing report categories

1. Navigate to the Settings area and click Administration.
2. Click System Settings. The System Settings dialog box appears.
3. On the Reporting tab, you can add, modify, delete, and sort the report categories. You can also assign a default category for any new reports.

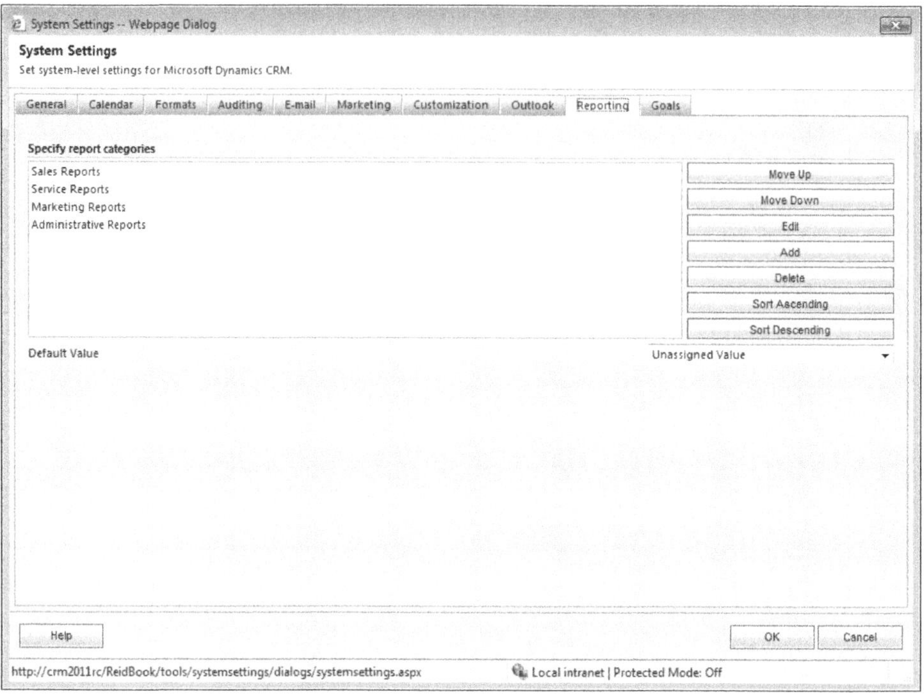

Remember the following when you edit report categories:

- Your changes will appear immediately in the user interface; you don't need to publish your changes.
- If a report belongs to just one category and you delete that category, you can still access the report by using the Available Reports filter.
- Microsoft Dynamics CRM currently ignores the order you set.

Customizing Dashboards in Microsoft Dynamics CRM

As we've already discussed, dashboards are a captivating way to display data and allow your Microsoft Dynamics CRM users to take immediate action on data available. Dashboards typically act as the home page for all users. Although users have the ability to change their landing page through their personal settings, we often find that most users like the visualization of data that the dashboard provides, assuming that the data displayed is useful to the user.

Seven dashboards come out of the box with Microsoft Dynamics CRM that focus on the main areas of the application. However, you will most likely need to edit these existing options or create new options, depending on what information needs to be presented to your end users. Follow these steps to view a list of existing dashboards and access the dashboard editor:

Accessing the dashboard editor

1. Navigate to Settings area, click Customizations, and then click Customize the System. The default solution opens.
2. Select Dashboards from the list of Solution components.

Actions on the Dashboard View

From the dashboard view, you can take several actions, including:

- **New** The New button allows you to create a new dashboard without using an existing dashboard as a starting point. We will get into more detail on creating a new dashboard later in this section.
- **Delete** You can delete dashboards in an unmanaged state using the Delete button on the dashboard ribbon.
- **Publish** Similar to all other entities, you must publish your dashboard changes before they are displayed to the end user. From the view, you can publish multiple dashboards simultaneously by selecting the dashboards you want to publish and then clicking the Publish button on the dashboard menu.
- **Show Dependencies** When you select to show the dependencies to the dashboard you can view the dependent components and the required components of the dashboard. This information is critical when exporting and importing solutions into other organizations. You can only select one dashboard at a time to display the dependencies for.
- **Managed Properties** From the Managed Properties dialog box, you can set whether the dashboard can be customizable when imported into a managed solution. This information then displays in the Customizable column of the dashboard view.
- **Set As Default** You can select one dashboard as the default view that users will see when they load the dashboard page. From there, users have the ability to set their own default from the Dashboard Management area of the Dashboard ribbon, as seen in Figure 13-16.
- **Save As** You may find instances where a user group asks for a new dashboard that is similar to an existing one but with one or two different components. Rather than creating a new dashboard and having to incorporate the same components and style, you can select an existing dashboard and click the Save As button. When you select this option, you will want to rename the dashboard and provide an updated description.

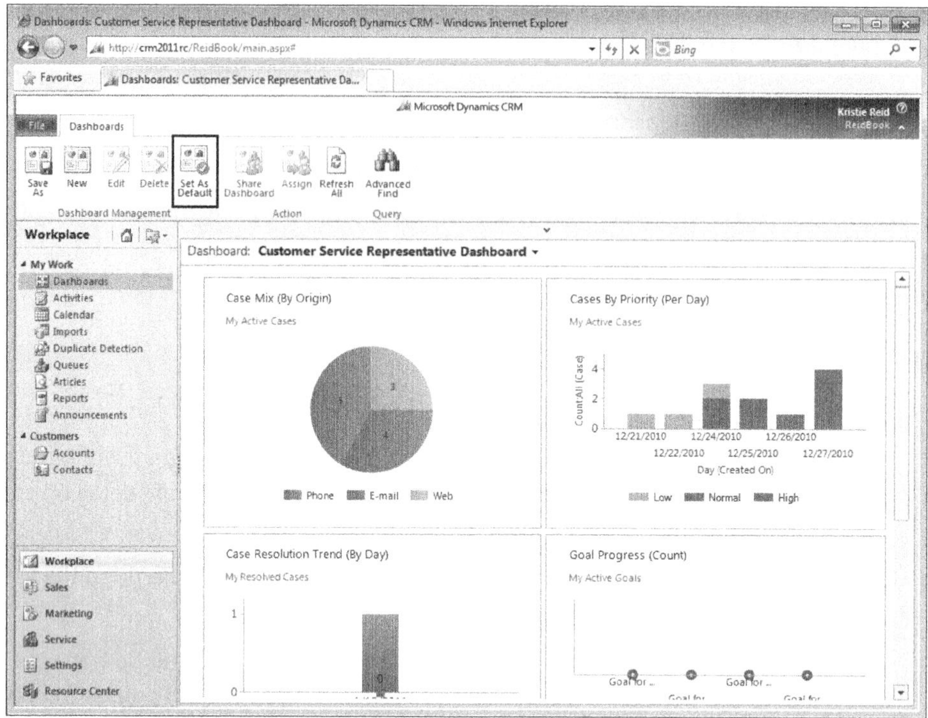

FIGURE 13-16 Set As Default button on the Dashboard ribbon

Tip Microsoft Dynamics CRM will let you have two or more dashboards with the same name. However, this would be very confusing for your end users so you will want to make sure that each dashboard has a unique name.

Next, let's look at how to create a new dashboard. After we finish, you can apply the same ideas to edit an existing dashboard.

Note Users can also create their own dashboards directly from the Dashboard ribbon, assuming that they have the appropriate permissions. However, from a security perspective the Dashboard ribbon acts a bit differently than other ribbons in that users will still be able to click the New button, even if they do not have permissions to create a user dashboard. However, they will receive a warning when they attempt to save the dashboard.

Creating a New System Dashboard

When you create a new dashboard, Microsoft Dynamics CRM will present you with a variety of dashboard layouts, including a description of the layout, as shown in Figure 13-17.

Dashboard Layouts -- Webpage Dialog

Select Dashboard Layout

Select a layout for your dashboard. You can use this as your initial outline, and then resize, add, or rearrange the components within this layout.

3-Column Regular Dashboard
3-Column Multi-Focused Dashb...
4-Column Overview Dashboard
2-Column Regular Dashboard
3-Column Overview Dashboard
3-Column Focused Dashboard

3-Column Regular Dashboard

This layout can accommodate components across three columns.

Create

http://crm2011rc/ReidBook/tools/dashboardeditor/dialogs/ Local intranet | Protected Mode: Off

FIGURE 13-17 Dashboard layout selection

Although you will be able to make almost unlimited adjustments to the layout that you choose, keep in mind that to maximize the effectiveness of a dashboard, you want to keep the dashboard visible on a single screen.

After you select the layout that you want to use, the New Dashboard window appears. Enter the name of the dashboard in the Name field. To configure the components that come with the dashboard layout, simply rest the mouse on the appropriate icon and select the component to insert, as indicated in Figure 13-18.

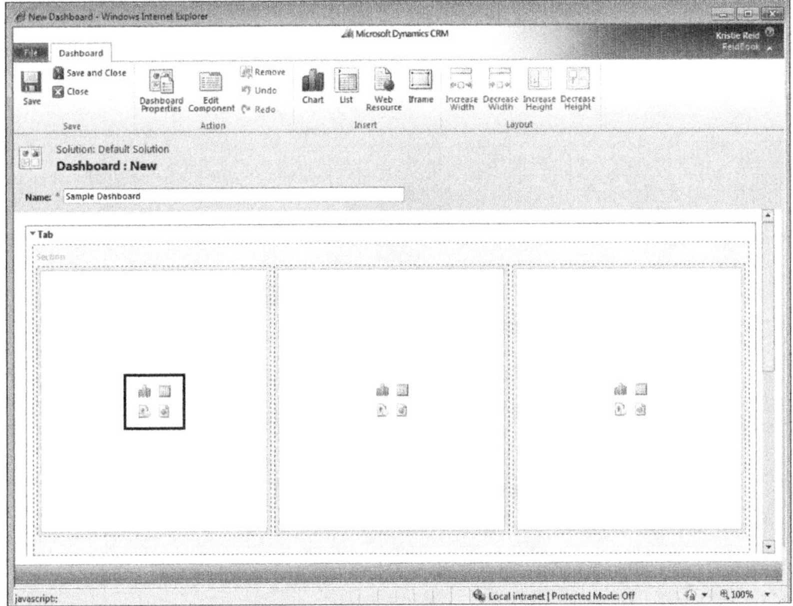

FIGURE 13-18 Inserting a component from the dashboard layout

You can insert the following components on a dashboard:

- Chart
- List
- Web Resource
- IFrame

Let's review each component type.

Chart

Charts are probably the most common dashboard component you will use—they provide simple visualization of the data you are displaying. When you insert a chart into a dashboard, you can customize the following features:

- **Record Type** Select the record type that you want the chart to display. This list will only display entities that allow charts to be associated with them.
- **View** Choose the view that the chart should pull the data from. When creating a system dashboard, only system views will be available. However, when users are creating a personal dashboard, they will be able to select the personal views that they have access to.
- **Chart** Select the chart that should display. Again, the list that appears here will only be from the system charts that have been created for the entity selected.

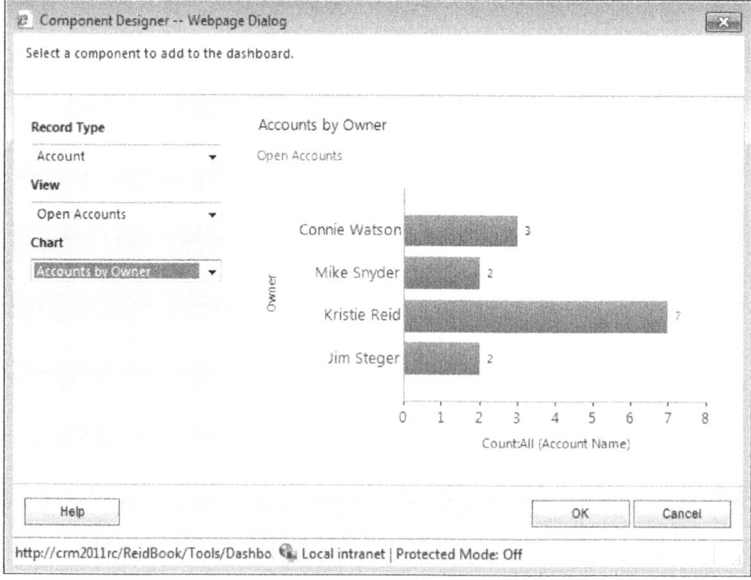

List

Lists are synonymous with views and display rows of records with columns of data as designed in the selected view. When you select to insert a list, you can customize the list by:

- **Record Type** Select the record type that you want the list to display. This list will only display entities that allow views to be associated with them.
- **View** Choose the view that the list uses to display data. The view selected will dictate the filter criteria and the columns that are displayed.

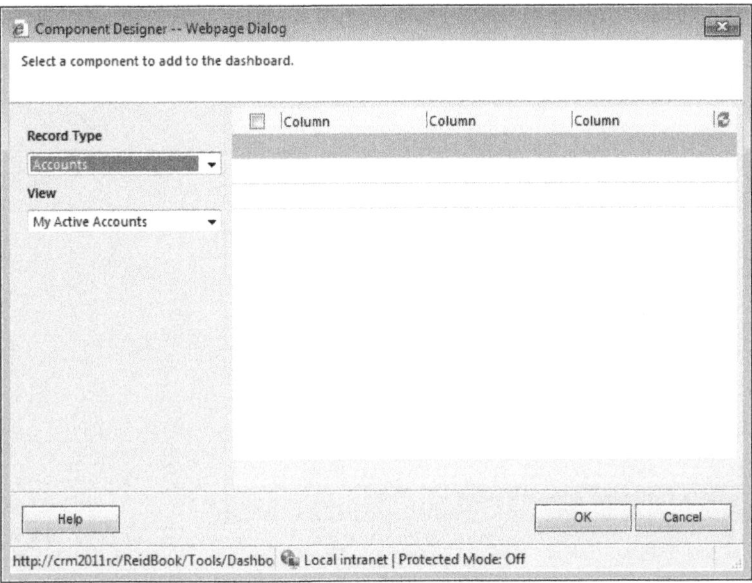

IFrame

IFrames on dashboards can be thought of in the same way as we discussed in Chapter 7, "Entity: Forms." When you insert an IFrame, you can set the following properties:

- **Name** Type the name of the IFrame, which will be stored with the *IFRAME_* prefix.
- **URL** Enter the address of the web page or resource that you want to reference in the IFrame.
- **Security** Indicate whether you want to block cross-frame scripting.
- **Visibility** Specify whether the control should be visible by default on the dashboard.

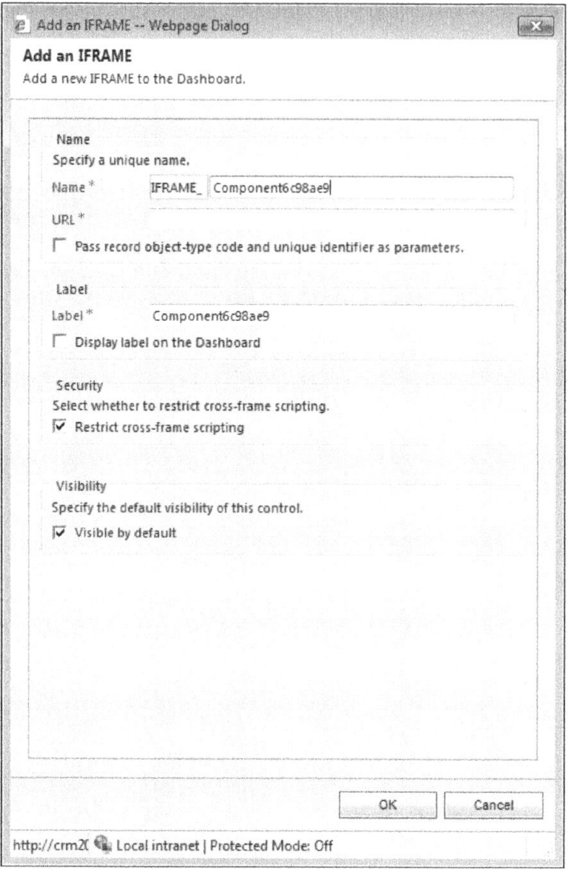

Note Clearing the Restrict cross-frame scripting option is not available for users creating personal dashboards.

Web Resource

You are already familiar with web resources from Chapter 11, "Solution: Web Resources." You can include web resources in your dashboards. Inserting a web resource onto a dashboard provides similar capabilities to when it is added to a form, as described in Chapter 7. The properties that you can set for your web resource as it relates to the dashboard include:

- **Web resource** Provide a lookup to an existing web resource you want to display.
- **Name** Enter a unique name for the web resource of the form.
- **Label** Provide a label for the web resource, which you have the option of displaying or hiding on the form.

- **Visibility** Specify whether the control should be visible by default.
- **Web Resource Properties** Pass custom parameters, enter alternative text, restrict cross-frame scripting, and pass record object-type code and unique identifiers as parameters, depending on the web resource type.

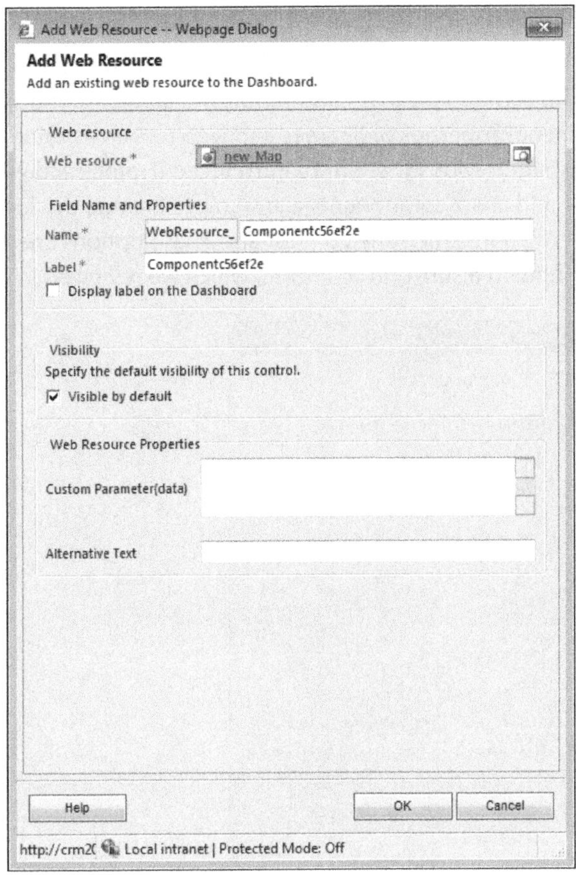

Editing Dashboards

After you have you dashboard set up, or if you are using an existing dashboard, several editing options are available from the dashboard ribbon. Let's go through each of the customization options on the dashboard ribbon:

- Actions
- Insert
- Layout

Actions

When editing a dashboard, the following actions are available:

- **Dashboard Properties** In the Dashboard Properties dialog box, which displays when you click the Dashboard Properties button, you can change the Name and the Description of the dashboard.
- **Edit Components** The Edit Component dialog box allows you to make changes to the properties of the component that control how the component displays to the end user. The component properties of IFrames and web resources bring up the same dialog boxes as described previously when we introduced IFrames and web resources. The properties for list and chart components allow you to change the format from what you can control when inserting the component. These options are the same as those available when adding a sub-grid to a form, which we reviewed in Chapter 7.

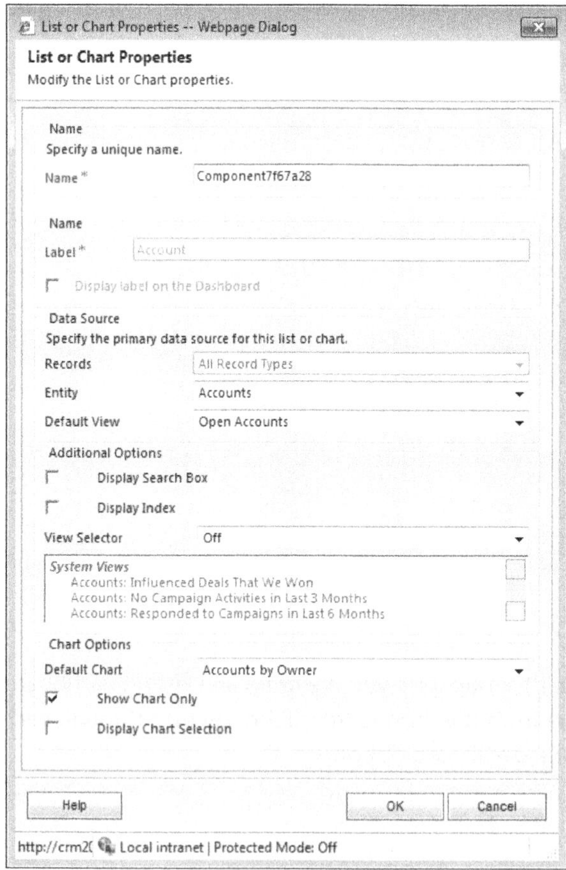

- **Remove** To remove a component from the dashboard, simply select the component and click the Remove button.

- **Undo/Redo** Similar to other Microsoft products, the dashboard designer of Microsoft Dynamics CRM allows you to undo and redo changes up until the point when you close the dashboard. You can also use the shortcut keys to undo your last change (Ctrl+Z) and redo the change (Ctrl+Y).

Insert

If the dashboard design that you select does not have enough components available, or if you remove a component and need to insert another one, you can insert charts, lists, web resources, and IFrames directly from the ribbon.

Layout

After you insert the components that you want to display on your dashboard, you may find that the information you are trying to display is larger or smaller than the space that you have available on your component. If this happens, you can use the layout options available to resize each component so that it displays nicely. Figure 13-19 shows the guidelines in the designer that you can use while changing the size and location of your components.

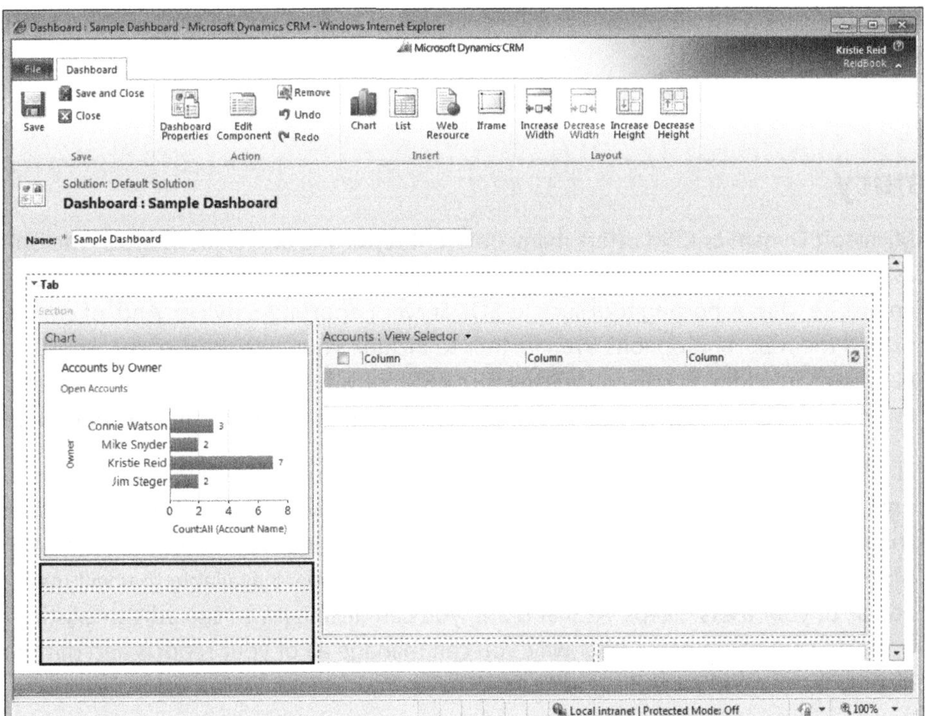

FIGURE 13-19 Dashboard layout guidelines

You want to make sure that the components fill all of the space available; therefore, you want to make sure that no guidelines remain to ensure that your layout will display nicely once the dashboard is complete. Use the following layout options to control the size of your components:

- **Increase Width** Increase the width to expand the component by one column. You will not have the option to increase the width of the component after it spans across the number of columns available.
- **Decrease Width** Decrease the width to contract the component by one column. You will only have the option to decrease the width of the component until it spans across only one column.
- **Increase Height** Increase the height of the component to make it display longer on the page.
- **Decrease Height** Decrease the height of the component to make it display shorter on the page.

Tip You also have the ability to move components to different areas of the dashboard. You can drag and drop the components to a different area, or you can use your arrow keys, which is what we find works best.

Summary

Microsoft Dynamics CRM offers many different reporting and analysis tools. The options available range from simple options such as views and Excel exports to a sophisticated enterprise-class reporting tool such as SQL Server Reporting Services. And, of course, you can extend the reporting options even further to include your own third-party reporting tool if necessary. In addition, Microsoft Dynamics CRM introduces visualization through dashboards to provide your users graphical and actionable information, all within the application.

The key to having all of these capabilities available to present data to your users is to use the right tools. When you receive a request for data, start by reviewing the tips introduced in this chapter to determine whether a report or a dashboard should be used. Determine whether Microsoft Dynamics CRM already has a report or dashboard available that will meet most, if not all, of your users' needs. At that point, you can decide if you can edit an existing resource or create something new. Either way, you can manage all of your reports and dashboards directly from the Microsoft Dynamics CRM user interface.

Part III

Processes

Chapter 14

Workflow Processes

In this chapter:

Microsoft Dynamics CRM includes a workflow module that you can use to automate your business processes based on rules, logic, and actions that you design. The functionality in Microsoft Dynamics CRM 2011 uses the Microsoft Windows Workflow Foundation, which enables users, administrators, and developers to design powerful business processes using the workflow tools. These tools include a user interface for creating and monitoring the workflow processes. In this chapter, we will review what is possible through that user interface to enhance your workflow rules.

Workflow Process Basics

Many companies try to adopt and implement standardized business processes to help their operations run more consistently. For example, the CEO might say, "All customer service cases must be resolved within 24 hours," or, "We're implementing a new sales process for all deals over $100,000." However, the communication of these business processes often gets delivered to employees in an ad hoc and unregulated manner. A process document may exist on a network file share, but people don't know that it's there. And some employees might rely on word-of-mouth information from coworkers to learn the processes for their jobs. Consequently, standardizing business processes can prove challenging for some companies, particularly larger organizations.

Microsoft Dynamics CRM workflow enables you to set up and define business process activities—including the proper sequencing—that employees should use when working with Microsoft Dynamics CRM data. As soon as a workflow rule is published, it is automatically applied when data that meets the specified criteria is entered into Microsoft Dynamics CRM.

Important Conceptually, you can think of Microsoft Dynamics CRM workflow as an application or service that runs in the background 24 hours a day, 7 days a week, constantly evaluating your Microsoft Dynamics CRM data and the multiple workflow processes in your deployment. When the workflow service encounters a trigger event, it fires the appropriate workflow processes to run the workflow actions. Typical workflow actions include sending an email message, creating a task, and updating a data field on a record.

By implementing workflow processes in your Microsoft Dynamics CRM deployment, you can enjoy the following benefits:

- Track and manage your customer data and processes consistently. Instead of relying on your users to remember the appropriate steps for processing data, you can create workflow processes that will automatically determine the next required steps and assign activities as necessary.
- Process your customer data faster, so that new sales leads or customer service requests are assigned and routed immediately upon record creation.
- Allow your users to focus on more valuable activities instead of having to perform a large number of manual, repetitive steps.

Organizations of all sizes can benefit greatly from workflow processes, so let's get into the details of using workflow in Microsoft Dynamics CRM. In the subsequent sections, you'll learn the following Microsoft Dynamics CRM workflow concepts:

- High-level architecture
- Running workflow processes
- Workflow security
- Understanding the workflow interface

High-Level Architecture

Windows Workflow Foundation provides a comprehensive programming model, run-time engine, and tools to manage workflow logic and applications. Microsoft Dynamics CRM workflow uses the Windows Workflow Foundation framework for its core infrastructure. Fortunately, the Microsoft Dynamics CRM workflow user interface abstracts users and administrators from needing to interact with Windows Workflow Foundation directly; therefore, you do not have to understand Windows Workflow Foundation to create workflow logic in Microsoft Dynamics CRM. However, the use of Windows Workflow Foundation as the platform for the user interface enables you to develop custom workflow components if the features available through the UI do not meet all of your business needs.

Another important component of Microsoft Dynamics CRM workflow is the Microsoft Dynamics CRM Asynchronous Processing Service that is automatically installed with Microsoft Dynamics CRM. The Asynchronous Processing Service executes long-running operations in Microsoft Dynamics CRM, including the workflow processes. The term *asynchronous* means that operations take place in a nonblocking manner so that the system can continue processing additional events without waiting for one action to complete. Conversely, *synchronous* actions need to complete entirely before the system proceeds to the next step.

Microsoft Dynamics CRM workflows execute asynchronously; consequently, the Asynchronous Processing Service must be running for any Microsoft Dynamics CRM workflows to execute.

Caution Because of the asynchronous nature of Microsoft Dynamics CRM workflow, you may notice a slight delay between the time that you apply a process and the time that the process is implemented. Depending on the workflow action, you may also have to refresh the record you're viewing to see new or updated values. As you will learn in this chapter, Microsoft Dynamics CRM provides multiple ways for you to monitor the execution of workflow processes as they are running.

Running Workflow Processes

Microsoft Dynamics CRM initiates workflow processes in one of three ways:

- Manually, by the user
- Automatically, from a trigger event
- From another workflow process

First, we'll discuss how users can manually execute workflows. Assume that you've already designed multiple workflow processes for the Opportunity entity. When users look at an Opportunity view, they can select one or more records, and then click the Run Workflow button located on the Opportunities ribbon, as shown in Figure 14-1.

When the user clicks the Run Workflow button, a dialog box appears, like the one shown in Figure 14-2.

In this dialog box, users can select one of the published, on-demand workflow processes to run against the records selected in the Opportunity view. After the user selects the process she wants to apply and clicks OK, Microsoft Dynamics CRM takes the actions specified in the selected workflow process for each of the selected records. Users can select and run only one workflow process at a time in this dialog box.

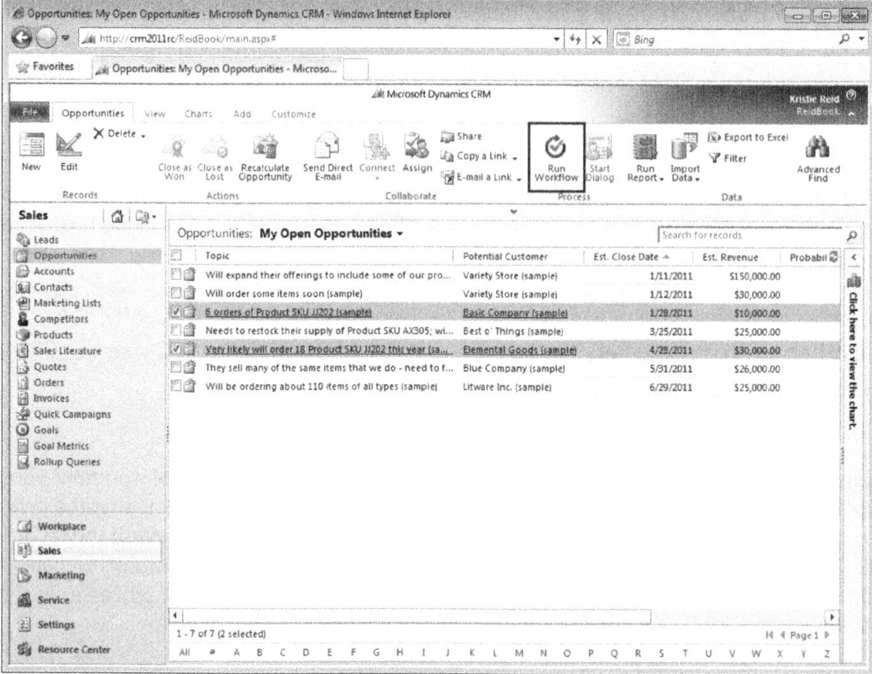

FIGURE 14-1 Executing workflow processes from the Opportunities ribbon

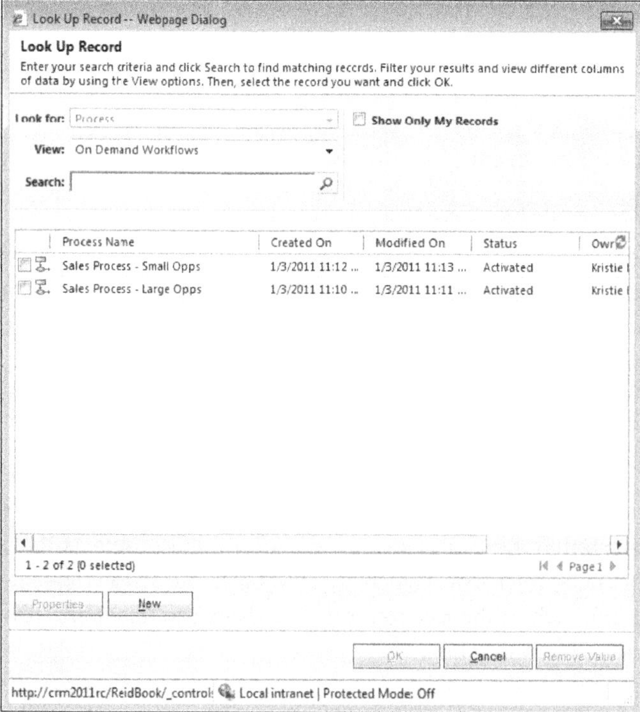

FIGURE 14-2 Run Workflow dialog box

Workflows also can be manually run directly from within a record, as shown in Figure 14-3.

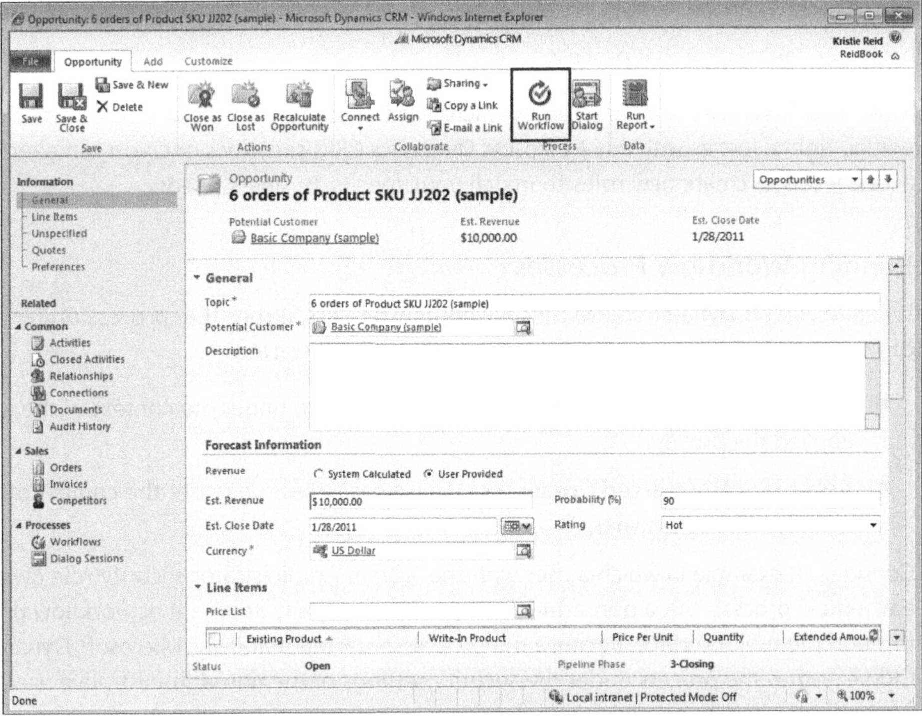

FIGURE 14-3 Accessing workflow processes from a record

In addition to manually applying workflow processes, Microsoft Dynamics CRM also can automatically run processes based on a trigger event you specify, or it can run them as a subprocess in another workflow process. As you might expect, designing workflow processes that run automatically provides you with more benefits than relying on a user to initiate the process.

Workflow Process Security

Just like the other features in Microsoft Dynamics CRM, you can configure detailed security settings for workflow processes. You can secure workflow processes from two perspectives:

- Creating and editing workflow processes
- Running workflow processes

Creating and Editing Workflow Processes

You configure security privileges to specify which users can create and edit Microsoft Dynamics CRM workflow processes the same way you configure security for other entities in

Microsoft Dynamics CRM, such as leads, accounts, and contacts, as described in Chapter 3, "Managing Security and Information Access." Each workflow process has an owner, and the owner of the workflow process, combined with a user's security role, determines which actions each user can take on that process.

Most default security roles created by Microsoft Dynamics CRM include basic workflow editing rights. Just as with any Microsoft Dynamics CRM security right, you can alter the access levels or create new roles to match your specific business needs.

Running Workflow Processes

When Microsoft Dynamics CRM runs a workflow process, it runs that process under one of two security settings, depending on how the process started:

- **Manually started processes** These processes run under the context of the user who applied the process.
- **Automatically started processes** These processes run under the context of the workflow process owner.

Consider an example in which a user with the System Administrator security role owns a workflow process, but a non-administrative user manually applies that workflow process through the user interface. Because the process is started manually, Microsoft Dynamics CRM executes the process under the security settings of the non-administrative user, not the user with the System Administrator role. If the workflow process actions require it to delete a record and the non-administrative user does not have permission to delete that record, the deletion step of the workflow process will fail. Therefore, you should confirm that a user has permission to execute all of the steps in a workflow process, including any child workflow steps, if you permit users to run that process manually.

On the other hand, when a trigger event automatically starts a workflow process, Microsoft Dynamics CRM uses the security credentials of the process owner.

Important The workflow process owner plays a key role because automatically started workflow processes run in the security context of the user who owns the process. However, if a user manually applies a workflow process in the user interface, the process runs under the context of that user's security credentials instead of under the security context of the process owner. If you're not sure how the process started, and consequently which security credentials it is using, you can view the workflow job owner with the monitoring tools explained later in this chapter.

If a workflow process runs correctly when started automatically but does not work properly when run manually, you can usually solve this problem by making sure the user who started the process has the security credentials necessary to execute all of the actions contained in the process.

Understanding the Workflow Interface

You can use the Microsoft Dynamics CRM Web client as the primary user interface for creating and managing workflow processes. This interface is extremely beneficial because it allows users of various skill sets to create and manage workflows, as long as they have the permissions to do so. Processes are accessed by navigating to Settings, and then Processes under the Process Center group. A familiar Microsoft Dynamics CRM view will appear, showing you the workflow and dialog processes, as shown in Figure 14-4.

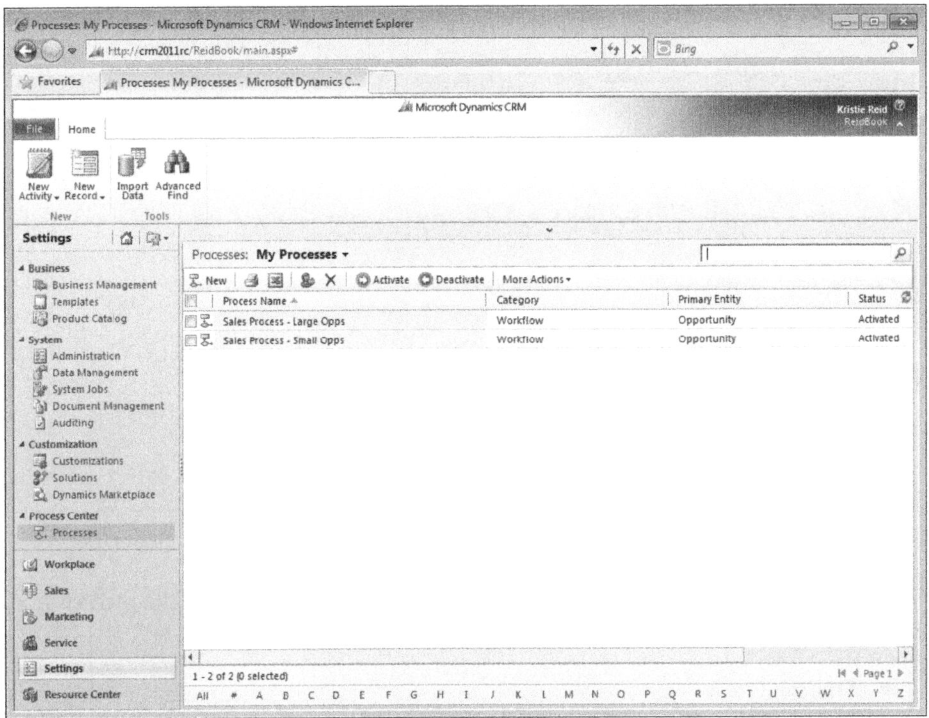

FIGURE 14-4 Process view

To create a workflow process, click the New button in the toolbar. Enter a process name, choose the entity to which the process applies, and select Workflow as the Category. You also can choose to create an original (blank) process or select an existing process template. If you create a new blank process and click OK, Microsoft Dynamics CRM displays the workflow editor tool (Figure 14-5).

In addition to creating workflow processes, you can use the Process view to perform other administrative tasks, such as:

- Assign
- Delete

- Activate
- Deactivate

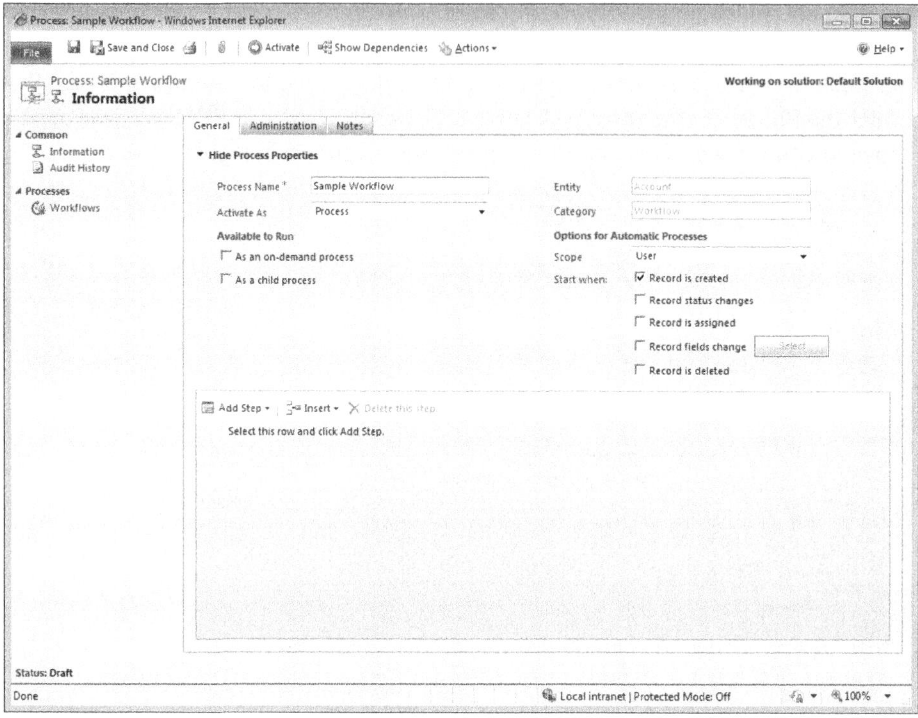

FIGURE 14-5 Workflow Process editor form

In addition to the administrative tasks, you also can make updates to the records and the view from the More Actions menu, including:

- Share
- Bulk Delete
- Enable/Disable Filters
- Save Filters to Current View
- Save Filters to New View
- Set View as Default View

After Microsoft Dynamics CRM runs a workflow process against a particular record, you can access information about that process in the System Jobs section or by clicking the Workflows link in the navigation pane of a workflow process (Figure 14-5). You will learn more about monitoring workflow processes later in this chapter.

Workflow Process Templates

Workflow templates provide a convenient mechanism for reusing common processes. Templates can save you time by simplifying the creation of workflow processes, and creating a workflow template is easy. Simply select the *Process template* option in the Activate As field when creating the workflow.

After you have created and activated a process template, you can select a template when you create a workflow process. When creating a workflow process, you can select a template only after you select an entity with at least one activated template. When the entity is selected, a list of activated templates for that entity will display in the template grid. Next, select *New process from an existing template (select from the list)* and select a template. When the workflow process record opens, it will contain all of the steps and settings from the saved template.

As you would expect, workflow templates can save you a lot of time if your system uses a large number of workflow processes that contain similar steps and actions.

Workflow Process Properties

When you create a workflow process, you must specify several parameters about the process:

- Basic workflow process properties
- Workflow process execution options
- Scope
- Trigger events

Basic Workflow Process Properties

The basic properties that can be changed on the General tab of the workflow process include the workflow's name and publishing type (either a process or a process template).

Tip The workflow editor allows you to enter duplicate workflow names for a given entity. However, this can be confusing when you troubleshoot or update processes, so try to provide unique, descriptive names for your processes. In addition, after the entity the process is associated with is selected, it cannot be changed, so make sure to think through the appropriate entity to associate the process with up front.

Using the Administration tab, you can update the owner of the process (important for security), add a workflow description, and choose the workflow job retention. The *Automatically delete completed workflow jobs (to save disk space)* option should be evaluated for each workflow to establish whether the completion of jobs is critical to maintain for auditing purposes. If not, we recommend that you select this check box to reduce the amount of space completed jobs consume in the database.

Finally, the Notes tab allows you to track notes about this workflow. We recommend you use this tab to note what changes were made with each version of the workflow whenever possible.

You will also notice a number of menu options on the workflow process editor, as shown in Figure 14-5. Most of these actions are similar to those taken on any entity within Microsoft Dynamics CRM, with the exception of Activate/Deactivate and Show Dependencies. The Activate button, which appears when the process is deactivated, activates the workflow, making it immediately available for use. The Deactivate button, which appears when the process is in an active state, deactivates the workflow, which immediately makes it unavailable for use.

Note Workflows can only be edited, including activation and deactivation, by the workflow owner. Therefore, before attempting to change a workflow, you must first assign the workflow to yourself, assuming you have the permissions to do so. Reassignment of a process will automatically deactivate the process. Keep in mind that if the workflow should be run as another user, you will have to reassign it back to that particular user, who will then have to activate the process, as no one but the process owner can do so.

The Show Dependencies button on the menu bar of the workflow process editor provides a list of all dependent and required components to the workflow, as shown in Figure 14-6. The dependent components are those that depend on this workflow and prevent you from deleting it while they depend on the workflow. The list of required components includes all entities and their fields upon which this workflow depends and should be included when exporting solutions.

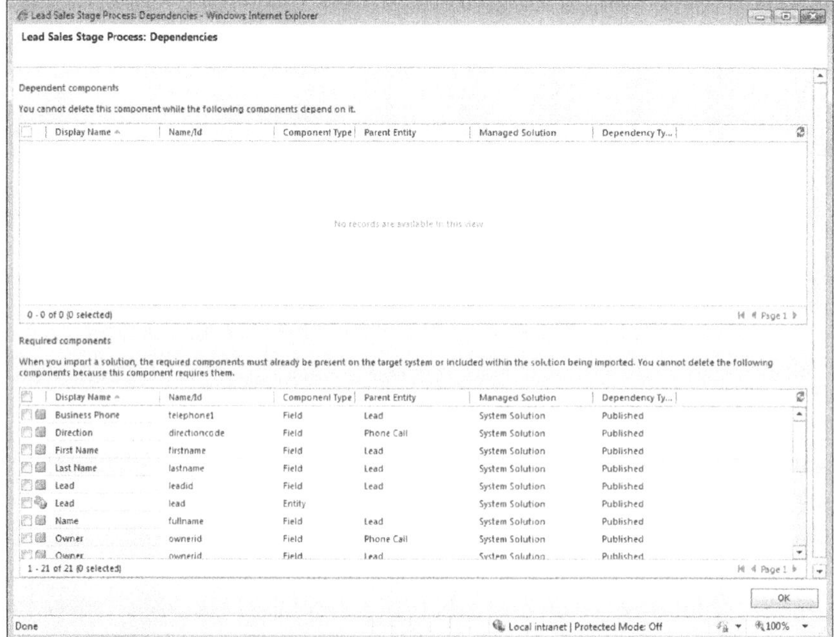

FIGURE 14-6 Process Dependencies view

Workflow Process Execution Options

When you create a workflow process, you need to specify how Microsoft Dynamics CRM can execute that process. As Figure 14-5 shows, you can configure multiple options to trigger the workflow process automatically. We cover the options for automatic execution in the section titled "Triggering Events" later in this chapter.

In addition to specifying automatic triggers, you can configure a workflow process with two other execution options:

- **On demand** Allows a user to execute a workflow process manually on a group of records or a single record
- **As a child workflow** Allows workflow process designers to reference the workflow process as a child in a different workflow process

You can mix and match these execution options appropriately, so you can create a large number of combinations based on how you want Microsoft Dynamics CRM to execute your workflow processes.

Scope

By setting the scope of a workflow process, you can further refine which records the process affects. The scope options are similar to those used in Microsoft Dynamics CRM security access levels:

- User
- Business Unit
- Parent: Child Business Units
- Organization

These scope options appear for workflow processes on user-owned entities such as leads, accounts, and contacts. For organization-owned entities such as addresses or products, Microsoft Dynamics CRM only provides an *Organization* scope option.

When running an automatic workflow process, Microsoft Dynamics CRM uses the combination of the workflow process owner's privileges and the scope of the workflow process to determine the records affected by the workflow.

Important The scope option applies only to workflow processes instantiated automatically by an event in Microsoft Dynamics CRM. Scoping a workflow process cannot elevate a user's rights. It can only further restrict the number of records affected.

Consider an example of how modifying the workflow scope affects the records on which a process runs: Say you have a workflow process that updates a lead, and a user named Alan owns that workflow process. If Alan has Organization-level update rights to leads, but the process's scope is set to User, only the lead records that Alan owns will be updated by this process, as limited by the scope of the workflow process. Likewise, if Alan's update access level is set to User but the workflow process's scope is set to Organization, the workflow process updates only leads owned by Alan as limited by the scope of Alan's security rights. Although he can run the workflow, the process will not complete because of the restriction of his security permissions. Workflow cannot elevate the privileges defined in Alan's security roles.

Tip When creating workflows intended to execute on any record in the organization, set the scope to Organization. If you are creating a personal workflow process to execute only against records you own, set the scope to User.

Trigger Events

When you create a workflow process, you must define the event that will trigger it. In other words, you must specify which actions in Microsoft Dynamics CRM will start the workflow process. For each process, you can specify one or more of the following triggers:

- ***Record is created*** Creating a new record of an entity
- ***Record status changes*** Changing the status (state) of a record
- ***Record is assigned*** Changing the owner of a record
- ***Record fields change*** Changing one or more values on a record
- ***Record is deleted*** Deleting a record

Most of these triggers are self-explanatory, but we want to clarify the *Record status changes* event. The *Record status changes* event refers to the status or state (schema name of statecode) of an entity, but not the status reason (schema name of statuscode). Table 14-1 displays some sample status and status reason values to illustrate the differences.

TABLE 14-1 Status and Status Reason Values for Select Entities

Entity	Status values	Status Reason values
Account	Active Inactive	Active Inactive
Case	Active Resolved Canceled	In Progress On Hold Waiting for Details Researching Problem Solved Canceled

Entity	Status values	Status Reason values
Lead	Open Qualified Disqualified	New Contacted Qualified Lost Cannot Contact No Longer Interested Canceled
Phone Call	Open Completed Canceled	Open Sent Received Canceled

Many people assume that the *Record status changes* event will execute when changing the status reason of a record. However, changing only the status value will trigger the workflow.

Tip If you want to trigger a workflow process from a change of the status reason attribute, use the *Record fields change* event and select Status Reason (statuscode).

With the *Record fields change* event, you can select one or more attributes of the entity for workflow to monitor. After you select the *Record fields change* event, click the Select button, and then select the attributes you wish to have monitored (see Figure 14-7).

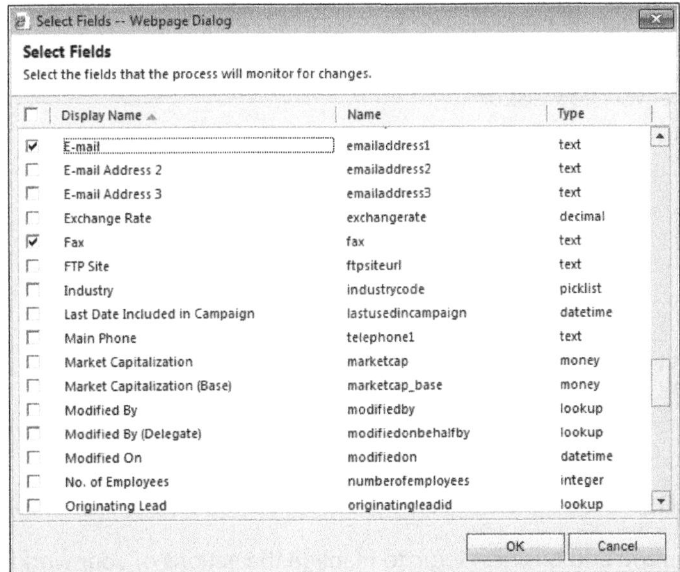

FIGURE 14-7 Choosing fields to monitor in a workflow process

Caution Updates to records happen regularly in the system. Consider this when choosing workflow processes using the *Record fields change* event to avoid unnecessary stress on the system. Further, avoid using *Wait* conditions in workflow processes triggered from this event.

Workflow Process Step Editor

This section covers how you create workflow logic and actions in the workflow process form using the step editor. On the step editor toolbar, you can add various step types, choose whether the newly entered step comes before (above) or after (below) the selected step, and delete steps. By default, steps are added below the selected step. Everything in this editor frame is contextual, meaning that Microsoft Dynamics CRM determines which actions you can take based on the step selected, which is highlighted in the user interface.

When you add any step (conditions or actions), a text box similar to the one shown in Figure 14-8 appears so that you can enter a step description.

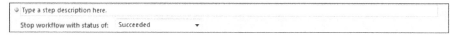

FIGURE 14-8 Step description

We strongly recommend that you take the time to enter a description, which can be referenced when monitoring workflow processes, during the selection of custom workflow actions, and in reporting. Adding a short and meaningful description greatly improves the overall process visibility to the organization. We'll cover the following Add Step choices available to you with the workflow editor:

- Check conditions
- Wait conditions
- Workflow actions
- Stages

Tip Be sure you select the correct row before removing a step. Click the desired row, and it will turn blue when selected.

Check Conditions

By using conditions, you can add business logic to manage the actions of your workflow process. You have the ability to create simple or complex logical statements that control when actions should be taken. Typical scenarios include sending an email message when a record status changes, creating different sets of activities based on the potential revenue of an opportunity, or updating a sales stage when all activities are completed.

After you open a workflow process, click Add Step, and select Check Condition, as shown in Figure 14-9.

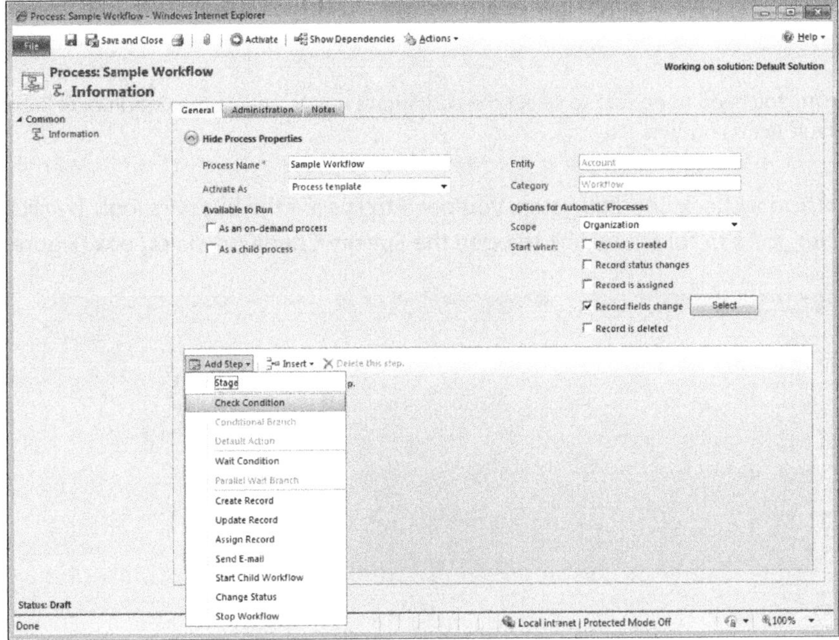

FIGURE 14-9 Adding a workflow check condition

You can create three different check condition branches:

- ***Check Condition*** The first *if-then* statement
- ***Conditional Branch*** An *else-if-then* statement displayed as *Otherwise-if-then* in the user interface
- ***Default Action*** An *else* statement displayed as *Otherwise* in the user interface

Figure 14-10 shows how these steps are displayed in the editor.

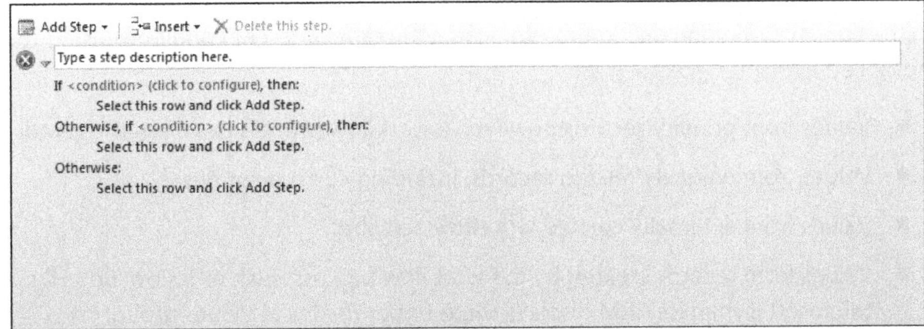

FIGURE 14-10 Check condition steps

Microsoft Dynamics CRM automatically determines which condition option you can insert into a workflow process, depending on which step you select in the statement box. For instance, you can use the Conditional Branch option only when adding a step with an existing Check Condition step.

Caution You need to be sure to select the condition's row to enable the Conditional Branch or Default Action options.

After you add a Check Condition step, you need to specify the business logic by clicking the *<condition> (click to configure)* link to open the Specify Condition dialog box (Figure 14-11).

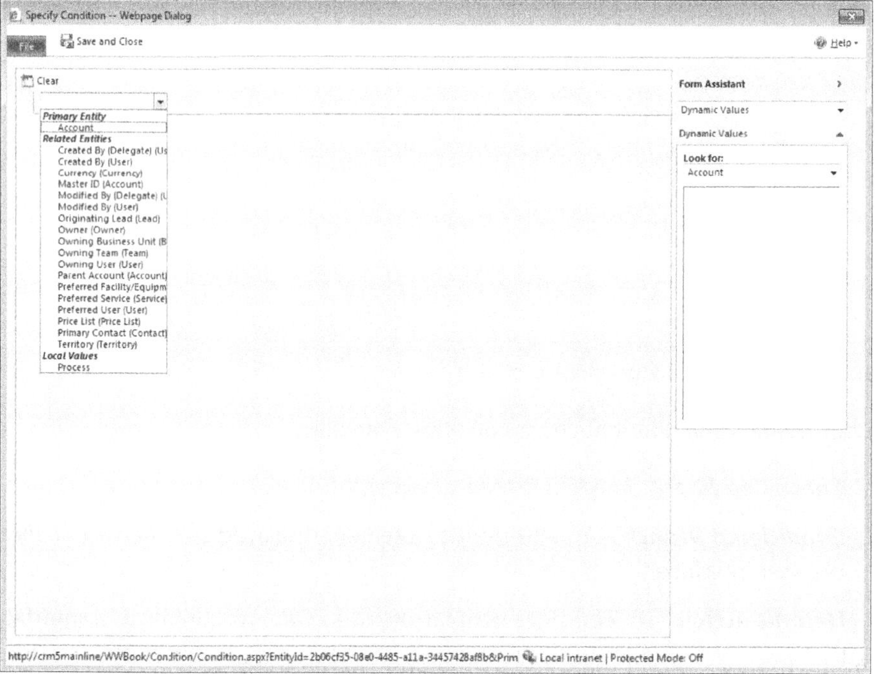

FIGURE 14-11 Specify Condition dialog box

In the Specify Condition dialog box, you can add many different conditions using the familiar Advanced Find interface, such as:

- Values from primary records on which a workflow process has been triggered.
- Values from uniquely related records, including custom entities.
- Values from externally created workflow activities.
- Values from records created by the workflow process, such as follow-up tasks. Microsoft Dynamics CRM displays these under the Local Values group.
- Special workflow conditions, such as activity count and execution time.

You may notice that the interface used to insert dynamic values in a check condition behaves a little differently from the interface for inserting dynamic values in entity records. In particular, you can insert dynamic values in a check condition by placing your cursor in the appropriate field and selecting the dynamic value in the Form Assistant. The user interface does not require you to click the OK button like it does when you insert dynamic values in an entity record.

Wait Conditions

Wait conditions enable you to incorporate time- or event-based dependencies to your workflow process. Common situations in which you can use wait conditions include sending an email message a specified amount of time before a service contract expires or just waiting a given amount of time before following up with a lead.

You create wait conditions the same way that you configure check conditions, including the Execution Time, Activity Count, and Activity Count Including Process conditions on the process. However, you have one extra option available when you configure the wait duration: By using the *Timeout* option, you can have the workflow step wait a specified period of time before continuing. Figure 14-12 shows a condition for a step that waits one month after the workflow is started before it proceeds to the next step.

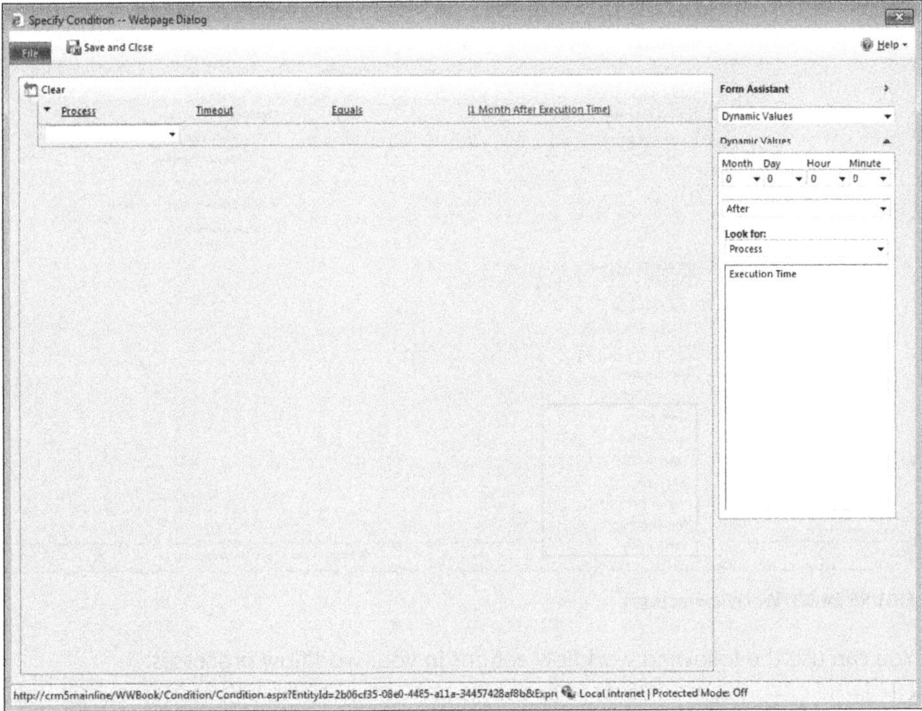

FIGURE 14-12 Wait condition using a timeout

Note One example of using the Activity Count option would be to send a reminder to an individual who owns an account that has open activities if the activities have not been completed within the expected period of time.

A parallel wait branch works similarly to the condition branch described earlier, so that conditions are compared similarly to an if-then statement.

Workflow Process Actions

Now that you understand conditions, we'll explain the workflow process actions that you can execute. Actions are the steps taken by the workflow process when the specified conditions are met. After you select a row, click Add Step to see the list of workflow actions available, as shown in Figure 14-13.

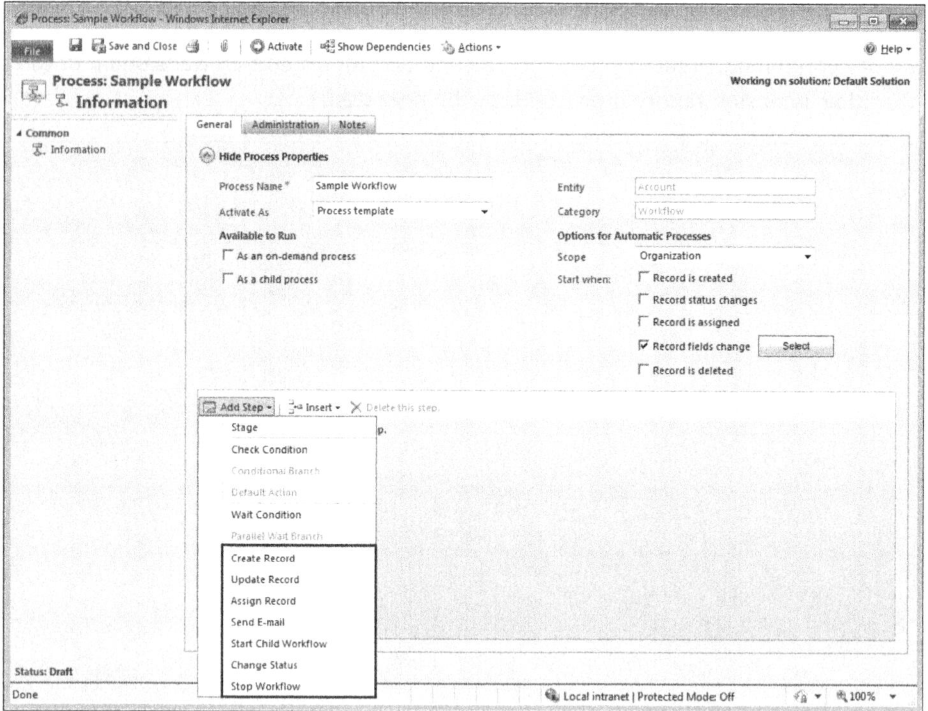

FIGURE 14-13 Workflow actions

You can use the following workflow actions in your workflow processes:

- Create Record
- Update Record

- Assign Record
- Send E-mail
- Start Child Workflow
- Change Status
- Stop Workflow
- Custom workflow actions

Note You will only see options for custom workflow actions in your system after custom workflow activities are registered.

Create Record

Use the Create Record action to create a Microsoft Dynamics CRM record, including activities and custom entity records. After you select this action, choose the entity type of the record you want to create, and click Set Properties to open a form in which you can specify default attribute values for the newly created record. Figure 14-14 shows the empty Task form that appears when creating a Task record in a workflow process.

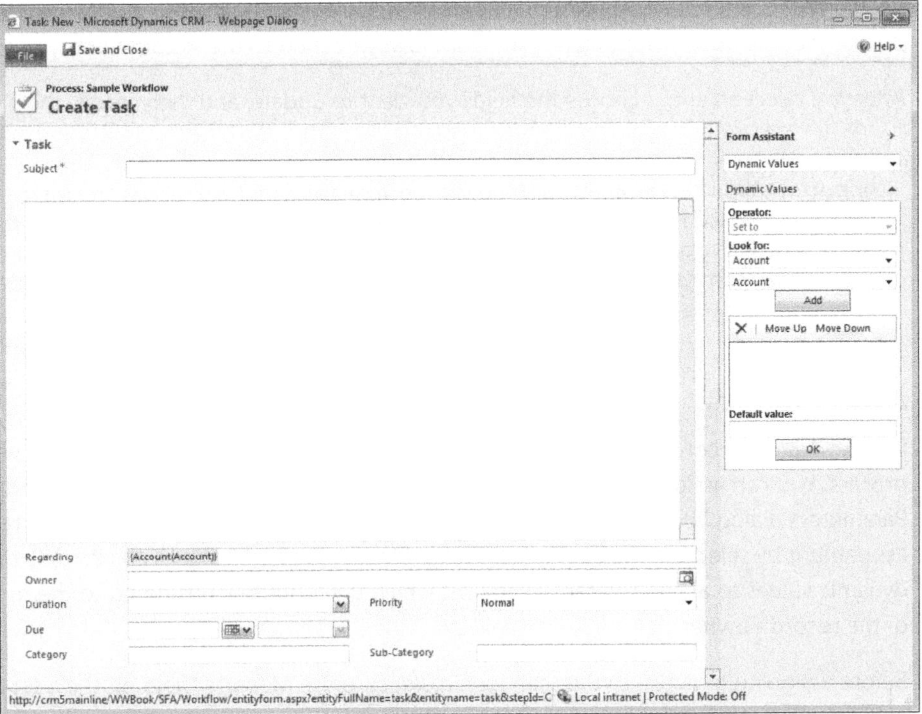

FIGURE 14-14 Workflow Create Task dialog box

Enter data in the various entity fields so that Microsoft Dynamics CRM workflow automatically creates the record with the values you specify. In some situations, you may want the same data to appear for all of the created records. In other cases, you will probably want Microsoft Dynamics CRM to populate the fields with dynamic data, depending on your business rules. Dynamic values are explained in detail later in this chapter.

Update Record

By using the Update Record action, you can update one or more fields when a workflow condition is met. For example, you can create an Opportunity workflow process that automatically changes the Opportunity's Priority field to *High* if the estimated value of a deal is greater than $100,000.

You can use the Update Record action to update data values in the record on which the workflow process is running, as in the preceding example, or in records of other entities related to the primary workflow entity. For example, you can create a workflow process that updates the Relationship Type field of an account to a value of *Prospect* if someone creates an opportunity for that account. Microsoft Dynamics CRM automatically determines which related entities you can update. For the most part, you can update values in related entities only if the entity has a primary relationship to the workflow entity. Because Account is the primary entity in relation to the Opportunity entity, Microsoft Dynamics CRM lets you update fields on the Account form in Opportunity workflow processes. However, the inverse is not true. You cannot update the value of an Opportunity for workflows attached to the Account entity.

After you select an entity, choose the fields you want to update, and then specify the new values.

Important Updating an entity will trigger any plug-ins or workflow processes registered to the entity. We recommend diagramming your process flows to see what effects running the workflow will have on other processes. You should be aware if a workflow updates a record that then triggers a series of plug-ins or other workflows to ensure that you are not triggering unnecessary processes or starting an infinite loop of updates.

Assign Record

Use the Assign Record action to change the owner of the record referenced in the workflow process. You can assign records to a user or team using the lookup on the Edit Assign Step Parameters dialog box, or you can use dynamic values to perform more advanced record assignment by selecting the Set Properties option. Figure 14-15 shows an example of using dynamic values to assign the record against which the workflow is running to the manager of the record's owner.

Before assigning a record to the manager, make sure the Manager field on the User form contains data for each user. If a manager isn't specified, the workflow will generate an error when it tries to complete the assignment.

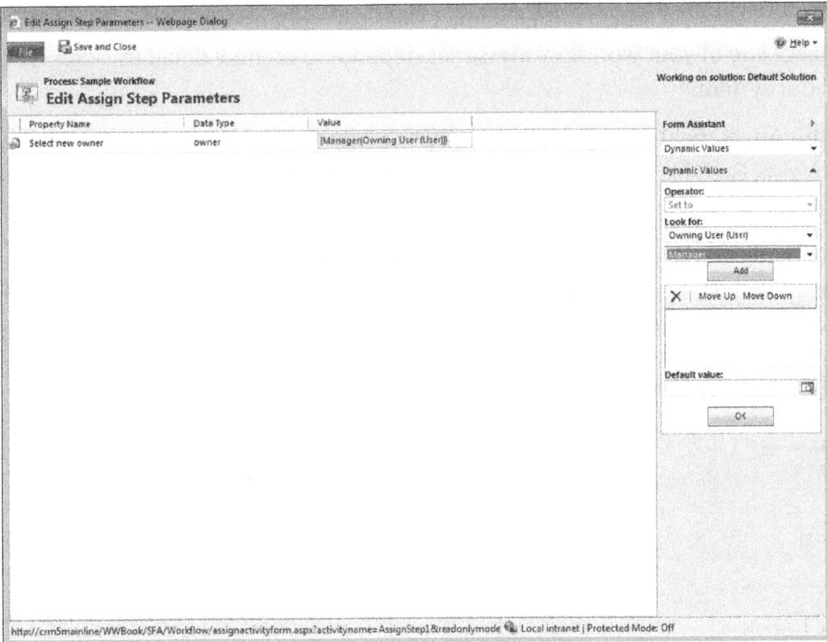

FIGURE 14-15 Workflow Edit Assign Step Parameters dialog box

If you assign a record to the manager or to a user, Microsoft Dynamics CRM changes the owner of the record when the workflow runs.

Send E-mail

Use the Send E-mail action when you want to send an email message as part of your workflow process. Select the Send E-mail action, and then specify whether you wish to create a new message or use an existing template. When you click Set Properties, the dialog box shown in Figure 14-16 appears.

From here, you can configure the key attributes of the message, such as the recipients, subject, and body. The following are some of the important details and constraints related to sending email messages with workflow:

- You can select an E-mail template if the entity of the workflow process offers a template or if entities related to the primary workflow entity or created by the workflow offer a template. You will need to specify the email message recipient (*To*) and sender (*From*) values. Failure to provide recipient and sender values will generate an error when the workflow executes.
- Although Microsoft Dynamics CRM sends the message as HTML instead of plain text, the workflow email editor toolbar does not include buttons to insert images or hyperlinks. However, you can select images and hyperlinks in a Web browser and then copy and paste them into the Description box (Body) of the email message.

- For email tracking, Microsoft Dynamics CRM can append the tracking code to the Subject line of your workflow messages depending on how email tracking is configured in your system.
- In the Attachments tab, you can specify as many file attachments per email message as you wish. Each file can only be as large as the maximum file size specified in the system settings.
- You may encounter formatting differences between the email text shown when configuring the workflow compared to the actual message sent. Send yourself a test email to verify that the email text is generated correctly before finalizing the workflow process.

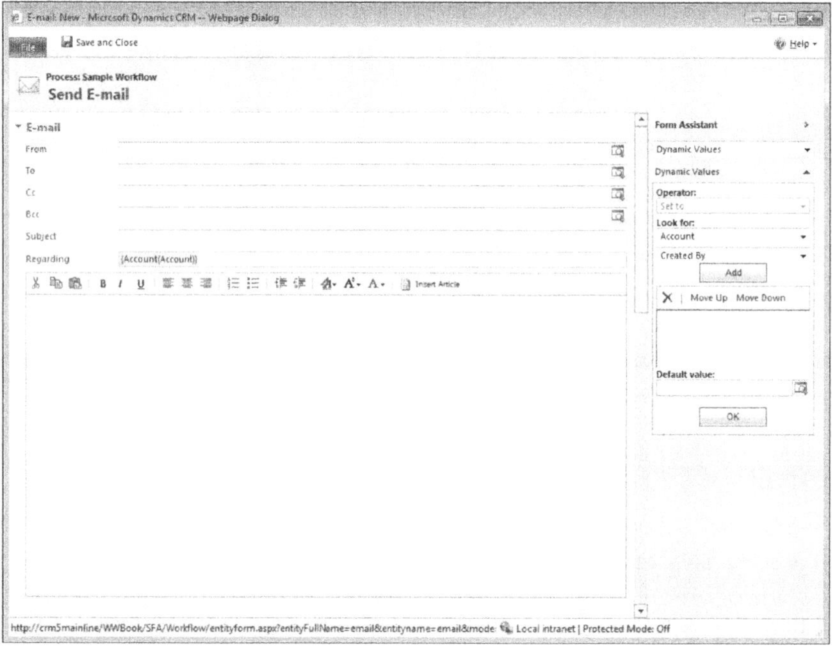

FIGURE 14-16 Send E-mail Set Properties dialog box

Tip You can use the email recipient fields (To, CC, BCC) to add multiple individuals, including dynamic values. However, when you add a dynamic value to one of these fields, you'll notice that Microsoft Dynamics CRM hides the lookup button in that field, preventing you from selecting a specific record, such as a contact or user. If you want to send an email message to a set of recipients that includes at least one dynamic value and one static record, don't worry—we have a solution for you.

Assume you want to create a workflow email message that includes a dynamic value to CC the account owner, but you also want to CC a user named Alan Brewer. To accomplish this, first add a dynamic value to the CC field that includes the account owner. After you do this, the lookup button in the CC field disappears. Next, add a second dynamic value to the CC field but do not actually select a dynamic field in the Dynamic Values box. Instead, simply select the user Alan Brewer using the Default value lookup button (Figure 14-17) and click OK.

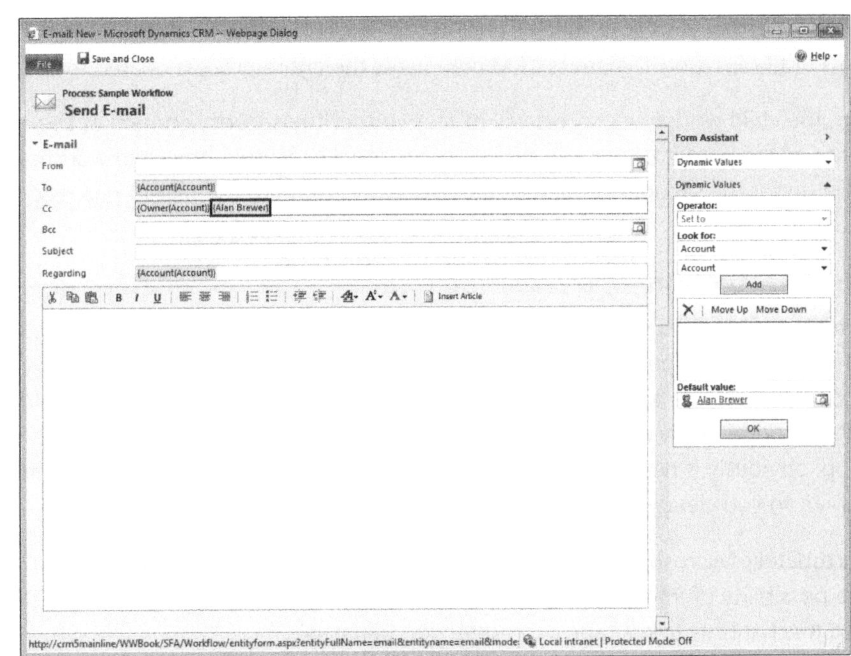

FIGURE 14-17 Including dynamic and static values in an email recipient field

When Microsoft Dynamics CRM runs this workflow process, it will always include Alan Brewer as a CC recipient because it won't find a dynamic value for that field and Alan Brewer is the default value.

Start Child Workflow

By using the Child Workflow action, you can execute an entirely separate workflow process as an action in the original workflow process. You can reference a workflow process as a child only if it has the *As a child workflow* option selected in the Available to Run section.

When you start to develop a large number of workflow processes, you may find that multiple processes perform the same subset of actions. To help make workflow processes easier to manage, you can create a workflow process that performs this subset of actions, and then have all other processes run this subset workflow process as a child workflow. Then, if you need to change the subset of actions, you have to edit only the subset workflow process for the new logic to be applied immediately to all of the workflow processes that reference this rule.

When you're using child workflow processes, remember that child workflow runs *asynchronously.* Therefore, the parent workflow process will execute the child workflow process and then continue to the next step without waiting for the child workflow to finish its logic. The simplest way to ensure that execution in a workflow process is synchronous is to rewrite the process to avoid using a child workflow. If you require a child workflow to execute synchronously, use a custom workflow activity in the child workflow. When a workflow process executes a custom workflow activity, it does not proceed to the next step in the workflow process until Microsoft Dynamics CRM completes the entire process related to the activity.

Finally, the child workflow process will execute under the security context of the executing instance of the parent process. In the case of manual execution, the child workflow process will run under the security context of the user who triggered the parent process.

Loop Detection

When you use child workflow processes, you might accidentally create a situation in which a workflow process can't ever complete because it's stuck in a loop. Or you might accidentally create a loop by designing a workflow process that updates a field on your record triggered by changes to that field. If a workflow process gets stuck in an infinite loop, obviously it negatively affects the performance of your Microsoft Dynamics CRM server, so you clearly want to avoid these situations.

Fortunately, Microsoft Dynamics CRM includes loop detection logic to help minimize the possibility of infinite loops occurring in the system. Microsoft Dynamics CRM uses two mechanisms to manage loop detection behavior:

- Depth counter
- Time expiration boundary

Microsoft Dynamics CRM automatically tracks a variable known as *depth counter*, which increments each time it executes a process. By default, Microsoft Dynamics CRM allows the workflow process to continue up to eight times before automatically halting the process. However, you may, for example, have a workflow that each year updates a contract's renewal date. In this situation, you would not want the workflow to stop operating on that record after eight successive actions. Microsoft Dynamics CRM handles this situation by using a concept known as the *time expiration boundary*. If the workflow is still active and hasn't been executed for a specified period of time, Microsoft Dynamics CRM resets the depth counter to zero.

Even though Microsoft Dynamics CRM provides this behavior, you should always carefully examine your business logic and test your complex workflow processes in a development environment to avoid infinite loops.

Change Status

Use the Change Status action to change the status (statecode) and status reason (statuscode) of a record. You can change the status of the record that triggered the workflow process instance, a related record, or a record created from within the workflow process.

Tip One case where we often use workflow is to automate the process of creating activities. For example, you may want to allow a user to run a workflow manually to create and complete a task when he updates the contacts associated with an account. To do this, you must first write a Create Record step to create the task and then follow that step with a Change Status step to mark that task as Complete. This process is shown in Figure 14-18.

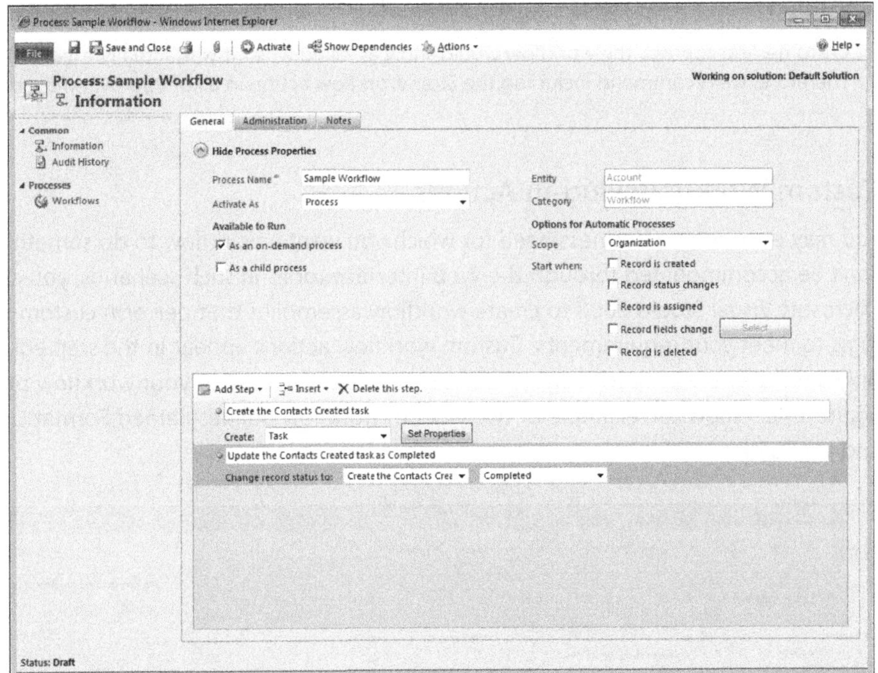

FIGURE 14-18 Updating the status of an Activity created within the workflow process

The same steps must be taken when creating an appointment activity to mark the time as Busy.

Stop Workflow

A workflow processes all of the conditions and actions that you configure, and then it considers the process finished. However, you may face a situation in which you want to stop a workflow somewhere in the middle of its process, typically when a condition is not met. You can use the Stop Workflow action in such situations. When you insert a stop action, you can select from one of the following two options:

- ***Succeeded*** Immediately stops the workflow process with a status of *Succeeded*
- ***Canceled*** Immediately stops the workflow process with a status of *Canceled*

Best Practices By including a stop workflow action in all of your processes, you can make sure that Microsoft Dynamics CRM closes all of your processes completely. A great example of when you would definitely want to use this step is when evaluating criteria from multiple entity types. For example, you have a workflow that updates the related account when the Potential Customer field of an opportunity is an account. If an opportunity is created with the Potential Customer field set to a contact, you should prevent the workflow from running. If you do not use the Stop Workflow step, anytime the workflow process is run against an opportunity where the Potential Customer is a contact, the workflow would show as failed when it was actually executed properly. Therefore, we recommend including the Stop Workflow action in all of your workflow processes.

Custom Workflow Plug-in Actions

You may encounter a business need for which you want a workflow to do something that can't be accommodated through the Web interface tools. In such scenarios, you can use Microsoft Visual Studio 2008 to create workflow assemblies that perform custom business logic to meet your requirements. Custom workflow actions appear in the step editor only after they are properly registered against the entity used in your workflow process. Figure 14-19 shows an example of two custom workflow utilities named Format Line Breaks and Url Builder.

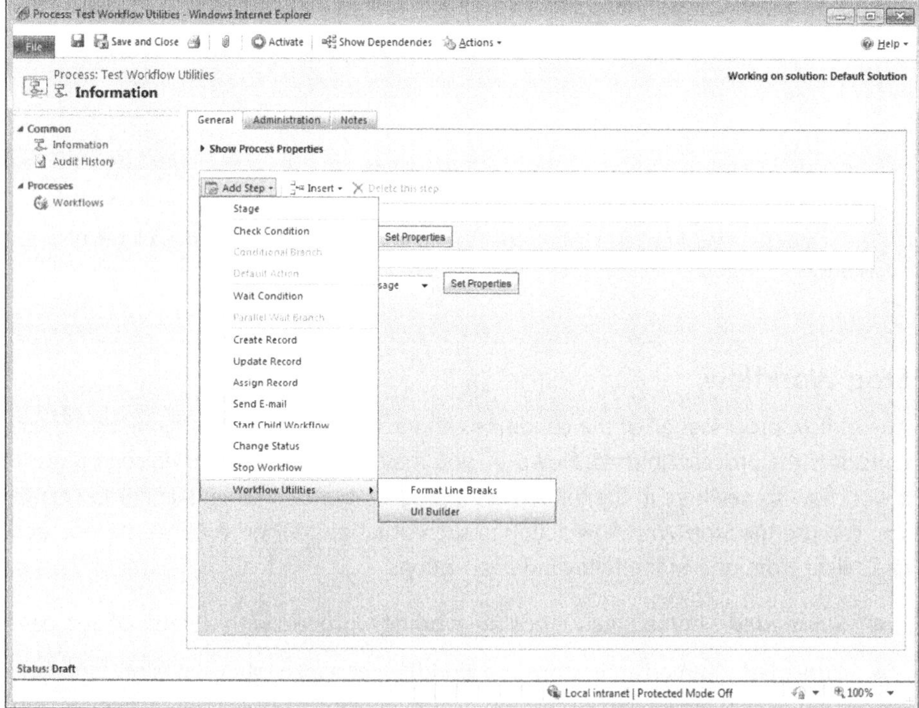

FIGURE 14-19 Custom workflow assembly actions

More Info Currently, you cannot use custom workflow actions with Microsoft Dynamics CRM Online. This option applies only to on-premise or partner-hosted deployments of Microsoft Dynamics CRM.

Stages

Stages act as groups for workflow steps, and you can add a stage to encapsulate common business steps. To add a stage to a workflow process, click Add Step, and then click Stage. In the blue background box, you can then add a stage description. Just as with steps, we recommend you take the time to describe each of the stages that you add.

Note If you add a stage to a workflow process, all steps in that process must be part of a stage. Microsoft Dynamics CRM informs you of this requirement when you add your first stage to a new workflow process.

In Microsoft Dynamics CRM, you can add stages to any entity in workflow. If you want, you can add wait conditions to each stage so that Microsoft Dynamics CRM won't proceed to the next stage until the workflow process satisfies the wait conditions. Figure 14-20 shows a sample workflow process with stages.

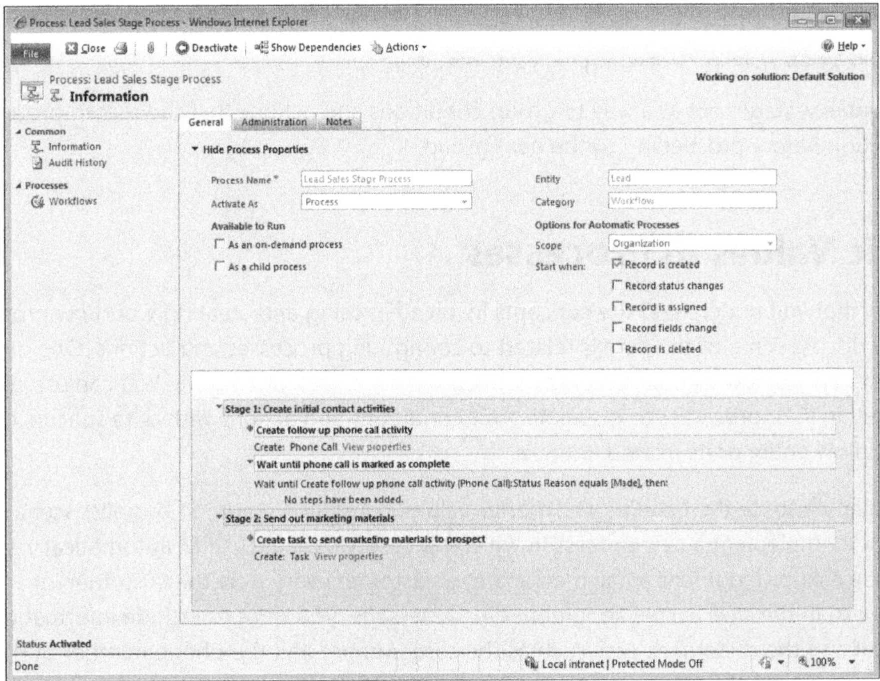

FIGURE 14-20 Sample workflow process with stages

In this example, the workflow process creates a new Phone Call activity after a Lead is created. The last step of the first stage is to wait until that Phone Call activity is closed before moving to Stage 2 (see Figure 14-21).

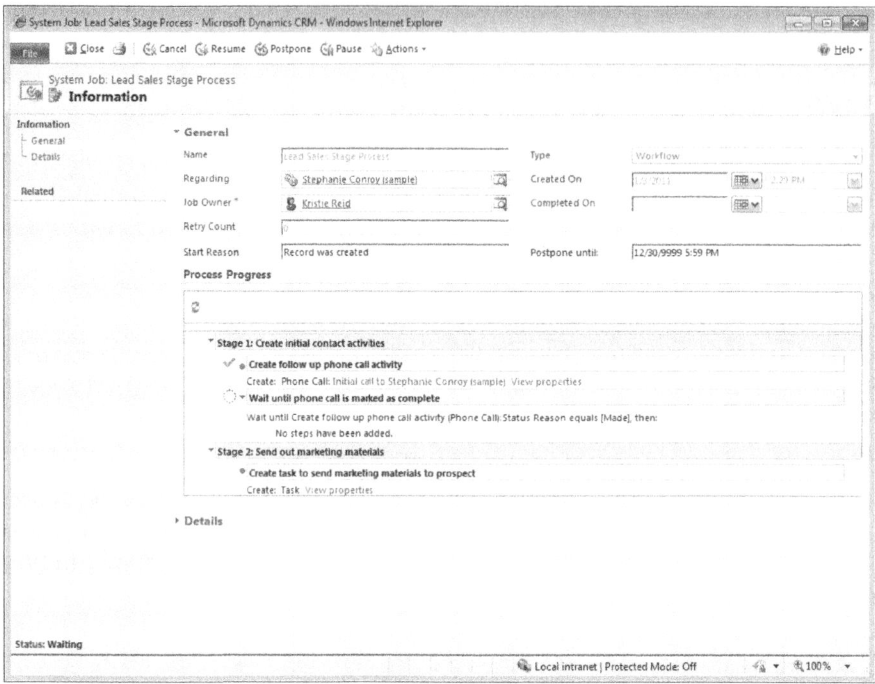

FIGURE 14-21 Workflow waiting to progress to next stage

Essentially, stages act as a way to group conditions and actions that the record progresses through before proceeding to the next group.

Dynamic Values in Processes

Now that you understand the concepts involved in using and creating workflow processes, let's discuss some of the details related to configuring processes and actions. One of the most important workflow features that you will use is *dynamic values*. You can use dynamic values in your processes to populate your conditions and actions with data specific to the workflow entity or its related entities.

To help illustrate the benefits of dynamic values, consider a common business scenario. You want to implement a new process in which Microsoft Dynamics CRM automatically sends a case acknowledgment email message to a customer every time the customer logs a service request. In the case acknowledgment email message, you want to include information specific to the customer's case such as the case number and the phone number of the case owner. Because the information you want to include in the message changes for each case, you must use dynamic values in the Send E-mail workflow action. We explain the details behind setting dynamic values shortly, but Figure 14-22 shows the final Send E-mail workflow configuration. The highlighted fields include the dynamic data.

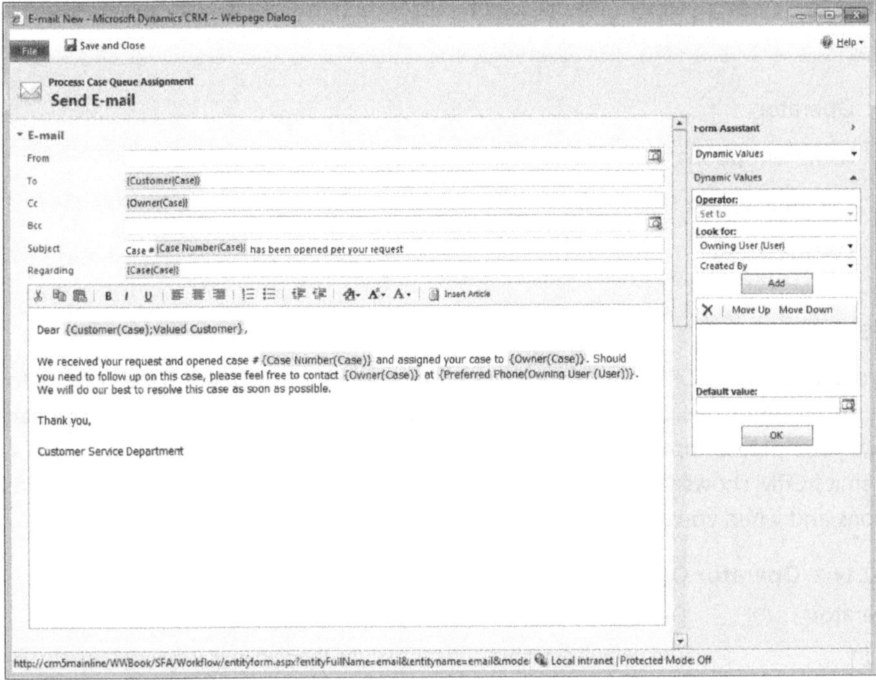

FIGURE 14-22 Dynamic values used in a Send E-mail workflow action

Note The preceding example assumes that cases are always owned by a user, not a team as indicated in the {Preferred Phone(Owning User (User))} dynamic value. Natively, there is no phone number associated with a team. You may also want to include a generic phone number as a default value to ensure that this element always contains data.

You access dynamic values in processes from the Form Assistant located on the right side of the form as shown in Figure 14-22. Microsoft Dynamics CRM automatically changes the dynamic values choices based on multiple criteria. To insert a dynamic value in a workflow process, select a field on the form where you want the dynamic value to appear, use the Form Assistant to select the value, and then click OK.

Tip Because the dynamic values Form Assistant automatically updates the options depending on your context, we must admit it can cause a little confusion when you initially start working with workflow processes. However, you will quickly become comfortable using dynamic values in all processes. One other thing to be aware of is that when using Dynamic Forms in an area such as the body of an email message, you may need to change the focus to another field and then move the focus back to the body to clear the dynamic values Form Assistant.

In addition to including dynamic values in the form, you also can use dynamic values to update data fields even if the attribute does not appear on the entity form. You can access non-form attributes on the Additional Fields tab.

In the Form Assistant pane, you can see the following aspects of dynamic values:

- Operator
- Look for options
- Dynamic Values box
- Default value

Operator

Microsoft Dynamics CRM automatically updates the operator values based on the form field with the current focus. So, if you select a numeric field on the form, Microsoft Dynamics CRM shows you operator options specific to numeric fields; when you select a date field, Microsoft Dynamics CRM shows you options specific to date fields. Table 14-2 shows the operator options and when you can apply them.

TABLE 14-2 Operator Options

Operator	Description
Set to	The default operator. Simply assigns the dynamic value to the field. For *DateTime* fields, additional time options are displayed.
Increment by	Can be used to increase the current value by the selected dynamic value. Available only for numeric fields for the Update Record action.
Decrement by	Can be used to reduce the current value by the selected dynamic value. Available only for numeric fields for the Update Record action.
Multiply by	Used to multiply the current value by the selected dynamic value. Available only for numeric fields for the Update Record action.
Clear	Removes the current value from the field. Available only with the Update Record action.

Important The *Set to* operator is the only option displayed unless you are using the Update Record action.

When you select a date field, Microsoft Dynamics CRM displays different operator options, as shown in Figure 14-23. By using the date-specific options, you can define the dynamic value for dates to be a certain amount of time before or after a date field.

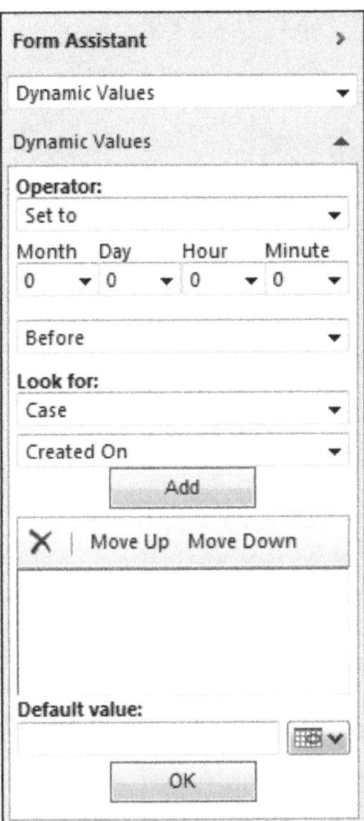

FIGURE 14-23 Date-based dynamic values options

Look for Options

Microsoft Dynamics CRM splits the Look for options into entity and field lists. The entity list displays the current primary entity, all related entities, a workflow option, and any custom assembly steps configured in the workflow process (Figure 14-24). The list of fields is contextually driven by the choice of the entity list and displays only those fields of the data type available for the field currently in focus. Almost all fields are available, including custom attributes.

If you select the Process option in the Look for picklist, as shown in Figure 14-24, the user interface displays these special attribute choices (depending on the field with focus):

- ***Activity Count*** The current number of activities associated with the primary entity, excluding any created by the workflow process.
- ***Activity Count Including Workflow*** The current number of activities associated with the primary entity plus any activities specifically created by the workflow process.
- ***Execution Time*** The amount of time elapsed on the current workflow step. The execution time value resets each time a step is taken.

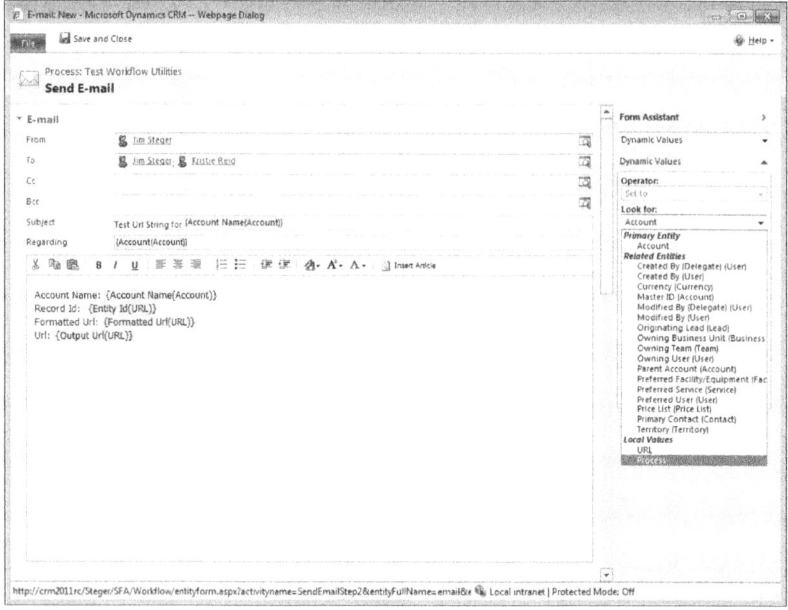

FIGURE 14-24 Accessing primary entity, related entity, custom assembly steps, and local values in dynamic values

If you configure a wait condition and select the Process option, Microsoft Dynamics CRM will give you a fourth option, Timeout. If you select Timeout, you can also access a special Duration dynamic value in addition to the typical Before and After values (Figure 14-25). By using the Duration option, you can specify an amount of time the workflow process should wait before it proceeds to the next step.

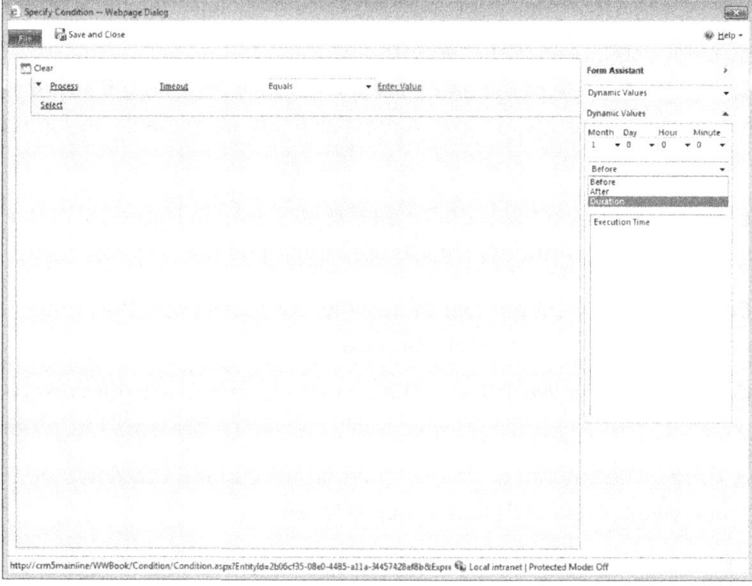

FIGURE 14-25 Accessing the Duration option for a Timeout wait condition

Tip For wait conditions, you will almost always want to use the Timeout option to ensure that the workflow process waits the correct amount of time before proceeding to the next step.

Dynamic Values Box

The dynamic values box stores the values you add. Most of the time, you will have only one value; however, the design allows for multiple values should one of them be null. A common use for this technique is choosing a customer value for an opportunity or case. Because the customer of an opportunity can either be an account or a contact, you may want to configure dynamic values to accommodate either scenario (Figure 14-26). In this example, Microsoft Dynamics CRM will try to populate the top value in the box (Account Name) as the dynamic value. If no account name value exists because the customer of the opportunity is a contact, Microsoft Dynamics CRM will try to populate the dynamic value with the next value in the box. If that value doesn't exist either, workflow will populate the dynamic value using the default value that you specify.

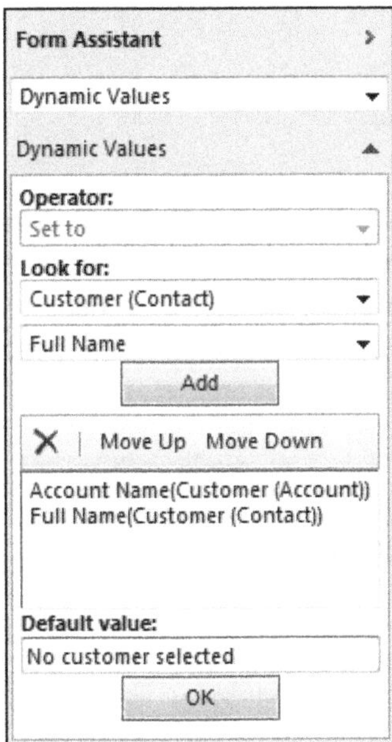

FIGURE 14-26 Multiple values selected in the dynamic values box

Default Value

If your dynamic value doesn't return any data from the database, you can use the default value to ensure the field contains some data. The example in Figure 14-26 shows that if an Account Name from the account or Full Name from the contact do not exist, the user will be notified of this with the result of No customer selected. You should strongly consider specifying a default value unless you are certain the data field chosen will always have data populated. Default values do not apply to workflow wait conditions.

Monitoring Workflow Processes

As we explained previously, the Microsoft Dynamics CRM Asynchronous Processing Service runs constantly behind the scenes, evaluating your workflow processes, Microsoft Dynamics CRM data, and events. System jobs (such as workflow processes) can have one of the following status reasons:

- Canceled
- Canceling
- Failed
- In Progress
- Pausing
- Succeeded
- Waiting
- Waiting for Resources

You can use the Microsoft Dynamics CRM Web interface to monitor workflow process jobs in any of these statuses from the workflow record, the related Microsoft Dynamics CRM record, or System Jobs. This flexibility provides you with the information you need to quickly determine which jobs have been executed and also to help you troubleshoot any failures.

In this section, we review the following:

- Monitoring workflow jobs from the workflow process record
- Accessing workflow jobs from a Microsoft Dynamics CRM record
- Accessing workflow jobs from System Jobs
- Reviewing the log details on an existing workflow process instance
- Taking action on existing workflow processes

Monitoring Workflow Jobs from the Workflow Process Record

The workflow process record contains a convenient Workflows link that lists all executed instances of the process in the system, including their status, as shown in Figure 14-27.

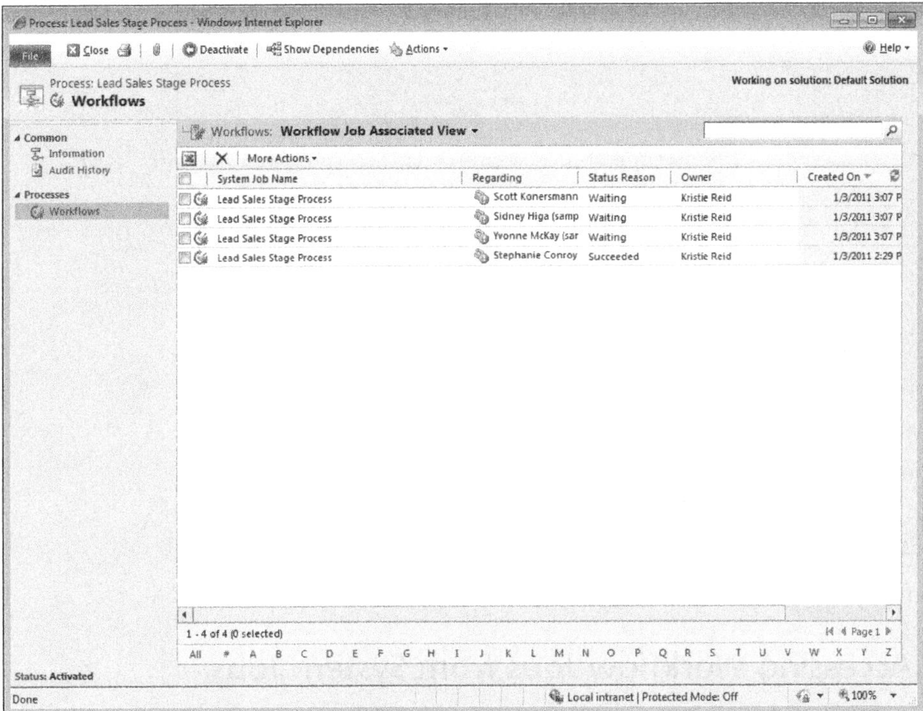

FIGURE 14-27 Reviewing workflow instances from the workflow process record

Because workflow security behaves similarly to the other entity, you have access to view instantiated workflows from the workflow process record only if you have Read privileges on the Process entity.

Accessing Workflow Jobs from a Microsoft Dynamics CRM Record

Microsoft Dynamics CRM conveniently lets you view and access any workflow processes running against a record directly from the record. You can click the Workflows link (Figure 14-28) in a record to show all workflow processes that have been executed or that are executing against the record.

Caution If a user opens a record in Microsoft Dynamics CRM, she can view a list of the workflow jobs related to that record in the Workflows associated view if the user's security role includes *any level* of Read access to the System Job entity. So, even if a user has only User level access to read System Jobs records, she can view all of the workflow processes running on the record from that record's Workflows view. This security behavior is unique because you would expect that this user would only see the system jobs that she owns. This exception exists to allow users to see all jobs to provide backward compatibility with the Microsoft Dynamics CRM 3.0 Sales Processes. Fortunately, if a user tries to open the workflow job and view the details, Microsoft Dynamics CRM will not let the user view that record if her security role doesn't allow it.

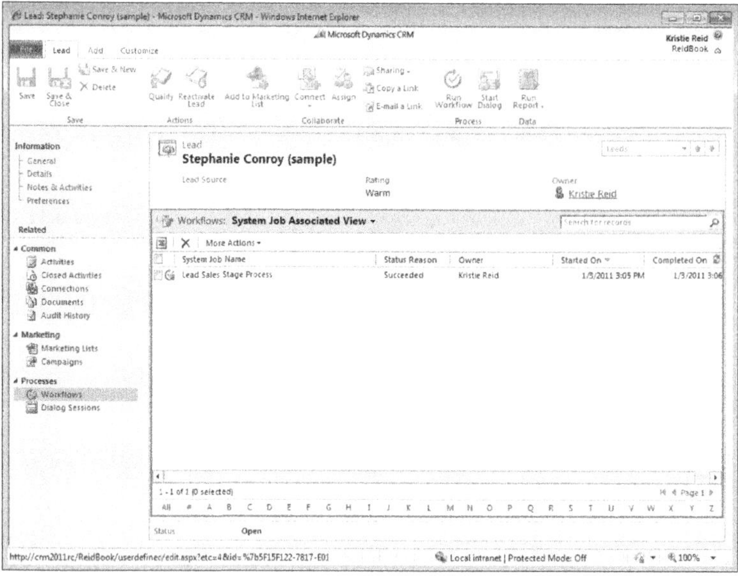

FIGURE 14-28 Workflows associated view from a record

Accessing Workflow Jobs from System Jobs

You can also view all instantiated workflow processes from the System Jobs link in the Settings area. Any user with the Read privilege on the System Job entity is able to access this area. In this view, an administrator can monitor all asynchronous jobs executed against Microsoft Dynamics CRM. To view only workflow processes, enable filters under the More Actions menu and select Workflow in the System Job Type column, as shown in Figure 14-29.

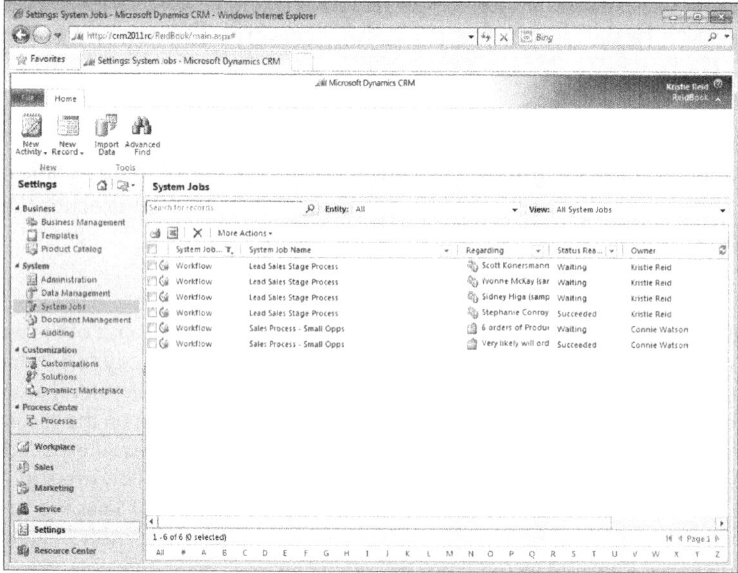

FIGURE 14-29 Workflow process instances in the System Jobs view

Reviewing Log Details

Regardless of where you access the executed workflow processes, you can review the details of any step by resting the mouse on the icon to the left of each step (see Figure 14-30).

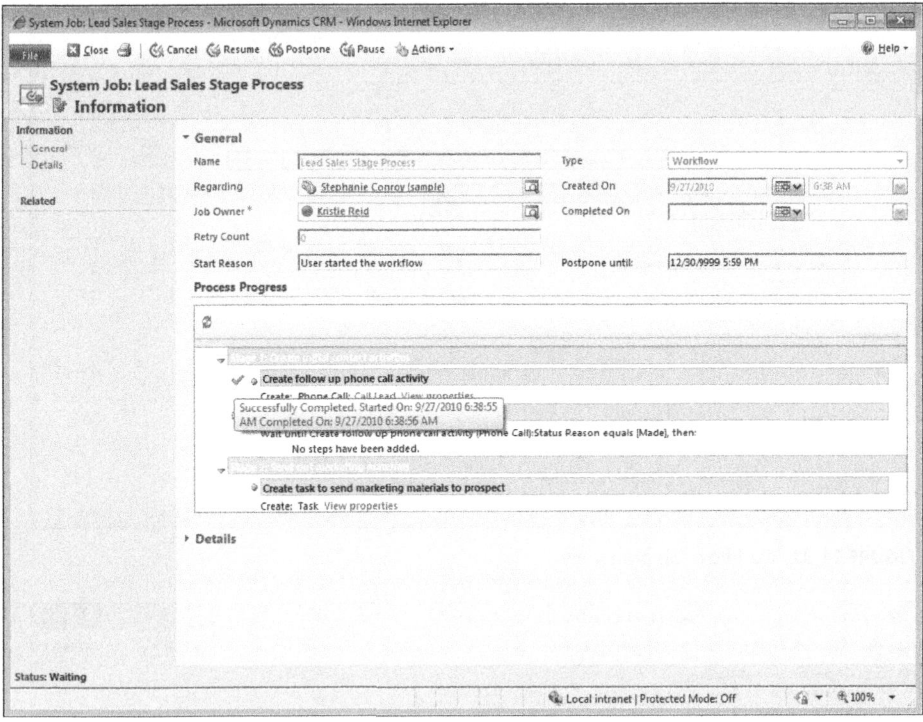

FIGURE 14-30 Accessing workflow log details from the step's tooltip

If your workflow process includes a large number of steps, resting your mouse on each step can be tedious. Fortunately, if you access the print view of a workflow job you can view all of the workflow details in a single layout. Figure 14-31 shows a sample print view, and you can see that it includes the details of each step.

To assist in identifying why jobs have failed or have a status reason of Waiting for reasons other than a wait step, additional information is available in the Details section, as shown in Figure 14-32.

The Retry Count displays the number of times that a job has attempted to run. The Postpone until field displays when the workflow will attempt to rerun the workflow process. This field can be edited. A user-friendly message of why the workflow did not complete successfully also is displayed to help identify what occurred. If that information is not enough, the Details tab includes the full XML error and exception that was produced by Windows Workflow Foundation.

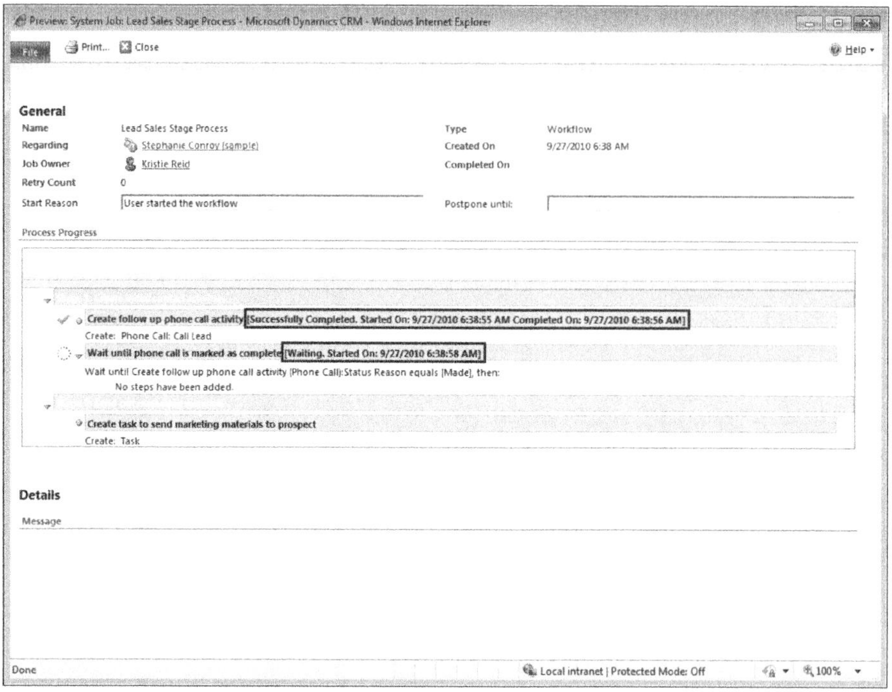

FIGURE 14-31 Workflow job print view

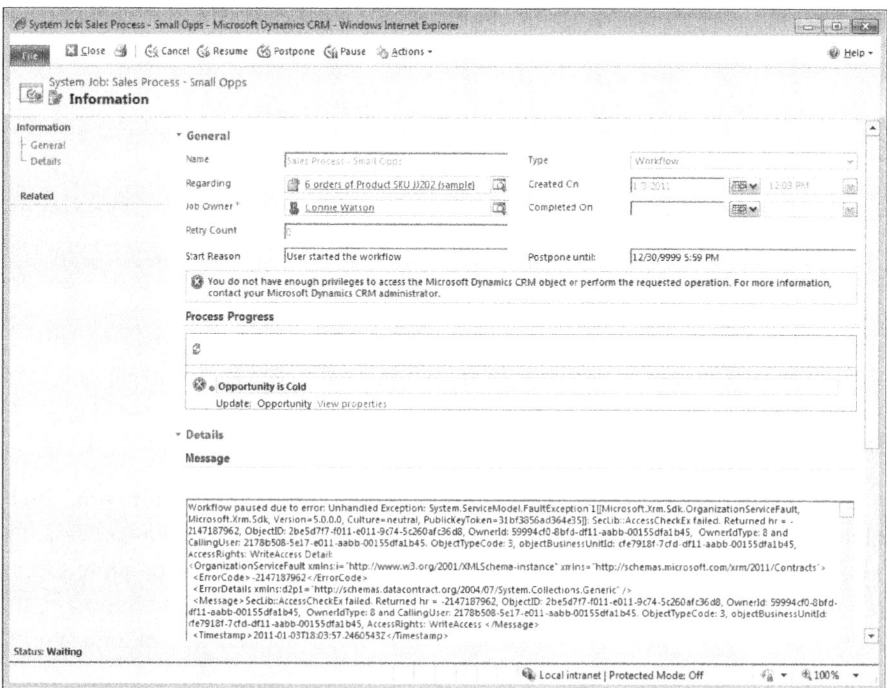

FIGURE 14-32 Workflow print details

Taking Actions on Existing Workflow Jobs

When you view a workflow process, provided that you have permissions to read and write to the system job, you can take the following actions:

- **Cancel** You can terminate an instance. No further steps will be executed.
- **Resume** You can resume a paused instance. If the Asynchronous Service paused the instance because of an error, you must correct the error before resuming.
- **Postpone** You can delay the execution of the instance until a future date and time.
- **Pause** You can manually pause an instance at any time.

Importing and Exporting Processes

Just as with most of the Microsoft Dynamics CRM customizations and settings, you can import and export workflow processes from one Microsoft Dynamics CRM system to another. Therefore, you can create and test all of your workflow processes on a development system and deploy them to your production environment.

If you are using the default solution, all workflow processes—even draft processes—will export as part of that solution, so you will have everything you need when you import it into a separate organization. However, if you are using solutions—managed or unmanaged—for your processes, you will need to make sure that all of the components related to your process are included in the solution. In addition, any entities that are included in your solution will need to be published to ensure that any form or field updates are available for the process to use once imported into another organization.

Fortunately, Microsoft Dynamics CRM warns you of any dependencies when adding a process to a solution. The warnings also are displayed throughout the export process to ensure that the solution can be imported correctly later, so that you understand which customizations need to be published and which components are required to successfully import the solution. When importing solutions, you also have the ability to activate any processes after the import process is completed by selecting the *Activate any processes and enable any SDK message processing steps included in the solution* check box, as shown in Figure 14-33.

When you import workflow processes into a system, be mindful that some references may be specific to the original system. Some potential workflow import issues include the following:

- **Missing entities or attributes** Microsoft Dynamics CRM will not allow you to import a process that includes references to custom entities or custom attributes that don't exist in the target system or is not part of the solution.
- **Missing custom workflow activities** Microsoft Dynamics CRM will not allow you to import a process that references a custom workflow activity that does not exist in the target system or is not part of the solution.

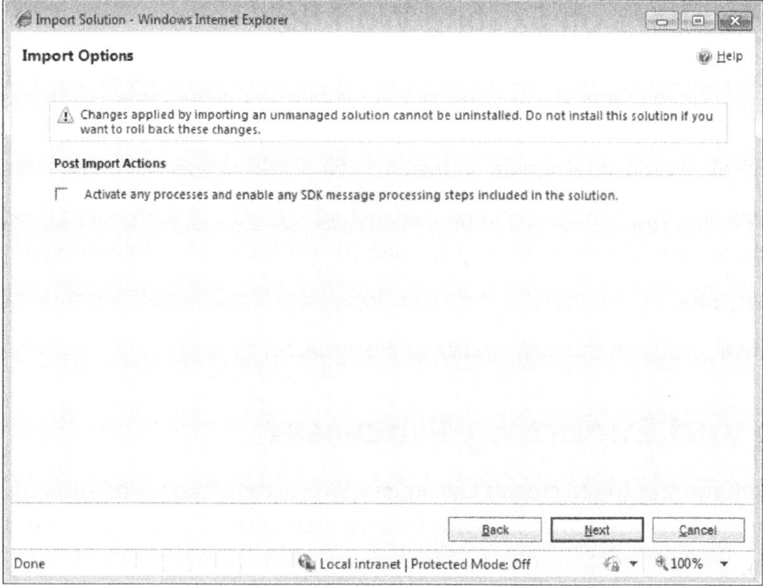

FIGURE 14-33 Solution import option to activate processes

- **User references** If workflow processes include references to specific users, Microsoft Dynamics CRM will maintain the user reference if you import the process to a target system on the same Microsoft Active Directory domain. If you import workflow processes between two different domains or into a Microsoft Dynamics CRM instance that does not contain the specified user, you need to update all of the user references manually before you can publish the imported process. You will receive a warning at the end of the solution import indicating that the user is missing and the process will remain deactivated.

Workflow Process Examples

Now that you understand the concepts and details related to Microsoft Dynamics CRM workflow processes, a few examples can show you how to pull everything together in real-world workflow processes. This section demonstrates the following common scenarios:

- Creating a business process for a new lead
- Escalating overdue service cases

Creating a Business Process for a New Lead

Assume your company would like to use a standardized process to handle each lead created in Microsoft Dynamics CRM. However, the business process varies depending on the source and location of each prospective client. The sales manager gives you the following requirements:

- If the lead comes from the web, send the lead an email message to acknowledge the request.
- For all leads (regardless of origin), create a phone call follow-up activity due one day after the lead is created assigned to the owner of the lead.
- Wait 14 days and determine whether the lead is still open. If yes, create a follow-up task due one day later to reconnect.
- Wait 30 days and evaluate the lead's status again. If it's still open, disqualify the lead.

This example will demonstrate the following features in workflow:

- Using conditions to create different sets of activities
- Using the Send E-mail action to send an email message
- Using the Create Activity action to generate activity records for the lead's owner
- Using the Wait condition to perform subsequent checks on the record

Creating the process

1. Log on to the Microsoft Dynamics CRM Web application, click Settings, and then click Processes.
2. Click New on the Processes grid toolbar. The Create Process dialog box appears.
3. In the Create Process dialog box, type **New Lead Process** in the Process name field, select Lead in the Entity list, and select Workflow as the Category. Ensure that *New blank process* is selected, and click OK.

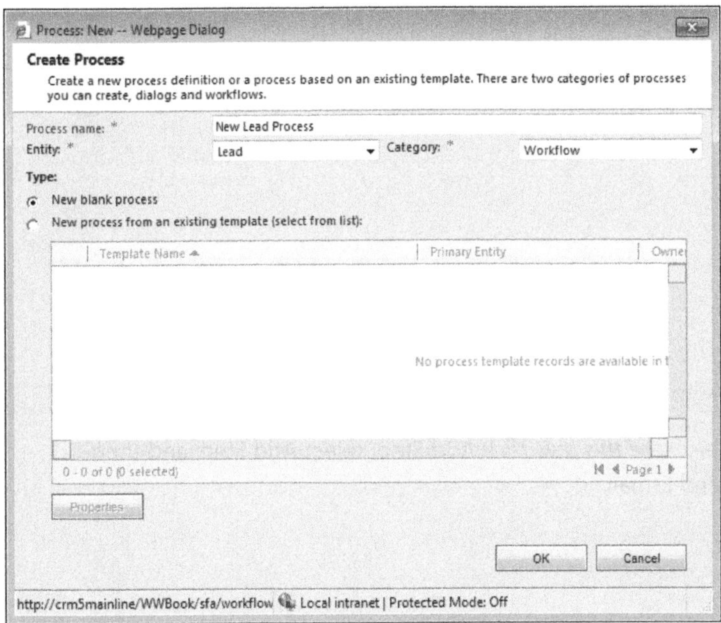

4. On the workflow process record, update the Scope of the workflow to Organization under the Options for Automatic Processes section. This option is used to make the workflow run on all leads entered in the system.

Note The following steps assume that After Step is selected for the Insert type. With this option selected, Microsoft Dynamics CRM creates each new step after the currently highlighted step.

Sending the response for website leads

1. Click Add Step, and click Check Condition.
2. For the step description, type **Check for Web lead**, and then click the *<condition> (click to configure)* link.
3. In the Specify Condition dialog box, create a condition as shown in the following image, and then click Save and Close.

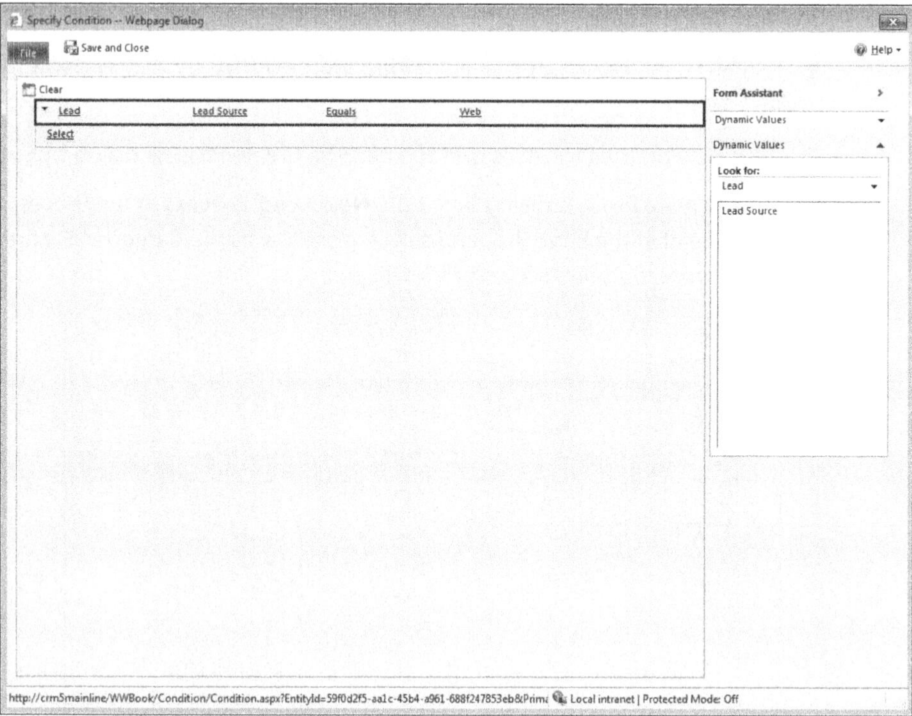

4. Click *Select the this row,* click Add Step, select Add Step, and then click Send E-mail.

5. For the step description, type **Send Web Template E-mail**. To use one of the default templates provided by Microsoft Dynamics CRM, select Use Template, confirm that Lead is selected, and then click Set Properties.
6. In the Send E-mail Using Template dialog box, click the To field to set the focus, and then in the Form Assistant panel, select Lead in the Look for field list. Click Add, and then click OK. This will use dynamic values to send the email message to the Lead.
7. Select Lead Template from the Template Type field. Microsoft Dynamics CRM will display all of the E-mail templates that apply to the Lead entity. Select the Lead Reply-Web Site Visit from the E-mail Templates list.
8. Click the Regarding field to set the focus, and then in the Form Assistant panel, select Lead in the Look for attribute list. Click Add, and then click OK. Your page should resemble the one in the following image. Click Save and Close when done.

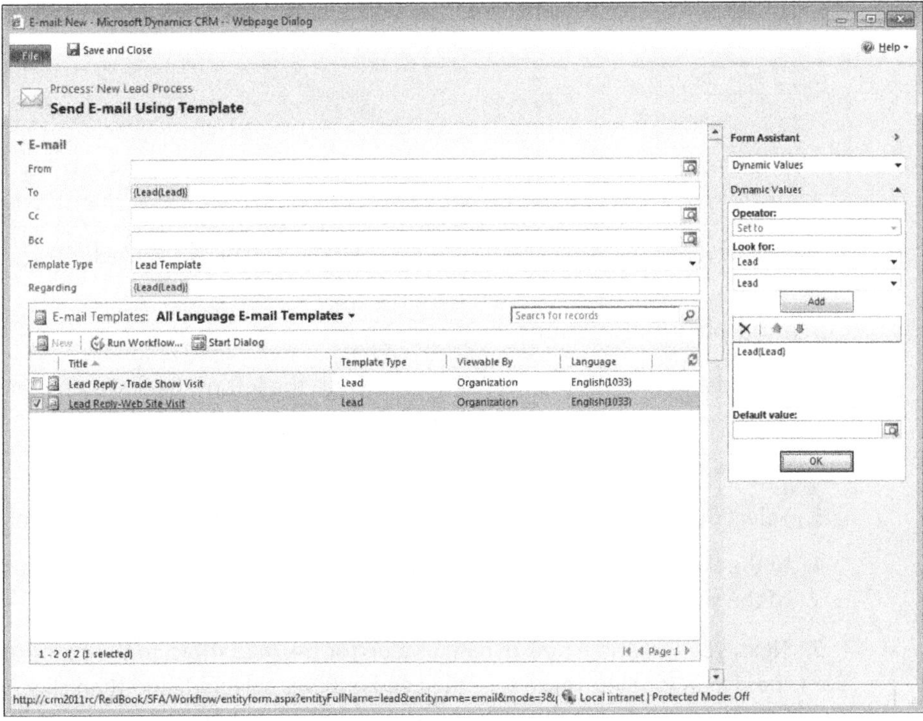

Your process should now look like Figure 14-34.

The next step is to add the common actions shared by all leads from the sales manager's process requirements. You want to create a phone call activity so that someone from your company attempts to qualify the leads.

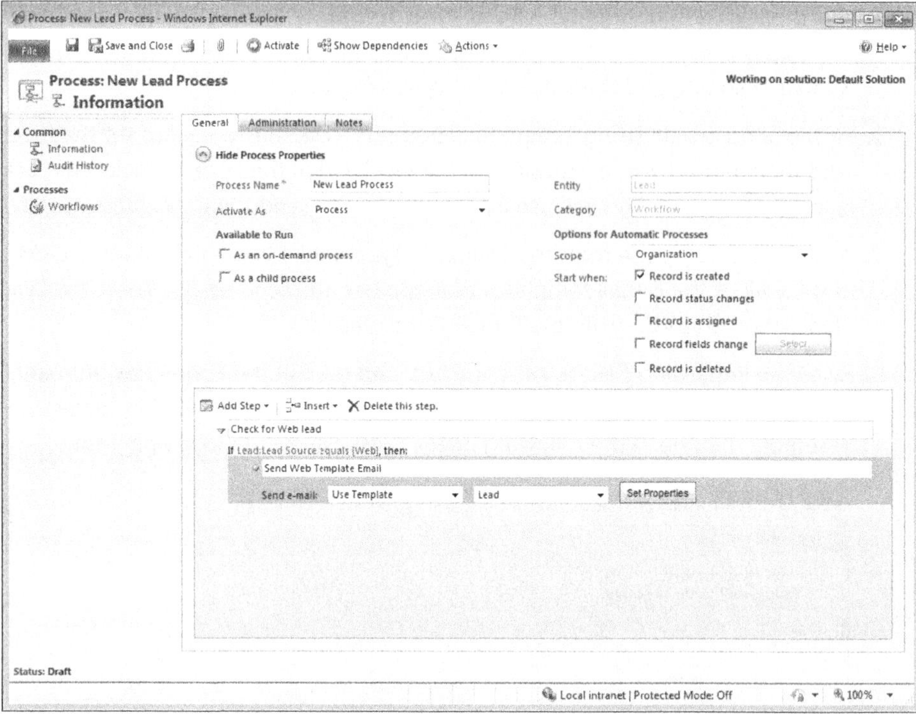

FIGURE 14-34 Workflow process after Web lead condition and actions are entered

Creating phone call actions

1. To add a phone call activity, click the area to the left of the first step name to select that step, click Add Step, and then click Create Record.
2. For the step description, type **Create phone call activity**.
3. Select Phone Call from the Entity list, and then click the Set Properties button.
4. In the Subject field, type **Follow up on new lead -** . Leave the cursor at the end of the space in the field.
5. Next, you will add a new dynamic value for the lead topic. In the Form Assistant, for the dynamic value, make sure the Lead entity is selected, and then click Topic in the field list. Click Add. Microsoft Dynamics CRM will add the dynamic value (highlighted in yellow) to your subject.
6. Type **No topic** in the Default Value box, and then click OK.
7. Click the Due field. You want this phone call to be made quickly, so give it a due date one day after the date the lead was created. In the Form Assistant, click 1 day,

and select After in the picklist. Next, select the Lead entity and the Created On field, and click Add. Leave the default value blank, and then click OK.

8. Next, follow a similar process to add dynamic values for the Phone Number, Sender, and Owner fields, as shown in the following image. Click Save and Close to complete.

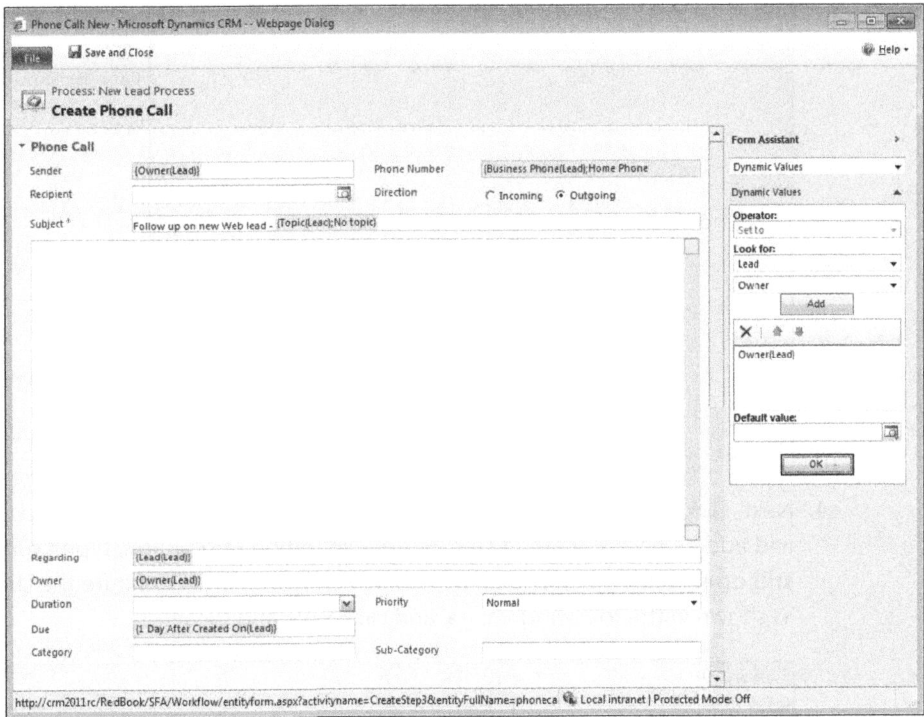

In the last sequence of steps, you will add some additional follow-up activities and cleanup steps. You will add a wait condition step to make the process wait for 14 days. Then, you will check to see whether the lead is still open. If it is, you will create a task to reconnect with the lead and assign it to the lead's owner. Then, you will add a final wait condition step with the duration of one month. If the lead is still open after one month, you will close the lead.

Adding the follow-up steps

1. Click the area outside of the phone call step to highlight it, click Add Step, and then click Wait Condition.
2. For the step description, type **Lead cleanup**, and then click the <*condition*> (click to configure) link.
3. In the Specify Condition dialog box, create a condition as shown in the following image, and then click Save and Close.

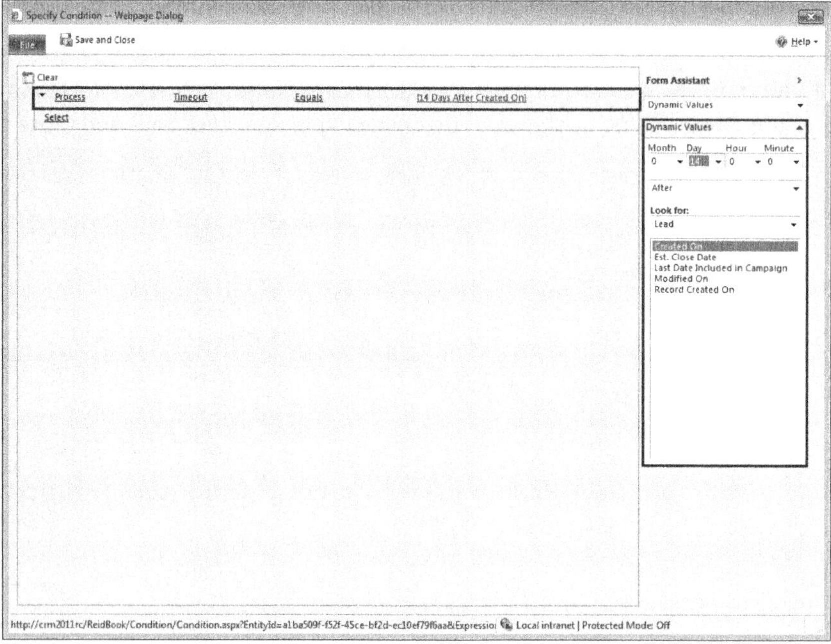

4. Next, click the *Select this row and Add Step* text under the timeout check you added and add a Check Condition step. For the condition description, type **Confirm lead is still open**. Click the *<condition> (click to configure)* link. Configure the check condition, as shown in the following image, and click Save and Close.

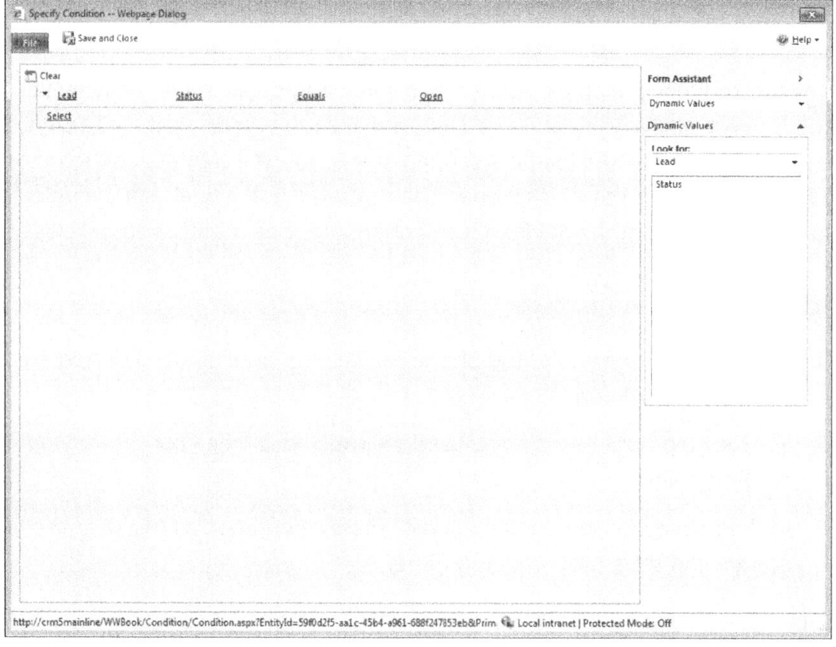

5. Click the *Select this row and Add Step* text under the check condition you added. Click Add Step, select Create New Record, and select Task in the picklist. Give the step a description of **Create follow up task to reconnect with lead**.
6. Click Set Properties and configure the task as follows:

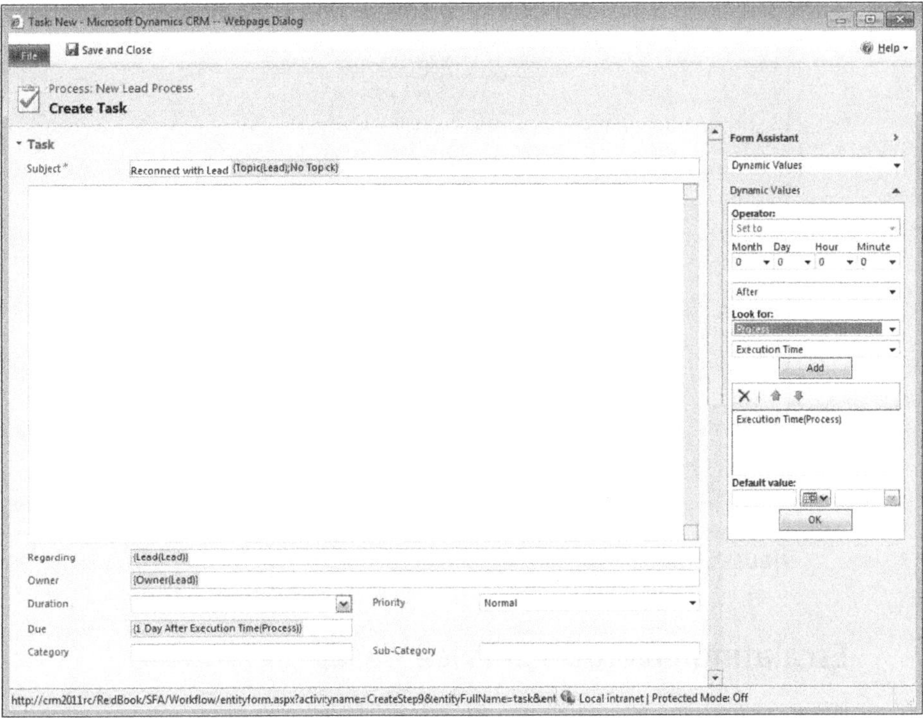

7. Select the task step and add another wait condition with the duration of 1 month. Give it a description of **Wait 1 more month**. When you configure the wait condition, make sure you select workflow timeout equals a duration of 1 month after the follow-up task was created. Click Save and Close.
8. Click *Select this row and Add Step*, and then add another check condition. For the condition description, type **Confirm lead is still open**. Click the *<condition>* (click to configure) link and configure the picklists to check if the Lead Status equals Open. Click Save and Close.
9. Click *Select this row and Add Step*, click Add Step, and add a Change Status action. Give it a description of **Disqualify lead**. Select the Lost option and activate the new process. The final workflow process should appear as shown in Figure 14-35.

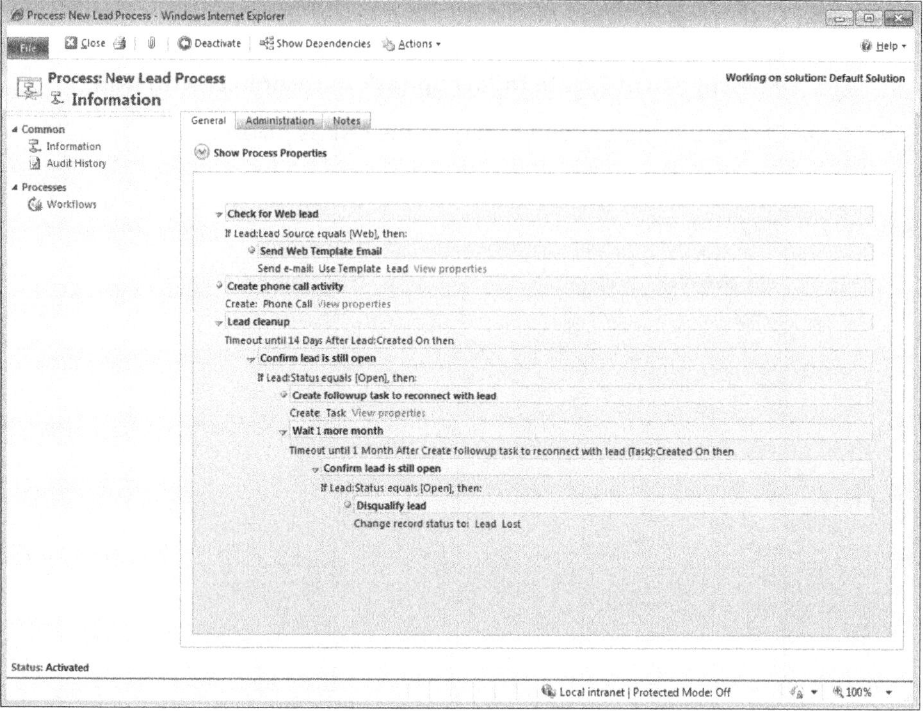

FIGURE 14-35 Activated new lead process

Escalating Overdue Service Cases

Every company would like to provide a quick turnaround time when responding to and resolving their customers' support cases. For the purposes of this example, assume that the organization would like to ensure that it responds to all cases within one day. After one day, they will check to see whether the case is still open. If it is, they will email the case owner's manager and create a queue item so the case can be handled by another individual or team. They will then wait another day to see whether the status changes. If it does not, they will send another email message to the manager of the case owner and assign the case to the Level 2 Support Team. This loop will continue until the case is resolved. Figure 14-36 shows the process graphically.

In addition to creating conditions and actions, this example will highlight additional features in workflow:

- Using the Stop Workflow action
- Using the Start Child Workflow action
- Creating a looping process

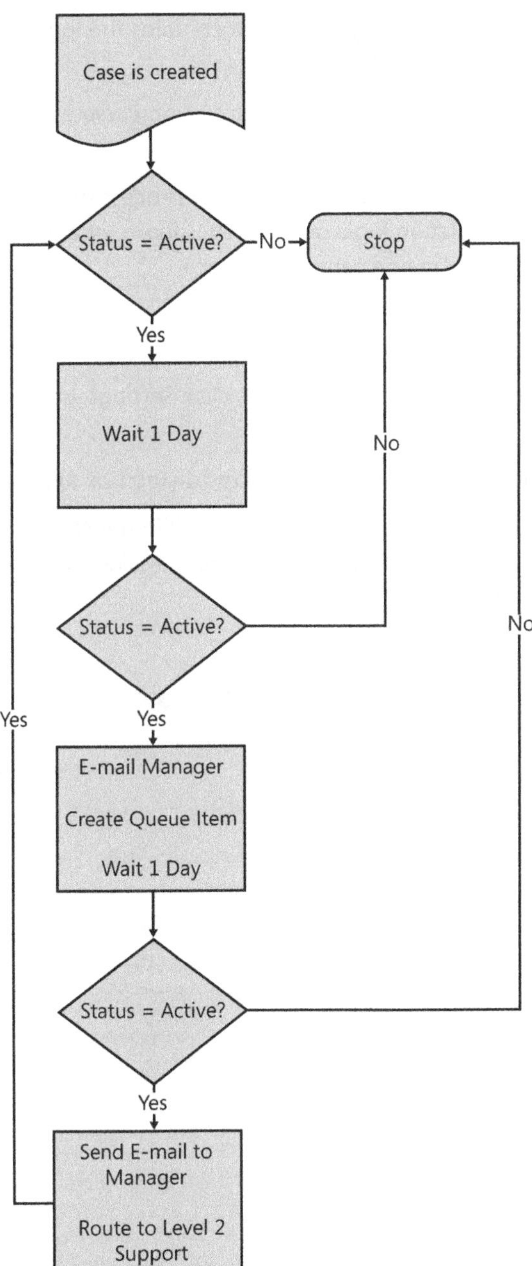

FIGURE 14-36 Case escalation logic

By now you should be familiar with the basics of creating a workflow, so we focus only on the new actions used for this example. You will create three workflow processes for the case entity in the following order:

- **E-mail process** A manual process that sends an email message to the case owner's manager.

- **Escalating logic process** A child workflow process that contains the logic for the case escalation. This process calls itself, creating a loop.
- **Create process** A process that is triggered from the *Record is created* event and calls the escalating logic child workflow process.

You will manually create the email message as a separate workflow process because you want to use this message twice in the escalation logic process. By using a separate process, you also can make changes to the message in one centralized place.

Creating the email process

1. Log on to the Microsoft Dynamics CRM Web application, click Settings, and then click Processes.
2. Click New on the Processes grid toolbar. The Create Process dialog box appears.
3. In the Create Process dialog box, type **Case Escalation - Email** in the Name box, and select Case in the Entity list and Workflow as the Category. Make sure *New blank process* is selected, and then click OK.
4. Create a process that matches the following figure:

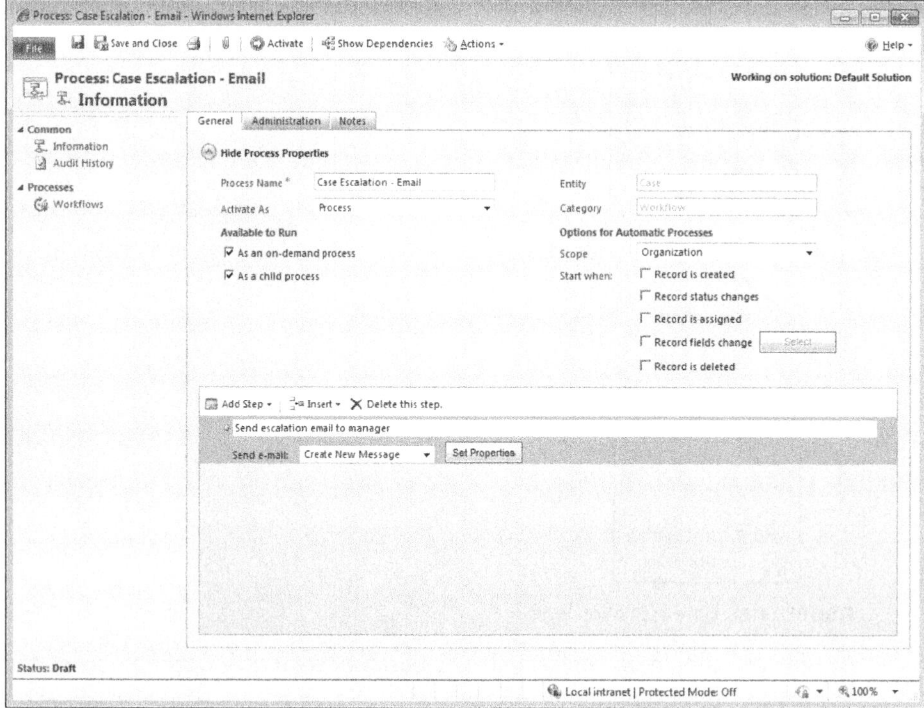

5. Click Set Properties and create an email message with the following parameters:

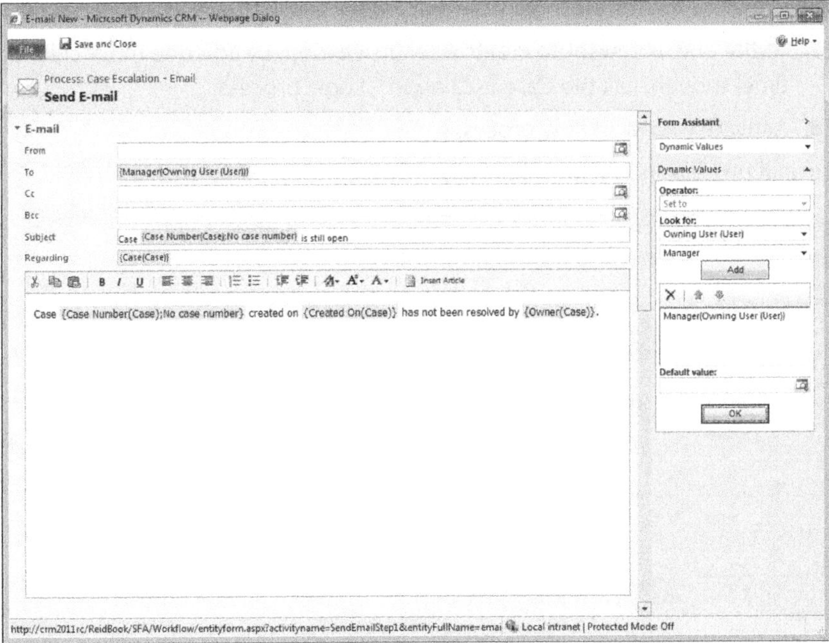

6. Activate the process.

The next step is to create the main escalating logic. Use the flow chart from Figure 14-36 as the blueprint. This workflow appears to be very simple, but notice that at the end, the workflow process calls itself, creating a loop.

Use extreme care when creating a loop in workflow, especially one that calls additional child processes. You can accidentally create a situation in which the workflow process enters an infinite loop. An infinite loop will create performance bottlenecks until it is terminated manually or by the Microsoft Dynamics CRM loop detection. Test the process in a development environment. If you find yourself in an infinite loop, immediately terminate the step, deactivate the process, and correct the problem.

Creating the escalating logic process

1. Create a workflow process for the Case entity called **Case Escalation - Logic**.
2. Change the scope to be Organization, uncheck the *Record is created* trigger, and set the Available to Run option to be As a child workflow.
3. Add a Wait condition and set it for one day from when the case was created, and then add a check condition immediately after that to check whether the Case Status is still Active.
4. For the actions of this condition, add the child email process. Click Add Step, and then click Start Child Workflow. Select Case Escalation – Email from the list.
5. Add a default condition to stop the process if the case is not active.

6. Continue to add the logic shown in Figure 14-36.
7. At the end, you want to create a recursive loop, so add one more child action. This time, though, call the Case Escalation - Logic process.
8. Activate your workflow process.

The final process should look like Figure 14-37.

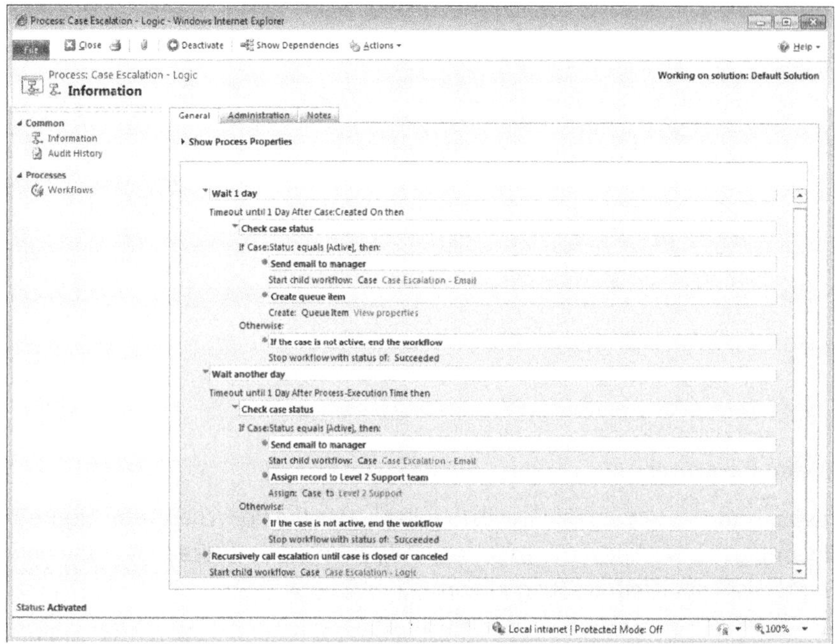

FIGURE 14-37 Case escalation logic process final steps

The last step is to initiate the Case Escalation - Logic process each time a new case is created. You will build a process based on the case's Create event that calls the Case Escalation - Logic process through the child action.

Summary

Microsoft Dynamics CRM includes powerful workflow functionality that you can configure to automate standardized business processes. You configure and manage workflow in the Microsoft Dynamics CRM user interface, so users and administrators can quickly create complex business rules without being required to have any programming knowledge. Furthermore, you can create workflow processes for most of the entities in Microsoft Dynamics CRM, including custom entities. By using workflow processes, you can specify criteria and business logic for how Microsoft Dynamics CRM should execute the process. In addition to configuring the workflow trigger event, you can insert conditions and actions in each process. Workflow processes follow the Microsoft Dynamics CRM security model, so you can configure the processes and security roles for your organization to restrict user access.

Chapter 15
Dialog Processes

In this chapter:

Microsoft Dynamics CRM 2011 introduces a dialog module to handle instances where you want to add wizard or call script functionality to the application. Similar to workflows, dialogs are processes that guide a user through a series of steps in an automated manner. Both system administrators and users can create dialog processes if they have a security role with the appropriate privileges. When a user runs a dialog from a record, the dialog process can capture information that can be stored in Microsoft Dynamics CRM entities and retrieve information already stored in the system. Further, dialog processes can kick off workflows to automate actions in Microsoft Dynamics CRM after the dialog session is complete.

Note This chapter assumes that you have already reviewed Chapter 14, "Workflow Processes." In particular, the "Dynamic Values in Processes" and "Importing and Exporting Processes" sections in that chapter are relevant to dialog processes. The information from those sections is not repeated in this chapter.

Dialog Process Basics

Many companies are interested in call-scripting capabilities to help their employees follow a consistent process for collecting information. This flow often includes decision points and different lines of questioning based on the answers provided. Microsoft Dynamics CRM uses dialog processes to handle this type of functionality. A dialog process is a series of screens, including prompts and responses, that guide a user through a business procedure. With dialog processes, you can collect information, confirm or view data already captured in the system, and see instructions for interacting with a customer or process.

In this chapter, we'll discuss the following concepts as they pertain to Microsoft Dynamics CRM dialog processes:

- Starting dialog processes
- Understanding the components of dialog pages
- Configuring security for dialog processes
- Understanding the dialog interface

Starting Dialog Processes

Microsoft Dynamics CRM initiates a dialog process in one of two ways:

- Manually, by the user
- As a child process of another dialog

As long as an entity has at least one active dialog process that can be run on demand, users can manually initiate dialogs from the entity ribbon of view or record. Dialog processes can only be run for one record at a time, unlike workflow processes, which can be run on multiple records simultaneously. When users select the record on which they want to run a dialog process, they can then click the Start Dialog button in the ribbon, as shown in Figure 15-1.

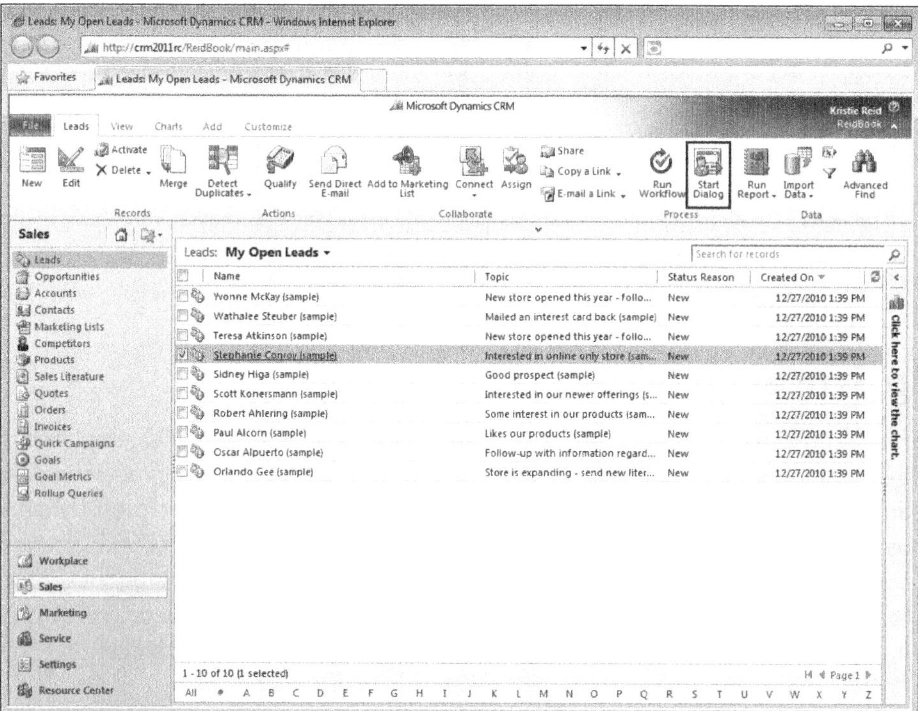

FIGURE 15-1 Accessing dialog processes from the view ribbon

Users can also start dialog processes directly from a record, as shown in Figure 15-2.

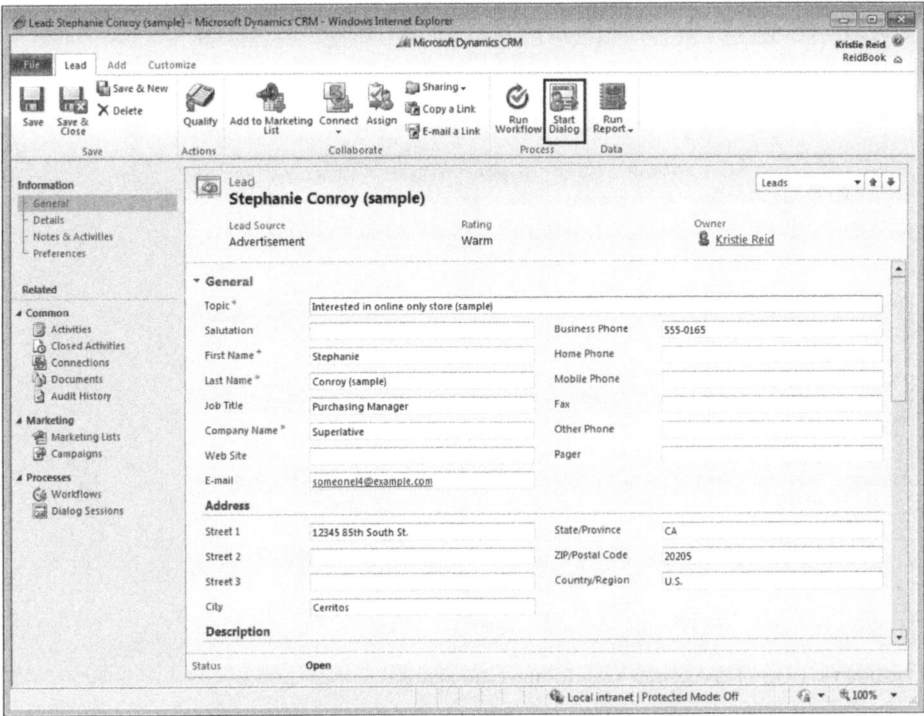

FIGURE 15-2 Accessing dialog processes from a record

After the user clicks the Start Dialog button, a list of the active, on-demand dialog processes for the entity appears, as shown in Figure 15-3.

After users select the appropriate dialog process and click OK, the dialog process begins and the pages created with the dialog interface appear.

Note Dialog processes can only be initiated on an existing record. This means a dialog process cannot be started without first selecting a record in Microsoft Dynamics CRM.

Because all dialog processes are associated with a URL that can be called to start the dialog process, you can also choose to customize your application by adding a button to the entity ribbon that kicks off a dialog process. Figure 15-4 shows an example on the Lead form, where a new button has been added to kick off a new lead dialog process. Adding a button in the ribbon eliminates users from having to select the correct dialog process, thus saving them a step. This approach is especially useful for companies that want to emphasize an important process or that use several dialog processes for an entity.

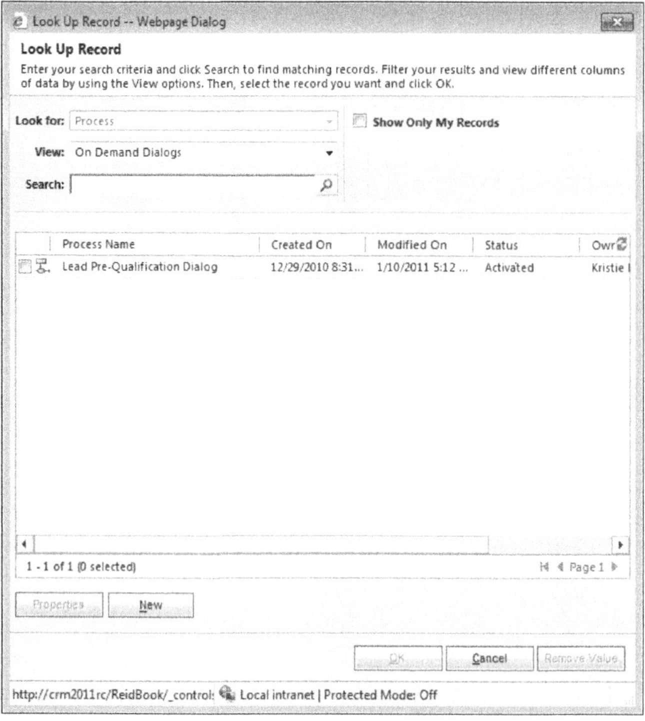

FIGURE 15-3 List of dialog processes for the Lead entity

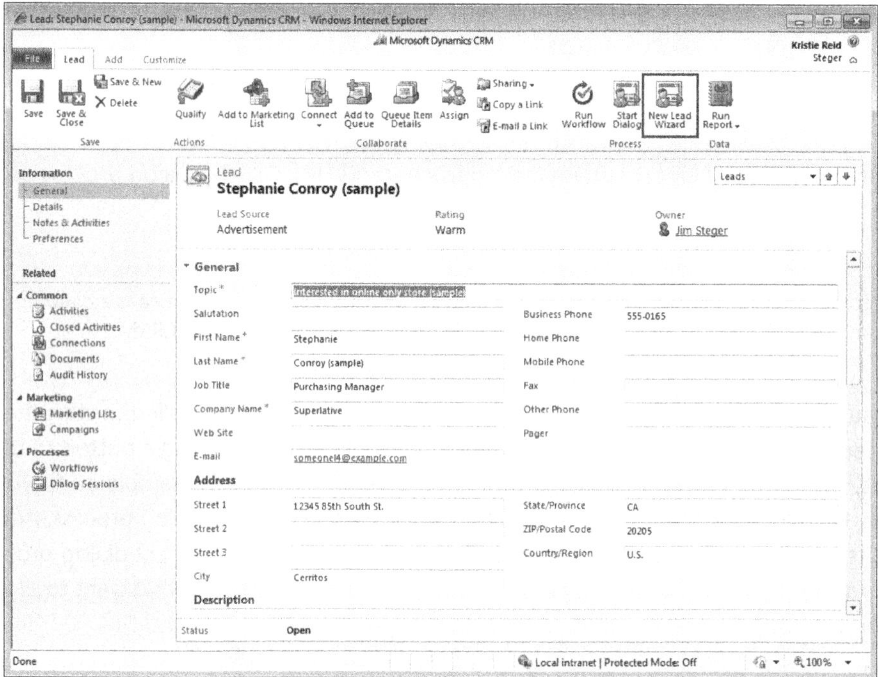

FIGURE 15-4 Custom button to start a specific dialog process from the Lead form's ribbon

Understanding the Components of Dialog Pages

Although the layouts of the pages are not as configurable as other forms in Microsoft Dynamics CRM, dialog processes offer several areas for displaying information. Each dialog page contains the following components:

- Page Header
- Prompt and Response
- Tip Text
- Comments

Figure 15-5 shows these sections in the dialog page.

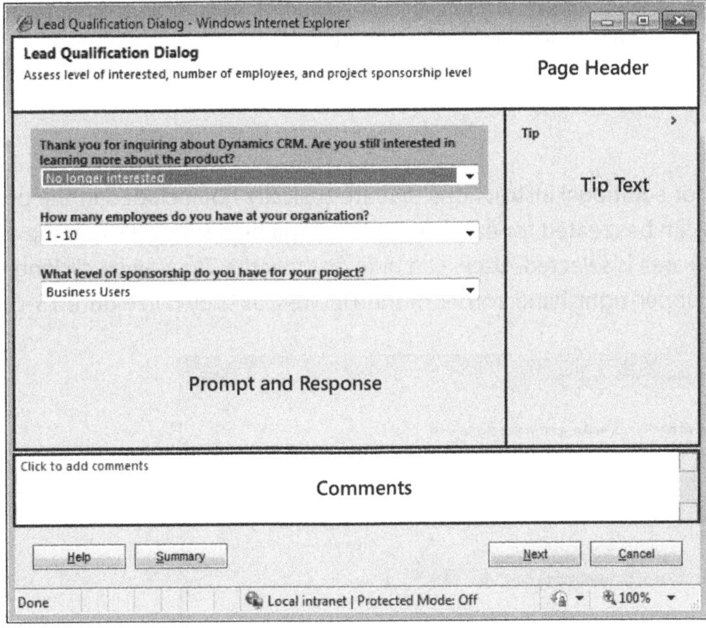

FIGURE 15-5 Configurable areas of a dialog page

Page Header

The page header area displays the name of the dialog process along with the name of the dialog page.

Tip For longer dialog processes, it's helpful to display the current step number so that users know which page they're viewing. Although you cannot automatically display the dialog page numbers, Microsoft Dynamics CRM allows you to name each page, so you can enter the page number as part of your title. Keep in mind that the total number of pages might change depending on the number of decision points in your dialog process. Therefore, it might not be possible to include the page number in the dialog header.

Prompt and Response

Each dialog page can contain one or more prompt and response areas. Prompts guide the user through a process by indicating what users should be asking or entering into the dialog page. The prompt text provides an area to include static text, dynamic values, Microsoft Dynamics CRM data, or links to other web pages. At least one prompt is required for each page. However, responses are not required for each prompt.

Responses allow users to enter information in the dialog page. This information can then be used to identify the next step in the dialog process or be stored or updated in Microsoft Dynamics CRM.

Tip When designing a dialog process, try to limit the number of prompts and responses for each page, so users don't have to scroll through the page.

Tip Text

The Tip area is used for additional instructions that are typically not included in the prompt script. A separate tip can be created for each prompt and will be displayed when the associated prompt and response area is selected. Users can hide or show the Tip area by clicking the view arrow located in the upper-right-hand corner of the Tip area, as shown in Figure 15-6.

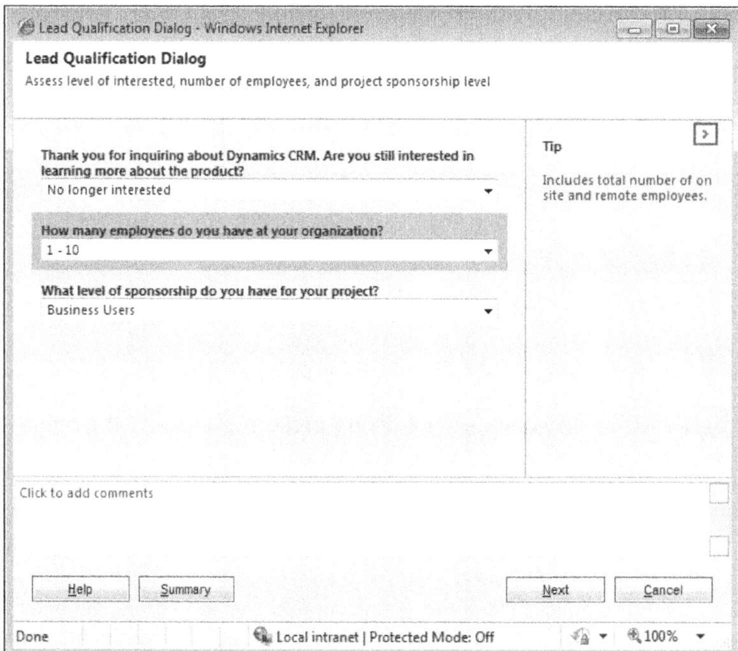

FIGURE 15-6 Arrow button used to hide or display the Tip area

Comments

The final area available on the dialog pages is for comments entered by users as they progress through the dialog process. Comments entered in this area on any dialog page persist throughout the entire dialog process. This is very useful in the case of a call script where the person who is providing the information may disclose details that are collected on another dialog page. In this scenario, the user collecting the information can type those details in the comments section and then use them to complete the responses on the appropriate dialog page as it is displayed.

In addition to these display areas, each dialog page includes the following buttons:

- **Help** Takes the user to the Microsoft Dynamics CRM help page.
- **Summary** Displays the dialog session. We'll discuss session monitoring for dialog processes later in this chapter.
- **Previous** Advances the user to the previous dialog page. This option is only available if the user has proceeded to a second page of the dialog session.
- **Next** Advances the user to the next dialog page. This option is hidden when the user has proceeded to the last page of the dialog session.
- **Finish** Exits the dialog pages. This option only displays when the user has completed the dialog session.
- **Cancel** Cancels the dialog session before the user has reached the end of the process. When this button is selected, the dialog session will be closed with a Status Reason of Canceled.

Important Users should be trained on the implications of using the Previous button in a dialog session. If the user goes back to previous pages, all of the responses captured in the subsequent pages will be deleted. This is to ensure that any branching or logic that follows will not be affected.

Configuring Security for Dialog Processes

Just like the other features in Microsoft Dynamics CRM, you can configure detailed security settings for dialog processes. You can secure dialog processes from two perspectives:

- Creating and editing dialog processes
- Running dialog processes

Creating and Editing Dialog Processes

Dialog processes and workflow process map to the same entity in Microsoft Dynamics CRM. Therefore, the same security privileges control creating and editing both types of processes. For additional information, see Chapter 14.

Running Dialog Processes

Although the permissions for creating and editing processes are identical for workflow and dialog processes, the privileges required to run those processes are different. To run a dialog process, users must have a security role with create, read, and write access to the Dialog Session entity. Dialog sessions are owned by the user who initiates them.

Understanding the Dialog Interface

You access dialog processes by navigating to the Settings area, and then clicking Processes. The Process view shows processes of all types, including dialogs, workflows, dialog templates, and workflow templates. You can enable filtering in the grid to show only dialog processes by filtering the Category column, as shown in Figure 15-7.

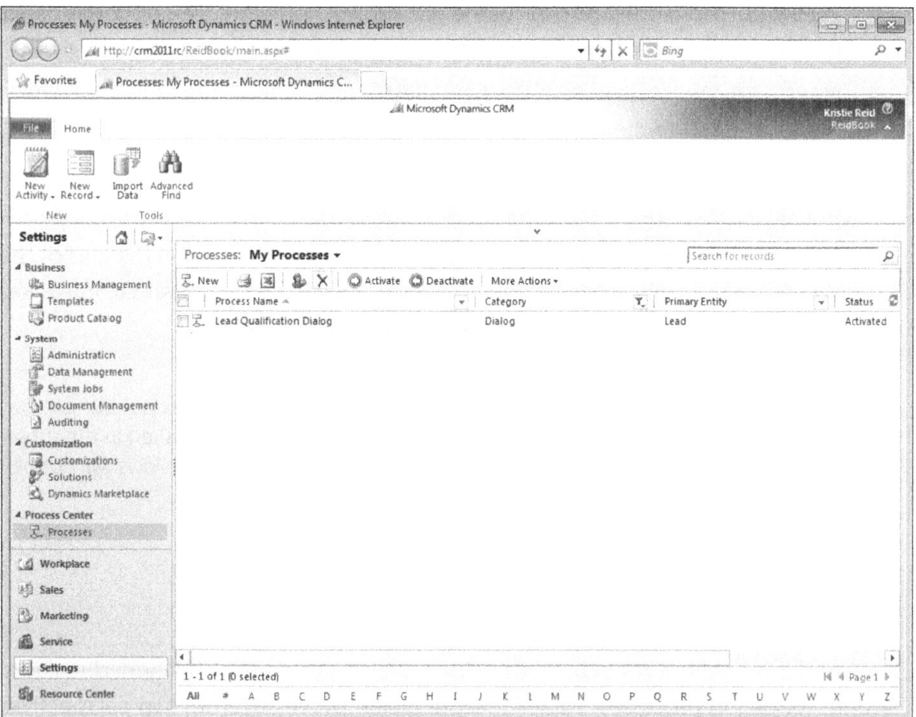

FIGURE 15-7 Process view filtered to show only dialog processes

To create a dialog process, click the New button in the grid toolbar. Enter a process name, select the entity to which the dialog should apply, and select Dialog in the Category field. You can create the dialog from an existing template if you have one, or you can leave the *New blank process* option selected. Click OK to launch the Process form, shown in Figure 15-8.

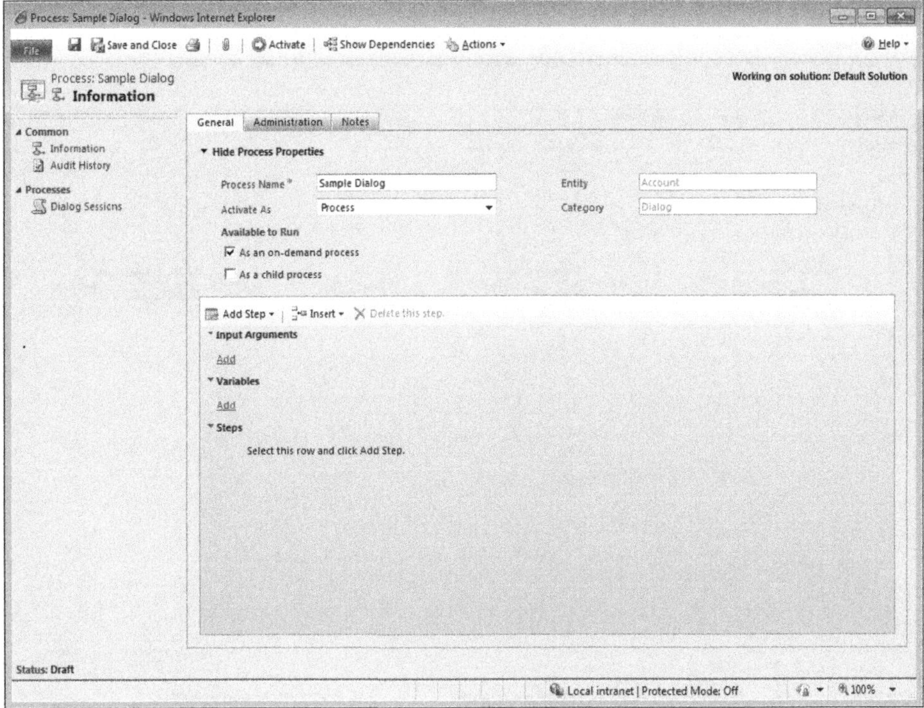

FIGURE 15-8 Process form

In addition to creating dialog processes, you can use the Process view to perform other administrative tasks, such as assigning, deleting, activating, or deactivating a process. The Process view displays only processes and process templates. After a dialog process is run on a particular record, you can access information about that session from the dialog process record or from that specific record. We will go into additional details about monitoring dialog processes later in this chapter.

Dialog Templates

Dialog templates provide an easy way to replicate dialog processes. To create a dialog process that can be used as a dialog template, choose to activate the process as a Process Template in the Activate As field on the Process form. After creating a template, you'll be able to select it when creating a process from an existing template for the specified entity, as shown in Figure 15-9.

When you create a process from an existing template, all of the properties, including input arguments, variables, and steps from the selected template will be copied to your new process. Similar to workflow templates, dialog templates can save a lot of time if your organization uses a number of similar processes. Of course, if the dialog processes are exactly the same, creating a single child process which gets called from other dialog processes might be the best design option to consider.

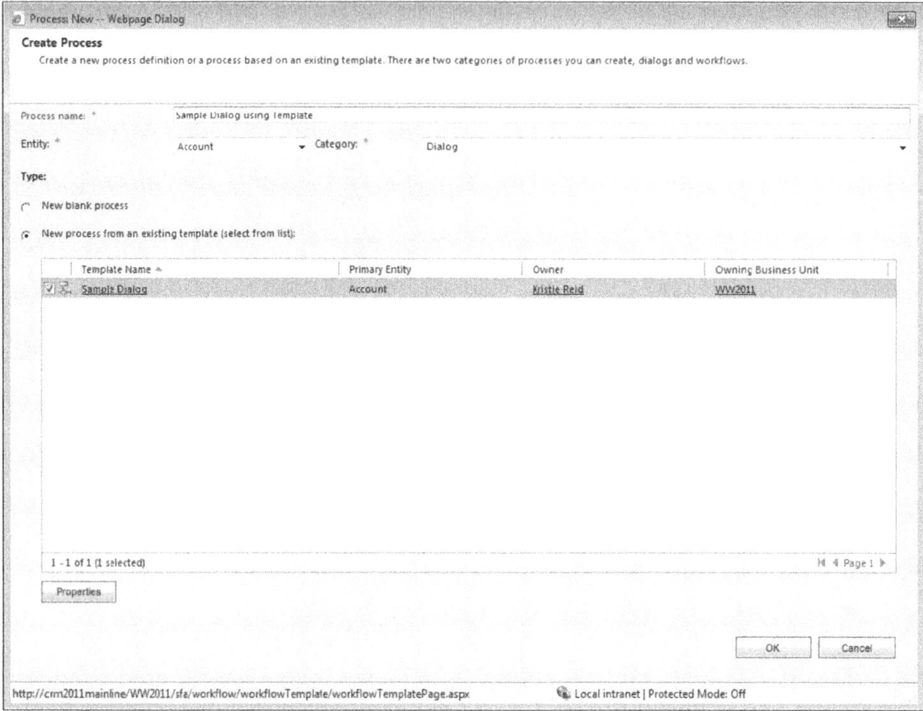

FIGURE 15-9 Template list in the Create Process dialog box

Dialog Properties

When you create a dialog process, you must specify several parameters about the process:

- Basic dialog process properties
- Dialog execution options
- Input arguments
- Variables
- Steps

Basic Dialog Process Properties

The basic properties that can be changed on the General tab of a dialog process include the dialog's name and publishing type, either a process or a process template. Similar to basic workflow process properties, the additional tabs on the Process form allow you to change the process owner and add a longer description or notes when appropriate.

Dialog Execution Options

Dialog processes can be run on demand or as child processes. Child processes are very useful for dialogs that are repeated across several call scripts. For example, the first questions asked when a customer calls a company are typically intended to identify the customer and route the call to the correct department by obtaining an account number, address information, and reason for the call. Based on this information, the customer would be connected to the appropriate department, at which point another process would start. Because these pages would be the same for each inbound call, it would be beneficial to create a single dialog process for inbound calls, which then starts the appropriate child process based on the information provided by the customer. With this approach, if those initial questions change, you would only need to update one dialog process.

Caution You must select at least one option to run the dialog. If you attempt to activate a dialog without identifying it as an on-demand or child process, Microsoft Dynamics CRM automatically selects makes the process available on demand, meaning the process will appear in the list of dialogs that can be started from a record or view.

Input Arguments

Input arguments are parameters that will be passed into a dialog from another process. As such, input arguments can only be used in dialogs that run as child processes. After you have entered input arguments, the *As a child process* option cannot be cleared until the arguments are removed.

For each input argument, you must enter a name, data type, and default value. Input arguments can have the following data types:

- Single Line of Text
- Whole Number
- Floating Point Number

Important Within the input arguments, the Name field must be populated with alphanumeric characters or the underscore. No spaces or special characters can be used. When the argument has the Single Line of Text data type, up to 256 characters can be entered. Whole numbers must fall between -2,147,483,648 and 2,147,483,647. Floating point numbers can contain up to five decimal places.

Figure 15-10 shows the property dialog box used to create and change input arguments.

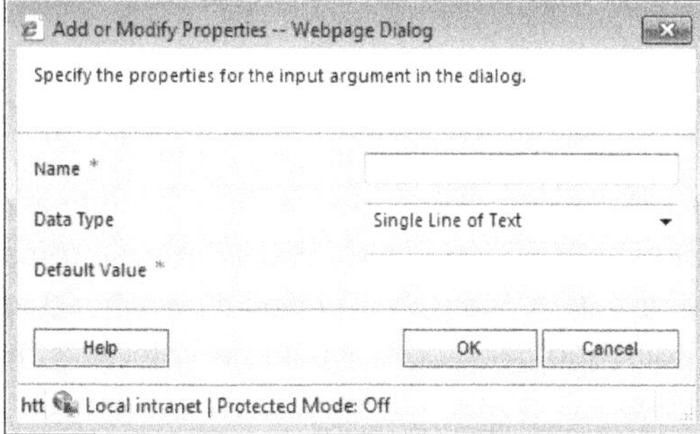

FIGURE 15-10 Add or Modify Properties dialog box for input arguments

After creating input arguments in a child dialog process and activating the process, the child dialog can be called from another dialog process. During that call, you can pass information collected in the parent process to the child dialog. To do this, click Add Step in the editor toolbar and select the Link Child Dialog step. Select the step after it's added to the editor, then select the entity and child dialog you want to call. Click the Set Properties button and set each of the input arguments to the appropriate response from the parent, as shown in Figure 15-11.

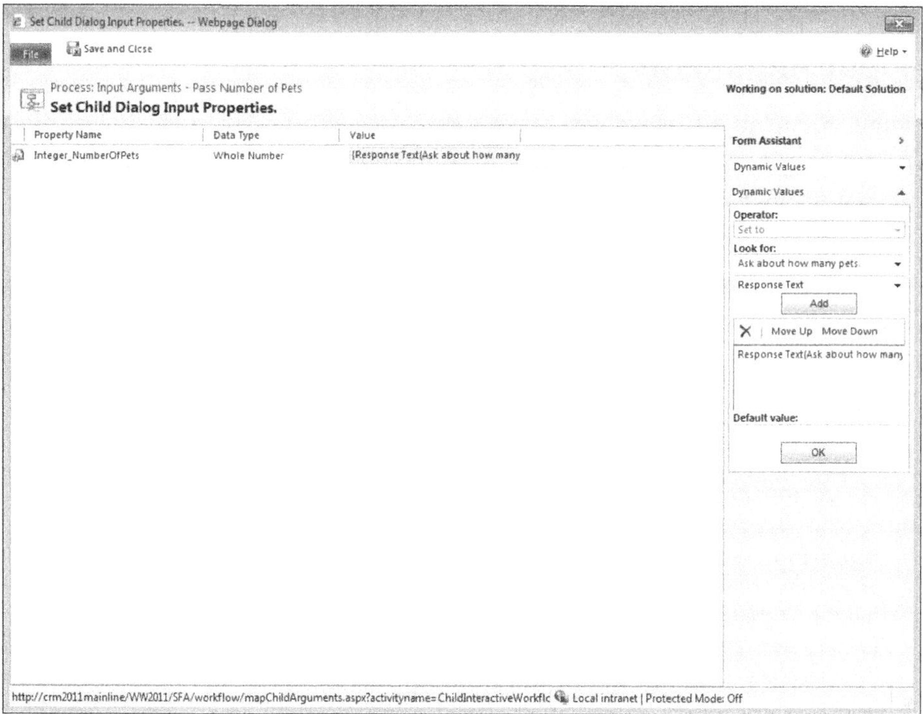

FIGURE 15-11 Setting input arguments for a child dialog

The input argument values can also be updated using the Assign Value step, which we discuss in the "Steps" section later in the chapter.

Variables

Variables are parameters that are stored and passed within a dialog process. Unlike responses, which can also be used throughout a dialog process, variables can be manipulated during the dialog process. For example, you could use variables to score a lead as responses are collected during a dialog process. Using the Assign Value step, you can perform calculations after each response to determine the final score for the lead.

For each variable, you must enter a name, data type, and default value. Variables have the same available data types as input arguments:

- Single Line of Text
- Whole Number
- Floating Point Number

Values are assigned using the Assign Value step discussed in the next section.

Steps

After the basic properties, input arguments, and variables of your dialog process are configured, you can create the steps of the process. Microsoft Dynamics CRM provides the following options for setting up dialog process steps:

- Stage
- Page
- Prompt and Response
- Check Condition
- Conditional Branch
- Default Action
- Query CRM Data
- Assign Value
- Create Record
- Update Record
- Assign Record
- Send E-Mail
- Start Child Workflow
- Link Child Dialog
- Change Status

- Stop Dialog
- Workflow Utility

Stages

When used in dialog processes, stages serve the same purpose they do in workflows, allowing you to group steps in the process. To add a stage to a dialog process, click Add Step, and then select Stage. As always, be sure to name your stages appropriately so that you and others who view the dialog process understand the purpose of each stage.

Note If you add a stage to a dialog process, all steps in that process must be part of a stage. Microsoft Dynamics CRM informs you of this requirement when you add the first stage to a dialog process.

Figure 15-12 shows a dialog process with stages. In this example, the first stage is used to confirm that a case is still open. If the issue is resolved, the case is closed. If not, the dialog proceeds to the second stage, where users are reminded to notify the customer that the case has been escalated to a second-level support team.

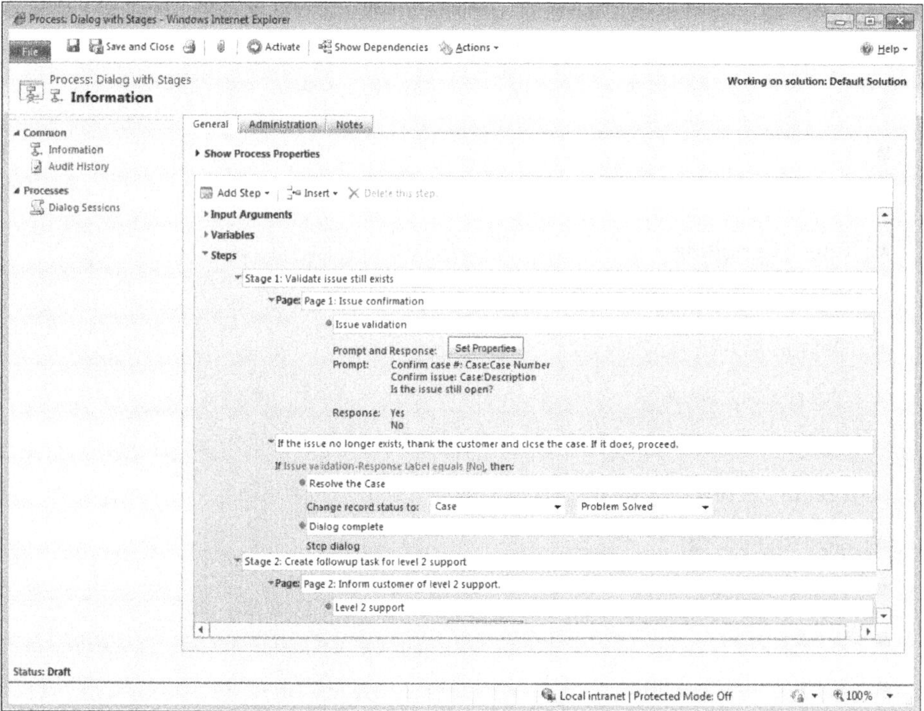

FIGURE 15-12 Dialog process with stages

Pages

Pages are the screens users will see when running dialog processes. Each page must consist of at least one prompt, created by adding a Prompt and Response step. You will not be able to activate a dialog process until it contains at least one prompt. To create a new page, click Add Step and select Page. Enter a name for the page, which will be displayed when a user steps through the dialog process.

Prompt and Response

A prompt is the text that displays on a dialog page, typically a question or script that should be used in conversations with customers. A response is a data point captured in a dialog page based on the information requested in the associated prompt. Figure 15-13 shows an example of the setup dialog box of a prompt and response page.

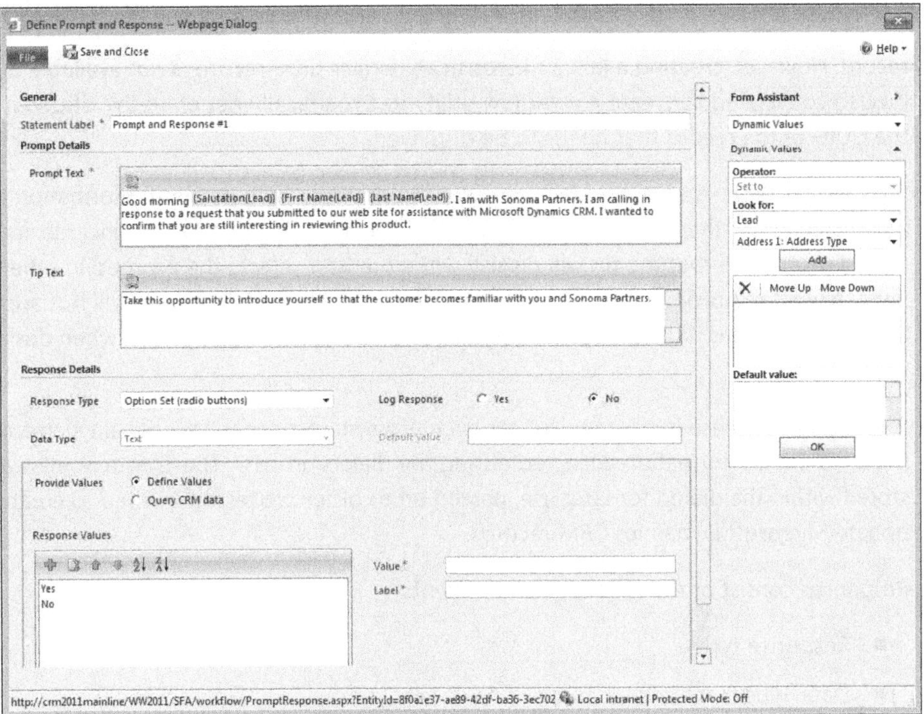

FIGURE 15-13 Define Prompt and Response dialog box

Prompts can be used to display the exact call scripts you want users to reference when talking to customers. Alternately, prompts can be used to provide instructions about how to step through the dialog pages. You can also use dynamic values in prompts. The use of dynamic values is detailed in the "Dynamic Values in Workflow" section in Chapter 14.

In addition to text, you can also add links in your prompts. When adding links to a prompt, you need to set a display name for the link as well as the correct URL, as shown in Figure 15-14.

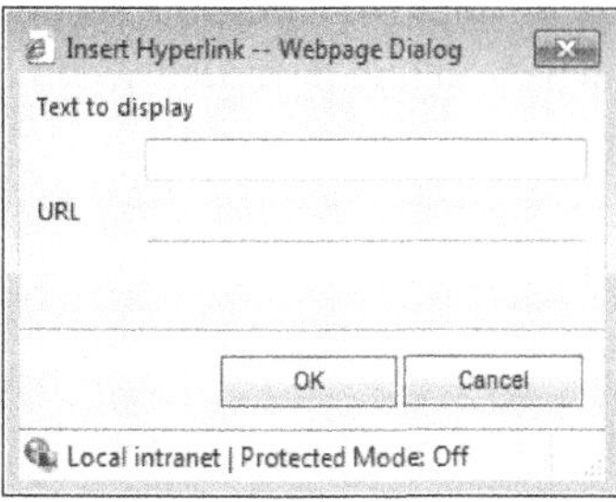

FIGURE 15-14 Insert Hyperlink dialog box

For example, you can include a link that the user reading from the dialog can provide to a customer during a call, or you can include a link to another Microsoft Dynamics CRM record. However, creating a link a Microsoft Dynamics CRM record is not available out of the box, so you'll need to create a workflow utility to dynamically generate the URL so it includes the GUID of the record that needs to be displayed.

For each prompt, you can also include a tip that provides help or other information to assist users when the prompt is selected in a dialog session. Tips also can include links. It is important to note that the tip will display when the user selects the prompt. In other words, if you have three prompts on a dialog page, the tip for the third prompt will not appear until the third prompt is highlighted. This feature is important to keep in mind when designing your pages.

Although a response is not required for each prompt, responses are critical when a user needs to enter information collected during the dialog process. These data points can be stored within the dialog for later use, passed on to other processes, or used to create or update Microsoft Dynamics CRM records.

Responses consist of the following components:

- Response Type
- Data Type
- Log Response
- Default Value

Currently, responses can have the following response types:

- None
- Single Line

- Option Set (radio buttons)
- Option Set (picklist)
- Multiple Lines (Text Only)

As the name indicates, the Multiple Lines (Text Only) option only supports text responses. For the remaining response types, the following data types are supported:

- Text
- Integer
- Float

Note Once you have selected the response data type and saved the prompt and response, you cannot edit the data type. Therefore, it is important to think through the design of your page before creating each prompt and response.

When using Option Set (radio buttons) or Option Set (picklist) as the response type, you need to provide the values for those options. To define option set values for a response, add response values by clicking the green plus icon and updating the Value and Label fields as appropriate, as shown in Figure 15-15.

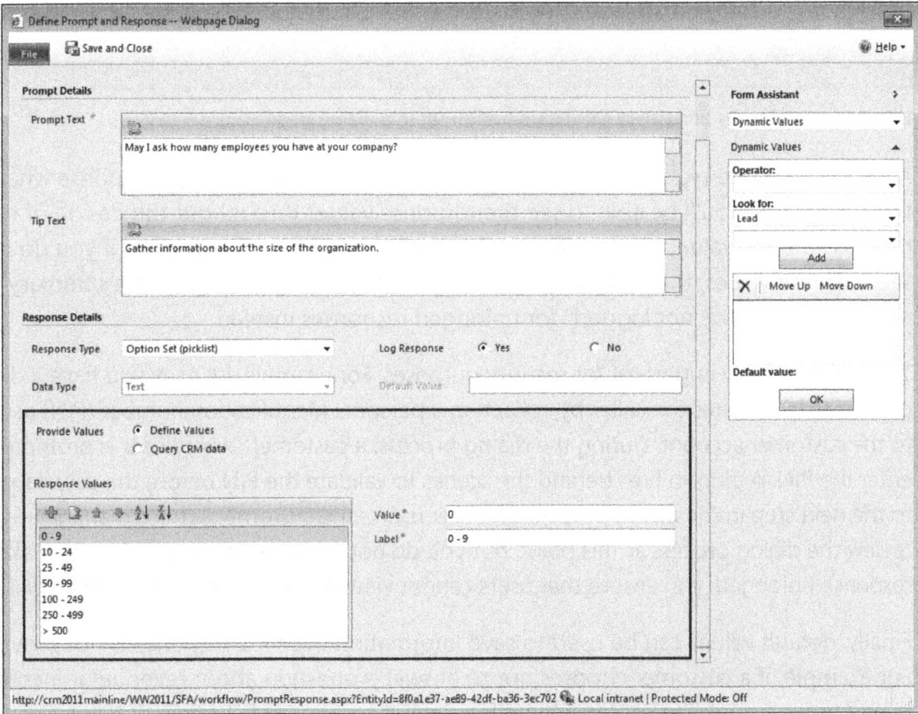

FIGURE 15-15 Defining values for an Option Set (picklist) response using the Define Values option

As an alternative to defining the option set values in the response, you can also use the *Query CRM data* option to generate options. We'll get into the details of using the Query CRM Data process later in this chapter, but for now, Figure 15-16 shows how the results of a Query CRM data option set displays to the end user to show a customer's open cases.

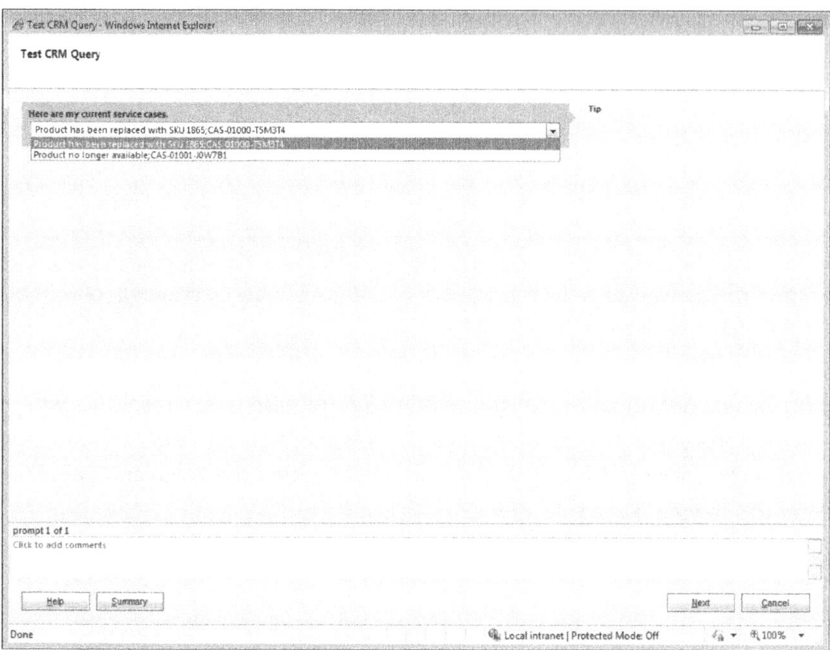

FIGURE 15-16 Results of a Query CRM data option set in a dialog page

After the response type is set, you must determine whether to log the response when the dialog runs. You'll be able to see the response values throughout the design of the dialog process, and the values can be displayed to users in the dialog pages, but if you do not log the response values, they will not be displayed in the dialog summary. The summary page will show "Response not logged" for unlogged responses instead.

This feature is very important for security purposes. For example, let's say you have a dialog process that validates the caller by collecting a personal identification number (PIN) associated to the customer account. During the dialog process, a customer service user is prompted to enter the PIN. A plug-in fires behind the scenes to validate the PIN before the user can proceed to the next step in the dialog process. Another user—the customer service manager—wants to review the dialog process at this point, but you do not want her to see the PIN. By making the response unlogged, you ensure that users cannot view the response outside of the dialog pages.

Finally, default values can be used to save information even if a response is not provided. For example, if a customer chooses not to answer a question about revenue or income, the dialog process could be configured with a default response of "Prefers not to answer."

Check Conditions

Using conditions in dialog processes is similar to using conditions in workflow processes. In a dialog process, conditions are typically used to identify the next step or section of call script users should be directed to based on a response. For example, as part of a dialog process, a user is prompted to verify the address information currently stored for a customer account. If the address information is incorrect, the process directs the user to a page on which he can update the address information. If the address is correct, the user is directed to the next step of the dialog process.

Query CRM Data

Recall the example in a previous section about displaying a customer's open cases in a dialog page, so the user working through the dialog process can select from a list of open cases. In this scenario, you want to display Microsoft Dynamics CRM data in the dialog process. This allows the user to see relevant records from Microsoft Dynamics CRM without having to leave the dialog session. By using Microsoft Dynamics CRM as the option set values in the response definition, you can also associate the dialog session to a record and reference fields from that record elsewhere in the dialog process or related child processes. The Query CRM Data feature is used for this purpose.

To use the Query CRM Data action, click Add Step and select Query CRM Data, as shown in Figure 15-17.

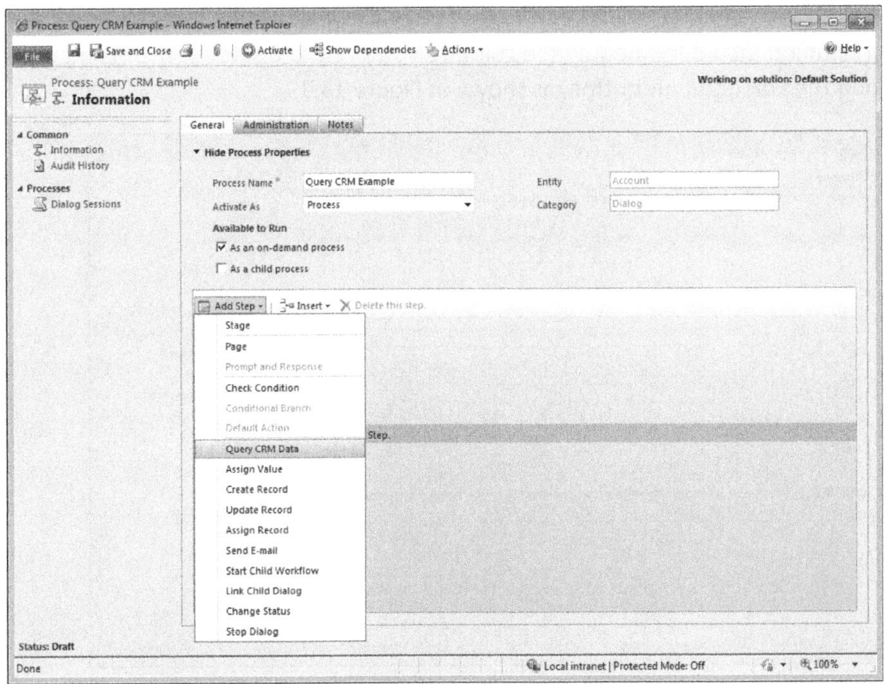

FIGURE 15-17 Creating a Query CRM Data action

The first step to creating this action is defining a query. As you will notice in Figure 15-18, the interface to define the query is very similar to Advanced Find.

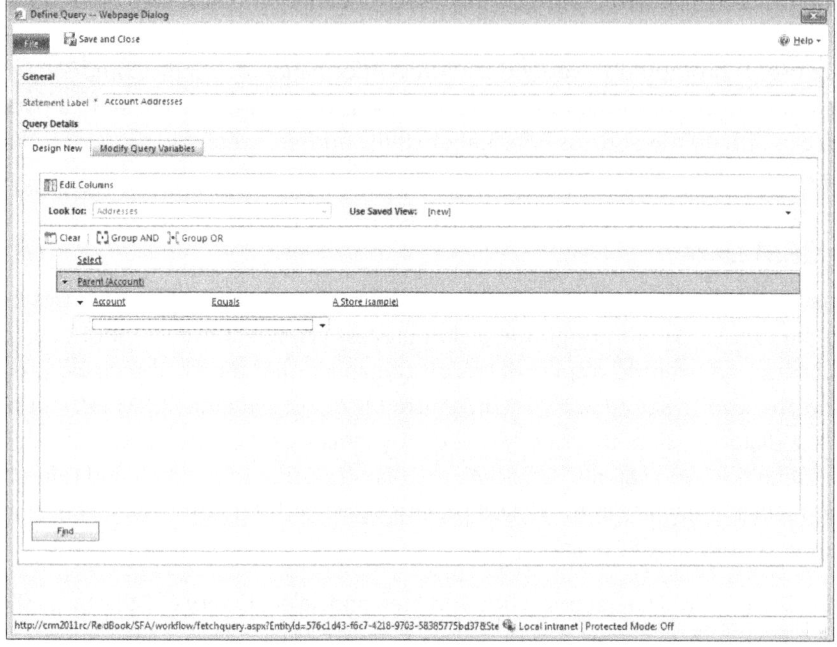

FIGURE 15-18 Define Query page for the Query CRM Data action

After defining the query, identify the columns you want to display in the dialog process by clicking the Edit Columns button, as shown in Figure 15-19.

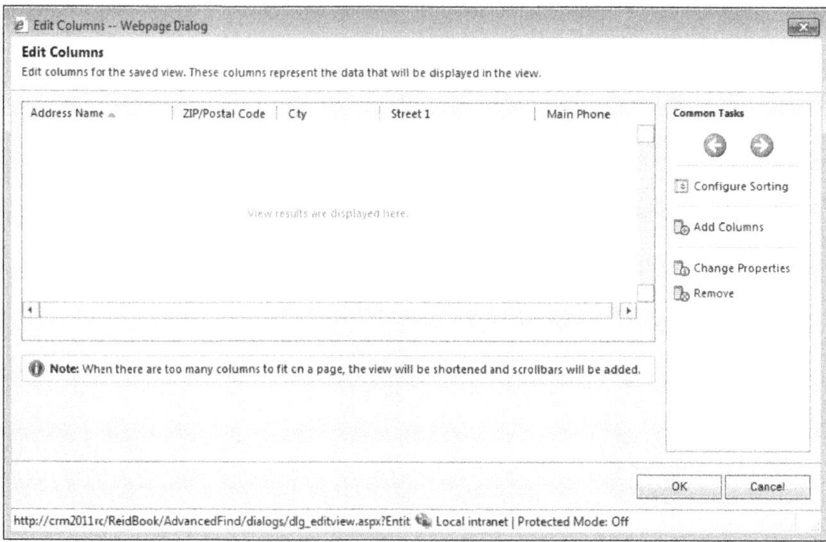

FIGURE 15-19 Edit Columns dialog box used to change the columns displayed in query results

Although the details of how to use Fetch XML are beyond the scope of this book, it is important to note that you have access to view and edit the Fetch XML used for the query on the Modify Query Variables tab, as shown in Figure 15-20.

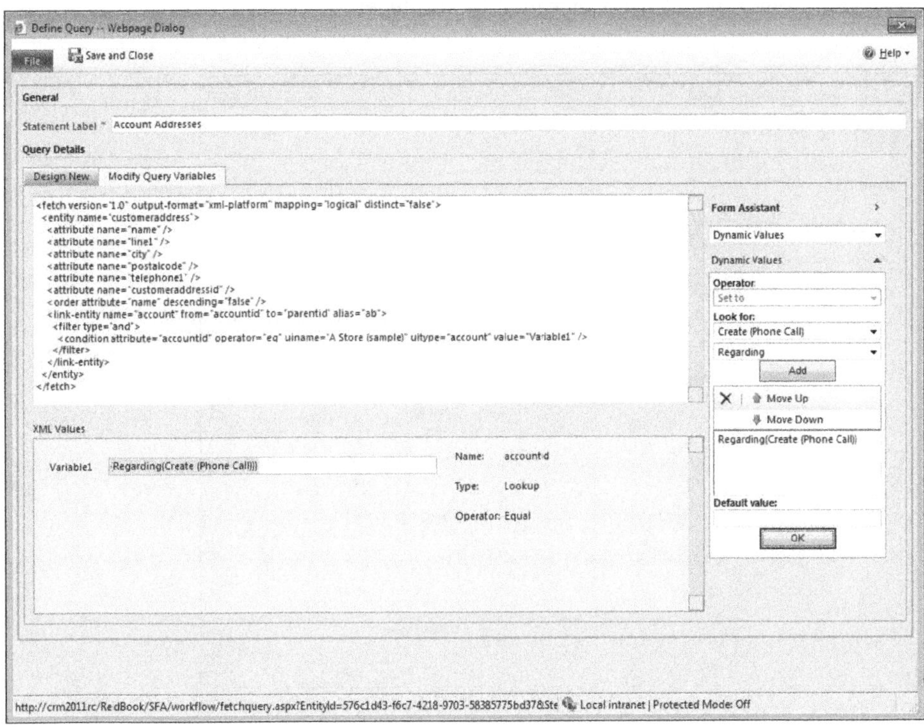

FIGURE 15-20 Fetch XML as shown on the Modify Query Variables tab of the Define Query page

Tip While creating your search criteria in the Define Query page, you'll notice that you have no way to narrow your criteria by the record on which the dialog process is running without using a specific GUID. Don't worry, we have a workaround for you: The example in Figure 15-20 shows how to use the GUID of the account in the Regarding field of a phone call activity that is created as soon as the dialog process is started. To do this, create a basic query in the query designer that populates a placeholder account record, as shown in Figure 15-18. Then, on the Fetch XML tab, we replaced the GUID in the Variable1 field with the Regarding value from a phone call created earlier in the dialog process. After editing the Fetch XML, be careful not to return to the Design New tab; doing so will delete the changes made to the Fetch XML.

Assign Value

The Assign Value action allows you to update the values stored in input arguments and variables. You have the ability to update the values statically (for example, increase the number by five) or dynamically (for example, increase the number by the results entered in a response). Figure 15-21 shows the Assign Value dialog box that is used to dynamically update the value of input arguments and variables.

Important The dynamic value and the input argument or variable you want to update must have the same data type. For example, if you are using an option set to update the lead score variable, which is a whole number, the data type of the option set created in the response values of your prompt and response page must be an integer.

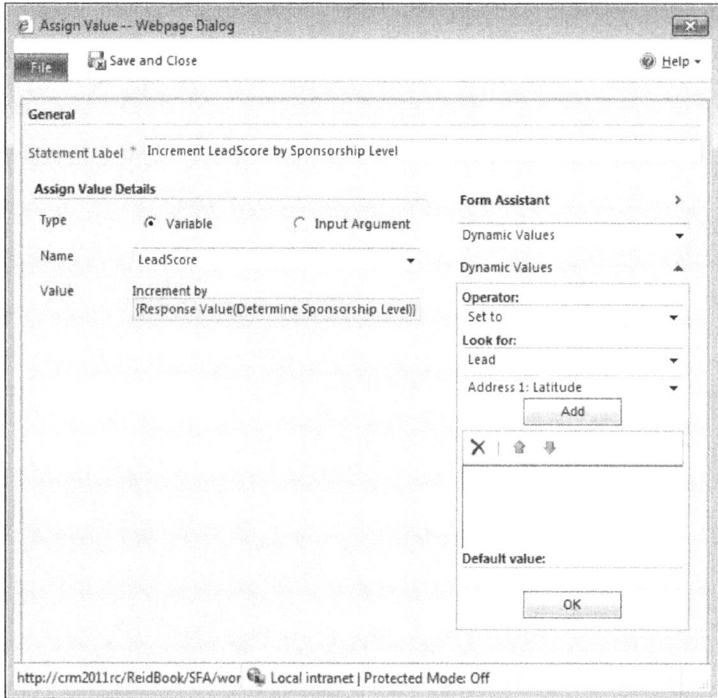

FIGURE 15-21 Assign Value dialog box

When assigning values to input arguments and variables that have the Single Line of Text data type, you have the following assign options:

- Set To
- Append With
- Clear

When assigning values to input arguments and variables that have the Whole Number or Floating Point Number data types, you can select from the following assign options:

- Set To
- Increment by
- Decrement by
- Multiply by
- Clear

Create Record

The Create Record action is used in the same manner for dialog processes as it is for workflow processes. When creating a record, you can assign values to the fields in the record with static information, dynamic values from the primary entity or related entities, or with data that is collected in the dialog process, including input arguments, variables, response values, and process conditions. This is very powerful because the information that is collected before and during a dialog process can be stored in Microsoft Dynamics CRM for future reference. No more asking your customers for the same information over and over again!

Update Record

By using the Update Record action, you can update Microsoft Dynamics CRM records with information collected during the dialog session. The records that can be updated include the primary entity on which the dialog process is running, any related entities, and any records that were created during the dialog session.

Think about the example where the first step of the dialog is to confirm the address information on the customer account. If the data in Microsoft Dynamics CRM does not match the information provided by the customer during the dialog session, the user can immediately update the address information on the customer account before proceeding.

Assign Record

Use the Assign Record action to update the owner of the record on which the dialog process is running, or on any related entities or records created during the dialog session. You can assign the record to a user or team directly in the process editor, or you can use a dynamic value in the assignment step by clicking the Set Properties button and using the Form Assistant in the Edit Assign Step Parameters page, as demonstrated in Chapter 14. You can assign records with a static user or team or dynamically from users or team stored on the primary entity or related entities, or with data that is collected in the dialog process, including new records created in the process.

Send E-Mail

Sending an email from a dialog takes the same form as sending an email from a workflow. As such, you can create a new message from scratch or use the available E-mail templates before setting the properties on the Send E-Mail action. Like the other actions that can be taken from a dialog process, the email can be populated with static text, dynamic values, and dialog-specific data.

Start Child Workflow

Dialog processes can call workflow processes, which will then run asynchronously while the user proceeds through the dialog process. As you would expect, only workflow processes that are configured to run as child processes can be run from a dialog session. The workflow must also be associated to the primary entity of the dialog process or a related entity.

Link Child Dialog

Similar to child workflow processes, child dialog processes can also be called from a dialog process. The child dialog must be associated to the primary entity of the dialog process or a related entity. The power of input arguments comes into play in the Link Child Dialog action, allowing you to pass data captured in one dialog session to another.

Let's recall our previous example, in which a standard series of questions is shared across several case-related processes. The first question inquires about the nature of the call, which the user working through the dialog process selects from a list of call reasons. Depending on the response, different child dialog processes are called. Figure 15-22 shows this process.

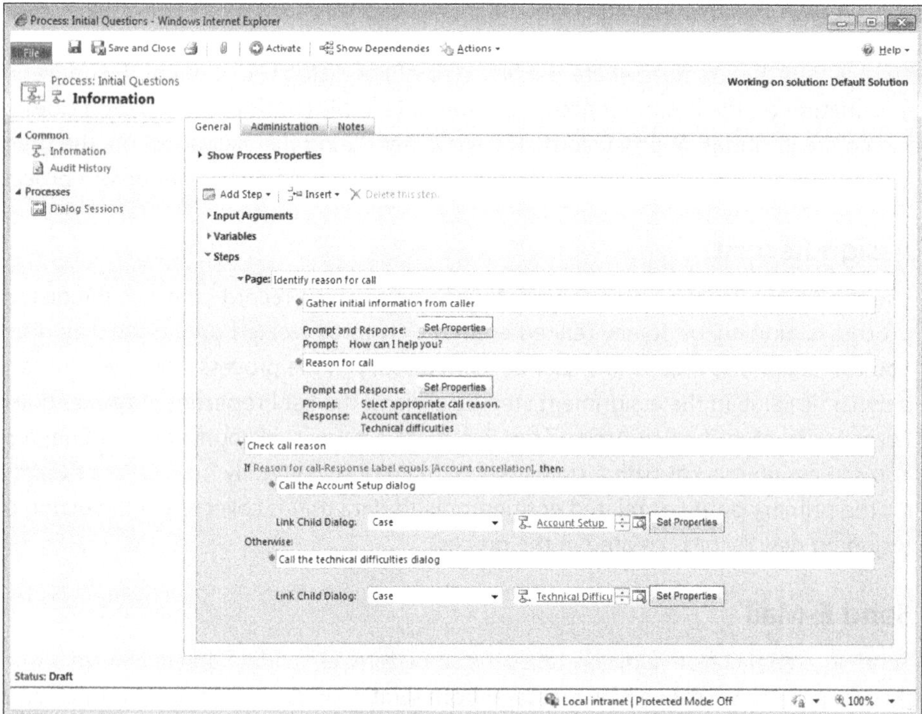

FIGURE 15-22 Dialog process that links to two child dialogs

Using input arguments, you can pass the information collected during the questions in the parent dialog process to the associated child processes.

Change Status

You can use the Change Status action to change the status of the record on which the dialog process is running, a related record, or a record created during the dialog process.

Stop Dialog

After the user working through the dialog process clicks the Finish button on the last page, the process is considered complete and the associated dialog session has a status of Completed. If the user exits the dialog any time before that, the dialog session will show a status of Canceled. However, you might find that you need to stop a dialog before the dialog process is complete. In this scenario, you can use the Stop Dialog action. Unlike workflow processes, dialogs cannot be stopped for multiple reasons. Using the Stop Dialog action will update the status of the dialog session to Completed.

Monitoring Dialogs

You have probably guessed that dialog processes run synchronously, as opposed to workflow processes, which run asynchronously. Dialog sessions can only be in one of the following statuses:

- In Progress
- Canceled
- Completed

You can use the Microsoft Dynamics CRM web interface to monitor dialog process jobs in any of these statuses during a dialog session or from the dialog process record or the related Microsoft Dynamics CRM record. Unlike workflow, dialog sessions do not appear in the System Jobs view.

Note Although you have the ability to monitor dialog processes in similar ways to workflow processes, it is important to understand that you cannot take any actions on those processes outside of dialog pages. Because dialog sessions are initiated by users, only the user who starts the dialog can follow the process to completion, or cancel the process by closing the dialog pages. When the dialog process is canceled, there is no way to resume the dialog.

In this section, we'll review the following:

- Monitoring dialog sessions
- Reviewing the summary of a dialog process

Monitoring Dialog Sessions

The dialog process record contains a Dialog Sessions link that lists all executed instances of the process in the system, including their status, as shown in Figure 15-23.

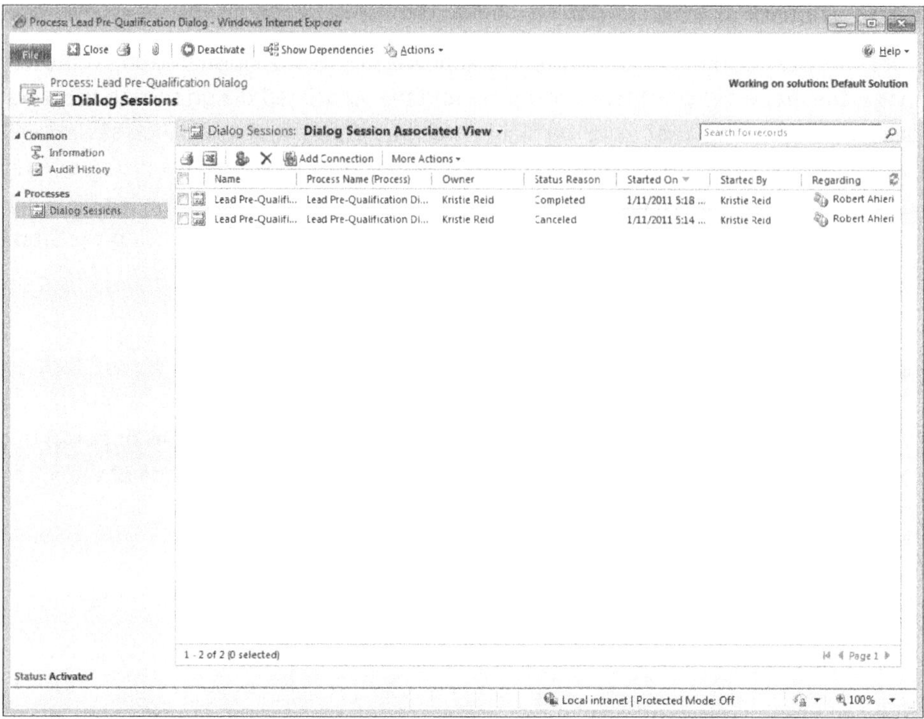

FIGURE 15-23 Reviewing dialog sessions from the dialog process record

Similarly, Microsoft Dynamics CRM also lets you view and access any dialog session running against a record directly from the record by clicking the Dialog Sessions link on the record to show all dialog processes that have been executed or that are executing against the record.

Reviewing the Summary of a Dialog Processes

To view additional details about the dialog process, you or the user running the dialog process can access the summary of the dialog session. This information is made available by opening a dialog session record or while progressing through the dialog process by selecting the Summary button, as shown in Figure 15-24.

Important As you can see, the responses to each prompt are available for review in the summary. As we described, you can opt to not log some responses so that they do not appear in the summary. This option should always be used when gathering personal information that should not be shared with other users during a dialog process.

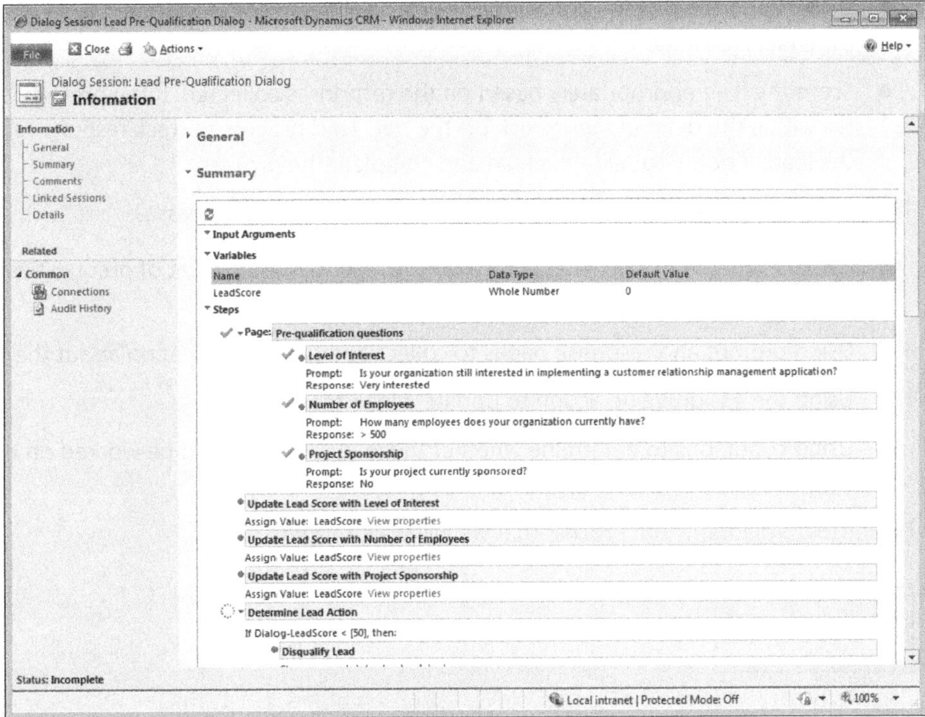

FIGURE 15-24 Dialog session summary

Dialog Process Example

Now that we have reviewed the concepts behind dialog processes, let's look at an example to tie all of these actions together. This section demonstrates a scenario in which the user prequalifies a lead based on information captured on a web form.

Prequalifying a Lead

Obtaining qualified leads is a primary goal of most sales organizations. Sales managers carefully consider the factors that determine whether salespeople should spend their time contacting a lead and how leads are distributed to their sales team. Assume that the standard process to prequalify a lead includes the following steps:

- Confirm that the person who submitted a lead is still interested in your product or service.
- Identify the number of employees in the lead's company to ensure that the eventual opportunity is large enough to pursue.

- Understand the project sponsorship level to validate the commitment level of the potential customer.
- Score the lead appropriately based on the responses collected. If the preceding criteria fall within the defined range, kick off the new lead process to track responsiveness to the lead. If not, disqualify the lead and complete the process.

This example will demonstrate the following features in dialog processes:

- Using a variable to calculate a score for the lead, based on a set of prequalification questions.
- Using prompt and response pages to collect additional information about the lead.
- Using the Assign Value action to update a lead score field.
- Using conditions to determine whether the lead record should be worked on through the initiation of a child workflow or deactivated.

Figure 15-25 diagrams the process that we will walk through.

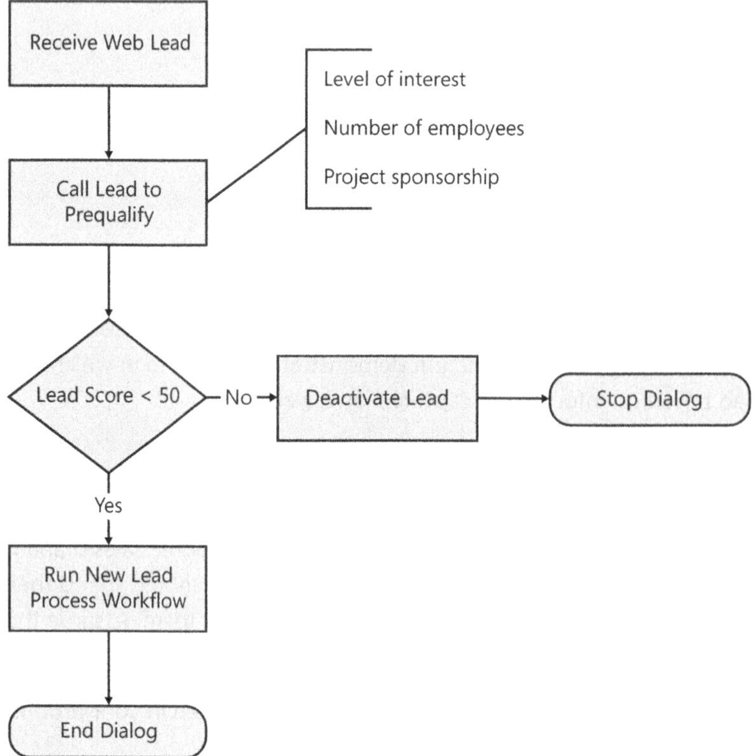

FIGURE 15-25 Lead prequalification logic

Creating the process

1. Navigate to the Settings area and click Processes.
2. Click New in the Process grid toolbar. The Create Process dialog box appears.
3. In the Create Process dialog box, type **Lead Prequalification Dialog** in the Process Name field, select Lead in the Entity field, and select Dialog as the Category. Ensure that the *New blank process* option is selected, and click OK.

After the dialog process is created, you will want to set up all of your input parameters and variables. For this example, we will set up a variable to track the lead score based on data collected during the dialog process.

Creating a lead score variable

1. In the process editor for the process you just created, click Add under the Variables section.
2. Type **LeadScore** in the Name field, select Whole Number as the Data Type, and enter **0** as the Default Value. Click OK.

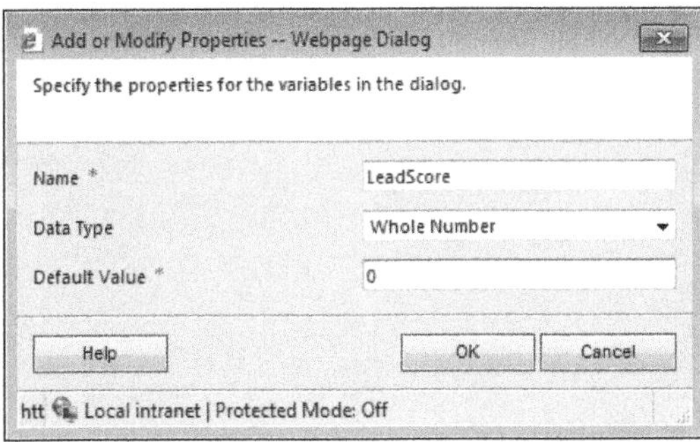

Next, we will create the prompt and response pages to collect additional information about the lead. Each response label will be given a numeric value that will then be used to increment the lead score variable we just created.

Creating the prompt and response page to with the prequalification questions

1. In the process editor, click Add Step, and select Page. For the step description, type **Prequalification Questions.**
2. Click the *Select this row and click Add Step* area. Click Add Step and then click Prompt and Response. For the step description, type **Level of Interest**.
3. Click Set Properties next to the Prompt and Response step. In the editor page that appears, verify that the Statement Label field contains Level of Interest, carried over from your step description.
4. In the Prompt Text area, type **Is your organization still interested in implementing a customer relationship management application?**

5. Select Option Set (picklist) in the Response Type field and select Integer from the Data Type field.
6. Leave the Define Values option selected in the Provide Values field, click the plus icon in the Response Values area, and enter the following Response Values:
    a. Value = 0, Label = No longer interested
    b. Value = 10, Label = Somewhat interested
    c. Value = 20, Label = Very interested
7. Click Save and Close.

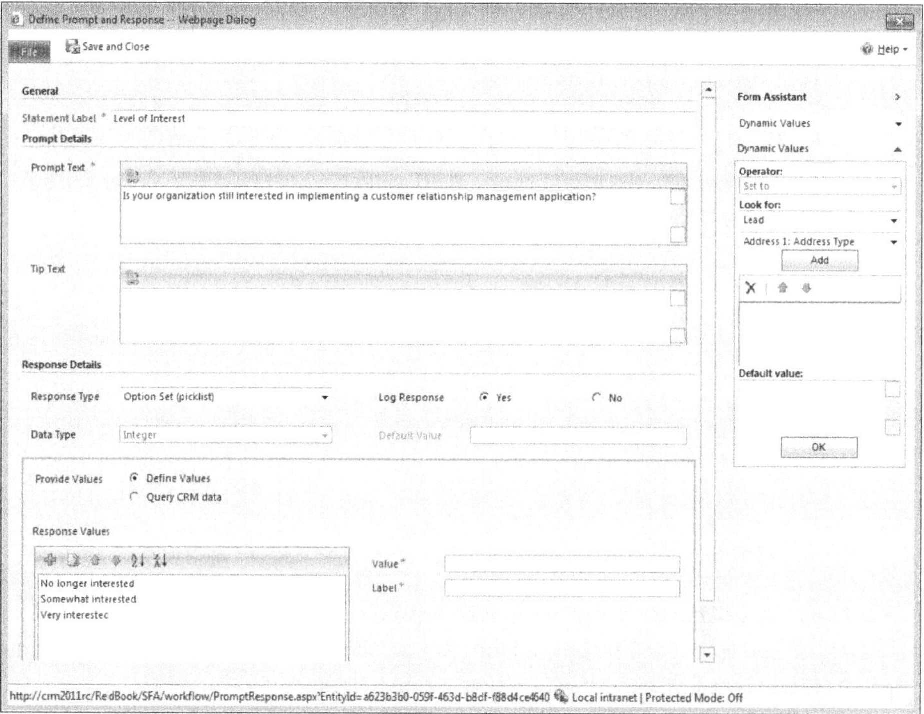

8. Click Add Step, select Prompt and Response, and name the step **Number of Employees**. Enter the following values in the prompt and response definition:
    a. Prompt Text   How many employees does your organization currently have?
    b. Response Type   Option Set (picklist)
    c. Data Type   Integer as the Data Type
    d. Response Values

        Value = 0, Label = < 25

        Value = 5, Label = 25–49

        Value = 10, Label = 50–99

Value = 20, Label = 100–499

Value = 40, Label = > 500

9. Select Save and Close.
10. Click Add Step, select Prompt and Response, and name the step **Project Sponsorship**. Enter the following values in the prompt and response definition:
    a. Prompt Text Is your project currently sponsored?
    b. Tip The goal of this question is to validate that the project is sponsored by an individual within the organization who can approve the project budget.
    c. Response Type Option Set (picklist) as the Response Type
    d. Data Type Integer as the Data Type
    e. Provide Values Define Values
    f. Response Values

       Value = 0, Label = No

       Value = 10, Label = Yes
11. Select Save and Close.

At this point, your dialog process should look like the one shown in Figure 15-26.

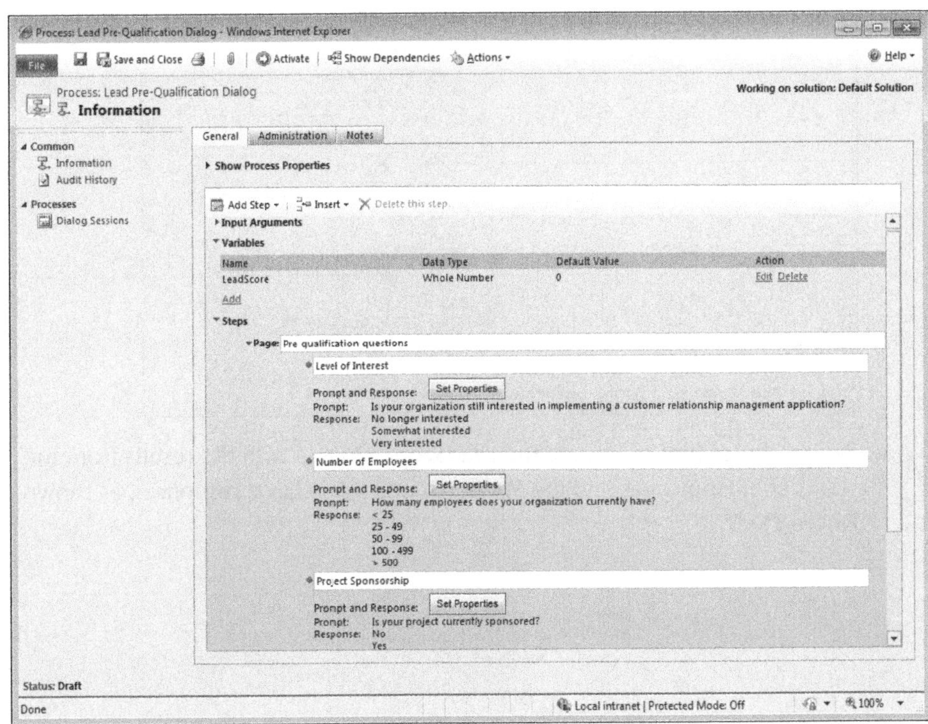

FIGURE 15-26 Prequalification dialog with prompt and response pages

After the responses are collected, you will use the values stored for each response to calculate the lead score.

Calculating the lead score based on the responses

1. In the process editor, highlight the Page step and click Add Step. Select Assign Value and type **Update Lead Score with Level of Interest** in the step description.
2. Click the Set Properties button next to the Assign Value step. Confirm that the LeadScore variable is selected in the Name field. Click in the Value field. In the Dynamic Values area, select the *Increment by* operator, then select the Level of Interest response value in the Look for field. Click OK to add the dynamic value to the Value field, and then click Save and Close.

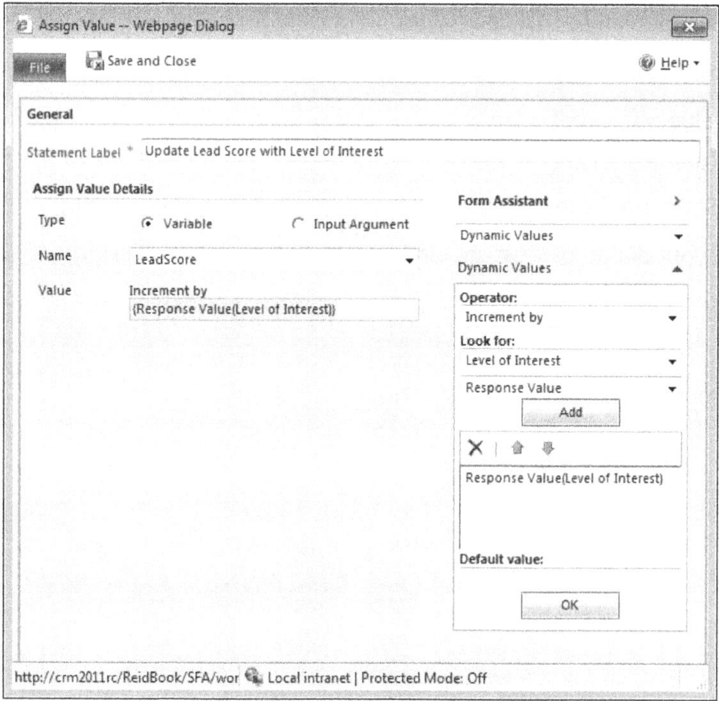

3. Repeat these steps to update the LeadScore variable with the results from the Number of Employees and the Project Sponsorship Level responses, as shown in Figure 15-27.

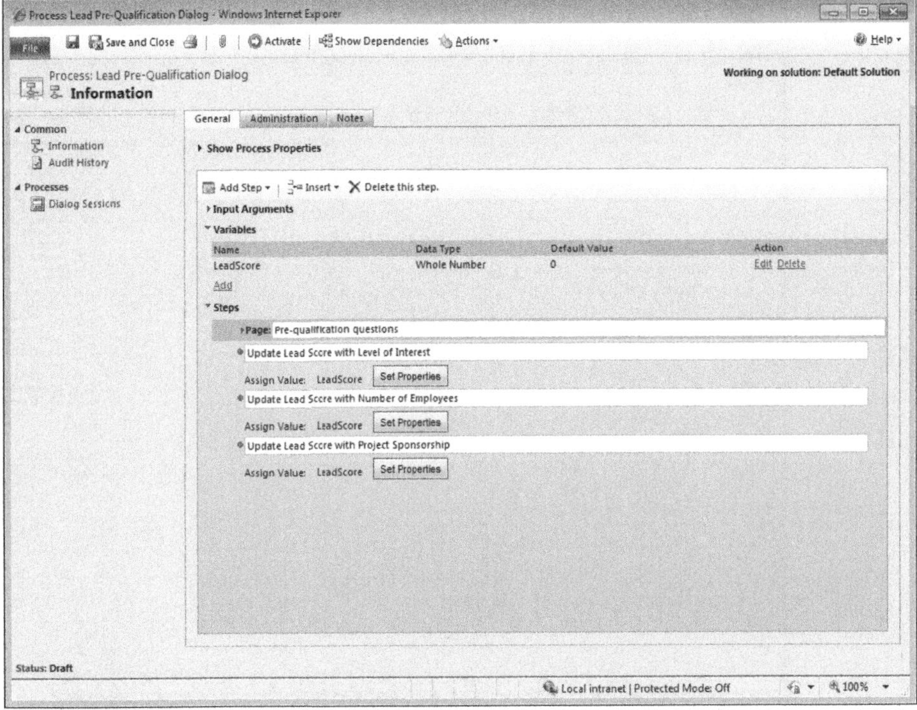

FIGURE 15-27 Prequalification dialog with Assign Value steps

After the lead score is calculated, the dialog process will determine the next step for the lead. If the score does not match the required minimum, the dialog process will end. If the minimum score is met, another workflow is kicked off and the lead is assigned to an account manager.

Creating the prequalification logic

1. In the process editor, highlight the final Assign Value item and click Add Step. Select Check Condition and type **Determine Lead Action** in the step description.
2. Click the *<condition> (click to configure)* link. In the Specify Condition dialog box, create the condition shown in the image on the following page, and then click Save and Close.

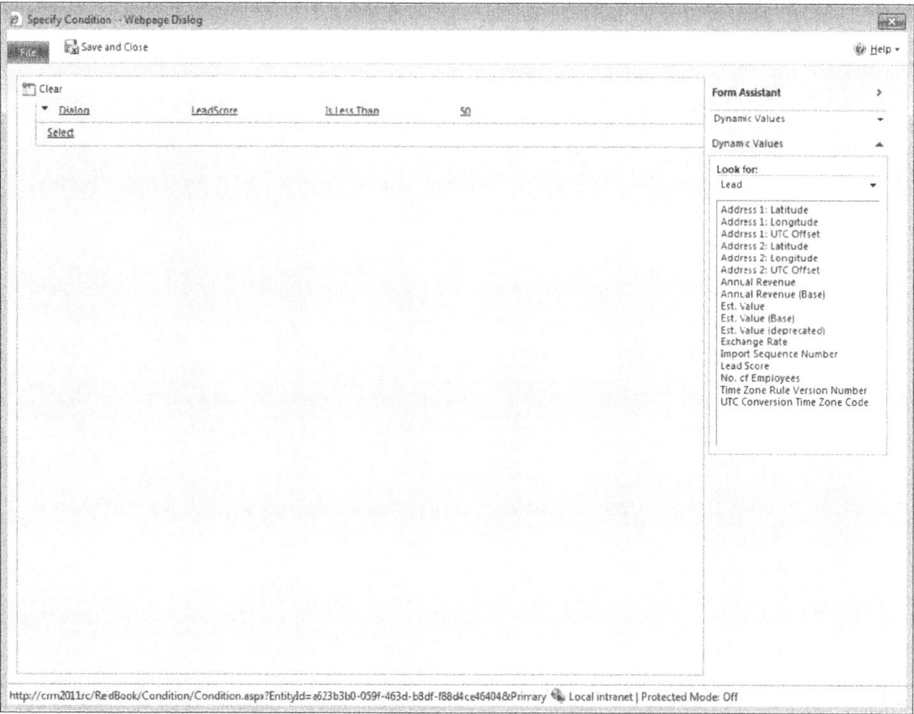

3. Click Select this row, click Add Step, and then click Change Status. Type **Disqualify Lead** in the step description and select Lost as the Lead Status.

4. Click Add Step, and then click Stop Dialog. Type **Complete Dialog** in the step description.

5. Select the If step, click Add Step, and then select Default Action. Click Select this row and then click Add Step, then select Start Child Workflow. Choose the New Lead Process workflow created in Chapter 14. This workflow will have to be changed slightly to be kicked off manually rather than when a lead is created.

6. Click Add Step, and then click Page. Type **Notify user of assigned Account Manager** in the step description. Click Select this row, click Add Step, and then select Prompt and Response. Type **Closeout call** in the step description. Set the property of the page and enter the following information into the prompt and response definition.

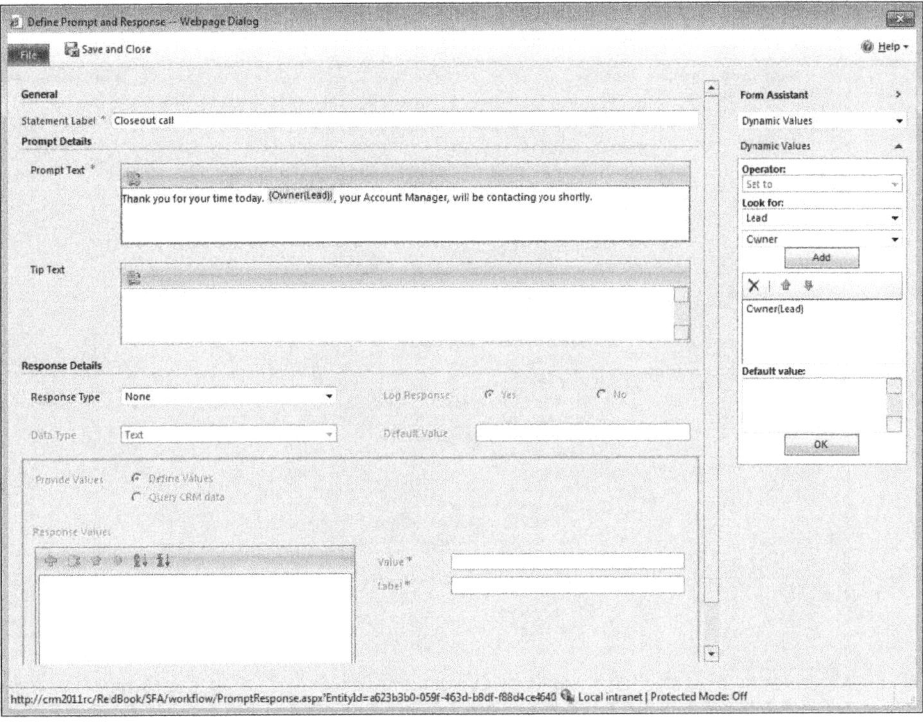

7. Click Save and Close.
8. Highlight the Page step, click Add Step, and then click Stop Dialog. Type **Complete Dialog** in the step description.
9. Click Activate to activate the dialog process.

Your process will look similar to what is shown in Figure 15-28.

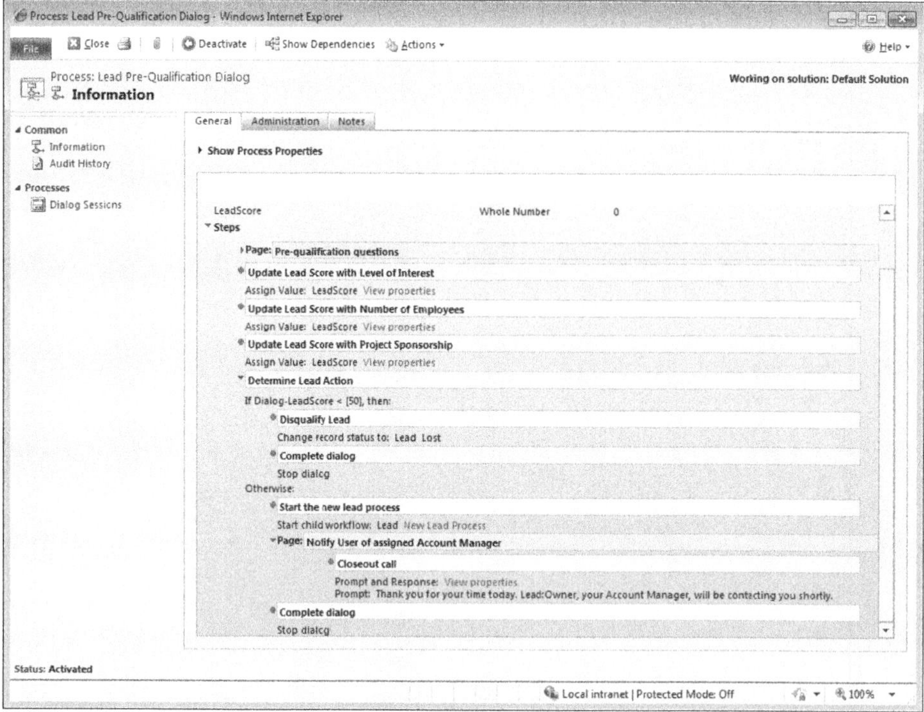

FIGURE 15-28 Activated prequalification dialog process

Summary

Microsoft Dynamics CRM now includes dialog functionality you can use for call scripting or for managing user interactions within a process. Although many features of the dialog processes are similar to those presented in workflow processes, dialogs allow for user interaction. Dialog processes can be created by system administrators and users with the appropriate security privileges. In addition to managing call scripting functionality, dialog processes can be used to lead users through a series of questions to collect additional information without making that information required on Microsoft Dynamics CRM forms.

Index

Symbols and Numbers

A

D

E

F

G

H

I

J

L

M

N

O

P

Q

R

S

T

W

X

About the Authors

Mike Snyder

Mike Snyder is co-founder and principal of Sonoma Partners. Recognized as one of the industry's leading Microsoft Dynamics CRM experts, Mike is a member of the Microsoft Dynamics Partner Advisory Council and is a virtual technical specialist for Microsoft. In addition, he has been recognized by Microsoft as a Microsoft Dynamics CRM MVP for the past three years. He co-authored several books about Microsoft Dynamics CRM for Microsoft Press that have sold more than 50,000 copies worldwide. Before starting Sonoma Partners, Mike led multiple product development teams at Motorola and Fortune Brands. Mike graduated with honors from Northwestern's Kellogg Graduate School of Management with a Master of Business Administration degree, majoring in marketing and entrepreneurship. He has a bachelor's degree in engineering from the University of Notre Dame. He enjoys ice hockey and golf in his free time.

Jim Steger

Jim Steger is co-founder and principal of Sonoma Partners. He has been developing solutions for Microsoft Dynamics CRM since the version 1.0 beta. Jim is a Microsoft Certified Professional and has been a Microsoft Dynamics CRM MVP since 2009. Jim has co-authored numerous books about Microsoft Dynamics CRM for Microsoft Press. Before starting Sonoma Partners, Jim designed and led various global software development projects at Motorola and ACCO Office Products. Jim earned his bachelor's degree in engineering from Northwestern University.

Kristie Reid

Kristie Reid is a consulting director with Sonoma Partners. She is based out of Denver, Colorado, and has been delivering Microsoft Dynamics CRM solutions since the 1.2 version of the product. While at Sonoma Partners, she has led more than 75 different CRM projects ranging from complex ISV developments to large-scale enterprise integrations. Kristie also authored a security whitepaper about Microsoft Dynamics CRM on behalf of Microsoft. Prior to joining Sonoma Partners, Kristie led software implementation projects at Quiznos, Cap Gemini, and PricewaterhouseCoopers. Kristie earned her Master of Business Administration and Master of Information Technology from the University of Denver and her bachelor's degree in finance and international business from Ohio University.

About Sonoma Partners

This book's authors—Mike Snyder, Jim Steger, and Kristie Reid—are executives at the Chicago-based consulting firm Sonoma Partners. Sonoma Partners is a Microsoft Gold Certified Partner that sells, customizes, and implements Microsoft Dynamics CRM for enterprise and midsize companies throughout the United States and Canada. Sonoma Partners has worked exclusively with Microsoft Dynamics CRM since the version 1.0 prerelease beta software. Founded in 2001, Sonoma Partners possesses extensive experience in several industries, including financial services, professional services, healthcare, and real estate.

Sonoma Partners is different from other Microsoft Dynamics CRM partners:

- We write the books for Microsoft. Consequently, we know the product inside and out, and our relationships with Microsoft product team will save you tons of time and headaches down the line.
- We offer a cost guarantee on all of our deployments. We can do this because of our experience completing more than 400 Microsoft Dynamics CRM deployments.
- We offer clients our unique, prebuilt intellectual property that consists of a full library of tools, utilities, controls, and solutions that you can plug and play in your deployment, saving clients thousands of hours of development time.
- Sonoma Partners offers prebuilt solution templates for professional services, financial services, healthcare, franchise management, and real estate.

In addition to the multiple books we've written for Microsoft Press, we share our Microsoft Dynamics CRM product knowledge through our email newsletter and online blog. If you're interested in receiving this information, you can find out more on our website at *http://www.sonomapartners.com.*

Even though our headquarters is in Chicago, Illinois, we work with customers throughout the United States and Canada. If you're interested in discussing your Microsoft Dynamics CRM system with us, please don't hesitate to contact us! In addition to working with customers who want to deploy Microsoft Dynamics CRM for themselves, we also act as a technology provider for Independent Software Vendors (ISVs) looking to develop their solution for the Microsoft Dynamics CRM platform.

Sometimes people ask us where we got our name. The name *Sonoma Partners* was inspired by Sonoma County in the wine-producing region of northern California. The wineries in Sonoma County are smaller than their more well-known competitors in Napa Valley, but they have a reputation for producing some of the highest-quality wines in the world. We think that their smaller size allows the Sonoma winemakers to be more intimately involved with creating the wine. By using this hands-on approach, the Sonoma County wineries can deliver a superior product to their customers—and that's what we strive to do as well.

Lightning Source UK Ltd.
Milton Keynes UK
UKOW06f0007160813

215371UK00006B/20/P